Personnel Management
A Comprehensive Guide to Theory and Practice

3rd Edition

Edited by

STEPHEN BACH AND KEITH SISSON

Industrial Relations Research Unit
University of Warwick Business School

Blackwell
Publishing

© 2000 by Blackwell Publishers Ltd
a Blackwell Publishing company

350 main Street, Malden, MA 02148-5018, USA
108 Cowley Road, Oxford OX4 1JF, UK
550 Swanston Street, Carlton, Victoria 3053, Australia
Kurfürstendamm 57, 10707 Berlin, germany

First published 2000 by Blackwell Publishers Ltd
Reprinted 2001, 2002

Library of Congress Cataloging-in-Publication Data

Personnel management: a comprehensive guide to theory and practice/edited by
Stephen Bach and Keith Sisson.—3rd edn.
    p.cm.
  Rev. ed. of: Personnel management: a comprehensive guide to theory and practice in
Britain/edited by Keith Sisson.
  Includes bibliographical references and index.
  ISBN 0–631–21294– (hardback) — ISBN 0–631–-21292–2 (paperback)
  1. Personnel management—Great Britain. I. Bach, Stephen, 1963– II. Sisson, Keith.

HF5549.2.G7 P47 1999
658.3'00941 21—dc21   99–043569

A catalogue record for this title is available from the British Library.

Set in 10 on 12pt Baskerville
by Kolam Information Services Pvt Ltd, Pondicherry, India
Printed and bound in the United Kingdom
by MPG Books Ltd, Bodmin, Cornwall

For further information on
Blackwell Publishing, visit our website:
http://www.blackwellpublishing.com

Contents

List of Contributors   vii

List of Figures   ix

List of Tables   xi

Preface   xiii

Part 1   Personnel Management in Context   **1**

1.   Personnel Management in Perspective
     Stephen Bach and Keith Sisson   3

2.   Personnel Management in the Lean Organization
     Karen Legge   43

3.   Personnel Management in the Extended Organization
     Trevor Colling   70

Part 2   Planning and Resourcing   **91**

4.   Manpower or Human Resource Planning – What's in a Name?
     Sonia Liff   93

5.   Recruitment and Selection
     Sue Newell and Viv Shackleton   111

6.   Still Wasting Resources? Equality in Employment
     Linda Dickens   137

Part 3   Employee Development   171

7.   Towards the Learning Organization?
     Ewart Keep and Helen Rainbird   173

8.   Management Development
     John Storey and William Tate   195

9.   Managing Careers
     Helen Newell   218

Part 4   Pay and Performance   239

10.   From Performance Appraisal to Performance Management
      Stephen Bach   241

11.   Remuneration Systems
      Ian Kessler   264

12.   Managing Working Time
      James Arrowsmith and Keith Sisson   287

Part 5   Work Relations   315

13.   Discipline: Towards Trust and Self-discipline?
      Paul K. Edwards   317

14.   Direct Participation
      Mick Marchington and Adrian Wilkinson   340

15.   Management and Trade Unions: Towards Social Partnership?
      Stephanie Tailby and David Winchester   365

List of Contributors

James Arrowsmith, Research Fellow, Industrial Relations Research Unit (IRRU), University of Warwick Business School

Stephen Bach, Lecturer in Industrial Relations, IRRU, University of Warwick Business School

Trevor Colling, Senior Research Fellow, Department of Human Resource Management, De Montfort University

Linda Dickens, Professor of Industrial Relations, IRRU, University of Warwick Business School

Paul K. Edwards, Professor of Industrial Relations and Director of the Industrial Relations Research Unit, University of Warwick Business School

Ewart Keep, Deputy Director of SKOPE, University of Warwick Business School

Ian Kessler, Lecturer in Management Studies and Fellow of Templeton College, University of Oxford

Karen Legge, Professor of Organisational Behaviour, University of Warwick Business School

Sonia Liff, Senior Lecturer in Industrial Relations and Organisational Behaviour, IRRU, University of Warwick Business School

Mick Marchington, Professor of Human Resource Management, Manchester School of Management, UMIST

Helen Newell, Lecturer in Industrial Relations and Personnel Management, IRRU, University of Warwick Business School

Sue Newell, Professor of Innovation and Organisational Analysis, Nottingham Business School, Nottingham Trent University

Helen Rainbird, Professor of Industrial Relations, University College Northampton

Viv Shackleton, Convenor, Organisation Studies Division, Aston Business School, University of Aston

Keith Sisson, Emeritus Professor of Industrial Relations, IRRU, University of Warwick Business School

John Storey, Professor of Human Resource Management, Open University Business School, The Open University

Stephanie Tailby, Principal Lecturer, Bristol Business School, University of the West of England

William Tate, Independent consultant

Adrian Wilkinson, Professor of Human Resource Management, Loughborough University Business School

David Winchester, Senior Lecturer in Industrial Relations, IRRU, University of Warwick Business School

List of Figures

1.1   Change in the use of different forms of labour over the past five years   20

5.1   The traditional, 'psychometric' view of the selection process: fitting
a square peg into a square hole   112

5.2   Selection methods used by employers   120

5.3   Comparison of the validity of a 'good' and 'poor' selection method   121

6.1   Discrimination: definition and remedies   149

9.1   Types of internal managerial labour market   222

9.2   Models of careers   226

10.1   Conflicts in performance appraisal   251

10.2   A typology of rater motives and manipulative rating behaviour   252

12.1   Percentage of full-time male employees usually working 46 or more
hours a week   288

12.2   Percentage of full-time female employees usually working 46 or more
hours a week   288

14.1   The escalator of participation   343

15.1   A typology of employer regimes   369

List of Tables

1.1	Twenty-seven points of difference between personnel management and HRM	12
1.2	Percentage of workplaces using 'new' management practices and employee involvement schemes	22
1.3	The significance of sector	24
1.4	The significance of workforce size	25
1.5	The significance of occupation	26
1.6	Workplaces by gender	26
1.7	Key legislative developments 1990–1999	32
1.8	Models of HRM/IR: the current stereotypes	34
1.9	The 'new' European social model	35
3.1	The changing structure of the UK contract catering market, 1989–1993	73
3.2	Subcontracting in establishments, 1990 and 1997	75
3.3	Employment in selected business services, 1989–1998	76
3.4	Share of local government contracts held by top ten companies, by service	80
5.1	Personnel specification for a secondary-school head of English (following Rodger's seven-point plan)	115
5.2	Application of a situational interview technique	124
6.1	Equal treatment practices, by formal equal opportunities policy	140
6.2	Relevant key European provisions	147
6.3	Key aspects of UK legislation	148
6.4	Discrimination claims to industrial tribunals, 1995–1996	155
7.1	Stages in the development of a learning organization	176
7.2	Characteristics of a learning organization	177
8.1	Priority accorded to management development	205
8.2	Amount of formal training	206
10.1	Features of performance management	245
10.2	Developments in performance management since 1991	260

12.1   Reasons for part-time working   292
12.2   Men and woman employed part time as percentage of each
       category's total employment, 1985 and 1995   295
12.3   Part-time work, by sector   296
12.4   Use of temporary agency workers and fixed-term contracts, by
       occupation   296
12.5   Types of shift pattern by numbers of employees   298
12.6   Percentage of employees by type of flexible work arrangement,
       spring 1997   302
12.7   Flexibilities possible by agreement under the Working Time Regulations   306
14.1   Contrasting meanings of participation   351
15.1   Trade union presence, membership, recognition and collective
       bargaining coverage, 1984, 1990 and 1998   370

Preface

Like its two predecessors, this volume is very much in the industrial relations tradition. Its treatment of the subject is, therefore, very different from the standard personnel management texts in two major respects. First, whereas most of these regard personnel management as being more or less synonymous with the techniques and activities associated with, if not necessarily performed by, specialist personnel managers, this collection is primarily concerned with personnel management as a system of employment regulation: the ways in which people in work organizations are selected, appraised, trained, paid, disciplined and so on. Second, and perhaps even more importantly, although it raises and throws considerable light on a great many policy issues – in particular, the significance for personnel management of the wider economic, political and social context – the book is not directly prescriptive as most textbooks in the area tend to be; the objective is to understand the ways in which people in work organizations in Britain are actually selected, appraised, trained, paid and disciplined, rather than with offering seemingly 'universal' solutions to the problem of managing the employment relationship. The aim, as well as contributing to the growing debate about this key aspect of management, is to meet the demands of teachers and students, at every level, for the breadth and depth of description, explanation and analysis they have come to expect in other areas of industrial relations.

Also like its predecessors, this volume is composed of original essays that bring together theoretical and empirical knowledge and understanding. Each chapter is stamped with the views of the authors, who are experts in their field. Each emphasizes analysis and explanation as well as description. Each focuses on trends over recent years and says something about likely future developments.

In the preface to the first edition, it was suggested that breaking with tradition was never easy. A major problem was to overcome what was perhaps the most unfortunate legacy of the prescriptive tradition that had dominated the study of personnel management in the past, namely the lack of information about what actually happened in practice. The hope was expressed that younger scholars would begin to follow the example of the contributors to, and take up the challenge of, writing descriptively and analytically about personnel management.

In the event, it was not just young scholars who responded. The result is that, although some areas, such as human resource planning, remain relatively under-researched, there has been a massive improvement in the quantity and quality of information that is available about personnel management. Indeed, such is the burgeoning amount of material, a major problem for the contributors has been to digest this information, much of it contradictory, and to present a coherent analysis.

Although much is the same, the structure and themes are somewhat different from the first two editions. Instead of one chapter offering an overview of trends and developments in personnel management, there are now three, reflecting our aim of achieving a better understanding of how apparently independent developments fit together, in the form of the 'lean organization' and the 'extended organization', dramatically altering the context in which personnel management is conducted. The chapters in the other three sections are concerned with more long-standing themes: planning and resourcing; employee development; managing performance; and work relations. However, reflecting developments since the last edition, chapter 7 uses the concept of the 'learning organization' to bring together material on training and development dealt with in two chapters in the second edition. The notions of 'empowerment' and 'partnership' are also used to explore developing trends in involvement and participation. There is also greater recognition of the significance of managers and professional workers as employees, which is reflected in a chapter on managing careers as well as management development.

There are fewer chapters than in the second edition. As well as the aim of achieving greater integration, this was prompted by two other considerations. One was the desire to keep the size of the book to manageable proportions. This did not just reflect the concern of the publishers, it needs to be emphasized, but also of teachers and students who complained about the sheer bulk of the second edition. The other was our view that a number of the chapters in the second edition had a timeless quality to them. In the circumstances, there seemed little point in asking contributors to update them for the sake of it, especially as in some cases we wanted them to take on more challenging tasks.

As well as the authors, and their colleagues who commented on the chapters, many people helped to make this book possible. Special thanks are due to Val Jephcott and Katy Woodfield for undertaking the substantial amount of secretarial work associated with such a project, and to the team at Blackwell, especially Catriona King, Bridget Jennings, Rhonda Pearce, Paula Jacobs and Joanna Pyke, for keeping us on track. We would also like to acknowledge the institutional support of the Industrial Relations Research Unit, whose Centre for International Employment Relations Research is funded by the UK Economic and Social Research Council. It is when you attempt a project such as this that you really appreciate the benefits of IRRU's intellectual as well as administrative resources. Last, but not least, we would like to thank Caroline and Jan for their support and encouragement as the book progressed through its various stages.

Stephen Bach and Keith Sisson

Part 1

Personnel Management in Context

Personnel Management in Perspective

Stephen Bach and Keith Sisson

Looking back at the two previous editions of this book (Sisson 1989; 1994a) provides a good snapshot of the changing state of personnel management. It is easy to forget in the current avalanche of literature that, as late as 1989, there was very little analysis of and information about personnel management in practice. Indeed, the first edition felt it necessary to invite younger scholars in particular to 'take up the challenge of writing descriptively and analytically about personnel management' (Sisson 1989: xii). There was a general recognition that competitive pressures were forcing employers to review personnel practice, but there was only the beginning of a debate about whether personnel management was in transition and, if so, where it was going. By 1994, especially with the results of the third Workplace Industrial Relations Survey (WIRS) (Millward et al. 1992) available, there were few doubts that fundamental changes were afoot, but there were major questions about the degree to which these changes marked a fundamental break with past practice in the direction of the emerging human resource management (HRM) paradigm (Millward 1994: 127). By the end of the 1990s, and the availability of further evidence from case studies and surveys, notably the First Findings of the 1998 Workplace Employee Relations Survey (WERS) (Cully et al. 1998), it is much clearer that, while there has been a major restructuring of employment relations in the UK, few organizations have redesigned them in line with the commitment-seeking models of HRM. Instead, there appears to be massive variety of practice and great uncertainty about the destination or, rather, destinations to which personnel management is heading. The function is variously seen as 'in crisis', 'in a black hole', 'in uncharted territory' (Sparrow and Marchington 1998: 296–9).

A decade after the publication of the first edition is an appropriate time to offer a critical appraisal of the field of personnel management and to try to put things into perspective in advance of the detailed treatment of the different areas in later chapters. We do so here in four cross-cutting ways. First, we examine the manner in which personnel management as a subject has developed and the ways in which the main traditions have made their contribution. Second, we explore the changing conception of the personnel function and the extent to which it has shifted from being an operating to a strategic function. Third, we look at the practice of personnel management, drawing on the First Findings of WERS.

Fourth, we look at the prospects for personnel management and especially the challenge of Europeanization. Finally, in the light of the analysis, we offer our thoughts on the state of personnel management, together with some implications for practitioners and policy makers.

The Study of Personnel Management: at the Crossroads of Three Traditions

The first edition suggested that the study of personnel management was dominated by two traditions, the prescriptive and the labour process, with a third, industrial relations, emerging as researchers began to take a sustained interest in personnel management practice (Sisson 1989). The first, the prescriptive approach, is primarily concerned to provide a tool-kit for managers and personnel specialists and gives scant attention to the context in which personnel techniques are formulated and implemented or the underlying assumptions on which these recipes are based. In contrast, the labour process approach seeks to lay bare the controlling instincts of personnel management and is critical of the assumptions of the prescriptive approach. Finally, the industrial relations tradition sees personnel management as a system of employment regulation with personnel techniques marshalled as part of the 'continual negotiation of order'. Each of these traditions has evolved in important ways, engaging with a wider range of social science disciplines and policy concerns.

The prescriptive tradition

This has traditionally been the dominant approach within the literature. Aimed at managers, and at personnel managers in particular, its primary concern has been to equip them with the tools of people management by developing protocols of best practice in the key areas (recruitment and selection, appraisal, remuneration, training and development). Much of the literature is vocational, and has been shaped by the close link between the academic field of personnel management and the occupation of personnel management, a much tighter link than is the case in related fields such as industrial relations. The expectation that personnel specialists will be Institute of Personnel and Development (IPD) qualified, although not a licence to practice like law, medicine or accountancy, has been a major influence on the personnel management teaching and research agenda.

This vocational orientation has led to a neglect of the assumptions underpinning the approach. In essence, however, the underlying conceptual framework, although not always made explicit, is that although organizations may be increasingly diverse this has few implications for personnel management and a set of universal prescriptions are advocated. These derive from the human relations perspective which sees no fundamental conflict between management and employees, who seek rewards from employment in terms of job satisfaction, autonomy and self-development rather than being primarily motivated by financial self-interest (McGregor 1960). In the language of the 1990s, these ideas have been repackaged with employers encouraged to adopt commitment-seeking personnel policies which develop a robust psychological contract.

In recent years, such literature has divided into two main types. There has been a huge growth in airport lounge books which briefly outline the core elements of communicating/leading/culture change, etc., reflecting the increased attention being given to what are patronizingly termed 'softer' management skills. This genre takes it as self-evident that these concepts are easily defined and can be successfully introduced to a receptive workforce as long as the individual manager recognizes that these 'softer' skills are important for organizational success and is prepared to abandon any vestiges of a non-participative management style.

At the other end of the spectrum are more specialized texts, often linked to the IPD syllabus, which examine similar issues but in much greater depth with a growing appreciation of the significance of context. The existence of a more competitive environment and the inevitability of constant and unpredictable change is emphasized. Consequently, personnel managers need to be nimble footed to survive in the harsh corporate environment of the 1990s and demonstrate their value to the organization.

Especially important have been the growing links between personnel management and strategic management, especially how firms create and sustain competitive advantage, provided by the prominence of the resource-based view of the firm articulated by the notion of core competencies (Grant 1991; Prahalad and Hamel 1990). In contrast to the earlier focus of the strategy literature, exemplified by Porter (1980), which concentrated on the importance of a firm's positioning within an industry as the key source of competitive advantage, the resource-based view shifted attention towards the internal processes which enable a firm to develop competitive advantage. Successful firms were those that systematically identified and developed their core competencies, suggested Prahalad and Hamel, because these constitute unique firm-specific attributes not easily imitated by other firms. The manner in which firms identify, nurture and sustain their core competencies has been widely debated, alongside a recognition that this process is far from straightforward (Javidan 1998; Moingeon et al. 1998; Scarbrough 1998a). The approach none the less has made a critical difference to the conception of personnel management and is an important consideration in claims for its strategic status discussed later.

There are two main reasons for this. First, establishing a link with strategic management has helped to bring personnel management in from the cold. The reorientation towards internal processes, the training and development of staff and the nurturing of firm-specific knowledge, which are more important than the firm's external position, provide personnel specialists with an opportunity to demonstrate how they contribute to the bottom line. Second, the appeal of core competencies is that it provides a currency to describe and link personnel practices which have been characterized as a disparate set of activities or, in Drucker's (1961) memorable description, a trash can for activities which lack internal cohesion. This is especially attractive to personnel specialists during a period when organizations have become more fragmented as traditional hierarchies are eroded and organizational boundaries are blurred, leaving the personnel function vulnerable to 'externalization' and 'balkanization' (Adams 1991) and a diminishing organizational contribution.

Despite these developments, difficulties remain with the prescriptive tradition. Even in the more recent literature, strong normative concerns remain, and there is a concentration on a small number of personnel areas, such as training and recruitment which undermines the interest in integration. In contrast to their predecessors, authors contributing to the more sensitive prescriptive literature are alert to the difficulties of developing and implementing personnel policies, but these problems are seen as essentially remedial which a good dose of training or a focused communications campaign will resolve. Neither the questionable underlying assumptions about the character of the employment relationship, nor the extent to which personnel managers have the status and influence to design and implement strategic personnel policies, are explored effectively, and this neglect has frequently led to problems of personnel credibility.

The labour process tradition

The second approach has very different origins from the first being rooted in Marxist political economy. In contrast to the benevolent view of personnel management inherent in the prescriptive tradition, in which personnel specialists try to balance the interests of employees and managers, the labour process tradition adopts a much more critical stance. In this perspective, managers are agents of capital seeking to maximize profits by intensifying work and systematically reducing labour costs. Personnel managers, and the techniques they employ, are part of the armoury used to exploit the workforce (Braverman 1974: 87). Faced with resistance from the workforce, employers constantly have to devise ways of exerting managerial control. The best known typology of the forms that these controls can take was devised by Edwards (1979) who identified simple control by either a supervisor or manager: technical control in which control, especially over the pace of work, was embedded in machinery programmed by managers; and bureaucratic control in which formalized personnel policies, such as job descriptions or systems of job evaluation, provided the framework for the management of the workforce. Even if formal rules were not always observed, this was not necessarily detrimental to management interests if these breaches of personnel policy legitimized and reinforced overall managerial prerogatives (Burawoy 1979).

The labour process tradition has provided an important counterweight to the predominantly prescriptive literature and encouraged the emergence of more critical accounts of personnel management (Legge 1995; Mabey et al. 1998). Moreover, it has evolved to develop a more nuanced view of management control with greater recognition that managers in their role as employees are themselves subject to an increased range of controls and that they may have ambivalent feelings towards a range of 'new' management practices.

In addition, the forms of management control have been extended beyond Edwards's threefold categorization. First, and most pervasively, the increasing density and visibility of financial disciplines within organizations represents a form of indirect control which has an increasingly direct impact over employee behaviour with employees encouraged to identify a direct link between achieving financial and other targets and future employment security (Marginson et al. 1993). Ackroyd and Procter (1998) extend this analysis suggesting that because British manufacturing firms come close to Goold and Cambell's (1987) financial control model of management, in which control is exercised through tight monitoring of strategic business unit performance and achievement of cost targets, this gives rise to a particular pattern of labour management which they term the 'new flexible firm'.

Second, of increased importance is outsourcing in which managers contract out the 'problem' of management control to other organizations or use the threat of contracting out to wrest concessions or enhance performance from the workforce, as has occurred in large parts of the public sector over the last two decades. Personnel specialists have not only implemented such policies but have also been subject to market testing of personnel activity, especially in the public services (Bach 1999: 190). Moreover, the threat that work may be outsourced to reduce costs is an especially potent threat because of the prominence of financial controls within public and private sector organizations.

Third, and most influential in terms of discussion about the emergence of HRM, has been the suggestion that employers are trying to substitute traditional bureaucratic controls with forms of cultural control (i.e. commitment), often intended to establish a new form of psychological contract in which employees exercise forms of self-control either individually or through forms of teamworking. Writers in a broad labour process tradition agree that control through commitment is becoming more prominent and share a deep suspicion of managerial motives, but apart from these initial assumptions there is limited consensus about the impact of commitment-seeking strategies.

One strand of analysis suggests that, contrary to much popular discussion about the extended or virtual organization (see chapter 3) and a belief that bureaucratic forms of organization are in decay, essentially technical control linked to a relatively unchanged Taylorite division of labour continues to flourish, notwithstanding the gloss of the rhetoric of commitment. The difference between prescriptive and labour process accounts is perhaps at its starkest in the accounts of personnel practices at high-profile manufacturing plants such as Nissan's car plant in the north-east of England. Whereas Peter Wickens (1987), the former director of personnel, suggests that labour management comprised a tripod of teamwork, quality consciousness and flexibility, this has been reinterpreted as management through compliance (teamwork), blame (quality consciousness) and stress (flexibility) (Garrahan and Stewart 1992; Delbridge and Turnbull 1992: 61–8).

It has been argued that technological developments have allowed essentially similar types of bureaucratic and technological controls to be applied in expanding areas of service-sector employment, such as call centres. What unites these diverse controls (mystery shoppers, video/acoustic surveillance, etc.) is a fundamental managerial distrust of the workforce. Thus in examining a broad spectrum of personnel practice including forms of employee involvement such as total quality management (TQM), appraisal techniques, or performance-related pay, the spectre of enhanced management control is always lurking to entrap and control unsuspecting employees (see the discussion in chapters 10, 11 and 14). Moreover, it is suggested, local empowerment sits alongside tighter control via performance measurement and management (Gallie et al. 1998).

A second strand of labour process analysis has been influenced by the work of Foucault, leading to a shift of emphasis from direct workplace control to new forms of all-pervasive surveillance. Putting to one side differences in emphasis, there is a consensus that 'panoptican control', in which techniques of surveillance become diffused widely across society, is increasing (Townley 1994; McKinlay and Taylor 1996). Moreover, the emphasis is on the internalization by employees of managerial expectations reducing the importance of traditional forms of management control. From such a perspective many of the management techniques associated with human resource management, such as personality testing, teamworking and total quality management, are reassessed and give the lie to managerial rhetoric of 'empowerment'.

Although the labour process tradition has been important in sensitizing the personnel management literature to some of the naive assumptions of prescriptive accounts, it has a number of shortcomings, many of which have been extensively debated (Smith and Thompson 1998). A particular difficulty has been an overemphasis on the issue of management control. There is insufficient recognition that organizations have a variety of differing objectives of which management control is only one, and a tendency to underplay the 'negotiation of order' and the ability of employees to undermine managerial intentions despite the Orwellian assumptions of the Foucauldian writers that employees have been reprogrammed into docile automatons. Also the context is neglected: just as there is one form of best practice in the prescriptive tradition, so there is one form of capitalism.

The industrial relations tradition

In contrast to most prescriptive accounts of personnel management, the industrial relations approach has viewed personnel management as part of a system of employment regulation in which internal and external influences shape the management of the employment relationship. This shifts the emphasis away from a focus on the techniques of personnel management, within the organization, to a consideration of personnel practice, set within a wider historical, economic and social context.

The historical development and institutional context in which personnel management has evolved looms especially large. Whilst sensitive to the diversity of organizational practice, there is a widely held view that the evolution of personnel management in the UK has been influenced strongly by the underdevelopment of management and the systems of corporate governance with an orientation to short-term results. The ambiguous role and status of personnel specialists is attributed in part to the inhospitable context of the UK business system in which many of them operate (see, for example, Thurley 1981; Sisson 1989; Keep and Mayhew 1998). The most important features of this system can be summarized as:

- an overwhelming emphasis on shareholder value as the key business driver, as opposed to the interests of other stake-holders;
- institutional share ownership by investment trusts and pensions funds which encourages a focus on short-term profitability as the key index of business performance rather than long-term market share or added value;
- relative ease of takeover, which not only reinforces the pressure on short-term profitability to maintain share price but also encourages expansion by acquisition and merger rather than by internal growth;
- a premium on financial engineering as the core organizational competence, and the domination of financial management both in terms of personnel, activities and control systems, over other functions.

Furthermore, two key features of the UK's overall industrial relations system mean there are few, if any, of the countervailing pressures found in most other developed economies to encourage investment in human capital:

- a tradition of 'voluntarism' in virtually every area of UK employment relations (including vocational education and training), which means that the framework of rights and obligations (individual and collective) is much less than in other EU member countries;
- a highly decentralized and diverse structure of collective bargaining, deeply embedded in procedural rather than substantive rules, which means the UK does not possess the detailed multi-employer agreements, which supplement and extend the legislative framework in most other EU member countries.

A second and related distinguishing feature of the industrial relations tradition is a strong emphasis on empirical inquiry. Here there have been two significant developments. First, there have been studies building on the legacy of detailed workplace investigation of personnel management practice in terms of the 'negotiation of order' and the patterns of co-operation and conflict at the workplace (Edwards and Scullion 1982). The starting point was that the context of personnel management had altered significantly arising from a combination of intensified product market competition and labour market reforms (Marchington and Parker 1990; Scott 1994). However, there was no straightforward relationship assumed between personnel management practice and this more competitive context. Instead, detailed longitudinal case study evidence was gathered to illuminate the 'new' industrial relations and its application in unionized and non-unionized settings (Clark 1995; Ram 1994; Scott 1994).

In their different ways the case study research conducted by Scott (1994) in the food processing industry, Clark (1995) in the cable industry of Pirelli and Collinson et al. (1997) more generally, highlight the uncertainties associated with the spread of the new techniques and reveal the limitations of both the prescriptive and labour process traditions. All three studies examine far-reaching initiatives to break with traditional personnel management practice, and under specific circumstances forms of employee involvement and flexibility were well received by the workforce. None the less, considerable suspicion of management motives remained. At Pirelli, there was a measured retreat from 'full flexibility' and some of the problems could have been anticipated if more detailed consideration had been given to personnel issues earlier in the project (Clark 1995). Thus even in a company which explicitly eschewed short-termism, developing and implementing strategic personnel management remained a difficult enterprise.

Complementing the development of case study research has been the much greater use of survey methods. Initially, such surveys focused primarily on collective employment relations: this would be true, for example, of the Industrial Relations Research Unit's (IRRU) *Changing Contours of British Industrial Relations* (Brown 1981) and the first three Workplace Industrial Relations Surveys which followed. Increasingly, however the focus has shifted. For example, IRRU's two company-level industrial relations surveys (Marginson et al. 1988; Marginson et al. 1993) did much to illuminate personnel policies and practices as well as the structure and organization of large companies. Significantly, although not without its critics (see, for example, McCarthy 1994), the survey technique has become an established part of the approach of bodies such as the IPD and Industrial Society, as well as the specialist reports published by Industrial Relations Services and Incomes Data Services. The result is that probably more is now known about the practice of personnel management in the UK than any other country. Certainly this will be the case with the publication of the full results of 1998 WERS which covered most areas of personnel practice.

The industrial relations tradition, it can be argued, has made its contribution to understanding developments in the field of personnel management without capitulating to a narrow managerialist agenda as Kelly (1998) fears. This is not to suggest that it is not without its limitations, however. One criticism, which it shares with the prescriptive tradition, is a preoccupation with larger, well-organized workplaces, with the result that the position of women or employees in smaller, especially non-unionized firms, has not been adequately addressed. A second, which it also shares with the the prescriptive tradition, is that the relationship between workplace personnel policies and employees' domestic circumstances is rarely explored, although it is explicitly recognized as an important issue by employers and the government in their advocacy of 'family-friendly' employment policies (DTI 1998). A third, and perhaps the most substantial, criticism is that there has often been a failure to ask, let alone answer, the 'so what?' question in terms of the implications for practitioners.

Summary

The field of personnel management has expanded greatly over the last decade and there is more diversity of perspectives both within and across the three traditions. The basic conclusion of a decade ago – that the subject was dominated by the prescriptive tradition – remains intact, not least because of the importance of the IPD and its inherent vocational orientation. Not only does the IPD have over 85,000 members but it also provides accreditation for institutions of higher education based on their adherence to the IPD syllabus and requires members to update their knowledge continuously, providing further opportunities to shape the professional personnel management agenda. Even so, there are increasing signs of cross-fertilization between, indeed some integration of, the three traditions. The IPD has become a major sponsor of empirical research. Elements of the labour process and industrial relations traditions have become increasingly intertwined, making it difficult to pigeon-hole some contributions. Researchers from the industrial relations tradition have become more conscious of the need to spell out the implications of their work. The upshot is an increasingly rich body of knowledge and understanding.

The Conception of Personnel Management: from Operating to Strategic Function?

For much of the period since 1945, personnel management, rightly or wrongly, was regarded as an administrative function concerned with operational matters relating to recruitment and selection, appraisal, reward and training policies and practices directed towards the individual employee. If there was an area of employment relations seen as appropriate for strategic initiative, it was that of management–union relations. Here Flanders's (1964) investigation of *The Fawley Productivity Agreements* had a profound influence on the proposals for the reform of collective bargaining by the report of the Donovan Royal Commission in 1968 and the approach of such public bodies as the National Board for Prices and Incomes and the Commission on Industrial Relations.

However, during the 1980s and 1990s the focus shifted and became swept up in broader discussions about the emergence and character of HRM. This debate signalled a very different role for personnel specialists and held out the prospect of shifting from an operational to a strategic role. The shift is nicely portrayed in Storey's (1992: 35) now-famous contrast between personnel and industrial relations, on the one hand, with HRM on the other (see table 1.1). Even so, a continuing preoccupation has been the relatively low status of personnel specialists and the ambiguity of their role (Legge 1978; Watson 1977; Hall and Torrington 1998).

The coming of HRM

The meaning of HRM has been and is likely to continue to be a topic for heated debate. Its novelty included an emphasis on pursuing a strategic approach to the management of human resources, developed with the full backing of senior management, embracing a tight coupling between human resources and business policy and a coherent or inte-grated set of personnel policies and practices. In addition, HRM comprised a particular high-commitment route in which there would be organizational pay-offs if specific config-urations of personnel policies were adopted. These policies involved adapting and re-invigorating the repertoire of personnel management to achieve key objectives: securing the commitment of the workforce; ensuring highly flexible and innovative working practices; and establishing a high quality of work by developing a skilled workforce and maintaining quality working conditions.

The HRM agenda was an enticing and optimistic prospect. Even the criticism – that the comparison between an idealized model of HRM and the messy realities of personnel management was inherently biased and inevitably revealed personnel management in an unflattering light – could be neatly side-stepped. The whole point was that HRM was intentionally aspirational and the force of the argument was increased, not diminished, by a recognition that many practitioners were not going to reach the promised land (Guest 1990). One of the striking features of human resource management was the extent to which its language and values permeated discussion among practitioners and was used to justify policy initiatives. Its potency was exemplified by the extent to which key values, such as the importance of a strategic approach, were internalized, and personnel specialists frequently became defensive if their organization's practice fell short of the strictures of HRM. Moreover, the majority of personnel specialists appear to believe in HRM and these views are most pronounced among IPD members which suggests that the IPD has been prominent in promoting HRM to its members (Grant and Oswick 1998: 187–91).

The emergence and resonance of HRM can be linked to the broader political and economic context and the dominant ideological values of this period. For companies which

Table 1.1 Twenty-seven points of difference between personnel management and HRM

Dimension	Personnel and IR	HRM
Beliefs and assumptions		
1 Contract	Careful delineation of written contracts	Aim to go 'beyond contract'
2 Rules	Importance of devising clear rules/mutuality	'Can-do' outlook; impatience with 'rules'
3 Guide to management action	Procedures	'Business-need'
4 Behaviour referent	Norms/custom and practice	Values/mission
5 Managerial task vis-à-vis labour	Monitoring	Nurturing
6 Nature of relations	Pluralist	Unitarist
7 Conflict	Institutionalized	De-emphasized
Strategic aspects		
8 Key relations	Labour management	Customer
9 Initiatives	Piecemeal	Integrated
10 Corporate plan	Marginal to	Central to
11 Speed of decision	Slow	Fast
Line management		
12 Management role	Transactional	Transformational leadership
13 Key managers	Personnel/IR specialists	General/business/line managers
14 Communication	Indirect	Direct
15 Standardization	High (e.g. 'parity' an issue)	Low (e.g. 'parity' not seen as relevant)
16 Prized management skills	Negotiation	Facilitation
Key levers		
17 Selection	Separate, marginal task	Integrated, key task
18 Pay	Job evaluation (fixed grades)	Performance related
19 Conditions	Separately negotiated	Harmonization
20 Labour management	Collective bargaining contracts	Towards individual contracts
21 Thrust of relations with stewards	Regularized through facilities and training	Marginalized (with exception of some bargaining for change models)
22 Job categories and grades	Many	Few
23 Communication	Restricted flow	Increased flow
24 Job design	Division of labour	Teamwork
25 Conflict handling	Reach temporary truces	Manage climate and culture
26 Training and development	Controlled access to courses	Learning companies
27 Foci of attention for interventions	Personnel procedures	Wide-ranging cultural, structural and personnel strategies

Source: Storey, 1992: 35

had weathered the deep recession and harsh monetarist policies of the early 1980s there was little let-up as intensified competition in an increasingly global economy made the task of effective personnel management more urgent. Related pressures in the public sector arising from policies of privatization and compulsory competitive tendering presented similar challenges. The popularity of the term HRM came to symbolize not only a belief that major changes in product markets required a fresh management approach, but also that the supply-side revolution unleashed by successive Conservative governments allowed managers to exercise an unprecedented degree of strategic choice in shaping the employment policies of individual organizations. With trade unionism in retreat, employers had an opportunity to decide whether to (de)recognize trade unions and to develop a more direct relationship with the workforce with the establishment of new channels of participation and involvement. This was not always a comfortable message for personnel specialists whose role had been inextricably linked to the Donovan prescription of joint regulation of the workplace with trade unions. None the less there was no shortage of recipes to emulate, not least from the much-publicized policies of the growing number of Japanese inward investors. It was widely assumed that their systematic approach to employee resourcing and utilization, alongside intensive forms of employee involvement, ensured a highly committed and productive workforce (see Wickens 1987; Womack and Jones 1990).

The attraction of HRM also rested on continuing unease about the state of British management. Improving management practice became a major preoccupation and a set of principles by which many activities were evaluated and discussed (Scarbrough 1998b). For example, it became commonplace for politicians to talk about 'Britain PLC' using the metaphor of the firm to discuss the prospects and remedies for the economy. This managerialization of society stemmed from continued concerns about the implications for competitiveness of poor management practice (Constable and McCormick 1987; Handy 1987), the use of private sector industrialists to assess problems of public sector organizations who invariably advocated better management (Griffiths 1983; Sheehey 1993) and the increasing importance of management consultants as purveyors of good practice. The upsurge in business education, with a rapid expansion of MBA and business studies courses, not only provided a forum for the dissemination of HRM ideas but also the promotion of a particular (strategic) view of management.

Accompanying the question of why new approaches to personnel management were emerging, and whether they represented anything distinctive in the management of the employment relationship, were issues to do with the nature and extent of the changes taking place. With several new journals given over to understanding and assessing human resource management (Sisson 1990; Poole 1990), and the IPD sponsoring research, there was a proliferation of empirical material on HRM. The topics covered epitomized the individualistic and strategic thrust of HRM – performance related pay, forms of employee involvement, culture change – and many of the articles were by practitioners who were storming the citadels of academia (see, for example, Griffiths 1990; Yeandle and Clark 1989).

Systematic evidence of the take-up of HRM initiatives, however, remained limited. For example, Storey (1992) found that, while there was widespread experimentation with HRM initiatives in mainstream organizations in both the private and public sectors, there was much less evidence of integration and coherence. Survey evidence was also equivocal (Millward et al. 1992); it remained uncertain whether only fragments of HRM had been found because the WIRS3 survey did not explore a sufficiently broad agenda to capture the emergence of HRM or whether its results truly reflected the uneven development of HRM (Sisson 1993). Intriguingly, however, it emerged that only a fraction of personnel specialists had incorporated 'human resources' into their title and HRM practices were more likely to be found in unionized than non-unionized workplaces.

Sharp differences also emerged as to whether HRM was predominantly a 'soft' phenomenon which broadly followed Guest's high-commitment model or whether a harder cost minimization variant was dominant. There was a growing concern, strongly expressed in the second edition of this book (Sisson 1994a: 15; see also Legge 1995) that 'hard' HRM was being wrapped in the language of the 'soft' version as a means to manipulate and control the workforce. Workers' acquiescence arose less from the potency of these techniques and more from the changing balance of power at the workplace in which management was in the ascendancy against a backcloth of high levels of unemployment and fears about job security. The broader ramifications of the preoccupation of industrial relations researchers with HRM also troubled some commentators. They feared that HRM was an ideological and managerialist project which had no truck with trade unions and which aimed to bury the realities of the conflictual nature of the employment relationship (Hyman 1998: 190; Kelly 1998: 131).

By the late 1990s HRM had become increasingly tarnished. Critically, even if it had long been recognized that many organizations were not pursuing a high-commitment model, the assumption seemed to be that this reflected a failure of managerial will rather than anything more fundamental. As the decade progressed there was more acceptance of the argument put forward by Kochan and Dyer (1992: 1) in the USA and Sisson (1994a: 11–12; 43–4) in the UK that this was better explained in terms of the institutional and organizational constraints on the capacity of even the most senior executives to exercise unfettered strategic choice (see, for example, Cappelli et al. 1997; Bach 1999).

Other nostrums which came to be questioned included the emphasis on individualism. This sat especially uneasily with the growing importance attached to teamwork and social partnership (chapters 14 and 15). Individual performance related pay was subject to critical scrutiny and was continually found wanting (chapter 11). Similar difficulties arose with the push towards flexibility with a recognition that too great a pursuit of flexibility could stifle innovation; the shift away from formalized career structures could prove damaging (chapter 9); and the learning organization had a hollow ring to it (chapter 7). More generally, managers as well as employees became worn down and cynical about the continual restructuring, downsizing, sub-contracting, work intensification, long hours and contract culture that they were expected to endure. This appeared to be a far cry from the high-commitment model that was promised but rarely delivered. The world seemed far more complicated than the proponents of HRM were ready to admit and the assumed shift from hierarchies to markets, collectivism to individualism and control to commitment was less apparent than the simple dualism of HRM prescription suggested.

Again with the virtue of hindsight, it might be said that HRM emerged during a particular historical conjuncture and its sentiments were the managerial version of Mrs Thatcher's dictum that 'there is no such thing as society'. The cataclysmic electoral defeat of the Conservatives in May 1997 after 18 continuous years in office may not have denoted a wholesale rejection of deregulation, contract culture and anti-collectivism of this period, but it did bring the language of fairness, social partnership and greater engagement with the European Union to the fore.

So as the ebb tide of HRM recedes, can anything be salvaged? Several of the underlying ideas associated with HRM remain central to understanding developments in personnel management, despite the waning interest in specific techniques. Even if at times they were overblown, some of the preoccupations of HRM did reflect the changing context of employment. As we demonstrate below, much of the interest in performance-related pay, psychological contracts and the like reflected the increasing concentration on the role of managers both in terms of their responsibility for personnel practice and as employees. Senior managers recognized that managerial loyalty and performance could not be taken for granted, and had to be rewarded and controlled in similar ways to that of other staff.

Yet perhaps the most important legacy bequeathed by HRM has been a growing awareness of the links between the effective management of people and competitiveness. In one sense this is not novel. There have been numerous attempts to link personnel policies to business strategy before, but these models – whether concerned with the fit between different competitive strategies and personnel practice (Schuler and Jackson 1987) or the organization's stage of growth or market position (Miles and Snow 1984) – are based on personnel policies following business strategy. In Purcell's (1989) terms, personnel practices are 'downstream' decisions with all the attendant problems which can arise when the personnel consequences of business decisions are not sufficiently thought through, as many cases illustrate (see Clark 1995). In addition, these approaches have an overly rationalist view of strategy formulation and, by concentrating on the development of strategy, give insufficient attention to the implementation of these ideas, which frequently have a more lasting impact on performance than finding the 'right' answer (Pfeffer 1998: 14).

In contrast to these 'matching models', as they are often termed, the appeal of the core competencies literature discussed earlier is that, instead of personnel policies following in the wake of other business decisions and stemming from external circumstances, personnel considerations are elevated to become the primary concern of senior managers. Thus firms have tried to identify their core competencies. It is to this assumed link between specific bundles of high performance personnel policies and firm performance that much attention is increasingly focused. This represents a direct legacy of HRM and the suggestion by Guest (1989) that what marked out HRM from personnel management was not the pursuit of a strategic approach *per se*, but the particular 'fit' of personnel policies. The 'bundles' debate, as it has been termed, is ambitious in attempting to demonstrate not simply the business case for particular policies, but also the overall business case for 'managing people right'.

A series of influential studies across a number of industries have used a variety of measures of employee skills and motivation to suggest that there is a direct, measurable and positive link between personnel practices, firm performance and profitability (Arthur 1994; Huselid 1995; Ichinowski et al. 1996; Becker and Huselid 1998). This view has been enthusiastically endorsed by other high-profile commentators (Pfeffer 1998) even if caution is required because of the complexities of the linkages involved and high performance is defined largely in financial terms (Guest 1997).

Research findings are not confined to the USA. In the UK a positive link between the satisfaction of the workforce as whole and the organization's productivity and profitability has also been noted (Patterson and West 1998: 2), while the European Foundation's (1997) survey of the role of direct participation in organizational change suggests positive links for ten EU countries including the UK. The influence of this type of research on the policy community is also increasingly evident. The European Commission's Green Paper *Partnership for a New Organization of Work* (CEC 1997) endorses similar sentiments (see below) and the DTI (1998) *Fairness at Work* White Paper in slightly different language argues explicitly for a link between efficiency and social justice. Yet there is a paradox here between the growing recognition of the importance of the management of people for enterprise and national performance and the actual practice of personnel practice. As Pfeffer (1998) argues:

> Something very strange is occurring in organizational management. Over the past decade (numerous studies) have demonstrated the enormous economic returns obtained through the implementation of what are variously called high involvement, high performance, or high commitment management practices . . . But even as these research findings pile up, trends in actual management practice are, in many instances, moving in a direction exactly *opposite* to what this growing body of evidence prescribes . . . firms have sought solutions to competitive challenges in places and means that are not very productive – treating their businesses as portfolios of assets to be brought and sold in an effort to find the right competitive niche, downsizing and outsourcing in a futile attempt to shrink or transact their way to profit, and doing a myriad of things that weaken and destroy their organizational culture in efforts to minimize labour costs – even as they repeatedly proclaim that 'employees are our most important asset' (xv–xvi).

It is this gap between policy and practice which has continued to ensure that personnel specialists confront an ambiguous position within organizations. It is not the only source of ambiguity, however. Many of the underlying ambiguities of the role of personnel specialists remain and serve to weaken any move towards a more strategic approach.

Personnel management and ambiguity

Even though specialist personnel managers are to be found in only a minority of UK workplaces (around 17 per cent according to the 1990 WIRS (Millward et al. 1992: 27–38), their position has been pivotal to the conception of the function as a whole. From their origins in welfare work, personnel specialists have acquired a range of tasks including industrial relations, human resource planning and management development activities whose importance has shifted over time, reflecting changing economic and legal circumstances as well as managerial priorities (Hall and Torrington 1998). Yet personnel specialists in the UK have never seemed to be able to escape a preoccupation with the 'management of ambiguity' (Tyson and Fell 1986: 62–6) thereby undermining their capacity to contribute to the development of a more strategic approach.

Much of the ambiguity is implicit in the nature of personnel activities. Personnel management combines both operational and strategic dimensions. Not only is there a very wide range of activities – recruitment and selection, training and development, and appraisal and reward, to mention only the most obvious – but also a considerable number of detailed operations in each case. Much of this can be devolved to line managers, but the personnel manager is still expected to be the expert. Indeed, it is only by establishing expertise in operational matters that the personnel specialist is able to persuade senior managers that they have the capability to make a strategic contribution. The danger, of course, is that the more they are involved in operational matters the less they are associated with the strategic dimension.

The range of activities is reflected in the position of personnel specialists in managerial hierarchies. Personnel managers, far from being a single homogenous occupation, are involved in a variety of roles and activities which differ from one organization to another and, perhaps even more importantly, from one level to another in the same organization. One typology (Tyson and Fell 1986: 21–7) sees the range extending from 'clerks', who make up the majority and who are involved in basic operational matters to 'contract managers' who, are responsible for pay and, where appropriate, negotiations with trade unions to a small number of 'architects' at the pinnacle who are likely to be intimately involved in policymaking as a member of the senior management team and/or with a seat on the board of directors.

According to the 1992 CLIRS2, specialist personnel representation at board level was present in only 30 per cent of UK-owned companies (for further details, see Sisson 1994b). Though the significance of board representation has been questioned, along with a recognition of the importance of more informal sources of 'corridor power', Hall and Torrington 1998: 114), the CLIRS2 data none the less suggest companies with a main board personnel director were more likely, according to both personnel and financial respondents, to take personnel matters into account in strategic business decisions as well as to exhibit a number of other indices of strategic activity, such as personnel policy committees, regular meetings of personnel managers from business units and involvement in management development (Sisson 1994b; Purcell 1995: 78–9).

A second source of ambiguity stems from the role of personnel specialists in managing the inherent tensions within the employment relationship. Personnel specialists are required to establish a framework to direct and control labour, whilst mobilizing the discretion and initiative of employees which may be stifled by coercive supervision. Personnel specialists therefore face a continual dilemma because, as Hyman (1987: 42) notes, 'solutions to the problem of discipline aggravate the problem of consent, and vice versa'. These difficulties are exacerbated by the indeterminacy of the employment relationship: personnel practice cannot be fully specified and personnel specialists are required to enforce a set of employee obligations which may only be partially recognized by the workforce and other managers.

This is linked to a third source of ambiguity. Personnel specialists act in an advisory capacity and their authority is both mediated and limited by the actions of line managers who may not share the same aims and priorities. For example, the emphasis the personnel specialist may put on consistent and standardized rules to reduce the ambiguities of the employment relationship and ensure procedural fairness can appear to line managers to be unnecessary interference limiting their discretion. Moreover, because managing people is an element of every manager's job, the distinct 'people' expertise of personnel specialists can be easily discounted, especially as the outcomes of much personnel activity is difficult to quantify. Moves to measure the effectiveness of the personnel function can help to raise its standing and ensure that their priorities are more closely aligned to organizational objectives (IDS 1997: 2). However, conforming to the dominant organizational agenda can also result in the personnel function supporting the same short-term financially driven agenda at the expense of developing a more strategic approach.

A recent development adding to the complexity of relationships is the devolution of personnel responsibilities to line managers (Bach 1999: 185–90; Hall and Torrington 1998; Hope-Hailey et al. 1997). In theory, this gives line managers greater influence over personnel decisions while allowing specialists to concentrate on more strategic concerns. In practice, it has proved difficult to devolve a clearly defined workload to line managers (Hope-Hailey et al. 1997: 15; Hall and Torrington 1998: 52). For example, in civil service agencies, line managers are expected to play their role in staff selection and development by cultivating a learning culture, providing appropriate feedback and ensuring effective communication of the business plan, so that employees are aware of their contribution to the organization (Cm 3321 1996: 42). Yet line managers are viewed as much less influential than personnel specialists even in relation to these targeted activities (Development Division 1997: 12).

Personnel specialists, it seems, are not necessarily willing to abandon their operational role, especially as devolution increases the difficulties of measuring their contribution and may increase tensions with line managers. Line managers, while supporting devolution in principle, may be unwilling to undertake enhanced people management responsibilities, especially if they are uncertain they will get the necessary training and support (Development Division 1997: 23; Hall and Torrington 1998: 49). More positively, line managers have suggested that the contribution of personnel specialists has been enhanced when they are more focused on the requirements of individual business units. However, as a later section argues in more detail, too great an emphasis on the freedom of individual business units can create tensions, for example in the area of management development where it may be unclear whether managers are a corporate or unit resource, making it even more difficult to develop a strategic approach.

A fourth source of ambiguity has been attributed to the gender bias of personnel management. Women make up the bulk of personnel specialists, but are disproportionately represented in more junior jobs and categories of IPD membership (Gooch and Ledwith 1996: 112). The terminology used to describe routine personnel management roles such as 'handmaidens' and 'clerk of works' have low status connotations as does the general label 'Cinderella function'. Even HRM has been seen as a 'male' phenomenon in its attempt to escape the welfare strait jacket of personnel management (Townley 1994: 16) and it is not self-evident that the shift to HRM represents a more positive employment agenda for women (Dickens 1998). For example, Lewis and Taylor (1996: 121–2) found that family-friendly policies foundered within a large accountancy firm because the dominant male values of demonstrating commitment by working long hours had a corrosive effect on those individuals who worked shorter hours to ensure a better balance between work and family commitments.

Anticipating the argument of the next section, most of the changes discussed below have increased the ambiguities inherent in the job of personnel specialists as well as the tensions in the employment relationship, making it even more difficult to develop a strategic approach. The personnel function itself has been directly affected by the process of marketization as the traditional department is increasingly regarded as only one possibility of delivery (Adams 1991). The intensity of restructuring and merger activity and the increase in non-standard employment have increased perceptions of job insecurity. Managers themselves face fewer promotion opportunities and an intensification of controls over their work performance (Gallie et al. 1998). Waves of change management and quality improvement measures at ever-shorter intervals have given rise to 'initiative fatigue' and contributed to increased levels of employee and managerial cynicism (Dean et al. 1998; Doyle et al. 1997). Against this background, personnel specialists face an especially difficult task in maintaining their credibility with fellow managers and employees because they are implicated in many of these changes and frequently have to tell them that they are surplus to requirements. It is little wonder therefore that in some organizations HRM has been retitled 'human remains management'.

Summary

The coming of HRM promised a new dawn for personnel management in the UK. Not only was it extremely optimistic. Here was a model that also appeared to be able to meet the demand for economic efficiency and make a significant contribution to improving the quality of working life. No less important, the stress on the significance of the management of human resources to the competitive advantage of the organization appeared to give the personnel function the strategic dimension and status which so many commentators had been seeking, together with the means to achieve it by devolving responsibilities to line managers and demonstrating a measurable contribution to business performance.

In the event, proponents considerably underestimated the will and ability of senior managers to make the necessary changes. The UK's business system, with its overriding emphasis on short-term profitability, could hardly have been more hostile; while the ever-intensifying competition, far from driving firms up market, encouraged many simply to reduce their cost base through restructuring. Personnel managers, who continued to bear significant operational responsibilities, found themselves spending most of their time handling redundancies rather than fulfilling the dreams of the HRM agenda.

Even so, it can be argued, HRM has left an indelible mark. It is not just that HRM, in the sense of a particular model, remains as a guide to best practice, however unrealistic it may be. There is widespread appreciation that personnel management has to have a strategic as well as an operational dimension. In particular, there is a greater understanding of the importance of the need for coherence and integration of personnel policies and practices. This does not necessarily mean that senior managers will always act accordingly. Short-term pressures, both financial and operational, will continue to take their toll. At least, however, there is a glimmer of an understanding of what can be done given the will.

The Practice of Personnel Management: Restructuring rather than Redesign?

Our focus now turns to the practice of personnel management. As previous sections have pointed out, the direction of personnel management dominated debate in the 1980s and 1990s. Initially, it took the form of a comparison of HRM with personnel management. Subsequently, the focus shifted to the nature and extent of the changes taking place: whether their diffusion was as widespread as some pundits proclaimed; whether the changes taking place were better understood in terms of 'hard' or 'soft' approaches;

whether they represented a paradigm shift in management thinking or simply reflected the changing balance of power. Perhaps inevitably, the debate sometimes resembled the discussion about whether the glass was half full or half empty.

As the millennium approaches, the position looks much clearer. There have most certainly been fundamental changes in the practice of personnel management making it possible to talk in terms of a restructuring of employment relations. The most fundamental change has been the decline in joint regulation by collective bargaining. According to the First Findings of the 1998 WERS (Cully et al. 1998: 28), union recognition had fallen from 66 per cent in 1984 to 53 per cent in 1990; between 1990 and 1998 it fell a further eight points to 45 per cent. Meanwhile, the proportion of workplaces with no union members increased from 27 per cent in 1984 to 36 per cent in 1990 to 47 per cent in 1998. In the words of the authors of the First Findings (Cully et al. 1998: 28), 'This signals, clearly, a transformation in the landscape of British employment relations, particularly when con- trasted with the relative stability and continuity that has characterized the system for much of the post-war period'. There are no signs, either, that other forms of indirect or representative participation have taken their place. Only 28 per cent of workplaces had a joint consultative committee in 1998, which is the same as in 1990.

A second major change is the growth in the different forms of so-called atypical or non- standard forms of employment. Figure 1.1, which also comes from the First Findings of the 1998 WERS, gives a good overview. Most obvious is the growth in part-time work. Part- time employees account for around a quarter of the workforce and they make up the majority of the workforce in a similar proportion of the workplaces. Significantly, this figure is up from 16 per cent in 1990 (Cully et al. 1998: 6).

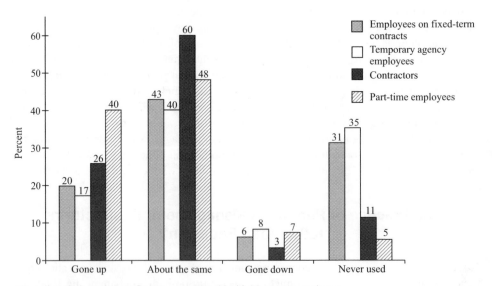

Base: all workplaces that are five or more years old with 25 or more employees
Figures are weighted and based on responses from 1,706 managers.

Figure 1.1   Change in the use of different forms of labour over the past five years

Source: Cully et al. 1998

For the most part, however, these changes have rarely been the result of conscious management decisions about managing employment relations, let alone their redesign. Indeed, the overriding impression that comes through from the both the case study and the survey evidence is of massive diversity, with little evidence of the take-up of some of the most basic of practices in many workplaces. As well as long-standing features of the UK business systems, two sets of circumstances are important in making sense of what has been happening: the changes in the patterns of employment and the developments in business strategies and structures which underpin them. Our task in this section is to expand on these seemingly bold conclusions.

The evidence for redesign

It is not difficult to find evidence of the redesign of personnel management. The personnel and management media offer a never-ending stream of cases for our digestion. Typically, however, they take the form of the presentation of so-called leading-edge thinking arising from the experience of one of the world's large multinational companies at one moment in time, or a development in Silicon Valley or somewhere equally remote. The problem with this type of literature, which takes us back to the discussion of the prescriptive tradition earlier, is not that advice is proffered or thought stimulated; rather that it can give a very false impression of what is happening in the vast majority of workplaces.

This is where the coming of surveys to personnel management has made its mark. They enable us to understand much better this general picture. Here the evidence from First Findings of the 1998 WERS about so-called 'new' management practices is extremely illuminating. The details are shown in table 1.2, grouped according to four main areas of activity: appraisal and reward, involvement and participation, training and development, and status and security. Although many of these practices are not new, as the team rightly point out, they have none the less come to be associated with change and offer the most robust set of data with which to make our points.

In the case of appraisal and reward, it will be seen that just over a half of non-managerial employees have some form of appraisal. Only one in ten of these employees has individual performance pay, however, raising major question marks about the amount of attention such arrangements have received in the prescriptive literature. More enjoy the benefits of share ownership (one in seven) and profit sharing (one in three), but they remain very much a minority.

In the case of involvement and participation, the signs of activity are greater. Thus, 37 per cent of workplaces reported regular meetings, 42 per cent said they had some kind of problem-solving group such as a quality circle and 45 per cent that they had used staff attitude surveys. Even so, this stills means that less than half of workplaces were affected. Only team briefing, with 61 per cent affected, was practised in a majority of workplaces.

The 1998 WERS First Findings also gives us a snapshot of the incidence of teamwork, which has figured prominently in models of changed practice. At first sight, the evidence for the incidence of teamwork looks pretty strong, as it did in the European Foundation's (1997) ten EU member country survey. Around two-thirds of workplaces (65 per cent) in the WERS reported that employees worked in formally designated teams. As in the case of the European Foundation's survey, however, only a handful (5 per cent of those with

Table 1.2 Percentage of workplaces using 'new' management practices and employee involvement schemes

Appraisal and reward

Most non-managerial employees have performance formally appraised	56
Individual PRP scheme for non-managerial employees	11
Employee share ownership scheme for non-managerial employees	15
Profit-sharing scheme operated for non-managerial employees	30

Involvement and participation

Workplace level joint consultative committee	28
Regular meetings of entire workforce	37
Problem-solving groups (e.g. quality circles)	42
Staff attitude survey conducted in last five years	45
Workplace operates a system of team briefing for groups of employees	61
Most employees work in formally designated teams	65

Training and development

Most employees receive minimum of five days training a year	12
Most supervisors trained in employee relations skills	27

Status and security

Guaranteed job security or no compulsory redundancy policy	14
'Single status' between managers and non-managerial employees	41
Workplace operates a just-in-time system of inventory control	29
Attitudinal test before making appointments	22

Base: all workplaces with 25 or more employees
Figures are weighted and based on response from 1,926 managers

Source: Cully et al. 1998: table 4

teams) had something resembling the semi-autonomous teamworking which has come to be regarded as the leitmotiv of new forms of work organization (see, for example, the review of the literature in Fröhlich and Pekruhl 1996: 79), i.e., respondents said team members had to work together, had responsibility for specific products or services, jointly decided how work was to be done, and appointed their own teams leaders. If, in Peters' (1987: 302–3) uncompromising words, 'the only possible implementers' of a strategy of quality production are 'committed, flexible, multiskilled, constantly re-trained people, joined together in self-managed teams', the UK clearly has a very long way to go.

Our next dimension is training and development. Here too the evidence is hardly supportive of a major shift. Despite the widespread importance attached to training by the Government, only 12 per cent reported that most employees received a minimum of five days training per year. Perhaps even more surprising is that only 27 per cent reported that most supervisors were trained in employee relations skills. Such skills have been found to be strongly correlated with both the more advanced forms of involvement and participation and with the estimated success of these schemes more generally (see, for example, European Foundation, 1997: 175–86).

The final cluster to be considered involves status and security. Here it will be seen from table 1.2 that less than half of workplaces (41 per cent) had single status arrangements between managerial and non-managerial employees and only 14 per cent guaranteed job security or had no compulsory redundancy policy.

Details of the combinations of practices are also illuminating (Cully et al. 1998: 11). There is some evidence of practices going together, the authors find, suggesting the development of a more strategic approach in the sense of the integration or 'bundling' of practices. Training, teamworking and supervisor training go together, as do individual performance pay, profit sharing and share ownership. Single status is associated with the first cluster but not the second, however, suggesting that direct participation and financial participation are seen as alternatives rather than complementary as might have been expected.

Perhaps even more telling, though, are the figures for the total number of practices. The practices listed, it hardly needs emphasizing, are far from being revolutionary. Indeed, most personnel texts assume them to be standard in today's workplace. Moreover, the figures also measure incidence only and not scope; as in the case of teamworking discussed above, therefore, they might be thought to exaggerate the significance. In the circumstances, the finding that only one in five (20 per cent) had half or more of the 16 practices and only one in 50 (2 per cent) had more than ten is a salutary reminder of the state of personnel management in most workplaces.

In themselves, these findings may elicit no more than a shrug of the shoulders. Crucially, however, as indicated earlier, it looks as if the 1998 WERS findings will also provide further evidence, to add to that available for the USA (see, for example, Becker and Huselid 1998; Osterman 1992; 1998; Pil and MacDuffie 1996) and Europe more generally (see European Foundation 1997) establishing a positive link between the adoption of these 'new' practices and performance. In the words of the team responsible for the 1998 WERS First Findings (Cully et al. 1998: 25), 'workplaces with a high number of "new" management practices were substantially more likely to report high productivity growth'.

The significance of the changing patterns of employment

Our attention now turns to the two sets of considerations which help to put both the changes in and diversity of personnel management practice into relief. The first of these is the changing patterns of employment. These patterns are many and varied, but four stand out: the ongoing shift from manufacturing to services; the shrinking size of workplaces; the polarization of the occupational structure; and the feminization of the workforce.

As the first column in table 1.3 confirms, the UK is very much a service economy: less than one in five workplaces are in manufacturing. The changing balance between public and private services also comes through: for example, a significant proportion of employees in health are now in the private sector. The composition of the workforce, column 3 suggests, is also critically affected. Part-time working is much less prevalent in manufacturing, whereas it is the predominant pattern in sectors such as hotels and restaurants. Levels of pay and productivity are also related to sector as columns 5 and 6 clearly show. Not only do sectors such as hotels and restaurants have the largest proportions of workplaces with employees earning less than £3.50 per hour, they also are characterized by some of the lowest levels of productivity.

Table 1.3 The significance of sector

	Distribution of workplaces by sector (%)	Workplaces with no part-time employees (%)	Workplaces with most employees part-time (%)	Low paying workplaces (%)	High productivity growth workplaces (%)
Manufacturing	18	36	1	5	34
Electricity, gas, water	–	51	0	0	55
Construction	4	39	0	1	49
Wholesale and retail	18	14	43	8	51
Hotels and restaurants	6	3	55	48	29
Transport and communications	5	23	4	0	60
Financial services	3	20	5	0	62
Other business services	9	23	7	10	34
Public administration	6	9	1	0	42
Education	14	0	40	2	42
Health	13	1	50	17	34
Other community services	4	8	51	19	23
All workplaces	100	16	26	9	41

Base: all workplaces with 25 or more employees, except column 5, where it is all workplaces five or more years old with 25 employees

Figures are weighted and based on responses from 1,929 managers for column 1, 1,914 for columns 2 and 3, 1,890 for column 4 and 1,668 for column 5

Source: Cully et al. 1998: tables 1 and 10

The First Findings of the 1998 WERS do not give us a breakdown of union membership by sector. Fortunately a recent analysis of the Labour Force Survey data does (Cully and Woodland 1998). It shows that the decline of manufacturing and the shift to services have been associated with the decline of union recognition and collective bargaining.

One of the developments which the shift from manufacturing to services has contributed to is a shrinkage in the size of workplaces, which is the second dimension deserving our attention. A strong impression of the significance of the size of workplaces comes from table 1.4. Column 1 confirms the long-standing association between union membership and the size of workplace. Other things being equal, the larger the workplace the more likely collective bargaining and vice versa. In addition, more than twice as many smaller workplaces had a quarter of employees earning less than £3.50 an hour as opposed to 9 per cent in the case of larger ones. Productivity growth was also less (33 per cent against 42 per cent, 50 per cent and 56 per cent for workplaces with 100 to 199 employees, 200 to 499 employees and 500 or more employees respectively).

Smaller workplaces, it also emerges, are less likely to have the 'new' employment practices discussed in the previous section. The proportion with no practices (8 per cent) was four times that of larger workplaces, while the number with five or more (28 per cent) was only about half as many (Cully et al. 1998: 26).

Table 1.4   The significance of workforce size

Workplace size	Union density: % of employees who are members	Any union members: % of workplaces	Union recognition: % of workplaces	Low paying workplaces (%)	High productivity growth workplaces (%)
25–49	23	46	39	12	40
50–99	27	52	41	8	38
100–199	32	66	57	6	42
200–499	38	77	67	4	50
500 or more	48	86	78	2	56
All workplaces	36	53	45	9	41

Base for columns 1–4: all workplaces with 25 or more employees; for column 5 all workplaces five or
   more years old with 25 employees
Figures are weighted and based on responses from 1,889 managers for columns 1–3; 1,890 for
   column 4 and 1,668 for column 5

Source: Cully et al. 1998: tables 7 and 10

The occupational structure of the workforce, our third dimension, has also altered markedly. The First Findings of the 1998 WERS do not provide a breakdown by occupation, but data from LFS in table 1.5 are instructive. They show that blue-collar workers in manufacturing represent a dwindling minority as manufacturing shrinks. The largest single groups are managers and administrators (4,306,000) followed by clerical (4,096,000). The two groups of professional and professional and technical amount to 5,517,000, whereas craft and related accounts for 3,370,000. More people are employed in personnel and productive services (2,986,000) than are plant and machine operators (2,589,000).

Arguably, the main divide is no longer between blue collar and white collar but between managerial and professional groups, on the one hand, and non-managerial employees on the other. Much of the interest and target of HRM, it can be argued, is the managerial and professional group. Significantly, for example, the focus of many of the WERS questions is implicit recognition of this: managers are expected to be subject to individual performance pay, appraisal, a special status and security, whereas for other employees it is more of an open question. Surprising as it may seem, occupation is not so relevant so far as membership of trade unions is concerned (see column 2 of table 1.5). Crucially important, however, is the pattern of regulation: even if they are members of trade unions and/or professional organizations, managers and professional employees are typically covered by individual contracts rather than by collective agreements.

The fourth and final dimension to be considered is gender. The growth in the proportion of women in the labour force reflects the shifts in sector and occupation discussed above. As is clear from table 1.6, the distribution remains skewed. Manufacturing and construction have relatively few women, whereas sectors such as retail or hotels have most workplaces with a preponderance of women.

In terms of its implications for personnel management, the most critical variable is working time. Nearly half the women in work do so part time. Other studies (see, for

Table 1.5   The significance of occupation

	Employment (%)	Union membership (%)
Managers and administrators	16	20
Professional	10	50
Associated professional and technical	10	46
Clerical	15	25
Craft and related	12	34
Personal and protective services	11	28
Sales	8	9
Plant and machine operators	9	38
Others	8	26

Source: column 1 *Labour Market Trends*, November 1998; column 2 *Labour Market Trends*, July 1998

Table 1.6   Workplaces by gender

	Workplaces largely male: > 75% male	Workplaces largely female > 75% female	Workplaces mixed (%)
Private sector	32	22	46
Public sector	14	49	37

Base: all workplaces with 25 or more employees
Figures are weighted and based on responses from 1,914 managers

Source: Cully et al. 1998: figure 2

example, the review in Gallie et al. 1998) tend to confirm that training and development opportunities are less for part-time employees as are pay levels and other benefits.

To summarize, there have been fundamental and interrelated changes in the patterns of employment which help to explain much of both the restructuring and diversity of personnel management which is to be observed in the UK. The decline of joint regulation, for example, can be associated with the reduction in the manufacturing workforce, along with highly unionized sectors such as coal, and a shrinking in the size of workplaces more generally. The growth in part-time work and the feminization of the workforce reflects the expansion in the service sector. The growing interest in HRM can be related, above all, to the increasing proportion of managers and professional workers in the workforce.

Yet it would be wrong to read off the practice of personnel management from a single set of structural variables. There are a number of cross-cutting dimensions which other reports, such as The *Employment in Britain Survey* (Gallie et al. 1998), suggest are contributing to the enormous diversity of practice. Take training, development and security, for example. A part-time female employee of one of the large retail chains might be expected to enjoy greater *de facto* security and training and development opportunities than her counterpart in a small family-owned store. Less expectedly, the same is likely to be true of the comparison with male full-time employees in some sectors of manufacturing or protection services; it may even be true of managers in these sectors. Much depends on the business systems, strategy and structure of employing organizations.

The significance of changing business strategies and structures

Underpinning the changes in both the practice of personnel management and the patterns of employment are specific business systems, strategies and structures. It is not just that those running organizations facing very different competitive considerations might be expected to take a different approach to personnel management. As a report from the Government of Canada and OECD (1997: 15–17) infers, there are good reasons for expecting the adoption of 'new' forms of work organization to be the exception rather than the rule. Such change can be seen as a form of investment in intangibles and so presents two major problems. One is that intangible investments are difficult to measure and therefore justify. The other, the so-called externality problem, is that organizations cannot guarantee that they will capture the returns made on intangible investments. For example, performance-enhancing organizational innovations require up-front training investments of both a general and firm-specific nature, which enterprises risk losing if employees leave before the returns can be captured. As the recent literature on innovation (see, for example, Pil and MacDuffie 1996) reminds us, because performance is initially likely to be worse with the new practices than the old, there is a strong temptation to prefer the incremental path to change, with the danger that individual practices are tried and rejected because they appear to be unsuccessful in themselves. In the circumstances, it is not surprising that many of the well-publicized cases of the introduction of new forms of work organization turn out to involve either green-field operations or a crisis situation.

The 1980s and 1990s also saw major changes in business strategies and structures, reflecting the underlying features of the UK's business system outlined earlier, which are important in understanding the patterns described in the two previous sections (for further details, see Sisson 1995). In the case of what might be termed the 'external face' of organizations there were considerable changes in the portfolio of many companies. For example, the second Company Level Industrial Relations Survey (CLIRS) found that, over the five years until 1992, more than two-thirds of companies with more than 1,000 employees in the UK reported cases of merger and acquisition and a similar number investment in new locations. Almost the same number, however, reported the closure of existing sites, nearly half divestment and 40 per cent the run-down of existing sites. Many of these changes were also associated with each other. Thus, the authors found that nearly three-quarters of the companies reported both growth and closure or run-down with 20 per cent citing growth only and eight per cent neither (Marginson et al. 1995: 20).

A second significant change is the growing internationalization of the UK economy. In the preparatory work for CLIRS in 1992, 975 companies were identified as having more than a 1,000 employees in the UK. Of these, 759 were UK owned and 216 overseas owned. Of the UK-owned companies, almost half (360) were themselves multinational including about one-third of the companies, discussed below, that had been privatized since 1979 (Marginson et al. 1995: 4; 20). Overall, then, almost seven out of ten large companies in the UK were multinational.

A third major change, externalization, involves the subcontracting of activities prev- iously performed inside the organization. This is closely associated in many people's minds with privatization and programmes of compulsory competitive tendering. As figure

1.1 has already confirmed, however, such developments are widespread and reflect the conventional wisdom that management should focus on its core activities, allowing much greater play for the market in areas of so-called ancillary services such as catering, cleaning and distribution.

There have also been significant changes on the inside of organizations, reflecting the revolution in information processing facilities. One, divisionalization, involves the break-up of the large-scale hierarchical organization into a number of semi-autonomous or quasi businesses responsible for most, if not all, activities within their jurisdiction. Examples include teams working under cellular manufacturing, executive agencies and trusts in the case of public services, the break-up of major companies such as Courtaulds and ICI into separate and independent organizations and, in the case of MNCs, the coming of inter-national product or service divisions with responsibility for individual products or related products either on a European or worldwide basis. The second, budgetary devolution, involves the allocation of responsibility for managing activities within financial resources or targets to the lowest possible unit within the organization. A third development is a variant of the externalization discussed in the previous section. It involves seeing the organization as an internal market in which services are traded between purchasers and providers to ensure that different groups are more responsive to the needs of each other and that activities are cost effective. The NHS, which has been split into purchaser health author-ities and provider trusts, is the extreme example.

Both these external and internal changes are profoundly important in understanding why there has been a restructuring, but little redesign, of employment relations in the UK. For example, at the same time as the changing portfolios have reinforced many of the implications of the business system they have also led to shifts out of manufacturing and reductions in the size of many organizations as the result of divestment and externalization. Many more workplaces in the UK compete for investment within the multinational companies' internal market at the same time as they have to justify retaining activities in house through market testing. Meanwhile, divisionalization, devolved budgeting and internal markets have emphasized the importance of management by financial perform-ance. In the words of McKinsey (1988), the management consultants, discussing develop-ments in the electronics sector:

> Decentralisation to small units has limited the scale of ambition to that of the units rather than the company as a whole. 'Numbers driven' rather than 'issue driven' planning has reinforced a focus on short term results rather than long term investment to create major new businesses. The limited role of the centre in many UK companies has meant that the potential synergies and scale benefits of a large company – in creating a customer franchise, in product development and in attracting and developing highly talented management – have not been achieved (49).

Coupled with the changing patterns of employment described in the previous section, these developments have also made a significant contribution to the diversity of personnel management practice. For example, developments such as the externalization of activities, divisionalization and budgetary devolution have combined to encourage the fragmenta-tion of employment systems, leaving managers to cope in a contingent fashion in the best way they can. Critically, too, developments in the public sector mean that it no longer has the function of the model or 'good employer'.

Most fundamentally, the sheer pace and extent of the change in business portfolios has been a consideration in its own right. It has not only produced massive insecurity on the part of managers and employees alike, which is inimical to developing the long-term relationships of the HRM model, it has also made it very difficult to develop a consistency in approach of almost any kind. Indeed, organizations are littered with half-finished initiatives which have had to be interrupted because of takeover or merger or change of business direction or divestment, leading to considerable cynicism not only on the part of employees but the senior managers who are supposed to be implementing them (see, for example, Storey et al. 1997).

Last, but by no means least, it is also important to remember that the 1980s and early 1990s saw the few countervailing pressures even further reduced. Individual employment rights were whittled away and the role of trade unions curtailed. The Wages Councils which had provided a statutory floor of pay and conditions were also abolished and there was further reduction in the coverage of the multi-employer agreements which had fulfilled a similar function elsewhere. Indeed, such agreements all but disappeared in key sectors such as metalworking. Along with privatization, the decline of sector regulation means that there are few acknowledged standards or benchmarks for organizations to follow.

A Forward Look: the Challenges of Europeanization

Our decision to focus on the challenges of Europeanization in discussing future trends in personnel management practice may come as something of a surprise. Most commentators tend to stress the importance of the pressures of globalization and technological change, above all in terms of the implications of the ongoing need, in the words of the former US Secretary of Labor Robert Reich (1999), for business flexibility and labour agility. In focusing on universal developments, however, the significance of the immediate context tends to be ignored. This is especially dangerous in the case of the UK. It is difficult to escape the conclusion that, for practical purposes, the major challenges European integration poses are likely to be the dominant consideration for the foreseeable future.

The impact of EMU

From the point of view of personnel management, the main challenge that EMU presents arises not so much from the membership decision (for further details, see Sisson et al. 1999): any advantage that the UK might be expected to gain from staying out of EMU, in terms of keeping its relatively low wages and costs, is likely to be offset by worries on the part of investors about continuing transaction costs and the longer-run possibility of goods and services originating in the UK being penalized in the EMU countries. Rather it is that, regardless of membership, the UK is unlikely to escape the significant pressure for restructuring that the greater transparency of prices and costs, coupled with the development of a single capital market, will generate. Indeed, there are strong grounds for suggesting that the pressure in the UK is likely to be greater than in most other countries because of the presence of a large number of MNCs (see below), one of the loosest set of arrangements governing closures, and the relatively low levels of pay and productivity (see, on this point, Cressey 1998).

The automotive sector provides the most extreme case of the use of the 'coercive comparison' which is likely to become an increasing feature. Each of the UK operations of Ford, General Motors (Vauxhall) and BMW (Rover) has been required by headquarters management to make major changes in work organization, as well as redundancies, in order to guarantee investment for the foreseeable future.

The tight controls on public expenditure that EMU brings in the form of the Stability and Growth Pact will maintain the pressure on the Government to keep a firm grip on the public deficit. Indeed, as with restructuring, the change between Conservative and Labour administrations in 1997 has made very little difference. In theory, if the UK stays out of EMU, it will retain the ability to set an independent monetary policy and level of public-sector borrowing. In practice, however, the pressure on the Bank of England's Monetary Policy Committee to take into account, if not necessarily to track, the decisions of the European Central Bank means that the limits on exercising it are likely be enormous.

Equally, it is very difficult to envisage that the UK will be immune to the encouragement that EMU, together with moves towards further economic and political union, will give to the Europeanization of industrial relations. Most obviously, having signed up to the social chapter, the UK will be affected by ongoing developments in the social dimension which are likely to be heavily influenced by the course that EMU takes including, for example, framework agreements at the EU inter-professional level, greater cross-national co-ordination of pay and conditions, though not collective bargaining, at the EU sector and inter-professional levels, and EMU social pacts linking pay moderation to investment in infrastructure to help promote employment.

Also important is that MNCs, as well as being the prime movers in the restructuring that EMU promotes, are likely to be a significant conduit through which policies and practice will flow from Europe into the UK as is already happening in the case of the automotive manufacturers. Greater cross-national co-ordination of pay and conditions, though not collective bargaining, at the Euro-company levels is a possibility. Again, there is an argument for suggesting that the UK will be more affected than other EU countries. As an extremely open economy, the UK is both home and host to a larger number of MNCs than any other EU member country. Significantly, of the 1,400 or so MNCs that will be required to have a European Works Council (EWC), around two-thirds (885 according to the latest figures from the TUC reported in EWCB 1998: 4) have operations in the UK. In the circumstances, it is difficult to envisage that the UK can be immune to the thinking and developments in other EU countries.

The end of voluntarism?

Even more fundamentally, the European connection signals the end of the voluntarism which has characterized UK employment relations for a century. Some idea of the amount of employment legislation recently introduced or about to be introduced which UK management has to come to terms with is shown in table 1.7. It is not just the sheer volume which is important, however. The nature and function of such legislation is critical.

The UK has never been wholly without legal regulation. From the end of the nineteenth century until the 1980s, however, such regulation had for the most part been auxiliary. In other words, legislation was primarily intended to support the voluntary actions of management and trade unions through collective bargaining. In the 1980s voluntarism took the form of support for management unilateralism as UK governments introduced a succession of measures to limit the role of unions and deregulate the labour market more generally. The key distinguishing feature of recent and imminent legislation is that it involves statutory regulation. Standards and entitlements are laid down in law and mechanisms other than collective bargaining, such as employment tribunals and/or the courts, are available to ensure compliance and redress.

A close look at table 1.7 shows that not all such regulation has its origins in Europe, the most obvious examples being the national minimum wage and a number of the provisions of the 1999 *Employment Relations Bill* (most notably those dealing with union recognition). Many of the most significant measures do, however, reflect the much stronger regulatory traditions of both the two main continental European models: the Roman–Germanic, covering the original six members of the European Economic Community, in which the statutory regulation of individual and collective employment relations plays the primary role; and the Nordic under which collective agreements are the central element of the system of regulation but receive statutory backing to give them the force of law (CEC 1989: 8–12).

It is not just a question of replicating national traditions at the EU level, however. There are very specific rationales for the EU social dimension which may be summarized as follows:

- fears about social dumping leading to downward pressure on labour standards as a result of MNCs relocating to low-cost countries;
- worries about a regional division of labour and its implications for EU cohesion;
- a concern to present a human face to the EU which will help to make the projected economic restructuring socially acceptable;
- the promotion of a European model, i.e. high skills, high quality, high technology and high productivity, which compares favourably with the US model of a highly deregulated system with hire and fire and low wage employment strategy.

In any event, the combination of legislation arising from EU initiatives and the Labour Government's domestic commitments adds up to the most far-reaching changes in the regulatory framework since the end of the First World War. Voluntarism, both in terms of the legislative framework and collective bargaining, has encouraged massive informality. It is not just that British management is unused to having to deal with this kind of detail as in, say, the Working Time Regulations. The timing is also critical. UK management is almost simultaneously going to have to deal with the requirements of regulations implementing EU directives on working time, parental leave and equality of treatment for part-time workers at the same time as implementing the NMW and the provisions envisaged in the *Employment Relations Bill*. One thing seems sure. There is going to be an increase in juridification in the sense of the involvement of the law and the courts in personnel management matters.

Table 1.7 Key legislative developments 1990–1999

Measure	Main provisions
Employment Act 1990	Repealed restrictions on employment of women and young people; secondary industrial action unlawful; tighter strike ballot procedures
Trade Union and Labour Relations (Consolidation) Act 1992	Consolidated existing collective and trade union law provisions
Management of Health and Safety at Work Regulations 1992	Required employers to assess risks to health and safety and take into account employees' health and safety capabilities when assigning tasks
Trade Union Reform and Employment Rights Act 1993	Employees' right to written terms extended; pregnancy and maternity rights improved in light of EU Pregnant Workers' Directive; check-off subject to three-yearly written consent; abolition of wages councils; redundancy and business transfer consultation requirements extended; independently scrutinized ballots for industrial action and union mergers
Sunday Trading Act 1994	Employees objecting to Sunday working given some protection
The Race Relations Remedies Act 1994	Abolished the ceiling on compensation in cases of race discrimination
The Deregulation and Contracting Out Act 1994	Made it no longer automatically unfair to select an employee for redundancy in contravention of a customary arrangement
Disability Discrimination Act 1995	Disabled people protected from discrimination in employment and access to goods and services
Collective Redundancies and Transfer of Undertakings (Protection of Employment (Amendment)) Regulations 1995	Extended requirement for information and consultation in the event of collective redundancies and business transfers to non-unionized employees
The Employment Protection (Part-time Employees) Regulations 1995	Part-timers given the same rights as full-time employees in a range of employment protection jurisdictions
The Occupational Pension Schemes (Equal Access to Membership) Amendment Regulations 1995	Sexual discrimination prohibited in occupational pension schemes
Asylum and Immigration Act 1996	Criminal offence to employ someone not having permission to live in UK
Health and Safety (Consultation with Employees) Regulations 1996	Extended requirement for information and consultation to non-unionized employees; Employers in non-union workplaces required to introduce arrangements for information and consultation
Sex Discrimination and Equal Pay (Miscellaneous Amendments) Regulations 1996	Industrial tribunals given power to award damages for unintentional indirect employment discrimination
Employment Rights Act 1996 and Industrial Tribunals Act 1996	Brought together existing employment legislation remaining unconsolidated after Trade Union and Labour Relations (Consolidation) Act 1992 in a more accessible form, taking into account, among others, the Sunday Trading Act 1994 and the Pensions Act 1995

Table 1.7 *Continued*

Protection from Harassment Act 1997	Criminal offence to pursue a course of conduct which amounts to harassment
Employment Rights (Dispute Resolution) Act 1998	Streamlined employment tribunal procedures and promoted alternative methods of resolving disputes including arbitration as a voluntary alternative to employment tribunal hearings
Public Interest Disclosure Act 1998	Known as the 'whistle-blowers' act, introduced protection to individuals raising genuine concerns at work about criminal acts, miscarriages of justice, illegality and danger to health and safety
Data Protection Act 1998	Implemented the EU Data Protection Directive when it comes into force in 1999 regulating the use of personal data held on computers
National Minimum Wage Act 1998	Introduced national minimum wage due to come into force in 1 April 1999 following detailed regulations
Working Time Regulations 1998	Implemented EU Working Time Directive and parts of EU Young Workers' Directive confirming working time as health and safety issue and setting limits on working hours
Human Rights Act 1998	Introduced the European Convention of Human Rights requiring legislation and court decisions to be compatible with convention
Teaching and Higher Education Act 1998	Amended Employment Rights Act 1996 to provide an entitlement for employees aged 16 or 17 to be permitted to take time off for training
The Employment Relations Bill 1999	Proposes a range of individual employment protections plus implementing EU Parental Leave Directive and providing for a statutory union recognition procedure
Transnational Information and Consultation Regulations 1999	Implement EU European Works Council Directive providing for transnational information and consultation arrangements in MNCs with 1,000 + employees in European Economic Area countries and at least 150 in two countries
EU Posted Worker Directive to be implemented December 1999	Covers rights of employees temporarily working in other EU countries
EU Part-time Work Directive to be implemented April 2000	Provides for removal of discrimination against and promotion of part-time work
EU Burden of Proof Directive to be implemented by July 2001	Burden of proof in indirect sex discrimination cases placed on employer
EU Social Partners' agreement on fixed term contracts (likely to become a Directive)	Provides for 'general principles and minimum requirements' regarding employees on fixed-term contracts

Other EU initiatives in pipeline include provisions for information and consultation in national-level undertakings; employee participation in companies registering under proposed European Companies Statute; extension of EU Working Time Directive to previously exempted industries

Source: ACAS Annual Reports, 1990–98

Towards a 'new' European social model?

Perhaps not surprisingly the highly charged debate over signing the social chapter and membership of EMU has tended to blind people to the fact that what has come to be known as the European social model is in the process of being significantly eroded, especially in countries such as Germany and Sweden. The earlier influence of the Roman–Germanic model with its emphasis on legal regulation has increasingly given way to the Nordic model of collective bargaining leading to the Maastricht Agreement on social policy process (for further details, see Hall 1994). Inevitably, the greater the role for collective bargaining and the more countries that have to be included in the net, the greater the need to shift from what the European Commission's 1997 Green Paper (CEC 1997: 14) describes as 'rigid and compulsory systems of statutory regulations to more open and flexible legal frameworks'.

The rationale has also shifted as the list of reasons for a social dimension implies. An increasingly important consideration is to meet the criticisms of the inflexibility of the traditional stereotype compared to the USA, while at the same time building on its strengths to develop competitive advantage (see table 1.8). In language reminiscent of the HRM debate, the European Commission's Green Paper *Partnership for a New Organization of Work* (1997), which is the clearest statement, says it is about

> the scope for improving employment and competitiveness through a better organization of work at the workplace, based on high skill, high trust and high quality. It is about the will and ability of management and workers to take initiatives, to improve the quality of goods and services, to make innovations and to develop the production process and consumer relations.

There is a need, says the Commission, to balance the employer's demand for flexibility with the employee's hopes for security. Equally important, education and training are increasingly seen not only as a way of helping individuals to become more adaptable in their present employment, but also of providing opportunities to acquire knowledge and skills, so that they can find alternative employment should the number of jobs be reduced in their present workplace.

The model, which is summarized in table 1.9, also shares common ground with the early work of Kochan and his colleagues in the USA (Kochan et al. 1986; Kochan and

Table 1.8   Models of HRM/IR: the current stereotypes

	Key features	*Outcomes*
The European model	Strong trade unions	Security
	Collective bargaining	Relatively high pay
	Legal regulation	Inflexibility; lack of competitiveness
	(*Employee rights*)	Unemployment
The US model	Weak trade unions	Insecurity
	Little collective bargaining	Relatively low pay
	Management regulation	Flexibility
	(*Management prerogative*)	Competitiveness
		Employment

Table 1.9 The 'new' European social model

Main ingredients	Outcomes
Flexibility	Quality people
Security	Quality goods and services
Education and training	Competitiveness
Direct participation ('empowerment')	'Good' jobs
Indirect participation ('partnership')	

Osterman 1994) in believing that, far from being mutually exclusive, direct and indirect participation are complementary. The involvement of employees, it is increasingly recognized, especially in semi-autonomous groups, is the key to ensuring continuous improvement. Indirect or representative participation is justified on managerial as well as moral grounds. In the absence of a representative voice, there is a danger that the views of employees are either not expressed, for fear of antagonizing managers, or are simply ignored. Implicit too is the view that the trust which managers espouse depends, above all, on the legitimacy of decisions. In the language of the European Commission's (CEC 1998a: 4) 'Social Action Programme' for 1998–2000 and the final report of the higher level group on the economic and social implications of industrial change (CEC 1998b: 9–10) 'partnership' or 'social dialogue' are seen as a prerequisite for achieving real change. To this end, the Commission is proposing that undertakings with 50 or employees should be required to inform and consult an 'independent and stable employee representative body' over a range of issues including 'changes in work organization and other decisions likely to significantly affect the employees' interests'.

The great attraction of the model is not just that its message is optimistic. Its prescription is apparently able to satisfy hitherto mutually conflicting objectives. For employees, with their long-standing demands for improvements in the quality of working life, it brings the hope of more challenging and rewarding jobs, together with on-going training and development opportunities. For management competing in an increasingly global market, it offers the prospect of ever-increasing levels of productivity, plus the opportunity to exploit sources of competitive advantage other than cost, such as the education and skills of the workforce, to produce high quality goods and services. For governments anxious to demonstrate that the 'third way' is more than rhetoric, it enables a programme of action to be built on the four so-called 'pillars' of: improving employability; developing entrepreneurship; encouraging adaptability in businesses and their employees; and strengthening the policies for equal opportunities.

Also important is that the model brings together the two dominant approaches to managing the employment relationship. It embraces much of the logic and thinking of the HRM model. At the same time, it recognizes the need for collective employee voice on both moral and managerial grounds, which is the essential feature of the collective bargaining or pluralist approach.

Even so, for UK management especially, the model represents a considerable challenge. Implementing the new working practices associated with the so-called 'high road', as the earlier discussion suggested, is going to be especially difficult in the UK. Embracing partnership is also likely to be problematic. The majority of UK workplaces, it needs to be remembered, are without any form of employee representation. Moreover, unlike the rest of Europe, the decline of multi-employer bargaining means there is no longer the scope for a dual system in which collective bargaining takes place outside the workplace between employers' organizations and trade unions, while inside the workplace some form of works council has responsibility for information and consultation.

For the time being, management can take some comfort from the fact that the Government is opposed to the key measure on national level information and consultation which the European Commission is hoping to bring in. Such opposition cannot be guaranteed in the longer run, however. The Government cannot sensibly go on introducing issue-specific employee voice mechanisms; separate arrangements have already been introduced for collective redundancies, health and safety, and working time, with another set to come with the implementation of the European Work Council Directive. In the light of the 1998 WERS findings, that even the most basic of personnel management practices are absent in many workplaces, a second-term Labour Government might see things differently, especially if British management is not seen to be making more serious efforts to improve its competitiveness.

Conclusion and Implications

It is easy to understand why many of our colleagues talk in terms of personnel management being 'in crisis', 'in a black hole', 'in uncharted territory'. Instead of simplicity, there is great complexity. The HRM model which many have seen as offering the new orthodoxy appears to be little more than a dream. It is not just that there is no one best way, however. Even the notion of one best way allowing for specific phases of operation or type of business looks suspect. Managing restructuring is likely to be the dominant on-going activity of personnel managers for the foreseeable future as it has been for the past decade. To complicate matters further, they are not going to have the relatively free hand they have enjoyed in the past. They have to come to terms with a raft of employment legislation and more active policy support for a social model which embraces collective information and consultation.

Against this, it can be argued, along the lines of Torrington (1998), that things were ever thus in the real world of personnel management: it was just that commentators were not as aware of the complexities as they are (or should be) today. More positively, when things are put in perspective, there is a case for suggesting that the study of personnel management emerges in a better state than it ever has been, with each of the three traditions making a valuable and developing contribution to understanding. There is also a widespread appreciation that personnel management has to have a strategic as well as an operational dimension. In particular, there is a greater understanding of the importance of the need for coherence and integration of personnel policies and practices both with one another and with business strategy. The increase in legal regulation will help to keep personnel management high on management's agenda. Public policy support for employability, family-friendly working arrangements and partnership is likely to do the same, helping to supply some of the 'meta standards' that Sparrow and Marchington (1998: 306–9) have called for. For those who find it comforting to have one, there is even a new orthodoxy (dubbed as the new European social model) which neatly combines much of the HRM and collective bargaining or pluralist approaches. Indeed, as the need for greater balance comes to be recognized, it looks as though it could be the decade of flexibility and fairness, security and employability, empowerment and partnership and individualism and collectivism.

There is even a positive side to the practice of personnel management especially relevant to practitioners. Perhaps most fundamental are the implications of the First Findings from the 1998 WERS on the incidence of 'new' working practices and their relationship with productivity growth. Not only do they offer further support for the positive relationship between changes in traditional working arrangements and productivity emerging from other studies. The implication of the findings on incidence is that there is significant scope for reaping the benefits of such investment in the UK. Only a fraction of workplaces (2 per cent), it will be recalled, have ten or more 'new' practices and yet their management is 'substantially more likely to report increases in productivity' (Cully et al. 1998).

The implications for policy makers of the state of personnel management in the UK are also more clear-cut than they ever have been. If they are serious about promoting partnership, the knowledge economy and so on, policy makers have to do more to help bring them about. It cannot be said too often that, left to their own devices, British management will find it difficult to make significant investments in human capital because of the major structural constraints within which they have to work. This not only means that the government will have to use the financial and legal means at its disposal in key areas such as training and development and information and consultation to lay down a very clear direction in which it wants management to go. More challengingly, it means a serious review of some the features of the UK's business system, in particular, corporate governance arrangements, which are so inimical to investment in human capital.

References and further reading

Ackroyd, S. and Procter, S. 1998: British Manufacturing Organisation and Workplace Relations Some Attributes of the New Flexible Firm, *British Journal of Industrial Relations*, **36**(2), 163–83.

Adams, K. 1991: Externalisation vs Specialisation: What is happening to Personnel. *Human Resource Management Journal*, **1**(4), 40–54.

Arthur, J. B. 1994: Effects of human resource systems on manufacturing performance. *Academy of American Management Journal*, 37, 670–87.

Bach, S. 1995: Restructuring the Personnel Function: The Case of NHS Trusts, *Human Resource Management Journal*, **5**(2), 99–115.

Bach, S. 1999: Personnel Managers: Managing to Change? In S. Corby and G. White (eds), London: Routledge, *Employment Relations in the Public Services*, 177–98.

Becker, B. and Huselid, M. 1998: High performance work systems and firm performance; a synthesis of research and managerial implications. *Research in Personnel and Human Resources*, **16**(1), 53–101.

Braverman, H. 1974: *Labor and Monopoly Capital*. New York: Monthly Review Press.

Brown, W. (ed.) 1981: *The Changing Contours of British Industrial Relations*. Oxford: Basil Blackwell.

Burawoy, M. 1979: *Manufacturing Consent*. Chicago: University of Chicago Press.

Capelli, P., Katz, H. and Osterman, P. 1997: *The New Deal at Work*. Boston: Harvard Business School Press.

CEC (Commission for the European Communities) 1989: *Comparative Study on Rules Governing Working Conditions in Member States*. SEC (89), Luxembourg: Office for the Official Publications of the European Communities.

CEC (Commission for the European Communities) 1997: Green Paper, *Partnership for a new organisation of work*. Bulletin of the European Union, Supplement 4/97, Luxembourg: Office for the Official Publications of the European Communities.

CEC (Commission for the European Communities) 1998a: *Social Action Programme 1998–2000. Commission Communication*. Luxembourg: Office for the Official Publications of the European Communities.

CEC (Commission for the European Communities) 1998b: *Final report of the higher level group on the economic and social implications of industrial change*. Luxembourg: Office for the Official Publications of the European Communities.

Clark, J. 1995: *Managing Innovation and Change*. London: Sage.

Collinson, M., Edwards, P. and Rees, C. 1997: *Involving Employees in Total Quality Management*. London: Department of Trade and Industry (summary).

Cm 3321 1996: *Development and Training for Civil Servants: A Framework for Action*. London: HMSO.

Constable, R. and McCormick, R. 1987: *The Making of British Managers*. London: British Institute of Management.

Cressey, P. 1998: European Monetary Union and the impact of UK industrial relations. In Kauppinen, T. (ed), *The Impact of EMU on Industrial Relations in European Union*, Helsinki: Finnish Industrial Relations Association.

Cully, M., O'Reilly, A., Millward, N., Forth, J., Woodland, S., Dix, G. and Bryson, A. 1998: *The 1998 Workplace Employee Relations Survey. First Findings*. London: DTI.

Cully, M. and Woodland, S. 1998: Trade union membership and recognition 1996–97; an analysis from Certification Officer and the LFS. *Labour Market Trends*, July, 354–64.

Dean, J., Brandes, P. and Dharwadkar, R. 1998: Organisational Cynicism. *Academy of Management Review*, **23**(2), 341–52.

Delbridge, R. and Turnbull, P. 1992: Human Resource Maximisation. In P. Blyton and P. Turnbull (eds), *Reassessing Human Resource Management*, London: Sage.

Development Division 1997: *The Changing Role of the Human Resource Function: Main Report*. London: Cabinet Office.

Dickens, L. 1998: What HRM means for Gender Equality. *Human Resource Management Journal*, **8**(1), 23–40.

Doyle, M., Buchanan D. and Claydon. T. 1997: Beyond the Recipe: The Next Course? *QWL News*, June, 10–15.

Drucker, P. 1961: *The Practice of Management*. London: Mercury Books.

DTI (Department of Trade and Industry) 1998: *Fairness at Work*. White Paper presented to Parliament. Cm 3986.

Edwards, P. and Scullion, H. 1982: *The Social Organisation of Industrial Conflict: Control and Resistance in the Workplace*. Oxford: Blackwell.

Edwards, R. 1979: *Contested Terrain: The Transformation of the Workplace in the Twentieth Century*. London: Heinemann.

European Foundation 1997. *New Forms of work organisation. Can Europe realise its potential? Results of a survey of direct employee participation in Europe*. Luxembourg: Office for the Official Publications of the European Communities.

EWCB 1998: Revised figures on EWCs in UK. *European Works Council Bulletin*, Issue 18, November/December.

Flanders, A. 1964: *The Fawley Productivity Agreements*. London: Faber and Faber.

Fröhlich, D. and U. Pekruhl 1996: *Direct Participation and Organisational Change – Fashionable but Misunderstood? An analysis of recent research in Europe, Japan and the USA*. EF/96/38/EN. Luxembourg: Office for the Official Publications of the European Communities.

Gallie, D., White, M., Cheng, Y. and Tomlinson, M. 1998: *Restructuring the Employment Relationship*. Oxford: Oxford University Press.

Garrahan, P. and Stewart, P. 1992: *The Nissan Enigma*. London: Mansell.

Gooch, L. and Ledwith, S. 1996: Women in personnel management. In Ledwith, S. and Colson, F. (eds), *Women in Organizations*, Basingstoke: Macmillan.

Goold, M. and Campbell, A. 1987: *Strategies and Styles*. Oxford: Blackwell.

Government of Canada and the Organisation for Economic Cooperation and Development. 1997: *Changing Workplace Strategies: Achieving better outcomes for enterprises, workers, and society.* Report of the International Conference organized by the Government of Canada and the Organisation for Economic Cooperation and Development, Ottawa, Canada, 2–3 December, 1996, Quebec: Government of Canada and OECD.

Grant, D. and Oswick, C. 1998: Of Believers, Atheists and Agnostics: Practitioner Views on HRM. *Industrial Relations Journal*, **28**(3), 178–93.

Grant, R. 1991: The Resource-Based Theory of Competitive Advantage: Implications for Strategy Formulation. *California Management Review*, **33**(3), 114–35.

Griffiths, R. 1983: *NHS Management Inquiry*. London: DHSS.

Griffiths, W. 1990: Kent County Council: A Case of Local Pay Determination. *Human Resource Management Journal*, **1**(1), 100–7.

Guest, D. 1989: Personnel and HRM: Can you Tell the Difference? *Personnel Management*. **21**(1), 48–51.

Guest, D. 1990: Human Resource Management and the American Dream. *Journal of Management Studies*, **27**(4), 377–97.

Guest, D. 1997: Human Resource Management and Performance: a Review and Research Agenda. *International Journal of Human Resource Management*, **8**(3), 264–76.

Hall, L. and Torrington, D. 1998: *The Human Resource Function*. London: Financial Times/Pitman.

Hall, M. 1994: Industrial Relations and the Social Dimension of European Integration: Before and After Maastricht. In R. Hyman and A. Ferner (eds) *New Frontiers in European Industrial Relations*. Oxford: Blackwell Publishers.

Handy, C: 1987: *The Making of Managers*. London: NEDO.

Hochschild, A. 1997: When Work Becomes Home and Home Becomes Work. *California Management Review*, **39**(4), 79–97.

Hope-Hailey, V., Gratton, L., McGovern, P., Stiles, P. and Truss, C. 1997. A Chameleon Function: HRM in the 1990s. *Human Resource Management Journal*, **7**(3), 5–18.

Huselid, M. 1995: The Impact of Human Resource Management Practices on Turnover, Productivity and Corporate Financial Performance. *Academy of Management Journal*, **38**(3), 635–72.

Hyman, R. 1987: Strategy or Structure: Capital, Labour and Control. *Work, Employment and Society*, **1**(1), 25–55.

Hyman, R. 1998: Industrial Relations in Europe: Crisis or Reconstruction? In T. Wilthagen (ed.), *Advancing Theory in Labour Law and Industrial Relations in a Global Context*, Amsterdam: North-Holland.

Ichinowski, C., Kochan, T., Levine, D., Olson, C. and Strauss, G. 1996: What Works at Work: Overview and Assessment. *Industrial Relations*, **35**(3), 299–333.

Ichinowski, C., Shaw, K. and Prennushi, G. 1997: The effects of HRM practices on productivity; a study of steel finishing lines. *American Economic Review*, **87**(1).

IDS 1997: *Measuring Personnel Effectiveness*. IDS Study 618 London: IDS.

IRS 1999: *The Ethical Business*. Management Review 12, London: IRS.

Javidan, M. 1998: Core Competence: What Does it Mean in Practice? *Long Range Planning* **31**(1), 60–71.

Keep, E., and Mayhew, K. 1998: Was Ratner right? – product market and competitive strategies and their links with skills and knowledge. *Employment Policy Institute Economic Report*, **12**(3).

Kelly, J. 1998: *Rethinking Industrial Relations*. London: Routledge.

Kochan, T. A., Katz, H. C. and McKersie, R. B. 1986: *The Transformation of American Industrial Relations*. New York: Basic Books.

Kochan, T. and Dyer, L. 1992: Managing Transformational Change: The Role of Human Resource Professionals. *Proceedings of the Conference of the International Industrial Relations Association*, Sydney, 1992, Geneva: International Industrial Relations Association.

Kochan, T. and Osterman, P. 1994: *The Mutual Gains Enterprise: Forging a Winning Partnership among Labor, Management and Government.* Boston: Harvard Business School Press.

Legge, K. 1978: *Power, Innovation and Problem-Solving in Personnel Management.* London: McGraw-Hill.

Legge, K. 1995: *Human Resource Management.* Basingstoke: Macmillan.

Lewis, S. and Taylor, K. 1996: Evaluating the Impact of Family-Friendly Employer Policies: A Case Study. In S. Lewis and J. Lewis (eds), *The Work-Family Challenge*, London: Sage.

McCarthy, W. 1994: Of Hats and Cattle, or, the Limits of Macro-survey Research in Industrial Relations. *Industrial Relations Journal*, **25**(4), 315–22.

McGregor, D. C. 1960: *The Human Side of the Enterprise.* New York: McGrawHill.

McKinlay, A. and Taylor, P. 1996: Power, Surveillance and Resistance: Inside the Factory of the Future. In P. Ackers, C. Smith and P. Smith (eds), *The New Workplace and Trade Unionism*, Routledge: London.

McKinsey & Co/NEDO 1988: *Performance and Competitive Success: Strengthening Competitiveness in UK Electronics, A report prepared by McKinsey Co.* London: McKinsey and Co.

Mabey, C., Skinner, D. and Clark, T. 1998: *Experiencing Human Resource Management.* London: Sage.

Marchington, M. and Parker. P. 1990: *Changing Patterns of Employee Relations.* London: Harvester.

Marginson, P. 1998: The Survey Tradition in British Industrial Relations Research: an Assessment of the Large-Scale Workplace and Enterprise Surveys. *British Journal of Industrial Relations*, **36**(3), 361–88.

Marginson, P., Armstrong, P., Edwards, P. and Purcell, J. with Hubbard, N. 1993: The Control of Industrial Relations in Large Companies. *Warwick Papers in Industrial Relations*, 45, Coventry: IRRU University of Warwick.

Marginson, P., Edwards, P. K., Armstrong, P. and Purcell, J. 1995: Strategy, Structure and Control in the Changing Corporation: A Survey-Based Investigation. *Human Resource Management Journal*, **5**(2), 3–27.

Marginson, P., Edwards, P. K., Martin R., Purcell, J. and Sisson, K. 1988: *Beyond the Workplace: Managing Industrial Relations in Multi-Establishment Enterprises.* Oxford: Basil Blackwell.

Miles, R. and Snow, C. 1984: Designing strategic human resource systems. *Organizational Dynamics*, Summer, 36–52.

Millward, N. 1994: *The New Industrial Relations.* London: Routledge.

Millward, N., Stevens, M., Smart, D. and Hawes, W. 1992: *Workplace Industrial Relations in Transition.* Aldershot: Dartmouth.

Moingeon, B., Ramanantsoa, B., Metais, E. and Orton, J.-D. 1998: Another Look at Strategy–Structure Relationships: The Resource-based View. *European Management Journal*, **16**(3), 297–304.

Osterman, P. 1992: How Common is Workplace Transformation and How can we explain who adopts it? Results from a National Survey. *Industrial and Labor Relations Review*, **47**(2), 173–88.

Osterman, P. 1998: Changing work organisation in America. What has happened and who has benefited? *Transfer*, **4**(2), 195–213.

Patterson, M. G. and West, M. A. 1998: People Power. *Centre Piece*, **3**(3), 2–5.

Patterson, M. G., West, M. A., Lawthorn, R. and Nickell, S. 1997: Impact of People Management on Business Performance. *Issues in People Management No. 22*, London: IPD.

Peters, T. 1987: *Thriving on Chaos: Handbook for a Management Revolution.* London: Macmillan.

Pfeffer, J. 1998: *The Human Equation.* Boston, MA: Harvard Business School Press.

Pil, F. K. and MacDuffie, J. P. 1996: The adoption of high-involvement work practices. *Industrial Relations*, **35**(3), 423–55.

Poole, M. 1990: Human Resource Management in International Perspective. *International Journal of Human Resource Management*, **1**(1), 1–15.

Porter, M. 1980: *Competitive Strategy: Techniques for Analysing Industries and Competitors*. New York: Free Press.

Prahalad, C. K. and Hamel, G. 1990: The Core Competences of the Corporation. *Harvard Business Review*, May/June, 79–91.

Purcell, J. 1989: The Impact of Corporate Strategy on Human Resource Management. In J. Storey, *New Perspectives on Human Resource Management*, Routledge: London.

Purcell, J. 1995: Corporate Strategy and its Link with Human Resource Strategy. In J. Storey, (ed.), *Human Resource Management: A Critical Text*. London: Routledge.

Ram, M. 1994: *Managing to Survive*. Oxford: Blackwell.

Rees, C. 1998: Empowerment Through Quality Management: Employee Accounts from Inside a Bank, a Hotel and Two Factories. In C. Mabey, D. Skinner and T. Clark, *Experiencing Human Resource Management*, London: Sage.

Reich, R. 1999: Three-legged trick to square vicious circle of job losses. *Guardian*, 5 January.

Scarbrough, H. 1998a: Path(ological) Dependency? Core Competencies From an Organizational Perspective. *British Journal of Management*, **9**(3), 219–32.

Scarbrough, H. 1998b: The Unmaking of Management? Change and Continuity of British Management in the 1990s. *Human Relations*, **51**(6), 691–715.

Schuler, R. and Jackson, S. 1987: Linking Competitive Strategies with Human Resource Management Practices. *Academy of Management Executive*, **1**(3), 209–13.

Scott, A. 1994: *Willing Slaves?* Cambridge: Cambridge University Press.

Sheehey, P. 1993: *Inquiry into Police Responsibilities and Rewards, Cm 2280*, London: HMSO.

Sisson, K. 1989: Personnel Management in Perspective. In K. Sisson, *Personnel Management in Britain*, Oxford: Blackwell Publishers.

Sisson, K. 1990: Introducing the Human Resource Management Journal. *Human Resource Management Journal*, **1**(1), 1–11.

Sisson, K. 1993: In Search of HRM?. *British Journal of Industrial Relations*, **31**(2), 201–10.

Sisson, K. (ed.) 1994a: *Personnel Management; A Comprehensive Guide to Theory and Practice in Britain*. Oxford: Blackwell.

Sisson, K. 1994b: HRM and the Personnel Function. In J. Storey (ed.), *Human Resource Management: A Critical Text*, London: Routledge, 87–109.

Sisson, K. 1995: Organisation Structure. In S. Tyson (ed.), *Strategic Prospects for HRM*, London: Institute of Personnel and Development, 56–80.

Sisson, K., Arrowsmith, J., Gilman, M. and Hall, M. 1999: A preliminary review of the industrial relations implications of economic and monetary union. *Warwick Papers in Industrial Relations*, Number 62. Coventry: Industrial Relations Research Unit.

Smith, C. and Thompson, P. 1998: Re-Evaluating the Labour Process Debate. *Economic and Industrial Democracy*, **19**(4), 551–77.

Sparrow, P. and Marchington, M. 1998a: Introduction: Is HRM in Crisis? In P. Sparrow and M. Marchington, *Human Resource Management. The New Agenda*. London: Financial Times/Pitman.

Sparrow, P. and Marchington, M. 1998b: Re-engaging the HRM function. Re-building work, trust and voice. In P. Sparrow and M. Marchington, *Human Resource Management. The New Agenda*, London: Financial Times/Pitman.

Storey, J. 1992: *Developments in the Management of Human Resources*. Oxford: Blackwell.

Storey, J., Edwards, P. K. and Sisson, K. 1997: *Managers in the Making. Careers, Development and Control in Corporate Britain and Japan*. London: Sage.

Thurley, K. 1981: Personnel Management in the UK – a Case for Urgent Treatment? *Personnel Management*, **13**(8), 24–9.

Torrington, D. 1998: Crisis and opportunity in HRM: the challenge for the personnel function. In P. Sparrow and M. Marchington (eds), *Human Resource Management. The New Agenda*, London: Financial Times/Pitman.

Townley, B. 1994: *Reframing Human Resource Management*. London: Sage.

Tyson, S. and Fell, A. 1986: *Evaluating the Personnel Function*. London: Hutchinson.

Watson, T. 1977: *The Personnel Managers*. London: Routledge.

Wickens, P. 1987: *The Road to Nissan: Flexibility, Quality, Teamwork*. London: Macmillan.

Womack, J. P., Jones, D. T. and Roos, D. 1990: *The Machine That Changed the World*, New York: Rawson Associates.

Yeandle, D. and Clark, J. 1989: A Personnel Strategy for an Automated Factory. *Personnel Management*, **21**(6), 51–5.

2

Personnel Management in the Lean Organization

Karen Legge

One of the most distinguishing features of this collection is the attention given to the different contexts of personnel management. 'Lean organization' is a term which has come to be widely used in the discourse of managing people in recent years and carries a number of significant connotations in a Western materialist society such as the UK. Following Derrida (1978), the meaning of any word or phrase is derived from a process of deferral to other words that differ from itself – difference should be understood as the absence of deferred meaning as well as the difference of opposed meanings. Hence 'lean' is the opposite of 'fat' but different from 'thin'. Both 'fat' and 'thin', in our society, carry negative connotations. Both, for example, imply an undesirable state of potential physical, psychological and social unhealthiness. With 'thin' we have overtones of starvation, anorexia and poverty; 'fat' conjures up images of ugliness, greed, self-indulgence and heart attacks. 'Lean', in contrast, carries with it positive notions of healthiness (not over or underweight), of quality (the most expensive, better cuts of meat are advertised as 'lean') and of what counts as aesthetically pleasing in a fashion-conscious world. Leanness is what the consumer wants or aspires to. That a deferred connotation of leanness is meanness should not be overlooked either, nor the fact of its ambiguity, carrying both positive (mean machine) and negative (unkind, selfish actions) messages.

This chapter explores several issues. First, what is lean organization and why is it fashionable, in theory at least, in the 1990s Anglo-American cultures? The question 'what' is lean organization has two facets: what is it supposed to be like in theory and what is it actually like in practice? Second, in addressing these questions, the chapter will consider the implications of lean organization in theory and in practice for a range of organizational stakeholders, in particular management and other employees. Third, from this analysis will be derived an assessment of the enacted and potential roles of personnel management in different settings and their relationship to organizational performance.

What Is Lean Organization?

Although the ideas associated with lean organization have been around since the early 1980s, being clearly signalled in the writings of the 'excellence' school with their talk of 'simple structures, lean staff', 'simultaneous tight-loose properties' (Peters and Waterman 1982) or of 'giants learning to dance' (Kanter 1989), the phrase 'lean organization' is very much associated with the work of Womack et al. (1990) in their much-cited book, *The Machine that Changed the World*. Based on the International Motor Vehicle Program (IMVP) of comparative research, Womack et al. (1990) identified a new way of making things that they termed 'lean production'. Effectively lean production and, by extension, lean organization, is about organizing in such a way that value is added by minimizing waste, whether of materials, time, space or people and by developing responsiveness to major stakeholders, most of whom – whether employees, suppliers or purchasers of goods or services – are defined as customers. In other words, lean organization proposes simultaneously to cut costs and enhance quality.

How exactly is this to be done?

In theory, lean ways of organizing, suggest Rees et al. (1996: 73), involve the marrying together of the hardware of total quality management (TQM) quality procedures and associated 'Japanese' production processes (e.g. just in time (JIT), statistical process control, supply-chain management, total productive maintenance, material resources planning, zero defects/right first time, benchmarking) with the 'software' of 'high commitment' human resource management (HRM) and work practices (e.g. careful recruitment and selection, with emphasis on traits and competency, extensive use of systems of communication, teamworking with flexible job design, emphasis on training and learning, involvement in decision making with responsibility, performance appraisal with tight links to contingent pay). Also involved is the use of information and communication technologies, associated with business process engineering, making it possible to move from function-centred to process-centred organization, from differentiated specialists to multi-disciplinary teamworking, from 'unresponsive' bureaucracy to flatter hierarchies.

A complementary framework for conceptualizing lean organization is that developed by Kinnie et al. (1996). They define leanness in terms of three different perspectives, each linked to a different phase or type of activity. Stage 1 sees leanness as a transitional phase, where the focus is on becoming lean, via downsizing, delayering and changes in the contractual status of employees. Stage 2 concentrates on leanness as an outcome, and on the characteristics of the lean organization in its search for structural flexibility. Highlighted here are business process re-engineering and lean production. Stage 3 focuses on leanness as a process and considers the part played by TQM, kaizen, teamworking and just in time systems. As the authors point out these are not discrete stages as there is considerable overlap in the issues considered under Stages 2 and 3 – after all lean production subsumes TQM and JIT, even if they are considered as outcomes from a Stage 2 perspective and as processes from a Stage 3 perspective.

Both Rees et al.'s (1996) and Kinnie et al.'s (1996) conceptualization of the lean organization is what might be termed the 'Japanese' model involving the tripod of lean production techniques, business process re-engineering and 'high commitment' HRM. It is debatable to what extent this model can be applied to manufacturing in the UK, let alone to services. Indeed, based on an analysis of the largest 200 British-owned firms (size measured by capitalization), Ackroyd and Proctor (1998) suggest that, descriptively speaking, a different form of lean organization exists in the bulk of British manufacturing industry. They emphasize that the typical British manufacturing firm has grown through merger and acquisition, comprising a large number of decentralized production facilities producing a very wide range of 'cash cow' goods for retail in mature markets. These are firms that favour tight control of financial performance from the centre, with a good deal of operational freedom allowed to plant management. In terms of production systems and working practices, there is little evidence of high levels of investment in advanced technology or of multiskilling or of high commitment HRM practices. Rather, the characteristics of the typical British manufacturing firm are as follows.

- Production is organized as cellular manufacture as it facilitates the calculation of marginal costs and the identification of unprofitable activities, while limiting the need for employees to develop a broad spectrum of skills.
- Advanced manufacturing technology is little used, except as additions to existing configurations of equipment.
- Labour flexibility is achieved by teams of semi-skilled workers performing a range of specific tasks and given some on-the-job training.
- Employees do not enjoy privileged status or high employment security, but compete with sub-contracted labour and alternative suppliers.
- Production operations are considered as dispensable, separate segments, about which calculations of cost are regularly made.
- Management takes the form of intensified indirect control based on the allocation of costs.
- The high surveillance management regimes associated with what are termed Japanese lean production methods involving TQM, JIT and so forth are not typical of British manufacturing as they exaggerate the quality of information typically available and the willingness and ability of managers to appraise such information, even if available, given the much reduced ranks of middle management and supervision.

This model of lean organization lacks the coherency and logic of its Japanese counterpart. Instead, it smacks of a policy of 'asset management' rather than 'value added', to use Capelli and McKersie's (1987) well-known distinction. Even where working practices are used that are associated with Japanese-style lean organization, such as teamworking, the motivation for their introduction may be pragmatic rather than due to any concern for strategic and operational integration. This is the form of leanness, motivated exclusively by concerns of cost-cutting, is often accused of 'cutting muscle' rather than fat, of giving rise to the stressed-out anorexic organization.

In comparing the Japanese and UK models of the lean organization, it is easy to see why both, whether in theory or practice, have become so fashionable in the 1990s. If we consider the Japanese model, a similar range of factors to those attributed to the rise of HRM discussed in chapter 1 seem relevant, increased globalization of markets and intensification of competition, the Japanese 'Janus' (the Japanese model being that an exemplar and a threat) and models of excellence and the now almost-taken-for-granted ideologies of the enterprise culture (Legge 1995), underwritten by New Labour's penchant for the work ethic as a cure-all for society's ills. In particular, though, in a world of intensified competition, 'lean' organization, based on the tripod of lean production, business process re-engineering and high commitment HRM is seen, in theory at least, as combining tight cost controls with meeting or exceeding the requirements of the customer. Even where the market niche is acknowledged as distinctly downmarket (e.g. the *Sun*, McDonald's hamburgers) quality is still an issue. Where profit margins are low, profitability depends on volume combined with cost minimization. This, in turn, depends on the ability to maintain close control of product/service specification, such that quality will be maintained at a level preferred by consumers against competing products/services at a similar price (i.e., that it represents value for money). Lean organization, by promising tight cost control simultaneously with TQM and responsiveness to both internal and external customers, appears a logical route to profitability.

The 'asset management' model of much of British manufacturing, as identified by Ackroyd and Proctor (1998) has a logic less to do with responding to international competition in the long term than with short-term profitability. As they state:

> The loss of manufacturing capacity from Britain suggests that the traditional ways we had of organising manufacture were not profitable. However, that some considerable capacity for manufacturing has been retained at the end of the twentieth century suggests that economically viable ways of organizing manufacturing have been rediscovered.

It is debatable whether the pragmatic use of ever tighter cost controls, cellular manufacture in small, downsized and decentralized production plants and a team-based flexible use of labour, enabled by weakened unions and a deregulated labour market, counts as much more than a particular 1990s variant on asset management in response to a UK business culture of short-termism. Yet the model of leanness that Ackroyd and Proctor (1998) present *is* a logical response to the considerations making for UK short-termism discussed in chapter 1. Such considerations place a premium on behaviours and investments that have a quick pay-back and act to inhibit long-term thinking and investment. Whether, in the long term, this should be seen as 'leanness' or 'anorexia' (Turnbull and Wass 1997) or even any radical new way of working is open to question. Certainly Roach (1996: 82) has argued, in relation to similar practices in the US that the result is likely to be 'increasingly hollow companies' unable to maintain let alone expand market share in a growing global economy.

A further variant on the UK model of leanness is that offered by the so-called 'extended' organization (see Colling in this volume). This is where attention is paid to the elimination of overhead as waste and non-core activities are subcontracted out to cheaper suppliers. Certainly the UK model would not meet the criteria Rees et al. (1996: 70–1) set out for a leanness that 'involve(s) a qualitative change in the way work is organized and managed'. They suggest that, in theory at least, leanness as an 'organizational blueprint' has the following characteristics:

- it is grounded in a socio-technical perspective which promotes an holistic view of the organization of work;
- it emphasizes a new 'organizational logic' in the interaction of key variables;
- it subverts hierarchical authority in favour of the dictates of the production or service delivery process.

However, Rees et al. (1996: 74) recognize that, in implementing change, organizations can rarely just transfer one blueprint for another. The dynamics of change produce actions and end states that may differ substantially from the prescriptions in the normative model. There are likely to be questions about the timing of the adoption of key components of leanness; vested interests in existing organization design, working practices and control systems; problems of organizational unlearning of old ways and logics, and the influence of organizational contingencies (history, culture, size, sector, union/non-union dimension) on how leanness emerges in practice.

Lean Organization in Theory and in Practice

A number of commentators have stressed that, in assessing the relationship between leanness and organizational performance, it is necessary to enter some caveats about the research base from which subsequent comments will be derived (Williams et al. 1992; Oliver and Wilkinson 1992; Brown and Reich 1997). In particular, Whitfield and Poole (1997: 75) have pointed to four reasons for retaining 'a degree of scepticism': the issue of the direction of causality in correlational studies; the narrow base on which existing research has been undertaken; the reliance on self-reports from senior management and an absence of reports from junior and middle management, employees and their representatives; the lack of conclusive evidence as to whether leanness is indeed cost effective; and debate over whether labour productivity (as opposed to market share or operating profit) is an appropriate proxy for organizational performance. Perhaps most importantly from the point of view of this chapter, we presently lack much information about the role of HR professionals in implementing leanness and the implications of leaner ways of working for HR policies and practices, in terms of the contribution they might make to overcoming some of the potential adverse aspects of the lean organization (Kinnie et al. 1996: 39–40).

Nevertheless, given the research studies we have, what tentative conclusions may be drawn about the theory and practice of lean organization and, consequently, of HR specialists' roles with regard to its implementation? The rest of this section concentrates on the impact on organizational stakeholders of three aspects of HRM: delayering and downsizing, lean production, including TQM and JIT, and business process re-engineering.

The theory of lean organization

Let us first look at the logic of delayering and downsizing lean production, TQM and JIT, and business process re-engineering and at what their advocates believe they might achieve – before considering the research evidence of their impact on organizations and their major stakeholders.

DELAYERING AND DOWNSIZING

Delayering (reducing the number of levels in the hierarchy to achieve a flatter organization and greater customer responsiveness) and downsizing (cuts in staff numbers at all levels, to cut costs) are some of the most visible signs of a strategy aimed at slimming the organization or 'shedding its fat'. Some commentators suggest that delayering and downsizing should only be considered as part of a strategy to achieve a lean organization if this embraces a holistic rethinking of the organization of work. Rees et al. (1996: 70–1), for example, argue that when headcount reduction is an accountancy-driven response to economic difficulties or to a downturn in demand it should not be seen as part of a 'non-cyclical and irreversible' change in working practice and organization, but rather as a centuries-old practice in response to adverse trading conditions. Indeed, they suggest that it is debatable whether the sort of downsizing tactic of business concentration and disposal to improve the return on capital is facilitative of other aspects of lean organization, such as empowerment and teambuilding, as the latter rest precisely on high levels of employee commitment that are likely to be undermined by redundancy. However, it has also to be recognized that delayering and downsizing are likely to be part of a strategy of business process re-engineering, are implicit in the assumptions of lean production about eliminating waste, and are likely tactics in the UK model of lean organizations.

LEAN PRODUCTION, TQM AND JIT

Lean production systems, as stated earlier, rest on the principle of eliminating anything that does not add value to the end product. Technically, it is characterized by the absence of indirect workers, buffer stocks and the rework typical of mass production and by the presence of re-skilled, multitasked workers using flexible equipment, organized on cellular lines for small-batch, just-in-time, right-first-time production with rapid changeover. In theory, at least, this system is designed to deliver variety and quality without the high costs of craft production methods and, indeed, with cost advantages over mass production 'because it uses less of everything compared with mass production – half the human effort in the factory, half the manufacturing space, half the investment in tools, half the engineering hours to develop a new product in half the time' (Womack et al. 1990: 13). Lean production also involves an integrated production chain, involving a close partnership with suppliers, reinforcing lean production in final assembly. In theory, at least, the post-Fordist reuniting of conceptual and manual tasks in the context of high-trust teamworking in assembly empowers the direct worker, enhancing autonomy and responsibility particularly for quality control at the point of product or service delivery (Abernathy et al. 1983; Piore and Sabel 1984; Tolliday and Zeitlin 1986 cited in Rees et al., 1996: 77). Let's elaborate and clarify for a moment.

Given the emphasis on the elimination of anything that does not add value, lean production systems are extremely fragile as there is no slack in the system. Hence the symbiotic relationship in lean production of total quality management (TQM) and just-in-time production (JIT). First some definitions. TQM may be defined as developing an all-encompassing organizational culture and associated work practices that aim to produce products and services that will meet the needs and expectations of customers. The philosophy that underpins TQM is that all employees in a sense are each other's customers and, including stakeholders such as suppliers, should work towards a continuous improvement (kaizen) in process design and product quality (see Legge 1995: 218–20). JIT may be defined as a system in which production is pulled through the plant in accordance with configuration of final market demand rather than pushed by predetermined production schedules. Hence the exact quantity of defect-free goods is produced just in time for sale in the market; subassemblies are produced just in time for final assembly; and brought-in components and materials arrive from the supplier just in time to be made into subassemblies (Turnbull 1988).

TQM and JIT may be seen as the cornerstones of lean production systems, but, given their fragility, requiring certain preconditions of production management and employee relations systems if they are to work in practice as in theory (Oliver and Wilkinson 1992: 19–31). First, if goods are to be produced just in time in fluctuating market conditions, then the system requires the ability to produce in relatively small batches. While small batches may be expensive in terms of set-up times, large batches incur the cost of tying up large amounts of capital in inventory. Hence, in deciding what is the smallest, economically viable, batch size, set-up times are crucial and the pressure is to reduce them as far as possible. This may be done by investing in multipurpose machinery and tooling with quick change dies, pre-kitting, calibrated machine tools, automatic stop devices and so on. Apart from such 'technical' solutions, reducing set-up times calls for changes in the social systems as setting up is included in the job description of direct production workers with the elimination of a separate (craft) grade of tool setters. All this has implications for operator training.

Second, JIT systems require a relatively simple unidirectional workflow achieved by cellular manufacture. Without this there arises three different causes of stock accumulation: complexity, inflexibility and uncertainty. Complexity of workflow is likely to give rise to bottlenecks and to an inevitable stock accumulation as materials that are stationary as work-in-progress or buffer stocks tie up capital while gaining no added value. Inflexibility, that assumes set-up times as given and derives economical batch sizes from this, ties up stock in long runs. Uncertainty encourages stock accumulation via buffer stocks, unless quality-assured supplies can be guaranteed along the complete value chain. This argues for a high-trust collaborative relationship with suppliers, TQM throughout the organization and standardization of work tasks to allow for the required degree of synchronization.

Third, in this context, it is easy to see the importance of TQM to lean production and its symbiotic relationship with JIT. Faulty raw materials, components or subassemblies, given absence of stock, will halt the system. But importantly the relationship is a two-way one. The very fragility of the JIT system is an aid to achieving continuous improvement as any malfunction of equipment, materials or workers, in the absence of inventory, is instantly highlighted by bringing the system to a stop. This necessitates that the problem is examined and rectified rather than being allowed to fester, protected by inventory. Further, given the definition of quality implied here – 'quality at the right price' – the elimination of waste, integral to JIT, is another aspect of achieving quality. Conversely, achieving 'zero defects', itself implies the elimination of waste, for example, the time and costs associated with reworking parts, rescheduling production and dealing with customer complaints and warranty claims. In addition, quality reduces costs by eliminating indirect grades of quality inspectors and increasing throughput. It allows production processes to be simplified because defective parts no longer need to be re-routed round rectification loops, while less waste assists in the elimination of buffer stock to guard against quality problems (Turnbull 1988: 8–9).

These requirements of lean production assume certain employee relations systems. The drive to eliminate waste and seek continuous improvement relies heavily on employee input, whether achieved through employee involvement and empowerment – or work intensification. As already said, reducing set-up times requires operators to acquire new skills as their job descriptions expand. Cellular technology is generally considered to require teamworking and intra-team flexibility to achieve maximum effectiveness. TQM similarly argues that 'empowered' employees, within facilitating management control systems, should take responsibility for quality and engage in kaizen activities. The fragility of the system argues for employees' numerical and temporal flexibility (particularly in relation to overtime) as allowable short-term buffers in response to larger than anticipated fluctuations in demand than can be coped with by the kanban system or any system break-down (Legge 1995: 222–3).

In summary, a number of beneficial outcomes theoretically derive from lean production: more efficient use of working capital, reduction in lead times and, hence, potentially greater customer responsiveness, improvements in quality, reductions in waste and an empowered direct workforce.

BUSINESS PROCESS RE-ENGINEERING

Business process re-engineering (BPR), in theory at least, presents the epitome of lean organization in that its logic is to cut out anything within the organization or along its supply chain (people, structures, technologies, materials) that does not add value. It involves examining all the activities of an organization, reformulating objectives and redesigning business processes to achieve these objectives, regardless of existing work practices and organizational boundaries. The radicality of the approach is conveyed by the violent language of its major protagonists, Hammer and Champy: 'Don't automate, obliterate' (Hammer 1990); 'On this journey we ... shoot the dissenters' (Hammer 1993: 71). 'It's basically taking an axe and a machine gun to your existing organizations' (see Strassman 1994 and Hammer 1994 cited in Willmott 1995: 89). In theory this involves using the potential of information and communication technologies (ICTs) to enable the redesign of work processes to achieve market responsiveness while substantially reducing costs. This, again in theory, means a move from function-centred to process-oriented organizing practices; from linear/sequential work organization towards parallel processing and multidisciplinary teamworking; towards integrating previously fragmented tasks so that fewer people take less time to perform the process in question. If the inevitable corollaries are massive downsizing and delayering, in theory at least, the up side is contained in a rhetoric of responsiveness and flexibility (customer sovereignty and the elimination of bureaucracy) and empowerment (Willmott 1994; 1995; Grey and Mitev 1995).

Lean or Anorexic Organization?

In theory then, lean organization should deliver a promised land of efficiency combined with customer responsiveness, enhanced value-added and employee empowerment. But, in practice, is this promise delivered?

Delayering and downsizing in practice

The motives for introducing delayering and downsizing point to their likely effects on employees. Both strategies aim for cost reduction through lower overheads, speedier communication and decision making through a reduction in bureaucracy, and greater entrepreneurship and responsiveness to customer demands. Such concerns were particularly evident in the delayering and downsizing programmes of the privatized industries in the 1980s, when such tactics were seen as an integral part of culture change programmes aimed at converting state-owned bureaucracies into champions of the enterprise culture. That delayering and downsizing have been widespread in UK industry in the 1980s and 1990s there can be little doubt. In a survey conducted by Roffey Park Management Institute (in two parts, Holbeche 1994 and 1995), examining the effects of delayering on employees' working conditions and career development, the first part (1994) indicated that of 200 UK-based organizations 95 per cent had undertaken delayering in the last three years or were about to do so (Holbeche 1994 cited in Kinnie et al. 1996: 12). An Institute of Management/Manpower survey (1995) of long-term UK employment strategies revealed that over half of the companies had restructured since 1994 and, in more than 70 per cent, one or more layers of management had been removed. Further, few organizations in privatized industries, manufacturing and financial services had escaped downsizing in the 1980s and 1990s (Sparrow and Marchington 1998).

The effects of delayering and downsizing are not confined to those who lose their jobs, whether through voluntary or compulsory redundancy or early retirement. Those who remain are affected by the accompanying restructuring of roles, responsibilities and the psychological contract between employees and employers. The inevitability of this restructuring follows from the fact that a similar workload has to be covered by fewer people and, in the case of delayering, with less supervision. As Sparrow (1998: 125) points out, when an organization designs out a layer of the hierarchy, it has to reallocate decisions that were once made by the eliminated jobs and this generally results in increasing the responsibilities and complexity of lower-level jobs. These jobs additionally have become more self-managed as direct supervision becomes physically impossible. On the positive side there is evidence that if this leads to genuine empowerment (see below), employees' satisfaction, commitment and motivation may increase. Certainly, with regard to delayering, in a survey conducted in the late 1980s, Dopson and Stewart (1993) found that the majority of middle managers interviewed felt positively about the way their jobs had changed: they were now closer to top management and the strategic and policy arena; they had a clearer area of responsibility and more control over resources, they felt they had more legitimacy and freedom to take decisions. Similarly, the Roffey Park Survey referred to earlier also found some evidence that when flatter structures worked well (usually accompanied by team-based, cross-functional working and genuine increase in employee autonomy) there was some increase in employee satisfaction (Holbeche 1995, cited in Kinnie et al. 1996).

In contrast to these findings, there is abundant evidence that delayering, and particularly downsizing, are perceived negatively by employees. In most surveys, employees report increased workloads, greater pressure of work and reduced morale (Dopson and Stewart 1993; Holbeche 1994, 1995; Kettley 1995; Vielba 1995). This may be accompanied by longer working hours on the part of middle management and professional workers as they seek to demonstrate loyalty and commitment in the hopes of either avoiding demotion or redundancy in the next wave of delayering/downsizing or of improving their chances of achieving the diminished prospect of promotion. Indeed, research suggests that reduced career development opportunities, or even the downgrading of one's job in the new structure, is a major reason for low morale in delayering exercises (Holbeche 1995; Inkson and Coe 1994; Ezzamel et al. 1996). In the case of both delayering and downsizing, there may well occur a disruption to the employee's psychological contract, that is, the set of reciprocal expectations between an individual employee and the organization (e.g. the organization offers security, in return the employee offers loyalty; the organization offers a career structure, the employee offers conformity and acceptance of authority) (see Herriot and Pemberton 1997; Stiles et al. 1997). When this occurs, and if there is no attempt to negotiate a new one, there may result what has been termed the 'survivor syndrome', when employees feeling shock, disbelief, betrayal, animosity, guilt and fear exhibit a reluctance to take on new responsibilities and work to minimum standards, become narrow-minded, cynical and risk averse and, not surprisingly, mistrustful of senior management (Brockner 1998; Rice and Dreilinger 1991 cited in Kinnie et al. 1996; Herriot 1998; Sparrow 1998). These reactions are exacerbated when employees cannot see any convincing strategic goal behind the delayering and when they perceive the situation to be handled unfairly (Holbeche 1994, 1995; Guest and Peccei 1992 cited in Kinnie et al. 1996). That these negative perceptions are likely to be the norm is supported by Evans et al. (1995) finding that much downsizing is usually not undertaken as part of a broader strategic repositioning. Other studies suggest that it may be undertaken as a fad (in times of uncertainty organizations tend to follow the trend in an attempt to feel secure) or to send signals to other stakeholders, such as the City, that robust actions are being taken to maintain profitability (a message that runs counter to the signals about commitment which a company seeks to send to its staff) (Coupar and Stevens 1998). The low morale that is likely to result may be exacerbated by employees' perception that senior management are not taking the cuts they are enforcing on their subordinates (Cameron et al. 1991).

In these circumstances, it is not surprising that exercises in delayering and downsizing, apart from a short-term reduction in overhead costs, rarely succeed in achieving the hoped-for gains in productivity and responsiveness (Howard 1996; Wyatt Co. 1994, cited in Kinnie et al. 1996). In the case of delayering, an increase in inflexibility rather than responsiveness may occur. Thus Sparrow (1998: 125) points out that inflexibilities may result from the inadvertent cutting out of 'lynch pin' roles and the 'organizational memory' that resides within them. (An example of such a role in the health service is the hospital ward sister.) Further, those suffering from the survivor syndrome, following either delayering or downsizing, may exhibit less flexibility, responding to threat by becoming overly reliant on traditional, comfortingly familiar ways of doing things (Kinnie et al. 1996: 18). If downsizing cuts muscle rather than fat, a dangerous loss of competences may occur. Although, in the short term, the climate of fear and work intensification may enhance productivity, it can also undermine commitment to an extent that is injurious to high-quality production and, in particular, high-quality service.

Lean production, TQM and JIT in practice

Discussion of lean production in practice has tended to take a dichotomized view, depending on where the commentator stood in relation to the 'schools of excellence', 'second industrial divide', labour process and Foucaldian points of view. Those who fell in the excellence and second industrial divide schools saw lean production as a form of flexible specialization, necessarily involving teamworking and functional flexibility and, hence multiskilling and empowerment of direct operatives and the changing role of managers from controllers to facilitators. The reuniting of conceptual and manual tasks, an increase in employee responsibility and involvement in problem solving, the substitution of close supervision for team leaders and some group autonomy was seen to result in increasing employee commitment and satisfaction, pride in workmanship and quality, pride in having jumped through rigorous selection hurdles, satisfaction with the high levels of productivity believed to be achieved and, with it, enhanced job security (see e.g. Berggren 1993; Piore and Sabel 1984; Wickens 1987). Those who adhered to a labour process perspective and, perhaps under the influence of Foucault, newly sensitized to issues of surveillance and control, saw lean production as a management tactic inevitably involving enhanced management control and the standardization and intensification of work (e.g. Delbridge and Turnbull 1992; Garrahan and Stewart 1992; Graham 1993; McArdle et al. 1995; Parker and Slaughter 1988; Sewell and Wilkinson 1992). As chapter 1 points out, the contrast between the two positions is well illustrated by Wickens's (1987) and Garrahan and Stewart's (1992) contrasting accounts of lean production at the Nissan transplant car plant at Sunderland, UK. (For a more detailed discussion, see Legge 1995: 228–34.)

These contrasting assessments are typified by the different commentators' interpretation of kaizen and associated quality circle meetings. For the excellence school commentators such meetings empower the workforce to contribute their ideas to task and process improvement, thereby satisfying their esteem and self-actualization needs. By encouraging the exercise of collective autonomy such meetings represent an advance in worker participation and workplace democracy. For those within a labour process or Foucaldian tradition, kaizen committees symbolize the exploitation of labour, as management seek to expropriate workers' knowledge ('mine the gold in the workers' heads') in the interests of capital without direct return to the worker. Thus, kaizen is 'not an alternative to Taylorism but rather a solution to its classic problem of the resistance of workers to placing their knowledge of production in the service of rationalisation' (Dohse et al. 1985: 128).

However, more recently, two other interpretations have emerged, on the basis of empirical research, that recognize that both costs and benefits for the employee can be implicated in lean production. The first, which Rees et al. (1996: 76) term the 'contingency' approach, argues that the impact of lean production will vary according to organizational context. Thus, in relation to TQM, Wilkinson et al. (1997) not only found immense variation in the degrees of employee involvement in their respective companies, but that employee reactions to the schemes were highly influenced by management style. Further, shopfloor employees, middle management and unions were often ambivalent in their reactions to TQM. Employees, for example, might recognize that greater input into how their work was carried out and increases in autonomy at the point of production, however minor, had increased job satisfaction, even though they were aware that they were working harder. Middle managers might perceive the development of team leaders as a threat to their position, but recognize that the project of TQM gave them a chance to show their initiative, 'enrol' quality as an expertise in its own right and so increase their career prospects. In some contexts management may seek to use TQM to marginalize the unions, but in others use them in a way to build a high trust or 'partnership' relationship (IPA 1992). Wilkinson et al. (1997: 816) conclude 'There is a need to remove the blinkers and put TQM initiatives into the context of each organization, studying not only the market situation, the industrial relations history and the HR practices used, but how "quality" is understood and used by all the parties involved.' The second non-polarizing perspective that has emerged, again mainly with reference to empirical research on TQM, is that termed by Rees et al. (1996: 79) as the 'reorganization of control'. This perspective, while recognizing that the nature of production and task organization are crucial factors in determining the 'frontiers of control' (to use labour process terminology), accepts that the implications of leanness need not necessarily be negative for the employee (see, for example, Collinson et al. 1998). In both the Wilkinson et al. (1997) and the Collinson et al. (1998) studies, for example, most employees recognized that TQM was introduced to achieve managerial objectives, such as 'improve customer service', 'make the company more competitive', rather than to improve their quality of working life, and that pre-defined targets, managerial pressure and reports and appraisals had led to their working harder. The Collinson et al. (1998) study also found that TQM, generally speaking, had failed to improve trust between management and workers. Nevertheless, they found that most of their respondents enjoyed working as hard as they did; that the organizations where the workers were most likely to say that they were working harder and more subject to managerial monitoring were also those where trust in management and acceptance of quality programmes were highest; and that workers subject to output targets and most aware of the monitoring of their work were clearly the most, and not the least, likely to be favourable towards quality initiatives and to express trust in management. As a result, Collinson et al. (1998) conclude that employees had pragmatic expectations of TQM; that while they did not necessarily seek empowerment and retained a sense of distance from management, nevertheless they welcomed the principles of quality management and involvement in problem solving even though this involvement was limited to immediate work tasks. Rather than being characterized in terms of 'work intensification', the authors suggest that the idea of the 'disciplined worker' might more appropriately describe their situation and reactions.

In essence, these middle-range themes, supported by case study research, suggest that lean methods of working may simultaneously give rise to both greater responsibility, autonomy and job interest for employees but, at the same time, more intensive work in the context of tighter managerial control (see also Collinson et al. 1998; Dawson and Webb 1989). Geary (1994: 650) (cited in Rees et al. 1996: 79–80), summarizes this position well:

> although management may grant employees considerable freedom to be self-managing, it is a practice which has not diluted managerial control over the labour process: it has rather been redefined and exercised in a different form. It would seem that management has at once become both enabling and restraining.

This assessment rings true. The very fragility of lean production systems and the consequent need for employee flexibility and co-operation, delivers potential power into the hands of the employee and creates dependence on the part of management. The very contradictions in the system – empowerment versus exploitation, flexibility versus rigidity, autonomy versus standardization, teams as support and coercion – suggest the continued relevance of the paradox that confronts personnel management. That is, simultaneously it needs to achieve both the control and consent of employees, to mask the commodification of labour in order to most effectively extract surplus value, to favour hegemonic control (via selection, induction, culture change programmes, rewards) in order to achieve some measure of self-disciplining, if not fully fledged attitudinal commitment (see Legge 1995: 14–19 for a development of this argument).

Business process re-engineering in practice

There is evidence that in the 1990s many companies in the US and UK experimented with BPR. For example, a survey of 600 managers in 1994 showed that 69 per cent of American companies and 75 per cent of European companies claimed at least one re-engineering project (CSC Index report, 1994 cited in Kinnie et al. 1996: 21). Further, a UK survey found at the beginning of 1995 that 59 per cent of organizations surveyed were planning or undertaking BPR activities (Grint and Willcocks 1995: 101). Another survey of 96 companies from the financial services sector, undertaken in the second half of 1994, found that 75 per cent of respondents had undertaken some form of BPR (McCabe 1995). However, in spite (or possibly because) of the messianic terms in which its potentially revolutionary effect on organizations is proclaimed by its protagonists, there is little evidence that it delivers the results it promises. A survey in the CFO journal (1994, cited in Kinnie et al. 1996: 21) found that only 16 per cent of respondents were satisfied with their BPR programmes, whereas 68 per cent were experiencing problems. Even Hammer and Champy (1993), major protagonists, estimated that 50–70 per cent of re-engineering initiatives were not successful in achieving the desired performance breakthrough.

This combination of widespread experimentation combined with subsequent disillusion may be explained by both the nature of BPR and its effects. Several commentators (e.g. Grint 1994; Willmott 1994) recognize that BPR is less novel in its components than its sales pitch makes out. Grint (1994), for example, traces how each of its components have appeared as 'flavours of the month' in earlier management crusades. While some claim can be made that the novelty of BPR lies in bringing together earlier practices into a holistic framework, facilitated by ICTs, Grint suggest that the eagerness to experiment with BPR lies largely in its cultural and symbolic, economic and spatial, political and temporal resonances with our times. In other words it gives the message that large American corporations wish to hear as they struggle with competition from the far East: 'American industry is weak now because of rather than despite American culture'; the modern prince is the corporation in the globalized marketplace that through developing an alliance of allies from human and non-human elements can control its environment and the competing princes of other corporations; with the fall of the 'evil empire', 'radicality' washed clean of socialist connotations may be reclaimed by capitalism and shown to have roots in American culture (Grint 1994: 193–8). The subsequent disillusionment with BPR may, therefore, be partly as a result of unrealistic expectations. However, two other explanations carry weight: that, in its attempts at holism, BPR contains a mass of internal contradictions in relation to issues of competition, commitment, empowerment and technology (Grey and Mitev 1995; Willmott 1994, 1995); and that, in its implementation, a narrow technicist view of organizational change and neglect of the human dimension inevitably gives rise to failure (Willmott 1994; Mumford and Hendricks 1996; Oram and Wellins 1995).

Two examples of the internal contradictions of BPR must suffice. First, in relation to competition and change, BPR is presented as a solution to these challenges: via BPR the organization becomes more efficient, effective and responsive. But, as Grey and Mitev (1995) point out, BPR, by its advocacy and implementation of competitive techniques, *constitutes* (authors' italics) the competition which is then the problem that the organization must address. Similarly with change: the more BPR suggests that change is normality, the more, through its activities, it ratchets up the scale and pace of change. In both these ways, it could be argued that the logic of BPR is inherently self-defeating.

Second, there is the issue of commitment and empowerment. Empowering multiskilled work teams to make decisions at the operational level requires that they are sufficiently committed to the organization to exercise that discretion in the organization's best interests, as reflected in the managerially set targets to which they are subject. (Note, already, the seeds of a contradiction.) Yet, as Grey and Mitev and many others have pointed out, the logic of BPR is to displace employees with ICTs and to engage in both delayering and downsizing, both deleterious to generating attitudinal commitment. Grey and Mitev cite studies which show that in IBM, BPR led to one specialist replacing four generalists and that, in Ford, 500 people working in vendor payment were reduced to 125 as a result of BPR. The likely result of a philosophy of 'doing more with less' is redundancy and (for those that remain) work intensification. Given that the rationale for change is invariably conceptualized in terms of a need for effectiveness/profitability, employees may accept this work intensification if they perceive the alternative is bankruptcy and unemployment. In this case their commitment is likely to be behavioural rather than attitudinal and be based on fear. If, on the other hand, the organization is already highly profitable (as in many cases in the financial services sector) employees are being asked to face redundancy or work intensification for the profitability of others, which is likely to result in cynicism and the behaviours associated with the survival syndrome referred to earlier.

Given the dangers of introducing empowerment without commitment, it is not surprising to find that BPR (along with other forms of lean production) has a very limited conception of empowerment. As Willmott (1995) suggests, in BPR 'empowered' work is assumed simply to be the opposite of fragmented and degraded work. Often this can comprise working on integrated tasks made possible by the development of expert systems and relational databases rather than with any expansion of discretion or even enhanced variety in the task (Willmott 1994: 42). Terming this conceptualization of empowerment as 'functionalist humanism' where 'the idea [is] that human beings are essentially desirous of greater freedom from the restrictions of mechanistic, bureaucratic governance', Willmott contrasts it with what he terms 'democratic (anti)humanism', where empowerment is associated less with the assignment to 'enriched' or 'high involvement' jobs than with the expansion of processes of self-determination (author's emphasis). Self-determination is seen as the freedom to 'shape, change or abandon the framework within which decisions are identified and made' (Willmott 1995: 92). This latter form of empowerment is clearly not on the agenda of BPR, particularly as it advocates the importance of leaders (a 're-engineering czar' – unfortunate connotations as Grey and Mitev (1995: 13) point out) and a top-down approach in its design and implementation. Hence, in BPR 'empowerment is better typified as "false charity" – "charity" because [at least] it seeks to bestow the gift of greater discretion and involvement upon employees; and "false" because it is motivated less by any concern to ameliorate the structural inequalities that make such gestures possible than it is by a calculation that such a change will engender enhanced performance and profitability' (Willmott 1995: 93). Seen in this light, both Willmott and Grey and Mitev suggest that, in reality, empowerment should be seen as a process of 'managerial colonization' and the exercise of control. The same criticisms have been raised when empowerment has appeared as part of the teambuilding initiatives associated with lean production, TQM and so forth: employees have increased discretion at operational level, but subject to accountability to managerial standards derived from an agenda firmly set by management.

A second explanation of the failure of BPR initiatives lies in its design and implementation. As pointed out by several commentators (Grey and Mitev 1995; Willmott 1994; Oram and Wellins 1995) re-engineers tend to take a narrow technicist view of change, neglecting the human dimension and dismissing employee concerns as emotional, irrational or political – the latter implying some instrumental and illegitimate protection of 'turf'. The very title of the approach, 're-engineering', is redolent of its technicist orientation. This view is supported by some survey evidence. Grint and Willcocks (1995) found that four of the top five most significant barriers to BPR related to such issues as middle management resistance, lack of senior management support, the prevailing culture and political structure and employee fear and resistance. The most significant barrier was seen to be middle management resistance. This is hardly surprising when not only is delayering explicitly on BPR's agenda, but also the overthrow of the very functional structures that have traditionally provided an identity and career path for middle managers. Similarly, skilled and professional groups, like engineers and accountants, may perceive a threat to their occupational control and specialist identities as BPR requires them to fit in with a multifunctional group that determines and evaluates the contribution of each member. The assumption too that change must become a way of life and that, hence, all employees should be infinitely malleable, flies in the face of the evidence we have about stress and burn-out.

In the minority of cases, where organizations have claimed some success for BPR, this appears linked to such human/political issues as: top management support; gaining employees buy-in; project management; implementation style; communication processes and establishing the need and the levers for change, i.e. the clichéd but widely accepted formulae for the successful management of any change (Grint and Willcocks 1995: 107).

Personnel Management in the Lean Organization

In the 1980s, WIRS survey evidence suggested that personnel specialists, in a majority of establishments, were only marginally involved in the initiation and implementation of advanced technical change (Daniel 1987). At best, even when personnel considerations in the introduction of new technology were not ignored, the role played by personnel specialists appeared to be one of late-in-the-day facilitators of implementation, constrained by technical and financial parameters over which they had little say and to which they could merely react – see, for example Child and Tarbuck (1985); Clegg and Kemp (1986); MacInnes (1988); Marginson et al. (1988); Rothwell (1985); Willman and Winch (1985). This finding seemed surprising, even then. Not only was it clear that information and communications technologies (ICTs) had immense implications for employment related issues, including organizational and job design, employment, careers and skills (see Legge

1989), but ever since Mumford's early and seminal studies (1969, 1972) of the introduction of first generation computer operations into offices in the late 1960s and early 1970s, it has been conventional in the prescriptive literature to advocate personnel specialists' adoption of a proactive 'organizational diagnostician' or 'collaborative systems designer' role in managing technical change. This advocacy, in theory, should have been reinforced by the 1984 WIRS finding that, where personnel specialists were involved and at an early stage, employees' reactions to it were much more favourable than in cases of non- or late involvement (Daniel 1987; Legge 1993).

In analysing personnel specialists' involvement in managing the transition to lean organization, admittedly from an inadequate and patchy empirical research base (see Kinnie et al. 1996; Rees et al. 1996), it is often like watching a re-run of the old technical change movie. Again, there is the predictable advocacy of a proactive role to be played by personnel specialists (change agent, hidden persuader, interpreter, facilitator, champion) (Wilkinson and Marchington 1994; Rees et al. 1996); again, frequently, the picture is one of marginalization (see Legge 1995; Kinnie et al.; Rees et al. 1996; Storey 1992). The prevailing pattern is one of line management being the initiator and centrally involved in the development of lean organization, with personnel specialists tagging on in the rear. This is well summed up by two quotations from Storey's (1992) respondents. First, the director of manufacturing at Peugeot-Talbot UK stated:

> The central personnel function is now basically a co-ordinating activity. The personnel director leads for us in the formal negotiations with the trade unions. But on the major policy shifts in areas such as communications, management, quality, team building, problem-solving teams and the like, these are matters for the executive. (Storey 1992: 204)

Second, the personnel director of a manufacturing company acknowledged:

> I have to admit that TQM and the Top Management Workshops represent two of the main thrusts to our management development strategy and, to be honest with you, they are now major planks in our human resource strategy as a whole. You are correct in saying neither of them was launched by us. We sort of inherited them. (Storey 1992: 183)

Typically, the personnel specialist role seems one of reacting to and patching up problems in the best tradition of UK lean organization pragmatism and short-termism. For example, Ezzamel et al.'s (1996: 66–7) study found that involvement and teamwork initiatives tended to be tacked on to market-driven reorganizations of companies, in order to cope with the problems posed by delayering and decentralization, rather than being integrated with and in parallel to the strategic planning of the reorganization. Calás and Smircich (1993, cited in Rees et al. 1996: 93) suggest that personnel specialists are being called up to perform 'analgesic' functions for organizations, playing a feminized counselling and supportive role in helping the 'outplaced' and survivors to cope with the pain and stress created by downsizing and delayering. Why does this reactive and marginal role appear par for the course in the majority of UK organizations?

At first sight the case for the proactive involvement of personnel specialists in developing lean organization seems even more obvious and imperative than that for advanced technical change *per se*. In the case of technical change it is understandable that it may be seen as naturally the preserve of engineers and production management, with no necessary involvement of personnel specialists, short of assistance in managing potential training and industrial relations issues. As, in practice, much of the training may be designed and implemented by line management or by specialist external providers and as technical change is usually welcomed by employees as a guarantor of plant (and, at least, some jobs) survival, even these potential training and industrial relations roles are often attenuated (Legge 1993).[1] In contrast, the very fragility of lean production systems cries out for flexible, committed employees who will exercise their necessary discretion in the (managerially defined) organizational interests. In theory, this calls for expert attention to the nature of the employee–organization psychological contract and the development of an internally consistent 'bundle' of high-commitment human resource policies 'integrated with manufacturing policies under the "organizational logic" of a flexible production system' (MacDuffie 1995: 217). In Oliver and Wilkinson's (1992) terms – assuming the Japanese model of leanness – this means the proactive creation of high-dependency systems in place of the low-dependency system of traditional mass production. Maintaining employee commitment in a lean production organization, recognizing the mutual dependency between employee and organization in order to fulfil the psychological contract, is generally reckoned to involve such mutually reinforcing employee relations policies as:

- 'trainability' and commitment as key criteria in employee recruitment, selection and promotion;
- extensive use of systems of communication;
- teamworking with flexible job design;
- emphasis on training and learning;
- involvement in operational decision making with responsibility;
- performance appraisal with tight links to contingent rewards, including promotion;
- job security/no compulsory redundancies.

(see Huselid 1995; MacDuffie 1995; Purcell 1996; Whitfield and Poole 1997; Wood and Albanese 1995; Wood 1996).

If this logic, which stems from the Japanese model of lean organization, is adopted, various roles for personnel specialists may be proposed and, in various case studies (see, for example, Terry and Purcell 1997; Wilkinson and Marchington 1994), have been identified. For example, in their representative sample of 15 companies in private manufacturing and services and public sector services, Wilkinson and Marchington (1994) identified various roles played by personnel specialists, in relation to TQM, that reflect a more positive light than the prevailing picture of marginalization. Two high-profile roles are identified as being enacted in just under half the cases: that of change agent, a strategic role, and internal contractor, an operational role. The change agent role occurred where personnel were able to define TQM as synonymous with change and identify themselves as the best qualified to manage this process. Their initiatives were often presented as preparing the ground for a change to a more 'quality-oriented culture' or 'helping to create an organization culture and structure where TQM is possible' (Wilkinson and Marchington 1994: 41). Invariably, for this role to be feasible, the personnel function, or individual, operated at board level and had the ear and confidence of the chief executive of the company or site in question. A second high-profile role was that of the internal contractor.

Here the personnel function attempts to draw up and publicize standards for the delivery of personnel services to internal customers, specifying products (e.g., employment policies, services, information) and level of service (i.e., the time by which the service will be provided) on offer. Products and services might include offers and contracts concerning the administration of recruitment, induction and training, advice on dismissal and disciplinary procedures, liaising with outside training, recruitment and statutory bodies, all related to a particular 'customer'. This high-profile role not only supports the introduction of TQM but, by its emphasis on 'meeting or exceeding [internal] customer expectations', enacts the philosophy of TQM.

Wilkinson and Marchington (1994) further identify two other, lower-profile, roles that personnel specialists enact in relation to TQM programmes: that of 'hidden persuader', a strategic role, and that of 'facilitator', an operational role. The hidden persuader, which they identified in just two of their organizations, is where a highly placed individual specialist acts as the mentor or sounding board for senior line and specialist managers, achieving this *éminence grise* role largely through personal credibility and because personnel is seen 'as neutral and can take an overview of the change process without pursuing any specific and potentially divisive departmental objectives' (Wilkinson and Marchington 1992: 42). While exercising high levels of influence behind the scenes, often personnel's role is relatively invisible lower down the organization.

Finally, Wilkinson and Marchington (1994) identify the most frequently observed role, that of facilitator. This usually involved a role in training, recruitment, selection and induction, communicating the new management style and generally providing hands-on support for line management. In many respects, it may be viewed as indistinguishable from the routine practice of personnel management, representing what other managers would normally expect of personnel.

Rees et al. (1996), in a prescriptive mode, identify four somewhat similar roles available to personnel specialists: the supporter (similar to the facilitator); the interpreter; the champion and the monitor. The supporter role they see as personnel providing managers and other employees with the skills and resources to cope with lean organizations. A typical activity here would involve the training required for team working and, particularly, the selection of suitable people for the team leader role and their development from progress chasers to operations facilitators. In such activities, training involves not just skills acquisition but also 'attitudinal restructuring', (Wood and Albanese 1995) with implications for cultural change. Developing appropriate and supportive performance management and reward systems is another area highlighted (see Wibberley 1993).

The interpreter role has some resonances with that of 'hidden persuader', although operating throughout the organization rather than at senior management level. Rees et al. (1996: 90) see the role as contributing to the sense-making processes of organization (Weick 1995): interpreting what it means to be a lean organization at the strategic level (e.g. that generating commitment is essential to cushion the fragility of lean systems); placing apparently discrete and disconnected changes into perspective at the operational level. As they point out, when line management and employees are in the thick of implementing a stream of initiatives, changes in work practices and restructuring, it is easy for them to lose sight of the overall purpose of the change process and become disheartened and disillusioned in the face of inevitable set-backs. Personnel can provide a rationale and perspective facilitated by their own apparent position of neutrality and objectivity.

The two other roles Rees et al. (1996: 93) identify are that of champion of the workforce – 'not in the spirit of welfarism or a paternalistic ethos, but in the spirit of promoting and protecting a vital business resource' and that of monitor 'reflect(ing) back the human consequences of change in highly visible and measurable terms to the managers involved'. In a sense, these two roles are related. The essence of the 'champion of the workforce' role is to highlight the fact that the fragility of lean systems make them highly vulnerable both to production contingencies and employee lack of co-operation, and that, hence, generating and maintaining employee flexibility, commitment and trust is vital. As Wickens (1987: 38, cited in Kinnie et al. 1996: 92) put it:

> We have to recognize that eliminating waste – whether wasted time or wasted actions – does stretch the system and, if undertaken in isolation and taken to the extreme, can create significant pressures. It then becomes important to build in an appropriate staffing level and/or schedule paid overtime for these activities.

He adds that job security is essential to maintaining employee commitment to continuous improvement (Wickens 1993: 87). Yet, in developing this argument, personnel specialists need to be able to demonstrate in visible, quantifiable and, preferably, financial terms what the costs might be of employee lack of commitment, flexibility and so on, and what benefits and costs might accrue from treating employees as 'a vital business resource'. In other words, the champion and monitor roles need to be enacted within a 'conformist innovator' framework (i.e. demonstrating the relationship between the personnel function's activities and organizational success) (Legge 1978).

All these roles carry potential dangers for the credibility and position of personnel specialists. As Wilkinson and Marchington (1994) point out, the high profile and strategic contribution of the change-maker role carries commensurate high risks of discrediting the function if the TQM initiative fails, not to mention making enemies of those managers who perceive themselves to be losing out due to the promotion of leanness. The hidden persuader carries the opposite risk. Even if the TQM programme is highly successful, personnel's contribution in the organization as a whole may go unrecognized, particularly as publishing the role could undermine 'the very essence of its value' (Wilkinson and Marchington 1994: 43). The contribution of the facilitator, if it is seen as indistinguishable from 'normal' personnel activities, may be taken for granted and pass without recognition. The internal contractor role carries the double risk of internal public humiliation if promised targets are not met and, in the extreme, the contracting out of part or all of the function itself. In other words, the high-profile roles carry the risk of advertising public failure and consequent loss of credibility, the low-profile roles that of lack of recognition for personnel's contribution to success, combined with other functions, notably the line, claiming credit for their achievements (c.f. Legge 1978: 21–6). Conversely, while the operational roles of internal contractor and facilitator may be easier to acquire and gain more support from line management than the strategic roles of change agent and hidden persuader, they carry the risks of reactivity. In other words, they allow the initiators of lean organization to define the agenda and, hence, the role (or lack of it) for personnel, rather than personnel proactively shaping the strategic agenda (Wilkinson and Marchington 1994: 47). In this light, Rees et al.'s (1996) advocacy of the champion and monitor roles seems sensible. Championing the workforce is both a natural and distinctive role for personnel that cannot be readily colonized by other management functions. But it is essential that personnel also succeeds in demonstrating, in terms credible to other management groups, the bottom line of their contribution. However, this strategy is predicated on the assumption that their voice and contribution assist in developing an effective lean organization – if it is not successful, again achieving a high profile is only to draw attention to personnel's responsibility for failure.

Clearly, the role that may be played by personnel specialists in the development and maintenance of lean organization will depend on the context. In Wilkinson and Marchington's (1994) study not only did personnel specialists occupy more than one role (for example, all acted as facilitators, irrespective of other roles adopted), but on single-sites the personnel function might intervene at different levels on different occasions and over time, while in multi-establishment organizations, members of the personnel function are themselves located at different levels (corporate/division/site) and with different positions and statuses. Hence the roles that are enacted in different parts of an organization will vary. Further, the role that might be played by personnel will be influenced by such factors as whether the site is greenfield, non-unionized and, possibly, foreign owned, as compared to a brownfield, unionized UK plant (see Millward et al. 1992). In the former case the personnel specialist is likely to stand a better chance of playing a change-agent proactive architect role than in the latter, where the hard grind of a contract manager's role, to inch in minor concessions in an incremental manner in the face of union demarcations, might be all that is feasible (Newell 1991; Tyson and Fell 1986). The industrial sector is also likely to have a bearing on the role that personnel specialists may play. In manufacturing firms the emphasis is likely to be upon the 'hard' and quantifiable production aspects of leanness and, hence, with line initiation and personnel's marginalization. In service sector organizations, though, given the greater degree of staff/customer interaction, there is a greater chance that leanness will be defined in terms of customer responsiveness and the programme contain the 'softer', more qualitative, aspects of customer care and cultural change – if within the context of delayering and downsizing, as in the financial services sector. In this case, personnel specialists stand a better chance of playing a central role (see Rees et al. 1996: 84–5).

Obviously, then, personnel managers are not presented with a free choice about which roles they might choose to enact. Apart from the factors already mentioned, as Wilkinson and Marchington (1996: 44) point out, the existing style and status of the function will have a bearing: 'clearly a function which performs basic operational work is unlikely to suddenly become transformed by the onset of TQM into a strategic role'. Second, the role that can be played will be influenced by the origins of the TQM initiative and the instigators' ideas about what TQM is all about – marketing and operations managers are likely to differ in their conceptualizations and priorities. Third, the nature of the initiative provides a set of constraints and opportunities for personnel to offer/claim a more strategic approach to organizational change 'by pointing to past failures, and then seizing the "high ground" for themselves'. However, although the role adopted will be significantly influenced by the personnel function's existing position and status, this is not set in stone. One role may be used to demonstrate competence to senior management (e.g., internal contractor role) and then be used as a springboard to another (e.g., change agent) (Wilkinson and Marchington 1994).

This discussion of the roles personnel specialists might play in developing and maintaining lean organization has tended to assume the Japanese model of leanness. What conclusions might be drawn if, in contrast, we assume the UK model of leanness, as depicted by Ackroyd and Proctor (1998), a model predicated on short-term asset management and tight financial control? The first assumption is that personnel specialists would be unlikely to be found at plant level and have a very diminished presence at corporate level. Whether driven by the logic of pragmatism, financial control or even responsiveness to the market, a personnel function would be likely to be defined as overhead and, as such, a waste to be eliminated. In addition, it is unlikely that the costly, long-term high-commitment model of personnel management would be adopted in this context. In spite of some research indicating a relationship between bundles of high commitment human resource management practice and organizational performance (e.g. Huselid 1995; Mac-Duffie 1995), the research evidence is still not compelling. Purcell (1996), for example, sounds a sceptical note, arguing that not only are there problems of measurement (issues to do with research design, direction of causality and possibility of Hawthorne effects) in ascertaining this link, but that the 'best fit' personnel practices for low-cost producers might be direct labour control policies rather than expensive high-commitment ones (see also Arthur 1994). For a low-cost producer, particularly operating in mature markets, investment in training, intensive communications and guarantees of job security may be seen as both unnecessary and undesirable. If behavioural compliance is sufficient, why go to the expense of trying to secure attitudinal commitment? If this approach to leanness is adopted, it is difficult to see any significant proactive role for personnel specialists. If any survive at plant level, managing pragmatic hiring and firing, outsourcing labour, bolt-on sporadic training and fire-fighting with union representatives, along with 'house-keeping' tasks, is their likely fate.

Conclusion

Developing and maintaining a lean organization might be likened to walking a tightrope. Just as the high-wire acrobat has to perform a balancing act, so those managing this change have to be aware of the costs and benefits of leanness. If the perceived costs of downsizing, delayering and work intensification become too high to offset the perceived benefits of increased operational autonomy, some skill enhancement, and more extensive communications, then the employee commitment, desirable to buttress the fragility of lean systems, is unlikely to develop or survive. This balancing act is exemplified by the paradox embodied in lean systems: 'they require a continuous, proactive process of management to ensure their smooth running, but at the same time they stress a reduction in managerial intervention; an increasing devolution and decentralization of decision-taking authority – the empowerment of employees' (Rees et al. 1996: 86). Just as a tightrope walk is a journey across a chasm, so too the development and maintenance of leanness is a journey, a continuous quest for improvement. And, as danger lurks for the tightrope walker if momentum is lost, so too it does for management if impetus fails and necessary supportive resources become dissipated.

Clearly the nature of the roles personnel specialists can play in the achievement of lean organization are many and varied depending on context, including past history. While a reactive, facilitative role may be valuable in itself, it carries the danger of other interest groups setting the agenda of leanness and in ways that might neglect the human dimension in the headlong pursuit of technicist solutions. As outlined, a highly visible, proactive role carries its own risk if the development of leanness is painful or unsuccessful.

However, there is much to be said for personnel specialists adopting the role of the 'champions of the workforce', as Rees et al. (1996: 90–2) suggest. At one level, the way is clear as erstwhile contenders for this role – the unions – are often marginalized in the development of lean organization. Notwithstanding the WIRS 1992 finding that innovative HRM/Japanization initiatives are more likely to be associated with unionized rather than non-unionized organizations (at least as far as UK-owned plants are concerned) (Millward et al. 1992), trade unions' interests may be threatened by the move to lean systems. Not only is there the issue that the unitary ideology of lean organization runs contrary to unions' espousal of collectivism, but also, in practical terms, team leaders may usurp the role of shop steward as first port of call in seeking information and the raising of grievances, while managers' penchant for communicating directly with employees may bypass and erode union channels of communication (Rees et al. 1996). Further, unions, already on the defensive through legal, socio-politico-economic changes, declining membership, non- and withdrawal of recognition, reduced bargaining agendas and so forth, may find it difficult to confront the downside of changes presented as essential for organizational competitiveness and survival, while increasing employees' involvement, responsibility and general empowerment. Storey's (1992) identification of two parallel systems of innovative HRM-type initiatives and conventional bread-and-butter industrial relations in mainstream unionized organizations, with never the twain meeting, is indicative of this marginalization. As a senior personnel manager at Rover is quoted, with reference to the early 'Working with Pride' programme, 'The unions were invited to the party but they didn't seem to want to come. So the party went ahead without them' (Storey 1992: 250–1).

Yet, if personnel adopts the role of champions of the workforce, it would be in a rather different sense than that of the unions. Traditionally unions have championed the workforce as an end in itself: to achieve a larger (fairer?) slice of the profit cake and improvement of working conditions for its membership, irrespective of the interests of other organizational stakeholders. Personnel specialists would lose credibility seeking this role as, first and foremost, to have a voice at all, they need to be seen as unequivocally part of the management team. Hence championing the workforce, as discussed earlier, must be presented in terms of 'promoting and protecting a vital business resource' (Rees et al. 1996: 91). Whether this is best done in partnership with the trade unions, assuming the latter adopt a 'market unionism' or 'making Donovan work' stance (Martinez and Weston 1992), or unilaterally, will depend on history and context. Even Rover, more recently, has recognized that change can best be managed by social partnership and a more constructive approach to the employer–union relationship (Taylor 1994).

Finally there is the critical, unconstructed, pre-HRM, view of what personnel management's role should be in the development of lean organization. Particularly in relation to BPR, both Willmott (1994: 45) and Grey and Mitev (1995: 16) suggest that, with an eye to wider issues of social justice and the good life, personnel management should 'question the rationality of remedies that contribute to the disease for which they profess to dispense a cure' and 'raise a sane voice in protest, rather than connive at providing technical and ideological support for it' (i.e., for downsizing, delayering, stress, work intensification and so on). While such a 'deviant innovator' role (Legge 1978: 85–90) (that is, attempting to gain acceptance for a different set of criteria for the evaluation of organizational success and personnel's contribution to it) may be highly attractive to the academic commentator, its political feasibility in the present organizational climate is wishful thinking, unless it can be used as a sales pitch to the ethically sensitive customer. Hardly a Kantian position! However, voices are being raised that leanness may only serve to create 'hollow companies', so the tide may be turning, particularly as the icon of leanness, Japanese manufacturing industry, has recently lost its lustre (Roach 1996).

Note

1 However, it should be noted that the WIRS 1984 survey (Millward and Stevens 1986) found much higher levels of involvement of personnel specialists (80 per cent) and at a much earlier stage (30 per cent at the decision to change and the remaining 50 per cent immediately after the decision to change) in the case of organization change (defined as 'substantial changes in work organization or working practices not involving new plant, machinery or equipment). Given the centrality of new ICTs to many initiatives in developing leanness, the changes outlined in this chapter would probably fall somewhere between organizational change and advanced technical change, as defined in the WIRS 1984 survey (see Daniel 1987).

References and further reading

Abernathy, W., Clark, K. and Kantrow, A. 1983: *Industrial Renaissance: Producing a Competitive Future for America*. New York: Basic Books.

Ackroyd, S. and Proctor, S. 1998: British manufacturing organisation and workplace relations: some attributes of the new flexible firm. *British Journal of Industrial Relations*, **36**(2), 163–83.

Arthur, J. B. 1994: Effects of human resources systems on manufacturing performance and turnover. *Academy of Management Journal*, **37**, 670–87.

Berggren, C. 1993: Lean production – the end of history? *Work, Employment and Society*, **7**(2), 163–88.

Brockner, J. 1998: The impact of layoffs on survivors. *Supervisory Management*, February, 2–7.

Brown, C. and Reich, M. 1997: Micro-macro linkages in high performance systems. *Organization Studies*, **18**(5), 765–82.

Calás, M. and Smircich, L. 1993: Dangerous liaison: the 'feminine-in-management' meets globalization. *Business Horizons*, March/April, 71–81.

Cameron, K., Freeman, S. and Misha, A. 1991: Best practices in white collar downsizing: managing contradictions. *Academy of Management Executive*, **5**(3), 57–73.

Capelli, P. and McKersie, R. B. 1987: Management strategy and the redesign of work rules. *Journal of Management Studies*, **24**(5), 441–62.

Child, J. and Tarbuck, M. 1985: The introduction of new technology: managerial initiative and union response in British banks. *Industrial Relations Journal*, **16**(3), 9–33.

Clegg, C. W. and Kemp, N. J. 1986: Information technology: personnel, where are you? *Personnel Review*, **15**(1), 8–15.

Collinson, M., Rees, C. and Edwards, P. K. (with Inness, L.) 1998: *Involving Employees in Total Quality Management: Employee Attitudes and Organizational Context in Unionized Environments*. London: DTI.

Coupar, W. and Stevens, B. 1998: Towards a new model of industrial partnership: beyond the 'HRM versus industrial relations' argument. In P. Sparrow and M. Marchington (eds), *Human Resource Management, The New Agenda*, London: Financial Times/Pitman, 145–59.

CSC Index 1994: *State of Re-engineering*. (Report), CSC Index.

Daniel, W. W. 1987: *Workplace Industrial Relations and Technical Change*. London: Francis Pinter.

Dawson, P. and Webb, J. 1989: New production arrangements: the totally flexible cage? *Work, Employment and Society,* **3**(2), 221–38.

Delbridge, R. and Turnbull, P. 1992: Human resources maximization: the management of labour under just-in-time manufacturing systems. In P. Blyton and P. Turnbull (eds), *Reassessing Human Resource Management.* London: Sage, 56–73.

Derrida, J. 1978: *Writing and Difference.* London: Routledge and Kegan Paul.

Dohse, K., Jurgens, U. and Malsch, T. 1985: From 'Fordism' to 'Toyotism'? The social organization of the labour process in the Japanese automobile industry. *Politics and Society,* **14**(2), 115–46.

Dopson, S. and Stewart, R. 1993: Information technology, organizational restructuring and the future of middle management. *New Technology, Work and Employment.* **8**(1), 10–20.

Evans, M., Gunz, H. and Jalland, M. 1995: Avoiding the perils of downsizing. *The Financial Post,* 29 July.

Ezzamel, M., Lilley, S., Wilkinson, A. and Willmott, H. 1996: Practices and practicalities in human resource management. *Human Resource Management Journal,* **5**(3), 7–23.

Garrahan, P. and Stewart, P. 1992: *The Nissan Enigma. Flexibility at Work in a Local Economy.* London: Mansell.

Geary, J. F. 1994: Task participation: enabled or constrained? In K. Sisson (ed.), *Personnel Management: A Comprehensive Guide to Theory and Practice in Britain.* Oxford: Blackwell, 634–61.

Graham, L. 1993: Inside a Japanese transplant: a critical perspective. *Work and Occupations,* **32**(9), 147–73.

Grey, C. and Mitev, N. 1995: Re-engineering organizations: a critical appraisal. *Personnel Review,* **24**(1), 6–18.

Grint, K. 1994: Re-engineering history: social resonances and business process reengineering. *Organization,* **1**(1), 179–201.

Grint, K. and Willcocks, L. 1995: Business process re-engineering in theory and practice: business paradise regained? *New Technology, Work and Employment,* **19**(2), 99–109.

Guest, D. and Peccei, R. 1992: Employee involvement: redundancy as a critical case. *Human Resource Management Journal,* **2**(3), 34–59.

Hammer, M. 1990: Re-engineering work: don't automate, obliterate. *Harvard Business Review,* **68**(4), 104–12.

Hammer, M. 1993: Quoted in *Forbes Magazine,* Summer, 71.

Hammer, M. 1994: Re-engineering work is not hocus pocus. *Across the Board,* September, 45–7.

Hammer, M. and Champy, J. 1993: *Re-engineering the Corporation: A Manifesto for Business Revolution.* London: Nicholas Brearley.

Herriot, P. 1998: The role of the HRM function in building a new proposition for staff. In P. Sparrow and M. Marchington, (eds), *Human Resource Management, The New Agenda.* London: Financial Times/ Pitman, 106–16.

Herriot, P. and Pemberton, C. 1997: Facilitating new deals. *Human Resource Management,* **7**(1), 45–56.

Holbeche, L. 1994: *Career Development in Flatter Structures: Raising the Issues.* Report 1, Horsham: Roffey Park Management Institute.

Holbeche, L. 1995: *Career Development in Flatter Structures: Organizational Practices.* Report 2, Horsham: Roffey Park Management Institute.

Howard, C. 1996: The stress on managers caused by downsizing. *The Globe and Mail,* 30 January.

Huselid, M. 1995: The impact of human resource management practices on turnover, productivity and corporate financial performance. *Academy of Management Journal,* **38**(3), 635–72.

Inkson, A. and Coe, M. 1994: *Career Ladders.* London: British Institute of Management.

Institute of Management/Manpower. 1995: *Survey of Long Term Employment Strategies.* London: IM.

Involvement and Participation Association. 1992: *Towards Industrial Partnership: A New Approach to Management–Union Relations.* London: IPA.

Kanter, R. M. 1989: *When Giants Learn to Dance.* New York: Simon and Schuster.

Kettley, P. 1995: *Employee Morale During Downsizing*. The Institute of Employment Studies, Report 291.

Kinnie, N., Hutchinson, S. and Purcell, J. 1996: The People Management Implications of Leaner Ways of Working. Report by the University of Bath, *Issues in People Management, No. 15*, London: Institute of Personnel and Development, 6–63.

Legge, K. 1978: *Power, Innovation and Problem-Solving in Personnel Management*. London: McGraw-Hill.

Legge, K. 1989: Information Technology: Personnel Management's Lost Opportunity? *Personnel Review*, **18**(5) (monograph issue).

Legge, K. 1993: The role of personnel specialists: centrality or marginalization? In J. Clark (ed.), *Human Resource Management and Technical Change*. London: Sage, 20–42.

Legge, K. 1995: *Human Resource Management: The Rhetorics, The Realities*. Basingstoke: Macmillan.

MacDuffie, J. P. 1995: Human resource bundles and manufacturing performance: organizational logic and flexible production systems in the world auto industry. *Industrial and Labor Relations Review*, **48**(2), 197–221.

McArdle, L., Rowlinson, M., Proctor, S., Hassard, J. and Forrester, P. 1995: Total quality management and participation: employee empowerment, or enhancement of exploitation? In A. Wilkinson and H. Willmott (eds), *Making Quality Critical*, London: Routledge, 156–72.

McCabe, D. 1995: *Quality Initiatives in the Financial Services*. Manchester: Financial Services Research Centre.

MacInnes, J. 1988: New technology in Scotbank: gender, class and work. In R. Hyman and W. Streeck (eds), *New Technology and Industrial Relations*, Oxford: Blackwell, 28–40.

Marginson, P., Edwards, P. K., Martin, R., Purcell, J. and Sisson, K. 1988: *Beyond the Workplace: Managing Industrial Relations in Multi-Plant Enterprises*. Oxford: Blackwell.

Martinez, L. M. and Weston, S. 1992: Human resource management and trade union responses: bringing the politics of the workplace back into the debate. In P. Blyton and P. Turnbull (eds), *Reassessing Human Resource Management*, London: Sage, 215–32.

Millward, N. and Stevens, M. 1986: *British Workplace Industrial Relations 1980–84*. The DE/ESRC/PS1/ACAS Survey, London: Gower.

Millward, N., Stevens, M., Smart, D. and Hawes, W. R. 1992: *Workplace Industrial Relations in Transition. The ED/ESRC/PSI/ACAS Surveys*. Aldershot: Dartmouth.

Mumford, E. 1969: *Computers: Planning and Personnel Management*. London: IPM.

Mumford, E. 1972: *Job Satisfaction, A Study of Computer Specialists*. London: Longman.

Mumford, E. and Hendricks, R. 1996: Business process re-engineering RIP. *People Management*, **3**(9), 22–9.

Newell, H. J. 1991: Field of Dreams: Evidence of 'New Employee Relations' in Greenfield Sites. D. Phil. dissertation, University of Oxford.

Oliver, N. and Wilkinson, B. 1992: *The Japanisation of British Industry, New Developments in the 1990s* (2nd edn). Oxford: Blackwell.

Oram, M. and Wellins, R. 1995: *Re-engineering's Missing Ingredient: The Human Factor*. London: Institute of Personnel and Development.

Packwood, T., Pollitt, C. and Roberts, S. 1998: Good medicine? A case study of business process re-engineering in a hospital. *Policy and Politics*, **26**(4), October, 401–15.

Parker, M. and Slaughter, J. 1988: *Choosing Sides: Unions and the Team Concept*. Boston: Labor Notes.

Peters, T. J. and Waterman, R. H. Jr. 1982: *In Search of Excellence, Lessons from America's Best Run Companies*. New York: Harper and Row.

Piore, M. and Sabel, C. 1984: *The Second Industrial Divide*. New York: Basic Books.

Purcell, J. 1996: Human resource bundles of best practice: a utopian cul-de-sac? Paper presented to the ESRC Seminar Series, 'Contribution of HR Strategy to Business Performance', Cranfield, 1 February.

Rees, C., Scarbrough, H. and Terry, M. 1996: The People Management Implications of Leaner Ways of Working. Report by IRRU, Warwick Business School, University of Warwick, *Issues in People Management*, No. 15. London: Institute of Personnel and Development, 64–115.

Rice, D. and Dreilinger, C. 1991: After the downsizing. *Training and Development*, **45**(5), 41–4.

Roach, S. S. 1996: The hollow ring of the productivity revival. *Harvard Business Review*, **34**(6), 81–9.

Rothwell, S. 1985: Company employment policies and new technology. *Industrial Relations Journal*, **16**(3), 43–51.

Sewell, G. and Wilkinson, B. 1992: Empowerment or emasculation? Shopfloor surveillance in a total quality organization. In P. Blyton and P. Turnbull (eds), *Reassessing Human Resource Management*, London: Sage, 97–115.

Sisson, K. 1990: Introducing the Human Resource Management Journal. *Human Resource Management Journal*, **1**(1), Autumn, 1–11.

Sisson, K. 1993: In search of HRM. *British Journal of Industrial Relations*, **31**(2), 201–10.

Sparrow, P. 1998: New organizational forms, processes, jobs and psychological contracts: resolving the HRM issues. In P. Sparrow and M. Marchington (eds), *Human Resource Management, The New Agenda*. London: Financial Times/Pitman, 117–41.

Sparrow, P. and Marchington, M. 1998: *Human Resource Management, The New Agenda*. London: Financial Times/Pitman.

Stiles, P., Gratton, L., Truss, C., Hope-Hailey, V. and McGovern, P. 1997: Performance management and the psychological contract. *Human Resource Management Journal*, **7**(1), 57–66.

Storey, J. 1992: *Developments in the Management of Human Resources*. Oxford: Blackwell.

Strassman, P. 1994: The hocus-pocus of re-engineering, *Across the Board*, **34**(4), 35–8.

Taylor, R. 1994: *The Future of Trade Unions*. London: André Deutsch.

Terry, M. and Purcell, J. 1997: Return to Slender. *People Management*, **3**(21), 46–51.

Tolliday, S. and Zeitlin, J. (eds) 1986: *The Automobile Industry and its Workers: Between Fordism and Flexibility*. Cambridge: Polity.

Turnbull, P. 1988: The limits to Japanisation – just-in-time, labour relations and the UK automotive industry. *New Technology, Work and Employment*, **3**(1), 7–20.

Turnbull, P. and Wass, V. (1997) Job insecurity and labour market lessons: the (mis)management of redundancy in steel making, coal mining and port transport. *Journal of Management Studies*, **34**(1), 27–51.

Tyson, S. and Fell, A. 1986: *Evaluating the Personnel Function*. London: Hutchinson.

Vielba, C. A. 1995: Manager's working hours. Paper presented to the British Academy of Management Annual Conference, Sheffield University Management School, 11–13 September.

Weick, K. E. 1995: *Sensemaking in Organizations*. Thousand Oaks, CA: Sage.

Whitfield, K., and Poole, M. 1997: Organizing employment for high performance. *Organization Studies*, **18**(5), 745–63.

Wibberly, M. 1993: Does lean necessarily equal mean? *Personnel Management*, **25**(7), 32–5.

Wickens, P. 1987: *The Road to Nissan*. London: Macmillan.

Wickens, P. 1993: Lean production and beyond the system: its critics and the future. *Human Resource Management Journal*, **5**(2), 33–49.

Wilkinson, A., Godfrey, G. and Marchington, M. 1997: Bouquets, brickbats and blinkers: TQM and EI in practice. *Organization Studies*, **18**(5), 799–819.

Wilkinson, A. and Marchington, M. 1994: TQM: instant pudding for the personnel function? *Human Resource Management Journal*, **5**(2), 33–49.

Williams, K., Haslam, C., Williams, J. and Cutler, T., with Adcroft, A., and Johal, S. 1992: Against lean production. *Economy and Society*, **21**(3), 321–54.

Willman, P. and Winch, G. 1985: *Innovation and Management Control. Labour Relations at BL Cars*. Cambridge: Cambridge University Press.

Willmott, H. 1994: Business process re-engineering and human resource management. *Personnel Review*, **23**(3), 34–46.

Willmott, H. 1995: The odd couple?: re-engineering business processes; managing human relations. *New Technology, Work and Employment*, **10**(2), 89–98.

Womack, J. P., Jones, D. T. and Roos, D. 1990: *The Machine that Changed the World*. New York: Rawson Associates.

Wood, S. 1996: High commitment management and payment systems. *Journal of Management Studies*, **33**(1), 53–78.

Wood, S. and Albanese, M. T. 1995: Can we speak of high commitment management on the shop floor? *Journal of Management Studies*, **32**(2), 215–47.

Wyatt Company 1994: *Best Practices in Corporate Restructuring*. Toronto, Ontario: Wyatt.

3

Personnel Management in the Extended Organization

Trevor Colling

Business growth for much of the twentieth century has been achieved through the development of increasingly bureaucratic and integrated corporations. Subcontracting and alliances between small firms, which characterized Britain's early industrial development, appeared to have been consigned to history. As capital ownership became more and more concentrated, and as the size of workplaces grew, 'the visible hand of management replaced the . . . invisible hand of market forces' (Chandler 1977: 1). Organizing production in these larger enterprises required hierarchies of management capable of passing information and directions from executive level to the shopfloor. So inevitable seemed this parallel development of capitalist development and bureaucracy that they were considered practically synonymous. As Blau (1966: 38) put it, 'strange as it may seem, the free-enterprise system fosters the development of bureaucracy in the government, in private companies, and in unions'. Management science and the study of industrial relations has focused therefore on the assumption of managing within integrated, self-sufficient and hierarchically organized firms (Chandler 1962; Hannah 1976; Pollard 1965; Williamson 1981).

Amidst changes in the breadth, nature and sources of competitive pressures, however, classic bureaucracies appear to be fragmenting once again. New structures, termed variously 'virtual', 'networked' or 'extended', have begun to emerge. Production organized increasingly across national boundaries has stretched organizations and required adaptability in corporate structures and management styles. Information storage, diffusion and retrieval within firms has been improved by emerging telecommunications and computing technology, diminishing the requirements for extensive managerial hierarchies. In new markets, driven by technological or knowledge-based innovation, smaller, nimbler organizations have been able to compete effectively against slower-moving large corporations. Consortium-based or networked organizations have emerged in which specialist products and services are provided by organizations working together rather than by single entities. Support functions have been transferred to arm's-length companies or subcontractors and new services have been bought in rather than developed internally. Extreme examples, such as Nike, Amstrad, and Nintendo, do not own any manufacturing capacity at all. Networks of subcontractors assemble products and some core functions, including research and product development, are also outsourced (Foster and Plowden 1996: 105).

The reasoning that led many organizations to follow this path typically followed from a review of their 'core' activities, in some cases in the wake of relatively disastrous over-diversification in the 1970s and early 1980s, combined with a perceived need to get 'back to basics' and concentrate on 'core competencies' (Peters and Waterman 1982). The organization had little or no expertise, went the argument, in carrying out many of the ancillary or professional services described above. Not only that, it had little idea of the market rate for such activities. In practice, it tended to relate what it paid to its employees doing these activities to the arrangements for the core staff. At the very least, continued the argument, the organization should put the activities out to tender to establish their true market cost. Other things being equal, the organization should subcontract these activities to the 'specialists', who would be responsible for any research and development in their area, and concentrate its own energies and resources on the core products or services.

Much more substantial theoretical underpinning is to be found in the developing branch of economics known as transaction costs analysis (Williamson 1975; 1979; 1980; 1981b; 1985). On the basis of this, organization theorists explain oscillation between two broad models of hierarchies and markets with reference along the following lines. It is assumed that, in capitalist economies, production is organized most effectively through the market, but that this may not be possible in some circumstances. Bounded rationality occurs where imperfect information flows between economic actors resulting in ineffective decision making. Further complications arise when actors seek to advance their self-interests with guile or where there is the suspicion that they might do so. An imbalance of information or expertise within a purely market relationship may thus lead to exploitation of one party by the other, unless other control mechanisms are available. Opportunism is also likely where the number of competitors is limited, offering incentives to collude in anti-competitive behaviour to the disadvantage of buyers. Finally, where the process requires considerable investment, or can be expedited only through the use of valuable physical or human resources, then market transactions may be simply too risky. By implication, following this line of argument, the requirement for hierarchies has been diminished as competition has intensified and extended, as information flows between and within firms have improved, and as the risk of opportunistic behaviour has reduced accordingly.

In the UK, however, state policy has also played a decisive role in shifting the balance from hierarchy to market. In the 1980s and 1990s, classic public-sector bureaucracies, including British Gas, the Central Electricity Generating Board and British Rail, were fragmented and their constituent parts pitted against each other in open competition (Colling and Ferner 1995). The so-called 'flexible firm' model devised by the Institute for Manpower Studies (Atkinson 1984; Atkinson and Meager 1986) *de facto* became government policy: public service organizations were effectively required, as the result of provisions introduced for compulsory competitive tendering and market testing, to think in terms of a 'core' and 'peripheral' workforce each with very different terms and conditions of employment. Overall, promotion of an 'enterprise culture' throughout the 1980s produced an increase of two-thirds in the number of UK businesses, an average of nearly 500 additional firms every working day (Felstead 1993: 20).

This chapter focuses on the personal management implications of, arguably, the most significant of these developments, namely outsourcing or contracting out, under which key functions or support services are provided by third parties via contract. The chapter begins by reviewing the incidence of what will be termed here the 'extended organization'. Developments in the demand for business services, such as cleaning, catering, accountancy and legal advice, are examined and strong trends are identified towards outsourcing. The chapter then proceeds to consider the character of the relationships within and between firms subject to outsourcing. Although these are potentially varied, important factors stemming from the regulatory context in the UK, the structure and dynamic of business services markets and the motives of buyers engaged in outsourcing have tended to perpetuate arm's-length contractual arrangements. The third section considers the ramifications for employment and the personnel function of the predominantly low-trust relationships between firms which have been engendered. The fourth and concluding section discusses whether or not such arrangements will continue to prevail following recent and likely labour market reforms and the promotion of new contracting practice in the public sector.

The Incidence of the Extended Organization

Some organizational commentaries positing the end of hierarchy owe more to the conventions of prophesy than to close analysis. Perceived technological imperatives conjure visions of the boundaryless or virtual firm in which work and production is almost limitlessly fluid (see, for example, Hamel and Prahalad 1996). For sceptics like Goffee and Hunt (quoted in Flood 1998: 52), 'what is remarkable about the language of modern organizational analysis is the extent to which it describes a world which literally does not exist'. This section evaluates the extent to which outsourcing activity has spread by examining the evidence from case studies and surveys.

Case studies

The most significant shift towards contractual relations has occured in the public sector (Ascher 1987; Colling 1999; Harrison 1993). Government policy rolled out through the 1980s delivered radical extensions of contracting programmes through a variety of means. Management practice in the state sector has always carried an exemplar role and the extension of outsourcing across the economy is at least partly attributable to this. Private-sector organizations have always bought in goods and services to some degree, but they have only recently aspired to extending their organizations on a scale comparable with the public sector.

Local authority services have been subject to the most comprehensive contracting regimes. Competitive tendering was required first in 1980 for proportions of work carried out by highways and building maintenance functions. The Local Government Act 1988 required authorities to expose practically all of their ancillary services to competition. Professional and technical services (including finance, legal and personnel functions) were incorporated into the local government legislation in 1992. In the NHS, catering, cleaning and laundry services were opened to competition in 1983. Attempts to extend the practice here, however, have not relied upon compulsion through legislation (Whitbread and Hooper 1993). Rather, increasing ministerial pressure applied through the course of the 1980s was augmented by structural reform. Outsourcing of key ancillary, professional and scientific services increased following the creation of autonomous trusts and the concomitant requirement to manage budgets locally. In the civil service 'Competing for Quality' policies introduced in 1991 did not require outsourcing *per se*, but encouraged it explicitly. Managers required to review the efficiency of their operations subjected them to a process of prior options. Among the most favoured of these was competitive tendering and strategic outsourcing (where no in-house bid is sought). Combined with the creation of agencies, these measures have ensured the transfer of technical and research functions, facilities management and information technology support to private-sector companies.

Breaking into these new markets has not been entirely cost free for contracting companies. They have faced resistance from unions and public-sector managers and competition from existing in-house services. But the impact on the contracting sector has been enormous. The proportion of the contracting market accounted for by the public sector has grown inexorably since the early 1980s. Though there are significant differences between services, the trend illustrated in table 3.1 for contract catering is revealing.

Private-sector business remains the largest single group of customers by far, accounting for over half of the total market. In just four years, however, the proportion of public-sector clients more than doubled to nearly a quarter of the total, driven almost exclusively by growth in the education catering market, one of the key areas covered by the compulsory competitive tendering legislation. The importance of this market is particularly striking when it is recalled that education catering has been one of the most difficult areas for contractors to break into (Walsh and Davis 1993). In other words, the proportion of work deriving from the public sector may yet be dramatically increased.

Case study evidence from the private sector is somewhat piecemeal, but also points to an increase in outsourcing activity. In some cases, this has involved merely extending existing

Table 3.1   The changing structure of the UK contract catering market, 1989–1993

| | *Percentage outlets per sector* | | |
	1989	*1992*	*1993*
Business and industry	**82.6**	**72.7**	**53.4**
Independent schools	5.7	7.0	4.4
Public catering	1.4	4.4	15.1
Construction sites, oil rigs, Training centres	0.7	2.3	2.3
Approx public sector[a]	**9.6**	**13.6**	**24.8**
Health	2.9	3.6	3.0
State education	2.8	4.6	17.8
Local authorities	3.1	3.4	2.0
Ministry of Defence	0.8	2.0	2.0

[a]   Figure arrived at by totalling health, state education, local authorities and MoD

Source: Keynote 1994a

custom and practice. Subcontracting in clothing and construction has long been common, though patterns have changed in response to recession or heightened levels of competition (Evans and Lewis 1989; Druker 1994; Rainnie 1984; Ram 1994). Elsewhere, organizational change has been promoted by deregulation and has displayed elements of the models and procedures adopted in the public sector. European airlines, led by British Airways, have adopted a 'core airline' model in which security, catering and some aspects of aircraft maintenance are subcontracted (Colling 1994; ITF 1992; Warhurst 1994). In telecommunications, energy and water too, pressure to reduce costs has been met by an increase in the use of subcontractors for ancillary services and for some core tasks (Ferner et al. 1994; Ferner and Colling 1993; Starks 1993).

The survey evidence

A MULTI-SECTOR PHENOMENON

Such impressions are confirmed by survey data. At the end of the 1980s, the Advisory Conciliation and Arbitration Service (ACAS 1988) reported that subcontractors were used by 77 per cent of firms and the Warwick Company Level Industrial Relations Survey (CLIRS) discovered the practice in 83 per cent of establishments (Marginson et al. 1993). The 1998 Workplace Employee Relations Survey (WERS) suggests that the great majority of employers (90 per cent) now contract out one or more service (Cully et al. 1998: 9). Significantly, proportions of employers involved are now similar in the public and private sectors, confirming accelerated take-up of the practice in the latter.

Running these findings in sequence would suggest further that the incidence of contracting has increased over the period (from 77 per cent to 90 per cent). Temptation to do so should be resisted, however, because the populations involved are varied and the findings relate to different levels of analysis. Debate about the rate of change has been heated. Early findings suggesting radical changes to organizational structures (e.g., Atkinson and Meager 1986) were contested fiercely (e.g., Hunter and MacInnes 1991). Marginson blamed imprecise survey methodologies and the skewed presentation of results for offering a misleading impression of the rate and nature of changes to employment structures (Marginson 1991; Marginson and Sisson 1988). The CLIRS study, by contrast, specifically tested for shifting attitudes to contracting and found the majority of establishment (61 per cent) suggesting there had been no change in company policy in the preceding five years.

Close scrutiny of available data highlights change which is cumulatively significant rather than cataclysmic. The CLIRS survey revealed that 39 per cent of establishments had changed their policy on subcontracting in the previous five years, hardly a negligible proportion (Marginson and Sisson 1988: 88). Indeed, it assumes added significance when it is considered that such changes led to one or more service being contracted out in the majority of cases. The focus on establishment level figures, justified properly on the grounds that it reveals the 'actual extent of subcontracting at local level' (Marginson and Sisson 1988: 86), tends to eclipse other prominent findings that company policy (as opposed to establishment practice) had changed in over half (56 per cent) of the sample. Respondents at this level emphasized, once again, that the majority of these changes had led to increased levels of subcontracting activity. Recent WERS data appears to confirm that this lag between changing policy and practice is now being overcome. One quarter of all employers surveyed in 1998 said that their actual use of subcontracting had increased (Cully et al. 1998: 9).

Preliminary findings presented in table 3.2 indicate growth in all four of the areas for which longitudinal data was available at the time of writing. The majority of establishments now subcontract cleaning and buildings maintenance services whilst the proportion of those buying in security increased by two-thirds.

The growth of business services

The relative decline of manufacturing industry and the growth of the 'new service economy' is an established and general phenomenon (Gershuny and Miles 1983). Across Europe, over 60 per cent of the workforce now work in service industries (Eurostat 1993).

Three distinctive aspects of the UK experience, however, highlight further the development of outsourcing. First, having begun in the early 1960s, substantially earlier than most other developed economies, the trend towards services is particularly advanced in the UK (Dunne 1988; Temple 1994). Second, the shift accelerated in the early 1980s, with the result that the UK economy is now more dependent upon services than most of its major international competitors, with a greater proportion of the workforce (69 per cent) employed in service occupations (Eurostat 1993). Finally, there are key differences in the kinds of services being developed. Whereas service growth elsewhere has been fuelled by tourism, restaurants and distribution, business services have been disproportionately important in the UK (Eurostat 1993). The percentage share of total UK employment accounted for by business services more than doubled between 1954 and 1991 from 9 per cent to 22 per cent (IRRU/IER 1993). More than half of that growth occurred in the final ten-year period between 1981 and 1991 and coincided with reductions in public-sector employment.

Detailed analysis of business services statistics is a difficult exercise because the growing importance of the service sector to the economy is only now being reflected in official statistics (Allen and Du Gay 1994). Much of the official data available are derived from

Table 3.2 Subcontracting in establishments, 1990 and 1997

Activity	Percentage establishments		Percentage change
	1990	*1997*	
Cleaning of buildings and premises	41	59	44
Security	21	35	67
Catering	17	—	
Building maintenance	46	61	33
Printing/photocopying	18	—	
Payroll	8	—	
Transport of documents/goods	30	39	30

Source: Millward et al. 1992; Cully et al. 1998

Table 3.3   Employment in selected business services, 1989–1998

	1989 (1,000)	1993 (1,000)	Percentage change	1998 (1,000)	Percentage change
Canteens/catering	173,821	179,769	3	203,854	13
Computing	172,359	183,787	7	388,214	111
Legal	473,047	187,723	−60	223,414	19
Accounting	—	161,322	—	157,559	−2
Market research/consultancy		144,110	—	189,227	31
Recruitment/personnel			—	508,482	—
Investigation/security			—	111,820	—
Industrial cleaning	362,574	411,268	13	411,311	0
Sewage/refuse	48,835	82,715	69	72,133	−13

Source: Office for National Statistics, unpublished data 1999

VAT returns and are therefore limited and in need of very careful interpretation (Business Monitor PA 1003). Labour Force Survey (**LFS**) data do now define service industries more closely. Identifying trends over time is still bedevilled by gaps in early data sets and by changes in the application of standard industrial classifications (**SICs**), but it does offer impressionistic evidence. Table 3.3 traces employment growth in a selection of business services provided usually on a contract or outsourced basis. Based on unpublished data from the Office of National Statistics, which applies 1992 SICs consistently, it suggests continued, if uneven, growth through the 1990s. Ancillary services, such as canteens, refuse collection and cleaning, grew steadily over the period as a whole. Catering grew more strongly in the second half of the period since 1993, whilst for cleaning and refuse the earlier period from 1989 was stronger. But it is the data for professional and technical services which are most startling. Recruitment and personnel services are the largest single employer among the sample and the strongest growth over the period is provided by computing services.

The strong suggestion from the industrial economics literature that little of this employment growth is genuinely new further confirms the resurgence of subcontracting (Dunne 1988; Temple 1994). Beyond areas like computing, where the development of new technology is clearly a factor, much of the rise in employment in these areas can be attributed to the transfer of jobs, whether directly or indirectly, from in-house functions to the vendors of business services.

The Character of the Extended Organization

Subcontracting does not lead inevitably to particular types of employment relationships. The structures through which employment is managed, the priorities which managers seek to meet, and the responses of employees themselves are influenced critically by the character of the extended organizations within which they work. A range of contractual relationships are possible with variations carrying implications for approaches to employment within them (see, Felstead 1993; Sako 1992).

At one end of the spectrum, emphasis attached to competition between providers and the close scrutiny of contractual terms and performance will tend to foster low-trust or 'distanced' relationships. Contracts are allocated primarily on the basis of price competition and subsequent buyer–vendor relationships are characterized as arm's length. That is, the respective parties will retain information and conduct operations with close reference to formally constituted contracts. Security of tenure for vendors is likely to be weak with buyers preferring short contract periods to allow for frequent market testing. Under these circumstances, operating costs will be tightly controlled by the buyer (to counteract opportunistic behaviour) and by the vendor (to maximize profit margins). Managers will be inclined to monitor labour utilization closely to ensure compliance with stipulated performance criteria and to minimize short-run costs.

At the other extreme, 'engaged' models infer a different set of inter-firm relationships characterized by some degree of mutual dependency (Beaumont et al. 1996). Market mechanisms are less important and may be absent altogether. Buyers may choose to reduce the number of service contractors, selecting some as 'preferred suppliers'. A broader range of attributes than price alone will be considered during the evaluation of bids, though this may still be important. Contracts are augmented by joint approaches to strategic and operational issues manifest in anything from mixed project teams to shared equity arrangements. As bureaucratic and financial ties are increased, the formal content of contracts diminishes, is less prescriptive in nature, and is relied upon less. Greater security is built into the contract through longer terms and guaranteed levels of demand. Performance monitoring is not prohibited by such arrangements, but may be less formal or delegated to the vendor. These kinds of arrangements provide opportunities to take longer-run approaches to employment matters. Pressures on pay and other labour costs are weakened in the relative absence of cost pressures overall and some measure of employment security is afforded by longer contract terms.

Choices between these options are not made in a vacuum, but are conditioned by 'existing social, structural and cultural constraints and facilitators' (Lane and Bachman 1994: 3). Discussion now shifts to how these are configured in the UK and their consequences for emergent contractual relationships. Three sets of factors are highlighted – the regulatory context, prevailing market structures, and buyers' motives. With some variation between services, these pressures tend to foster low-trust, market-driven approaches to outsourcing.

The regulatory context

Contractual relationships are influenced by legal regulation of business and employment relationships. Preferred models and practice are promoted actively in some countries. Integral to German law, for example, is a conception of the state which confers an obligation to impose general legal standards on society, including economic entities (Lane and Bachman 1997: 243). Lawyers play key roles in German companies and individual managers are well versed in the Legal Code. Contract law specifically is founded upon a series of articles requiring ethical standards in contract construction and an emphasis on mutual responsibility. German courts have played important roles in protecting weaker parties against the use of contracts to impose unreasonable standards or penalties by large companies.

In the UK, however, minimal state involvement in commercial and employment practice has long been the norm – a convention referred to as voluntarism or *laissez-faire* (see Clark 1996). In general terms, law has developed with the priority of protecting individuals from the unreasonable use of power by the state. The rights of individuals to contract as they see fit has been interpreted as a critical index of such freedom and firms have been left to arrive at voluntary agreements with suppliers and business partners. Standard terms are less common in the UK than elsewhere and grounds on which British courts intervene in contractual disputes are much narrower. Mutual or wider social interests are viewed as extraneous. Decisions tend to revolve instead around the internal coherence of the contract and whether and how it can be enforced. Assumptions that contracts reflect equal status and power pervade decision making and there are few protections for potentially vulnerable parties as a consequence.

Imperatives to allow firms to organize their own resources have tended to leave employees affected by business contracts with few protections too. Where low priority is accorded to job security, as in the UK, employers are able to expedite redundancies relatively cheaply and this tends to be reflected in bidding strategies. Firms are able to submit low bids on the assumption that savings in labour costs will restore profit margins in the medium term. European law counteracts such strategies to some degree. The Acquired Rights Directive protects the terms and conditions of staff affected by business transfers. For precisely this reason, British Governments have been reluctant to implement it. The Directive's transposition into British law, the Transfer of Undertakings (Protection of Employment) Regulations 1981 (TUPE), was limited for several years by a failure to acknowledge its application to public-sector transfers. Successful legal challenges in the European Courts obliged the government to amend the regulations in 1993, but notably few attempts have been made to lift continuing confusion about the precise circumstances in which protections are available.

Though less direct in its nature, financial systems also have an impact upon contractual relationships. As chapter 1 has already pointed out, in the UK these cohere around a stock market which is notoriously short-termist in approach. It has become commonplace to observe that managerial attention is focused disproportionately on short-run financial returns. Competitive strategies are defensive, aimed at maximizing profitability and dividend payments in order to fend off hostile takeovers. Conversely, the opportunities to extend market positions through acquisition, rather than organic growth, are exploited more often in the UK than in mainland Europe. As later sections discuss, this kind of activity has been a particular feature of the development of business services markets.

Each of these aspects of the regulatory context tends to foster arm's-length contracting relationships. Low levels of state involvement in the construction of contracts permits wide variation in their terms and opportunistic behaviour by buyers and vendors. This is maximized, of course, where contractual terms are cloaked in secrecy as is often the case in the UK. Felstead's (1993) attempts to study franchise contracts were frustrated by the refusal of two-thirds of the companies approached to provide copies. In many cases, even prospective franchisers were required to pay non-returnable deposits before they could inspect agreements (Felstead 1993: 95). Priorities accorded to short-term returns by financial systems may also be internalized. The scope for inter-firm co-operation is reduced for fear of revealing financial information to potential predators or competitors. Even where consortium bidding is common, there are few examples of the sort of shared financial arrangements presupposed in the engaged contracts model.

Market structure

Regulatory mechanisms are mediated by prevailing market structures and dynamics. 'Small numbers bargaining' refers to circumstances where limited numbers of suppliers are able to compete for contracts. It is problematic because of the risk of collusive and opportuntistic behaviour. With some variation between services, trends within the business services sector in the UK has tended to diminish, rather than broaden, competition between suppliers and this too might be seen to encourage low-trust relations with buyers.

The business services sector in the UK is not marked generally by the effective growth of small businesses. Entrepreneurial behaviour is apparent. The number of companies offering business services nearly trebled between 1981 and 1991, from 43,000 to 120,000 (Central Statistical Office 1992). Two-thirds of these companies are small, with turnovers less than £100,000, and a third are very small indeed, with turnovers under £34,000 (Keynote 1994b). But this picture is misleading for two reasons. First, some of this growth is accounted for by the fragmentation of large organizations such as GKN, NatWest and Thames Water (Shutt and Whittington 1987). Public organizations have also 'spun off' their in-house functions to allow them to compete for work outside their organizational boundaries (Paddon 1991). Second, small businesses have tended not to develop significant market shares and those that have been successful have come very quickly to the acquisitive attention of their larger competitors. Research looking at the award of contracts in local government, for example, found that successful private companies were relatively large enterprises. Over half employ over a hundred full-time staff and a third have turnovers in excess of £10m per annum (BMRB International 1995). Parent companies such as Granada, Rentokil, BET, and Securicor now have turnovers in excess of £500 million, putting them among the largest 200 companies in the UK (Extel Financial 1994).

The internationalization of service markets, partly driven in Europe by the creation of the internal market, has added an extra dimension to these trends. The European Union's Public Procurement directives are beginning to open up very valuable new markets for UK contractors in Germany, Italy and France (Paddon 1993). They have also stimulated substantial interest in the UK market from major international competitors (Digings 1991). UK contractors now face competition from European companies such as CGEA, Electrolux, and ISS International and, increasingly, from US and Japanese companies seeking to position themselves in the European market. These large companies wield significant influence in the marketplace. Table 3.4 illustrates the share of local government contracts awarded to the top ten companies in each service area. The majority of contracts continue to be awarded to in-house workforces, hence the small share of available contracts overall revealed in column one. Of those contracts awarded to the private sector, however, well over half in each case has gone to the largest companies. As noted above, the contract catering market is particularly concentrated with practically all private-sector contracts being held by just eight companies.

Table 3.4   Share of local government contracts held by top ten companies, by service

Service	Share of available contracts (% by value)	Share of contracts awarded to the private sector (% by value)
Building cleaning	15.2	56.1
Refuse collection	22	78
Education and welfare catering (top eight companies)	14.5	98.6
Ground maintenance	15.2	73.8
Vehicle maintenance	11	69.7

Source: LGMB 1994

Buyer motives

Motives held by buyers will affect critically the kind of contractual relationships established with vendors. Generalization on this point is difficult because objectives can be mixed and are rarely proclaimed publicly. In abstract terms, however, five key reasons for outsourcing can be deduced (see Harrison and Kelley 1993; Hunter 1998).

First, 'capacity subcontracting' refers to situations where demand is characterized by peaks and troughs. Where demand outstrips the capacity of in-house resources, additional production will be sourced through external suppliers. In some instances this might be viewed more properly as insourcing (where it involves the casual employment of temporary employees, for example). But it can be regarded as outsourcing where it happens rarely or when the work is usually conducted in-house.

Second, where elements of production are too sophisticated, and required too rarely, to warrant a continued in-house presence, then 'specialization subcontracting' may be adopted. Professional and technical services will be covered primarily by these sorts of arrangements, though catering may also be included. Employers' attempts to gain access to innovations in information technology have contributed to the boom in outsourced computing services.

Third, 'power subcontracting' refers to attempts to bypass internal obstacles to change by rendering these 'someone else's problem' (Atkinson 1986). This approach has been prevalent in parts of the public sector in response to pay restraint or industrial conflict. That limits on civil service pay increases might be obviated for those transferred to the private sector was referred to as an explicit objective of market testing, for example (Oughton 1994). More usually, however, outsourcing has been threatened or used to weaken employee resistance to restructuring. Early instances of privatization, involving refuse collection in the London boroughs, for example, were explicit attempts to restructure industrial relations (Ascher 1987; Colling 1995) and similar patterns are evident now among groups previously thought immune, including administrative staff and care workers.

Fourth, though often related to 'power subcontracting', cost reduction can be a distinct motive. Vendor firms are often able to realize economies unavailable to the buyer. For example, large catering firms extract preferential purchase terms from food producers and retailers and may undertake to pass these savings on to the buyer. In IT, savings can often be made from hardware and software purchases, a large proportion coming from preferential licensing arrangements enjoyed by some IT vendors. In labour-intensive services, however, wage and employment costs are a primary target.

Finally, fads and fashion undoubtedly play a part and many have begun to point to an 'outsourcing bandwagon' (Lonsdale and Cox 1998: 55). Distinctions in business education between analysis and prescription have been blurred and observers of outsourcing have been accused frequently of promoting the practice (see Pollert 1991). Consultants have also played important roles in spreading the practice, persuading clients of the merits of outsourcing by referring to the promise of cost savings and undertaking to take fees only as a proportion of savings achieved.

Partly because of the influence of public-sector models, evidence suggests that buyer motives for outsourcing tend to be 'cost' and 'power' based. In a survey undertaken by Harrison and Kelley (1993: 219), for example, only one-third of managers claimed specialization or capacity reasons for outsourcing, whilst one-fifth said their primary objective was explicitly to lower labour costs. Other evidence suggests organizations realise cost savings even where this has not been an explicit objective. More than 50 per cent of organizations outsourcing information technology services cut costs as a result and the figure is even higher in the public sector (83 per cent) (Pritchard 1998: 14). These factors are reflected frequently in contractual arrangements. Fitzgerald and Wilcocks (1994), in their review of the types of contracts used in information technology outsourcing, found little evidence of obligational forms of contracting. Contracts were usually short term, over 95 per cent specified periods less than five years and nearly one-third of companies embarking upon outsourcing had cancelled or renegotiated contracts within these periods. Over a quarter of these were given to new vendors and just over a fifth were brought back in-house (28–22). Asked to describe their arrangement, half said it was contract rather than trust based. Those claiming to have trust-based relationships said the trend was towards contract.

The Challenges of the Extended Organization

It has been argued that, in the UK, a constellation of factors tend to foster low-trust or distanced relationships between the parties to agreements extending the organization via outsourcing. Employment relationships are inevitably affected by this sort of environment. Evidence from the public sector points to reduced employment and job insecurity, fragmented pay systems, and work intensification (Cabinet Office 1996; Colling 1999; Walsh and Davis 1993). Two aspects of the challenges arising from such developments are discussed now. First, the medium-term consequences for the 'psychological contract' arising from the transfer process itself. Second, changes to organizational structures which have potentially longer-term consequences for the personnel function itself and, thereby, for the future regulation of employment relationships within extended organizations.

The psychological contract between employees and their organization is changed critically by the management of the initial transfer process. In the worst-case scenario, identification of units as a candidate for outsourcing can lead directly to withdrawal of investment and cost-reduction strategies, including redundancies, in preparation for transfer (Kessler and Coyle-Shapiro 1997). At best, claims by employers that 'people are our strongest asset' are undermined in circumstances where they choose to pass employees on to third parties, and many involved in outsourcing acknowledge that the process is fundamentally disempowering. As one commercial manager from Integris UK (quoted in Pritchard 1998) put it: 'Outsourcing is a decision people do not make for themselves. You choose who you work for but when you are outsourced, that choice is taken away from you.'

Communication and the extent to which employees are involved in key decisions assume particular importance in such circumstances. Outsourcing in 'arm's-length' contexts, however, undermines the will to establish effective procedures. Buyers may not be inclined to invest the effort required into areas which they have deemed already to be non-core and vendors may not be prepared to do so until they see some reasonable prospect of being awarded the contract. Where competition between potential vendors is significant, there will be limits on what they are willing to say to staff (for fear of giving away information to competitors) and what they are able to say (because important questions relating to breadth and quality of services may be decided late in the tendering process).

These considerations, in turn, affect critical questions about the timing and sequencing of discussions with the workforce. Intuitively, early contact might be thought most helpful. Where tendering periods are protracted and uncertain, however, this may be counter-productive, serving merely to heighten anxiety, diminish morale and increase staff turn-over. Consequently, it is claimed that private-sector employees sometimes find out about outsourcing decisions 'on the morning they meet their new employer' (Executive Director, Hoskyns quoted in Hassell 1994: 39). But such approaches preclude any possibility that employees might have a say in the shape, award and operation of the contract. Instead, their marginalization is confirmed and they are simply handed over *en masse* like so much furniture. Squaring this circle has led some to compromise solutions.

> An approach that seems to have worked well is to decide immediately who the key people are who need to be kept on board, and level with, and only with, this handful of people. Offer them whatever it takes to keep them and make sure they do not leak the news. Once a deal is close to consummation, then, and only then, the rest of the affected individuals can be informed. (Laribee and Michaels-Barr 1994: 7).

There are practical problems with this approach as well. Can you really expect the rumour mill not to turn? On what basis do you select your 'chosen few'? More important, such techniques may be just as damaging as others to trust and morale. How are employees excluded from the chosen few to relate subsequently to managers responsible for such decisions? What, for that matter, are they to make of colleagues who collude in such an arrangement? In short, outsourcing is extremely competitive; arm's-length environments undermine the psychological contract and foster predominantly low-trust relationships.

Challenges subsequent to transfer impact potentially on the personnel function itself and on its capacity to develop and sustain coherent approaches to employment. These stem from the organizational structures through which contracts are managed. Displacing hierarchical authority makes it difficult to assert and rely on the kinds of bureaucratic controls which have typified British personnel management (Guest 1998: 50). Where organizational relationships are predominantly market driven, flexibility and discretion are at a premium and authority pushed to lower levels. Each one of the four traditional models of personnel management identified by Sisson (1994) is undermined in this context.

First, establishment control is about founding personnel procedures and principles and ensuring compliance with them subsequently. Within buyers' organizations, the decision to outsource affects the scope for this sort of personnel activity *ipso facto*. After all, why buy a dog and bark yourself? Motives for outsourcing may include recognition of third-party expertise, for example, and such buyers will expect vendors themselves to manage employment effectively. The practice of buyers ensuring minimum employment standards through contractual arrangements, termed 'contractual compliance', has been discouraged strongly in public-sector environments and is rare elsewhere. But even where this happens, establishing and monitoring procedures will be delegated to the vendor. Organizational fragmentation within vendor organizations also renders personnel influence fragmented and partial. Maintaining contracts with a range of companies requires flexible and adaptive organizational forms. Larger firms are characterized by divisionalization, that is the identification of separate markets according to the characteristics of growth and profitability and their replication through internal divisions in the organization. Where this is pursued to a significant degree, divisionalization tends to 'drive down questions of style and non economic issues and positively encourage different approaches to employee relations in different segments of the business' (Purcell 1989: 76). Caterco, a contract caterer studied by the author, maintained broad-framework procedures and employment contracts across its business divisions, but variations between them were apparent in pay, training, communications and employee involvement (Colling 1997).

Second, traditional industrial relations responsibilities, accrued by personnel specialists as joint custodians of collective agreements, are diminished by outsourcing. Integral to public-sector models of outsourcing, for example, has been the objective of weakening trade unionism. Though de-recognition has been rare, due largely to the impact of TUPE and the retention of contracts by public sector bodies, impact upon the scope and depth of collective agreements has been considerable (Colling 1999). Centralized or corporate negotiations involving senior personnel advisers have been displaced increasingly by negotiations at service level about the shape and resourcing of specific contracts and these have been led usually by line managers. Among private-sector vendors, many operate predominantly on a non-union basis and line managers are accustomed to considerable discretion. Buildings maintenance, for example, shares many of the characteristics of the wider building industry described by Druker (1994). Though claiming some influence over the terms and conditions of non-manual staff, personnel functions are hardly involved at all in the employment of manual staff and self-employed contractors and '[the] physical and cultural difference between the office and the site is considerable' (7).

The possession of specialist knowledge and skills emphasized within the professional tradition continues to some extent, particularly in relation to employment law and TUPE. Everything depends, however, upon the circumstances in which such expertise might be brought to bear. In market-driven organizations, personnel services are delivered through service-level agreements and these militate against a proactive role for personnel specialists. Because line managers are empowered to specify and pay only for those services they deem useful, there is a danger that personnel advisers are confined, or confine themselves, to a residual role only, such as sweeping up legal wrangles left in the wake of line managers.

In the welfare tradition, the personnel department takes up specific problems and grievances on behalf of employees. In fragmented organizations, managed predominantly through the line, this sort of role, amplifying the voice of individual employees, may be significant. This is especially so where formal systems of representation are underutilized or absent. Problems arise, however, because the authority of personnel specialists is weakest, and the contact between them and employees least frequent, in precisely this sort of environment. In circumstances such as these, personnel functions may be confined to low-level, individualized casework, leaving untouched the systems and procedures from which it is generated.

Does any of this actually matter? Possibly not. Yet evidence now coincides of discomfort to employees subject to outsourcing and of considerable dissatisfaction among the buyers of outsourced services. Nearly half of all employees find the process of outsourcing stressful and this diminishes only slightly following transfer. Fears about role change and job security in new environments have been reported by one-third of surveyed employees (Pritchard 1998). On average, 57 per cent of civil servants affected by market testing reported worsened employment conditions including higher workloads, inadequate resources and diminished employment security (Cabinet Office 1996: 47).

Separate surveys of buyers found only 50 out of 1,000 companies experience entirely unalloyed benefits (PA Consulting, cited in Lonsdale and Cox 1998). Most organizations (39 per cent) indicate a neutral outcome, that is the benefits being balanced by drawbacks and other surveys have found one-third of companies reporting few benefits and one-quarter stating that outsourcing failed entirely to meet the objectives established for it.

The 'win–win' notion that distanced employment relationships, possibly yielding cost savings in the process, can increase organizational capabilities, has provided outsourcing's considerable rhetorical appeal. Yet, potentially, the process threatens key elements of the employment relationship and the foundations required for real innovation and development. The key point, as Sisson and Marginson (1995: 117–18) observe, reflecting the comments of a former CBI Employment Affairs Director (Gilbert 1994), is that externalizing the problems associated with managing the employment relationship does not mean that the problems disappear. Issues such as performance and quality, and training and development, remain fundamentally important. Furthermore, the introduction of such an obvious status divide associated with the 'core-periphery' model also runs counter to the trend towards team working and can be bad for performance. Peripheral workers have a lesser reason to show commitment to the contracting organization and may, in consequence, require greater degrees of supervision and control than other staff, which sits uneasily with the desire to shift away from traditional control mechanisms. Like so many of the seeming panaceas, market-driven organizational structures which degrade specialist personnel expertise are unlikely to provide the conditions required for rebuilding a secure base for the employment relationship in the future.

Discussion and Conclusions

The relationships within and between organizations described here are still in their infancy. They are likely to remain for some time to come, but they will change inevitably. What implications will this have for personnel practitioners and how should they respond?

If the development of extended organizations to date has been driven by reform of the public sector, there are few indications that it is likely to abate. The current Labour Government is committed to extending the scope for public–private partnerships rather than reducing it. The Private Finance Initiative, established by previous Conservative Governments, is to continue and will offer the private sector roles in building and managing public sector facilities. Subcontracting will also remain on the agenda in various forms. At organizational level, political and policy resistance to the concept has largely fallen away. Local authority work, for example, is now being transferred to the private sector in organizations once doggedly determined to retain direct workforces. Liverpool has contracted out its refuse collection services, Sheffield has awarded a ten-year contract to CSL to run its finance and IT services, and Capita has taken on Lambeth's revenues, benefits, and cashiering services for seven years (Pike 1997).

It would be understandable if personnel practitioners, faced with this secular trend, simply embraced the market. The argument set out here, however, is that to do so in the current circumstances carries consequences for employees, for the personnel function itself, and ultimately for the organizations involved. Without effective regulation, employees face forms of employment which are subject to frequent change, which are less secure and over which their influence is diminished considerably. The consequences for the personnel function cannot be separated from these tendencies. Arguably, settling for advisory roles, offering line managers only that information which they ask for, ultimately serves ill both the personnel specialist and their organization. As Sparrow and Marchington (1998: 22) argue, personnel specialists 'have to focus on the competency of the total pool of human capital within the organization'. Such a role requires a degree of corporate authority and the capacity to integrate and co-ordinate employment across widely differing circumstances.

Without change in the regulatory environment described here, however, there is little reason to believe that such roles will emerge independently. If arm's-length contractual arrangements and cost-reduction strategies have proved commercially successful in the past, at least in the short run, it may not serve their self-interest for companies to structure themselves differently or to heed pleas for revitalized roles from individual management functions.

Yet some current policy developments promise change and may provide levers for personnel practitioners within extended organizations. First, the dynamics within the influential public sector markets may be changing. A new regime based on achieving 'best value' is to replace compulsory competitive tendering in local government (DETR 1998). Parallel developments are likely in other services. Reviews of current market-testing policies are being conducted by the NHS Executive and the Cabinet Office is revising its guidance to civil service departments in line with 12 new guiding principles (Butler 1997; Cabinet Office 1997). Two factors may help to distinguish this kind of regime from previous ones: organizations will be able to determine for themselves whether and how the private sector should be involved in service provision; and services will be audited to ensure that best value is being achieved, but such judgements will be based on a broader range of criteria than price alone. Performance targets may also be determined in conjunction with communities and service users affected, and may thus turn on measures of effectiveness as well as efficiency.

Second, contracting behaviour may be affected by complementary labour market reforms. In areas where semi- and unskilled manual workers predominate, competitive strategies based on crude reductions in labour costs will be made more difficult by the National Minimum Wage provisions. New individual rights to formal representation may offer trade unions toe-holds in non union-contracting organizations and further stepping stones to formal recognition for bargaining purposes. Contract compliance mechanisms (that is, the ability of public organizations to require from their suppliers particular employment and management standards) may be permitted once again, following a review of the relevant sections of the Local Government Act (James 1997: 4). Clarification and the extension of TUPE protections are also likely. Revisions to the European Acquired Rights Directive were pushed through by the UK in June 1997. These had the effect of including the public sector for the first time and protecting the pension rights of employees affected. Key questions concerning the definition of a transfer of undertakings will await independent revision of TUPE.

The potential to move outsourcing away from arm's-length practices towards more engaged models characterized by mutual dependency is obvious. To the extent that holistic approaches to service provision are encouraged, subcontracting arrangements founded on capacity or specialization rather than cost may emerge. Strengthened employment rights may also buttress employees, their representatives, and personnel specialists within organizations and require their greater involvement in contract management procedures. Following several years of market dogma and deregulation, this developing scenario offers personnel practitioners more opportunities to influence employment practice in extended organizations than they have enjoyed for some time.

Acknowledgement

I am especially grateful to Jon Reese at the Office for National Statistics for collating and supplying the data used in table 3.3.

References and further reading

Advisory, Conciliation and Arbitration Service (ACAS) 1988: *Labour Flexibility in Britain: The 1987 ACAS Survey.* Occasional Paper 41, London: ACAS.

Allen, J. 1988: Towards a Post-Industrial Economy? In Allen, J. and Massey, D., *The Economy in Question*, London: Sage. 91–136.

Allen, J. and Du Gay, P. 1994: Industry and The Rest: The Economic Identity of Services. *Work, Employment and Society*, **8**(2), 255–71.

Armstrong, P. 1989: Limits and Possibilities of HRM in an Age of Management Accountancy. In Storey, J. (ed) *New Perspectives on Human Resource Management*, London: Routledge.

Ascher, K. 1987: *The Politics of Privatisation – Contracting Out Public Services.* London: Macmillan.

Atkinson, J. 1984: Manpower Strategies for Flexible Organizations. *Personnel Management*, August, 28–31.

Atkinson, J. 1986: *New Forms of Work Organization.* IMS Report No. 121. IMS: Brighton.

Atkinson, J. and Meager, N. 1986: *Changing Working Patterns – How Companies Achieve Flexibility to Meet New Needs.* National Economic Development Office: London.

Beaumont, P., Hunter, L. and Sinclair, J. 1996: Customer–supplier relations and the diffusion of employee relations change. *Employee Relations*, **18**(1), 9–19.

Blau, P. 1966: *Bureaucracy in Modern Society.* New York: Random House.

BMRB International 1995: *CCT: The Private Sector View.* London: Department of the Environment.

Butler, P. 1997: Private Investigations. *Health Service Journal*, 12 June, 20.

Cabinet Office 1996: *Competing for Quality Policy Review: An Efficiency Unit Scrutiny*. London: HMSO.

Cabinet Office 1997: *Government's Twelve Guiding Principles for Market Testing and Contracting Out*. News release CAB 114/97, 4 November.

Central Statistical Office 1992: *Distributive and Service Trades SDA 29*. Business Monitor. London, HMSO.

Chandler, A. 1962: *Strategy and Structure: Chapters in the History of the Industrial Enterprise*. Cambridge, MA.: MIT Press.

Chandler, A. 1977: *The Visible Hand: The Managerial Revolution in American Business*. Cambridge, MA: Harvard University Press.

Clark, I. 1996: The state and new industrial relations. In Beardwell, I. (ed), *Contemporary Industrial Relations: A Critical Analysis*, Oxford: Oxford University Press.

Clawson, D. 1980: *Bureaucracy and the Labour Process: The Transformation of US Industry 1860–1920*. London: Monthly Review Press.

Colling, T. 1994: Privatisation, Competition and the Management of Human Resources in British Airways. Paper at workshop on *Privatisation and the Management of Human Resources*. IRI, Rome, June.

Colling, T. 1995: Renewal or Rigor Mortis? Union Responses to Contracting in Local Government. *Industrial Relations Journal*, March.

Colling, T. 1997: Organising in the Disorganised State: The Prospects for Public Service Unionism in Outsourced Environments. Employment Research Unit Annual Conference – *The Insecure Workforce*. Cardiff: Cardiff Business School, September.

Colling, T. 1999: Tendering and outsourcing: working in the contract state. In Corby, S. and White, G. (eds): *Employee Relations in the Public Services: Themes and Issues*, London: Routledge.

Colling, T. and Ferner A. 1995: Privatisation and Marketisation. In Edwards, P. K. E. (ed.), *Industrial Relations in Theory and Practice*, Oxford: Blackwell.

Cully, M., O'Reilly, A., Millward, N., Forth, J., Woodland, S., Dix, G. and Bryson, A. 1998. *The 1998 Workplace Employee Relations Survey. First Findings*. London: DTI.

Decker, D. 1995: Market Testing – Does it Bring Home the Bacon? *Health Service Journal*, 19 January, 26–7.

Department of Environment, Transport and the Regions (DETR) 1998: *Modernising Local Government: Improvising Services through Best Value*. London: HMSO.

Digings, L. 1991: *Competitive Tendering and the European Community: Public Procurement, CCT and Local Services*. London: Association of Metropolitan Authorities.

Druker, J. 1994: 'Someone Else's Problem': Subcontracting and Change in Industrial Relations Management in the the Construction Industry. Paper at British Universities Industrial Relations Association Annual Conference, Worcester College, Oxford, 1–3 July.

Dunne, J. 1988: The Structure of Service Employment in the UK. In Barker, T. S. and Dunne J. (eds), *The British Economy After Oil: Manufacturing or Services*, London: Croom-Helm.

Escott, K. and Whitfield, D. 1995: *The Gender Impact of CCT in Local Government*. London: HMSO.

Eurostat 1993: *Services: Annual Statistics 1990*. Luxembourg: Office for the Official Publications of the European Communities.

Evans, S. and Lewis, R. 1989: Destructuring and Deregulation in Construction. In Tailby, S. and Whitson, C. (eds), *Manufacturing Change – Industrial Relations and Restructuring*, Oxford: Blackwell.

Extel Financial 1994: *Major UK Companies Handbook*. London: Extel Financial.

Felstead, A. 1991: The Social Organization of the Franchise: A Case of 'Controlled Self Employment'. *Work, Employment and Society*, **5**(1), 37–57.

Felstead, A. 1993: *The Corporate Paradox – Power and Control in the Business Franchise*. London: Routledge.

Ferner, A. and Colling, T. 1993: Electricity Supply. In Pendleton, A. and Winterton, J. (eds), *Public Enterprises in Transition*, London: Routledge.

Ferner, A. Terry, M., Berry, J., Gilman, M., Maina, B., Athina, N. and Tong, Y. M. 1994: Developments in Industrial Relations/Human Resource Management in Telecommunications: Britain. Draft paper for the International Telecommunications Research Network.

Fitzgerald, G. and Wilcocks, L. 1994: Relationships in outsourcing: contracts and partnerships. Paper presented at 2nd European Conference on Information Systems, Nijenrode.

Flood, P. C. 1998: Is HRM dead? What will happen to HRM when traditional methods are gone? In Sparrow, P. and Marchington, M. (eds), *Human Resource Management: The New Agenda*. London: Pitman.

Foster, C. and Plowden, F. 1996: *The State under Stress: Can the Hollow State be Good Government?* Buckingham: Open University Press.

Gershuny, J. and Miles, I. 1983: *The New Service Economy*. London: Frances Pinter.

Gilbert, T. 1994: An Employer's View: Employment Relations 2000: Proceedings of a Conference to Launch the Centre for International Employment Relations Research. *Warwick Papers in Industrial Relations* No. 50, Coventry: Industrial Relations Research Unit.

Guest, D. 1998: Beyond HRM: commitment and the contract culture. In Sparrow, P. and Marchington, M. (eds), *Human Resource Management: the new agenda*, London: Pitman.

Hamel, G. and Prahalad, C. 1996: Competing in the new economy: managing out of bounds. *Strategic Management Journal*, **17**, 237–42.

Hannah, L. 1976: *The Rise of the Corporate Economy: The British Experience*. London: Methuen.

Harrison, A. 1993: *From Hierachy to Contract*. London: Policy Journals.

Harrison, B. and Kelley, M. 1993: Outsourcing and the Search for Flexibility. *Work, Employment and Society*, **7**(2), 213–55.

Hassell, N. 1994: Testing market testing. *Management Today*, April, 38–42.

Hunter, J. 1998: *Selling disempowerment: the impact of outsourcing upon staff in the IT industry*. Unpublished MA thesis. Leicester: De Montfort University.

Hunter, L. and MacInnes, J. 1991: *Employer's Labour Use Strategies – Case Studies*. Employment Department Research Paper No. 87, London: HMSO.

Industrial Relations Research Unit and Institute for Employment Research (IRRU/IER). 1993: *The Changing Context of Industrial Relations in Britain*. Unpublished Statistical Series.

Industrial Relations Services (IRS) 1994: Procord Provides Outsourcing Model. *IRS Employment Trends*, August, 565, 4.

International Transport Workers Federation (ITF) 1992: *The Globalisation of the Civil Aviation Industry & Its Impact on Aviation Workers*. London: ITF.

James, M. 1997: Armstrong Unveils Plans to Bolster Employees' Rights. *Local Government Chronicle*, 24 October, 4.

Kessler, I. and Coyle-Shapiro, J. 1997: Employee Perceptions: Overlooked in Outsourcing? Annual conference of the British Universities Industrial Relations Association, University of Bath, July.

Keynote 1993: *Contract Cleaning: A Market Sector Overview*. London: Keynote.

Keynote 1994a: *Contract Catering: A Market Sector Overview*. London: Keynote.

Keynote 1994b: *Corporate Services in the UK*. London: Keynote.

Lane, C. and Bachmann, R. 1994: Risk, Trust and Power: The Social Constitution of Supplier Relations in Britain and Germany. Paper at the Work, Employment and Society Conference, University of Kent, 12–14 September.

Lane, C. and Bachman, R. 1997: Co-operation in inter-firm, relations in Britain and Germany: the role of social institutions. *British Journal of Sociology* **48**(2), 226–54.

Laribee, J. and Michaels-Barr, L. 1994: Dealing with personnel concerns in outsourcing. *Journal of Systems Management*, January, **45**(1), 6–12.

Local Government Management Board 1992: *CCT Information Service: Survey Report No. 6*, November. London: LGMB.

Local Government Management Board 1994: *CCT Information Service: Survey Report No. 10*, December. London: LGMB.

Lonsdale, C. and Cox, A. 1998: Falling in with the outcrowd. *People Management*, 15 October, 52–5.

Marginson, P. 1988: Centralised Control or Establishment Autonomy. In Marginson, P., Edwards, P. K., Martin, R., Purcell, J. and Sisson, K., *Beyond the Workplace: Managing Industrial Relations in the Multi-Establishment Enterprise*, Oxford: Blackwell.

Marginson, P. 1991: Change and Continuity in the Employment Structure of Large Companies. In Pollert, A. *Farewell to Flexibility*, Oxford: Blackwell.

Marginson, P., Armstrong, P., Edwards, P., Purcell, J. and Hubbard, N. 1993: The Control of Industrial Relations in Large Companies – An Initial Analysis of the Second Company Level Industrial Relations Survey. *Warwick Papers in Industrial Relations* No. 45, Coventry: Industrial Relations Research Unit.

Marginson, P. and Sisson, K. 1988: The Management of Employees. In Marginson, P., Edwards, P. K., Martin, R., Purcell, J. and Sisson, K., *Beyond the Workplace: Managing Industrial Relations in the Multi-Establishment Enterprise*, Oxford: Blackwell.

Millward, N., Stevens, M., Smart, D. and Hawes, W. 1992: *Workplace Industrial Relations in Transition*. Aldershot: Dartmouth.

Oughton, J. 1994: Market testing: the future of the civil service. *Public Policy and Administration*, **9**(2), 11–20.

Paddon, M. 1991: Management Buy-Outs and Compulsory Competition in Local Government. *Local Government Studies*, May/June, 27–53.

Paddon, M. 1993: EC Public Procurement Directives and the Competition from European Contractors for Local Authority Contracts in the UK. In Clarke, T. and Pitelis, C. (eds), *The Political Economy of Privatisation*, London: Routledge. 159–85.

Peters, T. J. and Waterman, R. H. 1982: *In Pursuit of Excellence: Lessons from America's Best Companies*. New York: Harper and Row.

Pike, A. 1997: Council services to face value challenge: companies believe they will still win business once tendering rules are changed. *Financial Times*, 29 May.

Pollard, S. 1965: *The Genesis of Modern Management*. Harmondsworth: Penguin.

Pollert, A. 1988: The Flexible Firm: Fixation or Fact? *Work, Employment and Society*, **2**, September. 281–316.

Pollert, A. 1991: *Farewell to Flexibility*. Oxford: Blackwell.

Pritchard, S. 1998: Outsourcing – the insider guide. *Independent on Sunday*, 2 August.

Public Services Privatisation Research Unit (PSPRU) 1992: *Privatisation – Disaster for Quality*. London: PSPRU.

Purcell, J. 1989: The impact of corporate strategy on Human Resource Management. In Storey, J. (ed.), *New Perspectives on Human Resource Management*, London: Routledge.

Purcell, J. and Ahlstrand, B. 1994: *Human Resource Management in the Multi-Divisional Company*. Oxford: Oxford University Press.

Rainnie, A. 1984: Combined and Uneven Development in the Clothing Industry: The Effects of Competition on Accumulation. *Capital and Class*, **22**, 141–56.

Ram, M. 1994: *Managing to Survive: Working Lives in Small Firms*. Oxford: Blackwell.

Rees, G. and Fielder, S. 1992: The services economy, subcontracting and the new employment relations: contract and catering and cleaning. *Work, Employment and Society*, **6**(3), 347–68.

Sako, M. 1992: *Prices, Quality and Trust: Inter-Firm Relations in Britain and Japan*. Cambridge: Cambridge University Press.

Shutt, J. and Whittington, R. 1987: Fragmentation Strategies and the Rise of Small Units: Cases from the North West. *Regional Studies*, **21**(1), 13–21.

Sisson, K. 1993: In Search of HRM. *British Journal of Industrial Relations*, **31**, July, 201–10.

Sisson, K. 1994: Personnel Management: Paradigms, Practice and Prospects. In Sisson, K. (ed.), *Personnel Management*, Oxford: Blackwell.

Sisson, K. and Marginson, P. 1995: Management systems, structures, and strategy. In Edwards, P. K. E. (ed.), *Industrial Relations: theory and practice in Britain*. Oxford: Blackwell.

Sparrow, P. and Marchington, M. 1998: Introduction: Is HRM in crisis? In Sparrow, M. and Marchington, M. (eds), *Human Resource Management – A New Agenda*, London: Pitman.

Starks, M. 1993: Producer Choice in the BBC. In Harrison, A. (ed.), *From Hierarchy to Contract*. London: Policy Journals.

Temple, P. 1994: The Agents of Change – Notes on the Developing Division of Labour. In Buxton, T., Chapman, P. and Temple, P. (eds), *Britain's Economic Performance*, London: Routledge.

Walsh, K. and Davis, H. 1993: *Competition and Service – The Impact of the Local Government Act 1988*. London: HMSO.

Warhurst, R. 1994: Converging on HRM? Towards a New Consensus in European Airlines Industrial Relations. Paper at *British Universities Industrial Relations Association Annual Conference*, Worcester College, Oxford, July.

Whitbread, C. and Hooper, N. 1993: NHS ancillary services. In Harrison, A., *From Hierarchy to Contract*, London: Policy Journals.

Williamson, O. E. 1975: *Markets and Hierarchies*. New York: Free Press.

Williamson, O. E. 1981: The Modern Corporation: Origins, Evolution, and Attributes. *Journal of Economic Literature*, Vol. 19, 1537–68.

Williamson, O. E. 1985: *The Economic Institutions of Capitalism: Firms, Markets, Relational Contracting*. New York: Free Press.

Part 2

Planning and Resourcing

4

Manpower or Human Resource Planning – What's in a Name?

Sonia Liff

The term 'human resource planning' has become dominant only relatively recently. For much of the post-war period the term 'manpower planning' was more commonly used. Some writers have speculated that recent name changes in the personnel field may be simply cosmetic (Guest 1987). Others might see evidence of political correctness in the rejection of the term 'manpower'. But although some writers use the term 'human resource planning' in much the same way as earlier authors used 'manpower planning', for most this name change does signal a significant difference in both thinking and practice in this field. The reason for the change comes as much from wider thinking about the nature of planning in the business field as it does from any specifically human resource issues. Manpower planning approaches derive from a rational, top-down view of planning in which well-tested quantitative techniques could be applied to long-term assessments of supply and demand. Apart from debates about whether strategies are ever formulated and detailed in this explicit fashion (see Whittington 1993 for a review of approaches), it is generally accepted that the increased uncertainty of the environment, the degree and frequency of change required as a response to competitive pressures, and more complex organizational structures and labour markets make such an approach less appropriate.

This chapter explores the significance of this changed context for human resource planning. It also looks at the, albeit very limited, evidence for changes in personnel practice in this field. It then moves on to look at the link between human resource planning and corporate strategy. Are human resource plans determined by corporate strategies and, if so, in what ways? Do they need to be tightly integrated with such strategies and, if so, how can this be achieved? Or can human resource strategies have a degree of independence – or indeed lead a corporate strategy. The name 'human resource planning' is again important here with its implied link with a resource-based view of the firm. This approach sees strategy making as starting from the internal resources of the firm. External market opportunities are assessed in relation to these distinctive internal resources to identify an effective competitive strategy which should be hard for others to imitate (Prahalad and Hamel 1990).

Plans may be comprehensive and persuasive in theory but can they be implemented effectively? Again this has sometimes been seen as a technical issue of translating strategies into policies, procedures and practices which can then be monitored and refined. In practice two types of issues have dogged efforts to translate human resource plans into effective practice. The first of these has often been seen as a 'technical' problem revolving round the refinement of measurement and predictive techniques. The move away from formalized, quantitative techniques might seem to side-step this problem. In practice it will be argued that it just reveals a deeper issue – the need to remember the 'humanness' of human resources. Knowledge, skills and abilities are not easy to measure and, even when they have been assessed, the ways in which they will be used in practice are dependent on individuals' motivation, commitment and the context in which they are operating. The second set of issues relates to the role of the personnel function and the status of human resource issues within the organization, reviewed in chapter 1. Unless the significance of human resource issues is recognized and taken account of, plans are unlikely to be formulated, let alone implemented. Here the linguistic link with human resource management, with its emphasis on line management ownership of people issues, may again be significant.

Finally, the chapter assesses the direction likely to be taken by human resource planning in the future. One issue of particular relevance in assessing the contexts in which it is likely that HR planning will have more or less significance is the role of HR specialists within an organization and, more broadly, the status accorded to human resource issues.

Manpower Planning in Theory

In the context of the post-war boom, where large organizations experienced stable growth, manpower planning was seen as both desirable and possible. The intention was to assess the supply of, and demand for, different types of labour and develop plans to reconcile the two. In order to do so organizations needed to take stock of the manpower resources currently at their disposal and predict how these were likely to change over the planning period (through recruitment, training, turnover or retirement). Changes in the external labour market were likely to be relevant to this consideration and might be assessed directly to give a broader understanding of changes in labour supply. Forecasting demand required an understanding of the business plan and the competitive environment in which it operated. Plans and policies which might emerge from such a process typically focused on recruitment and selection, training, career planning and pay.

For most writers this process has been seen as a linear. For example Hercus (1992: 405) gives the following list:

1 Forecasting HR requirements for an organization to achieve its business plan/objectives.
2 Forecasting HR available for meeting these needs, as well as an internal and external environmental scan of the organization.
3 Identifying the gaps between what will be needed and what will be available and develop HR action plans involving staffing, appraisal, compensation and development to meet these needs.

4 Implement and monitor the HR action plans, regularly evaluating progress at the senior management/board level.

Despite the use of the term HR in the above list this approach remains within the mainstream of manpower planning approaches. Hendry (1995: 191) provides a list with similar elements. However, he develops this somewhat by suggesting that the process is circular, rather than linear, and that change can be initiated at any point in the cycle. His model of the manpower planning cycle is as follows:

- analysing the current manpower resource;
- reviewing labour utilization;
- forecasting the demand for labour;
- forecasting supply;
- developing a manpower plan.

This approach makes the plan more responsive: for example a change could be initiated in response to a recognition of a skill shortage in the labour market or the decision to open a factory on a greenfield site. It contrasts with the notion of a stand-alone plan initiated at one point in time and, reviews notwithstanding, one which could be expected to last for a fixed planning period.

How were these activities to be carried out? A wide range of, mainly quantitative, techniques were developed based on different assumptions (O'Doherty 1997 reviews these in more detail). In terms of assessing changes in internal supply there are two main approaches. The first models the organization as one in which the organizational structure is stable with fixed numbers of particular types of jobs. As employees leave, either to retire or to jobs elsewhere, vacancies occur and those below can be promoted. The rate at which this is likely to occur can be modelled mathematically on the basis of age data and the points of time at which employees are most likely to leave or stay. The latter, for example, suggests that after an initial peak the tendency to leave decreases relatively predictably with length of service. The alternative model sees changes driven less by vacancies and more by the numbers of people at various levels of the organization. Promotion here is seen to be the result of someone reaching a particular level and having served the required period within it. This approach can be modelled by studying the career history of current and recently retired employees.

Forecasting demand is usually seen in terms of the need to assess the consequences of business plans for human resource needs. Thus if it is proposed that production of a particular product be expanded the associated human resource needs within particular occupational and skill levels can be predicted. Such predictions are likely to be most reliable in circumstances where production methods are unchanged. In practice this is rarely the case and assessment needs to be made in relation to, say, the planned purchase of more automated technology.

More qualitative techniques also have their place in this approach. These include detailed internal assessments of individuals considered suitable for future promotion to particular positions (succession charts) and surveys of the attitudes of groups of employees towards benefit packages and promotion opportunities. Broader external scanning of competitors' plans for expansion or contraction might also be relevant to assessing the supply of labour. Approaches also vary in the time-horizon that they use as the planning period; however, the quantitative approaches tend to require, or be more appropriate for, a longer time-horizon than the qualitative ones.

Manpower Planning in Practice

The extent to which and the ways in which such techniques were used and continue to be used has received surprising little study. Indeed Greer et al. (1989: 111) comment that 'the HRP literature has relied heavily on anecdotal evidence'. The UK research which does exist tends to have been carried out some considerable time ago and to consist of case studies of large companies (IPM 1975; Manpower Services Commission/National Economic Development Office 1978). Such contexts are most likely to favour the identification of evidence which supports the use of long-term quantitative techniques. However, even here there seems to be a gap between widespread claims and relatively limited activity. One US study is worth quoting because it provides the baseline for some comparative data which will be discussed below. This is a survey by Greer and Armstrong (1980) of human resource planning practice at the end of the relatively stable 1970s. Greer and Armstrong (1980) found evidence of reasonably widespread use of complex (in their terminology 'sophisticated') quantitative techniques for both supply and demand forecasting. For example Markov or network flow models (which map the flow of individuals within an organization) were used by over 20 per cent of companies and operations research techniques by nearly a quarter. In relation to demand forecasting 30 per cent used regression analysis techniques.

Human Resource Planning – Evidence for a Changed Approach

It is clear that the term 'human resource planning' has always been used in preference to 'manpower planning' by some writers and that others have changed their terminology without a significant change in approach. However, there is evidence of the term 'human resource planning' being used deliberately to signal a different orientation and of some limited change in practice.

The IPM (no date) *Statement on Human Resource Planning* uses the term in preference to manpower planning to 'indicate that planning the people side of the business involves more than demand/supply balancing'. They stress that human resource plans should be 'systematic', 'continuing', 'an integral part of corporate planning' and encompass the 'widest range of personnel policies'. Integration with business strategy will be considered below. What is worth highlighting here is that the process is envisaged as becoming both more tentative, via the stress on the need to reassess plans on a continuous basis, and more comprehensive, via the suggestion that plans need to move beyond matching supply and demand to consider issues such as effective ways of managing human resources to achieve organizational goals. The more rapidly changing environment thus makes the planning process more complex, and less certain, but does not make it less important or significant.

In contrast, as one would expect from the broader perspectives of human resource management, planning is envisaged as more central and vital to contemporary organizations.

This broadening of human resource planning to take in most areas of personnel practice is not universally accepted. Reilly (1996) does not deny the changed planning context, nor the changes in approach that this implies, but wishes to retain a narrow definition as 'a process in which an organization attempts to estimate the demand for labour and evaluate the size, nature and sources of supply which will be required to meet that demand' (p. 4). He argues that it is important to maintain a distinction between considering human resources at the aggregate level, the proper arena for planning in his view, and policies which apply to specific individuals. A rather different argument might be that since downsizing has been a dominant feature of organizational change, at least until relatively recently (Reilly cites evidence that 90 per cent of large organizations restructured in the early 1990s, almost always involving job losses, and two-thirds expected to do so again in the near future) there is good reason for human resource planners to maintain a focus on matching labour demand and supply.

What evidence is there that organizations are actually changing their approach to planning in this field? Many of the questions asked by Greer and Armstrong (1980) were replicated in a later US survey reported as Greer et al. (1989). In contrast to the earlier survey Greer et al. (1989) found evidence of widespread use of *qualitative* techniques. The use of Markov and related techniques had dropped to 6 per cent of companies and of operations research techniques to under 5 per cent. Regression analysis for demand forecasting had dropped to 9 per cent of firms. These are all significant declines on the figures quoted earlier. Interestingly the survey also reports a significant increase in the rating given by respondents as to the importance of human resource planning to the personnel function and the company.

UK data is again partial and inconclusive. In the late 1980s some commentators claimed to see a revival of interest in manpower planning as a result of impending demographic change (Bell 1989). A survey in 1988 (Cowling and Walters 1990) did not look at techniques used in detail but found that over 60 per cent of those companies that responded claimed to be carrying out the identification of future training, retraining and development needs on a formal and regular basis. This is taken as evidence of a broader, more pro-active approach in line with the change from traditional manpower planning towards human resource planning as defined by the IPM. This seemed to be most common in the private sector, perhaps suggesting inertia, continued attachment to existing approaches, or resistance to change in the public sector. Reilly (1996) claims to be drawing on extensive experience of human resource planning in UK companies in his account of how planning can be used. However, he does not provide any data about these companies nor on the frequency with which specific techniques are used or applied to particular purposes and so sheds little light on extent of use in practice. He does argue that the decision to go down a planning route cannot be reduced to structural factors such as the size of an organization. Instead he suggests it might derive from an ideological commitment on the part of management, from the culture of business or its subunits, or from the type of occupations employed. Reilly (1996) does go on to make a useful distinction between planning for substantive reasons (to have an effect) and planning because of the process benefits (closer to scenario planning). A recognition of the latter aspect of planning perhaps underlines the significance of keeping a separation between the planning process and the policies which would be needed to put any specific plan into practice.

The reality of links between corporate/business strategy and a changed approach to human resource planning has proved particularly hard to disentangle. Hercus (1992) surveyed UK practice with respect to human resource planning in a number of case studies within the type of large organization which was the subject of much of the earlier research. He found evidence of planning in these organizations but there was considerable variation in the degree of integration with business plans and the definition he was working with remained close to earlier models of manpower planning. Similarly Rothwell (1995) says that 1990 WIRS data shows that the proportion of all managers who claimed to be involved in manpower planning (41 per cent) was one of the highest of all employee relations activities. However, she notes that follow-up case study work found little practical difference between those employers claiming to operate strategically and those operating on an *ad hoc* basis; this scepticism is shared by Sisson and Timperley (1994). In contrast, revisiting companies that had been the subject of earlier research, Storey (cited in Hall and Torrington 1998) argued that those who had not done so previously were taking a more strategic view of human resources. Perhaps the most one can say with any confidence is that many UK companies continue to express a commitment to the ideas of human resource strategy and planning. How this translates into their practice, however, is less clear.

Corporate Strategy and Human Resource Plans – Push, Pull or Fit?

Under the manpower planning model there was a weak link with broader business planning activities. Clearly the business plan was the starting point but this was seen as relatively static allowing manpower plans to develop fairly autonomously. The stress on the quantitative aspects of human resources (numbers in post at various levels and succession planning as opposed to motivation and performance management) further reinforced this separation. This weak link is reflected in many of the traditional criticisms of personnel as not sufficiently aware of the bottom line and not business focused (e.g. Drucker 1961). In an increasingly competitive environment for business (and for managers) this is no longer a tenable approach.

The move (rhetorically and practically) from personnel to human resource management reflects this closer integration (Guest 1987). In 'hard' HRM models there is a stress on showing that human resources are being used cost effectively to fulfil business objectives. In 'soft' HRM the stress is on the way in which human resources themselves represent a key asset for the business which can ensure its competitive success. Either way the link between investment in human resources and the way in which they are utilized needs to be demonstrated explicitly.

In practice in the UK relatively few examples of soft HRM being applied at the practical (as opposed to rhetorical) level have been found. Consequently, the dominant model of the link between business plans and HR plans see HR as the 'dependent variable' – fleshing out the personnel implications of pre-determined business plans, implementing appropriate policies to fulfil the requirements identified. The consequence of this position is that there is no one best way of managing human resources. Instead there is a way that is appropriate to a particular business strategy. One consequence of this derivative approach is that typologies of human resource approaches are not identified in their own right but vary with a particular writer's approach to business strategy. Thus Schuler (1989) provides clusters of HR policies appropriate to Porter's typology of business strategy. Miles and Snow (1984), drawing on their own approach to strategy, group human resource policies in a different way.

So, for example, Schuler (1989) suggests HR policies that would be appropriate to a company pursuing an 'innovation' strategy (in Porter's terms). These include performance targets based on longer-term and group achievements, jobs which allow for the development of broad skills linked to broad career paths, and compensation packages that stress internal equity and encourage commitment to the organization. In contrast, Miles and Snow (1984) have a business strategy typology which includes a 'prospector' strategy involving the search for new product and market opportunities but not necessarily requiring innovation at the organizational level. This leads them to suggest human resource policies based on a sophisticated assessment of skills requirements at all levels and their recruitment from the labour market via a range of selection techniques.

The notion of 'fit' does not in itself necessarily imply a dependent role for human resource planning. An alternative could be for discussion between those developing the business strategy and those with responsibility for the human resource planning to result in some modifications to the business plan in recognition of human resource issues, internal or external. This might occur, as is discussed further in the next section, because of the difficulties of implementing what might be seen as the ideal business strategy, for example the skills currently available to the organization do not make a quality-enhancing strategy viable in the short term. More radically, an assessment of the current human resource could be a key element to be considered when developing the business strategy itself. Rather than simply looking externally for a market opportunity or competitive position, this view suggests than such options be appraised in the light of an assessment of human resource strengths and weaknesses – a practical expression of the phrase 'people are our most important resource'. Such a view might be thought to be increasingly relevant at a time when more organizations are said to be competing on their knowledge base (e.g. Starbuck 1992).

Prahalad and Hamel (1990) drew attention to the power of this approach in their development of the concept of core competencies. These are the skills the business has at the organizational level as a result of their human resources. It is what a company does well, rather than any particular individual or department, and typically involves the integration of particular capabilities across the organization. If such core competencies can be identified, and if they correspond to something which is valued by customers, then the organization can identify a business strategy to which it is particularly well suited and which is hard for others to imitate. The enthusiasm with which these ideas were taken up in the strategy literature of the early 1990s notwithstanding, it has proved difficult for organizations to utilize this approach in practice. The difficulty, in part, seems to be in finding a way of defining core competencies at anything other than a rhetorical level. In terms of human resource planning one would expect such an approach to be combined with a methodology for auditing employee skills and how they interacted so that areas could be identified for strengthening or development (Javidan 1998). Liff and Scarbrough

(1994) identified companies in the UK who were interested in trying to develop the ideas of core competency but who had been unable to develop any information systems and had made little progress towards their objectives. A major problem appeared to be the difficulty in finding ways to connect the kinds of skill requirements identified at a strategic level – for example, winning new markets – with an assessment of skills held by individuals within the workforce. More generally, and in line with the earlier discussion about the presence or absence of HR planning, the literature on the relationship a company *should* seek between its corporate and HR strategies is far more extensive than the literature detailing what that relationship is in practice.

There are good reasons for not being too surprised by the lack of clear evidence for a fit between human resource and business strategies. It derives from difficulties with the strategy process itself. As will have been evident the notion of fitting an approach to human resources into a corporate or business strategy reverts back to a rational planning model whereby the environment can be analysed and the organization's relationship with it predictably controlled. While this remains a common feature of prescriptive textbooks, it is based on precisely the same assumptions which were said to make traditional manpower planning inappropriate. Many writers have argued that strategies are, in contrast, emergent and partial and that the identification of coherent, successful strategies is often only a *post hoc* reconstruction (see Whittington 1993). If this is the case then one would expect to see a more interactive relationship between those responsible for business and human resource strategies.

Consequences of a Broader Agenda – the Need for Internal Coherence

In the section above the terms 'human resource' plans and strategies were being used almost interchangeably. This could be seen as part of the debate over whether to expand the remit of human resource plans beyond the reconciliation of labour supply and demand as suggested by the IPD. It is also indicative of a claim that what is needed from a plan is not just a set of mechanical techniques capable of delivering a specified number of people, but rather a coherent approach to managing human resources. When the scope of the planning process was narrow the manpower plan could arguably be derived directly from the business strategy. If a wider remit is deemed necessary, then this is an argument for the development of a human resource strategy as a stage between the business strategy and the human resource plan. The human resource strategy should ensure that the broader human resource plan not only matches the business plan but is also internally consistent. If it is, then it should be possible to identify a typology of approaches to managing human resources.

Hendry (1995) develops this approach through the elaboration of different types of what he calls employment systems. 'Without an understanding of a firm as an employment system, human resource practices and HRM cannot be considered as strategic' (Hendry 1995: 227). These employment systems show how choices over a wide range of issues come together to provide distinct, coherent approaches to managing labour in different circumstances. The starting point for the development of these employment systems is the distinction between internal and external labour markets. However, these are not seen narrowly as simply indicative of recruitment points of entry (chapter 5). Instead they encompass a range of approaches to securing labour and skills at a manageable cost. This, for example, includes not only issues of allocation (the traditional concern of manpower planners) but also the structure of jobs themselves (e.g. breadth, form of control).

There are many different models that have been developed by writers working within a labour market tradition. Hendry's (1995) model which delineates four main types of employment systems/labour markets will be described briefly here. The first two systems he describes are the classic internal and external labour markets. In the internal labour market (ILM) jobs are flexible and broadly defined but are clearly under the control of the employer. The intention is to develop firm-specific skills and to allow individuals to develop through their experience of work. Skills will be learnt from other employees and will be rewarded by increasing seniority. Long service is valued as well as more narrowly defined merit, and employment security is high. Career progression is controlled by the employer as are rewards which tend to be individualized. In contrast the open external labour market (ELM) is characterized by jobs that are narrow and unskilled. What skills are required are readily available in the labour market and training is minimal. Deployment is tightly controlled by the employer and job security is low. Pay rates will be determined by local factors but are likely to include a strong incentive element.

The other two types of employment systems can be seen as an elaboration of these well-established models. The first of these he calls the 'occupational labour market' (OLM). OLMs have the external orientation of ELMs but involve the skill recognition and development and associated rewards of the ILM model. The most obvious application of this system currently is in relation to (some) professional employees, although it also shares characteristics with the craft model. The externally facing element derives from the control that the profession (or craft) has over the content of training and access to employment, and indeed over the scope of jobs. Such jobs tend to be well paid and security high but people may be said to have a primary commitment to their occupation rather than to any particular employer.

The fourth type of employment system, 'the technical/industrial labour market' (TILM) offers different kinds of compromise. It shares many characteristics with the ELM in terms of the types of jobs, rewards and overall levels of security. However, some of the most extreme aspects have been ameliorated by detailed agreements, often with trade unions. This system has developed around Fordist/Taylorist forms of work organization where assembly line systems dictate semi-skilled but narrow and highly paced jobs. Wages are attached to jobs and vary with grades. Management has power over allocation and overall employment levels but this power is constrained by tightly negotiated agreements over the details of working arrangements and by rules governing promotion and redundancy which tend to be linked to seniority.

Finally Hendry (1995) identifies HRM as a potentially emergent fifth system intended to address the limitations of both the internal labour market and the technical/industrial labour market which have both proved too inflexible. The key feature of this system he sees as 'commitment'. The approach involves putting greater responsibility for performance on to the work group but also gives employees a greater voice within the organization. He accepts that such an employment system, in so far as it exists at all, still has many contradictory features.

From a system to a strategy? – constraints on choice

These employment systems are, of course, ideal types and may well not appear quite in their 'pure' form in any particular organization. More importantly an organization may well be operating more than one employment system – typically in relation to different types of employee. What turns such a system into a human resource strategy is when it can be shown to be chosen to fit with the business strategy. It is important to ask, therefore, to what extent managers articulate such employment systems and whether they are actually amenable to change in the way that would seem to be required of a strategy.

Hendry (1995) believes from his case study work that far more small- to medium-sized employers identify with this approach than would say that they undertook formal manpower planning. He claims managers were able to state clearly how they recruited, promoted and remunerated their employees and give reasons for these choices rooted in the labour and product markets in which they operated. Their approach is distinguished from a formal planning process in that it is more tentative and incremental. However, this would only make it not strategic if one accepts the classic rational model as the only form of business planning.

For some writers there seems to be a functionalist assumption that employment strategies will almost automatically come into line with changed production needs (Doeringer and Piore 1971; Piore and Sabel 1984). None the less, some constraints on developing or changing an employment system seem to be inherent in their descriptions. These relate to the power of professional groups and trade unions. This is not to say an employer could not seek to influence these but that there are limits to the extent to which this can be achieved unilaterally. Similarly, broad labour-market conditions will influence the viability of pure external labour markets. But it also seems likely that the integrative strength of such systems will also be a difficulty when an organization tries to change its approach.

Rubery (1994) makes a rather more complex argument which exposes both the multiple constraints on employers' ability to choose an employment system and the lack of simple coherence of direction that environment and business strategy exert on the choice of employment system. She argues that there are always good reasons for an organization to move towards an internal labour market although, drawing on Osterman (1984), she notes that firms often strenuously resist moving in this direction. These reasons derive primarily from issues associated with employees' input to the productive process but go far beyond the conventional stress on retaining firm-specific skills to include 'to capture returns on training, to ensure a hard-working, motivated labour force, to unleash productive capacity to improve the effective performance of the organisation, and to meet the demands of organised labour or reduce the likelihood of the development of collective organization of the workforce' (p. 45). Competitive and production conditions are also argued to militate in favour of a stable and committed workforce in most circumstances.

Rubery (1994) goes on to argue, however, that there are a range of factors constraining their achievement of this goal. Indeed she argues that the observed differences in employment systems is a consequence of these constraints rather than of differing employment needs. The major factors that constrain employers' choice are financial and organizational. On the financial side either the costs involved, or the pressure to demonstrate short-term financial returns, could mean that the investment required to undertake training, improve pay, or guarantee employment security may not be available. Organizational constraints include the difficulty small or decentralized organizations have in providing promotion opportunities. There is also the time needed to change HR systems and for the workforce to accept the messages the organization intends to convey by them. All this might lead to the conclusion that there is little point in trying to align human resource approaches with business needs. In fact Rubery (1994) argues, on the basis of extensive empirical research, that it is the model that is over simplistic and restrictive, especially its assumptions about what employment practices are required to deliver a stable and committed workforce. Employers have found a wide variety of means to achieve the same ends which include a more segmented approach to the labour market, such as targeting those with restricted alternative employment opportunities, and assessing people's expectations about promotion opportunities and pay, rather than assuming that these had to be set at an absolute level.

Demographic diversity – implications of a changed labour market

Most commentators focus on the increasingly competitive market that firms face in selling their products or services. Less attention is usually given to the consequences of changes in the labour market. Yet, as Rubery's (1994) examples make clear, these have led to significant changes in the terms on which employees are seeking work and their orientation to work. Conventional manpower models may no longer be appropriate not only because the structure of jobs is changing but also because sections of the workforce, most notably women with dependants, are engaging with the labour market in different ways. The increase in part-time work and non-linear careers are evidence of this (see chapter 9). These patterns of work may represent positive choices on the part of some employees to achieve a different balance between work and home or they may be decisions forced upon them by inadequate or unaffordable care for the young, sick or elderly. For similar reasons assumptions about the points in people's working lives when they will seek, expect, or alternatively not welcome, promotion or other increased demands may be breaking down. More generally different generations may have different senses of what constitutes a good lifestyle which may place greater or less emphasis on the funds necessary to acquire more material possessions or the time to spend away from work.

In a wider sense a more diverse workforce may require employers to rethink the way they currently structure jobs (make-up of tasks, etc.), to reassess the qualifications and experience they ask for, and the selection techniques used. This may be in part a decision forced on organizations by equality legislation (chapter 6) but may also be seen as the best way to satisfy their human resource needs. Once in employment such employees may not respond in the same way to HR policies as white able bodied males and may need different approaches to ensure their retention and motivation. These issues, and their significance for human resource planning, have been addressed more fully in the USA than in the UK (Avery et al. 1996). Even so such analyses tend to treat workforce diversity in an 'add-on' way which requires employers to consider some new issues but not fundamentally change what they are doing. In contrast Powell (1998) suggests that diversity should lead to a more basic reconsideration of how to assess the central concern of human resource planning –

the process of matching people to jobs. The argument is that matching has traditionally been thought of in terms of selecting those who fit in with the organization's current workforce profile and share their values. This is increasingly recognized as potentially detrimental to non-traditional employees: either excluding them altogether or only accepting them on condition that they assimilate within the dominant culture. But the argument is that such an approach is detrimental to organizations as well as to potential employees. Breaking with an over-cohesive workforce can, it is suggested, be beneficial in stimulating thinking about new approaches and market opportunities.

Implementing Human Resource Strategies

Returning to issues about matching labour supply and demands reduces the level of abstraction which pervades much of the discussions about the relationship between business strategy and human resource strategies. In practice there are different ways of managing people to deliver the same business goals. Even once a general approach has been agreed there are many steps involved in translating that into a viable practical human resource plan. What data is needed on the current and available workforce and how can it be obtained? How can probable changes in the workforce (retirement, turnover or different needs in terms of working arrangements or remuneration) be identified? How can the organization's needs for both a certain quantity and quality of labour be modelled? For example, all this data would be needed in order to determine whether a job security commitment could be given (with any realistic chance of the organization being able to fulfil it), whether it would be valued, and indeed what would count as such a commitment in the eyes of employees.

In a complex planning environment these information needs cannot be reduced to the type of mathematical techniques popular in the 1960s and 1970s. In particular there has been a shift from reconciling numbers of employees available with predictable stable jobs towards a greater concern with skills, their development and deployment. In part this is evidence of a greater recognition of the distinctive contribution employees make to the delivery of a business strategy, as discussed above. But it is also a response to the rapidly changing nature of jobs and production methods. Hendry (1995) notes the curious absence of discussion of skill within manpower planning and goes so far as to say that a skill supply strategy is a fundamental distinguishing feature of human resource plans.

Approaches to understanding skills

One of the good reasons why skills do not appear in the quantitative manpower models is that it is very difficult to pin down what they are. Most organizations have long kept records of employees' qualifications and the training courses they have attended. But, apart from skills which are not used being subject to deterioration over time, there are issues about the ways in which formal training is translated into skilled practice and the multiple routes by which skills can be acquired which do not involve training courses or result in qualifications. Neither is it simple to define the skills required to undertake a job since tasks can be carried out in different ways and it may not be apparent to employers that a higher level (or different mix) of skill could be more effective.

These two dimensions of skills, the capabilities of employees and the requirements of jobs, add a new dimension to the traditional manpower planning concern with reconciling supply and demand for labour. The significance of this issue for the UK workforce can be seen in part through a skill survey carried out within the ESRC's Social Change and Economic Life Initiative (Penn et al. 1994). In this study respondents were asked to report on their personal skill attainment. This was classified by the researchers as 'own skill' and measured by indicators such as training undertaken, qualifications achieved, and experience gained. Respondents were also asked to assess the skills required in their current job. This was classified as 'job skill' and assessed in terms of the extent of discretion exercised, numbers supervised, and qualifications required at appointment. On the basis of this data Rose (1994) reports that 40 per cent of respondents experienced a significant mismatch between their skills and those required in their current jobs. This study also demonstrates the difficulty of defining the skill requirements of a job separately from the those held by the employee since those respondents who were asked to define a skilled job most often did so by reference to the requirements it would place on the job holder.

These two dimensions do not cover fully the complexity of the issues facing employers attempting to measure skills as an input to a human resource plan. The most obvious additional issue is the potential discrepancy between the skill abilities of an employee and their performance in practice. While it is common to identify low-quality or low-productivity performance as evidence of a skill gap (Darrah 1994) there are a range of other explanations that need to be considered. At the individual level these include motivation and commitment. But there are also a range of relevant organizational issues including the equipment available, the quality of supervision and the way in which work teams function.

There is one further dimension of skill which is often dismissed as a distortion which should be capable of removal. This is some times referred to as the 'political' dimension (Cockburn 1983). Its significance was apparent in the discussion of occupational labour markets above. This is where a professional or craft group have been able to control the definition of the skill requirements of a particular job. The managerial dismissal of this aspect of skill as a distortion is based on the view that skill requirements are inflated and owe more to controlling entry, and hence wage levels, than they do to the requirements of the job. However, we could note that precisely the same arguments could be applied to employers' motivations for reducing the assessment of skill requirements. These conflicting assessments about *real* skill levels and requirements do not operate only at the level of the occupational group. A repeated theme in the literature on appraisal is that employees will be unwilling to identify or accept that they have training needs if they anticipate that performance levels will be used as a basis for allocating rewards or punishments (see chapter 10).

Attempts to implement skill supply strategies

Liff (1997) described three organizations who were developing computer or paper-based information systems to inform decision making about workforce skills. Their experiences illustrate both the potential relevance of this information base to a range of business and human resource strategies and the difficulties in practice of developing such an information system. The three companies shared a strong commitment to developing a link between their business strategy and their human resource strategy. They could all be said to be operating a form of hard HRM. Although this did not translate simply into a desire to minimize the costs associated with the workforce, there was a strong emphasis on both cost effectiveness and on ensuring that human resources were utilized in the most effective way. Within each of these organizations a group of managers (predominantly but not exclusively within the HR function) had identified improved data on the *match between* employee skills and job requirements as a key element in allowing the human resource strategy to deliver what was required of it by the business plan.

The specifics of the cases were, however, quite distinct. In the first case the company had traditionally had a strong commitment to training. Increased financial pressures, restructuring and substantial job losses had meant that training now needed to be assessed and presented in a new light. Assessing job skill needs and individual skill attainment meant that training could be targeted more effectively on those who needed it and where it could be expected to have the most benefit. Rethinking skill categories to look for common elements (potentially addressing the political dimension of skill) meant that differences in training times and methods which might exist, say, between departments or occupational groups could be addressed if the skill requirements could be shown to be analytically similar.

In the second company the primary concern was with deployment. A commitment had been made to the workforce to preserve employment security as part of a wider package which included restructuring and pay restraint. However, the extent of restructuring meant that this commitment could not be translated simply into allowing everyone to remain in their current job. Here the significance of data on job and individual skills was to see how people might be deployed into new positions, either directly or with some training input. Again, rethinking skill categories across departments was vital in order to ensure the maximum scope for such reallocation.

The third company was also concerned with deployment but in a rather different context. They had also experienced significant job losses, particularly among older experienced workers. They were in a high-skill design and manufacturing business and were anticipating the start of a major new project. In this case a system which could match project skill requirements against the skills of the existing workforce was seen as making a vital contribution to an assessment of how the current workforce could be effectively deployed on this new work and of what additional human resources might be needed in order to be able to deliver the project to the required standard.

For these various reasons all three companies were trying to design information systems which would help them align their human resources to a predefined business plan. They were clear about the purposes such systems were expected to serve and what was needed to deliver them. They approached their task within a mindset not dissimilar to that of quantitative manpower planners. A structure needed to be designed for the information system, data needed to be collected and input, and then it could be expected to begin demonstrating its use. Of course they anticipated some teething problems when it would be necessary to modify the system to some extent, but it was expected that such problems would be primarily technical in nature (to do with refining categories or matching processes).

What they did not appear to have anticipated was the problems they experienced in collecting what they saw as accurate data. This occurred both at the level of skill definitions where managers resisted the identification of generic skills across traditional boundaries, and at times the allocation of people suggested by such reassessments. Even more common was the problem of getting 'accurate' assessments of employees' skill levels either directly or from their line managers. From the perspective of those constructing these systems employees were consistently overestimating their skill levels. If one views these problems from the perspective of a neutral data collection process applied to organizational processes which are in the interests of all its members then such problems are indeed surprising. Such a perspective is quite common in the perscriptive personnel and computing literature but rare in organizational life. In practice individuals were concerned to maintain a positive view of their capabilities and levels of performance, despite formal assurances that this would not be linked to pay or grading, and managers were concerned to maintain their departmental power bases.

Despite the expressed desire to rethink skill categories those developing the systems faced problems which derived from the way the systems were designed. Because they were trying to develop systems that would capture what was in existence, and to test and refine them against their own knowledge of the organization, they inevitably tended to reproduce categories which reflected the existing organizational structures. They also found that they had to apply all kinds of knowledge that could not be built into the system to interpret its findings. For example, if the system was asked to identify people who could fill a particular vacancy it might produce the name of someone who did not get on with others in the team or someone who was in the middle of a divorce and who would be unlikely to respond well to a transfer. Thus in moving from the abstraction of HR strategies into the reality of plans managers were finding that they needed to confront not just technical problems of information systems design but importantly employees' attitudes towards being assessed and quantified and the limitations of viewing people as simply bundles of skills.

These examples give some flavour of what HR plans (as opposed to manpower plans or human resource strategies) might involve in practice. The concern is no longer simply with the numerical matching of numbers of people to job slots. But it remains very much about the process of matching labour supply and demand. Two things are distinctive. First, a recognition at the macro level (as opposed to the level of individual employees) of the significance of skills and performance and of the shifting nature of jobs in most organizations. Second, a recognition of the need to locate assessments of labour supply and demand within the broader context of an approach to human resource management, although this was more apparent by its absence in the case studies.

Conclusion: Where Next for Human Resource Planning?

As has been seen the literature on manpower/human resource planning covers an enormous range of approaches and perspectives. It can involve the use of mathematical techniques to assess the demand for, or supply of, labour at the macro level (e.g. Mangan and Silver 1983) or it could involve a more pragmatic assessment of different approaches to finding staff for an organization experiencing recruitment difficulties (e.g. Atkinson 1989). It can be seen as implementing the human resource aspects of a business strategy developed with consideration primarily for product market issues. Or it can mean the development and implementation of a human resource strategy integral to the business strategy. In what contexts are these different approaches likely to be tried and where might they be found useful and effective?

Where human resource plans are simply putting into effect the relevant bits of a preexisting business plan then (assuming the business plan itself is sensible) their success will depend on the compatibility of the business requirements with the relevant labour market, the compatibility of existing HR policies, and the degree of financial and other resources available for implementation. So, for example, the location of a new retail or service business close to an affluent neighbourhood may make sense in terms of customer demand, but may cause problems in terms of employee resourcing, particularly if an additional part of the strategy involves minimizing labour costs. This suggests that treating human resource issues as an afterthought to strategy making may succeed but may also prove highly problematic. Similarly there are probably still some contexts where quantitative techniques are relevant but what little evidence there is suggests that their use is declining. This does not need to be equated with a move away from any systematic approaches, however. The use of computer modelling within human resource information systems could provide new insights into human resource allocation and utilization. But the company examples described above appear to show that this requires managers to think in terms of skills rather than just numbers of employees and to recognize that skill is a concept not amenable to simple quantification. More generally, there could be a case for recognizing that human resource planning would benefit from a multidisciplinary approach combining economic, quantitative and behavioural methods (Edwards et al. 1983).

For HR planning to be strategic it needs to take place within an organization where human resource issues are seen as central to business strategy. However, this is not normally the case, certainly in the UK where financial considerations are invariably predominant. This situation may exist even in organizations which by other measures look as though they are acting strategically in relation to human resources. For example, a US study of subsidiaries of Fortune 500 companies (Martell and Carroll 1995) found evidence of 'strategic integration' between the human resource and strategic planning processes. But when asked to rate the importance of different functional areas to the implementation of strategy, 37 per cent of general managers rated HRM as extremely important compared with 73 per cent saying the same of marketing.

A factor which is arguably both a symptom and cause of the lack of importance given to human resource issues is the traditionally low status of HR specialists, as discussed in chapter 1. Various typologies exist (e.g. Storey 1992) which show that the human resource function may be treated in a purely administrative capacity, carrying out decisions made by others, or as having delegated powers only to regulate existing agreements. These are of course not the only possibilities and Storey includes a role where specialists act as advisors or indeed where they might be full members of the strategic decision-making team. It might seem reasonable to speculate that it would be only in the latter case that HR planning could be fully strategic. However, there is no reliable data with which to establish whether, or indeed where, that is the case. HR representation at board level has been treated as a proxy measure for involvement in strategy making. On this measure the picture looks relatively good with some surveys estimating that around two-thirds of UK organizations have HR representation at board level (Hall and Torrington 1998). However, the board member may well not be an HR specialist and simply having access to making an input to strategy making does not ensure that it will be made effectively in practice.

With the growth of human resource management there is a different scenario for how HR issues might assume a greater importance. Here line managers assume greater responsibility for the management of HR and hence, in the ideal case, become more aware of the ways in which such issues are central to achieving business goals. Again the evidence is lacking as to whether such an integration of roles results in integrated thinking about human resources and business objectives rather than simply line managers being overloaded and having inadequate specialist knowledge. However, it seems unlikely that such a change in allocation of responsibility will in itself be sufficient. Instead, strategic human resource planning is most likely to be seen as desirable and possible in a context where employees are seen as key elements to achieving a business strategy based on employee skills or high levels of service. Even in this context it is unlikely to be realized in practice without an integrated approach to employee relations which takes a soft HRM form. This is not just because in such a context the significance of human resource planning would be apparent to management but also because, without it, the degree of trust and the co-operation needed for data gathering and restructuring will not be present on the part of employees.

References and further reading

Atkinson, J. 1989: Four stages of adjustment to the demographic downturn. *Personnel Management* August, 20–4.

Avery, R. D., Azevedo, R. E., Ostgaard, D. J. and Raghuram, S. 1996: The implications of a diverse labour market on human resource planning. In E. E. Kossek and S. A. Lobel (eds), *Managing Diversity: Human Resource Strategies for Transforming the Workplace*, Oxford: Blackwell.

Bell, D. 1989: Why Manpower Planning is back in vogue. *Personnel Management*, July, 40–3.

Cockburn, C. 1983: *Brothers: Male Dominance and Technical Change*. London: Pluto.

Cowling, A. and Walters, M. 1990: Manpower Planning – Where are we today? *Personnel Review*, **19**(3), 3–8.

Darrah, C. 1994: Skill Requirements of Work: Rhetoric versus reality. *Work and Occupations*, **21**(1), 64–84.

Doeringer, P. B. and Piore, M. J. 1971: *Internal Labour Markets and Manpower Analysis*. Lexington, MA, D. C. Heath.

Drucker, P. 1961: *The Practice of Management*. London: Mercury Books.

Edwards, J. E., Leek, C., Loveridge, R., Lumley, R., Mangan, J. and Silver, M. (eds) 1983: *Manpower Planning: Strategy and Techniques in Organisational Context*. Chichester: John Wiley and Sons.

Greer, C. R. and Armstrong, D. 1980: Human Resource Forecasting and Planning: A state of the art investigation. *Human Resource Planning*, **3**(2), 67–78.

Greer, C. R., Jackson, D. L. and Fiorito, J. 1989: Adapting Human Resource Planning in a Changing Business Environment. *Human Resource Management*, **28**(1) 105–23.

Guest, D. 1987: Human Resource Management and Industrial Relations. *Journal of Management Studies*, **25**(5), 503–21.

Hall, L. and Torrington, D. 1998: *The Human Resource Function: The Dynamics of Change and Development*. London: Pitman Publishing.

Hendry, C. 1995: *Human Resource Management: A Strategic Approach to Employment*. Oxford: Butterworth-Heinemann.

Hercus, T. 1992: Human Resource Planning in Eight British Organisations: A Canadian Perspective. In B. Towers (ed.), *The Handbook of Human Resource Management*. Oxford: Blackwell.

IPM (Institute of Personnel Management) 1975: *Manpower Planning in Action*. London: IPM.

IPM (no date): *Statement on Human Resource Planning*. London: IPM.

Javidan, M. 1998: Core Competence: What does it mean in practice? *Long Range Planning*, **31**(1), 60–71.

Liff, S. 1997: Contructing HR Information Systems. *Human Resource Management Journal*, **7**(2), 18–31.

Liff, S. and Scarbrough, H. 1994: Creating a Knowledge Database – Operationalising the vision or compromising the concept? In R. Mansell (ed.), *Management of Information and Communication Technologies: Emerging Patterns of Control*, London: Aslib, The Association for Information Management.

Mangan, J. and Silver, M. 1983: The demand for and supply of labour. In J. Edwards et al. (eds), *Manpower Planning: Strategy and Techniques in Organisational Context*, Chichester: John Wiley & Sons.

Manpower Services Commission/National Economic Development Office, 1978: *Case Studies in Company Manpower Planning*. London: NEDO.

Martell, K. and Carroll, S. J. 1995: How Strategic is HRM? *Human Resource Management*, **34**(2), 253–67.

Miles, R. E. and Snow, C. C. 1984: Designing Strategic Human Resources Systems. *Organisational Dynamics*, **13**, (summer), 36–52.

O'Doherty, D. 1997: Human Resource Planning: Control to Seduction? In I. Beardwell and L. Holden (eds), *Human Resource Management: A Contemporary Perspective*, London: Pitman Publishing.

Osterman, P. (ed.) 1984: *Internal Labour Markets*. London: MIT.

Penn, R., Rose, M. and Rubery J. (eds) 1994: *Skill and Occupational Change*. Oxford: Oxford University Press.

Piore M. J. and Sabel, C. F. 1984: *The Second Industrial Divide: Possibilities for Prosperity*. New York: Basic Books.

Powell, G. N. 1998: Reinforcing and Extending Today's Organizations: The simultaneous pursuit of person–organization fit and diversity. *Organizational Dynamics*, **26**(Winter), 50–61.

Prahalad, C. K. and Hamel, G. 1990: The Core Competence of the Corporation. *Harvard Business Review* (May/June), 79–91.

Reilly, P. 1996: *Human Resource Planning: An Introduction*. Institute for Employment Studies Report 312, Brighton: IES.

Rose, M. 1994: Job satisfactions, job skills and personal skills. In R. Penn, M. Rose and J. Rubery (eds), *Skill and Occupational Change*. Oxford: Oxford University Press.

Rothwell, S. 1995: Human Resource Planning. In J. Storey (ed.), *Human Resource Management: A Critical Text*, London: Routledge.

Rubery, J. 1994: Internal and External Labour Markets: Towards an Integrated Analysis. In J. Rubery and F. Wilkinson (eds), *Employer Strategy and the Labour Market*, Oxford: Oxford University Press.

Schuler, R. S. 1989: Strategic Human Resource Management and Industrial Relations. *Human Relations*, **42**(2), 157–83.

Sisson, K. and Timperley, S. 1994: From Manpower Planning to Strategic Human Resource Management. In K. Sisson (ed.), *Personnel Management: A Comprehensive Guide to Theory and Practice in Britain*, Oxford: Blackwell.

Starbuck, W. 1992: Learning by Knowledge-Intensive Firms. *Journal of Management Studies*, **29**(6), 713–40.

Storey, J. 1992: *Developments in the Management of Human Resources*. Oxford: Blackwell.

Whittington, R. 1993: *What is Strategy and Does it Matter?* London: Routledge.

5

Recruitment and Selection

Sue Newell and Viv Shackleton

Escalating global competition coupled with increasingly sophisticated customer expectations means that the growth, or even survival, of a firm is difficult. It is no longer sufficient to be effective in selling a particular product or service or to rely on past reputation. Organizations need to respond to a rapidly changing global environment. Yet when we talk about 'organizations' we are obviously talking about the people who make up organizations, since by definition an organization cannot act. Continued success is dependent on attracting and retaining high-quality individuals who can respond effectively to this dynamic environment.

Thus, perhaps ironically in an age of increasingly complex technology, organizations are stating that 'employees are our greatest asset'. This implies that there can be 'wrong' people; individuals who are not going to contribute to organizational success and who may even harm the organization. Clearly, there are differences between individuals, for example, people differ in their physical appearance. But there are also psycho-social differences between people – in terms of abilities, personality, motivation and emotions. Given that jobs and organizations differ in terms of what they require, some individuals will be more suited to some jobs and organizations than others. Hiring the 'right' people is of paramount importance and this is dependent on effective recruitment and selection procedures, which aim to select the 'right' individuals and reject the 'wrong' ones.

One of the earliest management writers, F. W. Taylor (1911), stressed the importance of selection for the particular job – 'the best man for the job' (Taylor's sexist language would not be acceptable these days). He bemoaned the typical way in which individuals were selected, based on who you knew or who was first in the queue. Ability to do the particular job was not systematically assessed. Taylor instead introduced the idea that people should be selected for their particular skills and abilities which should be tested prior to the selection decision. Despite this early emphasis by Taylor, it is evident that many organizations still fail to adopt even the most basic recruitment and selection procedures which would allow them to attract suitable candidates (recruitment) and then make good predictions about the likely 'fit' between particular individuals and the organizational and job requirements (selection).

Recruitment and selection involves making predictions about future behaviour so that decisions can be made about who will be most suitable for a particular job. Predictions must always be couched in terms of probabilities because the future is unpredictable. However, informed judgements can be made (like actuaries deciding insurance premiums), rather than uninformed guesses (like crystal-ball gazers). This requires a systematic process of assessment of both individual differences and organizational requirements. Recruitment and selection can be viewed as a process by which the organization tries accurately to match the individual to the job and can be compared to completing a jigsaw puzzle. Recruitment and selection is a process of selecting the correct jigsaw piece (the 'right' individual) from the incorrect pieces (the 'wrong' individuals) to fit into a particular hole in a jigsaw puzzle. We will refer to this model as the 'psychometric' or traditional approach to recruitment and selection. It focuses on the job and presents the recruitment and selection process as a systematic and objective process which follows a logical sequence of events. The psychometric approach has been the dominant perspective and underpins the good practice model of recruitment and selection espoused, for example, by the Institute of Personnel and Development (IPD 1995).

In this perspective, jobs are defined in terms of their tasks (job description) and the characteristics of the person who will be able successfully to carry out these tasks (person specification). Recruitment is a process of attracting individuals who might meet this specification. Selection is the process of measuring differences between these candidates to find the person who has the profile which best matches the person specification as indicated by the job profile or description. In figure 5.1, candidate C would be chosen, being the best match for the particular 'hole'. This process resembles an obstacle course with the organization putting up increasingly difficult obstacles for the candidates to overcome. Each obstacle represents a competence, which is deemed necessary or desirable for the job incumbent. The most important obstacles are those competencies which are deemed essential for the effective performance of the job. The individual who can demonstrate the greatest number of essential competencies is given the job. Thus, if the job involves forecasting sales orders then the 'right' individual is going to be highly quantitative so that they have the ability to manipulate a variety of statistical data in order to understand sales trends.

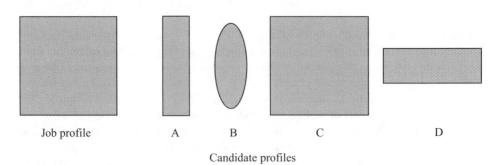

Job profile   A   B   C   D

Candidate profiles

Figure 5.1   The traditional, 'psychometric' view of the selection process: fitting a square peg into a square hole

The first half of this chapter is concerned with examining the recruitment and selection process as viewed from the dominant prescriptive psychometric approach, outlined above. Based on this approach, the key stages in the recruitment and selection process are outlined and the different methods of recruitment and selection assessed. We then go on to examine the limitations of the psychometric perspective in the context of increased uncertainty and competition facing organizations. We outline the advantages of viewing the recruitment and selection process from an exchange perspective which views the recruitment and selection process as the outcome of a process of exchange and negotiation.

The Recruitment Process

Organizational review and job analysis

Recruitment is the process of attracting people who might make a contribution to the particular organization. Recruitment is often stimulated when an existing employee leaves. Frequently, however, this situation is seen as a tight problem, that is, one with a fixed solution (like $2 + 2 = 4$). The organizational response is to try and replace the individual with a replica of that person. However, a more systematic response may be to review thoroughly the particular requirements, putting this into the wider context of both the organization and its environment. Perhaps, for example, the employee had supervisory responsibilities. This could present an opportunity to reallocate some of this authority in order to empower a particular group. However, the tasks undertaken by the departing employee may no longer be essential because of changes in the environment. In addition, recruitment may be necessary because of organizational expansion. Here, as well, the prescriptive literature suggests that it is important to take a helicopter view of the situation and ensure that there are not better alternatives to recruitment from an organizational perspective. For example, automation may preclude the need to recruit additional staff.

Thus, the first stage in the recruitment process involves a systematic review of the organization's requirements. A strategic or helicopter perspective is advocated to ensure that parochial concerns do not dominate the decision process. For example, in the short term, the individual department where the problem or opportunity has arisen may wish to simply replace a departing employee, or expand the number of employees in the face of higher workloads, or in order to keep staff numbers up, or using more political language, to empire build. This, however, may not be in the best interest of the whole organization.

The prescriptive literature suggests that following organizational review, a thorough analysis of the requirements of the job should be established, often termed 'job analysis'. This is necessary because, even in those situations where an individual is simply being replaced, there may still be changes in job requirements, especially if the individual being replaced has been with the organization for some time. There are a number of techniques that can be used for undertaking job analysis (see, for example, Greuter and Algera 1989), but essentially they all require the collection of systematic data about the particular job from existing incumbents and colleagues. This usually involves interviews, questionnaires or diaries.

First, using interviews, job holders may be asked to describe their main tasks and responsibilities. However, there may be bias in what is recalled because job analysis is used for a variety of purposes, including salary decisions, so job holders may have a vested interest in inflating the worth of their job. Another interview technique is to focus on 'critical incidents'. Job holders are asked to recall specific incidents of either good or poor job performance. This provides an indication of the most important aspects of the job and provides an insight into how good and poor job holders are differentiated. Another commonly used technique is the repertory grid. There are many versions of this, but a common one is to ask respondents to think of five or six job incumbents they have worked with. Names are not asked for, in order to preserve anonymity. The five or six people are assigned letters, A to E, for example. The interviewer asks the respondent to choose three of them and describe how two are similar, and one is different from the third, in the way they work. For example, 'A and B are willing to stay on at work to complete an urgent task, while the other person, C, doesn't', might be a typical answer. This information forms a construct. Later on, respondents rate A to E in terms of overall effectiveness at the job. For example, if A and B are rated more effective performers than C, and other respondents provide similar examples (assuming this type of work commitment is also referred to in critical incidents) then it is reasonable to conclude that a key competence which distinguishes good from poor performers has been established.

Second, structured questionnaries have been developed to collect data about specific jobs. The most well-established is the Position Analysis Questionnaire (PAQ) developed in the USA by McCormick et al. (1972), which consists of nearly 200 items which are categorized under six headings: information input; mediation processes; work output; interpersonal activities; work situation and job context; and miscellaneous aspects. Saville and Holdsworth (1995) have developed a similar structured approach in the UK, called the Work Profiling System (WPS).

Third, job holders can be asked to keep a diary recording their activities. This overcomes problems of incomplete memory, but can be very time consuming.

Finally, in contrast to other methods which rely on self-reporting by the job holder, it is helpful to carry out some direct observation to reduce bias and inaccuracies. While observation itself may alter the behaviour of people, as demonstrated by the classic Hawthorne Studies (Roethlisberger and Dickson 1939), it can nevertheless provide additional data and provide the job analyst with a better understanding of what the job entails. Moreover, although the job holder has the most intimate knowledge about what the job involves, peers, subordinates and superiors can be valuable sources of information and provide an alternative perspective, as the vogue for '360 degree' feedback illustrates (see chapter 10). Data from these other sources can be collected in similar ways to those obtained directly from job holders.

Job description, person specification and competencies

Once the job analysis data has been collected, the next stage is to develop a job description. This describes what the job involves: the purpose of the job; the tasks that are to be undertaken, together with an outline of the expected performance standards; the duties and responsibilities; and the reporting relationships. In addition, the job description will include details of remuneration, benefits, working conditions and hours. The job description identifies the particular demands of a job and emphasizes those aspects which are crucial to success. In some cases a distinction is made between a job description and a job specification. The job description is a statement of the tasks, duties, objectives and standards, while a job specification identifies the skills, knowledge and qualities required to perform the described job. The job description is thus job oriented, focusing on the work itself, while the job specification is worker oriented, focusing on the psychological and behavioural requirements of the job. Ideally, for the selection process, both a job description and a job specification should be drawn up and reviewed against the job. Survey evidence, drawn from the responses of 165 employers (IRS 1996: 12), indicates that almost two-thirds of employers reported that they always reviewed the job description against the aims of the job before proceeding to the recruitment stage, in line with personnel best practice.

The job description and job specification provide the necessary information to move to the next stage of the job analysis process, which is to develop a person specification. This converts the job specification into human terms, specifying the kind of person needed to perform the described job. Inferences are made about the psycho-social characteristics that are necessary for a successful job holder. There are two frameworks, which are well-established, to help with this process. The oldest is the Seven Point Plan, developed by Rodger (1952) which provides seven headings under which to categorize those personal qualities considered to be essential or desirable. An example is shown as table 5.1. A similar framework was developed by Munro Fraser (1978) and consists of five categories: impact on others; acquired knowledge or qualifications; innate abilities; motivation; and emotional adjustment.

These two approaches are still commonly used by firms in the UK (Mackay and Torrington 1986) and obviously have considerable overlap. Both stress the need to relate the personal characteristics specified to the prior identification of job demands and both can be used as the basis for designing a structured interview approach. More importantly, however, both suffer from a heavy reliance on personal judgement to determine what human qualities are associated with successful performance. They are not therefore politically or socially neutral (Watson 1994). Because of this inherent difficulty, an alternative approach has been gaining prominence, which emphasizes job competencies rather than personal qualities.

Table 5.1 Personnel specification for a secondary-school head of English (following Rodger's seven-point plan)

1 Physical make-up: no specific requirement (teachers come in all shapes and sizes!)
2 Attainments: good honours degree in English plus a teaching qualification; at least 7 years teaching experience in secondary schools, preferably including some management experience
3 General intelligence: good general intelligence
4 Special aptitudes: high verbal ability plus an ability to impart knowledge to students working at a variety of levels; leadership ability to integrate the members of the English department
5 Interests: in the arts generally and an interest in enthusing students and staff to take an interest in the arts
6 Disposition: dependable and sociable to both students and staff
7 Circumstances: no specific requirement, although must be prepared to work some evenings both for parent consultations and staff meetings

Job competencies focus on behaviours rather than personal characteristics. Organizations adopting a competency approach seek to define a series of effective individual behaviours, usually in the context of promoting superior organizational performance (Boam and Sparrow 1992; Dale and Iles 1992). So, for example, it is not a question of determining that the job demands someone with self-confidence, but that the job requires someone who can perform in front of 120 MBAs and deliver a lecture which is well received. While this specific behaviour need not have been demonstrated before, the key is to identify other situations which can be used as evidence that the individual possesses the competence successfully to engage in this behaviour. A well-known example of an attempt to use such an approach is the case of British Petroleum (BP). Faced with major challenges to its business in the early 1990s, BP sought to identify the key behaviours to support high performance and a shift in the corporate culture. The competencies which emerged from repertory grid and other analysis identified 67 essential behaviours which were clustered into a framework termed OPEN: Open Thinking, Personal Impact, Empowering and Networking. These competences fed into graduate recruitment and other personnel practices (Sparrow and Bognanno 1993).

While in theory this competency approach looks significantly different from the person specification approach, in practice there is considerable overlap. This is because there is still a translation process, which moves from the specific behaviour required to its root source in terms of the subsequent identification of traits, motives, attitudes, skills and aptitudes, and which still requires subjective judgement. Thus, a behavioural competence has been defined as 'an underlying characteristic of a person which results in effective and/or superior performance' (Boyatzis 1982). So while the difference lies essentially in the premium that is placed upon observable behaviour, nevertheless the problem of the underlying causes of psychological make-up remains the same. Consequently, traditional psychometric instruments may be used to obtain evidence of these competences during the selection process (Sparrow 1997). However, as this discussion indicates, moving from behavioural competencies to personality traits is certainly not straightforward (Fletcher 1992).

Recruitment Methods

Once the job analysis is completed and the job specification or behavioural competencies are identified, the next stage is to consider how to attract people who meet the requirements. A key decision is about whether to recruit internally or externally.

Internal recruitment may have a number of potential advantages. Recruits will already understand something about how the organization operates and so socialization and learning may be significantly reduced; it will be cheaper, as expensive advertising and recruitment consultancy fees are avoided; it may be able to relieve an organizational problem of too many employees in another area; and it may provide motivation to existing employees who can see new opportunities available within the wider organization. It is more likely that such an approach would be found among organizations which are keen to develop and nurture their own internal talent, along the lines advocated by proponents of a 'soft' human resource management approach. For these reasons it is not surprising that almost 97 per cent of employers routinely attempt to fill vacancies from internal sources before seeking external applicants, although this practice is far less common in the public sector (IRS 1996: 13). However, there may be disadvantages, for example, bypassing the opportunity to bring in new blood with experience from other organizations; or leaving a gap elsewhere in the organization which needs to be filled. In addition, internal recruitment can be potentially unfair and discriminatory, since it tends to perpetuate a workforce from the same sources as already exist and may therefore reinforce existing organizational inequalities.

External recruitment brings in individuals from outside. However, as organizational boundaries become more permeable with the rise of inter-organizational networking the definition of internal versus external recruitment becomes more problematic. The advantages of internal recruitment are basically the disadvantages of external recruiting. Most of the rest of this section will concentrate on methods to recruit individuals from outside the organization's boundaries where the emphasis is on finding ways to inform potentially 'good' employees of the job opportunity and encourage them to apply.

Sources of external applicants

Because internal methods are often not sufficient to supply a suitable pool of applicants, most organizations make use of external sources to attract potential recruits. There are many such sources, including employee referrals, employment agencies, 'walk-ins', and educational establishments. When existing employees are encouraged to find future employees this is termed 'employee referrals'. This may be merely asking employees to inform relations, friends or acquaintances, or it may involve a financial reward for the existing employee if a new recruit they have encouraged to apply, finally accepts a job. The advantage of this method is that the new recruits are likely to have a better understanding of the culture and values of the organization, and the nature of the work on offer, than the average recruit, which allows employers to make use of these tacit skills. Employers therefore benefit from the knowledge and skills that these workers have already acquired in the community and they may be more amenable to management control, not least because the existing workforce may take on some of the responsibility for ensuring the effective performance of those workers they have recommended (Manwaring 1984). As Ram's study of small Asian-owned firms in the West Midlands clothing industry shows, for these workers faced with very limited job opportunities, at least this form of recruitment avoided having to go through interviews or other formal recruitment methods (Ram 1994: 76–7). Of course, reliance on referrals may run up against equal opportunity problems if certain groups have a less than equal chance of hearing about vacancies, but this benefits employers seeking out disadvantaged, and therefore cheap, sources of labour.

Employment agencies are a very popular source of recruits with IRS (1996) survey evidence suggesting that they are used by more than three-quarters of employers, although fewer public-sector employers make use of them. Approximately half of employers use agencies to recruit staff with specialist skills, whilst other frequently cited reasons included when temporary staff were sought or because a vacancy needed to be filled quickly (IRS 1996: 9–10). Employment agencies vary from small local enterprises, specializing in one sort of employee, such as clerical workers or computer specialists, to international head hunters engaged in recruiting senior managers for multinational companies. Some specialize in temporary help while others search for more permanent placements. Head hunters will often search and select, that is, draw up a short-list to present to their client, who has the final say on who should be appointed. There are also public employment agencies in many countries, including Britain.

A 'walk-in' is where an applicant simply walks into the employer's premises, often as a result of seeing an advertisement in the window. Many shops and quick-food outlets recruit in this way. Like employee referrals, it is quick, cheap and can be very effective in terms of retention. Employees often stay longer than do those who come via different routes (Decker and Cornelius 1979). As with employee referrals, care needs to be paid to the issue of equal opportunities.

Increasingly, organizations are targeting recruitment towards particular educational institutions. This may be in addition to other methods. Companies that recruit graduates, particularly those in short supply such as software engineers, or where the market is fiercely competitive, such as accountancy, often set up good relations with university departments in selected universities. This helps them to advertise their company as well as to be able to position themselves to recruit early and 'the best'. In addition, the services of university careers offices and the facility of the milk-round interview are well known and much used by frequent recruiters of graduates, at least in the UK.

Methods of attracting applicants

There is some overlap between sources of applicants, discussed earlier, and methods of attracting applicants. But there are ways that organizations can increase the pool, notably by advertising. The most common medium for recruitment advertising is local newspapers, which was used almost universally by employers in the IRS survey (1996: 8). This contrasts with national newspaper advertisements which were used by approximately three-quarters of employers, mainly for professional and managerial posts (IRS 1996: 9). Trade and professional journals are often the medium of choice for specialist posts, but the long lead-times on such media means that forward planning is required. Preparing advertisements, particularly for managerial or professional jobs, is a specialist skill. For this reason, many organizations outsource this work to advertising firms or recruitment agencies, rather than attempt it themselves. Radio and television are expensive and are far less frequently used methods, but they reach a large audience. Recently a British university advertised for students with prime-time television advertisements.

The Internet is playing a more important role in recruitment. It advertises jobs and serves as a place to locate job applicants. Web sites can provide Internet users with information on the type of work the company is involved in and the job opportunities that are available. Interested parties can respond by e-mail. This has the advantage of a quick turnaround time and reduces the amount of paperwork that would normally be associated with written job applications. The Internet allows an organization to reach a larger and broader range of applicants than traditional methods. Williams (1997) suggests that the biggest decision for employers is not whether to use the Internet for recruitment, but how to utilize fully its potential. An example of the potential of the Internet is provided by Cisco Systems Inc. in the USA, which set up the world's first recruitment web site. It set up an 'opportunities page' to advertise all vacancies. These were categorized by department and location, to make finding appropriate jobs easier. A tailored search program was developed which enabled users to enter key words describing their desired positions. Applications could be sent via electronic mail. The results were very successful. Cisco believes that one of the major advantages of using the Internet as part of its recruitment strategy was that it could reach candidates who were not actively seeking work. Certainly it resulted in quicker and less expensive recruitment. The opportunities page received 64,000 visits in 1996, resulting in several thousand applications.

Both because of skill shortages and to improve customer services, some organizations have looked beyond the usual pool of candidates. The do-it-yourself chain of B&Q stores, for example, has targeted an older age group, the over 50s, as employees. It finds that these recruits are more conscientious and reliable, such as in the time they arrive for work, and are better with customers than younger staff. Similarly, in the USA, McDonald's has looked to new groups to hire, such as retired people and mothers with young children. It offers flexible working hours to attract these groups (Dreyfuss 1990). Forward-looking employers try to see recruitment from the applicant's point of view and choose methods that are likely to attract and retain suitable employees by adopting equal opportunities initiatives (chapter 6) or by adapting working hours (chapter 12).

The Selection Process

Following the recruitment of a pool of applicants employers need to make a choice between candidates. The most common method used for this selection remains the interview (see figure 5.2). However, increasingly firms are recognizing the importance of selection decisions and are applying other methods that can improve the success of the process. In evaluating which methods are effective, three basic criteria are normally applied, at least when seen from the traditional, psychometric perspective on recruitment and selection. These are reliability, validity, and usefulness.

Reliability

Reliability essentially refers to the consistency of a method used to select individuals. While there are numerous types of reliability three are most important when considering selection methods. The first comprises 'testee' reliability. For example, if a person uses a tape measure to measure a desk, it needs to be reliable and give the same reading each time, regardless of whether it is used in the morning or evening. It would be of little value if the tape was made of a material that was highly sensitive to variations in temperature, yielding different readings as the temperature changed. The same is true of any selection methods – if they are going to be of value, they need to provide the same information over time, at least if they are measuring an ability or personality trait that is considered to be relatively permanent. Thus, if the results of a personality inventory indicates an extrovert personality, it should generate the same result six months later. If there is such consistency over time then the inventory can be said to be measuring this trait reliably. This type of reliability is commonly referred to as test-retest reliability.

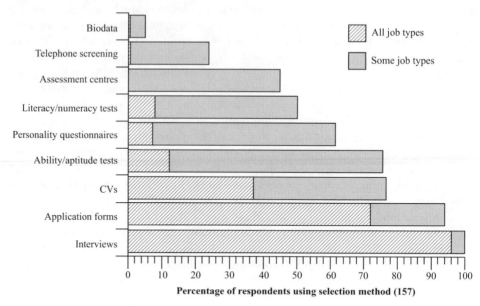

Figure 5.2 Selection methods used by employers

Source: IRS 1997

Second, there is 'tester' reliability. Using the tape measure analogy again, the measurement process can only be described as reliable or consistent if two people measuring the same desk come up with the same answer. If one person finds that it is 80 cm in length and the other 85 cm then the measuring process is not very reliable. Similarly, in terms of selection, if two people interview a person for a job, but one concludes that the candidate is suitable while the other concludes that they are not, the selection method is not reliable. Third, there is 'test' reliability. Sticking with the tape measure, if it is a reliable instrument there should be consistency between the distance between three and four centimetres and between seven and eight centimetres. That is, any part of the tape measure which indicates a centimetre should be the same as a different part of the tape measure which measures a centimetre. The same logic applies to a personality measure. If there are a number of questions which all relate to the assessment of the personality dimension of extroversion, all these items should have the same (or at least very similar) scores for the measure of extroversion to be reliable.

Reliability is typically presented in terms of a correlation coefficient, r, that is, the correlation between two scores, whether those are the scores of the same individual at different points in time, the correlation between the results of two testers, or the correlation between two items on a test which measures the same underlying dimension. A perfect positive correlation would provide a score of $r = 1.0$. This would mean that there was a totally predictable relation between the two scores. For example, taking a group of individuals, all of their scores might differ on a particular personality trait, but if for any given individual the scores on one of the measurements (scores on a personality scale at time 1), were identical to the scores on the other measurement (scores on the same personality scale at time two), the correlation would be 1.0 and the trait could be said to be measured reliably. In reality, in the domain of human behaviour, such perfect correlations do not exist. Nevertheless, what is required are significant deviations from randomness (total randomness being indicated by a score of $r = 0$) so that employers can be confident that the assessments used to make selection decisions are reasonably reliable or consistent.

Validity

There are a number of different types of validity, but from the point of view of considering selection methods, the most important is termed predictive or criterion-related validity. That is, establishing the relationship between the predictors (the results from the selection methods used) and the criterion (performance on the job). For a selection tool to be considered valid it must discriminate between candidates in terms of subsequent performance in the job. Those candidates who were predicted to be good potential employees, on a selection method, should subsequently perform well, while those predicted to be poor should perform less well. So again, a correlation is required but this time between the predictor (the selection method) and the criterion (the job performance). The 'pure' method of establishing this relationship is to measure applicants during selection and, based on whatever method(s) are being used, make predictions based on this about future performance. However, applicants are not chosen on this basis, but either all or a cross-section of applicants (i.e. those predicted to be poor performers as well as those predicted to be good) are taken on. This is necessary in order to be certain that those who were predicted to be poor actually are weak performers on the job. Thus, after a period in the job, performance is measured and the correlation established between the selection method prediction and the job performance criterion measure. The two graphs in figure 5.3 demonstrate the relationship between two different selection methods and subsequent performance. The aim is to avoid the selection of either 'false positives' – people predicted to be 'good' but who were subsequently 'poor'; and vice versa, i.e. 'false negatives'. In figure 5.3, the team-working score, derived from a group exercise used during the selection

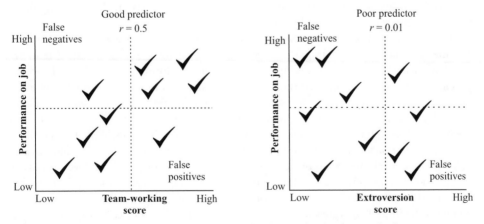

Figure 5.3 Comparison of the validity of a 'good' and 'poor' selection method

process, is a fairly good predictor of subsequent performance. This is because those who were given high marks on this exercise subsequently did well on the job while those who were given low marks did poorly, and there are few either false positives or false negatives. On the other hand, the extroversion score, derived from a personality measure, bears no relationship to subsequent job performance. There are as many false positives and negatives as there are true hits, i.e. high scorers who subsequently did well and low scorers who subsequently did poorly.

There are practical difficulties with this process of validating selection methods, such as the need to get results from a fairly large number of individuals. This is difficult in jobs where there are only a small number of people recruited over time. Research on selection method validation has therefore focused on areas where large groups are regularly recruited, such as to the army or the civil service. The more obvious problem is the reluctance of decision makers to agree to employ individuals who are predicted to be poor performers, just so that this can be proved!

The concurrent method of validation is sometimes used to avoid this difficulty with current employees used to validate a new selection method. The assumption behind this approach is that existing employees demonstrate variable job performance. If the new selection method can discriminate between good and poor performers, it should be able to discriminate in the same way between job applicants. In this case, the new selection method (e.g. a group exercise) is used with current employees who are scored on their performance on the exercise. This score is related to some measure of job performance, the criterion. If it is able to discriminate between good and poor performers then it is assumed to be a valid predictor and is used for selection purposes.

There are also problems with this validation process. The motivation of current employees is likely to be quite different to that of candidates, which may affect the scores. Candidates are likely to try harder than those already employed because they want the job. Also, current employees are already a restricted sample as they have been previously selected by some method. So they may, on average, be 'better' than the average candidate. More importantly, it does not prove that the differences in team skills, as measured by the group exercise, were evident prior to employment. It might be that they were learnt by employees as a by-product of their work. If this were to be the case, then using this method for selection would still be discriminating unnecessarily between individuals on a predictor that is not an essential prerequisite for the job.

One other issue that is particularly important when discussing issues of predictive or concurrent validity relates to the criterion or performance measure, rather than the selection method itself. This is because measuring job performance is difficult. There are problems related both to the subjectivity of measurement and to the focus or level of the measurement. In terms of subjectivity, a very common criterion measure used in validation research is supervisors' ratings of employee performance. However, as chapter 10 notes, these ratings are subjective and prone to rater bias. Second, in terms of the focus or level, Smith (1994) argues that there are at least three levels which need to be considered: the individual job level; the group or department level; and the organization level. It may be that an individual is functioning effectively as an individual but not at group or organizational level because of their reluctance, for example, to share information with other group members. Smith (1994) argues that it is necessary to consider all three levels in developing a criterion measure of performance. Unfortunately, much research and practice does not follow this advice, but rather uses very limited measures of the criterion, namely supervisor ratings.

While it is essential to understand these issues of reliability and validity, it is also true to say that very few organizations systematically assess the reliability and validity of the selection methods they use. When psychometric tests are used there is a tendency to rely on the evidence presented in the test manual on reliability and validity. To some extent this is justified by meta-analysis research, in which validity coefficients are pooled from many studies, thus producing reliability and validity data which have general applicability, providing the test is being used on a similar population to that established through the meta-analysis. However, good practice would suggest that it is always desirable to try and validate the selection method(s) used systematically, rather than rely on intuition. Organizations that fail to evaluate are much more likely to 'satisfice' – sticking to the established methods because they have no evidence that they are not working effectively – rather than optimize to get the best possible solution.

Selection Methods

A variety of methods can be used to make selection decisions, but the first thing to note is that the interview remains the most common method, often used alone, although increasingly combined with additional methods (Shackleton and Newell 1991; figure 5.2).

Interviews

Selection interviews have had a very bad press because research evidence seemed to suggest that this was a very ineffective way of making decisions. None the less interviews retain their appeal as a selection technique and virtually all employers use interviews for all categories of staff. However, as we discuss below, employers seem more aware of their limitations and are trying to use them more carefully, and for some groups, such as graduates, interviews are being complemented by a variety of other selection techniques (IRS 1997). An early study reported by Kelly and Fiske (1951) used an interview to predict the success of graduate students in psychology. The results were that neither one- nor two-hour interviews added to the validity of predictions made simply by using background information about the students. Moreover, when research examined whether two or more interviewers interviewing the same candidate came to the same conclusions, the evidence was equally negative – essentially there was little consistency or reliability. However, more recently the focus has been on investigating the interview process itself and this has helped us to understand why the interview, at least in its typical unstructured format, is a bad predictor. Essentially, unstructured interviews are bad predictors because the information which is extracted is different for each individual and differs between interviewers, and so comparisons between candidates cannot be made.

Different questions are asked of each candidate even by the same interviewer. Across interviewers there is even more variation in the type of questions asked. Under these circumstances it is almost inevitable that subjective biases make the interview both unreliable and invalid. Thus, stereotyping an individual as belonging to a particular group and assuming that they then have all the characteristics associated with that particular group is common; making decisions very quickly, within the first four minutes of the interview, based on superficial information such as physical characteristics, accent, or the type of newspaper read, is typical; and overrating the importance of negative information is high. However, understanding the sources of unreliability and invalidity has also helped to develop interviews which are much less likely to suffer from these subjective biases, although it must be recognized that these biases can never be totally eliminated.

Much work has been devoted to developing interview formats which minimize these subjective biases. The basic ingredient of these developments is to provide structure, so that interviews are more specifically job related, and are standardized, so that the same topics are covered with all candidates. The best known of these structured interviews are the situational interview, the patterned interview and the content analytical interview. In the situational interview, applicants are asked to describe what they would do in a number of hypothetical situations. This approach is based on the assumption that intentions are good predictors of behaviour (Latham et al. 1980). The situations that are used are extracted using a critical incident job analysis. The responses of the candidates are evaluated by experts using behaviourally anchored rating scales that are anchored by examples of good, average, and poor answers taken from existing employees' responses. In general, situational interviews have proved to be valid (Weekley and Gier 1987). Robertson et al. (1991) provide an example of a situational interview to assess adaptability or flexibility (table 5.2).

Another structured approach, the patterned behavioural description interview, asks for specific examples of past behaviour (Janz et al. 1986). The approach begins with a critical incident job analysis and with questions designed to ensure that applicants demonstrate how they have reacted to situations with similar characteristics. For example, if the critical

Table 5.2   Application of a situational interview technique

Two young people have approached the organization for finance to set up a new venture making and selling equipment to enable home-computer users to translate games easily between different models of computer. They are enthusiastic and talented but freely confess that they have no business, manufacturing or selling experience. What would you advise them?

Scale points

Low
Contact someone else (e.g. accountant) for information on cash flows
Tell them not to go ahead – too risky, no market

Medium
Recommend information to them
Tell them to recruit businessperson
Tell them accountant will prepare cost reports
Arrange for them to see organization's experts
Ask them to talk more once they have thought some more about it

High
Say the organization is enthusiastic about them as customers
Ask them about legal side of game translation
Do they have a prototype?
Contact Patent Office
Seems a big area of growth at the moment
Advise on information sources: DTI, venture capital, organization's accountants

Source: Robertson et al. 1990

incident analysis of a teacher's job revealed that dealing with difficult parents was an important part of the job, then an interview question might be, 'Tell me about the most difficult parent you have had to deal with in the last year'.

The content analytical interview is based on the view that talented people talk differently. The focus is on the exact content of each interviewee's responses. The questions may range widely from biographical details, to situational-type questions, to behaviour-based items. Questions about personal values and satisfactions such as 'What makes you feel important?' might be asked. For the interviewer, job performance categories are used to sort out the most important questions and the 'listen fors'. Each question is an item, like a questionnaire, and is scored separately before totalling all items. Interviews are often conducted over the telephone, since it is what is said that is being listened for. Although good validity has been reported with this method (Hill and Parker 1996), it requires the interviewer to follow a script and have the interview tape recorded. Many object to these constraints.

Research has shown that increasing the structure of the interview significantly increases predictive validity. But there is little or no increase in validity after a certain level of structure has been achieved, a level which all three of the above methods achieve (see Huffcutt and Arthur 1994; McDaniel et al. 1994). Indeed, it has been argued that over-structuring the interview can be a problem, as the unstructured interview can serve legitimate functions which the structured interview cannot (Dipboye 1994). In an unstructured interview, the interviewer can provide more realistic information about the job, with the candidate able to ask questions which relate to his or her personal needs, values, interests, goals and abilities. Through this process, the applicant and the interviewer can negotiate a mutually agreeable 'psychological contract'. Second, the unstructured interview can operate as a preliminary socialization tactic with the applicant learning about the culture and values of the organization (Dipboye 1997). These issues will be addressed more fully in the final section of this chapter.

The conclusion from this discussion relates to the job and organization itself. Where jobs are highly prescribed, where there is knowledge about how work needs to be carried out, and where there is clarity about what constitutes good performance, then a structured interview may be more appropriate because prediction is possible and structured interviews are better predictors. However, when an organization is competing in a turbulent environment and there is considerable uncertainty about what is required of individuals, a less structured approach may be more appropriate. This does not mean abandoning structure altogether. Using job and organizational analysis as a basis for designing interview procedures and standardizing, to some extent, both the questions and the rating procedures is helpful. But abandoning all 'slack' during the interview is unlikely to be effective because it ignores the other purposes of interviewing candidates which extends beyond assessing job competencies. As Judge and Ferris (1993: 23) argue: 'calls for structured interviews may be misplaced if the true goal, and utility, of the interview lies not in selecting the most technically qualified, but the individual most likely to fit into the organization'.

Psychological testing

Psychological testing has gained in popularity in the UK, especially for graduate and management-level candidates (Shackleton and Newell 1991; IRS 1997). Throughout the

1990s there was a substantial increase in their usage and they have become an integral part of the search for greater objectivity in selection. Essentially, two types need to be distinguished: personality tests and cognitive or ability tests. Cognitive tests provide an assessment of an individual's intellectual abilities, either in terms of general intelligence (IQ, or g) or specific abilities (such as verbal, numerical, spatial abilities or abstract reasoning). Personality tests provide an assessment of an individual's general disposition to behave in a certain way in certain situations. It is important to differentiate between these two types of assessment test.

COGNITIVE TESTS

The seminal piece of work on the use of cognitive tests in selection was undertaken by Hunter and Schmidt (1990). Using meta-analysis, these researchers were able to demonstrate that although the many studies on the predictive validity of tests appeared to be inconsistent, when adjustments were made for various factors (e.g. differences in sample sizes, restrictions in the range of scores from those involved) results were in fact remarkably consistent and proved that cognitive tests were valid predictors in a wide range of job situations. In other words, general intelligence predicts at least some of the performance variation in most job situations. Moreover, such tests are relatively simple to administer and score, albeit the person using such tests needs to be properly trained (see Bartram and Lindley 1994). There are two caveats to this general conclusion. First, for most jobs the range of intelligence of those applying for the job is likely to be very restricted. It is rare to have someone with an IQ of 90 applying for the job of a head teacher; similarly, it is probably rare for a person with an IQ of 140 to apply for the job of caretaker. The consequence of this is that a measure of cognitive ability may not differentiate much between the various candidates. Second, cognitive tests can be biased against certain groups. For example, it is well documented that Black Americans tend to score lower than Whites on tests of cognitive ability, and women tend to score higher on verbal ability than do men. This certainly raises issues of both social and ethical concern, which will need to be carefully considered when selecting particular tests.

PERSONALITY MEASURES

In most UK selection situations, the personality measures used are of the self-report type. There is considerably more controversy over the use of personality measures, than there is cognitive tests, so much so that they have been dismissed by some as being totally useless for selection purposes (Blinkhorn and Johnson 1990). The fact that there has been much less increase in usage of personality tests than cognitive tests over the course of the 1990s has been interpreted as a reflection of the concerns that have been raised about the validity of these tests, in comparison to other types of test (IRS 1997: 13). Certainly the results of early meta-analysis studies appeared to suggest very low criterion-related validity (Schmidt et al. 1984). More recently, research has shown that personality measurement can be useful but only when specific personality constructs are linked to specific job competencies (Barrick and Mount 1991; Robertson and Kinder 1993; Tett et al. 1991). Much of this work has been based on using the 'big five' personality factors of extroversion, neuroticism, conscientiousness, agreeableness, and openness. Certainly one of the problems with research on personality measurement has been that very different systems of personality description have been used, making it difficult to compare results. There is now a growing consensus around the five-factor model of broad traits (Goldberg 1993) and the use of Costa and McCrae's (1992) personality inventory which measures these five factors. Studies have demonstrated that these dimensions can be systematically related to different job dimensions. For example, conscientiousness is linked to a tendency to set goals which may be related to performance in jobs where there is discretion in the activities that can be undertaken; and openness to experience appears to be related to training success (Cooper and Robertson 1995). However, it is unlikely that personality tests alone will ever be good predictors of future job behaviour. This is because job situations often present strong situational pressures which mean that differences between individuals' behaviours are minimized. Second, it is highly likely that the same job can be done in very different, but equally successful, ways by individuals with different personalities. This does not mean that personality measures have no place in the selection process, as some have argued. Rather, it raises the question of how such measures are best used within this context.

While technical issues to do with the predictive validity of different types of psychometric test are important, there are also ethical issues raised about the use of such tests. Most importantly, individuals who have taken a test, whether cognitive or personality, have a right to the results of those tests under the code of ethics of both the British Psychological Society and the Institute of Personnel and Development. Yet Newell and Shackleton (1993) found that, especially when tests were used as part of the selection process, this did not happen in a significant minority of companies. Not only is this ethically bad practice, it also suggests that these tests are being used in ways which are unlikely fully to exploit their potential as part of the selection process, especially with respect to personality tests. The premise that there is a particular personality profile which is necessary to do a particular job effectively, is very problematic. Indeed, such an approach is more likely simply to confirm existing stereotypes and build in stagnation. Instead, it is more useful to use the results of the personality assessment to feedback and discuss with the individual how, given their particular personality characteristics, they would cope with different aspects of the job and how they would fit into the organization culture. Such a discussion, as part of an interview, allows the individual to think through more clearly their values and expectations in relation to the job and organization, so that a two-way exchange is produced. This approach would also make it less likely that individuals would fake their answers on personality measures in a bid to present a particular self-portrait. Knowing that there is no 'right' answer and that there will be an opportunity to discuss how personality impacts on the individual's approach to work is likely to encourage more open and honest responses from candidates.

Assessment centres

An assessment centre (AC) is not a single selection method, nor is it a place. Rather an AC refers to the utilization of a number of different selection methods over a specified period (typically one to four days) in order for multiple assessors to assess many candidates on a range of identified competences or behavioural dimensions. While ACs incorporate a variety of methods, often including interviews and psychometric tests, a core element is the simulation of actual work tasks in order to observe job-related behaviours (Cooper and Robertson 1995). For managerial jobs, in-tray exercises and group decision-making exercises are particularly common, at least in ACs in Britain. The in-tray exercise provides a candidate with a range of correspondence (memos, letters, reports) and he or she is required to make decisions in order to prioritize and deal with various problems in the material, under a very tight time schedule. Such an exercise is used to assess the individual's planning and problem-solving abilities. In group decision-making exercises, individuals are put together in small groups and required to either discuss a particular issue and come to a group consensus or solve a particular problem through a group decision process. Again, problem-solving abilities may be assessed, but in addition interpersonal and leadership skills can be evaluated in these situations.

Despite growing use of ACs, especially for graduate and managerial jobs (Shackleton and Newell 1991; IRS 1997: 15), there is also increasing evidence of their limitations. Jones et al. (1991) concluded that despite the validity of different components of an AC, the overall AC validity was surprisingly low. A key problem appears to be that managers, acting as assessors, are not able to accurately assess cross-situational abilities from the different exercises. So while managers are required to rate candidates on different competencies or dimensions for each exercise, these ratings appear to be largely defined by the overall task performance of the candidate on the particular exercise, rather than by specific behaviours demonstrated during the activity (Iles 1992). Correlations between the same dimensions measured across exercises are very low, while correlations between different dimensions measured within an exercise are much higher (Robertson et al. 1987; McCredie and Shackleton 1994). When the ratings from different exercises are combined into the overall assessment rating (OAR), it appears that assessors typically do not consider the whole range of dimensions, but instead rely on only a small number, and often those dimensions which empirically have less predictive validity. Finally, a number of studies have demonstrated a low correlation between the OAR and a variety of criterion measures of on-the-job performance (Payne et al. 1992).

Despite this somewhat negative evidence there are two important points to be made. First, designing and developing an AC has the potential to improve the validity of selection, but simply putting together a series of exercises and running them over two days, using a group of untrained assessors, does not guarantee that decisions will be improved. For example, Gaugler et al. (1987), using meta-analysis, found that the validity of ACs improved when a larger number of exercises were included, when psychologists rather than managers acted as the assessors, when peer evaluation was included as part of the assessment process, and when the assessee group contained a larger proportion of women.

Second, many of the problems identified with respect to ACs need to be looked at from a broader perspective than simply their criterion-related validity. A key benefit of using an AC is that it gives the potential recruit an extended opportunity to find out more about the organization. In particular, because many of the exercises are simulations of the kind of work that will be involved if the person is selected, the individual has a much better opportunity to develop realistic expectations about the job and the organization. This is more likely to occur, however, if this two-sided exchange of information is intentionally built into the programme. Otherwise, exercises could potentially be chosen which bear very little resemblance to the job or organizational context. Thus, not only is the organization given an opportunity to find out more about the potential recruits, but also to provide more information to these individuals so that a more mutually beneficial negotiation can take place. But this requires the adoption of an exchange rather than a psychometric view of the recruitment and selection process.

Recruitment and Selection: Limitations of the Psychometric Approach

The opening section of this chapter considered the importance of recruitment and selection in the light of the increasingly competitive environment. Employing people who can respond to the challenges of such environments is crucial. As noted earlier, adopting a more systematic approach to recruitment and selection to reduce bias and errors is useful. Yet, ironically, it could be argued that globalization and organizational requirements of flexibility, innovation, and commitment make the best practices advocated earlier somewhat problematic and suggest a need for an entirely new perspective on recruitment and selection.

First, considering the degree of change, organizations often require employees to be generalists rather than specialists, able to take on a variety of different roles which require a range of skills and competencies. Even where individuals are recruited for a particular position with a specified job description, it is highly likely that the job will change. Thus, the best practice prescription of doing a thorough job analysis to identify the task and the person requirements of the particular job may be difficult or inappropriate. There is not a fixed 'jigsaw hole' to fill, especially in the long term.

Second, alongside flexibility, is the need for innovation. Identifying opportunities for change and designing creative solutions is crucial for the survival of many organizations. This creative ability is about challenging the status quo and encouraging people to think and act differently. Following best practice guidelines leads to selection on the basis of whether candidates can do particular jobs efficiently and whether they fit the organizational culture. Rather than encourage innovation, traditional selection approaches may stifle creativity.

Third, increasingly organizations are operating in a global rather than a national arena. Considering the array of national differences it is unlikely that organizations will be effective if they simply try to replicate their home-base operation abroad (Bartlett and Ghoshal 1989). Rather, to manage this diversity requires recruiting and selecting people with very different backgrounds and experiences at all organizational levels. However, job analysis is backward looking. If the current job holders are all of the same race or nationality, for example, this may mean that individuals from different backgrounds will be excluded because they do not fit the existing profile of a competent employee. Alternatively, during the selection process, individuals from different nationalities may respond very differently to particular selection methods so that they are disadvantaged (Shackleton and Newell 1994), again reducing their chances of being selected.

Finally, ensuring the quality of all products and processes is now an essential prerequisite for organizations (Bolwijn and Kumpe 1990). Quality is assured by introducing a set of processes (e.g. ISO 9000) which will guarantee quality of output. Nevertheless, it is ultimately the people involved in these processes who will determine quality, whether of a product or service, reflecting their level of commitment to the organization. Yet it is very difficult to assess and select for commitment because showing commitment to an organization will at least partly depend on the organization reciprocating that commitment to the individual. Employee commitment is under severe strain in an era of downsizing and short-term contracts. Consequently, recruitment and selection cannot be seen in isolation from the subsequent interactions between the individual and the organization. Emphasizing the 'right' selection decision ignores how subsequent interactions will influence how far the decision was right. An exceptional individual may become disillusioned or demoralized by their subsequent treatment within the organization and so either leave or not contribute fully. Subsequent evaluation may then lead to the inference that the selection decision was faulty, which paints a distorted view of the problem.

Thus, there are problems with the traditional best practice view of recruitment and selection, in particular in so far as it tends to assume that there is one best way to do a particular job, as illustrated by the person specification. Just because the previous job incumbent did the particular job in a certain way, the assumption will typically be that it is necessary to find a similar-shaped 'jigsaw piece' to replace that individual. In practice this can result in unfair discrimination because a number of irrelevant non job-related selection criteria may be introduced into the selection decision. Recruitment and selection is about discriminating between individuals, but based on relevant and fair criteria like ability, rather than irrelevant criteria like gender, race, age or disability. However, given the 'one best way' assumption, unfair discrimination and prejudice can be the result. Using the traditional approach to selection, the tendency is then to perpetuate the status quo, which restricts certain groups who have been previously underrepresented in particular jobs, for example, black women in senior management positions (see chapter 6).

This psychometric view of recruitment and selection also presents a very static picture of the job. It underestimates the degree of change within organizations and the influences on individuals. It overestimates the personal criteria which influence job performance and underestimates the role or situational demands. Thus, in many jobs role expectations are so strong that the individual has limited flexibility in how they behave. Finally, this psychometric approach assumes that it is possible to measure psychological differences between individuals in the same objective way as physical differences between individuals can be assessed.

The assumptions of the traditional, psychometric, approach to recruitment and selection may therefore no longer be appropriate (if indeed they ever were) and a different approach is required. Herriot's (1984) view of recruitment and selection presents a very different metaphor of the process – an exchange or negotiation between two parties, the employing organization and the potential recruit. Both of these parties have a set of expectations related to their current and future needs and values. Recruitment and selection is portrayed as a series of episodes in which increasing amounts of information are exchanged to determine whether there is indeed compatibility between the organization and the individual. Negotiation is possible because neither the organization nor the individual is seen as having fixed characteristics, although the underlying values and needs of both sides are seen as being more stable. The outcome of this process, if successful, is that a viable psychological contract is negotiated which encapsulates congruence between the expectations of both parties. However, if the process of negotiation breaks down, because the parties are unable to develop a sense of congruence, this can also be construed as positive (or in Herriot's terms, 'valid negative'). The organization avoids employing someone who will not fit with the culture and the candidate avoids taking on a new job for which they are not suited.

The recruitment and selection process from the exchange perspective

From the exchange perspective, recruitment begins with the employing organization articulating its expectations of the particular type of employee it is recruiting and realistically communicating this information to potential applicants. They compare this information with their own personal expectations and ambitions and therefore only those individuals with a fairly close match to the organizational requirements will apply. This approach to recruitment is clearly very different from the one typically found which could rather be described as the 'glossy' approach. That is, firms present recruitment material, especially to the competitive graduate market, which presents little more than a glossy, exaggerated image of both the organization and the potential career opportunities for the successful candidates. In each company there are apparently no limits to the individual's career progression and they can be a senior manager within months, if determined and hard working. This type of recruitment brochure makes it very difficult for prospective candidates to differentiate between firms, preventing informed decisions about suitable and unsuitable prospective employers.

The justification for adopting this type of approach is that an employer aims to attract the 'best' people and therefore it does not want to deter good candidates from applying by presenting more realistic information, which includes some of its shortcomings. For example, the realistic picture may be that most people will not progress to senior executive levels, especially not within the first few years of their careers. But the company may fear discouraging good recruits when competitor companies are advertising a limitless career trajectory. It is seen to be too risky to be more realistic, i.e. to risk putting off those who will not fit the particular job and organizational environment.

In the traditional approach, this attempt to impress the best candidates continues. The selection process is seen as a one-way process of decision making, with the organization selecting the candidate on the basis of collecting as much valid and reliable information about that person as possible. It does not see the need to reciprocate and allow candidates realistic information about the job, enabling them to make an informed decision. Even the usual final question at the interview, 'Do you have any questions?', is often treated as another opportunity for the organization to assess whether the individual can ask 'something sensible' rather than as a genuine attempt to provide the candidate with information.

The obvious problem with this traditional approach is that new employees' expectations will not match the reality of the situation found. While it is clear that expectations are modified in the light of circumstances (Arnold 1985), there is a high turnover level arising from this approach, especially for individuals with little or no experience of employment who tend to have more unrealistic expectations. Brennan and McGeevor (1987) found that 58 per cent of graduates had changed jobs at least once within the first three years of employment, often because of unmet job expectations.

Adopting the exchange approach means that the recruitment and selection process involves a genuine exchange of valid and reliable information between both parties, with the organization providing ample opportunity for the candidates to really understand the culture, the job and the opportunities available. Recruitment is seen as a process of providing as much information as possible to attract applicants most suited to the job and work environment, rather than to attract the maximum number of 'good-quality' applicants. Selection between candidates, if necessary, is then a process whereby more information is exchanged between the two parties in order to establish whether there is a fit between the two sets of expectations. Where the fit is found to be lacking, negotiation will take place to see if any adjustment is possible in both the individual's and the organization's expectations. 'Fit' refers to the fit between the individual and the organization, as well as fit between the individual and the particular job.

Conclusion

Both the traditional psychometric view of recruitment and selection and the exchange model emphasize fit between the person and the job environment. But in the former case it is based on fixed dimensions of both the job and the person, with the organization having the sole prerogative to assess the fit. From the exchange perspective, fit is the outcome of a process of exchange and negotiation. Moreover, in the traditional view, fit is assumed between personal characteristics of the individual and the technical demands of the particular job (person–job fit). In the exchange model, fit relates to the matching of expectations and needs of the individual with the values, climate and goals of the organization (person–organization fit).

Smith (1994) distinguished between three types of individual characteristics that relate to job performance: 'universals', which refer to characteristics that are relevant to all jobs; 'occupationals', which refer to characteristics relevant to particular jobs or occupations; and 'relationals', which refer to characteristics relevant in a particular work setting. This typology suggests that it is important to match characteristics of people with the characteristics of particular work settings, and research has indeed shown that people who fit the work setting are more satisfied and committed compared to people who do not feel they fit (O'Reilly et al. 1991). Schneider (1987) proposed his attraction–selection–attrition (ASA) model to consider the process through which this fit between personality and organizational environment is established. People with similar personalities will be attracted to particular types of organization and individuals with characteristics which are similar to those existing in the organization will be more likely to be selected. Moreover, individuals with characteristics which are different to the dominant characteristics will be more likely to leave. However, in a study of the relation between organizational climate and recruiter's perceptions of the 'ideal' personality of new recruits, Van Vianen and Kmieciak (1998) found very little evidence to support the idea that recruitment and selection created homogeneity of personality. Rather they conclude that organizational climate is mainly created by homogeneity of behaviour (especially socialization into the organization) and not homogeneity of personalities. The key implication is that 'assessment of person–environment fit in selection should not be based primarily on personality–climate fit but on the fit between the person's needs and organizational practices' (Van Vianen and Kmieciak 1998). Such a view of recruitment and selection fits much more easily within an exchange view of the process than within the traditional psycho-metric view.

The problem with the traditional approach is two-fold. First, through the recruitment and selection process messages about the organization's culture and values are inevitably communicated to candidates. However, the messages communicated are likely to be inaccurate and unrealistic so that the new employee begins with false expectations about the congruence between their own values and attitudes and those of the organization. Second, and following from the first point, where congruence between the values, goals and attributes of the individual and the organization is lacking there is likely to be lower levels of satisfaction, performance, and commitment, on both sides, and higher levels of employee stress, absenteeism and turnover (Chatman 1991; Schneider 1987).

Given these problems there is now a growing recognition that increasing person–organization fit during selection can improve work-related outcomes (Bowen et al. 1991). Yet this requires a very different view of the selection process in which candidates can focus on learning about their jobs and the organization, beginning the process of organizational socialization (Anderson and Ostroff 1997). In this sense, recruitment and selection is a process of assessment and socialization, not an isolated episode. Criterion-related or predictive validity of recruitment and selection methods is then not the only, or even the most important, basis for evaluating the process. Rather, it is necessary to consider how recruitment and selection methods influence newcomer expectations and behaviour (Iles and Mabey 1993; Robertson et al. 1991). This is why some methods, which may have limited predictive validity in the traditional sense, are nevertheless useful because they do enable individuals to develop an accurate picture of what to expect.

Allowing new employees to gain a realistic understanding of the job and organization culture and using recruitment and selection as the basis for negotiating a robust psycho-logical contract starts the process of organizational socialization. It is certainly more likely to lead to the recruitment of individuals who are willing to give long-term commitment to the organization than is seeing recruitment and selection as a management decision-making process related to a one-sided prediction of future, narrowly defined, job success.

References and further reading

Anderson, N. and Ostroff, C. 1997: Selection as socialisation. In N. Anderson and P. Herriot (eds), *International Handbook of Selection and Assessment*. Chichester: John Wiley.

Arnold, J. 1985: Tales of the unexpected: Surprises experienced by graduates in the early months of employment. *British Journal of Guidance and Counselling*, **13**(3), 308–19.

Barrick, M. R. and Mount, M. K. 1991: The big five personality dimensions and job performance: A meta-analysis. *Personnel Psychology*, **44**, 1–26.

Bartlett, C. A. and Ghoshal, S. 1989: *Managing Across Borders: The Transnational Solution*. Boston MA: Harvard Business School Press.

Bartram, D. and Lindley, P. A. 1994: *Psychological Testing: The BPS 'Level A'* Open Learning Programme. Leicester: BPS Books.

Blinkhorn, S. and Johnson, C. 1990: The insignificance of personality testing. *Nature*, **348**, 671–2.

Boam, R. and Sparrow, P. (eds) 1992: *Designing and achieving competency: A competency based approach to managing people and organizations.* London: McGraw Hill.

Bolwijn, P. T. and Kumpe, T. 1990: Manufacturing in the 1990s – Productivity, flexibility, and innovation. *Long Range Planning*, **23**, 44–57.

Bowen, D. E., Ledford, G. E. and Nathan, B. R. 1991: Hiring for the organisation, not the job. *Academy of Management Executive*, **5**, 35–51.

Boyatzis, R. E. 1982: *The Competent Manager: A Model for Effective Performance.* New York: John Wiley.

Brennan, J. and McGeevor, P. 1987: CNNA graduates: their employment and their experience after leaving college. London: CNAA Development Services Publication, No. 13.

Chatman, J. I. 1991: Matching people and organisations: Selection and socialisation in public accounting firms. *Administrative Science Quarterly*, **21**, 433–52.

Cooper D. and Robertson, I. T. (1995). *The Psychology of Personnel Selection.* London: Routledge.

Costa, P. T. and McCrae, R. R. (1992). Four ways five factors are basic. *Personality and Individual Differences*, **13**, 653–65.

Dale, M. and Iles, P. (1992). *Assessing management skills: A guide to competencies and evaluation techniques.* London: Kogan Page.

Decker, P. J. and Cornelius, E. T. (1979). A note on recruiting sources and job survival rates. *Journal of Applied Psychology*, **64**, 463–64.

Dipboye, R. L. 1994: Structured and unstructured selection interviews: Beyond the job-fit model. In G. Ferris (ed.), *Research in personnel and human resources management*, **12**, 79–123. Greenwich, CT: JAI Press.

Dipboye, R. L. 1997: Structured selection interviews: Why do they work? Why are they underutilized? In N. Anderson and P. Herriot (eds), *International Handbook of Selection and Assessment.* Chichester: John Wiley.

Dreyfuss, J. 1990: Get ready for the new work force. *Fortune*, 22 April, 165–181.

Fletcher, C. 1992: *Competency-based assessment techniques.* London: Kogan Page.

Gaugler, B., Rosenthal, D. B., Thornton, G. C. and Bentson, C. 1987: Meta-analysis of assessment center validity. *Journal of Applied Psychology*, **72**(3), 493–511.

Goldberg, L. R. 1993: The structure of phenotypic personality traits. *American Psychologist*, **48**, 26–34.

Greuter, M. and Algera, J. 1989 Criterion development and job analysis. In P. Herriot (ed.), *Assessment and Selection in Organizations.* New York: Wiley.

Herriot, P. 1984: *Down from the ivory tower: Graduates and their jobs.* Chichester: John Wiley.

Hill, J. and Parker, C. 1996: The salvation of the interview? Structuring interviewing, *Assessment Matters*, Spring.

Huffcutt, A. I. and Arthur, W. 1994: Hunter and Hunter (1994) revisited: Interview validity for entry-level jobs. *Journal of Applied Psychology*, **79**, 184–90.

Hunter, J. E. and Schmidt, F. L. 1990: *Methods of Meta-Analysis: Correcting Errors and Bias in Research Findings.* Beverly Hills, CA: Sage.

Iles, P. A. 1992: Centres of excellence? Assessment and development centres, managerial competencies and HR strategies. *British Journal of Management*, **3**(2), 79–90.

Iles, P. and Mabey, C. (1993). Managerial career development techniques: effectiveness, acceptability and availability. *British Journal of Management*, **4**, 103–18.

IPM (Institute of Personnel Management) 1995: *The IPM Code on Recruitment.* London: IPM.

IRS (Industrial Relations Services). 1996: Policy and practice in recruitment: an IRS survey *Employee Development Bulletin*, **81** September, 5–13.

IRS 1997: The state of selection: an IRS survey. *Employee Development Bulletin*, **85** January, 8–13.

Janz, T., Hellervik, L. and Gilmore, D. C. 1986: *Behaviour Description Interviewing: New, Accurate, Cost Effective*. Boston, MA: Allyn and Bacon.

Jones, A., Herriot, P., Long, B. and Drakeley, R. 1991: Attempting to improve the validity of a well-established assessment centre. *Journal of Occupational Psychology*, **64**(1), 1–21.

Judge, T. A. and Ferris, G. A. 1992: The elusive criterion of fit in human resources staffing decisions. *Human Resource Planning*, **15**, 47–67.

Kelly, E. L. and Fiske, D. W. 1951: *The prediction of performance in clinical psychology*. Ann Arbour: University of Michigan Press.

Latham, G. P. 1989: The Validity, Reliability and Practicality of the Situational Interview. In R. W. Eder and G. R. Ferris (eds), *The Employment Interview*, Newbury: Sage.

Latham, G., Saari, L., Pursell, E. and Campion, M. 1980: The Situational Interview. *Journal of Applied Psychology*, **65**, 422–7.

Mackay, L. and Torrington, D. 1986: *The changing nature of personnel management*. London: Institute of Personnel Management.

McCormick, E. J., Jeaneret, P. R. and Mecham, R. C. 1972: A study of job characteristics and job dimensions based on the Position Analysis Questionnaire (PAQ). *Journal of Applied Psychology*, **36**, 347–68.

McCredie, H. and Shackleton, V. J. 1994: The development and interim validation of a dimensions based senior management assessment centre. *Human Resources Management Journal*, **5**, 91–101.

McDaniel, M. A., Whetzel, D. L., Schmidt, F. L. and Maurer, S. D. 1994: The validity of employment interviews: A comprehensive review and meta-analysis. *Journal of Applied Psychology*, **79**, 599–616.

Manwaring, T. 1984: The extended internal labour market. *Cambridge Journal of Economics*, **8**(2), 161–87.

Munro Fraser, J. 1978: *Employment Interviewing*. London: MacDonald and Evans.

Newell, S. and Shackleton, V. J. 1993: The use (and abuse) of psychometric tests in British industry and commerce. *Human Resource Management Journal*, **4**(1), 14–22.

O'Reilly, C. A., Chatman, J. and Caldwell, D. F. 1991: People and organisational culture: A profile comparison approach to assessing person-organisation fit. *Academy of Management Journal*, **34**, 487–516.

Payne, T., Anderson, N. and Smith, T. 1992: Assessment centres, selection systems and cost effectiveness: An evaluative case study. *Personnel Review*, **21**, 48–56.

Premark, S. Z. and Wanous, J. P. 1985: A meta-analysis of realistic job preview experiments. *Journal of Applied Psychology*, **70**, 706–19.

Ram, M. 1994: *Managing to Survive: Working Lives in Small Firms*. Oxford: Blackwell.

Robertson, I. T., Gratton, L. and Rout, U. 1990: The validity of situational interviews for administrative jobs. *Journal of Organizational Behaviour*, **11**, 69–76.

Robertson, I. T., Gratton, L. and Sharpley, D. 1987: The psychometric properties and design of assessment centres: Dimensions into exercises won't go. *Journal of Occupational Psychology*, **60**, 187–95.

Robertson, I. T., Iles, P., Gratton, L. and Sharpley, D. S. 1991: The psychological impact of personnel selection procedures on candidates. *Human Relations*, **44**(9), 963–82.

Robertson, I. T. and Kinder, A. 1993: Personality and job competencies: the criterion-related validity of some personality variables. *Journal of Occupational and Organizational Psychology*, **66**, 225–44.

Rodger, A. 1952: *The Seven Point Plan*. National Institute for Industrial Psychology, Paper No. 1.

Roethlisberger, F. J. and Dickson, W. J. 1939: *Management and the Worker*. New York: John Wiley.

Saville and Holdsworth Ltd 1995: *Work Profiling System* (WPS, updated version). London: SHL.

Schmidt, N., Gooding, R. Z., Noe, R. A. and Kirsch, M. 1984: Meta-analysis of validity studies published between 1964 and 1982 and the investigation of study characteristics. *Personnel Psychology*, **37**, 407–22.

Schneider, B. 1987: The people make the place. *Personnel Psychology*, **40**, 437–53.

Shackleton, V. J. and Newell, S. 1991: Management selection: A comparative study of methods used in top British and French companies. *Journal of Occupational Psychology*, **64**, 23–36.

Shackleton, V. J. and Newell, S. 1994: European management selection methods: a comparison of five countries. *International Journal of Selection and Assessment*, **2**, 91–102.

Smith, M. 1994: A theory of the validity of predictors in selection. *Journal of Occupational and Organizational Psychology*, **76**, 13–31.

Sparrow, P. 1997: Organisational competencies: Creating a strategic behavioural framework for selection and assessment. In N. Anderson and P. Herriot (eds), *International Handbook of Selection and Assessment*, 543–66, Chichester: John Wiley.

Sparrow, P. and Bognanno, M. 1993: Competency Requirement Forecasting: Issues for International Selection and Assessment. *International Journal of Selection and Assessment*, **1**(1), 50–8.

Taylor, F. W. 1911: *The Principles of Scientific Management*. New York: Harper.

Tett, R. P., Jackson, D. N. and Rothstein, M. 1991: Personality measures as predictors of job performance: A meta-analytic review. *Personnel Psychology*, **44**, 703–42.

Van Vianen, A. E. and Kmieciak, Y. M. 1998: The match between recruiters' perceptions of organisational climate and personality of the ideal applicant for a managerial position. *International Journal of Selection and Assessment*, **6**, 153–64.

Watson, T. 1994: Recruitment and selection. In K. Sisson (ed.), *Personnel Management: A comprehensive guide to theory and practice in Britain*, Oxford: Basil Blackwell.

Weekley, J. A. and Gier, J. A. 1987: Reliability and validity of the situational interview for a sales position. *Journal of Applied Psychology*, **72**, 484–7.

Williams, K. 1997: Surfing for jobs. *Management Accounting Journal*, **78**, 14–15.

6

Still Wasting Resources?
Equality in Employment

Linda Dickens

Introduction

It is a commonplace statement that people are the most important organizational asset. Human resources, we are told by many commentators, can provide organizations with competitive advantage. At the same time, however, we have continuing discrimination in the labour market on grounds of sex, race, disability, and a lack of equality of opportunity in employment. This prevents the full and effective utilization of all human resources. This chapter explores this apparent contradiction, arguing that, despite some progress, resources are being wasted, and offers an explanation of why this is the case.

In the next section action towards greater equality of opportunity in employment is considered in the context of data which reveal continuing employment disadvantage for particular groups in Britain. The initiatives which organizations might take to tackle this differential distribution of opportunities and rewards are outlined in the third section, drawing on guidance from the equality commissions. The fourth section considers the factors which might encourage an organization to adopt equality initiatives, identifying two main categories of reason why equality action might be taken: positive organizational self-interest (the 'business case' for equality) and penalty avoidance through compliance.

These potential motivating forces have not been sufficient to produce a universal adoption of equality initiatives, however. In the fifth section the unevenness of action is accounted for by considering the limited and contingent nature of the self-interest and compliance pressures, and the context for equality action, indicating the existence of countervailing pressures. Some organizations have taken equality initiatives but have achieved relatively little in terms of substantive outcomes. The sixth section discusses problems in translating the equal opportunity (EO) prescription into practice. It goes on to argue, however, that even if the good practice 'equality model' were to be implemented adequately, this would not necessarily produce equity in terms of distributional outcomes.

Much of the prescription in the employment equality area, it is argued, rests on an inadequate conceptualization of the problem, underplays the resistance which equality initiatives can generate and simplifies the reasons for it. The adoption and implementation of such prescription will deliver only limited progress. Although such progress is well worth achieving, the concluding section argues for the need to shift the emphasis away from measures designed to help members of the disadvantaged groups progress within existing organizations towards an approach centred on changing the nature, structure and values of organizations themselves.

Progress but Continuing Disadvantage in Employment

Signs of apparent progress towards greater equality of opportunity in employment can be seen in the large number of organizations declaring (in recruitment advertising and elsewhere) that they are an 'equal opportunity employer'; in the adoption of equal opportunity policies (EOPs); in the appointment of equal opportunity officers; in the growing membership of such campaigns as Opportunity 2000, Race for Opportunity, and 'positive about disabled people' (whereby companies displaying the 'two ticks' campaign logo agree, *inter alia*, to interview all disabled applicants who meet the minimum criteria for a job vacancy). Opportunity 2000 is a business-led campaign launched in October 1991 to 'increase the quality and quantity of women's participation in the workforce'. Race for Opportunity, also a business-led campaign, aims to encourage business to 'invest' in Britain's ethnic minority communities. Employment is one of its four key areas. It was set up in 1995 by 26 leading UK companies and a further 55 had joined by 1997 (IDS 1997).

Employers who participate in Opportunity 2000 set themselves qualitative or quantitative goals, undertaking to monitor and publicize progress towards those goals. They need not have an existing EOP but some of the first 61 members were private-sector organizations already well known for their EO initiatives. By 1998, membership had grown to over 350 public and private sector organizations, employing a quarter of the workforce. No single set of goals was proposed for Opportunity 2000 members: organizations declare their own objectives (some of which are rather general – for example, 'monitoring all recruitment and development practices for equal access and treatment') or set themselves qualitative or numerical targets (*EOR* 1992a: 20–3). The main areas where Opportunity 2000 organizations have focused their efforts include increasing the proportion of women in management and in non-traditional jobs (with an emphasis on training and development) and developing family-friendly initiatives (IDS 1996). Member organizations have shown achievements. The proportion of women senior managers increased in the National Health Service (NHS) from 18 per cent to 28 per cent in four years, and in British Airways from 13.5 per cent to 17.4 per cent in three years, while Abbey National doubled its proportion of women managers from 10 per cent to 20 per cent in four years (Hammond 1997: 17). On average, in 1996, Opportunity 2000 members offered eight family-friendly options: 70 per cent offered paternity leave, 65 per cent offered maternity arrangements above the statutory minimum and 30 per cent offered holiday play schemes (Business in the Community 1997).

Opportunity 2000 emphasizes a 'culture-change' model for developing equal opportunities and has sought to reinforce this recently by instituting awards for members under each of the five key aspects which its current model identifies, namely demonstrating commitment; making the investment; changing behaviour; communicating ownership; and sharing ownership. Prize-winning initiatives in 1998 under these headings were a careers open day run by the Foreign and Commonwealth Office; a job-share scheme in a components company; a structured EO programme in LWT; a development programme which attempted to retain and motivate valued staff in Barclays Telecommunication Services by restoring the balance between home and work life and to improve employees' adaptability; and a flexible benefits package for Price Waterhouse employees (Business in the Community 1998).

Employer initiatives specifically aiming to promote equal opportunities for ethnic minorities can also be identified. A survey of 750 subscribers to *Equal Opportunities Review (EOR)* found these most commonly included provision of guidance on race equality to selectors, ethnic monitoring of applicants and recruitment schemes to encourage ethnic minority applicants, such as placing job advertisements in ethnic minority publications and using ethnic minority images in publicity material (*EOR* 1993a: 14–20). Less common steps, taken by only a minority of respondents, included the setting of recruitment targets (usually reflecting local labour market composition) and pre-recruitment training schemes. Those surveyed might reasonably be expected to exhibit a predisposition to EO initiatives: of 166 respondents (a 22 per cent return), 63 per cent were from the public sector (mainly local authorities), 33 per cent were from the private sector (mainly finance and retail) and 4 per cent were voluntary organizations. A Commission for Racial Equality (CRE) survey of 168 large private sector companies and 149 subsidiaries found the most commonly adopted elements of racial equality programmes were ethnic monitoring (primarily of applicants) and procedures for dealing with racial harassment (IRS 1995).

Equality initiatives are being taken, therefore, but the evidence suggests that they are of limited breadth and depth. There has been a marked increase in the proportion of organizations claiming to have an equal opportunities policy. At the start of the decade, a majority of private-sector companies and almost half of all local authorities did not claim to have an EOP (*EOR* 1989: 13; EOC 1988). The latest WERS survey shows two-thirds of workplaces (64 per cent) now claim to have formal policies (Cully et al. 1998).

The existence of an EO statement or policy (and not all organizations recognize the difference) says little about what is actually happening in the organization. Adoption of a policy may have little impact, even at the minimal level of awareness of the policy's existence (Jewson et al. 1990; Colling and Dickens 1989). Surveys of self-declared EO employers have found that there may be little substance behind the declaration (e.g. EOC 1988; Hitner et al. 1981). In the NHS, for example, although 93 per cent of health authorities and boards investigated by the Equal Opportunities Commission (EOC) in 1990 stated they had an equal opportunity policy or statement, for many this amounted to little more than paying lip service to equality: 10 per cent had not committed their EOP to paper; 30 per cent had not communicated the policy to their employees; 60 per cent did not have an equal opportunities committee to plan or evaluate progress; and 75 per cent did not monitor their policy (EOC 1991). More recent research on equal opportunities policies in NHS Trusts shows marked improvement (*EOR* 1998g: 25–7) although among the 98 per cent of Trusts with a general EO policy statement there was wide variation in practice. Monitoring by gender, ethnic origin and disability was undertaken by nine out of ten trusts, but on job applicants only. Promotion, job termination and training were less well covered and only 30 per cent of trusts analysed pay data by gender. Thirty-five per cent did not produce a report on the monitoring data, which raises questions as to their utility, and only a minority had set any forecasts or goals for the representation of women, ethnic minorities or people with disabilities in their workforces.

CRE research into large private sector companies (IRS 1995) also revealed a gap between policy and action. Nine out of ten companies (employing some 7,000 people) had policies for racial equality but only around half had implemented, or were about to implement, an action plan to realize those policies.

WERS data (Cully et al. 1998: 13) indicate that a range of initiatives consistent with being an EO employer are more likely to be found in those organizations with a formal EOP than in those without. But among those workplaces with a formal EOP the specified practices were found only in a minority of cases, as shown in table 6.1. The most frequently cited was monitoring ethnic origin (48 per cent), the most infrequent (17 per cent) reviewing the pay rates of different groups. Twenty-seven per cent of workplaces claiming to have a formal written EOP had none of the six practices specified.

In some organizations, where the adoption of a policy is not seen as an end in itself, and equality initiatives have been taken, there have been achievements, although these may appear relatively small and the pace of progress extremely slow. In the Civil Service a Programme of Action to achieve equality of opportunity for women was implemented in 1984, followed by a second programme in 1992, with a similar programme for ethnic minorities being introduced in 1990. The representation of women in the top three grades of the Service increased from 28 (9 per cent) in 1984 to 53 (17 per cent) in April 1992 (Cabinet Office 1992: 3). The overall representation of ethnic minority staff in the Civil Service increased by half a percentage point in the two years to April 1992 to reach 5 per cent. While this figure is in keeping with the proportion of ethnic minorities of working age in the general population, ethnic minorities remained underrepresented in all management grades in the Civil Service, especially at the more senior grades (*EOR* 1993b: 9). Further programmes were introduced and further progress was made but data for 1997 indicated that while women make up over half (51 per cent) of all non-industrial staff in the Civil Service they are concentrated in the three lowest grades (90 per cent compared with 66 per cent of men); and although ethnic minority representation was slightly higher than in the economically active population as a whole (5.7 per cent compared with 5.3 per cent), only 10 per cent of ethnic minority civil servants are above the three lowest grades compared with over 20 per cent of white civil servants (*EOR* 1998a: 7).

Table 6.1 Equal treatment practices, by formal equal opportunities policy

	Formal equal opportunities policy Percentage of workplaces	*No policy Percentage of workplaces*
Keep employee records with ethnic origin identified	48	13
Collect statistics on posts held by men and women	43	13
Monitor promotions by gender and ethnicity	23	2
Review selection procedures to identify indirect discrimination	35	5
Review the relative pay rates of different groups	17	15
Make adjustments to accommodate disabled employees	42	16
None of these	27	67

Base: all workplaces with 25 or more employees
Figures are weighted and based on responses from 1,906 managers

Source: Cully et al. 1998: 13

EO is firmly on management agendas in a number of organizations, and a range of initiatives is being taken, with some examples of imaginative and often thoroughgoing approaches. Progress in terms of significant aggregate distributional outcomes (that is to say changes in the representation and distribution of various disadvantaged groups within organizations and in the workforce as a whole) however is less easy to identify. There clearly have been gains for some people in certain areas but this must be placed in the context of relatively little change in long-standing patterns of job segregation and pay disadvantage.

Labour market segregation and disadvantage

While having one of the highest rates of women's participation, the UK labour market is among the most gender segregated (Scott 1994; Perrons and Shaw 1995) and has one of the largest gender pay gaps in Europe (Rubery and Fagan 1995). Aggregate labour-force statistics show patterns of continuing disadvantage for women, with vertical and horizontal job segregation and continuing inequalities in pay and conditions. There has been considerable growth in female labour-force participation (women now constitute 44 per cent of persons in employment in the UK), but it has been growth of a particular kind, with much of it concentrated in part-time work in the service sector.

There is marked occupational, as well as industrial, segregation. In spring 1997 only just over half of men in employment worked in non-manual occupations, compared with 70 per cent of women in employment. Half of the women in employment are in just three occupational groups – clerical and secretarial; personal and protective services and sales – compared with less than a fifth of men. On the other hand women constitute very few of those employed in such groups as skilled engineering trades (2 per cent) or science and engineering professionals (10 per cent) and still only represent just under a third (32 per cent) of managers and administrators (Sly et al. 1998a: 102).

Women's pay position relative to that of men has improved but women who work full time still receive only 80p for every £1 earned by men. Women who work part-time earn 58 per cent of the average hourly earnings of men who work full time (EOC 1996). Whereas in 1998 one in five men earned £650 or more each week, only 4 per cent of women did (*EOR* 1998h: 30). At the other end of the pay ladder, while only 17.5 per cent of men earn less than £220 per week, this is the case for two in five women (*EOR* 1996: 34). Women (particularly those working part time) also receive fewer employment benefits than men.

The aggregate data available on the employment distribution and pay position of ethnic minorities are less detailed than those available for women and there is considerable variation between ethnic groups. Surveys and analysis have revealed considerable disparities in pay and working conditions to the detriment of black men (e.g. Brown 1984; *Labour Research* 1995a) and lower pay and fewer employment benefits for black women when compared with white women (Bruegel 1989; Bhavnani 1994: 85–91). A relatively small-scale investigation found that 'even when ethnic minority workers have higher education and training, their wages tend to be lower when compared with their white counterparts' and that 'ethnic minorities do not get promoted and in relative terms tend to stay on in lower grades relative to their education and qualifications' (Pirani et al. 1992: 40–1).

Labour Force Survey data (Sly et al. 1998b) reveal certain differences in the sectoral distribution of ethnic minority and white workers. For example, black women are more likely than women generally to work in the medical and health services, and within the Health Service black women are found in the least desirable sectors (Bhavnani 1994). Ethnic minority men are more concentrated in distribution, hotels, catering and repairs compared to their white counterparts. Self-employment is higher among some ethnic minorities than the corresponding white population (Moralee 1998: 125). Ethnic minority men are more likely to be in temporary and part-time jobs than white men; women from ethnic minorities are more likely than white women to be in temporary jobs, but are less likely to work part time (Dex and McCulloch 1995). Most marked, however, are differences in unemployment. Overall unemployment rates are significantly higher for ethnic minority groups. The unemployment rate for Black African men in 1997 was more than three times (25 per cent) that for white men (7 per cent). Pakistani/Bangladeshi men also have high rates. Black African and Pakistani women had unemployment rates (24 per cent and 23 per cent) four times those of white women (5.4 per cent) (Sly et al. 1998b: 601).

There are 3.9 million disabled people of working age in Britain (Sly 1996: 413). Of these 40 per cent were in paid employment compared with an economic activity rate of 83 per cent for the non-disabled population. Those people with disabilities who are in employment tend to work in a similar range of jobs to people without disabilities. They are slightly more likely to be self-employed (15 per cent compared with 12 per cent) and to be in non-manual occupations. The unemployment rates among people with disabilities are around two and a half times those for non-disabled people.

As well as the continuing disadvantage displayed in the survey statistics, discrimination by employers continues to be revealed by research studies, investigations by the equality commissions and in cases brought to employment tribunals. Even within organizations which declare themselves to be equal opportunity employers, discrimination may continue. Bradford Metropolitan Council, for example, one of the first local authorities to declare itself an EO employer, had legal action taken against it by the CRE in 1991 for persistent discrimination.

From an outcomes-oriented perspective, therefore, it would appear that EO initiatives have been too few or have achieved little in practice. Reasons for this are explored later. First, consideration is given to what is generally meant by EO initiatives, based on guidance issued by the equality commissions.

Equal Opportunity Initiatives

EO initiatives concern policy and practice designed to tackle the differential distribution of opportunities, resources and rewards (jobs, wages, promotions, employment benefits) among workers, based on their membership of a social group. There is no shortage of guidance on what to do and how to do it. Much comes from the two equality commissions – the EOC and the CRE – which publish codes of practice, guidance on developing and implementing EOPs, and on particular aspects such as ethnic monitoring. The Government has published a code of practice to accompany the relatively new Disability Discrimination Act (DDA) and a code of good practice on age discrimination is proposed for 1999. Guidance is offered, too, by employer bodies including the Institute of Personnel and

Development (IPD) and management consultants, as well as by such organizations as the Employers' Forum on Disability. The specialist press (such as *Equal Opportunities Review*) regularly publish examples of good practice.

The centre-piece of the equality commissions' guidance concerns the adoption of an EOP. As described by the CRE (1984: 8), this is a policy which aims to ensure:

> that no job applicant or employee receives less favourable treatment than another on racial grounds; that no applicant or employee is placed at a disadvantage by requirements or conditions which have a disproportionately adverse effect on his or her racial group and which cannot be shown to be justifiable on other than racial grounds, and that, where appropriate and where permissible under the Race Relations Act, employees of underrepresented racial groups are given training and encouragement to achieve equal opportunity within the organisation.

The EOC guidance is similar, presenting an EOP as ensuring no direct or indirect discrimination operates to the detriment of women or married people in any area of employment, including access to it, and that positive action measures (encouragement to apply, single sex and 'special needs' training, childcare provision, flexible hours, return to work schemes, etc.) are introduced.

On implementing EOPs, the CRE guidance (1983) is for the allocation of responsibility to a suitably qualified member of senior management; consultation with trade unions or employee representatives; a statement of the policy and publicity to all employees and job applicants; training and guidance on law and company policy to supervisory staff and other relevant decision makers; an examination of existing procedures and criteria for indirectly discriminatory effect, implementing change where this is found; and monitoring of policy through analysis of the composition of workforce and job applicants, and positive action/remedial action (e.g. language training), as permitted under the legislation.

The equality commissions' advice centres on developing fair procedures and fair practice, with some compensatory measures for members of disadvantaged groups. It emphasizes developing unbiased criteria and formal procedures, and guiding and training responsible staff to ensure that these are followed, with monitoring to be undertaken of process and outcomes. This forms the core of many EO initiatives.

Both commissions more recently have produced self-assessment standards to help employers develop equality policies and to measure how far the organization has progressed towards being an equal opportunities employer. The EOC's *Gender Equality Checklist* (1995) lists questions under six sections: commitment; awareness, information and monitoring; implementation; policy and procedures; reviewing and updating. The CRE's *Standard for Racial Equality for Employers* (1995) has three sections. The first sets out the case for action. The second provides a checklist grouped under three headings: commitment, action and outcomes. The third section is on measuring progress in six broad areas: policy and planning, selection, developing and retaining staff, communications and corporate image, corporate citizenship and auditing for racial equality. Five levels of achievement are detailed under each area. These standards have been designed to complement the commissions' statutory codes of practice of the 1980s, to provide a managerial tool for translating the provisions of the codes into action (Ollerearnshaw and Waldeck 1995).

Reasons for taking equality initiatives

A variety of external and internal factors can be identified which might encourage an organization to adopt the advice proffered and implement equality initiatives. These can be divided roughly into two categories: the positive pursuit of organizational benefits (self-interest or the business case for equality) and penalty avoidance through compliance.

This is not to deny that initiatives to promote greater employment equality can arise from a sense of social justice or moral responsibility. Key individuals in an organization, indeed, may be motivated by concerns for social justice. The role of John Moores in Littlewoods is often cited as such an example (Hackett 1988: 49; Hansard Society Commission 1990: 53). Recently, however, the Littlewoods Organization has emphasized the business advantages rather than the moral imperative of its equal opportunities strategies (*EOR* 1998f: 20). Although often posed as alternatives, business rationales for equality action may go hand in hand with social justice and/or compliance considerations. In practice, social justice or altruistic considerations probably have most purchase when operating in combination with the organizational self-interest or compliance factors discussed below.

ORGANIZATIONAL SELF-INTEREST

The new emphasis within the Littlewoods Organization on the commercial advantages of equality (and not merely its moral or legal necessity) reflects a broader development – the ascendancy of the business case for equality action (Dickens 1994; 1999). The positive organizational benefits of EO always formed part of the arguments for equality action but in the 1980s and 1990s this became the dominant mobilizing vocabulary. Organizational self-interest – the business case for equality – underpins and informs, for example, Opportunity 2000; the CRE's Racial Equality Standard; guidance from the Confederation of British Industry to its members (CBI 1996); exhortation and advice from the Government (e.g. DfEE *Equality Pays*, n.d.) and the IPD's position paper on managing diversity (IPD 1996).

A number of interlinked factors encouraging an interest in equality initiatives can be grouped under this heading of organizational self-interest: competition in the labour market; improving organizational effectiveness through efficient management of human resources and better employee relations; positive company image; and gaining from diversity. What they have in common is that EO is promoted as being in the best interests of the company, providing positive organizational benefits.

At certain times labour market changes have provided an external stimulus of this organizational self-interest kind. Concern in the late 1980s with the 'demographic time-bomb' (the decline in numbers of young people entering the labour market), and with skill shortages, led to increased consideration being given to 'non-traditional' recruits. The link to EO is that disadvantaged groups constitute an untapped or underutilized labour supply. Labour force projections indicate that women will form the major component of future labour supply. Black workers are disproportionately represented among the unemployed within every age and sex group, but particularly in the male 16 to 24 age group.

The emphasis is not only on widening recruitment, but also on better retention of existing staff. In some companies, either through experiencing labour market pressure or through copying action of competitors, this stimulated an interest in such initiatives as enhanced maternity provisions, career breaks and flexible working as cost-effective ways of holding on to valued female staff (*IRRR* 1990a: 2; Business in the Community 1993).

The efficient use of labour also concentrates on not wasting available resources by implicitly assuming that white, non-disabled men have a monopoly of talent, or that older workers have no contribution to make, and involves identifying untapped skills within existing workforces. There is evidence that part-time workers and workers from ethnic minorities, for example, are often overskilled for the jobs they do (e.g. Horrell et al. 1989).

IMPROVING ORGANIZATIONAL EFFECTIVENESS

Discriminatory practices are often attacked as part of a web of poor personnel procedures and bad management policies while EO is presented as good, professional management which encourages the efficient use of human resources. Organizations may gain from the development of a more professional approach to the management of people, but this rationale for EO action may have a particular appeal to personnel professionals within organizations. As Young notes (1987: 100), 'personnel managers stand to reap both the psychological rewards of establishing good practice and the material rewards of increased responsibility and resources within the organization'.

EO appears to fit well with the adoption of a human resource management approach which emphasizes valuing and developing people in pursuit of organizational effectiveness and which stresses the role of the individual and importance of involvement. This opens the way for arguments to be made about valuing all people, and valuing diversity, thus enabling equality action to be linked to the achievement of business goals (Dickens 1998; Miller 1996: 206). Similarly EO action is argued to support initiatives such as Investors in People and total quality management (IPD 1996: 1).

Where disadvantaged groups channel demands for social justice into industrial action (actual or potential), EO action may be instituted in a search for better industrial relations. The EOC (1986: 1) claims that other employee relations benefits which accrue to EO employers include 'an improvement in motivation and performance which, in turn, can reduce turnover levels'. It says 'employers have also found that by focusing attention on the treatment of all staff at work, the implementation of equal opportunities policies stimulates a healthy and more productive atmosphere and creates a better quality of working life.' Similar benefits are highlighted by the IPD drawing on reports of employer experience by Kandola and Fullerton (1994), and it notes 'other reported benefits include better decision-making, improved teamwork, greater creativity, better customer service skills, and improved quality of output' (IPD 1996: 6).

A further 'self-interest' pressure to EO action is concern for the organization's profile or image. Clearly a company's image can be harmed by its being found to have unlawfully discriminated, but, more positively, EO can be presented as a selling point for the organization. In local authorities political pressure from elected councillors, plus an awareness of diversity among recipients of council services, stimulated a number of EO policies. The CRE argues adopting EO policies can enhance an organization's attractiveness to investors as part of a package of ethical and good employer practices.

In some retail and other service sector companies, a need to have a staff more representative of the customer base has been an incentive to act. This may arise where the company is based in areas of high ethnic minority population or, more generally, where organizations are attempting to 'get close to the customer', understanding diverse customer needs in order to deliver the required quality of service to the client and so increase market share. Examples here include British Airways and British Telecom (Dickens 1994).

The concern may also be with how the organization is perceived by potential applicants and existing staff. In this case, equality action may be taken to project the image of a 'good employer' who 'puts people first', thereby presenting the company as a quality organization in order to become an 'employer of choice', able to attract and retain quality people. Particular organizations may be expected to have variants on this aspect of self-interest. For example, the BBC sees itself as holding others accountable and so must demand high standards of itself. It also perceives a need for a workforce representative of the community at large to contribute to diversity in programme making (*IRRR* 1990b), a way the organization can gain from having diversity among its employees.

The theme of organizational self-interest being served by recognizing that there is value added by having Blacks, women, etc. fully represented at all levels within the organization has been present in the American personnel management literature for a longer time than in the British. In the US there has been a move away from a concern with equal employment opportunity, seen as largely compliance based, towards valuing diversity (Copeland 1988a; 1988b). The idea is that organizations recognize the benefits that multiculturalism can bring to them, 'including, for instance, the challenging of stereotypical opinions and traditional assumptions...(T)he talents and attributes of people from different backgrounds and heritages are fully valued, utilized and developed' (Greenslade 1991). This argument has particular self-interest appeal to organizations operating in a context where minority groups are important customers and in a country, like the USA, where they constitute the fastest-growing segment of the population. However, the scope of diversity management in the US has widened beyond a focus on particular social groups to embrace everyone: 'to ensure that the full potential of all employees is being exploited and that barriers to their corporate development are removed' (Loden 1998: 19). In the UK 'diversity management' appears to be emerging as the label of choice (e.g. IPD 1996), although exactly what this means and the extent of its distinctiveness from equal opportunities may vary (Liff 1997; 1999).

COMPLIANCE AND PENALTY AVOIDANCE

The major external factor underpinning the compliance approach is equality legislation. There is extensive national legislation operating in the UK within the context of European law. This latter has been concerned particularly with equality between men and women since the Treaty of Rome did not explicitly cover racial discrimination. (The 1997 Treaty of Amsterdam, however, widens the scope for European equality action.) Tables 6.2 and 6.3 provide a summary overview of relevant European and national legislation. Table 6.3 merely sketches some key legal provisions and does not attempt to provide comprehensive coverage nor detail of the legislation. Figure 6.1 indicates how direct and indirect discrimination are defined in race and sex legislation and the legal penalties which apply when a claim of sex or race discrimination is upheld.

Table 6.2 Relevant key European provisions

Article 119 of the EEC Treaty. Directly applicable. Equal pay for equal work between men and women

Equal Pay Directive 1975 (75/117/EEC) Extends Article 119 to include equal pay for work of equal value

Equal Treatment Directive 1976 (76/207/EEC) Outlaws sex discrimination in all aspects of employment

Equal Treatment Directive (state social security) 1978 (79/7/EEC) Equality of treatment in all state benefits except pensions

Equal Treatment Directive (occ. social security) 1986 (86/378/EEC) Equality in occupational benefits except pensions (now overridden by the Barber case where ECJ ruled definition of pay under Article 119 includes pensions)

Equal Treatment Directive (self-employed) 1986 (86/613/EEC)

Protection of Pregnant Workers Directive (92/85/EEC) Requires 14 weeks paid maternity leave, right to return and protection from dismissal for all pregnant workers, regardless of service, and special health and safety provisions

Parental Leave Directive (96/34/EC) Individual non-transferable right to at least three months leave for childcare purposes following birth or adoption of child until up to eight years old. Entitlement to time off work for urgent family reasons

Burden of Proof Directive (97/80/EC) In sex discrimination cases, once facts are presented from which discrimination may be presumed, it falls on the employer to prove there has been no breach of the equal treatment principle

Part-time Work Directive (97/81/EC) Part-time workers to be afforded pro rata equal treatment with comparable full-time workers unless difference is justified on objective grounds. Barriers to part-time working to be reviewed

As table 6.3 indicates, the major legislative focus in Britain has been on sex and race discrimination. Legal intervention in the area of disability fell far short of outlawing discrimination until the DDA 1995. There is no legislation outlawing discrimination on the grounds of sexual orientation nor age[1] (although some limited protection is afforded indirectly), nor (in Britain) religion (where this does not overlap with ethnic or national origins). The legislative priorities are reflected in voluntary EO initiatives. The WERS Survey (Cully et al. 1998) found that among the two-thirds of workplaces with formal, written EOPs the areas covered included sex (98 per cent), race (98 per cent), disability (93 per cent), religion (84 per cent), marital status (73 per cent) and age (67 per cent). But other forms of discrimination exist (for example, class, sexual orientation) and some EOPs attempt to embrace other groups also. The main focus of this chapter is sex and race.

Individuals may complain of discrimination on grounds covered by the legislation and seek to enforce their statutory rights through the employment tribunal system. The equality commissions have statutory investigative powers as well as a role in aiding individual complainants and in giving advice and issuing guidance on the legislative requirements and the promotion of EO. The legislative threat therefore centres on the adverse publicity and the direct and indirect costs that a tribunal claim or commission investigation would involve.

Threatened or actual investigations by the equality commissions helped stimulate progress in a number of sectors in the early days of the legislation. In 1983, for example, the possibility of an investigation by the EOC in Barclays Bank led to reform of the bank's recruitment and selection practices, and an EOC formal investigation into Leeds Building Society helped stimulate a reconsideration of mobility requirements in the finance industry. CRE investigations into Yorkshire Passenger Transport Authority had spin-offs for other areas of passenger transport, including in London (Hackett 1988: 51). Its investigation policy was to target high-profile, household-name companies to provide examples likely to encourage more widespread action.

In the case of equal pay, the disruption to an organization's whole pay structure which a single claim potentially could involve is an added incentive for employers to take preemptive action rather than wait for legal challenge. The potential impact of the use of the law by an individual employee was demonstrated in supermarket retailing. In 1987 a checkout operative employed by the major food retailer, J. Sainsbury, compared her job to that of a warehouseman and claimed equal pay for work of equal value. The company agreed an out-of-court settlement and reviewed its pay structure, leading to an increased

Table 6.3 Key aspects of UK legislation

Equal Pay Act 1970 (amended by Equal Value (Amendment) Regulations 1983) Equal pay and other contractual conditions for men and women where engaged on same or similar work, work rated as equivalent by job evaluation, or where work is of equal value

Sex Discrimination Act 1976, SDA 1986 Prohibits direct and indirect discrimination in all areas of employment on grounds of sex or married status. Sex may be a genuine occupational qualification (GOQ) in specified circumstances (including for reasons of authenticity, decency and privacy; delivery of a personal welfare service; certain employment in a single-sex establishment). Special treatment permitted in respect of pregnancy and childbirth, and to encourage applications from, and to provide training for, underrepresented sex. Discriminatory terms in collective agreement or employers' rules rendered void

Social Security Act 1989 Equality in occupational benefit schemes (including health insurance and pensions)

Employment Rights Act 1996 Maternity rights (maternity leave, with pay; right to return after leave); time off for ante-natal care

Race Relations Act 1976 Prohibits direct and indirect discrimination in all areas of employment on grounds of race, colour, nationality, ethnic or national origins (includes some religious groups, e.g. Sikhs and Jews). Race may be a GOQ in specified circumstances (including authenticity, delivering welfare service). Special treatment permitted to encourage applications from, and to provide training for, underrepresented group. Particular action allowed by local authorities

Fair Employment (Northern Ireland) Act 1989 (not applicable in Great Britain) Outlaws discrimination on grounds of religious belief or political opinion. Employers required to register with Fair Employment Commission, to monitor religious composition of their workforce and, in the case of employers of over 250, applicants submit monitoring returns annually. Required to take 'affirmative action' where imbalances are evident, such action enforceable by the Commission

Disability Discrimination Act 1995 Prohibits direct discrimination and obliges employers to make reasonable adjustments to prevent any arrangements or physical features placing disabled people at a disadvantage. Applies only to employers with 15 or more employees

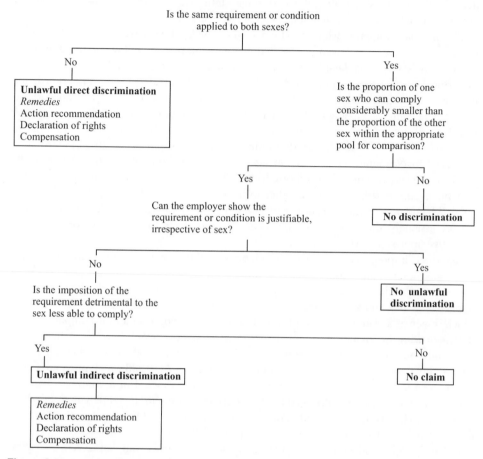

Figure 6.1   Discrimination: definition and remedies

Note: The same approach applies to determining direct/indirect race discrimination

salary bill for the company of 4 per cent above the annual wage settlement. Grading and pay structure revisions followed in other major food retailers.

The threat of numerous individual claims for equal pay has been a tactic used by some unions to persuade employers to review grading structures, for example, in respect of ancillary workers in the NHS and in parts of the electricity industry (Gilbert and Secker 1995; Donaghy 1995). A major regrading exercise in the local authority manual sector provided a good example of how the incorporation of equal value considerations into a grading structure (with value being attached, for example, to caring skills and responsibility for people) could improve women's relative pay position in terms of basic rates, if not take-home pay, since the latter can be distorted by differential bonus payments which favour male occupations (Dickens et al. 1988; LEVEL 1987). The local authority single-status agreement reached in 1997 was achieved in the context of the prospect of thousands of equal-value legal challenges over bonus payments and compulsory competitive tendering

(IRS 1997: 5). This equality-informed single-status framework agreement covers 1.5 million manual and white collar staff in local government.

The agenda-setting role which can be played by the legal framework can also be seen in the attention given to developing sexual harassment policies following the European Commission's Code on Dignity at Work and, importantly, some well-publicized cases involving high awards of compensation. It is also demonstrated by the attention being paid by many organizations to disability, and particularly the need for 'reasonable adjustments', following the passing of the DDA (*EOR* 1997a) and, negatively, by the continuing incidence of age preferences in recruitment (Worsley 1996: 18). There are a number of voluntary initiatives to tackle age discrimination and these are to be strengthened by a proposed government 'action plan on age' including a Code of Practice (DfEE 1998: 27–8). However, managers are reported as doubting 'whether age discrimination would ever be given the same priority as other forms of prejudice without legislation' (Worsley 1996: 23) and among the specialist readership of *Equal Opportunities Review* (mainly personnel professionals) the majority (86 per cent of respondents to a postal survey) favour a legislative approach (*EOR* 1998c).

Externally imposed standards with which organizations have to comply may be imposed by means other than legislation. For example, an organization can use its purchasing power to force those who deal with it to conform to minimum standards, whether in respect of health and safety measures or EO promotion. The Littlewoods Organization, which is seen as a leading-edge employer in the equality field, includes the company's EOP statement with the invitation to tender sent to its suppliers (*EOR* 1998f: 27). A number of local authorities used contract compliance effectively in the 1980s (*EOR* 1990: 26–8) but their ability to do so was limited by the Local Government Act 1988 which prevented non-commercial factors from being taken into account in the award of a contract. The Act allowed specific questions (approved by the Minister) relating to the employment of ethnic minorities to be asked of contractors but only a small number of local authorities used this limited provision (Commission for Racial Equality 1992: 30).

In Northern Ireland a limited form of legally backed contract compliance is in operation in respect of religious discrimination. Loss of government contracts is used as a legislative sanction of last resort where employers fail to comply with obligations under the Fair Employment Act 1989 (McCrudden 1991).

The existence of organizational self-interest and compliance-driven pressures of the kind outlined above may be necessary to produce action for equality, but, for reasons discussed in the next section, they may not be sufficient.

Non-adoption of EO Initiatives

Arguments that EO is good for business (organizational self-interest factors) or that discrimination is bad for business (the threat of penalties for non-compliance) clearly have not been sufficient to produce a universal adoption of thoroughgoing equality initiatives. In trying to account for this, the limitations and contingent nature of the self-interest and compliance pressures indicated above need to be recognized.

Business case arguments are contingent and variable. They will be experienced differently by (and within) different organizations and, indeed, pursuit of organizational self-interest may run counter to, rather than support, EO initiatives. Further, if the business case argument does promote an interest in EO, it may encourage only a partial, selective approach. The legal compliance threat, although present, has been generally weak in the UK in terms of risk of legal action and the penalties for discrimination, and it too is variable and contingent. Further, the broader context within which EO action is to be taken may contain pressures potentially detrimental to employment equality, alongside the potentially positive factors outlined in the previous section. These issues are now examined.

Organizational self-interest

The contingent and variable appeal of the self-interest arguments as between organizations can be seen, for example, in the case of changing demographics and labour-market composition. Even where skill shortages are perceived as problems, responses other than those favourable to promoting EO are possible, and are taken – for example, competing for scarce male labour through pay increases or by contracting out work (Atkinson 1989; Dickens 1989). Further, the segmentation of labour markets means that the various groups are not seen by employers as interchangeable. For example, a lack of skilled (male) labour will not necessarily lead to women being seen as a potential resource where skill is itself a male-gendered concept (Philips and Taylor 1980). Where equality initiatives are taken in response to labour-market pressure, they may not be secure when those pressures cease to apply. The 'defusing' of the demographic timebomb in the recession of the early 1990s led to some backsliding in the detail and extent of equality provisions – for example, removing guarantees of re-employment after a career break and cutting childcare facilities – even where these had been collectively negotiated (Colling and Dickens 1998).

An organization's capacity to respond to changing labour markets in ways likely to be beneficial for EO requires an awareness of the situation, which is often lacking, and adequate, qualitative human resource planning (see chapter 4). The effective and full utilization of the labour force also calls for investment in training. As chapter 7 indicates, UK organizations rarely score highly in these areas. Women and ethnic minorities (particularly those working part time) are often disadvantaged in access to training, whether provided by employers or the state (Clarke 1991; Lee and Wrench 1987; Green 1991; Green and Zanchi 1997) and the training provided may reinforce rather than challenge job segregation (Cockburn 1987; Felstead 1995: 180).

Part of the argument that EO makes good business sense is that it is cost effective. EO measures can be cost effective for an employer but this often calls for long-term assessment with account being taken of less easily quantifiable gains which may be difficult to evaluate and express in financial terms. As Humphries and Rubery note (1995: 13), 'it is because the costs to firms seem immediate and palpable while the benefits are more distant and less easy to capture that individual initiatives may produce only slow and patchy changes'. It is often at a level above that of the individual organization (or subunit) which bears the cost that the benefits of equality action may be reaped (Bruegel and Perrons 1995). The economic appeal of EO also may vary depending on the competitive strategy adopted by the organization. For example, investment in EO may make more (short-term) sense for an organization competing on quality/innovation than on cost.

Unfortunately, economic rationality does not necessarily point to EO practice at the level of the individual organization. There can be cost advantages to the individual employer, for example in the undervaluing of women's labour. It can be cheap to use ethnic origin, or other group characteristics or stereotypes, as screening devices in selection, a practice which helps reproduce patterns of gender and race segregation. Informal, word-of-mouth recruitment often constitutes indirect race and sex discrimination. But it offers cost advantages, as does exploiting disadvantaged labour market groups as a cheap, flexible workforce (Dickens 1992; Dex and McCulloch 1995; Fevre 1989; Wood 1986).

Because cost–benefit analysis as currently conceptualized is not always likely to favour the adoption of EO measures, an appeal to the 'bottom line' may not stimulate EO action, particularly as the cost of thoroughgoing EOPs can be high. The BBC estimated the short-term annual cost of its EO programme (covering race, gender and disability) at £2–2.5 million (*IRRR* 1990b). Any financial returns on cost in under four years were seen as unlikely and it was recognized that it would be impossible probably ever to show in accounting terms that the full cost of investment had been recouped. The BBC can point to other gains to justify its expenditure, such as the image of the company in the labour market and wider community, and a positive impact on quality of broadcasting output, but such compensating gains are not going to be perceived by, or be relevant to, all organizations.

Although smaller organizations will face smaller costs than those just cited, many of them, starting off with undeveloped personnel policies and practices and an absence of detailed personnel records, will have to bear considerable costs simply to get to first base.

The cost–benefit equation, however, is not static. Publicity given to successful tribunal claims and high awards against employers for discrimination, or to a formal investigation by one of the equality commissions, may have an impact, particularly on employers in the same sector. The cost–benefit equation will be affected also by the reaction of those who are discriminated against. Large costs may be incurred through not taking equality action where disadvantaged groups push their demands through industrial action, as black workers and women (and, indeed, black women) have done (e.g. Wrench 1987), or through seeking legal redress.

Trade unions, of course, can exert pressure for equality through collective bargaining, but, again, this is variable. Unions historically do not have a good record in tackling discrimination, and the exclusion strategies of unions against women and blacks have helped underpin job segregation and employment disadvantage (e.g. Boston 1987; Phizacklea and Miles 1987: 124). Although unions can apply positive pressure for EO through collective bargaining, thereby increasing the costs to employers of doing nothing, they also can exert countervailing pressure. Unions may defend the status quo by protecting the interests of male white workers, defining such interests as 'members' interests' and classifying the divergent interests of women or other disadvantaged groups as 'special', 'sectional' or even trivial (e.g. Lee 1987; Colling and Dickens 1989; Cunninson and Stageman 1993).

Recently, however, there have been more positive examples of trade unions campaigning and exerting pressure on employers for equality (e.g. Gilbert and Secker 1995; Donaghy 1995; Heery 1998; Colling and Dickens 1998; McColgan 1995) and a number of unions have taken initiatives to increase the proportion of women and other 'disadvantaged groups' within their governance and representation structures which may be expected to foster a greater preparedness to initiate and push for equality bargaining (Colgan and Ledwith 1996; SERTUC 1997). Unions can play a positive role for equality (Dickens 1999) but their ability to exert pressure for the adoption of equality initiatives depends on their organizational and bargaining strength which was weakened in the 1980s and 1990s.

Arguing for equality initiatives on the grounds that the promotion of greater employment equality makes good business sense may be problematic for EO achievement. Once the debate about equality is conducted in terms of what is in the company's best interests, EO initiatives can be contested and resisted as irrelevant or marginal to the best or real interests of the organization, as defined by those currently in positions of power, or as measured in terms of short-term contribution to the bottom line (Cockburn 1989). The evidence is that narrow cost–benefit analysis, especially if undertaken by line managers operating in decentralized business units within tight financial control, may block rather than promote equality action (Dickens 1998: 33–4; Wainwright Trust 1997).

Equality initiatives motivated by a search for organizational benefits can lead to the targeting of initiatives to reflect employer needs rather than the needs of the disadvantaged groups. These needs may coincide but matching is not guaranteed. An organization can benefit from a partial selective approach to equality, perhaps addressing only one particular problem; a general approach may be more costly, and thus less clearly in the interests of the organization. For example, enhanced maternity provision and career breaks targeted at women in higher grades, or 'high flyers', helps keep those women in whom training has been invested, thereby retaining scarce skills for the organization, and at the same time provides a positive image for the company. The extension of such provision to all women in the organization, including those in low-level jobs where no labour or skill shortages exist, although potentially a good move for EO, would be more costly, less attuned to the needs of the organization and, thus, can be argued against using the business case rhetoric. It is not surprising therefore to find that a number of business needs-driven initiatives (for example as reported by Opportunity 2000) show a greater concern with the 'glass ceiling' than the 'sticky floor' and that 'family-friendly' equality initiatives are often targeted within an organization rather than made universally available (Holtermann and Clark 1992). As Bruegel and Perrons observe (1995: 162), 'such targeting, however understandable, will barely help to loosen the gender order'.

Often, targeted EO initiatives seem to be about clearing the way for the advancement of individual blacks or individual women rather than about changing the position for significantly large groups of blacks or women within the organization (Cockburn 1991), and, of course, they do little for those outside the organization or only peripherally attached to it (Coyle 1995; Mason and Jewson 1992: 109).

Compliance and penalty avoidance

Turning to the second cluster of factors providing pressure for equality initiatives, those to do with avoiding penalties for non-compliance, we have already noted the weakening of the contract compliance lever. It is indisputable, however, that the enactment of equality legislation and key decisions by the national courts and, particularly in recent years, the European Court of Justice, have provided an important stimulus to action in respect of the removal of race and sex discrimination and in the area of equal pay between men and women. However, the nature and extent of that action varies.

Legislation can be a lever to wider reform, especially if it operates in conjunction with other factors. It provides an important statement of public policy as well as providing for rights and remedies and imposing duties. But the action stimulated by law as an external factor operating on organizations may be that of avoidance rather than compliance, with organizations seeking to minimize the likely impact of the law.

This happened, for example, in response to the original Equal Pay Act (Snell et al. 1981), with some employers ensuring that male and female workers were not employed on work that might be seen as the same or similar under the provisions of the Act. While this tactic is no longer open, following the equal value amendment, which allows comparisons of dissimilar jobs to be made, some employers have sought to protect themselves through adopting job-evaluation schemes. Formalizing and making explicit the basis for payment structures and pay differences through job evaluation can help expose and remove discrimination. There is, however, the risk that the introduction of job evaluation may serve to legitimate or obscure discrimination rather than remove it and make an equal pay challenge less likely to be made or to succeed. Outside the pay area, there is evidence of direct discrimination giving way to more covert, indirect discrimination (e.g. Collinson et al. 1990).

Even if compliance action is taken in respect of the law, little positive action is actually required from employers. The law requires an end to discrimination: it does not actually require that employers do anything to promote equality. Although an EOP might be a useful defence in any legal claim against an organization, the development of such a policy is not required by law. Apart from religious monitoring in Northern Ireland, there is no requirement for employers to audit or monitor their workforces (although case law indicates it is advisable to do so). Most forms of positive action to aid disadvantaged groups are prevented by the legislation, which equally protects white males, and which is concerned with halting present discrimination but does nothing to overcome the effects of past discrimination.[2]

Apart from the now little-used investigation powers of the equality commissions, rights in Britain are conferred on individuals to challenge discriminatory behaviour rather than responsibilities being imposed on administrative, employing, governmental and other organizations to take action to tackle disadvantage. The emphasis is on action by victims rather than action by power-wielders, an approach less likely to lead to EO action.

Although the legal requirements are limited, arguably the full potential of what compliance with the spirit of the law requires is not reflected in current practice. Potentially the concept of indirect discrimination is a far-reaching one, which could be utilized to tackle structural discrimination. But research shows a lack of understanding of the concept of indirect discrimination, and many companies which feel they have done enough to comply with the law have focused only on the more obvious direct discrimination. Similarly, in respect of equal pay for equal-value work, many organizations consider the changes they made at the time of the original equal pay legislation to be sufficient, despite the subsequent important legislative change. The new codes of practice on equal pay for work of equal value issued by the European Commission (1996) and the EOC (1997a) encourage and guide organizations to undertake pay system reviews to reveal any gender inequality or undervaluation of work typically carried out by women in comparison with that typically undertaken by men, something few employers do at present (Bevan and Thompson 1992: 5).

Although organizations may be vulnerable to legal challenge, in practice the risk appears small. Investigations by the equality commissions are infrequent (especially since judicial interpretation of their statutory powers restricted their scope for action) and individual applications to employment tribunals remain relatively scarce and meet with limited success, as shown in table 6.4.

As table 6.4 indicates, only a small proportion of cases is actually determined by a tribunal hearing and success rates for applicants are not very high. About one-third of race discrimination claims were determined by tribunals in 1995–6, with 16 per cent (109) being upheld. In 33 cases, awards were made: the median compensation award was £2,714. Eight people received awards of £8,000 and over. Just under 20 per cent of sex discrimination claims were determined by tribunals in the same period: 30 per cent of these (218) were successful and compensation was awarded in 77 cases. The median compensation was £2,708, with 13 people receiving awards of £8,000 and over. Compensation awards in discrimination cases include an element for 'injury to feelings' and average awards under this head, particularly in race discrimination and sexual harassment cases, increased following two Court of Appeal decisions in 1988 which made it clear that such awards should not be nominal (*EOR* 1992b: 30–5). Awards of compensation also increased following the removal of the statutory maxima in 1993 (sex) and 1994 (race). Some high individual awards have been made (*EOR* 1998e: 19); the median amounts, however, are still below £3,000 in both jurisdictions (and also under the DDA in its first year).

In 1995–6 110 equal pay claims were heard by tribunals: 36 (33 per cent) were successful. The large number of withdrawals under this jurisdiction may reflect the use of the legislation by trade unions as a tool in bargaining, as indicated earlier.

Where discrimination is found, the emphasis in the statute is on compensating the individual rather than requiring the employers to change their behaviour. There have been repeated but largely unsuccessful calls by the commissions and other bodies (e.g. EOC 1990; *EOR* 1997b) for the law to be strengthened, since the risk of a legal challenge at present is seen to provide an inadequate deterrent to discriminatory

Table 6.4 Discrimination claims to industrial tribunals 1995–1996

	Sex discrimination	Equal pay	Race discrimination
ACAS conciliated settlement	1464	128	405
Withdrawn	1508	456	656
Total not heard	2972	584	1061
Percentage of all cases	*81*	*84*	*61*
Case dismissed by tribunal	356	46	453
Otherwise disposed of	131	28	114
Case successful at tribunal	218	36	109
Percentage success rate*	*30*	*33*	*16*
Total cases heard	705	110	676
Total cases disposed of	3677	694	1737

* Proportion of heard cases which were successful at tribunal hearing

Source: Labour Market Trends, 1997: 152

behaviour, and for the enforcement procedures and mechanisms to be made more user friendly. What changes have been made reflect the requirements of European law, for example the removal of the ceiling on compensation awards following a decision of the ECJ in 1993. The government is considering proposals for new sex equality legislation made by the EOC following consultation in 1997 (EOC 1997b). The CRE also has proposed legal reform (*EOR* 1998d: 40).

Context and countervailing pressures

As well as indicating the sometimes weak and contingent nature of the organizational self-interest and compliance factors in providing pressure for EO action, we need to note that the context and external pressures can make it more or less likely that equality initiatives will be taken.

The context of the 1980s and early 1990s was not one particularly favourable to equality action. Public policy sent contradictory signals to employers on equality. The Conservative Government urged various EO actions on employers, supported EOPs and action plans, and as an employer (in the Civil Service) developed a number of equality initiatives. Yet it was found to be in breach of European equality law on more than one occasion, and opposed or weakened European Commission initiatives which many saw as beneficial to women. The Directive on pregnant workers which, among other things, extends the coverage and length of paid maternity leave, was adopted, with the UK abstaining, only in a weakened form after UK opposition. The adoption of Directives on atypical workers, which sought to extend pro rata rights and benefits to part-time and temporary employees, who are disproportionately women and ethnic minorities, was blocked by UK opposition (Jeffery 1995), as was the proposal for a directive on parental leave.

Deregulationary labour law policies pursued by Conservative governments since 1979 weakened statutory employment rights, pushing more women in particular outside employment protections (Dickens and Hall 1995). Although government ministers publicly deplored continuing race and sex discrimination, no government action was taken on the detailed legislative reform proposals made by EOC and CRE, and both agencies regularly complained of underfunding and inadequate resources to cope with an increasing demand for their services.

The change in government in May 1997 and Labour's signing up to the Social Chapter opened the way for the (revised) parental leave and part-time work Directives to be implemented in the UK, along with that on the burden of proof in sex discrimination cases. Implementation of the Working Time Directive will also, *inter alia*, improve the position of many women working part-time by introducing statutory paid holiday entitlement (Hall et al. 1998). A national minimum wage has been introduced (which will benefit women and ethnic minorities in particular); various family-friendly measures (mainly giving effect to minimum European requirements) are proposed, and the Government is developing a childcare strategy. In this respect the context for equality action may be seen as one which is becoming less inhospitable with the state prepared to act – to some extent – as regulator (Dickens 1999).

A context of economic recession is generally unfavourable to EO progress. Equality initiatives may seem a luxury in a time of job loss, reduced employment opportunities and financial restraint. Those employers, for example, trying to alter the ethnic composition of their workforces will find it particularly difficult to do so in a time of little or no recruitment. Indeed ethnic minority workers appear to have been disproportionately affected by recent job losses, in part a reflection of their particular regional and industrial distribution. Nor has organizational change and restructuring been gender neutral (Coyle 1995; Woodall et al. 1997).

In the public sector during the 1980s and 1990s, restructuring, growing commercialism and financial restraint provided reasons for limiting EO initiatives rather than building on them (*Labour Research* 1995b). As noted, the Conservative Government severely curtailed contract compliance in the public sector. It also imposed compulsory contracting out requirements on public-sector employers which led to a deterioration in women's jobs, hours and conditions (Escott and Whitfield 1995; EOCNI 1996). Equality initiatives came under threat from decentralization and fragmentation and from developments such as compulsory competitive tendering (CCT) and market testing (where equality measures may add to the cost of in-house provision when compared with external tenders). In June 1997 the Labour Government announced its intention to replace discriminatory CCT with a duty on employers to obtain 'best value' but the Green Paper was silent on the EO implications of the new regime (*EOR* 1998b).

This section has explored factors which may provide pressure towards the adoption of equality initiatives and sought to explain why, despite such factors, initiatives may not be taken. The next section looks at why achievements might be limited, even where EOPs are adopted.

Limited Achievements of EO Initiatives

It was noted earlier that equality initiatives in some organizations go no further than a declaration that they are EO employers. This may reflect complacency – a public declaration that there is 'no problem here'. The mere presence of ethnic minorities or women in an organization may be pointed to as evidence of no unfair discrimination or the existence of equality since many organizations fail to recognize that global numbers may mask marked disparities in distribution (Jewson et al. 1990: 11). Adopting a policy, therefore, does not necessarily indicate an intention to change the status quo. It can be seen, rather, as a declaration or symbolic ratification of current practice, an 'affirmation that customary behaviour conforms to the canons of acceptability' (Young 1987: 98).

Many organizations, however, do seek to go beyond applying the label and yet, as we have seen, there may be relatively little achievement in terms of distributional outcomes. In seeking to explain this relative lack of achievement when EO initiatives are taken, this section looks at the problems of translating EO prescription into practice, and, in particular, considers the inadequacies of much EO prescription.

The intention of EOPs can be neutralized through procedures being neglected, or by being followed in the letter but not in the spirit. As Jenkins (1986) found in recruitment and selection, 'espoused' models (what we say we do) and 'operational' models (what we actually do) can differ considerably. Part of the explanation for the inadequate translation of the EO prescription into practice is the distribution of power within organizations. Decision making may not be in the hands of the guardians of good practice, namely the personnel managers, who are likely to have developed the espoused model. Personnel managers, for example, are often marginal to selection decisions, with real power being vested in line managers (Collinson et al. 1990; Jenkins 1986). Some organizations appoint EO managers, who may or may not be based in the personnel department, but their power and status can be just as problematic and the EO function is often understaffed and under-resourced. 'They are sometimes beleaguered, lonely figures, who have to steer a course between trying to get line managers to understand how discrimination works and not being labelled a feminist or a loony lefty' (Hackett 1988: 52).

Line management is often found to be a site of resistance to equality initiatives (e.g. Opportunity 2000:1994) and, therefore, the current emphasis on devolving operational personnel activities to line managers is not good news for equality (Dickens 1998: 34). Line managers may resist the formalization, accountability and monitoring often required by EOPs as interference with their discretion in decision making. This can be reinforced because the personnel or EO function may be viewed as 'external' by line managers. Required changes can be seen as external imposition and threatening (especially in the case of EO) because they may be seen as a challenge to personal attitudes and traditional local norms or values. EO may be experienced as criticism of those in power: managers and others can be affronted by assumptions that they discriminate.

Problems with EO prescription

Focusing on the reasons why prescription may be translated inadequately into practice might suggest that adequate implementation would produce desired outcomes. This is not so. Fair procedures do not necessarily produce fair (distributive justice) outcomes, as Jewson and Mason (1986) and others have argued cogently.

This is demonstrated in the area of recruitment and selection where fair procedures require the assessment of individuals against relevant, job-related criteria rather than according to their membership of a particular social group. The emphasis is on suitability criteria (skills and technical ability to do the job) rather than acceptability criteria (attitudinal, behavioural, personality factors) which tend to interact with racial stereotypes and lead to discrimination (Jenkins 1986). Curran's (1988) work clearly demonstrates that in practice suitability and acceptability criteria may overlap. Both gender and a variety of personal attributes (social and tacit skills) in which gender (and possibly race) in embedded are regarded by many employers as specific and functional attributes and as requirements for the effective performance of particular jobs.[3]

Given the construction and current distribution of skills, attributes and qualifications in society, however, not all individuals will be able to demonstrate their suitability for the job to the same extent and the composition of the current workforce is likely to be reproduced (Webb and Liff 1988; Jewson and Mason 1986). Individuals within disadvantaged groups may be able to meet criteria developed around the usual incumbents – white able-bodied men – but, at best, this is EO as individual advancement rather than the advancement of social groups: it is an exclusive or selective equality which may aid a few honorary white men but leaves the position of the many untouched.

Implicit in much good-practice equality prescription is an argument that discrimination arises from actions of prejudiced individuals, that it is irrational behaviour, indicative of poor management practice, and that it can be curbed by detailed instructions, training and policing. This neglects the fact that organizational ends can be served by not following the prescription. Unfair discrimination can be rational and efficient for an individual and the organization either because of perceived cost advantages or in terms of control of the labour force (Maguire 1986; Manwaring 1983).

Since there can be an organizational rationality in continuing discrimination, it becomes rational for individuals within the organization to act in ways detrimental to EO. This is not necessarily a conscious process. Where sexism and racism have become institution-alized, it is simply adherence to normal practice – 'the way things are done around here'. An organization may have adopted an EOP but individuals will respond to signals (formal and informal) about what really matters in the organization and, therefore, what behaviour is likely to ensure success within it. This applies as much to those in personnel management as elsewhere (Collinson 1991: 58).

Local personnel managers may be transferred line managers with 'no allegiance to those principles and ideals of the personnel profession that could conflict with the more immedi-ate and short-term managerial priorities of profit and production' (Collinson 1991: 59). But even those who are professionals (members of the IPD) may elevate their organizational identity over their professional identity in order to be viewed as effective and to promote personal career progress. The alternative is what many EO managers experience: 'a...stressful role...(which)...offers little reward in terms of career development' (Hol-land 1988: 20). Managers prioritizing organizational loyalties, or seeing their personal success linked to so doing, will also find it rational to discriminate for reasons other than, or in addition to, individual prejudice.

Personnel managers and EO staff need to be seen to contribute to the core values of the organization but EO tends to be marginal in organizations rather than mainstream. In such circumstances it becomes possible, as Cockburn (1989) found, to argue the 'main aim' (what the business is really about) *against* EO. It may be advocated as good management practice but unless EO is a mainstream objective, priority will be given to other manage-ment practices which may conflict with the requirements of EO. This can be seen in a range of current personnel developments associated with human resource management which, despite the rhetoric, may be at odds with the promotion of equal opportunity (Dickens 1998; Woodall 1996). Monitoring and pursuing equal pay, for example, becomes more difficult in the context of the individualization of pay systems. Research points to 'an overall deterioration in gender pay equity under performance-related pay' (Rubery 1995). The organizational pursuit of flexibility and commitment (key policy goals of the HRM model) also impacts differently on women and men (Dickens 1998) and, as noted, attempts to impose an EO policy and monitor it from a central personnel department are hampered by increased decentralization in organizations and an emphasis on line management owning their own decisions.

A key implementation problem in respect of EO 'is that support for taking action designed to improve prospects for women, ethnic minorities and the disabled must come from an overwhelmingly white, male and non-disabled dominant group who may well regard equal opportunities as a threat' (Lovenduski 1989: 15). The threat comes in part from the fact that white men's characteristic career paths are implicitly predicated on the existence of 'unpromotable' categories, including women and blacks (Crompton and Jones 1984: 248). EO is not necessarily the win–win game portrayed in the prescriptive literature.

The threat is not simply to career opportunities. Work is a place where identities are shaped and lived out. For men, work can be an affirmation of their masculinity: equal opportunities, the entry of women into that work, or paying women equivalent wages, can seem like an attack on that identity. Few organizations have attempted to tackle the issue of gender conditioning (for one example, see Cameron 1987). The entry of 'outsiders' may be seen also as a threat to valued social organization and social group identity in the workplace (Salaman 1986). Such social organization is often homosocial (Lipman-Blumen 1976) and exclusion tactics include sexual harassment.

Sexual harassment is an issue which is increasingly on the EO agenda. But the link between sexual harassment and occupational segregation and the perpetuation of male power within organizations is not often acknowledged in the practitioner literature, the problem being presented rather as one of protecting individual women from deviant individual men. Those who seek to cross gender boundaries by entering non-traditional work often find their masculinity or femininity questioned (Cockburn 1987) or find themselves subjected to harassment (Purcell 1988: 174). Such pressures help keep women 'in their place' (Seddon 1983).

Masculinity is not only shaped by work; it is shaped too by men's power over women in the home. The promotion of equality in employment can challenge this power. The potentially revolutionary nature of the demands being made under the banner of EO should not be underestimated in seeking to locate and explain resistance to it. As Cockburn (1991: 63) argues, for example, the claim for equal pay for work of equal value 'potentially undermines the whole strategy of exploiting women sex-specifically'.

Of course, individual white men may not feel particularly powerful or see themselves as 'the problem'. One important criticism of racism awareness training, for example, is that it is experienced by whites as a personal attack, putting individuals in the dock on behalf of white society, and is thus resented, contributing to opposition to EOPs (see the discussion in Iles and Auluck 1989: 27–8). As Coyle (1989: 77) notes, however, although individual men may not feel powerful, 'men's strength lies in the way in which an ideology of gender, of expectations of masculinity and femininity, is lived out in the collective practice of an organization'.

But resistance to EO does not come only from white, non-disabled men. There may be resistance from within the disadvantaged groups which an EOP is designed to help, and this can be particularly dispiriting for the personnel or EO manager. Such resistance may arise through conflicting expectations of equal opportunities, a term which can mask multiple and conflicting meanings. There may be agreement at the symbolic level giving an illusion of common cause, but underlying differences in understanding and expectations can lead to feelings of betrayal (Young 1987: 4; Jewson and Mason 1986: 309). Opposition to EO initiatives may be occasioned through fear of backlash, or of being seen to have achieved a position based on grounds other than merit. Those few from disadvantaged groups who have made it within organizations may resist EO initiatives on the grounds that as they did it unaided, anyone should be able to.

Resistance may arise also because there are divisions between disadvantaged groups. The assumption of shared interest implicit in much universalistic EO prescription is misplaced. For example, seniority rules may advantage ethnic minority men in an organization where there is low turnover, but may not be of advantage necessarily to women with interrupted employment patterns. Certain groups, in particular circumstances, may have an interest in the EO prescription not being followed. Jewson and Mason (1986), for example, found in their study that the formalization of recruitment and selection in the name of EO damaged existing informal channels of communication valued by the ethnic minorities and there was resentment over the refusal of a new personnel manager to recognize traditional links with an Asian broker.

Divisions also exist within any one disadvantaged group and, consequently, interests may differ. Women are divided by class, ethnicity, age, sexual orientation, occupational status, etc. Ethnic minorities are far from homogeneous, as the difficulty even in finding an adequate definition and acceptable terminology demonstrates (Iles and Auluck 1991). Not only are there different groups (Asians, Africans, Chinese and so on), but the situation and experience of men and of women within these diverse groups also differ, and other factors contribute further to diversity of interests. Among people with disabilities there is great diversity depending on the nature of disability, as well as other factors such as their gender, ethnicity, etc. What all these diverse groups do have in common, however, is that they do not conform to the standard which informs and shapes formal and informal organizational structures and norms in Britain, namely, the white, non-disabled male.

Changing the Focus

The discussion so far indicates how problems of implementing equality initiatives and of obtaining substantive outcomes are rather more complex than suggested in much of the guidance literature and prescriptive equality models. The problems of obtaining desired substantive outcomes through procedural approaches have led some to argue for positive discrimination to effect distributional change. The 'radical' approach, outlined by Jewson and Mason (1986) in the context of a study of race discrimination, favours appointing candidates from disadvantaged groups regardless of the fact that they are less well qualified in order to achieve desired outcomes in terms of proportional representation of various groups in the occupational hierarchy.

This approach, however, has been criticized (e.g. Webb and Liff 1988) for sharing with the 'liberal' procedural approach, an acceptance of jobs and organizations as they are currently constructed. What is required is more than putting a black person into a white person's job (Jones 1973, cited in Iles and Auluck 1991). As Cockburn (1989) has noted, the radical approach focuses on gaining power not changing it: it is about attempting to advance disadvantaged groups within existing organizational structures whereas those organizational structures are what needs to be changed to better accommodate all.

The changing perception of disability provides a useful pointer to what is required. Leach (1989: 65) notes a shift in focus from physical defects or deficiencies to a recognition that most of the difficulties encountered by disabled people arise not from their impairment but from the systematic ignoring of their needs. This finds a reflection in the DDA's requirement for 'reasonable adjustment'. Access ramps, for example, can help those with certain physical disabilities play a full part in organizational life but are necessary only because buildings have been designed originally with only the physically able in mind. Similarly, positive action for equality of opportunity for women and ethnic minorities at present usually consists of special measures to help individuals in these groups compete for jobs designed with only white men in mind within organizations whose norms, values and structures are similarly shaped around the traditional incumbents and power holders, again, white men.

Initiatives such as job sharing, presented as an advance in EO for women, are such special measures focused on finding ways to enable women to cope with working patterns shaped around the typical domestic circumstances of men. Various flexibility initiatives such as home working or part-time working, which are often cited as evidence of an EO approach, may be double edged in that they are seen as atypical because they differ from the (male) norm (Dickens 1992). Developments such as career breaks and part-time work, while recognizing the current reality of women's lives, attempting to juggle waged work and domestic work, can be seen as initiatives which in practice take women out of competition for jobs or reduce labour-force attachment and thus save full-time jobs for men (Figart 1992: 43). They also help perpetuate the assumption that women bear the primary responsibility for caring for and raising children. Also, the more that women are granted various kinds of work flexibility to enable them to cope with motherhood and other domestic responsibilities the more they can be dismissed as different, less serious than male employees (Cockburn 1991: 92).

Opening flexible arrangements to men as well as women is preferable to seeing them as open to women only but, without further change, this may not solve the problem. Even if career breaks, for example, are open to, and taken by, both men and women (and they rarely are) they are likely to be taken for different reasons and to be regarded differently by the organization: as career enhancing if time out is taken to study, but career detracting if used for childcare, reflecting the low value currently placed on women's experience in household and family management despite the organizational, managerial and interpersonal skills involved.

The current focus is on helping ethnic minorities, the disabled and women to compete on equal terms with white, non-disabled men for jobs which have been shaped around the typical circumstances of white, able-bodied men. That is to say, there is a template for employment shaped around white, non-disabled men against which those seeking to get in and get on are measured. Rather than adopting this Procrustean approach with its focus on changing individuals to fit the template in order to obtain distributive justice, the template should be abandoned.

The 'valuing diversity' approach, discussed earlier, potentially might contain the seeds of this alternative approach in that it could open the way for different formal and informal organizational cultures and structures, reflective of diverse contributions, needs and attributes. At its most radical, the valuing diversity argument calls for an holistic, positive approach which recognizes and values (social group) differences and which challenges the nature of organizations as currently constructed. More problematically, however, some diversity approaches appear to involve dissolving rather than valuing differences (Liff 1997) and to herald a move away from redressing historical group-based disadvantage towards a focus on all individuals as individuals. As Miller argues (1996: 207), this threatens to sever the link between organizational strategies and the realities of internal and external labour market disadvantage.

This argument for a different focus, for what has been called by Cockburn (1989) a 'transformative EO strategy', concerned with the nature, culture, relations and purpose of the organization, should not be taken as an argument against attempting the kind of EO initiatives indicated earlier, which can produce gains for members of disadvantaged groups. Rather, the attempt here has been to explain why such initiatives generally fail to produce substantive change in the aggregate picture of disadvantage and discrimination, and to indicate the limitations of much current prescription.

The exhortation and guidance from official bodies and personnel management manuals tend to imply that the formulation and implementation of EOPs is relatively straightforward. Ambiguities in the concept of equal opportunities tend to be glossed over: the procedural emphasis is dominant but often with the promise of substantive outcomes in terms of change in the distribution of jobs. The application of professional models of good practice is advocated, which it is argued will produce benefits for employers and be cost effective. Adherence to such models is to be secured by monitoring, training and controls to counter prejudiced, irrational behaviour and traditional practice. The promotion of EO is presented as a technical problem for which technical solutions (monitoring systems, rational selection criteria, etc.) are appropriate.

What has been neglected, as Jenkins and Solomos argue (1987: 118), is the highly political nature of the process, the need for (and difficulty in achieving) sustained commitment for 'measures whose legitimacy, either in the nation at large or in the public domain of politics, cannot by any stretch of the imagination be regarded as either secure or consensual'. Considerable investment of time, labour and other resources is called for in a context where EO may appear to conflict with, rather than serve, what the company (or key people within it) define as its best interests; where discrimination may be organizationally and individually 'rational'; and where other objectives which are accorded more importance may run counter to equality initiatives.

Much EO prescription rests on an inadequate conceptualization of the problem; assumes unitary interests where divergent interests exist; pays inadequate attention to the resistance EO generates; and simplifies the reasons for it. Furthermore, what is called for generally focuses on helping individuals from disadvantaged groups get in and get on within existing organizations, with no real challenge being mounted to the nature, structure and values of the organizations themselves. More recent culture-change approaches to EO appear to represent progress here. In practice, however, the likely focus is the 'artefacts and creations' rather than more fundamental assertions and beliefs (Miller 1996: 207; Liff and Cameron 1997).

Without acknowledging through action that current organizational cultures, norms, structures, rules and notions of merit have been shaped around white, non-disabled men, and without a shift in focus away from, at best, helping people fit into jobs and organizations as presently constructed towards changing the construction of jobs and organizations to accommodate all, achievement will always fall short of equality in employment.

Notes

1   It may be possible to argue that age discrimination constitutes unlawful (indirect) sex discrimination (e.g. *Price* v. *Civil Service Commission* [1977] IRLR 291 EAT) but cases may not succeed because of difficulties in showing that the age requirement has a disproportionate impact on women and because employers can argue age discrimination is 'justifiable' (*Jones* v. *University of Manchester* [1993] IRLR 218 EAT).

2   Although the Fair Employment Act 1989 provides for 'affirmative action' to secure 'fair parti-
    cipation' in the employment of Protestants and Catholics, this goes little further than the sex and
    race discrimination legislation, adding redundancy selection in pursuance of affirmative action to
    the usual provisions permitting outreach recruitment and training provision for the under-
    represented group (McCrudden 1992: 179–81).

3   Although women's tacit skills may be sought by employers, they are rarely positively rewarded.
    This is part of the systematic undervaluing of women's work. The skills which tend to be
    recognized and rewarded as such (for example, in job evaluation) are those normally associated
    with work done by men.

References and further reading

Atkinson, J. 1989: Four Stages of Adjustment to the Demographic Down Turn. *Personnel Management*,
    August, 20–4.

Bevan, S. and Thompson, M. 1992: *Merit Pay, Performance Appraisal and Attitudes to Women's Work*. IMS
    Report No. 234, Brighton: Institute of Manpower Studies.

Bhavnani, R. 1994: *Black Women in the Labour Market*. EOC Research Series, Manchester: EOC.

Boston, S. 1987: *Women Workers and the Trade Unions*. London: Laurence and Wishart.

Brown, C. 1984: *Black and White in Britain*. London: Heinemann.

Bruegel, I. 1989: Sex and Race in the Labour Market. *Feminist Review*, **32**, summer.

Bruegel, I. and Perrons, D. 1995: Where Do the Costs of Unequal Treatment Fall? In J. Humphries
    and J. Rubery (eds), *The Economics of Equal Opportunities*, Manchester: EOC.

Business in the Community 1993: *Corporate Culture and Caring*. London: BIC.

Business in the Community 1997: *Opportunity 2000 Fifth Year Review*. London: BIC.

Business in the Community 1998: The 1998 Opportunity 2000 Awards. *Opportunity 2000 Update*,
    Spring.

Cabinet Office 1992: *Equal Opportunities for Women in the Civil Service: Progress Report 1991–2*. London:
    HMSO.

Cameron, I. 1987: Realising the Dividends from Positive Action. *Personnel Management*, October.

Clarke, K. 1991: *Women and Training. A Review*. Manchester: EOC.

Cockburn, C. 1987: *Two-Track Training*. Basingstoke: Macmillan Education.

Cockburn, C. 1989: Equal Opportunities: The Short and Long Agenda. *Industrial Relations Journal*,
    20(3), 213–25.

Cockburn, C. 1991: *In the Way of Women. Men's Resistance to Sex Equality in Organisations*. Basingstoke:
    Macmillan Education.

Colgan, F. and Ledwith, S. 1996: Sisters Organising – Women and their Trade Unions. In F. Colgan
    and S. Ledwith (eds), *Women in Organisations*, London: Macmillan.

Colling, T. and Dickens, L. 1989: *Equality Bargaining – Why Not?* London: HMSO.

Colling, T. and Dickens, L. 1998: Selling the Case for Gender Equality: Deregulation and Equality
    Bargaining. *British Journal of Industrial Relations*, **36**(3), 389–411.

Collinson, D. 1991: 'Poachers Turned Gamekeepers': Are Personnel Managers One of the Barriers
    to Equal Opportunities? *Human Resource Management Journal*, **1**(3), 58–76.

Collinson, D., Knights, D. and Collinson, M. 1990: *Managing to Discriminate*. London: Routledge.

CRE (Commission for Racial Equality) 1983: *Implementing Equal Employment Opportunity Policies*.
    London: CRE.

CRE 1984: *Race Relations Code of Practice*. London: CRE.

CRE 1992: *Annual Report 1991*. London: CRE.

CRE 1995: *Racial Equality Means Business – A Standard for Racial Equality for Employers*. London: CRE.

CBI (Confederation of British Industry) 1996: *A Winning Strategy – The Business Case for Equal
    Opportunities*. London: CBI.

Copeland, L. 1988a: Valuing Diversity I. *Personnel,* June, 52–60.

Copeland, L. 1988b: Valuing Diversity II. *Personnel,* July, 44–9.

Coyle, A. 1989: The Limits of Change: Local Government and Equal Opportunities for Women. *Public Administration,* Spring, 39–50.

Coyle, A. 1995: *Women and Organisational Change.* EOC Discussion Series No. 14, Manchester: EOC.

Crompton, R. and Jones, G. 1984: *White Collar Proletariat: Deskilling and Gender in the Clerical Labour Process.* London: Macmillan.

Cully, M., O'Reilly, A., Millward, N., Forth, J., Woodland, S., Dix, G. and Bryson, A. 1998: *The 1998 Workplace Employee Relations Survey: First Findings.* London: HMSO.

Cunnison, S. and Stageman, J. 1993: *Feminising the Unions: Challenging the Culture of Masculinity.* Aldershot: Avebury.

Curran, M. 1988: Gender and Recruitment: People and Places in the Labour Market. *Work, Employment and Society,* **2**(3), 335–51.

DfEE (Department for Education and Employment) 1998: *Action on Age.* London: DfEE.

DfEE n.d.: *Equality Pays: How Equal Opportunities Can Benefit Your Business.* London: DfEE.

Dex, S. and McCulloch, A. 1995: *Flexible Employment in Britain: A Statistical Analysis.* EOC Discussion Series No. 15, Manchester: EOC.

Dickens, L. 1989: Women – A Rediscovered Resource? *Industrial Relations Journal,* **20**(3), 167–75.

Dickens, L. 1992: *Whose Flexibility? Discrimination and Equality Issues in Atypical Work.* London: Institute of Employment Rights.

Dickens, L. 1994: The Business Case for Women's Equality: Is the Carrot Better than the Stick? *Employee Relations,* **16**(8), 5–18.

Dickens, L. 1998: What HRM Means for Gender Equality. *Human Resource Management Journal,* **8**(1), 23–40.

Dickens, L. 1999: Beyond the Business Case: A Three-pronged Approach to Equality Action. *Human Resource Management Journal,* **9**(1), 9–19.

Dickens, L. and Hall, M. 1995: The State: Labour Law and Industrial Relations. In P. Edwards (ed.), *Industrial Relations: Theory and Practice in Britain,* Oxford: Blackwell.

Dickens, L., Townley, B. and Winchester, D. 1988: *Tackling Sex Discrimination through Collective Bargaining.* London: HMSO.

Donaghy, R. 1995: Trade Unions and Equal Opportunities. In J. Shaw and D. Perrons (eds), *Making Gender Work,* Milton Keynes: Open University Press.

EOC (Equal Opportunities Commission) 1986: *Guidelines for Equal Opportunities Employers.* Manchester: EOC.

EOC 1988: *Local Authority Equal Opportunities Policies: Report of a Survey by the EOC.* Manchester: EOC.

EOC 1990: *Equal Pay for Men and Women: Strengthening the Acts.* Manchester: EOC.

EOC 1991: *Equality Management.* Manchester: EOC.

EOC 1995: *Gender Equality Checklist.* Manchester: EOC.

EOC 1996: *Pay: Briefings on Women and Men in Britain.* Manchester: EOC.

EOC 1997a: *Code of Practice on Equal Pay.* Manchester: EOC.

EOC 1997b: *Equality in the 21st Century: A New Approach.* Manchester: EOC.

EOCNI (Equal Opportunities Commission for Northern Ireland) 1996: *Report on Formal Investigation into Competitive Tendering in Health and Education Services in Northern Ireland.* Belfast: EOCNI.

EOR (Equal Opportunities Review) 1989: Discrimination at Work. BIM Finds. No. 24, March/April, 3.

EOR 1990: Contract Compliance Assessed. No. 31, May/June, 26–8.

EOR 1992a: Opportunity 2000. No. 41, January/February, 20–6.

EOR 1992b: The Rising Cost of Injury to Feelings. No. 41, January/February, 30–5.

EOR 1993a: Action for Race Equality: An EOR Survey of Employer Initiatives. No. 48, March/April, 14–20.

EOR 1993b: Limited Progress in Civil Service Race Action Programme. No. 48, March/April, 8–9.

EOR 1996: Narrowing of Gender Pay Gap. No. 70, November/December, 34.

EOR 1997a: Implementing the DDA. No. 72, March/April, 18–25.

EOR 1997b: Improving Equality Law: The Options. No. 72, March/April, 28–34.

EOR 1998a: Mainstreaming EO in the Civil Service No. 79, May/June, 7.

EOR 1998b: Best Value, Best Equality? No. 79, May/June, 20–7.

EOR 1998c: Tackling Age Bias: Code or Law? No. 80, July/August, 32–7.

EOR 1998d. CRE Proposals for Race Law Reform. No. 80, July/August, 40.

EOR 1998e: Compensation Awards '97. No. 81, September/October, 13–19.

EOR 1998f: Littlewoods: Increasing Diversity, Increasing Profits. No. 81, September/October, 20–8.

EOR 1998g: Equal Opportunities and Monitoring in the NHS. No. 82, November/December, 25–7.

EOR 1998h: Gender Pay Gap Widens – Slightly. No. 82, November/December, 30.

Escott, K. and Whitfield, D. 1995: *The Gender Impact of CCT in Local Government.* Equal Opportunities Commission Research Discussion Series No. 12, Manchester: EOC.

European Commission 1996: *A Code of Practice on the Implementation of Equal Pay for Work of Equal Value for Men and Women.* Luxembourg: Office for Official Publications of the European Communities.

Felstead, A. 1995: The Gender Implications of Creating a Training Market: Alleviating or Reinforcing Inequality of Access. In J. Humphries and J. Rubery (eds), *The Economics of Equal Opportunities*, Manchester: EOC.

Fevre, R. 1989: Informal Practices, Flexible Firms and Private Labour Markets. *Sociology,* **23**(1), 91–109.

Figart, D. M. 1992: Is Positive Action 'Positive'? Collective Bargaining and Gender Relations in the Irish Civil Service. *Industrial Relations Journal,* **23**(1), 38–51.

Gilbert, K. and Secker, J. 1995: Generating Equality? Equal Pay, Decentralisation and the Electricity Supply Industry. *British Journal of Industrial Relations,* **33**(2), 190–207.

Green, F. 1991: Sex Discrimintion and Job-Related Training. *British Journal of Industrial Relations,* **29**(2), 295–304.

Green, F. and Zanchi, L. 1997: Trends in the Training of Male and Female Workers in the United Kingdom. *British Journal of Industrial Relations,* **35**(4), 635–44.

Greenslade, M. 1991: Managing Diversity: Lessons from the United States. *Personnel Management,* December, 28–33.

Hackett, G. 1988: Who'd be an Equal Opportunity Manager? *Personnel Management,* April, 48–55.

Hall, M., Lister, R. and Sisson, K. 1998: *The New Law on Working Time: Managing the Implications of the 1998 Working Time Regulations.* London and Coventry: IRS and IRRU.

Hammond, V. 1997: Cultural Change and Equal Opportunities: Learning from Opportunity 2000. *Equal Opportunities Review,* No. 75, September/October, 14–22.

Hansard Society Commission. 1990: *Women at the Top.* London: Hansard Society for Parliamentary Government.

Heery, E. 1998: Campaigning for Part-time Workers. *Work Employment and Society,* **12**(2), 351–66.

Hitner, T., Knights, D., Green, E. and Torrington, D. 1981: Races at Work: Equal Opportunity Policy and Practice. *Employment Gazette,* September.

Holland, L. 1988: Easy to Say, Hard to Do: Managing an Equal Opportunity Programme. *Equal Opportunities Review,* No. 20, July/August, 16–21.

Holtermann, S. and Clark, L. 1992: *Parents' Employment Rights and Childcare.* EOC Research Discussion Series No. 4, Manchester: EOC.

Horrell, S., Rubery, J. and Burchell, B. 1989: Unequal Jobs or Unequal Pay? *Industrial Relations Journal,* **20**(3), 176–91.

Humphries, J. and Rubery, J. (eds) 1995: *The Economics of Equal Opportunities.* Manchester: EOC.

IDS (Incomes Data Services) 1996: *Opportunity 2000.* Study 597, March.

IDS 1997: *Promoting Racial Equality.* Study 625, May.

Iles, P. and Auluck, R. 1989: From Racism Awareness Training to Strategic Human Resource Management in Implementing Equal Opportunity. *Personnel Review*, **18**(4), 24–32.

Iles, P. and Auluck, R. 1991: The Experience of Black Workers. In M. Davidson and J. Earnshaw (eds), *Vulnerable Workers*, Chichester: Wiley.

IPD (Institute of Personnel and Development) 1996: *Managing Diversity*. London: IPD.

IRRR (Industrial Relations Review and Report) 1990a: Recruiting and Retaining Women Workers. Recruitment and Development Report 6, June London: Industrial Relations Services.

IRRR 1990b: Ethnic Monitoring – Policy and Practice. December, No. 478, 4–11.

IRS (Industrial Relations Services) 1995: Implementation of Racial Equality Policies Disappointing, Says CRE. *Labour Market Trends*, 578, 2–3.

IRS 1997: Historic Single Status Deal in Local Government. *Employment Trends*, 639, September, 5–10.

Jeffery, M. 1995: The Commission Proposals on 'Atypical Work': Back to the Drawing Board... Again? *Industrial Law Journal*, **24**(3), 296–9.

Jenkins, R. 1986: *Racism and Recruitment: Managers, Organisations and Equal Opportunity in the Labour Market*. Cambridge: Cambridge University Press.

Jenkins, R. and Solomos, J. 1987: Equal Opportunity and the Limits of the Law: Some Themes. In R. Jenkins and J. Solomos (eds), *Racism and Equal Opportunity Policies in the 1980s* Cambridge: Cambridge University Press.

Jewson, N. and Mason, D. 1986: The Theory and Practice of Equal Opportunities Policies: Liberal and Radical Approaches. *Sociological Review*, **34**(2), 307–33.

Jewson, N., Mason, D., Waters, S. and Harvey, J. 1990: *Ethnic Minorities and Employment Practice. A Study of Six Organisations*. Research Paper 76, London: Employment Department.

Kandola, R. and Fullerton, J. 1994: *Managing the Mosaic: Diversity in Action*. London: IPD.

Labour Market Trends 1997: Industrial and Employment Appeal Tribunal Statistics, 1994–95 and 1995–96. April, 151–5.

Labour Research 1995a: Black Men Paid Fifth Less than Whites. June, 4.

Labour Research 1995b: Disappearing Municipal Equality. March, 15–16.

Leach, B. 1989: Disabled People and the Implementation of Local Authorities' Equal Opportunities Policies. *Public Administration*, **67**, Spring, 65–93.

Lee, G. 1987: Black Workers and their Unions. In G. Lee and R. Loveridge (eds), *The Manufacture of Disadvantage*, Milton Keynes: Open University Press.

Lee, G. and Wrench, J. 1987: Race and Gender Dimensions of the Youth Labour Market: From Apprenticeship to YTS. In G. Lee and R. Loveridge (eds), *The Manufacture of Disadvantage*, Milton Keynes: Open University Press.

LEVEL 1987: *A Question of Earnings: A Study of Earnings of Blue Collar Employees in London Local Authorities*. London: London Equal Value Steering Group.

Liff, S. 1997: Two Routes to Managing Diversity: Individual Differences or Social Group Characteristics. *Employee Relations*, **19**(1), 11–26.

Liff, S. 1999: Diversity and Equal Opportunities: Room for a Constructive Compromise? *Human Resource Management Journal*, **9**(1), 65–75.

Liff, S. and Cameron, I. 1997: Changing Equality Cultures to Move Beyond 'Women's Problems'. *Gender Work and Organisation*, **4**(1), 35–46.

Lipman-Blumen, J. 1976: Toward a Homosocial Theory of Sex Roles: An Explanation of the Sex Segregation of Social Institutions. In M. Blaxall and B. Reagan (eds), *Women and the Workplace*, London: University of Chicago Press.

Loden, M. 1998, cited in Workplace Diversity – New Challenges, New Opportunities. *Equal Opportunities Review*, March/April, 18–24.

Lovenduski, J. 1989: Implementing Equal Opportunities in the 1980s: An Overview. *Public Administration*, **67**, Spring, 7–18.

McColgan, A. 1995: Equal Pay, Market Forces and CCT. *Industrial Law Journal*, **24**, 368–71.

McCrudden, C. (ed.) 1991: *Fair Employment Handbook*. London: Industrial Relations Services.

McCrudden, C. 1992: Affirmative Action and Fair Participation: Interpreting the Fair Employment Act 1989. *Industrial Law Journal*, **21**(3).

Maguire, M. 1986: Recruitment as a Means of Control. In K. Purcell et al. (eds), *The Changing Experience of Employment*, Basingstoke: Macmillan Educational.

Manwaring, T. 1983: The Extended Internal Labour Market. *Cambridge Journal of Economics*, **8**(2), 166–9.

Mason, D. and Jewson, N. 1992: Race, Equal Opportunity Policies and Employment Practice. *New Community*, October.

Miller, D. 1996: Equality Management – Towards a Materialist Approach. *Gender Work and Organisation*, **3**(4), 202–14.

Moralee, L. 1998: Self Employment in the 1990s. *Labour Market Trends*, **106**(3), 121–30.

Ollerearnshaw, S. and Waldeck, R. 1995: Taking Action to Promote Equality. *People Management*, **23**, February, 24–7.

Opportunity 2000 1994: *Third Annual Report*. London: Business in the Community.

Perrons, D. and Shaw, J. 1995: Recent Changes in Women's Employment in Britain. In J. Shaw and D. Perrons (eds), *Making Gender Work*, Milton Keynes: Open University Press.

Philips, A. and Taylor, B. 1980: Sex and Skill: Notes Towards a Feminist Economics. *Feminist Review*, Vol. 6.

Phizacklea, A. and Miles, R. 1987: The British Trade Union Movement and Racism. In G. Lee and R. Loveridge (eds), *The Manufacture of Disadvantage*, Milton Keynes: Open University Press.

Pirani, M., Yolles, M. and Bassa, E. 1992: Ethnic Pay Differentials. *New Community*, **19**(1), 31–42.

Purcell, K. 1988: Gender and the Experience of Employment. In D. Gallie (ed.), *Employment in Britain*, Oxford: Blackwell.

Rubery, J. 1995: Performance Related Pay and the Prospects for Gender Pay Equity. *Journal of Management Studies*, **32**(5), 637–54.

Rubery, J. and Fagan, C. 1995: Comparative Industrial Relations: Towards Reversing the Gender Bias. *British Journal of Industrial Relations*, **33**(2), 210–35.

Salaman, G. 1986: *Working*. Chichester: Ellis Horwood.

Scott, A. 1994: Gender Segregation and the SCELI Research. In A. Scott (ed.), *Gender Segregation and Social Change*, Oxford: Oxford University Press.

Seddon, V. 1983: Keeping Women in their Place. *Marxism Today*, July, 20–2.

SERTUC (Southern and Eastern Region TUC) 1997: *Inching towards Equality*. London: SERTUC.

Sly, F. 1996: Disability and the Labour Market. *Labour Market Trends*, **104**(9), 413–24.

Sly, F., Thair, T. and Risdon, A. 1998a: Women in the Labour Market: Results from the Spring 1997 Labour Force Survey. *Labour Market Trends*, **106**(3), 97–105.

Sly, F., Thair, T. and Risdon, A. 1998b: Labour Market Participation of Ethnic Groups. *Labour Market Trends*, **106**(12), 601–15.

Snell, M., Gluckich, P. and Porall, M. 1981: *Equal Pay and Opportunities*. Department of Employment Research Paper 20, London: HMSO.

Wainwright Trust 1997: *Decentralisation and Devolution: The Impact on Equal Opportunities at Work*. Standon: The Wainwright Trust.

Webb, J. and Liff, S. 1988: Play the White Man: The Social Construction of Fairness and Competition in Equal Opportunities Policies. *Sociological Review*, **36**(3), 532–51.

Wood, S. 1986: Personnel Management and Recruitment. *Personnel Review*, **15**(2).

Woodall, J. 1996: Human Resource Management: The Vision of the Genderblind. In B. Towers (ed.), *The Handbook of Human Resource Management*, Oxford: Blackwell.

Woodall, J., Edwards, C. and Welchman, R. 1997: Organisational Restructuring and the Achievement of an Equal Opportunity Culture. *Gender Work and Organisation*, **4**(1), 2–12.

Worsley, R. 1996: Only Prejudices are Old and Tired. *People Management*, January, 18–23.

Wrench, J. 1987: Unequal Comrades: Trade Unions, Equal Opportunity and Racism. In R. Jenkins and J. Solomos (eds), *Racism and Equal Opportunity Policies in the 1980s*, Cambridge: Cambridge University Press.

Young, K. 1987: The Space between Words: Local Authorities and the Concept of Equal Opportunities. In R. Jenkins and J. Solomos (eds), *Racism and Equal Opportunity Policies in the 1980s* Cambridge: Cambridge University Press.

Part 3

Employee Development

7

Towards the Learning Organization?

Ewart Keep and Helen Rainbird

The inadequacies of training and development and the need for reform of the institutional frameworks in the UK have been long-running issues in personnel management as our chapters in previous editions (Keep 1989, 1994; Rainbird 1994) have described in detail. The ability of organizations to develop the skills and knowledge to do present and future jobs, which roughly translated is what training and development is about, has been critically affected by the wider national vocational and education system. Justifying investment in intangibles such as training and development is not easy at the best of times. It is difficult to prove the benefits and there is always the fear that it will be the employees who will benefit, rather than the organization, because the skills make them a more marketable commodity in a free labour market. The essentially voluntarist approach, coupled with other features discussed in chapter 1, has made things even worse by creating something of a vicious circle which is akin to what economists term 'the prisoner's dilemma'. Organizations tend not to train for fear that other employers, instead of doing their share, will poach employees from them. In the circumstances, with short-term financial results so paramount, it is easy to persuade themselves that training and development are something of a luxury. More pragmatically, if they find they are short of a particular set of skills, they can solve the immediate shortage by recruiting trained workers or alternatively by subcontracting or using temporary workers – all of which are usually easier to justify in a crisis situation than the original investment in training and development. Furthermore, in the case of most occupations, employers in the UK are operating in a relatively low pay economy. This contributes to competitive strategies based on a 'low skills equilibrium' (Finegold and Soskice 1988) which has been used to characterize the UK economy.

The debate has taken on added urgency in recent years. An increasingly broader band of commentators and policy makers have urged a more general need for greater stress upon skills and knowledge as a source of competitive advantage, reflecting a number of interlinking trends said to be driving change in the way organizations in the developed world operate and compete. Thus it is argued that in the global marketplace organizations in developed countries can no longer compete solely or even mainly on the basis of price. Instead, they must offer a range of customized, tailor-made products and services.

Competitive advantage comes from the ability to offer high-quality, personalized service. At the same time, change in product ranges is massive and rapid. Organizations are ceaselessly having to learn to do new things, offer new services and to reorganize fundamentally the way they deliver to their customers, not least because product development lead times and life cycles are apparently becoming ever shorter (the example of personal computers and other consumer electronics is frequently used here). Finally, there is believed to be a massive and sustained shift throughout the developed world towards knowledge-intensive industries and a huge growth in the number of knowledge workers.

In the face of these changes, the only viable response, it is argued, at least for organizations located within the developed world, is to seek long-term competitive advantage via the utilization of the skills and knowledge of their employees. Their skills, viewed collectively, form the organization's core competences that provide it with features and attributes from which stem its unique competitive advantage. In order to develop and enhance these core organizational competences, organizations need to harness the power of organizational learning, and move from systems, processes and cultures that support individual learning towards higher levels of collective learning and skill acquisition. The aim is to achieve the 'learning organization' defined by Senge (1990: 4) as one 'where people continually expand their capacity to create the results they truly desire, where new and expansive patterns of thinking are nurtured, where collective aspiration is set free, and where people are continually learning to learn together'.

This chapter examines the concept of the 'learning organization' (LO) and explores whether it provides a viable blueprint for producing an integrated approach to training and development within organizations. Whilst it welcomes an approach that emphasizes the social context in which learning takes place as opposed to an emphasis on the individual, it finds the model of the learning organization at odds with the product market strategies of many organizations and weak in its conceptualization of power relations in the workplace. We also point to the absence of an institutional infrastructure in the UK capable of promoting more widespread investment in skills and the adoption of training and development practices which might contribute in some way towards meeting the goals of the learning organization.

The chapter is divided into six sections. We start with an analysis of the textbook model of the learning organization, examining the stages required to achieve this status as well as the theoretical assumptions about the nature of learning and business competition underpinning it. We then turn to the evidence based on individuals' experiences of training and survey evidence from companies and assess the extent to which this provides support for the existence of LOs. The third section discusses how the organizational barriers affect the ability of companies to adopt the model of the LO in their human resource strategies. The fourth section situates the objectives of the LO in the broader societal and economic environment in which companies operate and emphasizes the unsupportive institutional circumstances found in the UK. Finally, we conclude that although there is little evidence of the emergence of LOs or of product market strategies which would require such a commitment to learning there are nevertheless steps that can be made by organizations to create structures which are more conducive to promoting learning.

The Basic Concept

The LO has been seen by many as a significant development in the conceptualization of learning, skills and knowledge within an organizational setting. Between the late 1980s and the mid 1990s the concept of the LO rose to prominence and a considerable body of literature developed on the topic. The concept of the LO offers an idealized and, at first glance at least, highly attractive model of organizational development. In particular, it provides a broader strategic framework within which skills, training and development policies can be located, thereby providing training and HRM specialists with an approach for selling their wares to senior management. Instead of training and skills being a bolt-on extra, learning moves to centre stage and becomes the chief organizational principle around which business strategy and competitive advantage can be developed.

Put simply, there are said to be three different states of learning within an organization: individuals within an organization learning things; organizational learning – where the organization as an entity starts to develop ways in which it can learn lessons collectively; and the learning organization – where the central organizational goal is systemic learning. The nature of the changes required becomes clearer when we examine the five-stage model of development of a learning organization proposed by Jones and Hendry (1992). The first three stages of the model (Foundation, Formation and Continuation) are taken to represent a state of organizational learning. Stages 4 and 5 (Transformation and Transfiguration) represent progression and transition to becoming a fully blown learning organization (see table 7.1).

Although the different authors who have analysed the LO have produced varying checklists of criteria which may be taken to characterize an LO, the differences are ones of detail rather than fundamentals, and a broadly representative example is outlined in table 7.2. For a fuller treatment of these models and a very useful review of the LO literature, see Mabey et al. (1998).

The LO literature also relies heavily on a number of theoretical models of individual learning (most notably that developed by Kolb 1984). The central question for an LO is how to foster moves from single-loop learning to the more advanced states of double- and triple-loop learning and how to manage the collectivization of individual learning through cultural norms and new forms of organizational structure (such as project teams and quality improvement groups) (see Pedler et al. 1991; Jones and Hendry 1994; and Swieringa and Wierdsma 1992 for a detailed treatment of these issues).

A number of comments need to be made about these models. The first relates to what is perhaps the greatest strength of the concept – its emphasis on a systemic approach to learning within an organization. One of the marked counter-trends over the last decade has been an increasing emphasis on shifting more and more responsibility for training and development on to the individual employee, reflecting expectations that, given a process of almost continuous restructuring, the employer is less likely to benefit in the future than in the past. As has been suggested elsewhere (Keep 1997), this increasing focus on the individual is problematic, not least because it often appears to demand that the individual worker attempt to second guess, without access to reliable information, the demands of the wider economy and of current and future employers.

The LO literature's notion that learning and reflection need to be built into the routines and culture of management activities is also important, because the frequent inability to

Table 7.1   Stages in the development of a learning organization

---

Organizational learning

1   Foundation
Basic skills development, plus equipping learners with habits and enthusiasm to learn more.
Basic HRD strategies to motivate and build confidence for further learning

2   Formation
Organization encourages and develops skills for self-learning and self-development, helps individual learn about the organization and their place in it. Opportunity and resources are made available to meet demand for learning

3   Continuation
The learner and organization are becoming more innovatory, independent and self-motivated. HRD promotes learning on an individual basis, with tailor-made learning experiences

Step change/Paradigm shift
Learning Organization

4   Transformation
A complete change in the form, appearance and character/culture of the organization. HRM characterized by fairness, openness, flexibility, meritocracy. Ethical considerations important in general business management

5   Transfiguration
People come first and a concern for society's welfare and betterment
The organization represents a way of life to be cherished because of its values
Learning is at the centre of activities
Lack of concern about credentials
The organization is instructing and controlling itself by means of total involvement in the community
The organization is judged by the extent to which the people who make it up control and teach the organization how to learn, rather than vice versa
No formal appraisals

Source: Adapted from Jones and Hendry (1992)

achieve this goal has been one of the continuing failures of the UK training scene. In marked contrast to the much-vaunted Japanese approach to in-company training and development (Koike 1997), in UK organizations training all too often continues to be a marginal activity that is regarded as an optional extra rather than as an activity integral to the process of production. The LO concept is useful in posing questions about how organizations can go about building developmental and learning activities into the every-day fabric of what they do.

A less helpful aspect is the language in which some of the literature is couched and its underlying inability to confront the harsh realities that face many organizations. An example would be Jones and Hendry's (1992) description of the final stage of development in an LO (Transfiguration), where people come first and the organization is driven by a concern for society's general welfare and betterment, and where the emphasis is on people developing themselves as individuals and being allowed to do what they want to rather than what other people (perhaps their managers) deem appropriate (pp. 30–1).

The problem with this kind of 'communitarian' vision is that, however attractive it may appear to organizational development specialists, it has at best limited resonance with

Table 7.2   Characteristics of a learning organization

A learning organization:
- capitalizes on uncertainty as a source of growth
- creates new knowledge as a central part of competitive strategy
- embraces change
- encourages accountability at the lowest level
- encourages managers to act as mentors, coaches and learning facilitators
- has a culture of feedback and disclosure
- has a holistic, systemic view of the organization and its systems, processes, and relationships
- has a shared organization-wide vision, purpose and values
- has leaders who encourage risk taking and experimentation
- has systems for sharing knowledge/learning and using it in the business
- is customer driven
- is involved in the community
- links employees' self-development to the development of the organization as a whole
- networks within the business community
- provides frequent opportunities to learn from experience
- avoids bureaucracy and turf wars
- has a high-trust culture
- strives for continuous improvement
- structures, fosters and rewards all types of teams
- uses cross-functional work teams
- views the unexpected as an opportunity to learn

Source: Adapted from Marquardt and Reynolds (1994)

senior line managers facing the reality of short-term pressures to minimize cost and boost bottom-line performance. 'Transfiguration' is not merely not on their immediate agenda, it has very little to do with what most organizations, certainly in the private sector, but even much of the reformed public sector, are tasked with doing. Within the confines of the Anglo-Saxon model of capitalism, the full-blown LO model looks suspiciously idealistic and perhaps unrealistic. Indeed Scarbrough et al. (1998) suggest that one of the reasons for the recent eclipse of the LO concept by models of knowledge management is the former's failure to resonate with the competitive agenda in many organizations.

A related point is the LO concept's underlying assumptions about competitive strategy and organizational architecture. The implicit belief is that competitive advantage comes from customization, ceaseless innovation and high specification, high-quality goods and services delivered by flat, non-hierarchical organizations where workers enjoy considerable empowerment. The LO model sits poorly with Taylorism and Fordism.

As will be argued below, it is open to question if Fordism is dead, at least in large swathes of the UK service sector, or whether the force of Tayloristic systems of job design and work organization is yet spent. At the very least, it seems important to underline the fact that counter-balancing the language of delayering, devolved management, empowerment and stress on the problem solving, creativity and innovation of individual workers, are the persistence of work regimes based on command and control systems, scripted interactions with customers, routinization of work tasks and often high levels of surveillance (on the latter point see, for example, Collinson and Collinson 1997). The battle between these two opposite visions, a battle often being fought out within individual organizations, is of fundamental importance within UK management as it enters the twenty-first century. Although management gurus, futurologists and many proponents of the LO model imply that the triumph of empowerment and creativity over command and control (theory Y as opposed to theory X) is inevitable, the evidence adduced below and in other chapters in this volume suggests that this may not be so in all cases.

In any event, it is clear that many of the organizations who have been attracted to the idea of the LO have, in fact, been aiming more for enhanced organizational learning than for the full-blown model. This is hardly surprising given the requirements, in terms of value and culture change, that the textbook LO model demands. It is also apparent that the kinds of structural, procedural and cultural characteristics specified in the Marquardt and Reynolds model outlined earlier represent hurdles of varying heights for different organizations. Across a whole range of areas of managerial decision making, such as competitive and product market strategy, leadership style, organizational culture, job design, work organization, team design and operation, reward systems, control and reporting structures, management style and functions, appraisal and development systems, and information and participation procedures, any attempt to move towards higher levels of organizational learning will be encouraged or constrained by the prevailing norms, which will vary considerably between organizations.

A final point to make about this body of literature is that, as with many other areas of management writings, the bulk of what is available concentrates on definitional argument, model building, and is prescriptive. Broadly based, in-depth, longitudinal research of how the concepts and models play out in real-life organizations is in very short supply, and even detailed case studies are few in number (see Marquardt 1996 for examples of what is available). In the UK, many of the examples seem to come from within the NHS, and the leading private-sector company associated with the concept has been the Rover Group. This organization's recent problems suggest that the timescale for any project to become a learning company and witness concrete effects on the bottom line, may be lengthy.

Moreover, while the LO literature displays a detailed interest in theoretical models of workplace learning (such as that advanced by Kolb 1984; and Swieringa and Wierdsma 1992), their practical utility may be limited. As Ashton (1998: 68) observes, 'learning theories derived from experimental observations and studies of the cognitive process abstracted from the realities of the organizational context are of little relevance to the practitioner . . . struggling to understand the process of learning as embedded in organizational structures'. Unfortunately, the LO literature on the whole offers limited recognition, and in some cases none, to wider research that has been undertaken into what actually takes place in terms of learning in the workplace (for examples of which, see Maguire 1997; Tavistock Institute 1998a; Darmon et al. 1998; Eraut et al. 1998; Ashton 1998). As will be suggested below, there is much that can be learned from this detailed, fieldwork-based research.

The Nature and Extent of Training and Development

If large numbers of employers had succeeded in achieving the objective of becoming learning organizations, we would expect to find this reflected in a number of ways. First, we would find evidence that individuals were able to access formal training and informal learning opportunities in the workplace. Second, it would be possible to identify the adoption of training and development practices which could be considered as indicative of a commitment to the ideals of the learning organization. In this section, sources of evidence on individuals' experiences of training and development are examined, alongside survey evidence of company practices, updating the analyses we made in the second edition of this volume of vocational education and training provision for the young (Keep 1994) and the continuing training of adult workers (Rainbird 1994).

Individual experiences

There are two distinctive features of British provision of vocational education and training for young people. The first has been the tradition of early school leaving. Until very recently, the majority of young people left education at the age of 16 and entered the labour market. This contrasted with most other developed industrial economies, where a far higher proportion of the 16 to 18 year age cohort remained in education, accompanied by an earlier development of mass, as opposed to elite, higher education systems. The education system in England and Wales has been characterized by early selection and low participation (Finegold et al. 1990) although the Scottish education system with its broader curriculum has achieved significantly higher participation rates (Raffe 1991). Despite these observations, a combination of changes in employers' demand for young workers and a shift towards service-sector employment have contributed to decline in the proportion of 16 year olds entering work from 62 per cent in 1975 to only 9 per cent in 1992. This has been accompanied by a sharp rise in the numbers remaining in full-time education post-16: by 1994–95 72 per cent of 16 year olds and 59 per cent of 17 year olds were in full-time education (Evans et al. 1997: 50). One of the knock-on effects of this growth has been its effect on the student population in higher education. In 1979 just one in ten young people entered higher education. By 1997 this had risen to almost one in three (DfEE 1998a), and between 1980–81 and 1990–91 overall student numbers grew by 42 per cent, the growth of participation by women, mature and part-time students being particularly strong (National Commission on Education 1993: 293).

It might be assumed that employers would compensate for the relatively low levels of educational attainment which, historically, have characterized new recruits into employment by having effective systems of vocational training. On the contrary, weaknesses in education participation and qualification have been reinforced by the second major failure of vocational education and training (VET) provision: the failure of employers to offer structured training to young recruits. Provision in the form of the institution of apprenticeship existed primarily in manufacturing industry, but between 1970 and 1990 apprentice numbers plummeted from 218,000 to 53,600 (Keep 1994: 310). Although partly reflecting the decline in manufacturing employment, the proportion of apprentices in the workforce also declined during this period, with government training schemes, such as the Youth Training Scheme and Youth Training contributing to this outcome (Marsden and Ryan 1989). Outside manufacturing industry, and especially in the services sector, there has been little formal training for early school-leavers, the one exception being hairdressing.

Perceived weaknesses in the VET system, in the quantity and the quality of training, evident in young people's acquisition of vocational qualifications gave rise to a series of reforms to youth training which are documented in Keep (1994). Yet the persistence of weaknesses in foundation training delivered by a voluntary system are all too apparent, leading Harrison (1997: vii) of the IPD to argue:

> For many observers, the present system of education and training for young people is not delivering the quality foundation learning that all interested parties are committed to. Few of the National Targets for Education and Training for the year 2000 look likely to be reached. The funding systems that support and drive education and training provision are out of alignment with the objectives they seek to achieve. Sir Ron Dearing's recommendations for qualifications for 16–19 year-olds are not in themselves sufficient to solve the deep-seated problems afflicting the education and training system.

Two positive developments need mention. The first of these has been the reinstatement of apprenticeship as a model for work-based learning through modern apprenticeships (MAs), introduced by the Conservative Government in 1993. This has allowed public funding to support apprenticeship arrangements in the sectors where they have continued to exist and for their extension into new sectors of the economy, representing the creation of a relatively high-quality work-based education and training route. For a full review of the development and extent of modern apprenticeships see Maguire (1999). The second has been the provision under the Teaching and Higher Education Bill (1997) of a statutory entitlement for 16 and 17 year olds to have time off during working hours to undertake study or training leading to a relevant qualification.

The initial education and training of young people undoubtedly shape their attitudes towards learning throughout their working lives. The evidence suggests that, to date, this has been inadequate compared the experiences of their counterparts in other developed economies. There are therefore weaknesses in the foundations on which employers build their human resource development strategies. This has consequences, for managers' ability to adapt work organization to external competitive pressures, on the one hand, and for employees' own ability to learn and adapt, on the other.

So far, we have dealt with only the weaknesses in educational qualifications and initial vocational training in the UK workforce. If the objective is to achieve what Senge (1990: 1) defines as an organization 'where people continually expand their capacity to create the results they truly desire', then the evidence on individuals' experience of continuing training in employment requires examination. In an assessment of the nature and extent of continuing training (Rainbird 1994), the weaknesses of the British data on individuals' experiences was highlighted. The major source is the annual Labour Force Survey which records training received by the individual in the four weeks prior to the survey. Nevertheless, there may be differing perceptions of what constitutes training: employees may only consider formal off-the-job training in these terms and discount on-the-job instruction and forms of learning which are more closely related to the transmission of organizational culture. Indeed, it is important to distinguish learning from training. For example, Eraut et al. (1998) have demonstrated that, certainly as far as highly qualified workers are concerned, the work environment itself is significant in providing learning opportunities through problem-solving activities and learning from colleagues and mentors which are unrelated to formal instruction.

The Department for Education and Employment reports that a further education college or a university is the most common location for off-the-job training received by employees (DfEE, 1996). An analysis of the sources of access to training reported in the Labour Force Survey demonstrates that training on employers' premises accounts for approximately one-third of continuing training, with 40 per cent of men's and nearly 50 per cent of women's continuing training being provided by education institutions (Payne 1992).

Age, gender, ethnicity, educational background, hours of work and employment status exert considerable influence on individuals' access to learning, reinforcing patterns of inequality. Those lacking in initial educational qualifications are least likely to participate in continuing training at work and in adult education outside the workplace. As far as adults' experiences of workplace-related training is concerned Clarke's (1991: 41–2) analysis of the 1989 Labour Force Survey data concluded:

> The pattern of training provision for adult employees is a complex one with different groups of women and men having very different access to continuing training. Women part-timers in all occupations have substantially less access to training than full-time employees, both women and men. Since a high proportion of women spend at least part of their working life in part-time employment, and over two fifths of all women employees currently work part-time, this is a major source of disadvantage for women in the labour market. Other groups of adult workers who are disadvantaged in terms of training are manual workers (the majority of whom are men), employees in small workplaces (who are disproportionately women) and employees in the private manufacturing sector (the majority of whom will be men).

This complex pattern continues to exist (McGivney 1997; Blundell et al. 1996). The relatively disadvantaged groups when it comes to access to adult education and training provision appear to be women, those with literacy and numeracy difficulties, people with few or no qualifications, ethnic and linguistic minorities, older adults, people with special needs and disabilities and ex-offenders (McGivney 1997: 131). 'In other words, those who ostensibly have the greatest need participate the least' (McGivney 1997: 131). In 1997, the report of the National Advisory Committee on Continuing Education and Lifelong Learning was still able to observe that although there were many 'successful and imaginative elements of lifelong learning already occuring in the country' they did not add up to 'a learning culture for all'. One in three adults had taken no part in education or training since leaving school and a similar proportion reported that their employer had never offered them any kind of training (Fryer 1997: 1–2).

Survey evidence of company training practices

Unlike other countries which collect systematic data on training expenditure under the terms of their training legislation, there is little survey evidence in Britain on expenditure on training. Since the abolition of the Industrial Training Board's requirement on companies to complete levy returns, longitudinal industry-level data have not been collected.

(For a history of the Industrial Training Boards see Perry 1976 and Senker 1992.) The major national company training surveys are the Training in Britain survey (Deloitte Haskin & Sells 1989) and the Employers' Manpower and Skills Practices Survey (EMSPS) conducted by the (then) Department of Employment (see the series of working papers published by the Employment Department's Social Science Research Branch, for example, Dench 1993a and 1993b). In reviewing the findings of EMSPS, surveys of members conducted by the Institute of Personnel and Development and the Industrial Society, and research conducted by Felstead and Green (1994, 1996). Raper et al. (1997: 11) identify five major trends in company training practices:

1   the devolution of responsibility for training and development to line managers
2   the declining use of external, off-the-shelf courses
3   the increased use of in-company training
4   the increased use of on-the-job training, planned work experience and coaching
5   the influence of quality standards (such as BS5750 or ISO 9000) and health and safety regulations as motivators for training.

For a more detailed discussion of these changes and their implications for both line managers and training specialists, see Eraut et al. 1998, Tavistock Institute 1998, and Institute of Personnel and Development 1999.

Raper et al. (1997) report that the EMSPS survey found that managers perceived market competition and customer demand as the main influence on quality improvements, which might support the view that adaptability to changes in the market environment, a feature of the learning organization literature, was significant. Nevertheless, in specific areas legislation clearly plays a role and the more recent surveys show that training budgets have been cut. Managers have become more directly involved in training, not because of their commitment to the concept of the learning organization but because the shift from off-the-job to less expensive on-the-job training in the workplace has required it (Raper et al. 1997: 12).

Although at present there is little survey evidence which places training practices in the context of broader human resource policies, one yardstick is *Investors in People* the national training standard introduced in the wake of the *Training in Britain* survey of 1989 and reflecting its concerns about the nature and the extent of the training taking place. The very ambitious target was set of achieving 70 per cent or more of organizations with 200 or more employees and 35 per cent of those with 50 or more by the year 2000. Initially, take-up was very slow: by the middle of 1996, scarcely 10 per cent of organizations had achieved the target (Employee Development Bulletin 1996). By August 1998, however, 31 per cent of organizations with more than 200 employees and 16.8 per cent of organizations with more than 50 staff had gained IIP status, and many more (46.5 per cent of organizations with 200 plus employees and 26.2 per cent of those employing more than 50 people) had committed themselves to gaining IIP status (National Advisory Council for Education and Training Targets 1998: 74). Moreover, there is evidence to suggest that some organizations, although not signing up for the formal process, have none the less adopted the good practice laid down in IIP.

Further survey evidence will be available with the publication of the 1998 Workplace Employee Relations Survey in the autumn of 1999. The preliminary findings show that only 12 per cent of employers questioned reported that their employees received five days a year training and 27 per cent that most supervisors received training in employee relations skills (Cully et al. 1998: 10). This gives scant support to the view that the LO model has been adopted in the larger organizations (those with more than 25 employees) which are included in the survey. Given that these are the organizations which are most likely to have sophisticated HR and training practices, it can be assumed that these percentages would be even lower for smaller employers. In the words of the Tavistock Institute (1998a: 26), there was 'a significant gap between the language or discourse of companies who viewed themselves as learning organisations and regarded people as their most important asset, and the actual practices of these companies'.

Organizational Barriers to Learning

Our attention now turns to the considerable barriers to learning that exist within UK organizations and wider society. To begin with organizational barriers, key aspects of the people-management systems and structures of work organization and job design described in other chapters in this volume stand in the way of making learning the central pillar of organizational life and competitive advantage. Unless and until some of these are changed, more learning will often either be underutilized or wasted.

Work organization, people-management systems and competitive strategies

As Pevoto (1997: 212–13), reviewing another 'quick fix...cook book' on the learning organization, remarked:

> I keep asking myself why was this book written? What the world doesn't need is one more 'quick fix' book, or one more 'cook book' for how to make the organisation and its people work better. We have hundreds of those littering the shelves of authors, professors and libraries. I was reminded of the story of the farmer and the agricultural agent wherein the agricultural agent suggested the farmer attended a seminar on new farming methods, and the farmer replied, 'Why, I'm not farming now as well as I know how to'. The same could be said of organisations. Most are not managed or led now as well as people know how to.

This observation raises the important, and in much of the LO literature oft-ducked, issue of existing evidence on underemployment and the poor usage of existing levels of skills. The scale of the problem may be much larger than is generally held to be the case by employers and policy makers. In the UK, the evidence supplied by the Skills Survey (Green et al. 1997) suggests that underemployment and underutilization of existing qualifications held by employees may also be a reality for a substantial proportion of workers. The survey suggested that 32 per cent of degree holders believed themselves to be in jobs that did not require this qualification, 30.6 per cent of holders of sub-degree qualifications felt they were overqualified for their current jobs, and 22.4 per cent of workers with qualifications were in jobs where no qualification whatsoever was required.

These figures suggest that, in many organizations, before any more learning is attempted there need to be greater efforts to harness existing pools of expertise and knowledge.

In order to do this, issues concerning work organization and job design may need to be tackled. As research by Dench et al. (1998) has illustrated, despite the textbook models of worker empowerment and the demands by some employers for workers with better skills in communication, problem solving and creativity, in reality in many organizations 'the generally low level of autonomy allowed to employees especially in non-managerial roles and in less skilled jobs was a theme emerging from many of our in-depth interviews' (p. 58). Far from wanting self-monitoring, problem-solving innovators, Dench et al. (1998) conclude that, 'in reality most employers simply want people to get on with their job, and not to challenge things' (p. 61). In these organizations it continues to be the case that managers undertake the planning, thinking, design and decision-making elements of work, while the non-managerial workforce get on with following tightly defined procedures and taking orders from above. The scope for real organizational learning (and for the learning to be utilized productively) at all levels in the workforce is hence limited.

Another issue concerns power. Learning is, in essence, a political process in that it leads to change and the disorganization of existing patterns of influence and control. The problem is that, in some cases at least, it seems likely that the necessary change will disrupt the continuity of power relationships and hierarchies. A better-educated workforce made up of autonomous, polyvalent knowledge workers needs far fewer managers, and managers whose role is one of facilitator, not hander-out of orders. Much of the writing on learning organizations appears to assume that a huge change in the role of managers (for example Senge (1990) suggests that managers become servants of the workforce) is both possible and desirable. It is apparent that this is not likely always to be the case. Traditional models of management have cast managers as policemen and women, spies, controllers, dispensers of reward and punishment, sources of wisdom and expertise, order givers and arbitrators between competing claims. The new model of management tries to paint them as teacher, coach, mentor, facilitator, resource controller and 'servant' of the team.

It is not obvious that the majority of existing managers, recruited to perform the very different tasks of old model, possess the skills, behaviours and attitudes required to perform these new functions. Nor are the benefits for managers from such a dramatic change in roles clear. For example, if managers do become facilitators, with their ex-subordinates (now empowered) as the major source of competitive advantage, how do managers maintain their status and pay *vis-à-vis* the rest of the workforce?

This brings us to the wider problem of the LO's tendency to adopt, often implicitly rather than explicitly, a unitarist perspective. The emphasis on employers' and workers' mutual interest in learning in the learning organization model ignores the fundamental conflict embodied in the employment relationship between the employer and the employee. This is nowhere more evident than in management's desire to tap into the tacit skills of the workforce, which are embodied in collective knowledge of the production process, through mechanisms such as quality circles and suggestion schemes. Long ago, Marx (1976) recognized that tacit skills constituted a source of worker resistance to the degradation of manual work, commenting:

> The worker's continual repetition of the same narrowly defined act and the concentration of
> his attention on it teach him by experience how to attain the desired effect with the minimum

of exertion. But since there are always several generations of workers living at one time, and working together in the manufacture of a given article, the technical skill, the tricks of the trade thus acquired, become established, and are accumulated and handed down (p. 458).

If workers are to allow management to learn from this source of expertise it raises serious questions about the guarantees that will be given to employees in exchange. Although management literature points to the need for employee commitment to the organization, there is little evidence of an understanding that this requires a reciprocal commitment to the employee. Scarbrough et al. point out that the incentives needed to underpin employee commitment are rarely addressed. They cite a KPMG (Scarbrough 1998) survey of 100 leading businesses which found that 39 per cent of respondents said that their organization did not reward knowledge sharing and that this was considered one of the most important barriers to storing and sharing knowledge (p. 51–2)

The structures of work organization and job design prevalent in many UK organizations are not the only barrier to the LO concept. Given the choice between trying to get employees to work harder/longer or to get them to do more by working in smarter ways, the evidence suggests that many (perhaps most) British organizations appear to prefer the tried and tested route of increasing working hours.

British workers currently work the longest hours in the EU, with a third doing more than 48 hours per week, and the UK is the only EU member state in which the average length of the working week has increased over the last decade (Milne and Elliott 1999). In many UK organizations, a long-hours culture has become entrenched, with the standard response to increased market or customer pressures being simply to add further to the workload and working time of existing employees (Kodz et al. 1998). Evidently, long working hours render it more difficult for staff to find the time and energy to learn (the more so in organizations where the current norm is for more and more learning to be undertaken in the employee's own time rather than during working hours).

Perhaps the fundamental point is implicit in this example. The notion that a set of universalistic trends and competitive pressures is impelling organizations towards competition based on organizational learning is seriously flawed. Alternative avenues to competitive advantage remain viable, at least in the UK, and price-based competition continues to thrive above all in the service sector (see Keep and Mayhew 1998). The figures on underemployment and working time reflect the fact that many organizations, far from opting for the high skills route to competitive success (Keep and Mayhew 1996a, 1998; Regini 1995; Ackroyd and Procter 1998; Foundation for Manufacturing Industry/Department of Trade and Industry/IBM 1996), remain wedded to standardized, low-specification goods and services where the main factor of competitive advantage is consistent delivery of relatively simple goods and services at a low price. This Fordist or Neo-Fordist strategy is in turn reflected in Tayloristic forms of work organization that minimize the opportunities for creativity and discretion.

Not only that. If there is one thing the LO literature makes clear, it is that the whole project of becoming an LO is a long-term venture. It is not going to be accomplished in six months or a year. This means the organization has to maintain commitment, invest over a long time-period and stick with a strategy over several years. The evidence suggests that very few UK organizations are capable of this, reflecting the key features of the business system outlined in chapter 1. Merger and acquisition, rather than internal growth through

R&D activity, are the favoured route to 'success'. The evidence from the DTI's 1997 R&D scorecard international benchmarking exercise showed that in the last five years UK companies reinvestment of sales in R&D was the lowest in the G7 group of leading industrialized countries (*Guardian* 1997) (see also DTI 1997; Buxton 1998).

The pathology of failing to master the basics

A major problem in much of the prescriptive literature on the LO is its near-automatic assumption that those running relatively large, sophisticated organizations, well equipped with specialist managers, will be capable of mastering the basic technologies and processes upon which their firms' operations were based and of moving from simple single-loop learning (Kolb 1984) towards more complex and reflexive models of learning. The evidence of recent history suggests that such assumptions are not always correct, that even the most rudimentary single-loop learning is sometimes too demanding, and that in some cases managers are actually either incapable of or uninterested in mastering the basics of their trade, often with spectacularly disastrous results.

A few examples will suffice. British and Commonwealth started out life as a shipping company, but during from the late 1960s moved away from this into finance and brokerage activities. In the late 1980s the company decided to buy a US computer leasing company (an area of activity about which B&C knew little). A huge sum was expended purchasing a major US player, only to discover subsequently that the US company's figures were fraudulent and much of its business fictitious. B&C collapsed with losses of £500 million.

In the case of Barings Bank, the official inquiry (Board of Banking Supervision 1995) into its collapse makes it clear that the senior managers had at best limited, and at worst no, understanding of the operation of the futures markets in which Nick Leeson was trading and upon which they were ultimately willing to stake a sum in excess of the net worth of the company. The report not does make it clear whether the underlying cause of this fatal lapse was an unwillingness to learn or a lack of the intellectual capacity to master the topic. In any event, the consequences were spectacular.

To offer a final example of these problems from the field of personnel management, we need look no further than the privatized train-operating company, South West Trains. Apparently unaware of the experience in the docks and elsewhere in similar circumstances, the management decided to offer an enhanced redundancy package to their drivers in order to reduce headcount and save long-term costs. The terms of the package were attractive and many drivers decided to avail themselves of the offer. Having let the drivers leave, management discovered that there were now insufficient staff to cover all the timetabled train services. As a result, there were numerous train cancellations and the company was fined £1 million by the Office of the Rail Regulator for service levels in breach of the company's franchise agreement. The next year SWT had to offer £6,000 bonuses to drivers to give up their holiday entitlement in order to avoid further cancellations and fines.

The scale and consequences of these disasters suggest that in certain circumstances, which may be bound up with company culture, complacency and overconfidence, or the intellectual resources of senior management cadres, the barriers to learning can be profound. Moreover, while it could be argued that such examples of disastrous failure to master the basic building-blocks of a firm's activities/technologies/process/productive techniques are aberrations, there are much more widely applicable examples of senior managers failing to learn. One example would be UK management's heavy reliance on mergers and acquisitions as a source of competitive advantage. The balance of research evidence suggests quite clearly that, in the majority of cases, mergers fail to produce the expected benefits (Dickerson et al. 1995). Despite this evidence, the UK economy continues to witness a higher level of merger activity than any other developed country because of the significance of financial engineering in the UK's business system.

The UK – a Learning Society?

The ability of learning organizations to emerge would, in part, seem related to there being a supportive institutional environment within the wider society in which the organizations operate. It has been argued that some nation states (for example Japan), by virtue of elements of their societal organization, labour-market structures and cultural and historical inheritances constitute a learning society within which it is easier for individual organizations to improve and sustain organizational learning (Trivellato 1997).

The argument that societal influences are important seems a powerful one. Organizations exist within a wider societal environment, which may or may not be amenable to the improvement of organizational learning. While the external environment does not necessarily determine what happens, it does influence the likelihood of a given outcome, not least because managers and other employees have lives outside the organization and bring into employment perspectives, attitudes and expectations that are, at least in part, moulded by the culture and traditions of the wider society in which they live (Chisholm 1997).

In the UK, the notion of the learning society, region and city has become a popular one, and the creation of a learning society is now an element of official UK vocational education and training policy. Despite enthusiasm for the concept by policy makers, research undertaken for the Economic and Social Research Council's (ESRC) 'Learning Society' programme suggests that, in some respects at least, the UK has a long way to go before it becomes a learning society (Green 1998; Coffield 1997a 1997b; McGivney 1997; Keep and Mayhew 1996b). A number of structural and cultural characteristics, such as the enduring legacy of our class structure; short-termism; a relatively deregulated labour market that encourages high levels of labour turnover and the perception of labour as a commodity; a tradition of low-trust employee relations; a shareholder rather than stakeholder model of capitalism; and conceptions of management as doing/action rather than reflection and analysis, all suggest that the UK offers an environment that may be relatively hostile to the swift and easy development of high levels of organizational learning.

One example of these environmental factors is the generalized 'common sense' assumption within British society that intelligence and ability are distributed across the population so that a fixed proportion of any given age group will be capable of achieving high levels of learning and academic excellence (however defined). To some extent at least this belief is coupled with a normally unspoken belief that ability is in large part a reflection of social class, or as the following leaked Conservative Party election proposals by former minister

John Maples put it, 'while ABC 1s can conceptualise, C2s and Ds often cannot. They can relate only to things they can see and feel. They absorb their information and often views from television and tabloids. We have to talk to them in a way they understand' (*Financial Times*, 21 November 1994: 10).

Attitudes such as these go some way towards explaining the tendency for workers in manual occupations to receive little training. Besides the limited nature of the jobs they occupy, in many cases their managers may believe that training would be wasted on them. Obviously the vision that only a certain section (usually rather limited) of the population, and by implication the workforce, is capable of benefiting from training and development sits uneasily with the concept of an LO.

There are also two specific issues which have to be resolved if there is to be a more general move towards a learning society. On the face of it, these would seem to be more immediately amenable to the influence of policy makers. Yet there continues to be a reluctance to confront them, raising doubts about the seriousness of the commitment to 'joined-up policy', if not the concept of the learning society itself.

A question of partnership?

In the same way that the power relationship between the employer and the employee is rarely considered within the unitarist framework of the learning organization literature, the dynamics of workplace industrial relations are equally absent. Since the late 1980s there has been a surge in interest among British trade unions in training as an item on the 'new bargaining agenda' (Storey et al. 1993; Rainbird and Vincent 1996). Emerging in response to the recognition of the significance of skills to competitive strategy and, in the British context, the unions' progressive exclusion from authoritative decision making in training policy, this has been manifested in the development of demands for a worker's right to training and union involvement in workplace training committees. Since the election of the Labour Government in 1997, a discourse on social partnership on training and learning in the workplace has emerged in official documents such as the Green Paper *The Learning Age* (DfEE 1998b). This draws on experiences such as the Ford Motor Company's Employee Development and Assistance Programme and the UNISON/employer partnerships on employee development in the public sector (on the latter, see Munro et al. 1997) which have used joint approaches in initiating and managing learning programmes.

Despite the official discourse on social partnership on training, British management vehemently opposed the suggestion, in the new Labour Government's *Fairness at Work* White Paper published in 1998, that training should be a matter of collective bargaining. In the event, rather than emphasizing the significance of the joint regulation of training to large numbers of working people, government ministers compromised. The Employee Relations Bill published in early 1999 did not concede that the right to bargain on training should be included automatically where trade unions are recognized for the purpose of collective bargaining. Instead, it proposes rights to information and consultation on training which can be agreed on a voluntary basis, indicating that the government's consultations with employers and the CBI suggested that they were unready to accept a more extensive role for the trade unions in training.

Evidently, few British employers are disposed to European-style approaches to training and thus towards the forms of participation which would encourage joint approaches to learning. Some senior trade unionists, such as John Edmonds of the General, Municipal and Boilermakers' Union, have seen the incorporation of training into the bargaining agenda as a mechanism for moving the adversarial tradition of British industrial relations into the more co-operative forms of the 'European mainstream' (Storey et al. 1993). In contrast, Streeck (1992b) argues that it is essential for unions to maintain, alongside areas of co-operation on skill formation, a strong independent power base which can be mobilized when necessary (p. 252). The ideal of co-operation on learning embodied in the learning organization therefore requires a level of power sharing with employees and their representatives which is unanticipated in unitarist accounts. Indeed, the Tavistock Institute's (1998) review *Workplace Learning, Learning Culture and Performance Improvement* argues that despite the promise of stakeholder empowerment in much of this literature, the reality is of 'an agenda of powerholders interested in a more vibrant capitalism' (p. 9).

Paying for training

Government policy makers also seem to be reluctant to be precise in identifying responsibility for paying for training. In overall terms, they currently divide training/learning for adults into three categories: task-specific; general or transferable skills; and broader learning for intellectual development/leisure/wider adult life. The evidence suggests that, with few exceptions such as Rover and Ford, companies are willing to pay only for the first, are often wary of paying for the second (for fear that such skills will either be poached or will enable staff to leave), and usually have little or no interest in paying for 'blue-skies' learning under the third category (Metcalf et al. 1994).

The official position appears in the Green Paper, *The Learning Age*. This argues that '(i)ndividuals, employers and the state should all contribute, directly or through earnings foregone, to the cost of learning over a lifetime because all gain from this investment. Individuals enhance their employability and skills, businesses improve their productivity, and society enjoys wider social and economic benefits' (DfEE 1998b: 25). Yet the only aspect of workplace learning which is clearly identified for support on a shared basis between the state and employers is that of young people in work, modern apprenticeships being given as an example. For adults in work, it envisages the setting up of individual learning accounts whereby the state, the individual and (hopefully) the employer, will make contributions to a fund enabling individuals to undertake a course of study and training of their choice. In other words, the major initiative is aimed at employee development, with pump-priming support from the state for the first million individual learning accounts, rather than training that is directly related to current and future job needs. Moreover, the emphasis on individual responsibility evades the question of the institutional structures required to develop mechanisms for socializing the costs of investment, so that individual employers who do invest in training are not penalized by the poaching of trained workers by those that do not. A continued reliance on the market model seems unlikely to promote an 'ecology of skills' (Streeck 1992a) with incentives to organizations and individuals alike to invest in training and development, capable of allowing learning organizations to develop and thrive.

Conclusion

Perhaps the LO literature's greatest contribution to debates about learning, skills and knowledge is its implicit message that current obsessions with the individualization of learning are seriously misplaced and that the social and systemic dimensions of learning are the key determinants of how an organization successfully acquires, productively deploys, and develops its stock of skills. While interesting as a theoretical construct, however, the idea of the LO, may be of limited value in serving as a blueprint for skills policies in the majority of UK organizations. In particular, its lack of contact with the often harsh realities of cost and time pressures and external environmental constraints raises serious problems. Given the evidence presented above, it seems reasonable to argue that there is little chance of achieving any very high level of organizational learning in the following circumstances, all of which are too prominent in the UK: cost-based competition; standardized products and services; a heavy reliance on economy-of-scale advantages; low-trust relationships; hierarchical management structures; people-management systems that emphasize command, control and surveillance; an underlying belief that (whatever the overt rhetoric) people are a cost or a disposable factor of production; little slack or space for creativity; and a culture of blame where mistakes (particularly those of lower-status workers) are punished. Whether the majority of organizations will be able to surmount the cultural and environmental barriers that currently often prevent an effective collective approach to organizational learning remains to be seen.

Recognizing what is possible seems a crucial requirement if many organizations are to reap competitive advantage from a more concerted attempt to systematize and collectivize learning (Ashton 1998). Many organizations in the early to mid 1990s jumped on the LO bandwagon, at least in some cases without perhaps fully confronting what a wholehearted commitment to becoming an LO would imply for their competitive strategies, management structures and organizational culture. A first step might be to try to reorganize work systems and restructure job design in order to make better use of the existing stock of skills in the workforce. At present, in many organizations, a large stock of latent talent, skill and knowledge is being underutilized. A second and allied approach is to look for hidden pockets of undertraining and to identify those sections of the workforce who are currently being offered few if any opportunities to engage in learning. As Mabey and Salaman (1995) underline, it is crucial to try to make learning apply across the whole organization rather than simply in isolated pockets of (usually high-status) staff. There is copious research evidence (McGivney 1997) that tells us that structured learning opportunities tend to be concentrated on young entrants, managers and other workers with high levels of initial qualifications. Older workers, the outer layers of the flexible workforce, shopfloor and front-line staff and those with poor initial qualifications tend to lose out.

There are also a range of techniques that can not only boost the breadth of reach and effectiveness of structured learning opportunities within organizations, but which can also be deployed in support of cultural change within the organization that will assist in boosting the value of learning within the work routines of line managers and hence (in the longer term) within organizational strategy. These include better use of structured on-the-job training (Cannell 1997), mentoring and coaching, job rotation, visits, work shadowing, the development of high-quality teamworking practices, project work, and the better use of professional networks (for further details, see Eraut et al. 1998). Interestingly, in their review of the use of a wide range of informal and semi-structured devices whereby individuals learned in the workplace, Eraut et al. (1998: 41) note that 'very few of our positive examples resulted from organisation-wide strategies or initiatives. Most were relatively informal and initiated by middle managers, colleagues or the learners themselves.'

A final, crucial point concerns conceptions of the managerial task. For as long as managers in the UK see themselves primarily as doers, firefighters or as Action Man/Woman rather than as reflective practitioners, the scope for wide-reaching and permanent organizational change will remain limited. If learning at a fundamental and deep level is not at the heart of what it means to be a successful manager, it seems highly unlikely that organizational learning will easily take root within the organizations which these individuals manage and lead.

References and further reading

Ackroyd, S. and Procter, S. 1998: British Manufacturing Organisation and Workplace Industrial Relations: Some Attributes of the New Flexible Firm. *British Journal of Industrial Relations*, Vol. 36 No. 2, 163–83.

Ashton, D. 1998: Skill formation: redirecting the research agenda. In Coffield, F. (ed.), *Learning at Work*, Bristol: Policy Press, 61–9.

Blundell, R., Dearden, L. and Meghir, C. 1996: *Determinants of Effects of Work Related Training in Britain.* London: Institute of Fiscal Studies.

Board of Banking Supervision 1995: *The Report on the Collapse of Barings Bank.* London: HMSO.

Buxton, T. 1998: Overview: the foundations of competitiveness – investment and innovation. In Buxton, T., Chapman, P. and Temple, P. (eds), *Britain's Economic Performance*, 2nd edn, London: Routledge, 165–86.

Cannell, M. 1997: Practice makes perfect. *People Management*, Vol. 3 No. 5, 6 March, 26–33.

Chisholm, L. 1997: Lifelong Learning and Learning Organisations: Twin Pillars of a Learning Society. In Coffield, F. (ed.), *A National Strategy for Lifelong Learning.* Newcastle: University of Newcastle, 37–52.

Clarke, K. 1991: Women and learning. A Review, *Research Discussion Series*, No. 1, Manchester: Equal Opportunities Commission.

Coffield, F. 1997a: Nine Learning Fallacies and their Replacement by a National Strategy for Lifelong Learning. In Coffield, F. (ed.), *A National Strategy for Lifelong Learning*, Newcastle: University of Newcastle, 1–35.

Coffield, F. 1997b: A Tale of Three Little Pigs: Building the Learning Society with Straw. In Coffield, F. (ed.), *A National Strategy for Lifelong Learning.* Newcastle: University of Newcastle, 77–93.

Collinson, D. L. and Collinson, M. 1997: 'Delayering Managers': Time–Space Surveillance and its Gendered Effects. *Organisation*, Vol. 4 No. 3, 375–407.

Cully, M., O'Reilly, A., Millward, N., Forth, J., Woodland, S. and Bryson, A. 1998: *The 1998 Workplace Employee Relations Survey. First Findings.* London: HMSO.

Darmon, I., Hadjivassiliou, K., Sommerlad, E., Stern, E., Turbin, E. and Danau, D. 1998: Continuing vocational training: key issues. In Coffield, F. (ed.), *Learning at Work*, Bristol: Policy Press, 23–36.

Deloitte, Haskins and Sells, 1989: *Training in Britain. A Study of Funding, Activities and Attitudes.* London: HMSO.

Dench, S. 1993a: What types of employer train? *Employment Department Social Science Research Branch, Working Paper No. 3*, November.

Dench, S. 1993b: Why do employers train? *Employment Department Social Science Research Branch, Working Paper No. 5*, December.

Dench, S., Perryman, S. and Giles, L. 1998. Employers' perceptions of key skills. *IES Report 349*, Sussex: Institute of Employment Studies.

DfEE (Department for Education and Employment) 1996: *Training Statistics, 1996.* London, HMSO.

DfEE 1998a: *Labour Market and Skill Trends 1998/99.* Sudbury: DfEE.

DfEE 1998b: *The Learning Age. A Renaissance for a New Britain.* London: HMSO.

DTI (Department of Trade and Industry) 1997: *Competitiveness – our partnership with business – a benchmark for success.* London: HMSO.

Dickerson, A. P., Gibson, H. D. and Tsakolotos, E. 1995: The Impact of Acquisitions on Company Performance: Evidence from a Large Panel of UK Firms. *Studies in Economics*, No. 95/11, Canterbury: University of Kent (Department of Economics).

Employee Development Bulletin. 1996: 'Making capital out of Investors in People, EDB No 84, December, 11–16.

Eraut, M. 1994: *Developing Professional Knowledge and Competence.* Brighton: Falmer Press.

Eraut, M., Alderton, J., Cole, G. and Senker, P. 1998: Learning from other people at work. In Coffield, F. (ed.), *Learning at Work*, Bristol: Policy Press, 37–48.

Evans, K., Hodkinson, P., Keep, E., Maguire, M., Raffe, D., Rainbird, H., Senker, P. and Unwin, L. 1997: Working to Learn, a work-based route to learning for young people. *Issues in People Management*, No. 18, London: Institute of Personnel and Development.

Felstead, A. and Green, F. 1994: Training during the recession, *Work, Employment and Society*, Vol. 8, No. 2, 199–219.

Felstead, A. and Green, F. 1996: Cycles of training? Evidence from the British recession of the early 1990s. In Booth, A. and Snower, D. (eds), *The Skills Gap and Economic Activity*, Cambridge: Cambridge University Press.

Financial Times (1994): 21 November, 10.

Finegold, D. and Soskice, D. 1988: The failure of training in Britain: analysis and prescription. Oxford Review of Economic Policy, Vol. 4 No. 3, 21–53.

Finegold, D., Keep, E., Miliband, D., Ratte, D., Spours, K. and Young, M. 1990: A British Baccalaureat. Ending the Division Between Education and Training. *Education and Training Paper No. 1*, London: Institute of Public Policy Research.

Foundation for Manufacturing Industry/Department for Trade and Industry/IBM 1996: *Tomorrow's Best Practice: A Vision of the Future for Top Manufacturing Companies in the UK.* London: FMI.

Fryer, R. H. 1997: *Learning for the Twenty-First Century. First report of the National Advisory group for Continuing Education and Lifelong Learning.* November, Barnsley: Northern College.

Guardian (1997): 26 June.

Green, A. 1998: Core Skills, Key Skills and General Culture: In Search of the Common Foundation in Vocational Education. *Evaluation and Research in Education*, Vol. 12 No. 1, 23–43.

Green, F., Ashton, D., Burchell, B., Davies, B. and Felstead, A. 1997: An analysis of changing work skills in Britain. Paper presented to the Low Wage Employment Conference of the European Low Wage Employment Research Network, CEP, LSE, December.

Harrison, R. 1997: Foreword. In Evans, K. et al., Working to learn. A work-based route for young people. *Issues in People Management*, No. 18, London: Institute of Personnel and Development.

Institute of Personnel and Development 1999: *The Changing Role of Trainers*, London: IPD.

Jones, C. and Hendry, C. 1992: *The Learning Organisation: A Review of Literature and Practice.* London: HRD Partnership.

Jones, C. and Hendry, C. 1994: The learning organisation: Adult learning and organisational transformation. *British Journal of Management*, Vol. 5 153–62.

Keep, E. 1989: A Training Scandal? In Sisson, K. (ed.), *Personnel Management in Britain*, 1st edn, Oxford: Basil Blackwell, 177–202.

Keep, E. 1994: Vocational education and training for the young. In Sisson, K. (ed.), *Personnel Management. A Comprehensive Guide to Theory and Practice in Britain*. 2nd edn, Oxford: Basil Blackwell.

Keep, E. 1997: 'There's no such thing as society...': some problems with an individual approach to creating a Learning Society. *Journal of Education Policy*, Vol. 12 No. 6, 457–71.

Keep, E. and Mayhew, K. 1996a: Evaluating assumptions that underline training policy. In Booth, A. L. and Snower, D. J. (eds), *Acquiring Skills*, Cambridge: Cambridge University Press.

Keep, E. and Mayhew, K. 1996b: Towards a Learning Society – Definition and Measurement. *Policy Studies*, Vol. 17 No. 3, 215–31.

Keep, E. and Mayhew, K. 1998: Was Ratner right? – product market and competitive strategies and their links with skills and knowledge. *Employment Policy Institute Economic Report*, Vol. 12 No. 3.

Kodz, J., Kersley, B. and Strebler, M. 1998: Breaking the long hours culture. *IES Report 352*, Brighton: Institute of Employment Studies.

Koike, K. 1997: *Human Resource Management*. Tokyo: Japan Institute of Labour.

Kolb, D. 1984: *Experiential Learning*. Englewood Cliffs, NJ: Prentice-Hall.

Mabey, C. and Salaman, G. 1995: *Strategic Human Resource Management*. Oxford: Blackwell.

Mabey, C., Salaman, G. and Storey, J. (eds) 1998: *Strategic Human Resource Management; A Reader*, London: Sage.

Mabey, C., Salaman, G. and Storey, J. 1998: Learning Organizations. In Mabey, C., Salaman, G. and Storey, J. *Human Resource Management: A Strategic Introduction*: Oxford: Blackwell Publishers.

Maguire, M. 1997: Employee Development Schemes: Panacea or Passing Fancy? In Coffield, F. (ed.), *A National Strategy for Lifelong Learning*, Newcastle: University of Newcastle, 143–57.

Maguire, M. 1999: Modern apprenticeship: just-in-time or far too late? In Ainley, P. and Rainbird, H. (eds), *Apprenticeship. Towards a New Paradigm of Learning*, London: Kogan Page.

Marquardt, M. 1996: *Building the Learning Organisation*. London: McGraw-Hill.

Marquardt, M. and Reynolds, A. 1994: *The Global Learning Organisation*. Burr Ridge, IL: Irwin.

Marsden, D. and Ryan, P. 1989: Employment and training of young people: Have the government misunderstood the labour market? In Harrison, A. and Gretton, J. (eds), *Education and Training UK. Policy Journals*, 47–53.

McGivney, V. 1997: Adult Participation in Learning: Can We Change the Pattern? In Coffield, F. (ed.), *A National Strategy for Lifelong Learning*. Newcastle: University of Newcastle, 127–41.

Metcalf, H., Walling, A. and Fogarty, M. 1994: Individual Commitment to Learning: Employers' Attitudes. *Employment Department Research Series* 40, Sheffield: ED.

Milne, S. and Elliott, L. 1999: How rich and poor must both pay the price of a workplace revolution. *Guardian*, 4 January.

Munro, A., Holly, H. and Rainbird, R. 1997: *Partners in Workplace Learning. A Report on the UNISON/ employer Learning and Development Programme*. London: UNISON.

National Advisory Council for Education and Training Targets 1998: *Fast Forward for Skills*, London: NACETT.

National Commission on Education 1993: *Learning to Succeed. A Radical Look at Education Today and a Strategy for the Future*. London: Heinemann.

Payne, J. 1992: Motivating training. Paper presented to the Centre for Economic Performance's project on Vocational Education and Training, January.

Pedlar, M., Burgoyne, J. and Boydell, T. 1991: *The Learning Company*. London: McGraw-Hill.

Perry, P. J. C. 1976: *The Evolution of British Manpower Policy. From the Statute of Artificers 1593 to the Industrial Training Act 1964*. London: Eyre and Spottiswoode.

Pevoto, A. E. 1997: Book review, *The International Journal of Training and Development*, Vol. 1 No. 3, 212–13.

Raffe, D. 1991: Scotland v England: The place of home internationals in comparative research. In Ryan, P. (ed.), *International Comparisons of Vocational Education and Training for Intermediate Skills*. London: Falmer.

Rainbird, H. 1994: Continuing training. In Sisson, K. (ed.), *Personnel Management. A Comprehensive Guide to Theory and Practice in Britain*. 2nd edn, Oxford: Blackwell.

Rainbird, H. and Vincent C. 1996: Training: a new item on the bargaining agenda. In Leisinck, P., Van Leemput, J. and Vilrokx, J. (eds), *The Challenges to Trade Unions in Europe. Innovation or Adaptation*, Cheltenham: Edward Elgar.

Raper, P., Ashton, D., Felstead, D. and Storey, J. 1997: Toward the learning organisation? Explaining current trends in training practice in the UK. *International Journal of Training and Development*, Vol. 1 No. 1, March, 9–21.

Regini, M. 1995: Firms and Institutions: The Demand for Skills and their Social Production in Europe. *European Journal of Industrial Relations*, Vol. 1 No. 2, 191–202.

Scarborough, H., Swan, J. A. and Preston, J. 1998: *Knowledge Management and the Learning Organization: The IPD Report*. London: Institute of Personnel and Development.

Senge, P. 1990: *The Fifth Discipline: The Art and Practice of the Learning Organisation*. New York: Doubleday.

Senker, P. 1992: *Industrial Training in a Cold Climate: an assessment of Britain's training policies*. Aldershot: Avebury.

Storey, J., Bacon, N., Edmonds, J. and Wyatt, P. 1993: The 'new agenda' and Human Resource Management: a roundtable discussion with John Edmonds. *Human Resource Management Journal*, Vol. 4 No. 1, 63–70.

Streeck, W. 1992a: *Social Institutions and Economic Performance: Studies in Industrial Relations in Advanced Capitalist Economies*. London: Sage.

Streeck, W. 1992b: Training and the new industrial relations. A strategic role for the unions? Regini, M. (ed.), *The Future of Labour Movements*, London: Sage.

Swieringa, G. and Wierdsma, A. 1992: *Becoming a Learning Organisation*. Reading, MA.: Addison-Wesley.

Tavistock Institute 1998a: *Workplace Learning, Learning Culture and Performance Management – a report prepared for the IPD*. London: Tavistock Institute.

Tavistock Institute 1998b: Intermediate Report to EU DGXIII on European Observatory on Innovations in Vocational Training. London: Tavistock Institute.

Trivellato, P. 1997: Japan as a Learning Society – An Overall View by a European Sociologist. In Coffield, F. (ed.), *A National Strategy for Lifelong Learning*. Newcastle: University of Newcastle, 185–206.

8

Management Development

John Storey and William Tate

Just ten years ago the state of management development in Britain was roundly condemned in a string of influential reports (Mangham and Silver 1986; Handy et al. 1987; Constable and McCormick 1987). The findings and tenor of these were encapsulated in a sentence which suggested that management training and development in this country was typically too little, too late for too few. When compared with its major industrial competitor countries, British management training and development was judged to be sadly lacking. Since that time there have been two recessions, coupled with much downsizing and re-engineering. As the next chapter discusses in more detail, the idea of the 'end of career' has gained prominence as well.

Under these unpropitious circumstances, managers and management have been elevated, scrutinized and debated in the past decade to an extent perhaps never before matched. Deregulation, globalization and the associated restructurings have projected management and managers centre stage. Organizational learning and knowledge management have been hailed as the key elements in modern strategic management, as the previous chapter has already indicated. Consequently, it could be argued that the subject of management development is more vital than ever. Debate among practitioners and analysts about management development has been intense.

At one level there is scope for optimism. The findings from recent research based on a large, representative national survey conducted by the Open University Business School in conjunction with the Department for Education and Employment (DfEE) and the Management Charter Initiative (Storey et al. 1997b; Thomson et al. 1997) suggest that management training and development is in a more robust state than it was a decade previously when the critical reports on management development in the UK were published. None the less, important questions remain. How well diffused is this training and development? What are the skills, competencies, capabilities and expertise required of managers? What are the principal current techniques in management development and what evidence is there of their effective use? And finally, a question particularly pertinent for this book, what difference does the British context make to the way management development is practised?

These are the main issues addressed in this chapter. The first section discusses the nature of management development. This addresses matters such as how the activity is conceptualized and its various perceived purposes. It also reviews the changing ways in which management development has been viewed over time. The second section describes and assesses the main initiatives at national level. The third describes the key interventions and techniques deployed at organizational level. The fourth examines the factors which shape the extent and nature of the interventions at both levels, and the chapter concludes with a look at possible scenarios for development in the future. As well as the Open University Business School national survey already referred to, the chapter draws on recent empirical research to illustrate and underpin the analysis from the Warwick case-study based comparative study of management development in Britain and Japan (Storey, Edwards and Sisson 1997a).

The Nature, Meaning and Purpose of Management Development

Conceptualizations about what management development is are obviously closely inter-twined with what it is deemed to be for. As many senior managers can be heard to say, development is not (or at least ought not to be) an end in itself. There is an interesting tension in the provision of developmental opportunities. On the one hand, economic utility is frequently demanded: development must be shown to meet the needs of the business. To this end, there has been an increasing interest in attempts to evaluate the outcome of investments in management development activity. Yet, on the other hand, one finds much talk of the inherent value of developmental activity and even open declarations of will-ingness to take its beneficial outcomes on trust.

Another, equally fundamental, issue concerning the theory and practice of management development turns on the question of whether there is a known body of knowledge and set of generic skills which managers should be expected to have, much in the manner, say, of a qualified professional accountant, lawyer or doctor. The controversial competencies debate hinges on this point. If management is seen in this light, it raises the issue of whether the competencies approach is equally relevant to entrepreneurship and the management of dynamic business agendas involving uncertainty and change. There is also the issue of the relevance of competencies to the specific managerial needs and aspirations of particular enterprises and the requirement for specifications of competencies to be able to keep pace with – even anticipate – changing times and needs (Morgan and Hampson 1998).

Conditions of increasing instability and heightened international competition have made traditional industrial bureaucracies look problematical. Many commentators have now therefore come to associate management with proactive and innovative behaviour and some even link it with challenging norms to suit changing needs. From this viewpoint, modern managerial competences hinge around the capacity to foresee new developments. The ability to identify threats and opportunities has become salient as has the demonstra-tion of creativity and the capability of getting things moving and managing change, of being a self-starter rather than waiting on instruction – in other words, the competences of initiative, entrepreneurship and political acumen. Under the new unstable conditions, learning and development become especially critical. The implications for changes to required management skills have been examined by a number of authors (Weir and Smallman 1998; Witzel 1998).

There were some signs of a new role for management development in the 1980s and 1990s when it became increasingly common to treat management development as a device to bring about organizational change and in particular to engineer 'culture change'. Lippitt (1982), for example, talked of management development as 'the key to organisational renewal'. This link between culture change and management development has been particularly noticeable in the finance sector. Banks, building societies and insurance companies, where managers were traditionally unlikely to be innovators or risk takers, were all subjected to broadly similar treatment involving management development interventions (Smith 1987; Stemp 1987). Attempts to use management development as a tool to engineer wide-ranging culture change have also been reported from other sectors, such as hospitality (Beaver and Lashley 1998), retail (Nixon 1998) and telecommunications (Smith et al. 1986).

In the 1990s, the management development literature increasingly raised the problems of managing in downsized and lean organizations and the new career management challenges came to the fore (for example, Herriott and Pemberton 1996; Cianni 1997). There has also been continuing interest in how management development might be used to assist line managers in adjusting to new organizational circumstances (as, for example, in the report about Pearl Assurance by Heywood 1997).

The aim of using management development as a tool in pursuit of specific business agendas, such as quality, innovation, cost reduction and knowledge management has also survived (Alexander 1987; Tate 1997). Companies increasingly declare that their training activities are to be seen as explicitly linked with establishing company values such as 'existing for the customer'. Following the British Airways example, chief executives are now routinely drawn into training programmes to signal top-management commitment to the message being conveyed. Management development may also be used as a means to forge a common identity following a takeover or merger. It may also be used to create a distinctive identity following a demerger, as in the case of the break-up of The Burton Group.

If, then, these are among the wide-ranging and ambitious aims of management development, how has the phenomenon itself been defined? A much-quoted definition conceives of it as 'an attempt to improve managerial effectiveness through a planned and deliberate learning process' (cited by Mumford 1987: 29). But, interestingly, Mumford later averred that, despite an erstwhile attachment to this definition, his more recent empirical research and consulting activity had led him to conclude that it was defective. His main objection is that it overemphasizes the importance of deliberate planning in the process of management learning.

Learning, some suggest, has become increasingly distanced from teaching and training. Learning is now more likely to be viewed as having emergent, natural and personal 'inside-out' properties, rather than being the expected outcome from a planned 'outside-in' event. Learning is more 'chaotic' and unmanageable than hitherto supposed. It has been viewed as an aspect of the non-rational half of the management equation which may thus contribute more to organizational diversity than conformity (Tate 1995).

The fact that formal definitions are now out of favour serves to highlight the fashions and trends within the field of management development. As Pedler, Burgoyne and Boydell (1991) remind us, managerial training and development has evolved through a number of recognizable phases. Immediately following the Second World War, the perceived urgency of upgrading skills in order to meet productivity targets led to an emphasis on systematic training. The limitations of this planned, formalistic, approach, they suggest, led to the emergence of 'organizational development' (OD). Another reaction was the coming into favour of self-development methods and action learning.

These latter approaches have in turn been subjected to criticism. They are now some-times perceived as all very well for personal growth, but as less functional for moving forward the organization. This same point can be found embedded in the useful distinction between manager development and management development. The former can include all manner of educational and training experiences which enhance the individual. The latter more directly impacts on the functional capability of the managerial stock as a whole, and improves the collective management performance in a manner relevant to business needs. This chapter follows convention using the term 'management development' to embrace both manager training and development and higher-order management devel-opment activity.

The tension between two fundamental models of management development can be seen today and throughout its formative history. The first model sees appropriate management development as being provided in a formal top-down and highly structured manner. Authority and expertise are vested in the employer or the employer's agents, and are external to the learner, who is clearly on the receiving end of this wisdom. The process is most commonly manifested in formal training programmes. Associated with this approach are corporate training colleges (and more recently corporate universities), training depart-ments staffed with qualified trainers, a well-publicized programme of core and optional training courses, and an integrated system of appraisal which identifies both training needs and candidates for the training programmes. The opposite, informal model, devolves responsibility to the employee and emphasizes the virtues of self-development.

Another way of considering the profile of management development in a given organ-ization is to examine its level of 'maturity'. Burgoyne (1988) identifies six levels or stages in organizational management development. At the first level, there is no systematic devel-opment in any sense of the term. Whatever development of talent may happen to occur does so in a totally unplanned way. At the second level, there are isolated fragmentary activities, perhaps in sporadic response to identified acute problems. At the third level, various development activities occur and are, to some degree, co-ordinated and integrated with each other. At stage four, the integrated approach is taken further in that manage-ment development is treated strategically and plays its part in implementing corporate policies – for example, through human resource planning to meet the preordained corporate strategy objectives. At stage five, the practice becomes even more sophisticated in that management development in turn makes an input into corporate strategy formula-tion. The final stage is really an embellishment of number five: management development processes enhance the nature and the quality of corporate policy formulation and they are also used to implement these enhanced policies.

From the above, it can be seen that the range of development activity presents a series of options between formal or informal, off-the-job or on/in/through-the-job, employer managed or self-managed, for the present job or future positions, individually contextual-ized or organizationally contextualized. Having thus sketched the basic conceptual terrain, we turn now to a review and analysis of developments in the British context. We do this in the following two sections. The first of these describes the main national-level initiatives and the following one examines initiatives which have been taken at organizational level.

National-level Initiatives

A number of highly influential reports appeared in the mid to late 1980s (Constable and McCormick 1987; Handy et al. 1987; Mangham and Silver 1986) expressing acute concern about the state of management development and the quality of British managers. At that time there were approximately three million people in managerial jobs, with about one-third of these being in senior and middle-managerial posts. On average, it was found these three million received only about the equivalent of one day's formal training per year. The majority received no training. Worse still, of the 100,000 persons entering managerial roles each year, the majority had received no formal management education or training.

The Handy report (Handy et al. 1987) put this record in international context. Although some organizations were doing a lot for the development of their managers and were doing it well, the main competitor countries were doing more and doing it better. The Americans placed considerable emphasis on the provision of formal business education – especially MBA courses – in colleges and universities. In contrast, the Japanese output of MBAs was close to zero. Instead, they devised a successful formula of recruiting potential managerial talent from well-educated graduates from the elite universities followed by a highly systematic approach to in-company development. Britain, by contrast, followed neither the external nor the internal model, but toyed with elements of both. The overall conclusion was that Britain should not import wholesale any particular foreign system, but should provide some coherent and logical approach to fit its home circumstances.

Both the Handy et al. (1987) and the Constable and McCormick (1987) reports made a number of specific recommendations. The Handy report suggested that leading companies should commit themselves to a 'development charter' of good practice, including five days off-the-job training per annum for all managers. Other recommendations related to the provision of education. The most far-reaching of these was Constable and McCormick's call for the establishment of an apprenticeship or 'articles of management' approach in the form of a new national Diploma in Business Administration (DBA) and an expansion in MBA programmes. They suggested a target output of 10,000 MBA graduates per annum by the late 1990s. In broad terms, this target at least is now being met.

It was also recommended that access to both of these courses should be made more easily available to working managers through the wider provision of part-time, modular courses. The hallmark of these would be flexibility. Their character would be shaped by a careful melding of academic and work-based activity. The proposed direction of change could be said to favour vocationalism – applied learning for the many rather than theoretical learning for the few. Again, there are some signs that the trend has moved in this direction.

Mangham and Silver's research (1986) discovered that over half of British companies, of all sizes, were making no training provision for their managers. The lowest level of investment occurred at the more senior levels. However, difficulty was encountered in proving a link between the incidence of training and company performance. Few respondents were able to articulate the competencies which were required of senior, middle and junior managers, a fact which it was felt might offer an explanation.

All the reports carried implications for individual organizations, but in the main they raised questions of national policy. Little commented upon, however, is the fact that these reports sprang largely from a concern about the lack of supply of more skilled managers rather than a failure to make proper use of available skill. The seeming inability of organizations to utilize their talent – to liberate, foster, nurture, channel and retain it – was not part of their remit; yet this arguably is equally wasteful and economically damaging. The US guru Edwards Deming used to claim that organizations typically used as little as 15 per cent of what their employees were able and willing to offer in their work.

The Management Charter Initiative

National policy is an area in which Britain has been characteristically weak. However, following this particular cluster of reports the challenge to take action was in part at least taken up on this occasion. The most immediate response was the establishment of the Management Charter Initiative (MCI) in November 1987 by a consortium comprising the CBI, the British Institute of Management, and the Foundation for Management Education. The new body was named the Council for Management Education and Development (CMED), later becoming the National Forum for Education and Development (NFMED). In November 1987 CMED launched MCI as its operational arm. MCI is an employer-led initiative backed by the Department for Education and Employment and the Department of Trade and Industry.

MCI started out with three major items on its agenda: the founding of a mass movement of organizations prepared publicly to commit themselves to a code of good practice to promote the development and application of high standards in modern management (the Management Charter Movement); the construction of a set of management qualifications designed to provide recognizable steps of accreditation for professional managers (the Chartered Manager); and the formation of a Chartered Institute of Management with a Royal Charter to advance the 'profession' of management (the Chartered Institute).

This became a highly controversial agenda. There was considerable disagreement among the membership of the original Council for Management Education and Development, which took on a further twist when MCI subsequently became the Government's designated industry lead body for the development of standards (of competence) for the occupation of management. As part of a government initiative, other lead bodies were doing the same for other occupations. Various interested parties, such as the Association for Management Education and Development (AMED), contested the aspiration for codification and standardization of managerial competence. However, following this unsettled beginning, MCI survived, though progress on the three-fold agenda was variable (Silver 1991).

With the later appointment of MCI as the lead body for management, the heart of MCI's agenda concerned the definition of national standards of managerial competence. These tied in with the establishment of a nationally recognized hierarchy of vocational qualifications being developed in parallel by the National Council for Vocational Qualifications (NCVQ), again for all occupations, including management. Since 1990, MCI has been analysing, refining, codifying and publishing comprehensive sets of standards for the various national vocational qualification (NVQ) levels aimed at first-level, middle and senior managers.

The management standards are assessment focused; that is, outputs in the workplace rather than inputs during training and education are emphasized and measured. The standards can serve as a platform for training, recruitment and rewards and provide a yardstick against which to assess achieved and displayed competence (Tate 1995). One aspect of controversy has focused on the relationship between assessed competence and actual performance, rather in the manner in which it is argued that intelligence tests do not measure intelligence, only the ability to pass intelligence tests. The danger of equating the two concepts led Collin (1989) to caution that management education in the UK could 'become the vehicle for training people in the skills of test performance rather than for developing effective managers – essentially an open-ended activity'.

The emphasis is on demonstrated capability to do rather than the possession of knowledge or the amount of time spent on courses. Consistent with its emphasis on demonstrated competence rather than learning *per se*, part of the standards-based initiative is MCI's regional programme for the 'crediting of competence' via approved centres. The concept is commonly referred to as the 'accreditation of prior learning' (APL); but as MCI points out, this is inaccurate as it is managers' current competence rather than their prior learning that is given recognition. APL allows managers to receive formal credit for units of competence acquired via work experience or any other means. The fact that managers may be awarded qualifications (i.e. NVQs) as a result of producing portfolios of evidence and without formal study, or indeed any new learning, leads detractors to argue that APL misrepresents development and is a misuse of time. Protagonists claim that incidental learning does occur as a by-product of reflection during the APL experience.

The third element, the formation of a professional chartered institute, ran into the fiercest opposition. Established professional groups such as the then Institute of Personnel Management and the Institute of Industrial Managers were particularly alarmed. It would appear that this idea has now been quietly dropped.

The competency debate

The work of MCI to define and promulgate management standards in Britain is part of a much wider movement affecting not just management or even this country. Debate for and against the methodology has produced fierce arguments about whether managing can and should be specified precisely, and how best to develop and assess it. The competence movement has seen variants take root abroad, especially in the United States where it began in the state education system in the 1960s. In the late 1970s in the US (where the term is spelled 'competencies') McBer & Co were commissioned to conduct research into a generic model of management.

The more recent UK government-sponsored version of competence standards specifies, for individual managers at various degrees of seniority, a level that is deemed acceptable to employers. It is an output model, targeting what is demonstrated in work, rather than learning inputs. Higher and different levels of capability are possible and desirable, but not deemed vital to getting the work done. The national standards are arrived at by functionally analysing occupations (in this case managing) in successive levels of detail.

The US model stands in sharp contrast. This springs from an interest in the development of competence rather than its assessment. Definitions of competence are arrived at by analysing what distinguishes superior performers from average performers, rather than by looking at the content of the job. In the UK model, 'the standards do not deny that qualities, skills and knowledge are important, but consider that these are supplementary issues which follow on from describing work role expectations' (Mitchell 1991). Spelling apart confusion arises in Britain over these two different approaches for several reasons, not least because the US approach is preferred by many British companies, and it is advised on and implemented for them by some of the main UK consulting houses. The word 'competence' further carries overtones of bare adequacy and is also used in legal circles to equate with decision-making powers.

Some companies prefer to use alternative terms in place of competencies such as 'key success factors' (Guinness), 'management dimensions' (Safeway) or 'management capabilities' (British Airways). A select group of individual competencies are often labelled 'core', in that they are deemed to lie at the heart of the managerial role for a given employer (British Airways' list consists of customer orientation, business understanding, team working, communication, coaching and developing, and planning and achieving change). To add further confusion in the use of the word 'core', a parallel strand of corporate-level management has developed that explores the distinctive 'core competence' of a business, such as Sony's famed 'pocketability' (Walkman, Discman, etc.). In a radical restructuring, Birmingham Midshires Building Society reorganized its departmental functions around processes that it also termed 'core competencies', such as risk management and process delivery.

Which of the two basic approaches to individual manager competence should a company choose? If an employer does not wish to link capability with its employees gaining NVQs, it is free to adopt whichever approach it prefers and to generate its own list of competencies. The latter may be tailored not only to the particular company, but also to particular functions (i.e. crossing occupational and even national boundaries) or address particular concerns and needs of the business at that time. International and multinational companies may choose to disregard the British-based approach as too limited for assessment purposes. So decided Guinness Plc., but Unilever chose to support the national initiative.

The seeming virtues of the popular input model are offset by the fact that the result is not transferable across employers and does not link with national qualifications. Furthermore, the process of developing competencies this way is very time consuming and expensive. In Britain, through the work of MCI, many employers have found substantial benefit from having inexpensive and ready access to extensively researched definitions of what it takes to be assessed as competent as a generic manager. This holds the additional benefit for individual managers of transferability in employment through holding a nationally recognized qualification which all employers can understand.

There are positive aspects to the endeavour, but the inherent problem associated with a fixed list of competencies (in either model) in the sphere of management work is the extent to which the needed role behaviours are subject to such tremendous variation. The source of variability may lie in the divergent business strategies (Schuler and Jackson 1987) or in the periodic change in priorities required of managers and workers as paradigms of good practice change over time (Storey 1992).

As Mabey, Salaman and Storey observe (1998: 370–3), proponents can claim that such models provide the basis for developing, operating and binding an integrated human resource system horizontally, covering assessment for recruitment and selection, manpower and succession planning, career management, appraisal and performance management, training and development, and remuneration and reward. This integrating feature leads some practitioners to assume that all competencies lend themselves to all such personnel applications. That is not the case. Some personal qualities (drive, judgement and courage, for example) unsurprisingly find a home in companies' lists of desired managerial competencies; but they may tend to be applied more at the recruitment stage than to training.

Competence, as a concept, has proved widely popular. It is one of the big ideas of the last decade. Many benefits – to individuals and organizations alike – can be cited for its adoption. Yet critics continue to present fundamental, practical and philosophical objections to the approach, particularly the UK model. Objections by traditional business schools being pressured to make their management education more vocationally inclined reflect concern that the underpinning knowledge and theory could suffer. Some have a root dislike of genericism, as well as antipathy to job- rather than person-based development. Further objections include the belief that the job of managing is different from all other occupations and does not lend itself to fine analysis, fragmentation and prescription, except at the most elementary, foundation-skill level. Despite the range of criticisms, many blue-chip companies have placed competence methodology at the heart of their human resource strategy and make strong claims for its success.

Organizational-level management development methods

Evidence about the actual state of provision for management development at organizational level is still relatively sparse, but a few sources have become available in the late 1990s. The Open University Business School research (Storey et al. 1997b; Thomson et al. 1997) commissioned by the Department for Education and Employment (DfEE) and the Management Charter Initiative (MCI) uncovered, overall, a transformed picture when compared to the one described just ten years previously by Constable and McCormick (1987) and Handy et al. (1987). The priority given to management development by top teams in the late 1990s was much higher and the amount of training and development provided had also increased. Many of the major targets set by the reports in 1987 had been met: the amount of training offered to managers had increased and the expansion in the number of MBA graduates had been achieved. By 1997, only 4 per cent of larger companies reported doing no training, compared to a situation ten years previously when, according to Constable and McCormick (1987) 'somewhat over half of all UK companies appear to make no formal provision for the training of managers'. One of the interesting findings was the move towards a more rounded approach to management development in recent years with a more balanced apportionment of responsibility between the organization and the individual. In sum, this appears to be a success story of some magnitude.

As well as a statistically representative sample of 904 organizations covering all main industry groups and employment sizes, telephone interviews with 501 organizations with over 100 employees and a survey of 403 small businesses using a postal questionnaire, there were also in-depth interviews with various managers at 18 large case-study organizations, all of whom had participated in the Constable and McCormick (1987) survey a decade before. Finally, to counterbalance the 'company' perspective, there was a survey of 125 managers from a sample of the 501 companies and these 'users' were asked to reflect on their own first-hand experiences of management development.

Forty-three per cent of all respondents reported that their organization had a formal written statement or series of statements which promulgated a policy for management development. As expected, larger organizations, measured both by revenue and employees, were more likely to have such policies. Among the organizations with over 5,000 UK employees, 60 per cent had formal management development policies compared with 24 per cent of organizations with 100 to 299 employees. Among the small business sample, only 8 per cent of the 389 companies had explicit management development policies, but 42 per cent reported that they had informal policies for management development. National ownership of companies did not seem to impact as much as expected: 42 per cent of British-owned organizations had policies compared with 45 per cent of foreign-owned enterprises. Manufacturing organizations were the least likely to have such formal policies whereas government organizations were the most likely.

Although the vast majority of the large organizations participating in the face-to-face interview programme did have policy statements, it was notable that there was very little reference to such statements during the interviews. There were even instances of those responsible for corporate management development admitting that they simply did not use or draw on the formal statements – even in the case where new policies had been devised in the past few years. The message appeared to be that written policies and manuals were rather out of favour in the mid to late 1990s. They were somewhat sceptically viewed as statements of high intent. Likewise, procedures were accorded lower credence than heretofore; 'facilitation' and subtle 'interventions' were the new lexicon.

None the less, when subjected to various statistical tests, there was a very considerable correlation between the existence of a formal management development policy and many other positive aspects of management development activity in the organizations. Hence it was necessary to probe various aspects of policy. For example, who is responsible for the initiation and implementation of management development policy? It was found that central personnel with a score of 48 per cent were regarded as carrying the main responsibility, but if the board (23 per cent) and the chief executive (20 per cent) scores are combined, the balance of judgement could be that responsibility across senior management is fairly evenly split. In the 1986 study of those organizations which did have an explicit policy, 51 per cent reported that the responsibility for initiating it rested at the board level while 45 per cent attributed it to the personnel department. In broad terms, therefore, it could be said that not a great deal has changed on this point other than some switch of responsibility for management development towards central personnel.

When it comes to implementation, there was a marked difference in response patterns. Personnel and human resource specialists were the people who carried by far most responsibility. Also, as might have been expected, divisional and unit managers were also mentioned fairly strongly. In 1986, where explicit policies did exist, 60 per cent placed responsibility for implementation with the chief executive, only 17 per cent placed it with corporate personnel. The 1996 survey findings reveal personnel as carrying the main responsibility for implementation. This suggests a general shift towards a clearer allocation of management development implementation to specialists during the past decade.

Despite the generally healthy state of management development in the UK, it is noteworthy that 57 per cent of the sample did not have an explicit budget earmarked for this activity. Government organizations were the most likely to have a budget allocation (45 per cent), manufacturing organizations least likely (34 per cent). As expected, there was a size effect here: larger organizations were far more likely to have a dedicated budget (56 per cent of those with over 5,000 organizations compared with only 19 per cent of organizations with 100 to 299 employees).

A crunch question was how much relative priority does management development have now compared with ten years ago? To measure this, a 10-point scale was used where 1 stood for low priority and 10 stood for high priority. Using the mean (average) the perceived priority had markedly increased from a score of just 3.45 ten years ago to a mean of 6.02 today. The full pattern of results is shown in table 8.1

There was a sharp difference between the results for the past, present and future. Priority was expected to increase even further in the future with a mean here of 7.21. Put another way, 45 per cent saw their present priority as being in the top end of the range (the 7 to 10 categories), while only 22 per cent judged the priority to be at the lower band of 1 to 4. In contrast, the judgement about the situation ten years ago was that only 8 per cent of organizations gave high priority to management development while 63 per cent accorded it low priority. Almost three-quarters anticipate that in the future their organizations will accord management development a still higher priority and only 6 per cent expected it to have low priority. These are important differences. The survey clearly reveals the increasing importance of management development in British organizations since the previous surveys a decade ago.

The amount of training

The OUBS research project measured this by the number of formal training days per annum per manager. The average number across all size groups (including small businesses and all sectors of the economy) was 5.2 days per annum. This represents a very considerable amount of training and suggests that the target set over the past decade has actually been met. It represents a substantial increase compared with a decade ago and is a

Table 8.1 Priority accorded to management development

| Scale | *Percentages making judgements using a ten point scale* | | |
	Now	*Ten years ago*	*Foreseeable future*
1–2 (low)	7	34	2
3–4	15	29	4
5–6	33	20	20
7–8	34	6	54
9–10 (high)	11	2	19
Not stated	0	9	1

Table 8.2   Amount of formal training

Days	100–299	300–499	Percentages by employee size group 500–999	1,000–4,999	5,000 plus	Overall
No days	3	6	3	4	3	4
1–2 days	20	23	21	19	17	20
3–5 days	45	37	33	43	40	40
6–9	11	13	13	10	16	12
10–14	8	16	16	7	7	11
15 plus	11	2	8	7	6	7
Not stated	3	3	6	9	9	6
Mean	5.8	5.1	6.0	6.5	5.2	5.5

further confirmation that the broad-brush picture of optimism in relation to management training and development can be substantiated.

Table 8.2 shows the detailed breakdown for companies with over 100 employees. It reveals that, overall, some 24 per cent of organizations were claiming to provide over 10 days of training per manager.

A matter of some surprise here was the relatively little impact made by organizational size. Indeed, the very considerable amount of training provided by medium-sized companies – which was broadly on a par with the largest companies – is one of the notable findings from the survey. Similarly, there was little variation between sectors: in the middle-to-large companies, organizations in manufacturing, services, retail and distribution as well as holding companies with interests in diverse sectors, were all providing about five and a half training days per year. Foreign ownership of companies did not make a great deal of difference to the amount of training.

There is, of course, potentially a great deal more to management development than management training, but the more informal methods are notoriously difficult to measure. The approach adopted in this survey was to ask respondent's for their judgements about how sufficient the informal methods were in comparison with their desired optimal position for this kind of activity. The results broadly paralleled those found concerning the amount of training – that is, there is substantially more now than there was ten years ago. Respondents expected there to be even more in the future. When asked what were the most important drivers of the increase in management training and development, the main finding was that once again internal factors relating to company strategy and support of the board came out as the strongest whereas external influences such as Investors in People, NVQs and similar training targets were rated lower, as were operational factors such as cost of training, retention of staff or demand from managers. So, once again, the importance of top-level strategic choice was confirmed and emphasized as the critical factor.

The use of formal qualifications in management development has increased dramatically over ten years for all levels of manager. For example, among junior managers the use of formal qualifications as a path towards management development increased from 22 to 77 per cent and among senior managers from 20 per cent to 44 per cent. External formal qualifications in management were rated as having relatively little importance in the mid

1980s; this situation changed significantly by 1996 across all managerial levels. Business schools have met this demand with an increase in certificate, diploma and MBA courses. Even in small firms, the use of external qualifications and the use of formal management development methods such as external courses was high (between 70 to 80 per cent of all small firms used external courses to some extent). As for informal methods, most important were learning by doing the job and coaching. As expected, coaching, mentoring and in-company job rotation decreased with seniority.

UK companies are doing substantially more training than a decade ago and senior managers judge its consequences to be positive. Moreover, the analysis of associated variables reveals that senior managerial choice is far more important than such 'givens' as organizational size or sector. There are many small companies which have created sophisticated systems while there are much larger companies which have not done so despite their greater resources. What is interesting, and indeed almost paradoxical, is that this reported increase in training has occurred despite a marked shift in sentiment away from formal suites of training schedules and programmes towards coaching and individu-ally tailored career development. In the interviews, management development specialists were above all else keen to emphasize that they were performing their roles in a very different way and that the whole conception of what management development was about had shifted markedly. Under these circumstances, it would not have been at all surprising to record a decline, let alone a rise of any scale, in the amount of training. The explanation, we suspect, is that, in the main, the public agenda is set by the powerful voices of leaders in the large corporations. In consequence, downsizing, delayering and the drastic slimming, if not actual closure, of large central training departments dominate the headlines. Mean-while, among medium-sized companies a very different agenda is being played out. As our results show, the much-vaunted delayering has not been at all pronounced when a representative sample of the whole economy is taken. Equally, the amount of training in medium-sized companies has increased rather than having been cut back. Indeed, when an open-ended question was posed asking how, if at all, the methods of developing managers would change in the future, the overall response showed that a larger proportion talked about an increase in more formal programmes and external training (27 per cent of the total, unprompted) compared with only 15 per cent who referred to more informal methods such as job rotation and action learning.

STRUCTURED TRAINING

Sending managers on courses represents a relatively simple and yet high-profile way for management development to be seen to be happening. The efficacy and appro-priateness of such activity is dependent upon a range of factors. Many a training and development department has degenerated into a state where its function is merely to administer training-course programmes. Course details are circulated and the department simply handles the paperwork by matching nominees and volunteers to the available places. At worst there is no real investigation of whether the courses offered are really the ones which are most needed by the business, nor is there any proper investigation of who would benefit most from the courses. The handling of follow-through and impact is likely to be a further area of weakness in such cases. In these circumstances training may be seen as being offered as a substitute for effective management development.

The problems often associated with management training are fairly well known. Managers, especially at senior levels, may be reluctant to accept the idea that they have weaknesses which require rectification through training. Managers may maintain they are too busy to spend time away on a course. Training content and process may also come under attack. They may not be appropriately tailored or targeted to the particular audience. If they are provided in-house, then they may, conversely, be attacked as too simplistic and too insular. Finally, there is the seemingly perennial problem of transferring learning back into the work situation. Even if end-of-course measures do reveal considerable learning, there is no guarantee that this will be carried over into subsequent work behaviour. In the absence of such behaviour change, questions are inevitably raised about the value of this investment of time and money. In a thorough critique, a management development director who acts as purchaser of management training on behalf of a large insurance company concluded that what often passes for management training in Britain is largely atheoretical and fails to meet real needs (Mole 1996).

Self-development

Given the varied nature of managerial work and the wide range of individual strengths and weaknesses which every manager brings to it, there are some strong advocates of the view that formal training approaches are simply inappropriate. Moreover, in reaction to disappointment about the overall impact of formal training courses – and perhaps as a way to avoid their costs – enthusiasm for self-development has grown apace. Dunnell (1987) proselytized a self-development scheme at the insurance company Guardian Royal Exchange under the title Management Development on a Tight Budget. Others have preferred to emphasize the motivational effects of individuals devising their own development plans, taking responsibility for their own development and in effect 'owning' the problem. A popular idea has been the notion of 'learning contracts' (Boak, 1998), whereby company and individual act in partnership on the development question. Continuing professional development can also offer similar opportunities (Sadler-Smith and Badger 1998).

There are structural trends in employment that favour self-development. The traditional company values of reciprocated loyalty between employer and employee are breaking down. The 'psychological contract', as it is termed, is changing. Assumed long-term tenure is giving way to a more self-interested and shorter-term relationship. For most managers, one-company careers are less common. Learning is similarly affected; the concept of lifelong learning is a recognition that initial learning has a limited shelf-life and that continuous learning is needed to maintain employability in today's insecure job market. Both employer and employee now feel disposed to be flexible and to look after their own interests. In this changing scenario, self-planned and self-funded development fits with the need to acquire skills that can be used to aid mobility between employers, and perhaps cope with the world of self-employment. Transferable skills are becoming more valuable than dedicated ones. This may help employers, too, as they find merit in having managers with the confidence and ability to move on rather than hang on. Ironically, some employers are willing to pay for managers to attend expensive executive development courses at overseas business schools to boost their CVs and thereby make voluntarily severance more acceptable.

There are, however, some cautionary notes struck among the general enthusiasm for the concept of self-development. Some managers may not be really capable of self-development and where packages are provided those who need them least are paradoxically the ones most likely to make use of them. There are also attendant dangers of isolation of the individual manager's goals and skills from those needed by the organization if self-development becomes too heavily relied on. Consequently, Pedler (1986) suggests some form of group support to underpin self-development.

The main mechanisms of self-development might be regarded as comprising initial activity in self-awareness (e.g. through assessment or development centres), frequent feedback, and – where appropriate – familiarization with career development options including a realistic view of possible career paths; followed by the preparation of an individual development plan. Such a plan should ideally incorporate the preferences of the individual, objective assessments of his or her capabilities, and a realistic view of opportunities within the organization. The unfolding of events may involve ongoing lobbying (by subordinate and boss) relating to emerging opportunities and amended action plans to develop skills in preparation for desired options.

Increasingly, however, self-development has more to do with raising current job satisfaction and performance, together with making lateral moves, rather than with the next planned move up the company career ladder. Flatter organization structures, unpredictability in fast-changing environments, the fashion for outsourcing professional functions, coupled with a much weaker corporate hand on the development planning tiller, have replaced the sturdy vertical career ladder with an ill-defined crazy-paving through unclear organizational territory. In a growing number of companies, both the path and the development process are self-trodden and informal.

MENTORING AND COACHING

This next category includes development methods which are designed to combine the merits of informal self-development with more formal organizational support mechanisms. Mentoring, coaching and action learning have these features. A key distinction is drawn between informal and incidental learning. As Marsick and Watkins (1990) observe, the former refers to self-directed conscious attempts to learn using, for example, coaching or networking, and in these instances learning itself may be the main purpose. Incidental learning, by contrast, occurs as a by-product of everyday work-life; it arises out of work tasks where learning is not the main purpose. Marsick and Watkins (1990) argue that the quality of both types of learning can be enhanced by proactivity, by critical reflexivity and by creativity. Thus, as suggested also by Mumford (1989), an individual or group can plan work tasks so that one of the required outcomes is further learning. There can be an aim to foster collaborative learning, and this itself can be aided by the creation of a learning community with appropriate norms. Supportive climates will encourage managers to invite a focus on the way they formulate problems as well as the problem-solving phases.

A management mentor is a senior figure who, although not the direct line manager, takes a relatively long-term interest in the development of a promising younger manager. The mentor acts as a guide on development issues and can provide orientation with respect to longer-term career matters. A set of prescriptive guidelines is furnished by Clutterbuck (1987).

There are many articles which argue that recycling the experience of older senior managers is cost effective (Tack 1986). Other reports suggest that older managers who are left out of corporate training schemes may be found useful alternative roles as mentors (Skapinker 1987). But this contradicts Clutterbuck's (1987) advice which is only to use as mentors those managers who are currently highly active and who are at the height of their credibility, standing and influence. These people are more likely to be in their forties and early fifties rather than in their sixties.

It is widely understood that much valuable corporate knowledge is tacit; i.e. uncodified and located in individual manager's experience. It is argued that organizations should find means of holding on to their corporate memory, taking special care to safeguard it as managers approach the end of their careers. This calls for transferring this know-how, know-when and know-who to others, as well as making it explicit wherever possible. Mentoring fits well with this idea. Part-time contracts for exiting managers to provide consultancy to the employing organization are another way of meeting this need in a planned manner, which may also help develop the manager's portfolio for the next stage of life.

Coaching of senior managers has become a high-profile form of specialized consultancy, provided from both inside and outside the organization (Dutton 1997; Nowack and Wimer 1997). Board members are particularly attracted to this form of development since it insulates them from the rest of the company's development people and processes, and preserves their dignity. Coaching is completely personalized, and can focus on the key areas of concern to individual senior managers: style of management in relation to changes of culture, management of time and priorities, plans for career progression and the balance between work and the rest of life.

ACTION LEARNING

A range of varied approaches to developing managers can be put under the heading of action learning (Raelin 1997). Their common theme is the view that 'management' is a cluster of practices which can best be upgraded and honed by direct exposure to problem-solving situations. Much of the credit for bringing recognition to the concept of action learning is given to Revans, a business professor who made widely known his disenchantment with traditional business education methods. Revans pioneered an approach which engaged managers in programmes wherein they were assigned problem-solving situations, often in organizations other than their own, and for which they were given various types of support. For example, the participating managers would meet regularly with each other in a self-help group and with a facilitator. The analysis of issues was thus problem directed and closely aligned to felt need.

Whether tackled by individual or group, the key point is to move beyond debating possible solutions to problems and to try out favoured options as soon as possible. Learning is also designed to continue beyond the implementation of successful solutions through the explicit analysis of why something worked as it did. This idea echoes the notion of 'double loop learning' as popularized by Argyris and Schön (1978; 1981).

This 'learning by doing' is clearly adaptable to many situations and it can take many forms. One key mode adopted by Revans was to initiate an exchange programme which involved collaboration between a consortium of collaborating companies and universities.

The participants spent a period of months in their receiving organizations interspersed with university-based periods to discuss and analyse the problems they had encountered and their other experiences. The package was designed to constantly challenge each manager to review and reinterpret his previous experience.

Action learning is defined by Pedler (1991: xxii) as involving an approach which takes the task as the vehicle for learning. It is based on the premise that there is no learning without action and no sober and deliberate action without learning. He sees it as having three main components – people, who accept the responsibility for taking action on a particular issue; problems, or the tasks that people set themselves; and a set of six or so colleagues who support and challenge each other to make progress on problems. He sees the process as involving a 'learning spiral'. Out of previous activity emerges a new 'problem'. As Pedler (1991) observes, the ability to 'problematize', i.e. to construct appropriate questions which are neither too overwhelming not too trivial, is a crucial skill which influences a person's ability to learn through action. A second stage, 'ownership', relates to the acceptance of problems as having both a personal and public dimension. A third step involves building a 'set', or work group, that can help tackle problems. Other stages in the learning spiral entail various reworkings of the problem, dealing with conflict, and the handling of negative feedback. Significant learning events will involve an amendment in identity and a move on to new problems.

Summary characteristics of organizational-level management development provision in Britain

The provision of various forms of management development in Britain would appear to have increased in recent years, albeit from a very low base. Corporate provision has two main characteristics: it is varied and fickle. The first characteristic is a comment on the marked variation in activity between different organizations. It is very difficult to generalize about British management development because, in some companies, the provision is well planned, sophisticated, well resourced and extensive. In others, there is barely any provision of any kind at all. The second characteristic, fickleness, refers to the extreme nature of the degree of change in the provision of management development found in British companies. The Warwick study, which compared British and Japanese companies (Storey, Edwards and Sisson 1997), found that, even in the sophisticated British companies, management development programmes were highly susceptible to being chopped and changed around every few years as a succession of management development managers instituted their own 'new' programme (the researchers referred to this tendency as 'programmitis'). In contrast, in Japan, whatever the other merits and demerits of the systems might be, there was a remarkable degree of continuity in the way in which management development was provided. Older senior managers would have a sound understanding therefore of the development opportunities being offered to their junior managers; this was rarely found to be the case in Britain. In consequence, in the Japanese companies management development was routinized and part of the fabric of corporate life. Development of subordinates was also an accepted part, indeed a high priority, of the job of senior managers in a way that was not so in the British cases.

The relative instability of the British management development programmes and the relative sustainability of the Japanese had a number of aspects and consequences. The Japanese managers at all levels were able to describe the training and development systems in their companies; this often was simply not the case at all in the British companies. There were dramatic lurches in the British cases: elaborate suites of training courses were designed and refined for one period, only to be totally disbanded the next. Self-development would be the main emphasis at one time and then it would be more or less disregarded at another. As a consequence, line managers were confused and sometimes cynical.

Arguably, a key source of this crucial contrast can be traced to the market-oriented character of the British scene described by Dore. But it may not be quite so simple as that. Management development specialists in Britain were anxious to stress that their cue was taken almost entirely from 'the business strategy' or 'the needs of the business'. When they drew their mental models of the place of management development in diagrammatic form, they invariably placed business strategy/business needs at the centre or top of the figure. They tended to make a point of being rather dismissive of external influences emanating from government/civil service/MCI and, to some extent, business schools as well as other vested interests which they perceived as having wrong-headed or political agendas. Given this central focus on business need, it is easier to understand that adaptability was equally prized. There was little compunction about making a clean sweep of a suite of training programmes or the closure of a management training college. Self-development, mentoring and close attention to individual development needs would be happily stressed for a period of four or five years and then a new chief executive (or sometimes even the same one) would declare a need for a sea-change and so a new era of more systematic, programme-based provision would be launched to 'meet the needs of a new phase in the business'. What was going on here was as a result of a deep-seated conceptualization of management development as necessarily a second-order, downstream activity. The (turbulent) marketplace and the business strategies designed to engage with it were seen as unquestioningly paramount. In Japan, by contrast, there was less of a tendency to begin all conversations about the place of management development with a reaffirmation of the primacy of the market. There appeared to be a more securely based belief in the enduring value of growing managers in order to meet the changing character of market conditions.

Other findings from this study revealed aspects of organizational practice that were less expected. Thus, for example, wide functional experience was not a characteristic of Japanese managers. On the contrary, the British managers displayed this to a far greater extent. The study also produced some surprises, especially concerning the low levels of formal training recorded in Japan.

Distinctive conclusions also emerged as a result of talking to the subjects of development. Four themes emerged. First, the idea of a career may carry a different interpretation in Japan from that in Anglo-Saxon countries, with the personnel department typically moving managers without the individual having any real say in the process. The finding that Japanese managers do not think in terms of career paths is itself interesting and would not have been expected. What was, of course, well known was the careful planning conducted by Japanese companies, but very little was known about how managers themselves saw the process. It was found that they were in fact not particularly satisfied with the way in which this was handled. Apart from the evident implication that the

Japanese system is far from perfect, this highlights the nature of the management of managers: they were promised job security, but were expected to move between jobs as they were told.

Second, as against any expectation that Japanese managers will be particularly satisfied with the means used to assess their performance, there were no differences from the British sample. There is certainly some other published material pointing in a similar direction. Thus, it is well established that Japanese employees tend to report lower levels of job satisfaction than do employees in many Western countries. This is usually explained in terms of the high expectations which the Japanese may have, together with some tendency to be more self-critical than other peoples. This finding is different, however, in that managers were reporting not their own satisfaction but their assessment of company systems. The lack of enthusiasm about evaluation systems links to the third point: the extent to which there was an enterprise culture. The interviews were with quite senior managers, in some cases only a couple of steps away from the main boards of their companies. There was no active discontent, but neither was enthusiasm much in evidence. There was little sense of close identification with firms: managers were often critical of where their firms were going, of a lack of personal direction, and of career uncertainties. Their firms were important to them, but they retained a sense of distance and were not absorbed into an embracing enterprise culture.

With the exception of NatWest, the British firms were coming at this issue from a tradition of weak central policy. In Lucas and British Telecom there was a strong sense that far more organization of the management development function was required. In Tesco, managers recognized that a good deal had been done but still felt uncertainty about the future. Given the general situation on career planning in Britain, it is not surprising that NatWest managers were, in comparison, relatively satisfied. None the less, the frustrations mentioned above suggest that the organization may have to come to terms with another aspect of the British environment, namely, the image of the active manager as hero and the need to create an environment in which the individual can shape his (and sometimes her) destiny.

Factors Shaping the Provision and Effectiveness of Management Development

Most of the literature on management development is prescriptive. There have been relatively few attempts to model systematically the variables which influence the extent and impact of management development activity. A notable exception to this is the work by Thomson et al. (1997; 1998) and Storey et al. (1997) which, drawing on a large-scale national survey, used statistical techniques to locate the key causal factors. The most notable result from this analysis was that managerial choice rather than the range of independent variables such as organization size, sector or technology was the most crucial factor. Additionally, some pointers are available from the wider training and human resource development literature. For example, Pettigrew et al. (1988) analysed 20 companies and identified a number of factors which seemed to stimulate positively HRD initiatives. These included the circumstances where there was a commitment within an organization to work towards a business strategy requiring the management of increased complexity; situations where an internal labour market was embraced which facilitated an open skill and career structure; where training and development opportunities were recognized as helping recruitment where managers favoured an integrated approach to recruitment, learning and career development. Pettigrew et al. (1988) also identified the kind of factors which inhibited HRD. These included a preoccupation with immediate tasks; low levels of qualifications; and training regarded as a low-status activity.

The OUBS research found that, in total, it was not the structural variables (such as organizational size, sector affiliation, or company ownership) which mattered but rather the strategic policy choices made within the firm. Hence it revealed, for example, that where companies had opted for a formal policy statement on training and development they were far more likely actually to provide more training. Likewise, those organizations reporting that management development was accorded a high priority were the ones which did a lot more training. To exemplify, the average number of training days operated by companies which reported high priority for management development was 6.9 days, whereas those who reported that low priority was accorded to management development provided only 2.7 days. It was concluded that policy variables (such as priority given, construction of a policy statement, the organization taking responsibility for it, and views on what makes a good manager) are far more important than structural ones. High priority to structured training and development provision also correlated highly with the levels of satisfaction reported by the managers who were the consumers of these programmes.

The robustness of these variables was reconfirmed when measures were also taken of the outcomes from management development activity. Priority and policy were again revealed as critical. These are important findings and by no means entirely expected. How much confidence can we have in their validity? It is necessary to recognize the limitations of the study. The main measure of management development activity used in the above calculations was the amount of management training. This is a fairly crude measure though it does have the advantage of relative simplicity. In addition, the data is merely a snapshot offered by one respondent for each organization and as such provides something close to the 'official' management development perspective. There is also of course the danger that respondents are likely to offer accounts which reveal some consistency between, for example, the amounts of management training and the adjudged priority of management development as well as the judgement about the existence or otherwise of a formal policy on the subject. Some extra confidence in the findings, however, can be drawn from the fact that the accounts of 'users' tended to confirm the general direction of the causal connections.

Looking to the Future

We noted at the beginning of this chapter that recent research reveals evidence that activity in the area of managerial education, training and development has increased substantially compared with the situation a decade before (Storey et al. 1997; IDS 1997). The number of MBAs has increased fourfold, the Management Charter Initiative has established, reviewed and updated all the management standards. And managers in general have enjoyed greater exposure to a much wider range of learning opportunities. Interest in the subject has been fuelled by associated developments – for example, in the concept of the learning organization, in the idea of knowledge management and in the associated technologies of intranets and the Internet. At the same time, as we have also noted in this chapter, there is increasing uncertainty about the kinds of roles for which managers are being prepared.

One thing about the future seems fairly sure: computer technology will be even more critical. With computer processing power growing exponentially, it is hard to conceive of the managerial functions computers will undertake, say, five or ten years from now. The growth of artificial intelligence is such that computers are now talking to computers, monitoring and anticipating problems and solving them without managerial intervention. Monitoring supermarket-consumer buying patterns and controlling stock levels, and mass-producing cars to individual orders, are two examples.

It is hard to imagine any manager's job insulated from technology. Technology is affecting what managers are responsible for, how they carry out their duties, what they need to learn, and how they learn. Technology provides managers with new means of carrying out their daily tasks. Technology changes managers' relationships too, both their nature, and with whom they interface.

At the time of writing (early 1999) one key thrust in the leading companies – including the major management consultancies – is the development of in-house shared networks containing data, induction programmes, self-help training programmes, records of accumulated experiences and question-and-answer style computer conferencing. CD-ROMs (both off-the-shelf and custom designed for each organization's specific needs) and web-based material are also increasingly being used. These technologies are seemingly in tune with the current preference for distributed, asynchronous and tailored learning. At the same time, large organizations maintain an interest in, and a fascination with, the short 'executive' seminar programmes offered at the premium end of the market by the top American and European business schools for a select few.

Despite the emphasis on information technology as the medium for learning, the short, one-to-two-day management training event market also remains fairly buoyant. This is largely a consequence of the extent to which training has been outsourced by organizations. Large, in-house training departments remain out of favour – at least for the time being. Those which remain are having to adapt themselves by offering internal consultancy rather than standard training packages and they may also find it necessary to market their services outside the organization.

Finally, while we have noted the increase in provision and take-up of management development opportunities during the past decade it should be borne in mind that this growth has been built on a not-very-substantial initial base. Moreover, there is the question as to whether that provision is capable of matching the nature and scale of the new set of challenges facing managers now and in the future. Accordingly, there is no room for complacency.

References and further reading

Alexander, G. P. 1987: Establishing shared values through management training. *Training and Development Journal*, **11**(2).

Antonacopoulou, E. P. and Fitzgerald, L. 1996: Reframing Competency in Management Development. *Human Resource Management Journal*, **6**(1), 27–48.

Argyris, C. and Schön, D. 1978: *Organizational Learning: A Theory-action Perspective.* Reading, MA: Addison-Wesley.

Argyris, C. and Schön, D. 1981: *Organizational Learning.* Reading, MA: Addison-Wesley.

Beaver, G. and Lashley, C. 1998: Barriers to management development in small hospitality firms. *Strategic Change,* **7**(4), 223–35.

Boak, G. 1998: *A Complete Guide to Learning Contracts.* Aldershot: Gower.

Boyatzis, R. E. 1982: *The Competent Manager: A Model for Effective Performance.* New York: Wiley.

Burgoyne, J. 1988: Management development for the individual and the organisation, *Personnel Management,* June.

Cianni, M. 1997: Individual growth and team enhancement: Moving toward a new model of career development. *The Academy of Management Executive,* **11**(1), 105–15.

Clutterbuck, D. 1987: *Everyone Needs a Mentor.* London: IPM.

Collin, A. 1989: Managers' Competence: Rhetoric, Reality and Research. *Personnel Review,* **18**(6).

Constable, J. and McCormick, R. 1987: *The Making of British Managers.* Corby: British Institute of Management.

DfEE 1996: *Management Development – A Toolkit for Employers and Managers: Report to Department of Employment and Education.* London: DfEE.

Dore, R. 1989: *Japan at Work: Markets, Management and Flexibility.* Paris: OECD.

Dunnell, R. 1987: Management Development on a Tight Budget. *Personnel Management,* 48–51.

Dutton, G. 1997: Executive coaches call the play. *Management Review,* **86**(2), 39–43.

Handy, C. 1987: *The Making of Managers.* London: National Economic Development Office/Pitman.

Herriott, P. and Pemberton, C. 1996: *New Deals.* Chichester: John Wiley.

Holbeche, L. 1994: *Career Development in Flatter Structures.* Horsham: Roffey Park Management Institute.

IDS (Incomes Data Services) 1997: Management Development 10 years on. *IDS Management Pay Review,* No. 199: 21–4.

IM (Institute of Management) 1994: *Management Development to the Millennium: The Cannon and Taylor Working Party Reports.* Corby: IM.

Industrial Society 1997: *Management Development: Measuring Best Practice.* London: Industrial Society.

Lippitt, G. 1982: Management development as the key to organisational renewal. *Journal of Management Development,* **1**(2).

Mabey, C., Salaman, G. and Storey, J. 1998: *Human Resource Management; A Strategic Approach.* Oxford: Blackwell.

Management Charter Initiative 1994: *Management Standards.* London: MCI.

Mangham, I. and Silver, M. S. 1986: *Management Training: Context and Practice.* London: Economic and Social Research Council.

Marsick, V. and Watkins, K. 1990: *Informal and Incidental Learning in the Workplace.* London: Routledge.

Mitchell, L. 1991: *Competence Standards in Developing Managerial Competences: The Management Learning Contract Approach.* London: Pitman.

Mole, G. 1996: The Management Training Industry in the UK: An HRD Director's Critique. *Human Resource Management Journal,* **6**(1) 19–26.

Morgan, D and Hampson, I. 1998: The management of organizational structure and strategy: the new professionalism of management. *Asia Pacific Journal of Human Resource Management,* **36**(1), 1–24.

Mumford, A. 1987: *Developing Directors: The Learning Process.* Sheffield: Manpower Services Commission.

Mumford, A. 1989: *Management Development: Strategies for Action.* London: Institute of Personnel Management.

Nixon, B. 1998: Real time management development: a case study offering lessons for successful transformation. *International Journal of Business,* **1**(4), 222–8.

Nowack, K. and Wimer, S. 1997: Coaching for human performance. *Training & Development,* **51**(10), 28–32.

Pedler, M. 1986: Management Self Development. *Management, Education and Development*, **17**(1).

Pedler, M. 1991: *Action Learning in Practice*. Aldershot: Gower.

Pedler, M., Burgoyne, J. and Boydell, T. 1991: *The Learning Company*. Maidenhead: McGraw-Hill.

Pettigrew, A., Sparrow, P. and Hendry, C. 1988: The Forces that Trigger Training. *Personnel Management* **20**(12), 28–32.

Raelin, J. 1997: Action learning and action science are different. *Organizational Dynamics*, **26**(1), 21–34.

Sadler-Smith, E. and Badger, B. 1998: The HR practitioner's perspective on continuing professional development. *Human Resource Management Journal*, **8**(4), 66–75.

Schuler, R. S. and Jackson, S. 1987: Linking competitive strategies with human resource management practices. *Academy of Management Executive*, **1**(3), 209–13.

Silver, M. (ed.) 1991: *Competent to Manage – Approaches to Management Training and Development*. London: Routledge.

Skapinker, M. 1987: Cookson Seeks a Common Management Style. *The Financial Times*, 22 April.

Smith, D. 1987: Culture and Management Development in Building Societies. *Personnel Review*, **15**(3).

Smith, P. E., Barnard, J. M. and Smith, G. 1986: Privatisation and Culture Change. *Journal of Management Development*, **5**(2).

Stemp, P. 1987: Improving Management Effectiveness. *Management, Education and Development*, **18**(3).

Storey, J. 1992: *Developments in the Management of Human Resources*. Oxford: Blackwell.

Storey, J., Edwards, P. K. and Sisson, K. 1997a: *Managers in the Making: Careers, Development and Control in Corporate Britain and Japan*. London: Sage.

Storey, J., Thomson, A. and Mabey, C. 1997b: What a Difference a Decade Makes. Management Development Ten Years On. *People Management*, **3**(12), 28–34.

Tack, W. L. 1986: Management Recycling. *Sloan Management Review*, **27**(4), 63.

Tate, W. V. 1995: *Developing Corporate Competence: A High-Performance Agenda for Managing Organizations*. Aldershot: Gower.

Tate, W. V. 1997: Developing an Integrative Framework for Corporate Competence. Competence – A Source of Competitive Advantage? Paper presented to the 7th conference of the Centre for Labour Market Studies, University of Leicester.

Thomson, A., Mabey, C. and Storey, J. 1998: The determinants of management development; choice or circumstance? *International Studies of Management and Organisations*, **28**(1), 91–113.

Thomson, A., Storey, J., Mabey, C., Gray, C., Farmer, E. and Thomson, R. 1997: *A Portrait of Management Development*. London: The Institute of Management.

Weir, D. and Smallman, C. 1998: Managers in the Year 2000 and after: a strategy for development. *Management Decision*, **36**(1), 43–51.

Witzel, M. 1998: Redesigning management development in the new Europe. *EFMD Forum*, **1**, 6–12.

9

Managing Careers

Helen Newell

For managers especially, but also for other groups of employees, the career has been regarded as a fundamental element in the development process as well as non-work experience (see, for example, Sofer 1970; Scase and Goffee 1989). In the context of greater labour market flexibility, however, there have been repeated warnings, even from government ministers, that people cannot expect to remain in a job for life. Instead, the notions of employability and entrepreneurship are emphasized as alternatives to the lifetime career model. This, coupled with downsizing, rationalization and the impact of new technology, suggests significant changes for the way in which both organizations and employees have to view careers. Some authors, such as Handy (1976), have for many years argued that traditional careers are simply not compatible with new flat and flexible organization structures. Others believe that we should not and, indeed, cannot write off the traditional career. From research carried out in 33 leading private and public-sector organizations, for example, Guest and Mackenzie (1996) found that, while there had been substantial restructuring leading to a reduction in grades, there had not always been a reduction in hierarchy and many traditional career ladders remained intact. Nevertheless, it was clear from their research that, as the number of opportunities for promotion had decreased, the steps between jobs had increased, making it more difficult to move onwards and upwards. The ladders may still exist, in other words, but the rungs are fewer and further apart.

Critically, what also emerges from this strand of the literature is a change in perceptions of who should be responsible for careers. To some extent we can see a new model of the career developing, where individuals are expected to work for many organizations during their lifetime and place the responsibility for turning this pattern of jobs into a career upon themselves. In short, the individual is expected to own, plan and construct their own career, rather than relying on an organization to do this for them.

This chapter is concerned with the ways in which careers are perceived and managed and the extent to which they have changed, in particular in the light of recent organizational change discussed in chapters 1, 2 and 3. The first section outlines the major current areas of debate about careers and argues that an approach to careers which relies on individual employees playing a key role will require a much more strategic emphasis on training and development by organizations than currently exists in the UK. The second section looks at those factors which provide the context within which career management takes place. It suggests that careers need to be seen from the perspective of the individual as well as the organization, since careers are fundamentally about a relationship. The chapter focuses on the structural barriers and opportunities provided by the organization and the personal hopes and expectations of individual employees. It also examines the way in which careers are perceived in different countries. Managers' roles and practices are deeply embedded in their social and cultural environment and there are considerable differences across countries in traditional models of career management. The third section continues this theme of diversity in examining the differences between men and women's careers in the UK. All too often our model of careers is based on the experience of men, whereas women's experience of careers tends to be quite different from that of their male counterparts. The final section looks at some of the current trends in career management and, in particular, considers the usefulness of the concept of the psychological contract in helping us not only to understand, but also to manage and plan, careers in practice.

Current Issues in Career Management

In recent years there have been two main foci for debates about careers. The first concerns the problem of promotion opportunities in a context of flatter organizational hierarchies, low voluntary wastage and extensive restructuring, downsizing or rightsizing. There has been a shift away from the traditional model of narrow upwards mobility, where employees made their way up the promotion steps of a narrowly defined functional ladder. Even those middle managers in large organizations who always felt powerless, 'squeezed by the demands of implementing strategies they don't influence and the ambitions of increasingly independent-minded [subordinates]' (Kanter 1989: 310), did at least have a secure job and could expect, if not a rapid, then at least a steady rise up the hierarchy. Security in the future, Kanter argues, will come not from being employed, but from being 'employable'. In other words, individuals should concentrate on developing the skills and knowledge which will make them attractive to a range of organizations, rather than expecting to remain with one organization for life. In theory, this should bring with it not only greater responsibility for the individual (in deciding on the appropriate skills and knowledge to be developed) but also for the organization (in enabling or empowering the individual to develop or acquire these skills and knowledge). However, as we will see in the final section of the chapter, all too often this shift towards self-managed careers hardly represents a genuine move towards employee empowerment.

The second area of focus has been the growing acceptance by organizations that goals such as increased profit, better productivity or even survival are dependent upon the innovation and creativity of their human resources. Such behaviour, it is argued, requires a motivated and committed workforce which, in turn, is to be secured through the provision of satisfying work and careers. This again suggests a more strategic role in training and development for organizations since it relies heavily on the provision of opportunities for self-development (Sisson 1989). Unfortunately, recent research by Martin et al. (1998) suggests that, in so far as increased value is being placed on training and development, this is associated not with employer-initiated activities but with employee-driven demand as employees attempt to adjust to a climate of job insecurity by making themselves more employable.

The Context for Career Management

There are four major influences on the way in which careers are perceived by both organizations and individuals. At the most macro level, cultural norms and expectations play an important role. For example, in Holland, Australia and the USA the average tenure of workers is seven years, whereas in France, Germany and Japan, average tenure is over ten years (Goffee and Nicholson 1994). Despite the sweeping claims that the 'traditional' career in Britain is dead, research shows that managers at least still remain with the same organization for a considerable period of time (Guest and Mackenzie, 1996). One survey, for example, revealed that most of the managers in Lloyds Bank (96 per cent), British Telecom (88 per cent) and Hewlett Packard (60 per cent) had all worked for those organizations for at least the previous ten years and that some of those interviewed had worked there for the previous 20 to 25 years (McGovern et al. 1998). Patterns of labour market segmentation are also important, professional and occupational labour markets having quite distinctive characteristics of high or low mobility, development continuity or future uncertainty.

Two other important influences on careers are of course the organization and the individual themselves. A career has been defined as 'the evolving sequence of a person's experiences over time' (Arthur et al. 1989). This definition is useful in so far as it emphasizes change as well as stability and links the career to the individual rather than merely to the organization or to the individual, so that careers are viewed fundamentally as a relationship between one (or more) organization(s) and the individual. Both the organization and the individual are important and careers can be seen from the perspective of both parties. Derr (1986), for example, has defined careers in terms of external and internal careers. The external career he defines as the combination of opportunities and constraints which exist in a given organization, the organization's needs and the realities of the labour market. This includes not only the formal rules, policies and practices of the organization – the hard systems – but also the soft systems, such as organizational culture. From this, the organization's perspective, we are concerned with managing the career. In contrast, the internal career is concerned with unique personal career definitions, that is the hopes and plans of individual employees. Schein (1978) argues that it is subjective definitions (attitudes and experiences) which specify for the individual the meaning of success, what path should be followed to success and, by implication, what kinds of events will be stressful and disappointing. From this point of view, we are concerned with planning careers.

The external career

DEVELOPING MANAGERS

Organizations view careers in a variety of different ways. Some see them as a way of allocating jobs and providing training, i.e. the emphasis is on developing managers. Many managers would agree that they have learned most from the sequence of jobs they have done and from specific problems they have met within those jobs. Their career – the sequence of jobs they have held – has developed them. From this point of view, job moves are often seen as having a two-fold purpose: getting the right people into the right positions to achieve the organization's objectives and developing them through a sequence of jobs so that they learn from a variety of experiences. Unfortunately, these two aims are frequently incompatible. The best person for the job is not necessarily the one who will learn most from it. Nevertheless, it remains one of the most common approaches to career management. One other problem associated with this view of careers is the emphasis on short-term performance; the main consideration tends to be meeting current organizational needs, not planning for future needs.

CAREER LADDERS

Another way in which organizations view careers is as tracks or ladders, which take people up the management hierarchy. A successful career is thus one which takes the individual to the top of the ladder. This view of careers is particularly apparent in some organizations which have so-called 'fast tracks' for high fliers. When ladders are used to represent organizational hierarchies, they are often also associated with timetables. If a certain rung on the ladder has not been reached by a certain age, or after a certain length of time with the organization, then progress beyond that rung is effectively blocked (Lawrence 1984). Not only is the ladder concept increasingly inappropriate in many modern organizations with relatively flat structures and a need for flexibility, the use of fast-track schemes in particular can have harmful consequences for the organization. Employees who are not on the fast track become demotivated; the organization relies on early and often unreliable assessments of long-term potential; once on it, the fast track is a self-fulfilling prophecy; employees fail to obtain a good grounding in any one specialism because of frequent job moves; and fast trackers often seek to impress through the introduction of change without being in the job long enough to see through its implementation or to be held responsible for the consequences.

THE TOURNAMENT MODEL

Some organizations view careers as a type of competition: not all managers will have a successful career within the organization – only those who are successful in the tournament. As individuals make their way through the organization or each round of the tournament, the competition becomes progressively more selective. Being knocked out in an early round is a significant barrier to further progression. From this point of view, 'winning', which often has more to do with knowing the rules of the game than being a good and competent manager, is more important than the learning and development of either the manager or the organization.

'SINK OR SWIM'

Typically, in many British organizations the view of senior managers (who have often themselves not received any management development) has been that managers are born, not made. This has led to people being promoted into new positions without any particular preparation, training or development on the basis that, if they are good managers, they will 'swim' and if they are bad managers they will 'sink'. One of the conclusions drawn by Storey et al. (1997) in their comparison of careers in Japanese and British organizations is that 'to the extent that there was a generic British approach, it lay in a "sink or swim" attitude to early career development' (p. 28).

THE PROCESS OF CAREER MANAGEMENT

Another way of looking at careers from the organization's point of view, reflecting an approach adopted by Sonnenfeld et al. (1992), is according to their balance of external versus internal supply flows and group versus individual assignment flows. In terms of supply flows, some organizations are almost entirely closed, except for entry points at the bottom of the organizational hierarchy. They are said to have an internal labour market providing a well-developed career path within the organization. These organizations tend to see people as assets with a long-term development value rather than as costs. Other organizations are open at all levels. In terms of assignment flows, some organizations move individuals to new jobs on the basis of their individual performance, while others move people according to their contribution to group performance. Sonnenfeld et al. (1992) argue that, strategically, organizations that emphasize individual contribution expect individuals to contribute value on an on-going basis, subject to continuous assessment of some kind, whereas where group contribution is emphasized employees are seen as having intrinsic value. The authors use these two dimensions to construct a model of career systems (see figure 9.1). The two aspects of resourcing and results are combined to produce four typical career systems.

Organizations which recruit externally and promote exclusively on individual performance are labelled 'baseball teams'. Here the emphasis is on recruiting people with the right skills and any development of the individual tends to be on the job rather than through formal training programmes. There is a high rate of turnover and careers often consist of moves between organizations with employees in baseball teams often identifying with their profession rather than a particular organization. This would not only include professional organizations such as accountancy or legal firms, but also high-technology firms and consultancy organizations.

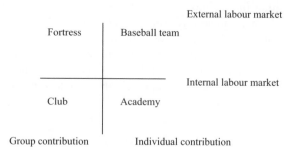

Figure 9.1   Types of internal managerial labour market
Source: Sonnenfeld et al. (1992)

Organizations that promote from within on the basis of individual performance are labelled 'academies'. Here people are recruited early in their career and the emphasis is on developing them over time. Such organizations are characterized by low levels of turnover and will often have fast-track career schemes. Organizations that might fall within this type are traditionally blue-chip organizations from banking, the civil service and the pharmaceutical industry.

'Clubs' will also promote from within, but promotion will be based on group contribution. A club places a high value on loyalty, equity and reliability. People move through the organization slowly and tend to have generalist rather than specialist careers. Many of the recently privatized utilities would have fallen within this category prior to privatization and it is likely to describe large areas of the remaining public sector, although the introduction of competitive forces may well mean that different career systems will be deemed appropriate.

Finally, in the 'fortress' organization, people are recruited externally and there are high levels of turnover, often redundancy and little commitment to employees. Many organizations fall into this category when they get into difficulties and it is often a transitional stage from being a club to another type. It is a common pattern for publishing firms, retail and hotel and catering.

The internal career

CAREER AND LIFESPAN DEVELOPMENT

In the past, emphasis on the external career has often neglected the fact that people do not passively respond to the opportunities and constraints presented by the organization, but actively seek experience of stability and change which meet their perceived needs and interests. The internal career is thus concerned with the hopes and plans of individual employees. It is the individual's attitudes and experiences which will determine the meaning of a successful career. Some writers have used the concept of career stages to explain how individual's views about careers change over time, different eras of adulthood being linked to different adult roles and associated values. The importance of each role (for example, launching a career, relationships, leisure development, the need for an integrated life-style) rises and falls over time, implying that organizations need to provide different opportunities for employees at different stages of their careers (Cytrynbaum and Crites 1989, Dalton 1989). In particular, Bartolome and Evans (1979), in their study of 532 male middle managers, found that half of them were dissatisfied with the way in which they were investing time and energy in their professional rather than their private lives. Not only did these managers have competing loyalties, but the importance attached to them also changed throughout their lives. Turning towards private life tended to lead to a decrease in work investment and vice versa. They predicted that this changing rhythm runs through the life of many managers and that it reflected psychological development as well as the structure of careers and families in modern industrial society.

In addition, Gunz (1989) argues that different individuals have different capacities to shift and change careers, to deal with career uncertainties and to cope with organizational disappointments. Some people welcome job change, look forward to working with new and different people and have the self-confidence and willingness to take risks, whereas other people do not. He visualizes careers as climbing frames: while some people climb up the frame by the approved route, some abandon the frame altogether and others will not climb at all, but simply hang on for survival.

CAREER ANCHORS

Schein (1978) argued that different people (even within the same organization) came to define their careers very differently in terms of an evolving image of their own talents, motives and values. He believed that people developed certain 'career anchors' at an early stage in their career which will govern their individual career paths. His original list consisted of five anchors:

- technical-functional competence;
- managerial competence (analytical, interpersonal, emotional);
- security and stability;
- autonomy and independence;
- entrepreneurial or creativity.

Later, he added the need for a basic occupational identity – service to others; power, influence and control; and variety – arguing that people could in fact have more than one career anchor at the same time. This helps to explain why some individuals see lack of promotion as a failure, while others do not seem to be bothered by it. Those with an anchor in general management often define progress and success in terms of formal promotions, while the person who is anchored in technical expertise cares more about her or his ability to remain challenged in that area. Here the sense of occupational career is much stronger than the sense of organizational career. Like Schein (1978), Herriot and Pemberton (1995) have highlighted the diversity of career preferences among managers. They describe how some managers prefer to get out and others to get on, while some withdraw their commitment from the organization but hang on to their jobs. Other writers have suggested similar typologies. Derr (1986), for example, suggests the following five orientations to careers:

1   getting high, where the individual derives excitement from the content of the work itself;
2   getting ahead, where the individual is motivated by the prospect of climbing the organization's career ladder;
3   getting secure;
4   getting free, where the individual seeks autonomy and independence;
5   getting balanced, where the individual seeks a balance between work and non-work activities.

Career management systems in international comparison

Managers' roles and practices are deeply embedded in their social and cultural environment. Although we noted above that, at least as far as women managers are concerned, there are many similarities in the barriers they face in careers, there are also considerable differences across countries in traditional models of career management. The preferred paths for advancement, the traits and behaviours required for promotion, are different. In one cross-national study, for example, Derr and Laurent (1989) found substantial differences in what managers from different countries perceived as being necessary for career success. While 88 per cent of American managers considered achieving results to be the key factor in promotion, this view was shared by only 52 per cent of French managers. The French managers believed that being labelled as high fliers was the most important determinant of career success, whereas in Germany it was technical competence and functional expertise that was seen to be important. In contrast, Lane (1989: 92) argues that 'generally it remains true to say that the promotion to top level posts of "gifted amateurs" remains a uniquely British phenomenon'. Favoured career paths also differ, especially the possibility of moving between organizations, industries or sectors.

Evans et al. (1989) have identified four different national models of careers: the Japanese; the Latin–European (France); the Germanic; and the Anglo–Dutch (the UK). The dominant career paths within each of these models is represented diagramatically in figure 9.2. The arrows inwards indicate where recruitment takes place, the arrows outwards where exit from the organization occurs. The horizontal and vertical lines indicate movement either across functions or within functional chimneys. It should be noted that these diagrams represent stereotypes reflecting the main patterns of homogenous practice in these countries; it is important to bear in mind that, within many countries, there will be marked differences particularly, for example, between the large, established organizations, small organizations and self-made entrepreneurs. The approach in each model reflects the underlying values of the society in which it is embedded and the different configurations of educational, political and economic institutions that impinge on management, and the different understandings of 'what management is all about' and therefore the different qualities that managers should bring to it. In addition, not only do the career systems described tend to operate only in large organizations, we must also be wary of seeing these models as more than a snapshot. If career management is changing rapidly in Britain, then it is likely to be changing in other countries and other cultures. Despite these limitations, however, the model is extremely useful in reminding us of the substantial differences between cultures in the way that careers are perceived and managed and thus in helping us to understand some of the difficulties that organizations face in developing so-called international managers.

THE ANGLO–DUTCH MODEL

Here management is seen as something separate, definable and objective – management ability is seen as a general and transferable skill, with a strong emphasis placed on interpersonal skills. The British variant in particular emphasizes empirical thinking and places a premium on personal experience. Selection of managers is thus based on the basic character of the individual in terms of personality and behaviour – a classical education and broad general approach to management. Managers climb up through functional or technical hierarchies over a period of about eight years to a general management job. There is a managerial culture based on a highly individualistic university education system and relatively narrow access to top-quality education, which emphasizes theoretical

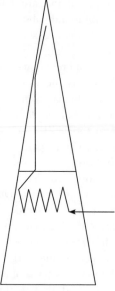

Potential development:
Functional ladders
• Functional careers, relationships and
  communications
• Expertise-based competition
• Multifunctional mobility limited to few
  elitist recruits, or non-existent
• Little multifunctional contact below level of
  division heads and Vorstand (executive
  committee)

Potential identification:
Apprenticeship
• Annual recruitment from universities
  and technical schools
• 2-year 'apprenticeship' trial
  – Job rotation through most functions
  – Intensive training
  – Identification of person's functional potential and talents
• Some elitist recruitment, mostly
  of PhDs

Functional approach to management development: the Germanic model

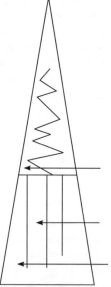

Potential development:
Managed potential development
• Careful monitoring of high potentials
  by management review committees
• Review to match up performance and
  potential with short- and long-term job
  and development requirements
• Importance of management
  development staff

Potential identification:
Unmanaged functional trial
• Little elite recruitment
• Decentralized recruitment for technical
  or functional jobs
• 5–7 years trial
• No corporate monitoring
• Problem of internal potential
  identification via assessments,
  assessment centres, indicators
• Possible complementary recruitment
  of high potentials

Managed development approach to management development:
Anglo–Dutch model

Figure 9.2 Models of careers

Source: Evans et al (1989)

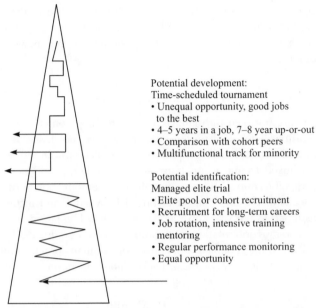

Potential development:
Time-scheduled tournament
• Unequal opportunity, good jobs
  to the best
• 4–5 years in a job, 7–8 year up-or-out
• Comparison with cohort peers
• Multifunctional track for minority

Potential identification:
Managed elite trial
• Elite pool or cohort recruitment
• Recruitment for long-term careers
• Job rotation, intensive training
  mentoring
• Regular performance monitoring
• Equal opportunity

Elite cohort approach to management development: the Japanese model

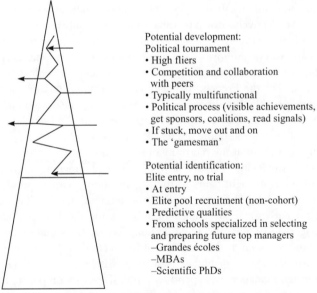

Potential development:
Political tournament
• High fliers
• Competition and collaboration
  with peers
• Typically multifunctional
• Political process (visible achievements,
  get sponsors, coalitions, read signals)
• If stuck, move out and on
• The 'gamesman'

Potential identification:
Elite entry, no trial
• At entry
• Elite pool recruitment (non-cohort)
• Predictive qualities
• From schools specialized in selecting
  and preparing future top managers
  –Grandes écoles
  –MBAs
  –Scientific PhDs

Elite political approach to management development: the Latin model

Figure 9.2 *Continued*

disciplines, little on-the-job training, a narrow definition of job responsibility and relatively short-term management driven by substantial shareholder influence. Promotion is often gained by moving between organizations, with management being seen as a profession. There is usually early promotion to management positions, commonly without experience of lower-line positions.

THE GERMAN MODEL

German managers are not seen to 'manage' but to 'manage something' – consequently they are selected primarily for their professional and expert knowledge. Interorganization mobility is not viewed as bad, but it is expected to take place within the same industry or sector or between linked technical functions (such as design, production, maintenance, engineering and quality control). Career mobility is therefore not particularly valued, because moving leads to the forfeiting of technical knowledge and in one career move you can forfeit as much as ten years on the career ladder. The German system relies on formalized apprenticeships, job rotation and training, even for graduates. Two- to five-year periods of on-the-job training, coupled with courses on company practices and policies and training partnerships with local technical or trade schools, form the core of the system.

THE LATIN MODEL

Here management is regarded more as a state of being than as a result of development processes within the company. It denotes identity more than activity or a set of capabilities. Managers are collectively known by the term *cadres*, legally recognized as grande école or university graduates with five years study after the baccalaureate, holding a position from which he can exercise authority over subordinates. The term *cadres* originally referred to a group of impartial technocrats, distinct from the owners but dedicated to the efficiency of the organization. For the French, management is an intellectual rather than an inter-personally demanding task. 'Emphasis is on formal learning, the development of "educated cleverness" numeracy, literacy and a stylish competence with the French language together with a high level of formal reasoning ability' (Lawrence 1992).

Qualifications are crucial at the recruitment stage and the strict recruitment criteria for managers leads to a small elite. This is followed by limited screening but high-performance monitoring until seven or eight years in the organization – career progression is then a competitive struggle along the lines of the 'tournament' model. The career route is determined at an early stage by choice of subjects for the baccalaureate – the most ambitious managers-to-be take the Bac-c option that includes mathematics and natural science, since these are seen as the best test of intellectual and reasoning ability. This is followed by a two-tier system of higher education, with the grandes écoles forming the upper tier. Typically, managers will spend two intensive years preparing for the entrance exams which are nationally competitive. Graduates usually develop an expertise in engineering disciplines and reach high positions in both public administration and industry. Barsoux and Lawrence (1990) found that 90 per cent of presidents and chief executives were graduates of the grandes écoles. The French model is famous for its system of *pantoufflage* – high mobility of civil servants in mid-career to posts at or near the top of private-sector organizations. Board directors tend to hold seats in both public and private sectors and to run both in the same bureaucratic style. There is therefore a strong expectation that managers will be geographically mobile and refusal will often lead to removal from the high-flier list. The main, indeed almost only, system of management development is one of grooming – for example, young graduates are sent on international assignments to serve as attachés to senior managers.

Careers and management development are currently the subject of much debate within France as they are in other countries. There are two main perceived problems with the system: it wastes potential by ignoring all those individuals who do not belong to the elite group; and it assumes that managers are automatically prepared for difficult and demanding careers just because they have been recruited from the best sources. Perhaps in response to these issues there has been a growth in the number of business schools in France during the 1980s.

THE JAPANESE MODEL

In Japan, there is much less focus on management development *per se*. In fact, Japanese organizations pay more attention to general capability development, irrespective of the kind of contribution, be it technical, or otherwise. Development is a long-drawn-out business, which includes a wide range of employees. Japanese organizations rely far more on the job experience and less on formal training days, the expectation being that they will change jobs at short notice. In Japan line managers have responsibility for the development of their subordinates and performance against this criterion is invariably recorded on each manager's appraisal review. Not only that. It is a criterion that is regarded as critical in judging managerial behaviour.

Research carried out by Storey et al. (1997), contrasting British and Japanese careers, suggested that, in the main, the Japanese treated training and development more seriously than the British organizations; they had much higher levels of educational attainment; they were far more likely to give weight to continuous development and to role models and mentors. The Japanese organizations were also more likely to have a series of planned assignments through which they gained early exposure to responsible positions. Importantly, in contrast to the many changes that have taken place in British organizations over recent years, the Japanese had been recognizably consistent over many years.

Even so, there are some problems with the Japanese model. In particular, Storey et al. (1997) noted that, although there was career planning, Japanese managers did not feel involved in the process. It was the organizations that owned the careers rather than the managers themselves.

The Difference between Men's and Women's Careers

Most of what we know about career development is based on the experience of men. Yet, during the past two decades, there has been a dramatic increase in the number of women pursuing management and professional careers (Davidson and Cooper 1992). In the UK, women made up 41 per cent of the workforce in 1984 and, by 1991, they accounted for over 11 million employees, their share of the employed workforce having risen to 44 per cent (Naylor and Purdie 1992). Not only do the data indicate that the workforce composition is moving towards a gender balance, but also that there is a significant change in the composition of those entering the workforce. In 1991, 70 per cent of married females were in the workforce and over 41 per cent of women with a child were in employment, compared to a mere 24 per cent in 1983. These data suggest that we should be wary of adopting career models based solely on the experience of men. Further, Burke and Davidson (1994) argue that not only will organizations be forced, because of labour supply issues, to look at women as a major source for managerial and professional employees, there are also business gains in terms of greater competitive advantage in actively seeking to attract women to the organization.

Current research evidence suggests that, while women graduates enter the workforce at levels comparable to their male colleagues and with similar qualifications, their career paths soon diverge (Burke and Davidson 1994). Although equally well qualified, educated and trained, and employed in similar numbers, their progress into senior management positions is not comparable. Even in two countries that would normally be thought to be very different, for example, Japan and the USA, women managers are subject to similar career barriers (Adler and Izraeli 1988; Chan 1988). Across countries, it seems, they experience credibility problems, blocked mobility, discrimination and fixed stereotypes. The latter embrace the beliefs that successful managers have male attributes; women do not have the commitment or motivation to manage; married women or mothers are unsuitable for jobs requiring foreign travel or long hours; men are more emotionally stable then women and are intellectually superior; and other employees, especially men, will not want to work for a woman (Arttachariya 1997).

But what accounts for the different experience that men and women have of organizational careers? While explanations for perceived differences between men's and women's careers vary widely, Fagenson (1990) argues that a combination of three factors – gender perceptions, organizational structures and organizational processes – help to explain women's limited ability to assume positions of significant power in the workplace. Gender perceptions lead to women's behaviour and limited representation in senior management being attributed to factors that are unique to women, i.e. women possess characteristics that are in conflict with the demands of their managerial role and are antithetical to their being promoted to the upper levels of their organization. In terms of organizational structure, it is argued that gender differences are accounted for by the greater opportunities provided for men, rather than women, to gain power, prestige and monetary rewards. Important here, for example, is women's occupational segregation, their token status, their exclusion from information networks and their limited access to mentoring relationships. Finally, in terms of organizational processes, promotion of women as managers, their training and the assessment and reward of their ability and performance are key personnel practices which affect the career success of women.

Current Trends in Career Management

In the introduction, we noted that there has been a growing acceptance that organizational goals are increasingly dependent on the innovation and creativity of human resources. Many senior managers believe that the only way that this innovation and creativity is to be harnessed is through increased employee commitment to the organization. Their implicit assumption is that, in order to be committed to an organization, its employees must share the organization's goals and values. This type of commitment has been labelled 'affective' commitment (Meyer and Allen 1984). While many managers strongly believe that there is a link between commitment and improved performance – the willingness to go the extra mile – research evidence does not support this. As Guest (1992) notes, the evidence indicates that there is only a small, positive and marginally significant correlation between performance and commitment. Similarly, the links between commitment and labour turnover, and commitment and absenteeism are also weak. In fact, job satisfaction appears to be more strongly related to performance than commitment is. This is further compacted by the fact that multiple and competing attachments are also possible (for example, many employees may be committed to individual managers, work groups, tasks, projects, families, professions) as Reichers (1985; 1986) has demonstrated.

Affective commitment is not the only type of organizational commitment. A second type, 'continuance' commitment, can also be identified (Meyer and Allen 1984). This comprises two separate elements. The first concerns the investments made by an individual in their present organization over time and the types of behaviour which tie individuals to organizations. The second concerns the lack of attractive alternatives to their existing job. Although individuals who are committed to their organizations in this way may remain with the organization over time, they do not necessarily share the goals and values of that organization nor do they display a willingness to exert considerable effort on its behalf. They may remain with the organization because they fear serious financial loss from leaving (for example, loss of pension) or because they have concerns about the loss of family or social ties which might result from geographical relocation. For some of these employees, decisions about the appropriate level of effort will be judged on an instrumental basis – what contributions are commensurate with the inducements provided by the organization. Others may feel that rewards are no longer commensurate with the investments they make, yet remain because there are no opportunities else where or because the costs of moving elsewhere are perceived to be too high. In this sense, the relationship to the organization might be defined as a 'negative attachment', characterized on the one hand by little intention to meet organizational demands and on the other by an intention to remain with the organization. Since life and work circumstances change, affecting or altering expectations over time, we might expect, in times of recession and rationalization, a move away from the affective type of commitment towards continuance commitment. One way of understanding why and how this occurs is through the concept of the psychological contract.

The psychological contract

The concept of the psychological contract, first used by Argyris (1960), defines what employees are prepared to give by way of effort and contribution in exchange for something they value from their employer, such as job security, pay and benefits or continuing training. It is thus concerned with each party's perception of their mutual obligations to each other and, traditionally, at least as far as middle managers are concerned, has been based on loyalty and commitment to the organization in exchange for employment security and career progression, linked to increases in status and rewards. Such perceptions may result from formal contracts, but more likely is that they arise implicitly from the expectations which each holds about the other. Herriot (1992: 8) links careers and psychological contracts by defining an organizational career as 'the sequence of renegotiations of the psychological contract, which the individual and the organization conduct during the period of his or her employment'.

As with the distinction between external and internal careers, the parties may hold very different expectations and therefore perceptions of what the obligations or terms of the psychological contract may be. However, since the organization itself cannot have perceptions about obligations (Kotter 1973), we need to focus on its representatives as being the source of messages regarding expectations and obligations. This means that not only will the personnel or human resource manager play an important role in forming expectations, but also that the employees' line manager may play an important role. Herriot et al. (1997) argue that, as a result, the psychological contract is often unclear.

In the face of increasing competitive pressures and tighter cost controls accompanied by restructuring, rationalization, and a reduction in hierarchies often with low voluntary wastage, organizations are no longer willing or indeed able to promise job security or promotion opportunities in this traditional sense (Goffee and Scase 1992). An expansion of role requirements and a reduction in support staff, coupled with the need to live with regular organizational change, has intensified the work of most managers and has done nothing to enhance any sense of comfort or stability. For some authors, this presents a very pessimistic future for managers. For example, Scase and Goffee (1989) describe changes in psychological contracts between managers and their employing organizations which have left managers feeling that they work harder and under tighter controls, without anything being provided in exchange. Furthermore, Herriot and Pemberton (1995) argue that this type of psychological contract supports a business strategy of survival through cost competitiveness, but that it will not ensure survival. It will cease to be a source of competitive advantage because it will not produce innovation. From their survey work, Herriot et al. (1997: 160) conclude that the 'major issue in analysing and negotiating contracts is not what is being offered by each party so much as what is a fair-exchange deal'.

The impact of restructuring

In a survey for the Institute of Management, Wheatley (1992: 4) concluded that management restructuring exercises in Britain 'are a real – and widespread – phenomenon; overall four fifths of the individual managers surveyed, and two thirds of the corporate respondents, had experienced one or more restructuring in part of their organization in the last five years'. Within Britain, there have been significant changes in both the number and the nature of managerial jobs. Those organizations which are most likely to have restructured and delayered are the utilities, rail and the government sectors, while professional and retail services are less likely to have gone through the restructuring process (Coulson-Thomas and Coe 1991). Wheatley (1992) found that four-fifths of the individual managers and two-thirds of the organizations he surveyed had experienced restructuring at least once in the last five years. This restructuring had personally affected three-quarters of the middle managers surveyed in terms of increased workloads and increased responsibility. In a further survey by Lockwood et al. (1992) the impact of these changes on middle management careers was considered and it was concluded that less than half the organizations had formal mechanisms for identifying future senior managers while, in the rest, succession planning remained an informal process. Despite this, 60 per cent of the employing organizations were satisfied that their career systems were adequate to meet future needs. This view was not shared by middle managers, however, 84 per cent of whom were concerned about the way in which their organizations managed careers, particularly in relation to future opportunities for promotion and developing new skills and knowledge or alternative career paths.

The lack of formal career management systems has also been highlighted in case-study research. In their case study of the impact of restructuring on middle management jobs in British Telecom, for example, Newell and Dopson (1996) found that, although formal career management processes existed in a sophisticated form on paper, in practice they had ceased to operate in a situation where reductions in wastage and turnover have simultaneously reduced opportunities for internal job moves and have led to a high degree of uncertainty over careers. The ensuing vacuum had been filled by a variety of responses from individual middle managers who relied heavily on what could be termed 'informal' systems of career planning.

In a further Institute of Management report, Benbow (1996) found that managers' 'angst' had reached an all-time high in the post-recession economy with managers working harder and longer than ever before. Eighty per cent of managers reported that their workloads had increased and 60 per cent that their workloads had increased greatly. Younger managers in particular reported a dramatic increase in workload. More than half always worked in excess of official hours and almost a further quarter did so often. Approximately 40 per cent worked at weekends and 54 per cent always or often worked in the evenings. Perhaps not surprisingly, then, older and more senior managers reported higher levels of job satisfaction than junior and younger managers. More than 50 per cent of the managers expressed concern over the demands of work on personal relationships, with those aged between 35 and 44 years experiencing the greatest difficulties in achieving a balance between work and home life.

Herriot and Pemberton's research (1997) also shows how far the reality of organizational practices is from the ideal model. They argue that if innovation is to be achieved whilst retaining the benefits of cost competitiveness, then there must be a change in the employment relationship. However, this change must be brought about through negotiation and compromise, not by way of an imposed deal. In the face of dramatic organizational change the process of balancing organizational and individual needs will be hard to achieve, leading to breaches of the psychological contract (Robinson and Rousseau 1994) as discussed in the next section. Other research by Herriot et al. (1997) suggests a mismatch between the expectations of organizations and their employees about reciprocal obligations at work (see, for example, Herriot et al. 1997). Whilst employees are clear about what matters to them – fair pay, safe hours and conditions and an element of job security – organizations are in danger of underestimating this transactional nature of the employment relationship, as well as falsely expecting loyalty when they have failed to keep their side of the contract.

Goffee and Nicholson (1994: 89) argue that the impact of rationalization and restructuring must be interpreted in light of the different experiences and priorities of managers and that there may be intergenerational differences with younger male managers 'nurturing a life outside of employment which will provide the skills and emotional satisfactions that work organizations cannot deliver'. They also suggest that women may be better placed than men when it comes to the renegotiation of the psychological contract. They argue that, whilst women have not lacked ambition, they have never expected to achieve their career aims through the orderly corporate careers anticipated by many men. Women are therefore more accustomed to career paths characterized by uncertainty and interruption and have developed work orientations more focused on intrinsic rewards than external benefits. But, as Liff and Ward (1998) point out, this approach overlooks the importance of power relations in the renegotiation process. Power is likely to affect the negotiation process in a variety of ways. Labour market power, for example, enables organizations to offer or impose a poor deal in the knowledge that individuals will be unable to go elsewhere; it also permits scarce individuals to threaten to leave unless they get a more favourable one. Personal power, in the shape of negotiating skills, may enable the organization's or the individual's representative to strike a better deal. An uneven distribution of power may persuade the more powerful party to leave the process and impose a deal instead of negotiating one. Similarly, it is important to understand the relative power of men and women in organizations. Liff and Ward (1998) studied founding a Opportunity 2000 company, with a good equal opportunities record (a target of 30 per cent of women in management positions by the year 2000 and the type of formal policies that one would expect to achieve this figure), and discovered that formal policies alone were not enough to overcome existing cultural barriers to equal opportunities. The case study highlighted some of the particular difficulties faced by women managers in any renegotiation process, problems largely related to a lack of power:

> They have problems presenting themselves as plausible candidates for promotion since the dominant organization model of those that succeed is strongly sex-typed male. Women are also differentially excluded from those networks through which they can make themselves known and learn about promotion processes. Crucially from the point of view of work family issues, they are denied access to information about ways in which they can balance their commitments by a combination of informal messages that such a combination is untenable and a significant degree of self censorship in their formal interactions with their managers ...Culture and informal processes are as important in determining women's success in promotion. (Liff and Ward 1998: 10–11)

Breach of the psychological contract

Violation or breach of the psychological contract occurs where one party perceives the other to have failed to fulfil promised obligations. Robinson and Rousseau (1994) argue that breaching the psychological contract may be a relatively common occurrence in organizations today, with almost 55 per cent of their sample claiming that their psychological contract had been broken by their employer. The research also showed that such a breach could lead to serious consequences, such as low job satisfaction, lower performance levels and intention to leave the organization, as well as eliciting feelings of anger and betrayal and eroding trust. Given that Robinson and Rousseau's sample was a cohort of MBA students (arguably more likely to resign after experiencing a violation than managers in general if only because of their enhanced marketability), other managers may very well find themselves in a double-bind situation whereby they are 'damned if they stay' but also 'damned if they leave' the organization. Case-study evidence (Newell and Dopson 1996) suggests that many managers feel that they are stuck in a situation which is continually demanding more in terms of hours and skills, without the support of proper training and development. However, studies also show that female managers leave their organizations at higher rates than male managers, not for family reasons, but because of lower levels of satisfaction with their job and with the organization, and because of less optimism than their male counterparts about progress in their current organizations. Evidence suggests that they are electing to set up their own businesses (Goffee and Scase 1985; Carter and Cannon 1992) or moving to equally demanding jobs in different organizations (Marshall 1995). Given that projections of the demographic make-up of the workforce of the future show that, of new workforce entrants during the next 20 years, only 15 per cent will be white males, this is a factor which should be of great concern. In putting forward their business case for the development of practices and policies that support the career aspirations of professional and managerial women, Burke and Davidson (1994) argue that organizations that create an environment where women and men are judged on their merit can expect to:

- attract the best talent;
- retain their investment and therefore make cost savings, since fewer women are likely to 'bail out';
- optimize potential and productivity, by reducing feelings of frustration and being stuck among women;
- attract and retain the best clients, thus improving market share;
- have a better quality of management, since it will promote an organizational culture that is merit based and the criteria for development and promotion are based on abilities, skills and performance.

Conclusions

Overall, then, there is little evidence to show that a new model for managing careers has emerged over the last 10 to 15 years. For the most part, what is happening is that traditional career management is continuing, albeit in a slightly augmented form. Employers want their employees both to be more flexible about their expectations of a career and, at the same time, to accept responsibility for managing their own careers. As McGovern et al. argue (1998), this shift towards self-managed careers hardly represents a genuine move towards employee empowerment.

Focusing on the psychological contract emphasizes the importance of the role of a variety of organizational representatives, not just personnel managers, in its formation. It also draws attention to the great dangers, above all in the case of managers, of organizations being seen to breach the contract.

So what are the implications? Herriot et al. (1997: 161) believe that:

the consequences of violation of the contract are so dangerous as to make it necessary for organizations to devote resources to discovering and agreeing what it is, and then keeping it wherever possible. If it is essential to change the contract, then the attempt should be made to involve the employees in re-negotiation, and to explain why the change is necessary.

Whilst explicit contracting over careers may lead to better trust relations, whether or not organizations have the time or the expertise to make this work, is questionable. As Herriot and Pemberton (1995) point out, the process of negotiation requires that each party be aware, to some degree, of what it wants and is willing to offer before negotiations can take place. The negotiation process therefore requires well-informed and well-prepared participants on both sides. Giving ownership of careers to employees, which often means no more than leaving career management to employees, might seem attractive, but it carries with it substantial dangers for the organization. If employees are to be successful in developing and negotiating careers, there are certain skills that they, as well as those in the personnel function, need to possess.

Unfortunately, little progress is likely to be made unless organizations accept at least some responsibility for their employees' careers. This, in turn, means taking steps towards a planned and integrated approach to the different aspects of career management, which clearly involves the various management development activities discussed in chapter 8. Thus Torrington and Hall (1998: 467) suggest that organizations can support and encourage individuals to manage their own careers by 'providing flexible and realistic career grids, honest feedback, opportunities for individual career exploration and planning'. Whilst one might wish to add to this list, particularly in relation to provision for training in negotiation skills, for many organizations these steps alone will provide a major challenge for the personnel function.

In their comparison of Japanese and British career and development systems, Storey et al. (1997) concluded that especially challenging for British organizations would be to find ways in which corporate and individual goals could be linked, including the development of systems through which different personnel policies, such as career management and management development, could be more closely integrated. A key element in the success of the Japanese system, they argued, is the successful integration of different aspects of the employment relationship. This implies, as Guest and Mackenzie (1996) have suggested, that the fashion in the UK for devolving responsibility for career management away from the centre of the organization may have to be reversed if there is to be any real progress, since the only way to monitor and update a career management system systematically is for this to be resourced and done centrally. From their research, Guest and Mackenzie found that it was often difficult to obtain a clear picture of what was happening in organizations because a policy of devolution meant that accountability had been left to local management, some of whom had used this to introduce their own preferred arrangements. Trends towards devolution, coupled with the lack of investment in training and development highlighted in previous chapters, suggest that, in terms of career management, British organizations still have a long way to go.

References and further reading

Adler, N. and Izraeli, D. (eds) 1988: *Women in Management Worldwide*. New York: M. E. Sharpe.
Argyris, C. 1960: *Understanding Organizational Behaviour*. Homewood Illinois: Dorsey Press.

Arthur, M. B., Hall, D. T. and Lawrence, B. S. 1989: *Handbook of Career Theory*. Cambridge: Cambridge University Press.

Arttachariya, P. 1997: *Women Managers in Thailand; Cultural, Organizational and Domestic Issues*. Ph.D. thesis, University of Warwick.

Barsoux, J.-L. and Lawrence, P. 1990: *Management in France*. London: Cassell.

Bartolome, F. and Evans, P. 1979: Professional Lives vs. Private Lives: Shifting Patterns of Managerial Competence. *Organizational Dynamics*, Spring, 2–29.

Benbow, N. 1996: *Survival of the fittest: a survey of managers' experience of and attitudes to work in the post-recession economy*. Corby: Institute of Management.

Burke, R. and Davidson, M. 1994: Women In Management: Current Research Issues. In Davidson, M. and Burke, R. (eds), *Women In Management: Current Research Issues*, London: Paul Chapman, 1–10.

Carter, S. and Cannon, T. 1992: *Women as Entrepreneurs: A study of female business owners, their motivations, experiences and strategies for success*. London: Academic Press.

Chan, A. 1988: Women Managers in Singapore: Citizens for tommorrow's economy. In Adler, N. and Izraeli, D. (eds), *Women in Management Worldwide*, New York: M. E. Sharpe.

Coulson-Thomas, C. and Coe, T. 1991: *The Flat Organization: Policy and Practice*. Corby: BIM Press.

Cytrynbaum, S. and Crites, J. O. 1989: The Utility of Adult Development Theory In Understanding Career Adjustment Process. In Arthur, M. B., Hall, D. T. and Lawrence, B. S. (eds), *Handbook of Career Theory*, Cambridge: Cambridge University Press, 66–88.

Dalton, G. W. 1989: Developmental View Of Careers In Organizations. In Arthur, M. B., Hall, D. T. and Lawrence, B. S. (eds), *Handbook of Career Theory*. Cambridge: Cambridge University Press.

Davidson, M. and Cooper, C. 1992: *Shattering the Glass Ceiling: The Woman Manager*. London: Paul Chapman.

Derr, C. B. 1986: *Managing The New Careerists*. London: Jossey-Bass.

Derr, C. B. and Laurent, A. 1989: Internal and External Careers: A theoretical and cross cultural perspective. In Arthur, M. B., Hall, D. T. and Lawrence, B. S. (eds), *Handbook of Career Theory*, Cambridge: Cambridge University Press, 454–71.

Evans, P., Doz, Y. and Laraurent, A. (eds) 1989: *Human Resource Management in International Firms*. London: Macmillan.

Fagenson, E. 1990: At the heart of women in management research: Theoretical and methodological approaches and their biases. *Journal of Business Ethics*, Vol. 9, 2267–74.

Goffee, R. and Nicholson, N. 1994: Career Development in Male and Female Managers – Convergence or Collapse? In Davidson, M. and Burke, R. (eds), *Women In Management: Current Research Issues*. London: Paul: Chapman, 88–92.

Goffee, R. and Scase, R. 1985: *Women in Charge*. London: Allen & Unwin.

Goffee, R. and Scase, R. 1992: Organizational Change and the Corporate Career: The Restructuring of Managers' Job Aspirations. *Human Relations*, April, 363–85.

Guest, D. 1992: Employee Commitment and Control. In Hartley, J. and Stephenson, G. M. (eds), *Employment Relations*. Oxford: Blackwell, 111–35.

Guest, D. and Mackenzie, K. 1996: Don't write off the traditional career. *People Management*, February, 22–5.

Gunz, H. 1989: The Dual Meaning of Careers. *Journal of Management Studies*, May, 225–50.

Handy, C. 1976: *Understanding Organizations*. London: Penguin.

Herriot, P. 1992: *The Career Management Challenge*. London: Sage.

Herriot, P., Manning, W. E. G. and Kidd, J. M. 1997: The content of the psychological contract. *British Journal of Management*, Vol. 8, 151–62.

Herriot, P. and Pemberton, C. 1995: *New Deals: The Revolution in Managerial Careers*. Chichester: Wiley.

Herriot, P. and Pemberton, C. 1997: Facilitating New Deals. *Human Resource Management Journal*, Vol. 7, No. 1, 45.

Kanter, R. M. 1989: *When Giants Learn To Dance*. London: Simon & Schuster.

Kotter, J. P. 1973: The Psychological Contract. *California Management Review*, Vol. 15, 91–9.

Lane, C. 1989: *Management and Labour in Europe: The industrial enterprise in Germany, Britain and France*. Aldershot: Edward Elgar.

Lawrence, B. 1984: Age Grading: The Implicit Organisational Timetable. *Journal of Occupational Behaviour*, Vol. 5, 23–35.

Lawrence, P. 1992: Management Development in Europe: A study of Cultural Contrast, Britain and France. *Human Resource Management Journal*, 11–23.

Liff, S. and Ward, K. 1998: *Distorted Views through the Glass Ceiling: The construction of women's understanding of promotion and senior management positions*. Paper presented to the 1st Gender Work and Organization Conference, Manchester.

Lockwood, J., Teevan, P. and Walters, M. 1992: *Who's Managing The Managers? The Reward and Career Development of Middle Managers in a Flat Organization*. Corby: Institute of Management.

McGovern, P., Hope-Hailey, V. and Stiles, P. (1998): The Managerial Career After Downsizing: Case Studies from the 'Leading Edge'. *Work, Employment &; Society*, **12**(3), 457.

Martin, G., Staines, H. and Pate, J. 1998: Linking Job Security and Career Development in a New Psychological Contract. *Human Resource Management Journal*, Vol. 8, No. 3, 20–40.

Marshall, J. 1995: *Women Managers Moving On: Exploring Careers and Life Choices*. London: Routledge.

Meyer, J. and Allen, N. 1984: Testing the side-bet theory of organizational commitment: some methodological considerations. *Journal of Applied Psychology*, Vol. 69, 372–8.

Naylor, M. and Purdie, E. 1992: Results of the 1991 Labour Force Survey. *Employment Gazette*, April, London: HMSO.

Newell, H. and Dopson, S. 1996: Muddle in the Middle: Organizational Restructuring and Middle Management Careers. *Personnel Review*, Vol. 25, No. 4, 4–20.

Riechers, A. E. 1985: A review and re-conceptualisation of Organizational Commitment. *Academy of Management Review*, Vol. 10, 465–76.

Riechers, A. E. 1986: Conflict and Organizational Commitments. *Journal of Applied Psychology*, Vol. 71, 508–14.

Robinson, S. L. and Rousseau, D. M. 1994: Violating the Psychological Contract: not the exception but the norm. *Journal of Organizational Behaviour*, Vol. 15, 245–59.

Scase, R. and Goffee, R. 1989: *Reluctant Managers: Their Work and Life Styles*. London: Unwin.

Schein, E. 1978: *Career Dynamics: Matching Individual and Organizational Needs*. Reading, MS: Addison-Wesley.

Sisson, K. 1989: Personnel in Transition? In Sisson, K. (ed.), *Personnel Management in Britain*. Oxford: Blackwell, 22–54.

Sofer, C. 1970: *Men in Mid-Career: a Study of British Managers and Technical Specialists*. London: Cambridge University Press.

Sonnenfeld, J. A., Peiperl, M. A. and Kottes, J. P. 1992: Strategic Determinants of Managerial Labour Markets. *Human Resource Management*, Vol. No. 27–4.

Storey, J., Edwards, P. K. and Sisson, K. 1997: *Managers in the Making: Careers, Development and Control in Corporate Britain and Japan*. London: Sage.

Torrington, D. and Hall, L. 1998: *Human Resource Management*. London, Prentice-Hall Europe.

Wheatley, M. 1992: *The Future of Middle Management*. Corby: British Institute of Management.

Part **4**

Pay and Performance

10

From Performance Appraisal to Performance Management

Stephen Bach

Assessment of performance has become a pervasive feature of modern life. Individuals are bombarded with opportunities to undertake assessment: on television programmes; on train or plane journeys; the adequacy of their local library; the cleanliness of a fast-food restaurant; and in the political process in which opinion polls, phone-ins, focus groups and referenda have become ubiquitous. Whether the request to assess an activity is welcomed or viewed as a source of irritation, the request to appraise a service is relatively uncontentious. By contrast, the growth of similar processes within organizations, especially performance appraisal, which is the focus of this chapter, has frequently generated controversy and failed to meet managerial expectations.

Performance appraisal of managers has long been a mainstay of personnel management practice and its spread to other occupations exemplifies the increasing uptake of the systematic and consistent approach to personnel practice touched on in chapter 1. The increasing use of performance appraisal, however, has been accompanied by greater awareness of its limitations. Within the prescriptive personnel management literature this critical awareness has spawned attempts to link individual performance appraisal to corporate objectives, exemplified by the interest in performance management, and the search for more varied forms of feedback and performance measures which involve the appraisee more fully (Bevan and Thompson 1992). Alongside these developments, there has been the emergence of a more critical literature which attributes the resurgent popularity of performance appraisal as a part of the panoply of techniques used by employers to elicit commitment and at the same time to exercise detailed control over employee behaviour (Townley 1993; Newton and Findlay 1996).

As well as its intrinsic importance, the reason for the focus on performance appraisal is that its evolution in recent years sheds light on many of the thorniest controversies surrounding human resource management. First, it has been suggested that the shift from performance appraisal to performance management is indicative of the emergence of a more strategic and integrated approach to personnel practice. However, as with other aspects of HRM, there may be a gap between the formal policy and actual practice of performance appraisal. Second, performance appraisal, and especially the emergence of performance management, is a microcosm of the debate about whether HRM is predominantly a 'soft' or 'hard' management style. The soft approach to performance management is associated with the development of resourceful employees, identifying training needs to ensure high levels of future performance. In contrast, a hard approach is primarily concerned with reviewing current performance against individual objectives and linking these ratings to individual pay. This type of reward-driven approach contrasts markedly with a developmental-driven approach.

Third, integral to the emergence and practice of HRM has been an emphasis on the integration of personnel polices to ensure internal consistency and 'fit' between personnel policies and business strategy. Performance management exemplifies these developments because its distinctiveness arises from an emphasis on linking corporate to individual objectives. In addition, performance appraisal, an activity that has always been undertaken by line managers, illustrates the dilemmas for personnel specialists of devolving personnel activities to line managers who may be indifferent to the priorities of personnel specialists.

The chapter starts by putting performance appraisal into the context of the growth in interest and coverage of systems of performance management. It proceeds to examine the forms and extent of performance appraisal and discuss the problems associated with it. It argues that the prescriptive literature concentrates on implementation problems which are viewed as remedial through proper training and communication. Radical critiques of performance appraisal, influenced by labour process and Foucauldian traditions, raise more fundamental questions about the purpose of performance appraisal but are too one dimensional in their assessment. The final part of the chapter examines recent attempts to overcome many of the problems of performance appraisal. In particular, it reviews the move to broaden the aims and process of performance appraisal by using so-called '360-degree' and 'upward' appraisal systems.

Performance Management: Origins and Outcomes

With the increased recognition of the problems that permeate most company appraisal schemes, discussed in detail below, there have been attempts to refashion appraisal to ensure that it contributes more fully to effective personnel practice. The most frequently mentioned development has been the shift from performance appraisal to performance management. Reflecting the importance attached to integrating personnel policies and business strategies, many employers have focused on the role of performance appraisal within a broader organizational context in which appraisal is only one part, albeit the key component, of a more systematic process of performance management. In common with many recent personnel initiatives, the key impetus for its development has been the more competitive environment in which firms operate. This has placed a premium on firms' ability to measure and improve the performance of their staff. This pressure has not been confined to the private sector: central government strictures to demonstrate value for money and clear accountability has ensured a strong interest in performance management across the public sector. Restructuring within organizations, with an emphasis on decentralized decision making and greater responsibilities placed on line managers for staff management, has lent itself to the use of performance management systems seeking to align individual and corporate objectives. Devolved decision making has often been accompanied by individual reward systems and performance management has provided the means to link rewards to performance (Bevan and Thompson 1992; Storey and Sisson 1993). Moreover, many organizations have viewed the introduction of performance management as a means to facilitate cultural change and establish and evaluate staff against a set of core competences, as is the case at KPMG (the professional services organization) (IRS 1999a).

Personnel practitioners also have a strong interest in promoting the use of performance management systems. When personnel managers have presided over ineffectual appraisal systems this has reinforced negative perceptions among managers that personnel is primarily an administrative and policing function concerned to collect appraisal forms whose relevance has been lost in the mists of time. In this light, personnel practitioner enthusiasm for performance management can be viewed as the latest in a long line of what Legge (1978) termed 'conformist innovation' strategies, in which personnel managers justify their activities in terms of the dominant financial nexus within organizations. Support for this interpretation can be found in the two most recent Institute of Personnel and Development (IPD) sponsored surveys of performance management (Bevan and Thompson 1992; Armstrong and Baron 1998). A key aim of the 1992 study was to test out the belief that performance management activities 'contribute significantly and measurably to organizational productivity and profitability' (Armstrong and Baron 1992: 1). Unable to establish the link in 1992, the IPD returned to the issue in their 1998 report, but the hoped-for link remained elusive.

This has not prevented the superiority of performance management over traditional appraisal being widely acclaimed. Advocates of performance management claim that its novelty resides in the cycle of integrated activities which ensure that a systematic link is established between the contribution of each employee and the overall performance of the organization. This strategic approach contrasts with the free-standing nature of performance appraisal, in which the outcomes of each individual appraisal are rarely linked to overall corporate objectives. Line managers, rather than personnel specialists, have the dominant role in the design and management of the performance management process and a premium is placed on ensuring effective communication and feedback is given to employees.

The consensus about why performance management has emerged as a key issue is not matched by agreement about its precise meaning. Storey and Sisson (1993: 131) suggest that, at its broadest, it can refer to any activity which is designed to improve the performance of employees and in its narrowest sense can be equated with individual performance-related pay. Bevan and Thompson (1992: 5) identify a number of components which they would expect to find within any organization claiming to operate a performance management system. These included: communicating clear objectives to employees; establishing departmental and individual objectives related to wider objectives; conducting formal reviews of progress towards targets; using these reviews to establish training needs and ensuring an overall evaluation of the whole process. This definition excluded individual performance-related pay (PRP), although most commentators suggest PRP is an integral part of performance management (Storey and Sisson 1993: 132; Lewis 1998).

This imprecision reflects the diversity of personnel practices incorporated under the performance management label. Bevan and Thompson (1992) in their survey for the IPD of 1,800 employers found that just under 20 per cent of them claimed to operate a performance management system. Alongside many of the components identified above, they found that organizations with formal systems of performance management were more likely to place heavy emphasis on communicating with staff and involving them through systems of total quality management. Performance-related pay was a common feature of these organizations alongside a strong emphasis on setting clear and quantifiable targets. None the less, this uniformity belies the variation in approach highlighted in the accompanying study (Fletcher and Williams 1992). In addition, it should not be assumed that these various components were fashioned into an integrated whole because both reports highlighted the uneven and piecemeal spread of performance management. As Fletcher and Williams (1992) note:

> But what was most striking about the origination of formal performance management systems was their often reactive nature ... This suggests an absence, in most organizations of an over-arching strategic rationale for the introduction of performance management. (p. 77)

In the most recent survey carried out for the IPD by Armstrong and Baron (1998), based on a survey of 562 personnel practitioners, it was reported that 69 per cent of organizations had a formal process of performance management. Although reflecting a smaller sample than the previous survey, and reliant on personnel specialists self-reporting, it represents a substantial increase in the growth of performance management. As important as its increased coverage was its changing character. One danger of the definitional malleability noted earlier is that it can disguise important changes in organizational practices which have occurred over the course of the 1990s. In particular, there has been a shift from an almost exclusive emphasis on reward-driven systems based on individual performance-related pay and quantifiable objectives towards more rounded systems of performance management with a stronger developmental focus. This was borne out by the survey results which showed that, although objective setting and annual appraisal remained the dominant features of performance management, the use of personal development plans was far more prevalent than performance-related pay (see table 10.1).

What are the main elements of this shift in emphasis and why has it occurred? First, there have been changes in the establishment and measurement of objectives linked to the reorientation of performance management, so that employee development is more prominent within the process. For much of the 1990s, objective setting was tailored to the requirements of individual performance-related pay systems requiring measurable individual objectives to ensure performance-related pay schemes operated as intended. But this brought its own difficulties, in particular, as chapter 11 observes, concerns about the narrowness of objectives and criticisms that the focus on achieving targets could impinge on teamwork. With less emphasis placed on reward-driven performance management, the requirement to generate precise ratings has diminished; in the IPD survey the proportion of respondents who provided an overall rating for performance had fallen since 1991 from 64 to 54 per cent (Armstrong and Baron 1998: 107). Linked to this trend, has been a modification to the exclusive focus on outputs and whether individual objectives have been met by incorporating consideration of inputs and how objectives are achieved. This change in emphasis is reflected in the increasing use of competences as part of the performance management process (see table 10.1 and IRS 1999b).

Second, organizations have broadened the establishment of individual and corporate objectives away from an almost exclusive focus on short-term financial targets towards a

Table 10.1 Features of performance management

Feature	Percentage
Objective setting and review	85
Annual appraisal	83
Personal development plans (PDPs)	68
Self-appraisal	45
Performance-related pay (PRP)	43
Coaching/mentoring	39
Career management	32
Competence assessment	31
Twice-yearly appraisal	24
Subordinate (180-degree) feedback	20
Continuous assessment	17
Rolling appraisal	12
360-degree feedback	11
Peer appraisal	9
Balanced scorecard	5

Source: Armstrong and Baron, 1998

so-called 'balanced scorecard' of key results areas. This approach is used at the Halifax financial services organization, for example (IDS 1997: 8). Each branch has targets set in four quadrants comprising: financial perspectives; internal process perspectives; customer perspectives; and staff development perspectives. The intention is to emphasize that performance is about more than financial results. But, curiously, no targets are set for staff development, which would appear to undermine the suggestion that targets in each quadrant are of equal importance.

Performance management has been broadened further to take into account comparisons with other organizations in the same or other sectors. In the public sector, this has been exemplified by the explosion across the public services of performance indicators and league tables. This adds a further dimension to performance management with, for example, teachers no longer only concerned with their own individual appraisal, but also required to consider their contribution to their school's overall performance in league tables. The Labour Government's plans for the public services continue this approach with a strong emphasis on benchmarking performance alongside proposals to link pay progression to appraisal for teachers (Treasury 1998).

These developments, which have anchored performance appraisal more firmly into a system of performance management, have recast but not eliminated many of the managerial dilemmas traditionally associated with measuring individual performance. Although Armstrong and Baron (1998) suggest that approaches to performance management have become more effective over the last decade, they still report that 37 per cent of their respondents viewed performance management as 'ineffective' or only 'slightly effective' in improving organizational performance (p. 109). For the time being, it seems, the pendulum has swung away from the focus on rewards towards a greater concern with development, but this is likely to provide only a temporary respite from continuing debate about the appropriate balance between development and rewards. A further tension is the continuing emphasis on the development of objective measures of performance, which has to be set aside a recognition that subjectivity may be an inevitable feature of performance management (Grint 1993). Most performance management systems are designed with the assumption that managers within organizations can establish clear unambiguous goals which can be broken down into individual components, are accepted by the individuals concerned and can be easily measured. The extent to which these assumptions are valid goes to the heart of the problems of performance appraisal, which forms the core component of all systems of performance management.

Performance Appraisal: Policy and Practice

Concerns about performance appraisal are not new, as McGregor's (1957) 'uneasy look' at appraisal illustrates. It has only been in the last decade, however, that criticism has included a more radical tinge, challenging many of the cherished assumptions of performance appraisal. Until recently, most criticism of appraisal has come from within mainstream management writing. For McGregor (1960), with his concern for the human side of enterprise, appraisal represented a judgemental and demotivating process. Similar concerns were voiced by Deming (1982), who suggested that appraisal was 'a deadly disease' which blamed individuals for problems systematic to organizations. Margerison (1976) went as far as to predict that appraisal would 'fall apart at the seams' (cited in Gill 1977: 66) due to a combination of managerial indifference, employee ambivalence and union opposition. This theme was reiterated by Fletcher (1993), who suggested that the days of standardized appraisals were numbered. But, despite these gloomy predictions, the use of performance appraisal has flourished.

Although the surveys conducted have often had low response rates (14 per cent in both IRS 1994 and Industrial Society 1997) and are not strictly comparable, the overall evidence indicates that there has been an increase in the incidence of appraisal schemes, although the increase has been much more modest than is usually claimed. In the first large-scale survey commissioned by the IPM, Gill et al. (1973) reported that 74 per cent of her respondents had an appraisal scheme in place for some of their workforce, a figure which rose to 82 per cent by 1977 and remained at that level in 1986 (Long 1986). In the 1990s, the total has continued to edge up with IRS (1994) and the Industrial Society (1997) reporting that up to 90 per cent of their respondents used an appraisal system for some of their staff and by 1999, the figure reported by IRS had almost reached 100 per cent (IRS 1999b). Storey (1992) also noted managerial interest in reinvigorating performance appraisal within the 15 mainstream organizations he examined. What accounts for this increased use of appraisal?

The purpose of appraisal

Respondents are sometimes asked why they have introduced appraisal schemes, encouraging bland responses such as 'to improve performance' or to 'identify training needs' with respondents frequently ticking a number of responses demonstrating that employers may have multiple objectives for appraisal systems (see, for example, IRS 1994, 1999b). The responses may account for the apparent paradox of the increasingly vocal criticism of appraisal accompanied by its increased usage. It is precisely the multiple and potentially conflicting objectives that employers seek of appraisal schemes, as revealed in survey evidence, which accounts for many of the implementation difficulties that arise for employers in their use (Beer 1981).

The increased use of appraisal systems has been linked to the extension of individual performance-related pay which, as chapter 11 suggests, shows little sign of subsiding. Bevan and Thompson (1992: 15), in their survey for the Institute of Personnel Management, had difficulties in pinning down the meaning of performance management, but found that it was closely associated with the use of individual performance-related pay. Consequently, it is often assumed that the growth of performance appraisal has resulted from the extension of performance-related pay. This assumption does not provide the full picture, not least because, as noted above, the biggest increase in the uptake of performance appraisal occurred during the 1970s.

In fact, there is little evidence to suggest performance appraisal has been introduced primarily to support individual performance pay. Long (1986: 15) reported that assessment of salary increases was not viewed as one of the main purposes of performance review and there had been virtually no change since 1977. For most organizations, reward policies are a less important influence on appraisal practice than broader issues of training and development (IRS 1994: 8; 1999b: 8). An Industrial Society (1997) survey reported that only 14 per cent of respondents included 'discussing performance reward' as an element of the appraisal system and only 12 per cent suggested that the main purpose of the appraisal system was 'to allocate performance increases fairly'. It is more plausible to argue that, in the early 1990s, the emphasis on performance-related pay shaped the type of scheme adopted rather than being a key influence on the increasing use of performance appraisal (see, for example, Storey 1992: 107).

An important influence on the increased use of appraisal has been the commitment of Conservative Governments in the 1980s and 1990s to introduce private-sector 'best practice' into the public sector as part of its attempt to enhance managerial control and increase efficiency (Winchester and Bach 1995). There had been little tradition of performance appraisal in the public services (see Long 1986: 7), reflecting the self-regulatory ethos of the professional staff that dominate the sector. The education sector is indicative of these developments, with the pre-incorporation university sector committing itself to appraisal from the mid 1980s in return for a substantial pay rise (Townley 1990). In the school sector, protracted discussions led to the introduction of appraisal from the early 1990s (Healy 1997). The establishment of appraisal within the public sector has been especially contentious because of its association with the command-and-control style of management seemingly favoured by Conservative governments. Appraisal has been viewed by employees and trade unions as a means to reinforce budgetary constraints and ensure conformity with government priorities.

Historically, the main purpose of appraisal schemes has been influenced by the dominant issues in personnel management practice. Thus, in the mid 1960s, when management by objectives (MBO) was being forcefully advocated, appraisal practice was strongly influenced by this approach with a focus on current performance (Gill et al. 1973). Individual performance-related pay also skewed appraisal systems towards a focus on recent performance. With the interest in core competencies, many organizations have become interested in defining performance against competencies, using the appraisal process to assess whether employees are exhibiting those aspects of behaviour deemed integral to corporate success. Storey (1992: 107) attributed much of the revived interest in appraisal within the organizations he examined as arising from the interest in developing organization-specific competencies. A further stimulus for organizations to revamp their appraisal systems has arisen from the interest in gaining external accreditation, such as Investors in People, discussed in chapter 7. The existence of an appraisal process is central to demonstrating that training and development needs are reviewed against targets at organizational and individual level (Investors in People 1998: 26).

The main purpose of performance appraisal has continued to oscillate between a concern with short-term performance as exemplified by MBO and PRP and a more developmental orientation. Irrespective of the formal approach adopted, a common use of performance appraisal has been as a means to discipline employees despite categorical advice that appraisal should not be used for disciplinary purposes (ACAS 1996: 24). None the less IRS (1994: 8) found that 18 per cent of respondents viewed identifying poor performance as a prelude to disciplinary action as one reason for introducing appraisal. In his study of trainee accountants, Grey (1994) notes that, although performance appraisal was presented as an aid for career management, in practice it was used to discipline employees and weed out poor performers in the annual 'cull'.

For personnel specialists, the increased use of appraisal is welcome because the establishment of an appraisal system represents the systematic collection of information about employees which provides the bedrock of all personnel practice. Unlike for line managers, who tend to view appraisal as a means to an end – whether it be to justify decisions, reward good employees or signal areas for improvement – for personnel specialists appraisal is an end in itself as it provides a range of data to implement personnel policies, including training and development need analysis, career planning and aspects of reward management. Appraisal data is a valuable source of information about the effectiveness of recruitment and selection and equal opportunity policies. In organizations such as County NatWest, for example, the persistence of personnel specialists in badgering recalcitrant line managers to complete their appraisal forms is indicated by the employment of a personnel trainee during the appraisal period to ensure high completion rates (Carlton and Sloman 1992: 93).

Who is appraised?

Performance appraisal has traditionally been associated with managerial staff because of its appropriateness in the range of available monitoring and control systems. Not surprisingly, the largest proportion of staff – usually in excess of 80 per cent – covered by appraisal are managers covering a broad spectrum of the managerial hierarchy. An important exception to this pattern are board-level directors. Long (1986: 9) reported that the coverage of appraisal arrangements for directors was almost half the figure for other managers. Little seems to have changed in the intervening decade with the Industrial Society (1997) noting that under half of board-level directors participate in an appraisal process. This finding appears to contradict the commitment of top managers to openness and empowerment, although support for these values has been viewed as integral to the recent development of 'upward' and '360-degree' appraisal (Ward 1997: 24).

One of the most trumpeted developments in performance appraisal has been its extension to cover a larger proportion of the existing workforce. In addition to the large swathes of public-sector professionals now covered by appraisal, its extension to semi-skilled workers has been viewed as an important initiative to develop the commitment of these workers to managerially defined patterns of behaviour. The harmonization of the conditions of employment of manual and non-manual workers, as exemplified by the 1997 single-status agreement in local government, can be seen in this light. Townley (1989) put a different gloss on these developments, suggesting that in essence appraisal is being used as a more subtle form of managerial control with tighter monitoring of manual workers' performance (Townley 1989: 104–5). This argument was based on the finding by Long (1986: 9) that between 1977 and 1986 appraisal had been extended to cover more secretarial and supervisory staff and most strikingly the proportion of skilled and semi-skilled employees had increased from 2 to 24 per cent. Although the robustness of Long's (1986) survey has been criticised (Newton and Findlay 1996: 42; Storey 1992: 107), by the second half of the 1990s survey evidence indicated that approximately one-third of semi-skilled workers were being included in appraisal arrangements (IRS 1994, Industrial Society 1997). The first findings from the 1998 WERS reported that 54 per cent of non-managerial employees had their performance formally appraised, although no information is yet available about the processes involved (Cully et al. 1998: 10).

With the changing composition of the workforce and the substantial increase in the use of part-time and fixed-term contract workers, discussed in chapter 1, the extent to which these groups are covered by appraisal is of increasing importance. With the trend to harmonize the working arrangements of part-time and full-time workers, one could expect that the proportion of part-time workers covered by appraisal arrangements will increase. There is limited evidence on the current proportion of part-time staff covered by appraisal arrangements and without knowing their occupational composition it is difficult to assess the significance of a figure of 55 per cent inclusion (Industrial Society 1997). More starkly, only 18 per cent of workers on fixed-term contracts were covered by appraisal arrangements, which suggests that a crucial segment of many organizations' workforces are excluded from formal personnel management systems.

What is appraised?

At the core of the appraisal process is the type of performance criteria used for rating individuals. In traditional appraisal schemes the personality traits of individuals were rated based on the 'commonsense' assumption that traits such as leadership skills and loyalty are important for effective performance. The use of personality traits has been subject to extensive criticism for their subjective characteristics and because of the difficulty of isolating the particular facet of personality responsible for effective job performance. The use of trait-based methods has continued to wane over the course of the 1970s and 1980s, although this does not preclude appraisers continuing to make judgements on the basis of personality traits, even if this is justified in terms of more acceptable performance criteria (Barlow 1989).

The dominant approach, particularly for managerial staff, continues to be the assessment of individuals against objectives established in the previous appraisal round (IRS 1994,

1999b; Industrial Society 1997). This approach is considered to allow a more objective discussion of performance and potentially allows individuals to have greater involvement in setting the performance criteria against which they will be judged. But, as Kessler (1994: 484–6) suggests, a formidable array of difficulties confronts managers in establishing agreed performance criteria. Especially in service industries, it may be difficult to establish tangible and quantifiable performance objectives, and this difficulty may be exacerbated in politically sensitive sectors such as health in which the key performance criteria for staff may be contested, as the debate in the health service about the significance of waiting lists testifies. For other occupational groups, such as clerical staff, the scope for individual discretion may be so limited as to render the establishment of targets a futile ritual.

Lewis's (1998) study of three differing financial services organizations highlighted many of these difficulties. At the high street bank and the building society, there was considerable unease about the manner in which objectives were set. Although officially a consultative process occurred between the area and branch manager, in practice branch managers had few illusions that objectives were imposed from the centre. Managers also expressed concern about the number of key performance targets they were expected to meet – about 20 at the building society – coupled with the narrow, short-term financial orientation of their targets.

A related concern is that individuals' tenacious pursuit of their own performance targets may lead them to neglect other aspects of their job or to focus on achieving their objectives to the detriment of teamwork or other important aspects of organizational performance. There is a heightened danger of this occurring in a context in which managers complain that they are being pressurized to achieve harder performance targets. These concerns have led some organizations to modify their performance criteria so that managers are assessed on the manner in which they achieve their targets as well as the targets themselves (IDS 1997).

These latter developments reflect a concern to develop performance criteria extending beyond a sole focus on objectives towards a more rounded focus on behaviour. Various dimensions of performance are linked to a series of behavioural statements and employees are rated according to the extent to which they demonstrate these behaviours. For example, at United Distillers employees are assessed against seven management competencies: commitment to results; leadership; interpersonal effectiveness; people development; problem solving; strategic awareness and capability; and international perspective (IDS 1997: 4). The best-known methods using this type of approach are Behavioural Observation Scales (BOS) and Behavioural Anchored Rating Scales (BARS). Managers might be asked to identify a key aspect of performance such as 'handling customer complaints' and examples would be devised of good, average and poor performance against this anchor with a numerical value attached to each statement. Managers are then able to rate each employee against each anchor which incorporates specific competencies.

Appraisal Under the Spotlight

The orthodox critique

Appraisal has become a mainstay of personnel management practice and has spread to sectors and occupational groups formerly excluded. But, despite this increased coverage, appraisal has not been immune from sustained criticism. The dominant critique of appraisal arises from within an orthodox management framework. These criticisms do not challenge the underlying managerially defined purpose of appraisal, but rather they seek to remedy the imperfections in the design and implementation of different appraisal systems.

A fundamental, and widely acknowledged, problem is that the appraisal process is used for a variety of conflicting purposes (Torrington and Hall 1995: 319; Marchington and Wilkinson 1996: 142). Appraisal can be used to motivate staff to improve performance by establishing clear objectives for the future and letting them know what is expected of them. This contrasts with an appraisal process which is primarily concerned with distributing rewards based on an assessment of past performance. Finally, the appraisal process can be more geared to development, with training needs identified to remedy deficiencies in performance revealed by the appraisal process. The difficulty is that, frequently, these different elements are blended together in an ill-defined manner. The appraiser is forced to adopt conflicting roles, cast as both a monitor and judge of performance, but also as an understanding counsellor (see figure 10.1). It is generally assumed that employees are unlikely to confide their limitations and anxieties about job performance to their appraiser (Newton and Findlay 1996: 43), not least because it could directly impact on their remuneration if merit-related pay is used or, at the very least, it could indirectly hinder their promotion chances.

It is well documented that managers are reluctant to judge employees and to assign poor ratings to them (Rowe 1964). This reluctance to transmit negative feedback to employees has been attributed to a variety of motives including: a concern that it could prove demotivating, a recognition that their own lack of support and guidance may have contributed to poor performance; and a more straightforward concern to avoid conflict

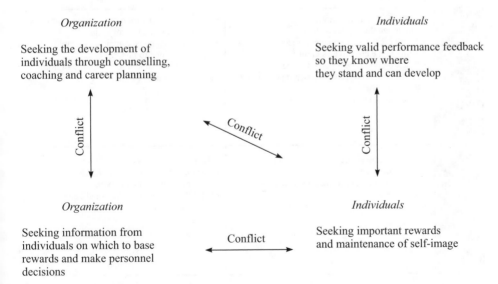

Figure 10.1 Conflicts in performance appraisal

Source: Beer 1981, Adapted from Porter, Lawler and Hackman

(Longnecker et al. 1987). Longnecker et al.'s (1987) study of 60 senior managers found that a variety of factors, other than the subordinate's actual performance, influenced the ratings managers allocated their subordinates (see figure 10.2). At County Natwest, human resource managers complained that 'Systematic overrating of staff is an ongoing problem' (Carlton and Sloman 1992: 87). As Grint (1993: 68) points out, the question of for whom this is a problem does not merit discussion. Compounding the managerial problems of rater bias is the existence of the inflation of performance feedback. In other words, even when poor ratings are allocated to employees, there is a tendency for supervisors to explain away lower ratings, diluting the impact of poor ratings (Waung and Highhouse 1997).

A variety of other distortions have been noted in the appraisal process which focus on the appraisal interview (Furnham 1993; Grint 1993). Given the problems of biased assessment raised in chapter 5 in relation to the selection interview, it is likely that similar problems will occur in appraisal interviews. The first problem is the 'halo effect' distortion. This arises when one attribute of the individual is used as the basis to rate the overall performance of the person, largely irrespective of the stated criterion. The reluctance of managers to be too harsh or overly lenient can result in an error of central tendency in which everybody is rated as average. This reluctance to differentiate between appraisee undermines the value of the appraisal process. A third problem is called 'recency bias'. Because managers rarely keep detailed notes about their appraisees, and are not very precise about rating all the behaviours they are required to judge, there is a tendency to base appraisal on the recent past, regardless of how representative it is of performance over the year. This shortcoming may be tempered by the shift within some organizations from appraisal as an annual process to a more continuous process of performance review (Armstrong and Baron 1998: 115).

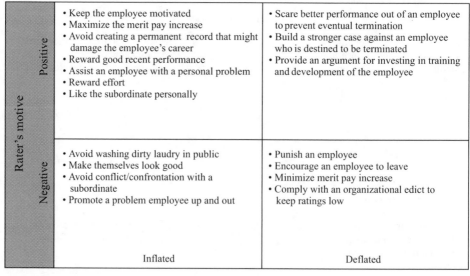

Rater's motive		Inflated	Deflated
	Positive	• Keep the employee motivated • Maximize the merit pay increase • Avoid creating a permanent record that might damage the employee's career • Reward good recent performance • Assist an employee with a personal problem • Reward effort • Like the subordinate personally	• Scare better performance out of an employee to prevent eventual termination • Build a stronger case against an employee who is destined to be terminated • Provide an argument for investing in training and development of the employee
	Negative	• Avoid washing dirty laudry in public • Make themselves look good • Avoid conflict/confrontation with a subordinate • Promote a problem employee up and out	• Punish an employee • Encourage an employee to leave • Minimize merit pay increase • Comply with an organizational edict to keep ratings low

Figure 10.2 A typology of rater motives and manipulative rating behaviour

Source: Adapted from Longnecker and Ludwig 1990

The appraisal interview is influenced also by the gender and ethnic origins of the appraisee and appraiser. Chen and DiTomaso (1996), surveying mainly American studies, suggest that women in similar jobs to men and performing to the same level gain similar ratings. However, they contend that gender impacts on ratings in two main ways. First, women gained better ratings when they were evaluated in 'women's' jobs and, second, cultural assumptions or implicit theories of performance criteria, i.e. the choice of performance standards actually used, may be unconsciously biased towards the values of white men. Many employees, especially women, complain of a competitive masculine culture at the workplace in which long hours are equated with loyalty and commitment to the organization with detrimental implications for appraisal ratings of those workers not prepared, or able, to demonstrate this level of 'commitment' (Lewis and Taylor 1996; Simpson 1998).

In these circumstances it is perhaps not surprising that it is widely argued that managers who undertake appraisals are, at best, ambivalent about the process and, at worst, outrightly hostile, viewing appraisals as generating unfair, subjective outcomes which are difficult to justify to individuals, demotivate staff and act as a lightning conductor for more generalized concerns about pay and promotion prospects (Barlow 1989). As one manager pithily remarked: 'Performance appraisal is a load of rubbish. You decide on the rating you want in the box and then make up a few words of narrative in the other sections to justify it' (Carlton and Sloman 1992: 86). A similar lack of enthusiasm among managers has been raised in other mainstream UK organizations with managers admitting that they 'go through the motions' of performance reviews because they suggested that appraisal lacked credibility (McGovern et al. 1997: 18; Storey et al. 1997: 182). One means to identify managerial commitment is to establish the percentage of appraisal forms which are completed, although even then high completion rates may reflect persistent badgering by the personnel department rather than line management enthusiasm (see, for example, Carlton and Sloman 1992: 93).

Few surveys pose this question. An exception is the Industrial Society's (1997: 9) which found that 64 per cent of organizations reported a more than two-thirds completion rate. This left 15 per cent of respondents who did not know how many appraisals were completed, 12 per cent who said that between one- and two-thirds were completed, and just 4 per cent admitting that less than one-third of appraisals were completed. A starker picture often emerges from case studies, with one personnel manager at a software firm admitting that over one-third of the workforce had never been appraised and that 85 per cent of staff had not been appraised for more than a year, although appraisals were meant to occur every six months (Howell and Cameron 1996).

Personnel specialists have adopted a variety of measures to reduce the subjectivity of the appraisal process and improve its credibility, assisted by a burgeoning applied psychology literature which has attempted to identify and eliminate 'leniency' (Kane et al. 1995; Waung and Highhouse 1997). One response, although unpopular with managers, has been to use forced distributions to prevent managerial leniency. The computer company Hewlett Packard used to use such an approach, but abandoned it because the perception amongst staff was that their rankings depended on the negotiation skills of their manager rather than their own performance. Instead, managers are provided with guidelines about the proportion of staff which would be expected to be in the top and bottom portions of the distribution (IDS 1997: 13).

Some authors have gone as far as to suggest that screening supervisory candidates for the tendency to rate leniently might be feasible (Kane et al. 1995). Within this type of applied psychology literature, the search for an objective appraisal process which eliminates rater bias continues. The extent to which the results of laboratory experiments of appraisal interviews conducted predominantly on students can be applied to complex organizations must remain doubtful. More generally, in response to concerns about the fairness of appraisal ratings, employers are investing greater efforts in checking the fairness and consistency of appraisal results (IRS 1999b: 16).

Greater recognition that the appraisal process is shaped by the behaviour of two parties has led more attention to be paid to the contribution of the appraisee in developing a more accurate appraisal process. Self-appraisal draws on a unique source of information and provides an additional perspective on performance. Opinion is divided on the validity of self-ratings with some studies continuing to show that subjects rate themselves higher than other raters (Furnham and Stringfield 1998: 525). In addition, responses differ by gender, with women tending to rate themselves less positively than do men and being less lenient than men in their self-ratings (Fletcher 1999: 39). Company practice at firms such as Shell suggests that, rather than overestimating their performance, staff often underestimate their abilities and that self-appraisal promotes individual responsibility and openness (IDS 1997: 6)

The most common response to problems of subjectivity and rater bias is to redouble training efforts to ensure that managers are trained in conducting appraisals, to recognize good and bad performance, and be aware of the sources of potential bias. Managers have also tried to refine their performance measurements to reduce subjectivity. Bowles and Coates (1993: 13) express some scepticism about the effectiveness of these type of measures, not least because in their own survey of 48 organizations the favoured remedies bore little relationship to the problems identified and were the same methods that had been used for many years with apparently limited effect. Despite some evidence that managers are concerned to rectify these deficiencies, it could be argued that, in the main, senior managers expend relatively little effort in making their appraisal process function effectively.

First, line managers are rarely held accountable for how well they conduct performance appraisals on their staff. For example, even in the largest US companies (the so-called Fortune 100) only 22 per cent of them evaluated how effectively their managers conducted appraisals (Thomas and Bretz 1994: 31). In the UK, the relative unimportance attached to performance appraisal is symptomatic of the lack of emphasis that organizations attach to people-management practices. Fewer than half the line managers in the seven organizations surveyed by McGovern et al. (1997) considered successful implementation of personnel policies to be an important or very important factor in their own performance appraisals.

Second, it might be expected that line managers would have a pivotal role in the design of the appraisal process, reflecting their direct involvement and the trend to devolving responsibility for personnel activities to the line, as discussed in chapter 1 (Hall and Torrington 1998). This appears not to be the case, however. Long (1986) attributed line management's lack of commitment to the appraisal process as arising largely from their exclusion, although she anticipated that this would change in the future. Instead, there appears to be a fatalistic acceptance by line managers of the subjectivity of appraisal as an inevitable part of organizational life (Storey et al. 1997: 181).

The conclusion to emerge is that within the practitioner-orientated literature there is a strong awareness of the limitations of performance appraisal and numerous suggestions on how to remedy this problem. The underlying philosophy that unites these accounts is essentially unitarist. It is assumed that employees and employers both derive equal benefits from appraisal and this is especially likely to be the case when the appraisal process is as open and objective as possible. Consequently, although appraisals can never be totally free from a subjective element, problems that arise can be remedied by effective training and clear communication of the objectives and importance of the appraisal process. In short, it is the implementation of appraisal that is at fault rather than more fundamental problems associated with the assumptions that lie behind performance appraisal.

The radical critique

It is these implicit assumptions about the purpose of performance appraisal that have increasingly been questioned as a more critical literature has emerged. These perspectives, in their differing ways, are centrally concerned with the problems of management control and the contribution of performance appraisal towards ensuring that employees adhere to management objectives (Barlow 1989; Grey 1994; Healy 1997; Newton and Findlay 1996; Townley 1993). These accounts reject most of the assumptions that underpin the practitioner-orientated analysis of performance appraisal. Instead of a concern to prescribe how appraisal can operate effectively, the focus is on understanding the actual practice of appraisal within the workplace with greater emphasis on its specific context. Unitary assumptions about the benevolent purposes of appraisal are replaced by a more radical ideology concerned to examine managerial objectives, especially tighter control over behaviour and performance, the potential to individualize the employment relationship, and the scope for managers to use appraisal as a veneer to legitimate informal management. Some of these authors, especially those influenced by Foucault's (1981) work, view trends in appraisal as part of a more sinister management regime to control all aspects of employee behaviour and eliminate scope for employee resistance.

A dominant thread running through these accounts is the emphasis placed on the manner in which appraisal is used to bolster managerial power and control. Barlow's (1989) study of a petrochemicals firm highlights many of the shortcomings of appraisal as perceived by line managers. But he departs from the prescriptive literature in suggesting that these problems do not undermine the utility of the appraisal system to managers. Indeed, quite the reverse is true, because it allows managers discretion to promote favoured individuals but, if challenged, to legitimize them by referring to the formal appraisal process. The spread of performance appraisal to manual workers, school teachers and university lecturers has similarly been interpreted as a means to increase managerial control over diverse occupational groups formerly immune from these processes (Townley 1989, 1990; Healy 1997).

Within many of these critical accounts there are strong leanings towards Foucault's (1981) conception of power, with appraisal used by managers as a form of disciplinary gaze (see especially Townley 1993; Grey 1994) which complement other forms of electronic and personal surveillance found in call centres and the like. The starting point for this literature is Foucault's (1981) discussion of Bentham's Panoptican, the model prison in which prisoners can always be observed by the prison guards, but the guards cannot be seen by the prisoners. Because prisoners would never know whether they were being observed, the Panoptican combines surveillance and discipline. For Townley (1993), the relevance to appraisal within the university sector is clear: 'Appraisal operates as a form of panoptican with its anonymous and continuous surveillance as seen in the articulation of a monitoring role,' (Townley 1993: 232). Grey (1994) pursues similar themes, suggesting that, for trainee accountants, the appraisal process is used as a form of disciplinary technology with those rated as satisfactory running the risk of being summarily dismissed in the annual cull.

Although these critical perspectives provide an important corrective to the prevailing prescriptive literature on appraisal, they are not beyond criticism. There is a tendency to assume that managerial intentions are necessarily translated into managerial actions, ignoring the issue of human agency (Newton and Findlay 1996). Although Healy (1997) illustrates how trade unions have collectivized some of the individualistic intentions of the appraisal, she none the less emphasizes the 'inevitable role of control in the system' (p. 217). Similarly many commentators would be hard-pressed to recognize the picture of 'panoptican control' of academics portrayed by Townley (1990). Both Barlow (1989) and Townley (1989) view the achievement of managerial objectives as straightforward. This is curious when, as noted earlier, the management literature is replete with evidence of the ambivalent feelings of line managers towards appraisal and commentators express exasperation at the leniency shown by managers in rating employees.

Within Foucauldian accounts, there is a particular problem because of the failure to acknowledge that scope for employee resistance to appraisal still exists, even within the Panoptican organization. As Healy (1997: 216) recognizes, a recurring theme among her school-teacher respondents was 'appraisal disdain', which she interpreted as a form of resistance. In the very different and seemingly high-commitment context of an American microelectronics company McKinlay and Taylor (1996: 293) demonstrate that peer review, intended as the centrepiece of managerial disciplinary technology, floundered as workers traded monthly scores to undermine the monitoring intent of the scheme.

Despite their limitations, these critical accounts have helped to challenge many of the traditional assumptions about performance appraisal and to advance understanding of why the anticipated benefits of appraisal emerge only rarely in practice. Critical perspectives highlight that it is not sufficient to assume that clearer objectives and training of appraisers will yield satisfactory results. The contested nature of appraisal, the specific managerial objectives sought and the nature of the context in which it is applied, all have an important bearing on the impact of the appraisal process. These insights have informed many of the current developments in performance appraisal.

The Democratization of Appraisal?

The adoption of multiple sources of feedback has been the most trumpeted development in performance appraisal in the last few years and has attracted overwhelmingly positive endorsement, even from those who are sceptical about the value of traditional appraisal (see, for example, Grint 1993). A variety of terms have been used to signify that the appraisal process is no longer the preserve of managers appraising their employees, but can incorporate performance feedback information from a variety of stakeholders in the organization, to ensure a more rounded view of overall performance is established. It is the combination of information from self-appraisal, subordinate appraisal, peer appraisal and feedback from other internal customers, with the possibility of including external suppliers and customers, which has been termed '360-degree' appraisal. The term can be misleading because the most novel part of the process, and the aspect which has attracted most attention, has been the appraisal by staff of their managers, i.e. 'upward' appraisal. It is less common to use other sources for appraisal. In particular, customer feedback is rare and may be actively discouraged, for fear that it would be the organization, not the individual, who was being assessed (Kettley 1997: 40).

The interest in 360-degree appraisal and especially upward appraisal can be attributed to three main factors. First, the adoption of human resource management techniques with the emphasis on empowerment and teamwork assign greater responsibility to employees and these systems are premised on the assumption that employees are a key source of competitive advantage. Upward appraisal is a logical extension of this management style which impresses on employees that their voice is important with their feedback contributing to the rating and performance improvement of managerial staff. The adoption of competency-based forms of performance management requires managers to be evaluated against how much they exhibit these competencies, and employees, because of their close proximity to their manager, are in the best position to make these assessments (Ward 1997: 23). It is more difficult for all staff to ignore the results of performance feedback when it is based on more than one person's judgement.

Second, reductions in the number of managerial layers have left managers with a broader span of control. In conjunction with more diverse working arrangements, such as project teams and increased workloads, it is considered inappropriate to rely solely on the judgement of a single manager who may not be sufficiently in touch with their staff to judge their performance or may only be aware of certain aspects of performance. With increased recognition that performance appraisals can be subject to legal scrutiny, one safeguard is to use multiple sources of feedback to deflect legal challenges (Redman and Snape 1992). This reason may become more important when legal force is given to the European Union Data Protection Directive and employees are allowed to view personal information held in manual form, such as appraisal forms, as well as electronic forms as at present.

Third is the belief that 360-degree appraisal overcomes many of the limitations of traditional appraisal systems. Advocates maintain that upward appraisal may provide a more accurate view of performance because subordinates are in closer contact with their manager and are more directly affected by the manager's style than is the manager's superior. For these reasons, the subordinate can observe and judge more accurately the performance of the individual manager and the extent to which the manager is adhering to, rather than paying lipservice to, the empowerment philosophy which has gained ground in many organizations. Upward appraisal therefore provides a direct source of information about whether managers are able to achieve results through their people (Kettley 1997). Even if upward appraisal is not objective, at least it replaces individual subjectivity with subjectivity of a collective nature (Grint 1993: 71).

There is a recognition that 360-degree appraisal may not be appropriate for all companies or for all groups of employees and the occupational psychology research has extended its focus to include the congruence of ratings and leniency bias among different raters (see, for example, Furnham and Stringfield 1998). A number of these studies suggest that multi-source feedback is more appropriate for rating certain characteristics than others. Not surprisingly, subordinates are able to rate delegation more accurately than their managers, but managers can rate their own know-how and innovative capacities more effectively than can their staff (Mount 1984 cited in Kettley 1997:5).

It has been suggested that 360-degree appraisal is commonplace within many UK organizations (Fletcher 1999: 39). Armstrong and Baron, however, reported that only 11 per cent of companies used this form of feedback as part of their approach to performance management (table 10.1), although many others were contemplating its introduction (Armstrong and Baron 1998: 313). As with many personnel management innovations, company practice is rarely as widespread as the advocates suggest. The literature on 360-degree appraisal is influenced by American experience and comes from accounts of a small number of innovators – British Petroleum, British Airports Authority, WH Smith and US multinationals such as Rank Xerox (Kettley 1997; Redman and Snape 1992; Ward 1997). It is hard to avoid the suspicion that many of the books and articles are rather self-serving because they are often thinly veiled marketing efforts for 360-degree appraisal, especially their own proprietary feedback instrument. This would appear to be confirmed by Kettley (1997: 50), who reported that more than half her case study companies made use of an external consultant to design and analyse the data generated, often at high cost.

The 360-degree feedback has been used as part of the performance appraisal process to supplement traditional sources of information, but more often it is used for developmental purposes to enhance managers' awareness of their strengths and weaknesses. Handy et al. (1996), reported that 71 per cent of companies used feedback solely for developmental purposes, compared to 23 per cent of organizations who used feedback to support performance appraisal, and only 6 per cent of companies linked the process to pay. Kettley (1997: 41–2) classified the manner in which 360-degree appraisal was being used in her case studies into three categories. The most common approach was to support personal development by enabling participants to gain feedback on how their behaviour affected others and on their strengths and weaknesses. This sometimes formed a one-off or fed into personal development plans. Second, feedback was used more directly as part of the appraisal process to add another dimension to the discussion. Of the two companies which used it in this way, only one made it a compulsory element of the performance appraisal system. Finally, two of the organizations had developed feedback systems in which the focus was on improving the working relationships and performance of the team. These applications indicate that 360-degree appraisal is overwhelmingly a managerial process used to enhance managerial skills.

A prominent issue in any discussion of 360-degree appraisal is anonymity, with the majority of organizations providing feedback on a confidential basis. This is primarily to reassure participants that there would be no repercussions as a result of their feedback and would thus encourage them to be more honest. It may be less threatening to participants to receive their feedback on an anonymous basis. Other employers, however, argue that named feedback is more useful because it allows the feedback to be contextualized and related to specific situations or relationships, and can reduce the scope for unconstructive personal comments. Irrespective of the approach taken, difficulties remain with 45 per cent of employers using 360-degree appraisal, suggesting that subordinates who provide feedback feel threatened and unable to be honest and 36 per cent of employers suggesting that it is threatening to participants (Handy et al. 1996).

These results suggest that this type of feedback is likely to prove effective only within relatively high-trust organizations in which managers are prepared to accept criticism and be open enough to alter their behaviour as a result of the feedback provided. As Kanouse (1998: 3) warns, multi-rater feedback can easily fail; for example, if a company is about to restructure and shed jobs, then feedback mechanisms can be viewed as a means to select employees for redundancy. The 360-degree appraisal mechanisms can be subject to the same problems as arise from more traditional performance appraisal – poor communications, untrained raters and conflicting aims for the scheme (Kanouse 1998: 3).

Most of the commentary on 360-degree appraisal is overwhelmingly positive, but some key issues are scarcely considered. In particular, it is not self-evident that the feedback does challenge the basic assumptions underpinning all appraisal systems, as is often claimed. The 360-degree appraisal shares with more traditional appraisal the assumption that performance improvements arise from measuring and rewarding the performance of individuals, but uses a different method (i.e. subordinate feedback) to measure it. None the less, the focus remains on variations between individuals rather than examining the context in which those individuals work which may have a greater impact on performance. The 360-degree appraisal is trumpeted as empowering, but it does not necessarily challenge existing power relationships and behaviour within organizations. Employers decide whether to use such a system and take all the key decisions about its design and operation. Subordinates' views form only one part of managerial assessment and are used primarily for developmental rather than pay purposes. Beneath the gloss of democracy, many of the traditional assumptions of appraisal remain intact. For example, a striking feature of the literature on upward appraisal is the concern expressed about how managers might be upset by negative feedback, but such concerns are rarely raised in relation to the reactions of employees. The implication is clear: employees remain subordinates and should accept criticism gracefully, but the same standards cannot be applied to managers because it might erode managerial prerogatives. Winstanley and Stuart-Smith (1996: 70) conclude bluntly that 'It is ludicrous to suggest that multiple or upward appraisal redresses the power balance'. The risk is that, if staff do not genuinely view 360-degree appraisal as empowering, then many of the negative responses to appraisal highlighted earlier could re-emerge.

Conclusion

This chapter has highlighted the paradox that, although performance appraisal is being used more extensively than ever before, there is a much greater awareness of its limitations. This has encouraged considerable change in practice and an emphasis on performance appraisal giving way to performance management. A representation of these trends is shown as table 10.2. This representation may be unrealistically optimistic, but the key point is that much of the shift in emphasis has drawn on the criticisms of traditional performance appraisal that have emerged not only from prescriptive literature but also from an emerging radical critique of performance appraisal. These criticisms have yielded positive benefits. Not only have they revealed some of the questionable assumptions embodied in traditional appraisal practice and hastened the search for alternatives, they

Table 10.2 Developments in performance management since 1991

From	To
System	Process
Appraisal	Joint review
Outputs	Outputs/inputs
PRP	Development
Ratings common	Less rating
Top down	360-degree feedback
Directive	Supportive
Monolithic	Flexible
Owned by HR	Owned by users

Source: Armstrong and Baron, 1998

have also illustrated the importance of the context in which performance appraisal is implemented. This has allowed much greater clarity in designing and implementing performance appraisal with an explicit consideration of the primary purpose of appraisal, and recognizing differences between hierarchical or peer-orientated approaches and reward- or developmentally orientated systems

The increasing number of studies also provide some pointers as to why performance appraisal appears to be more accepted in some organizations than others. Employer practices which genuinely sustain trust by promoting transparency and procedural fairness alongside respect for the individual are more likely to lead to appraisal systems which are accepted and valued by the workforce. In some organizations, notably large swathes of the public services characterized by low trust and suspicion of managerial motives, most employers will face an uphill battle in gaining acceptance of the value of performance appraisal (see, for example, Healy 1997). Yet, even here, performance appraisal can be made more palatable. Marsden and French (1998), in a survey of performance-related pay in the public services which reported predominantly negative views of individual PRP, nevertheless found much more positive attitudes towards the establishment of objectives within the appraisal process. In the private sector, and focusing on managerial responses to appraisal, Storey et al. (1997: 183) highlighted the much more positive attitudes towards appraisal when formal, written objectives were established, suggesting that managers welcomed the certainty of clear objectives.

It is the sustained criticism of the imprecision and lack of objectivity of performance appraisal, and a recognition that too much weight has been attached to the annual appraisal interview, which has generated a search for more rounded forms of assessment and ones less reliant on a manager's rating of their employees. The shift towards an element of self-appraisal, the more diverse criteria used within performance management systems and the interest in 360-degree appraisal all testify to the emergence of a broader approach to performance appraisal. It appears that organizations are trying to make a virtue out of the different perspectives on performance which different stakeholders bring to the appraisal process. There are signs that these developments reflect, as Grint (1993: 74) advocates, a partial abandonment of a single, objective measure in favour of a more reflexive and sceptical approach which grudgingly accepts diversity. A key challenge then becomes how employers reconcile and use the diverse feedback they are receiving from a number of sources.

These developments also suggest that, while performance appraisal will remain at the heart of personnel management practice, it is likely to be increasingly linked to a system of performance management, drawing on a wider network of performance measures from both inside and outside the organization. Some of these indicators arise from the scope to monitor performance more easily by deploying information technology, whether in a manufacturing context, a call centre or a social security office. Other forms of performance information will be generated from surveillance by fellow employees, customers or mystery shoppers. These developments, while often viewed negatively in Foucauldian accounts, potentially provide opportunities for a more nuanced approach which moves away from the rightly and increasingly much-criticized one-dimensional view of individual performance.

References and further reading

ACAS 1996: *Employee Appraisal*. London: ACAS.

Armstrong, M. and Baron, A. 1998: *Performance Management: The New Realities*. London Institute of Personnel and Development.

Barlow, G. 1989: Deficiencies and the Perpetuation of Power: Latent Functions in Management Appraisal. *Journal of Management Studies*, **26**(5), 499–517.

Beer, M. 1981: Performance Appraisal: Dilemmas and Possibilities. *Organizational Dynamics*, **9**(4), 24–37.

Bevan, S. and Thompson, M. 1992: An Overview of Policy and Practice. In IPM, *Performance Management in the UK: An Analysis of the Issues*, London: Institute of Personnel Management.

Bowles, M. and Coates, G. 1993: Image and Substance: The Management of Performance as Rhetoric or Reality. *Personnel Review* **22**(2), 3–21.

Carlton, I. and Sloman, M. 1992: Performance Appraisal in Practice. *Human Resource Management Journal*, **2**(3), 80–94.

Chen, C. and DiTomaso, N. 1996: Performance Appraisal and Demographic Diversity. In E. Kossek and S. Label (eds), *Managing Diversity*, Oxford: Blackwell.

Clark, G. 1995: Performance Management. In Mabey, C. and Salaman, G., *Strategic Human Resource Management*, Oxford: Blackwell.

Cully, M., O'Reilly, A., Millward, N., Forth, J., Woodland, S., Dix, G. and Bryston, A. 1998: *The 1998 Workplace Employee Relations Survey: First Findings*. London: Department of Trade and Industry.

Deming, W.-E. 1982: *Out of the Crisis: Quality Productivity and Competitive Position*. Cambridge: Cambridge University Press.

Fletcher, C. 1993: Appraisal: An Idea Whose Time Has Gone? *Personnel Management*, **25**(9), 34–8.

Fletcher, C. 1999: The Implications of Research on Gender Differences in Self-Assessment and 360 Degree Appraisal. *Human Resource Management Journal* **9**(1), 39–46.

Fletcher, C. and Williams, R. 1992: Organizational Experience. In IPM, *Performance Management in the UK: An Analysis of the Issues*. London: Institute of Personnel Management.

Foucault, M. 1981: *Power/Knowledge: Selected Interviews and other Writings*. Brighton: Harvester Press.

Furnham, A. 1993: Management: Nothing to Do with Ability – Some of the Pitfalls of Employee Appraisals. *Financial Times*, 23 July, 15.

Furnham, A. and Stringfield, P. 1998: Congruence in Job-Performance Ratings: A Study of 360 Degree Feedback Examining Self, Manager, Peers and Consultant Ratings. *Human Relations*, **51**(4), 517–30.

Gill, D. 1977: *Appraising Performance: Present Trends and the Next Decade.* London: Institute of Personnel Management.

Gill, D., Ungerson, B. and Thakur, M. 1973: *Performance Appraisal in Perspective: a Survey of Current Practice.* London: Institute of Personnel Management.

Grey, C. 1994: Career as a Project of the Self and Labour Process Discipline. *Sociology,* **28**(2), 479–97.

Grint, K. 1993: What's Wrong with Performance Appraisals? A Critique and a Suggestion. *Human Resource Management Journal,* **3**(3), 61–77.

Hall, L. and Torrington, D. 1998: *The Human Resource Function: The Dynamics of Change and Development.* London: Pitman.

Handy, L., Devine, M. and Health, L. 1996: *360 Degree Feedback: Unguided Missile or Powerful Weapon?* Ashridge: Berkhampstead.

Healy, G. 1997: The Industrial Relations of Appraisal: The Case of Teachers. *Industrial Relations Journal,* **28**(3), 206–20.

Howell, K. and Cameron, E. 1996: The Benefits of an Outsider's Opinion. *People Management,* 8 August, 28–30.

IDS (Incomes Data Services) 1997: *Performance Management.* London: IDS.

IRS (Industrial Relations Services) 1994: Improving Performance: A Survey of Appraisal Arrangements. *Employment Trends,* 556, March, 5–14.

IRS 1999a: Accounting for Performance at KPMG. *Employment Trends,* 672, January, 12–16.

IRS 1999b: New Ways to Perform Appraisal. *Employment Trends,* 676, March, 7–16.

Industrial Society 1997: *Appraisal.* No. 37, London: Industrial Society.

Investors in People 1998: *The Investors in People Standard.* London: Investors in People.

Kane, J., Bernardin, J., Villanova, P. and Peyrefitte, J. 1995: Stability of Rater Leniency: Three Studies. *Academy of Management Journal,* **38**(4), 1036–51.

Kanouse, D. 1998: Why Multi-rater Feedback Systems Fail. *HRFocus,* January, 3.

Kessler, I. 1994: Performance Pay. In K. Sisson (ed.), *Personnel Management,* Oxford: Blackwell.

Kettley, P. 1997: *Personal Feedback: Cases in Point.* Sussex: Institute for Employment Studies, IES Report 326.

Legge, K. 1978: *Power, Innovation and Problem Solving in Personnel Management.* London: McGraw-Hill.

Lewis, P. 1998: Managing Performance-Related Pay Based on Case Study Evidence from the Financial Services Sector. *Human Resource Management Journal,* **8**(2) 66–77.

Lewis, S. and Taylor, K. 1996: Evaluating the Impact of Family-Friendly Employer Policies: A Case Study. In S. Lewis and J. Lewis (eds), *The Work–Family Challenge,* London: Sage.

Long, P. 1986: *Performance Appraisal Revisited.* London: Institute of Personnel Management.

Longnecker, C. and Ludwig, D. 1990: Ethical Dilemmas in Performance Appraisal Revisited. *Journal of Business Ethics,* **9**(4), 961–9.

Longnecker, C., Sims, H. and Gioia, D. 1987: Behind the Mask: The Politics of Employee Appraisal. *Academy of Management Review,* **1**(3), 183–93.

McGovern, P., Gratton, L., Hope-Hailey, V., Stiles. P. and Truss, C. 1997: Human Resource Management on the Line. *Human Resource Management Journal,* **7**(4), 12–29.

McGregor, D. 1957: An Uneasy Look at Performance Appraisals. *Harvard Business Review,* **35**(3), 89–95.

McGregor, D. 1960: *The Human Side of Enterprise.* New York: McGraw-Hill.

McKinlay, A. and Taylor, P. 1996: Power, Surveillance and Resistance: Inside the Factory of the Future. In P. Acker, C. Smith and P. Smith (eds), *The New Workplace and Trade Unionism,* London: Routledge.

Marchington, M. and Wilkinson, A. 1996: *Core Personnel and Development.* London: Institute of Personnel and Development.

Margerison, C. 1976: A Constructive Approach to Appraisal. *Personnel Management,* **8**(7), 30–4.

Marsden, D. and French, S. 1998: *What a Performance: Performance Related Pay in the Public Services.* London: Centre for Economic Performance.

Newton, T. and Findlay, P. 1996: Playing God? The Performance of Appraisal. *Human Resource Management Journal* **6**(3), 42–58.

Porter, L., Lawler, E. and Hackman, R. 1975: *Behavior is Organizations*. New York: McGraw-Hill.

Redman, T. and Snape, E. 1992: Upward and Onward: Can Staff Appraise their Managers? *Personnel Review*, **21**(7), 32–46.

Rowe, K. 1964: An Appraisal of Appraisal. *Journal of Management Studies*, **1**(1), 1–25.

Simpson, R. 1998: Presenteeism, power and organisational change: long hours as a career barrier and the impact on the working lives of women managers. *British Journal of Management*. **9** (special issue), 37–50.

Storey, J. 1992: *Developments in the Management of Human Resources*. Oxford: Blackwell.

Storey, J., Edwards, P. and Sisson, K. 1997: *Managers in the Making: Careers, Development and Control in Corporate Britain and Japan*. London: Sage.

Storey, J. and Sisson, K. 1993: *Managing Human Resources and Industrial Relations*. Buckingham: Open University Press.

Thomas, S. and Bretz, R. 1994: Research and Practice in Performance Appraisal: Evaluating Employee Performance in America's Largest Companies. *SAM Advanced Management Journal*, Spring, 28–34.

Thompson, P. and Ackroyd, S. 1995: All Quiet on the Workplace Front? *Sociology*, **29**(4), 615–33.

Torrington, D. and Hall, L. 1995: *Personnel Management: HRM in Action*. London: Prentice-Hall.

Townley, B. 1989: Selection and Appraisal – Reconstituting Social Relations? In J. Storey (ed.), *New Perspectives on HRM*, London: Routledge.

Townley, B. 1990: The Politics of Appraisal: Lessons of the Introduction of Appraisal into UK Universities. *Human Resource Management Journal*, **1**(2), 27–44.

Townley, B. 1993: Performance Appraisal and the Emergence of Management. *Journal of Management Studies*, **3**(2), 221–38.

Treasury 1998: *Modern Public Services for Britain: Investing in Reform*, Cm. 4011, London: The Stationery Office.

Ward, P. 1997: *360-Degree Feedback*. London: Institute of Personnel and Development.

Waung, M. and Highhouse, S. 1997: Fear of Conflict and Empathic Buffering: Two Explanations for the Inflation of Performance Feedback. *Organizational Behavior and Human Decision Processes*, **71**(1), 37–54.

Winchester, D. and Bach, S. 1995: The State: the Public Sector. In P. K. Edwards (ed.), *Industrial Relations*, Oxford: Blackwell.

Winstanley, D. and Stuart-Smith, K. 1996: Policing Performance: the Ethics of Performance Management. *Personnel Review*, **25**(6), 66–84.

11

Remuneration Systems

Ian Kessler

Broadly defined as the way in which employees are rewarded at the workplace, remuneration has been seen to take various forms with important distinctions being drawn between intrinsic reward, for example self-esteem and fulfilling work, and extrinsic reward, reflected in monetary and non-monetary payments. Indeed, the way in which the notion of remuneration includes a range of different rewards is apparent in Bloom and Milkovich's (1992: 22) definition of it as a 'bundle of returns offered in exchange for a cluster of employee contributions'.

This chapter concentrates primarily on extrinsic monetary reward or pay which, as a central pillar of the employment relationship, has understandably attracted considerable attention from policy makers, practitioners, academics and other commentators since the emergence of industrial organizations. Naturally, the preoccupation of these parties with pay has taken various forms and been based upon differing assumptions and perspectives. None the less, the locus of interest has been relatively enduring. Thus, despite the heated debate and the seemingly endless search for new and better ways to pay employees, discussion and practice has essentially been a variation on the same theme and that is how to operationalize and balance the relationship between pay, the job, the person and performance (Mahoney 1989).

This chapter seeks to evaluate remuneration by reference to these three pay contingencies – job, person and performance – arguing that developments over recent years can be understood in terms of the shifting interest in and emphasis given to them. First, the chapter will define these contingencies more precisely and highlight how they have been institutionalized through certain structures, systems and techniques. Second, consideration will be given to the evolving pay agenda, highlighting developments in remuneration as reflected in past practice and present rhetoric. Third, evidence will be drawn on to assess and explain the current use and balance between the three.

It will be suggested that recent pressures have encouraged discussion on approaches to pay and, with varying degrees of explicitness, have generated a number of practitioner and policy-driven prescriptions. These prescriptions will not be viewed as particularly new in that they often involve a simple reworking of the well-established pay contingencies and a call for a shift in emphasis between them. More significantly, however, it will be noted that, according to the evidence, changes in practice around these 'new' prescriptions remains limited. This begs questions in turn about the durability of established pay practices.

Definitions and Types

Pay and the job

The job, defined as a stable configuration of organizational tasks and responsibilities, has traditionally formed the essential building block for the development of pay and grading structures. Such structures have been based upon the notion of relative job worth. Different approaches have been adopted to relative job worth (Mahoney 1983; Rubery 1997), the major contrast being drawn between externally driven market comparison and internal organizational comparisons sometimes conceptualized in terms of external and internal equity. The tension between these bases for comparison, given that jobs of similar internal worth may attract very different external market rates, has generated managerial difficulties and attempts to deal with them through such mechanisms as market supplements. However, the importance of internal comparison has been highlighted by a number of observers. Brown and Walsh (1994), for example, note that such comparisons often form the basis for employee perceptions of 'fairness', with any failure by management to acknowledge the significance of worker views running the risk of unleashing latent power to demotivate.

Job evaluation is the principal mechanism used to evaluate internal job worth. Thus, job evaluation is concerned with job size, not with the performance of individuals in the job. It seeks to evaluate job size not according to any absolute standards but in relation to other jobs in the organization. The process of evaluation is not objective in any scientific sense; personal judgements are inevitable and subjectivity will invariably creep in. It is, however, designed to be a systematic approach in that it involves the consistent application of a given set of rules. At the same time, the degree of subjectivity may vary according to the particular job evaluation technique used. Non-analytical schemes such as job ranking, paired comparisons and job classification are founded on whole-job comparisons and tend to be less formal and less structured in their application than analytical schemes including factor comparison and point factor rating plans involving the unpacking of jobs according to defined characteristics and their assessment against established scales.

An extensive prescriptive and descriptive literature can be referred to for details on job evaluation techniques and associated procedures (see, for example, Pritchard and Murlis 1992; Armstrong and Baron 1995). It is, none the less, worth noting that job evaluation schemes come in a tailor-made or more standard form. Clearly, bespoke schemes are more sensitive to particular circumstances and needs. Organizations can, for example, develop and identify their own job factors related to the occupational make-up of their workforce and deemed important for evaluation purposes. As for standard schemes, most of the major management consultancies have developed their own systems. The widely used Hay scheme, for instance, uses just three main factors – know-how, problem solving and accountability (Armstrong and Murlis 1991: 474). Although primarily concerned with relative internal worth, the use of such standard schemes does allow some linkages to market rates for jobs of a similar size as measured in the same way.

Pay, person and performance

The relationship between pay and the other two contingencies, person and performance, has mainly been presented in the context of payment system design and operation. Payment systems, as mechanisms driving pay movements, are based upon a number of different criteria. Two fundamental criteria distinguish pay systems: time and a broadly defined notion of performance (Brown 1989). As will be seen, person, as a pay contingency, has been related to both criteria in a number of ways.

Time-based pay rewards employees simply for time attended. It has a range of managerial advantages, such as low administrative costs, as well as certain employee benefits in the form of predictability and comprehensibility. However, in the absence of any incentive effect, it clearly relies on other techniques to manage staff performance. Time has often been harnessed to the job in that a given a job has attracted a given rate of pay in the form of a daily or hourly rate, a weekly or monthly wage or an annual salary. The creation of a pay and grading structure based upon job evaluation is often followed by a market pricing exercise as organizations utilize pay data from a range of sources including published surveys, 'pay club' surveys and advertisements, to position themselves in the labour market for those types of workers. Moreover, for many workers such rates have, in turn, been tied to the process of collective bargaining which has regularly increased those rates traditionally in line with the cost of living.

Time has also been linked to person often in the context of job-based grading structures. Thus, time served by the individual, or seniority in an occupation, have usually been the means for progression along fixed increments within grade. Such an approach overlaps somewhat with the issue of performance. The implied rationale for this form of progression is the supposed link between pay and personal development: length of time in post or experience encourages skill and knowledge formation which, in turn, lead to more efficient and effective job performance.

The link between pay and performance is more complex and raises three basic questions: whose performance is being assessed?; how is it being measured?; and how is it being rewarded? These questions imply a multidimensional model of performance pay systems. The first question concentrates attention on the unit of performance. As a standard definition indicates, performance pay can be seen as the explicit link to financial reward to individual, group or company performance.

The second question focuses on the evaluation of performance. It is in this respect that the distinction between person and performance becomes important. Generally performance can be seen in terms of inputs, what individuals or groups bring to the job, or in terms of various outputs often in the form of objectives and targets. It is as an input measure that 'person' again emerges as significant, for many of these inputs take the form of personal characteristics such as skill, knowledge and behaviour. These individual features and abilities might be seen as potential or 'promised' performance rather than achieved performance as reflected in harder output measures. This link between person and performance has a long history, underpinning traditional craft-based apprenticeship schemes with their emphasis on skills acquisition. However, it has taken a more modern form as competence pay which seeks to link skill along with other input measures of performance such as behaviour and knowledge to reward.

The third question concentrates on the performance–pay link. This directs attention to the distinction between a relatively fixed relationship, where a given level of output usually produces an automatic payout, and a less mechanistic link often founded on some assessment of individual performance. It also emphasizes the fact that the payment may be consolidated into base pay or remain an unconsolidated lump sum.

Drawing upon these dimensions, a number of types of pay systems are typically distinguished (Casey et al. 1991; National Research Council 1991). First, there are systems based on some form of appraisal or assessment of the individual employee. Related to inputs, these systems are referred to as merit, skills or competency schemes. Related to outputs, they are called individual performance related schemes. They often involve a payment which is integrated into base salary either in the form of a percentage increase or additional increments on a pay scale.

The second type involves bonuses which provide unconsolidated payments to the individual employee. These are founded on a relatively mechanistic relationship between pay and the individual in terms of units of production, targets or sales. They include the differing forms of piecework as well as other traditional systems such as sales commission. In the case of many piecework schemes, the pay–output link is established on the basis of time saved. Time and motion studies establish a standard time for the job with speedier production and naturally higher output generating the piecework payment.

The third type of pay system is bonuses which are mechanistically geared to the performance of the group, whether it be the work team, section department, establishment or company. These bonuses are often provided as unconsolidated payments and are paid on a collective basis to those within the measured unit. Collective bonuses include gain-sharing schemes, which relate pay to changes in the sales value or the added value of a designated group within the organization, as well as profit sharing and some forms of employee share ownership. Such profit-sharing and employee share-ownership schemes come in two broad types: 'approved' and 'non-approved'. Approved are those which conform to Inland Revenue conditions in terms of design and eligibility and, in doing so, qualify for certain tax benefits. The main schemes are profit sharing, based on the distribution of shares bought on the employees' behalf from a profit-sharing pool, and saving-related share options, allowing employees to buy shares at a fixed market prices from accrued savings. Non-approved schemes can be designed in any way but clearly do not attract any such tax benefits.

There are important areas of overlap between job, person and performance. For example, the reward of skills, knowledge or competencies is likely to be linked to their application on the job. In other words, such reward will still partly or wholly be linked to whether they improve the employee's performance in a meaningful output sense. Moreover, the linkages between these three criteria and reward are not mutually exclusive. It may well be the case that a job tied to time generates base pay, while personal features or performance, individual and/or collective, are the foundation for variable pay. However, emphasis given by policy makers, practitioners and commentators to these three contingencies has altered over time and attention now turns to some of these shifts.

The Evolving Pay Agenda

From the shopfloor to the office

The period since the Second World War has been marked by twists and turns in the interest shown by policy makers, practitioners and academics in the pay of different groups of employees. From the mid to late 1960s and through the 1970s, this interest was concentrated on the way in which manual workers, in both the private and the public sector, were rewarded. For white-collar employees, job and grade remained the stable bedrock of remuneration. Pay structures provided scope for progression within grade usually on the basis of seniority and between grade through promotion when individuals outgrew the job and were deemed equipped to fulfil a larger one. For manual workers in the private sector, however, payment systems were widely seen, certainly from a managerial perspective, as out of control. Performance pay, in the form of individual and group piecework covering some six million employees, was seen to have generated an instability in industrial relations which in turn was viewed as having a detrimental effect upon Britain's broader economic performance. Research suggested that these piecework systems had decayed in the face of workplace pressures, undermining ordered national bargaining, generating unregulated conflict and earnings drift and encouraging rigidities in workplace employment practices (National Board for Prices and Incomes 1966).

Subsequent developments in remuneration were in large part directed towards addressing the perceived weaknesses in piecework systems. The productivity agreements of the 1970s were based on attempts to establish a clearer reciprocal relationship between pay and broader organizational changes, while measured day-work schemes sought to establish a much more controlled, stable and fixed relationship between pay and output. Both approaches, however, met with limited success. The incomes policies of the period stimulated the use of productivity agreements as a means of bolstering earnings without always creating a geniune link to revised working practices. Some of the management difficulties which had bedevilled piecework schemes, in particualr those related to planning production and ensuring workflow, inhibited the operation of measured day-work, and such systems also ran the risk of simply replacing wage drift with effort drift. Indeed, faced with these difficulties, some organizations moved away from incentives for manual workers altogether (Smith 1989: 46–9; Tolliday 1991: 95).

In the public sector, the policy concerns were somewhat different, but none the less still clearly focused on the manual worker. Thus, problems were seen to revolve around low pay, particularly for employees in health, local government and the public utilities. The revision of pay systems, and particularly the negotiation local bonus schemes based on a closer link between pay and output measures of group performance, were seen as a way to improve the earning potential of public servants (National Board for Prices and Incomes 1967).

Over the years, however, there was a shift of interest from manual pay systems and structures to white-collar workers' reward, reflected in Smith's (1989: 61) observation that, 'The only group not experiencing the changes brought about by the reward culture are shopfloor employees'. The focus on non-manual pay may partly have arisen by default in that manual pay simply became less problematic as periods of high unemployment weakened the shopfloor union power which, along with weak management, had accounted for the decay of piecework schemes. More fundamental was the longer-term shift from manufacturing to service-based employment outlined in chapter 1.

The concentration of interest on non-manual pay is perhaps most forcefully illustrated by the growing attention devoted to individual performance-related pay (IPRP) in the late 1980s. As highlighted by Fowler (1988), IPRP at this time was viewed very much in terms of a link between pay and the achievement of individual outputs in the form of objectives or targets. It was seen as being applicable to an increasing range of white-collar workers at different levels within the organizational hierarchy. The third Workplace Industrial Relations Survey (Millward et al. 1992), for instance, found that between 30 and 40 per cent of establishments had merit pay for white-collar staff at various levels, compared to under 20 per cent of establishments with schemes for manual staff. Moreover, Cannel and Wood (1992) found that, while over a quarter of establishments in their survey of 360 organizations had introduced IPRP for non-manual employees within the last five years, the equivalent figure for their manual counterparts was only 6 per cent.

Certainly there were contrasting opinions on the value of such schemes. In the prescriptive literature, many of the leading management gurus were critical. Deming (1982: 102) referred to merit pay as a deadly sin, while Kanter (1989: 233–5) challenged the assumption that individuals alone are responsible for their own performance. However, leading policy makers were fairly vociferous in their support. The CBI (1988), for example, called for pay systems which 'focus on the performance and needs of individuals'. The Conservative Government was similarly supportive, reflected not least in their pronouncements on public sector pay. As the *Citizen's Charter* (1991: 35) stated: 'Pay systems in the public sector need to make a regular and direct link between a person's contribution to the standards of the service provided and his or her reward.'

Pressures for change

Alongside the factors encouraging an interest in the pay of non-manual workers, additional and perhaps more profound pressures built up in a cumulative fashion and recently crystallized in a broader pay agenda incorporating a wider range of occupational groups and covering many dimensions of pay. Three sets of pressures can be distinguished. The first set can be labelled organizational. They relate, in part, to organizational restructuring. The 'delayering' or 'flattening' of organizations has clearly weakened one of the key forms of reward, promotion, by severely reducing avenues for advancement. In addition, these factors include changes in job and work design. The pursuit of greater task flexibility, often within the context of team working, has challenged the notion of job as a tightly defined bundle of activities and responsibilities.

The second set of factors has taken the form of institutional changes, particularly in the industrial relations landscape, which may have unsettled some of the established pay moorings. As Rubery (1997: 341) points out, collective bargaining and the trade unions have often been seen as essentially conservative forces, seeking to defend established wage structures and prevent the erosion of existing rights and benefits. As chapter 1 has pointed out, over recent years both institutions have progressively been weakened and undermined with declining union membership and density and a narrowing in the coverage of collective bargaining (Purcell 1993). The period has also been characterized by attempts to deregulate the labour market which have involved the removal of those institutions, wages councils and other mechanisms such as the Fair Wage Resolution, designed to provide some minimal support for pay determination at the bottom end. Countervailing developments in the form of equal pay for work of equal value legislation have been slow to take effect, while the National Minimum Wage represents a very recent initiative.

A third set of factors can be viewed as managerial in that they derive from the interest in using pay to deal with new objectives, especially in circumstances characterized by the intensification of competition and the need for organizational efficiency and effectiveness. Of course, there is nothing new about managers using pay to pursue a range of goals but, arguably, shifts in the balance of power and the weakening of traditional institutional supports have given management greater discretion to advance their pay aims. For instance, while the break-up of multi-employer bargaining and the emergence of single-employer bargaining at different levels within organizations reflects a range of factors, not least changing company structure, it can also be seen as a managerial preference allowing trade-offs between pay increases and specific company needs or demands (Katz 1993).

A growing concentration of interest in managerial attitudes and behaviours has not, however, been matched by an analytical consensus on management orientation or their implications for approaches to pay. Arrowsmith and Sisson (1999) distinguish two such orientations, marketization and internalization, with very different pay consequences. Marketization suggests that employees are exposed to the full blast of competitive pressures, while internalization implies the need to shelter employees from such pressures both as a more efficient and effective means of regulating the employment relationship and as a way of developing firm-specific skill and deepening worker commitment to the organization. Differing views on the underlying purpose of similar pay systems have been predicated on adherence to these orientations. For example, profit sharing has been seen as a means of sharing organizational risk and uncertainty with employees or as a way of encouraging greater worker loyalty to and identification with the company. Similarly, there has been much debate about whether IPPR constitutes a high-commitment management practice or 'harder' judgemental mechanisms based upon translation of competitive business concerns into individual objectives (Wood 1996; Walsh 1993). A further perspective on such debates suggests that any given pay system can be structured and used in various ways rather than intrinsically supporting any particular orientation (Kessler and Purcell 1995).

It appears, therefore, that many of the supports and building blocs for the traditional systems of remuneration are under threat, while a range of new pressures is encouraging a re-evaluation of approaches to reward. The institutional structures which sustained established pay structures with their delicate balance of internal differentials and external relativities have been undermined with the diminishing significance of collective bargaining and union power. Such changes have weakened the institutional constraints upon managerial approaches to reward, yet at the same time increasing competitive pressures have forced changes in organizational structure and ways of working which have necessitated the search for new ways of rewarding. Established means of reward through promotion and career development opportunities have withered with the creation of flatter and downsized organizations. Moreover, the notion of the job, so crucial as the basis for grading structures and as a measure of fairness linked to relative internal worth, has been challenged in the search for greater task flexibility and new working relationships. These changes appear to have given rise to a new prescriptive discourse and rhetoric.

A Changed Agenda?

The normative, prescriptive and to some extent academic response to these recent developments has taken two forms. One has involved the articulation of a particular approach to reward, sometimes captured by the term 'new pay', rather than the adoption of any specific techniques or system. As Lawler (1995: 14) notes, 'The new pay is not a set of compensation practices at all but rather a way of thinking about the role of rewards systems in a complex organization.' The other has been based on a re-evaluation of the balance between, and the substantive character of, job, person and performance as they relate to reward.

A strategic approach

The articulation of a particular approach to pay under current organizational and environmental circumstances has been presented as a set of principles and values informing the design and operation of pay systems. A number of such principles and values, given varying degrees of emphasis and coherence by different commentators, have been highlighted. First, the approach is based on the belief that remuneration should be considered in a 'strategic' way, i.e. in relationship to and support of the pursuit of broader organizational objectives and developments. As Lawler (1995: 14) continues, 'The new pay argues in favour of a pay design process that starts with business strategy and organizational change.' The implication of such a statement is that approaches to pay in the past were somewhat detached from business needs.

Second, this 'new' thinking stresses the way in which reward can be used as integrative and unifying force, aligning employee and organizational goals. As Schuster and Zingheim (1992: xi) note, 'The new pay provides that organizations effectively use all elements of pay to help them form a partnership between the organization and its employees.'

Third, and partly related, a close link is proposed between organizational performance, individual performance and rewards. As Schuster and Zingheim (1992: xi) continue:

> By means of partnership, employees can understand the goals of the organization, know where they fit in accomplishing these goals, become appropriately involved in the decisions affecting them, and receive rewards to the extent the organization attains these goals and to the extent they have assisted the organization to do so.

The power of these strands as a means of understanding recent developments in pay is brought together by Gomez-Mejia (1993: 4) who states that:

> The emerging paradigm of the field is based on a strategic orientation where issues of internal equity and external equity are viewed as secondary to the firm's need to use pay as an essential integrating and signalling mechanism to achieve overarching business objectives.

This view of pay as being strategically integrated and aligned might be seen as part of and linked to the broader strategic human resource management agenda. Thus, the fit or matching frameworks relating human resource policies to various contingent factors such as competitive strategy (Schuster and Jackson 1987), stage of organizational life cycle (Kochan and Barrocci 1985) and organizational structure (Fombrun et al. 1984) have invariably included pay. It is also very much in tune with the general thrust of strategic human resource management with its emphasis on the need for personnel policies to be complementary as well as supportive of business strategy. Whether such thinking is genuinely 'new' is open to greater debate and perhaps ignores long-standing conceptualizations such as Lupton and Gowler's (1969) contingency model which applied similar principles of fit to pay issues on a more systematic and less normative basis (see below).

This strategic approach to pay, especially under the banner of 'new pay', initially emerged in the USA and the extent to which its rhetoric has been adopted in Britain should not be overstated. Certainly, elements of it have emerged. As Pritchard and Murlis (1992: 12) state in a prescriptive text:

> For most organizations, pay is one of the most important items of cost, and in many of these it is the largest single cost item. Increasingly businesses are recognizing the need to manage pay strategically.

Such views are echoed in another practitioner-oriented UK publication (Market Tracking International 1996: 2):

> There has never been a greater commercial imperative to link reward strategy and business strategy.

Moreover, aspects of this approach to pay have also been reflected in the comments of policy makers. The words of the Director General of the CBI strongly echo those quoted above and indicate an interesting shift, from earlier CBI calls for a link between pay and individual performance to an emphasis on a relationship between rewards and performance more broadly defined:

> The framework for reward needs to reinforce the steps that many employers have already been taking to link pay to individual, team and company performance, so that there is a clear link between wealth creation and pay rises... These approaches give individuals a sense of opportunity and of participation in the success of their company and the economy as a whole (Turner 1996: 21).

However, if the use of this overarching rhetoric in he UK should not be exaggerated, there has been much wider discussion of how pressure for change has necessitated a re-evaluation of established pay techniques.

Re-evaluating job, performance and person

The relationship between job, performance and person, as well as the systems and techniques linking them in the pay context, appear to have been subject to radical reappraisal. Dealing with each of these key terms in turn, it is perhaps the notion of the job which has been subject to the most rigorous examination, calling into question the viability of current grading structures and the job-evaluation systems upon which they are based. As the barriers between jobs crumble, and preoccupation with task flexibility continues, traditional job-evaluated grading structures are seen by management as problematic. Rooted in detailed job descriptions, a considerable number of narrow grades and senior-ity-based incremental progression, they have not only been seen as a highly bureaucratized and time consuming to implement and maintain, but also extremely rigid and mechanistic to operate.

One of the more widely touted approaches to striking some balance between task flexibility and a degree of role demarcation has been the creation of broad bands. In essence, this involves the replacement of the multitude of narrow grades with a smaller number of wider pay scales based on a simple minimum and a maximum with no intermediate incremental points. The effect is to subsume within a single band a larger number of different jobs. While providing an underpinning framework still based on the principles of job evaluation, and ensuring some consistency of treatment, this approach is seen to overcome the limits of traditional structures. The broader bands allow jobs to be placed on a basis of less detailed, generic descriptions, reducing related administration, but more importantly providing greater managerial discretion in the utilization of staff. More-over, the higher pay ceilings of such bands are seen to provide more scope for employees to be rewarded as they develop or grow in their jobs, while removal of increments also allows managers more freedom to link reward to general performance. The greater head-room provided has the added benefit of allowing management more discretion in responding to external labour market pressures for particular occupational groups within grade, rather than forcing them to institute some special treatment potentially undermining the integrity of the pay structure as a whole.

Broad bands still have to confront the issue of positioning and progression. In this respect, and more generally in relation to the development of pay systems, there appears to have been an increasing attention paid to systems of reward which are based upon input-performance and thus more closely linked to the person in the form of skills and or competencies, at the expense, to some extent, of the interest shown in output-based individual performance-related schemes in the late 1980s.

Skills and competencies are clearly distinguishable (Pritchard and Murlis 1992). Skills are concerned with practical abilities and expertise and may also be seen to cover mastery of certain bodies of knowledge. Competencies, in contrast, are related to underlying behavioural and attitudinal characteristics or traits required of the employee to carry out the job effectively. Competencies and skills can be used either singly or in combination for two main purposes. First, they can form the basis of or be built into job evaluation and in this sense overlap with the notion of the job. In this form, competencies in particular are adding a new dimension to the evaluation process by encouraging a consideration of the job not only according to what is involved, but also in relation to how it should be done. Second, they can be used to determine, wholly or in part, individual pay increases. In other words, employee pay progression can be tied to the achievement or acquisition of certain skills or competencies.

The perceived value or strength of relating pay to competencies or skills may in part derive from the weaknesses of output-related IPRP. One of the many concerns raised with such schemes is that, by focusing upon output achievements, they encourage a narrow and blinkered concentration on specific tasks to the neglect of daily behavioural requirements needed to perform the job in an all-round sense. In addition, however, positive benefits are seen to derive from such an approach. The pay link to competencies and skills is seen to allow individuals to be rewarded as they develop within the job in the absence of traditional avenues for promotion. In the context of rapidly changing work requirements and the emphasis on empowerment, a link between pay and ways of working may be viewed as more appropriate than a link between pay and the achievement of rigid performance targets set across a relatively long time-horizon. Moreover, the emphasis on individual competence is sometimes seen as supporting or furthering 'core' corporate competencies. In other words, having distinguished the competencies upon which the organization competes, appropriate individual competencies are then identified and articulated in various ways. Whereas in the 1980s it was corporate business objective which cascaded into individual targets, in the late 1990s the downward flow is from organizational to individual competencies.

As well as a shift in the emphasis given to different forms of individual performance as the basis for reward, increasing attention has also been given to other units as the basis for performance pay. Of these units, the team has achieved particular prominence in line with moves towards teamworking. Highlighting this interest, Armstrong (1996: 22) states:

> The significant part that teamwork plays in achieving organizational success has directed attention towards how employee reward systems can contribute to team effectiveness. The focus is now shifting away from individual performance related pay which has conspicuously failed to deliver results in many instances, and towards team pay and other methods of rewarding the whole team.

Team-based pay has a seductive attraction in that it would appear to encourage co-operative behaviour within groups, while also acting more covertly as a mechanism for managerial control by encouraging peer pressure to ensure standard performance at a high level.

In addition, there seems to have been some heightened interest in reward systems linked to company or plant performance. This interest has centred not only on systems linking pay to profit, but also on forms of gain sharing founded upon other measures of organizational performance. Such gain-sharing schemes are not new. Indeed, the Scanlon plan, measuring labour cost as a proportion of sales, and the Rucker plan, measuring labour costs against sales minus the cost of material and supplies, can be traced back to the 1930s. The renewed interest in them may in part be explained by the fact that the link between pay and these indicators of organizational performance is more meaningful and easy to identify with than a link with profit, which is often subject to forces beyond employee control. Indeed, essential to these schemes are forms of direct participation such as suggestion schemes and joint works committees, which allow employees to feed-in ideas to improve corporate performance. These features of gain sharing strengthen the 'line of sight' between employee action and measures of corporate performance used for pay purposes.

In summary, it can be suggested that a range of forces have encouraged discussion of new approaches to pay, which in its strongest form might be interpreted as a new pay rhetoric and set of prescriptions. The direction of this debate has been seen to rest on a number of propositions: that a more strategic approach to pay is needed; that a looser and more flexible definition of the job requires a move away from rigid and mechanistic grading structures based on highly bureaucratized job evaluation systems towards broad-banded structures; that pay linked to the person and in particular to individual competencies and skills is a more appropriate means of rewarding the empowered employee than pay related to objectives or targets; that, in the age of teamworking, rewards need to be associated with work-group performance as well as with corporate performance, and defined in a manner meaningful to employees. The next section considers the extent which the evidence supports these contentions, particularly by way of assessing the prevalence of the highlighted practices.

The Evidence

A more strategic approach?

The extent to which organizations have reward strategies can be evaluated in a number of ways. In the most basic sense, consideration can be given to whether they have a formal strategy. In a tighter sense, attention might focus on the substance of that strategy and particularly on whether it involves some attempt to relate rewards to business strategies and to other human resource policies and practices. In the strongest sense, attention needs to be given to whether the strategy is implemented and operated in a meaningful and effective way.

There is limited evidence available on the extent to which organizations have reward strategies in any of these senses. However, one of the few surveys conducted in the area (Industrial Society 1997b), covering almost 300 organizations, suggests that such strategies exist primarily in a weak form. While almost three-quarters (73 per cent) of the companies reported that they had formal written strategies, under half of these (47 per cent) agreed that they were efficiently linked to HR strategy, with just over one-half (57 per cent) feeling they met business needs effectively. It is perhaps a testament to questionable application of such strategies in any meaningful sense that under one-half (49 per cent) of the surveyed organizations agreed that employees understood their company's reward policy.

In considering whether organizations have reward strategies, attention inevitably focuses on the nature of decision making as it relates to remuneration. In common with more general discussions on organizational decision making, much of the debate has revolved around two important dimensions; first, the degree of choice organizations have in approaches to reward; and, second, how any choice has been exercised. Along the first dimension, notions of strategy, at least in a deliberate and purposeful sense, would assume organizations do have some scope to determine their approach rather than being constrained or driven by factors beyond their control. Along the second dimension, a contrast can be drawn between a strategic orientation to reward which derives from a top-down, ordered and relatively rational process and a less strategic orientation, where the process is seen as less ordered and rational and subject to internal and external pressures less easily controlled.

Using these distinctions, different approaches can be distinguished in reviewing the extent to which British organization have been able and willing to adopt reward strategies. Fluctuating market pressures often appear to have encouraged *ad hoc* and opportunistic approaches to pay. For example, the introduction by a number of organizations of IPRP in the late 1980s was often response to a tight labour market and seen as a way of bolstering pay rates to deal with recruitment and retention difficulties. A survey of local authorities, for example, found that the need to address such difficulties was one of the main reasons for the introduction for performance related pay (LACSAB 1990).

Constraints may also remain despite the appearance of choice. For example, although attention was drawn to a weakening of the traditional institutions of pay determination, the underlying rationale for such institutions may still exert a significant force for ongoing conformance. This is reflected in Arrowsmith and Sisson's (1999) survey of some 300 organizations across four major sectors – engineering, health, printing and retail – which found that, despite the breakdown of multi-employer bargaining, the sector still played a key part in shaping pay process and outcomes. Indeed, such findings lend some weight to an institutional perspective on pay developments as discussed by Gerhart, Trevor and Graham (1996) and might be seen to represent a form of so-called 'normative isomorphism' (DiMaggio and Powell 1983), or convergence, with key actors locked into similar technologies and labour markets continuing to view adherence industry pay standards as the best approach.

Examples are similarly available of coercive and mimetic forms of isomorphism. The developments in Civil Service pay illustrate their combined influence. Thus, while newly created executive agencies were given the freedom to develop their own pay systems, a recent review suggests that very similar schemes emerged with all of them linking pay to individual performance and most using pay ranges. This can be explained by the fact that the Treasury refused to sanction any system without such a pay–performance link, hence coercing them along this path. There was also evidence of agencies copying one another. 'In the form of "follow my leader" most new structures mimic those already introduced for higher grades and already introduced in early delegated areas' (PTC, 1996: 5).

In terms of how decisions on rewards are made, the rational, top-down and ordered approach to the selection of approaches to pay assumes its most sophisticated form in contingency theory (Lupton and Gowler 1969). Recognizing that a variety of objectives might be pursued through pay, it suggests that organizations need to follow a number of steps in adopting their approach: identify the specific objectives pursued; consider the pay systems and structures available to further these objectives; and, having identified the options, base the choice on the organization's internal and external circumstances.

The second approach viewing decision making on rewards as less rational, ordered or systematic is in tune with the assumption underpinning a number of analytical frameworks. The resource-based theory of the firm, for instance, might be seen to imply a complex, evolutionary or path-dependent understanding of how pay schemes emerge. Although there is little research work on how pay systems have evolved within a dynamic organizational environment, the case of one privatized company highlights the importance of a Civil Service past in explaining the distinctive way in which a performance-related pay system was designed and implemented (Kessler 1994). Moreover, Cappelli and Crocker-Hefter (1996) contrast the way in which the incentive system of US retailers Norstrom had developed over time to support a 'core competence' which revolved around selling fashion goods bought on impulse with the time–rate pay of Sears seeking to compete more on the basis of safe and reliable purchases.

Others falling within this second approach have highlighted the importance of reward as a managerial control mechanism and as such how it becomes subject to countervailing employee pressures designed to divert and subvert employer intentions (White 1981). The less rational approach to pay is also reflected in works which have stressed the significance of reward in symbolic terms. Such work overlaps in large part with pay as a means of control. Quaid (1993), for instance, seeks to illustrate the way in which job evaluation systems are a potent way of socially constructing reality to sustain a particular balance of workplace power, while Ahlstrand (1990) has noted how productivity agreements at Esso Fawley oil refinery have been used to protect and further the careers of certain managers long after such agreements were deemed to have any positive and tangible impact on corporate performance.

New grading structures and the role of job evaluation

The evidence suggests that, while organizations have been changing their pay and grading structures, the alterations appear to have been relatively modest. If anything, job evaluation has continued to play a slightly increased role in underpinning pay structures; although there has been some rationalization and simplification of grading systems, this has not been reflected in extensive use of broad banding.

Certainly job evaluation schemes are being revised, with case-study examples suggesting that organizations are seeking to address rigidity and bureaucracy. For example, as a means of rationalizing procedures, the National Grid Company moved from a jointly negotiated job-evaluation system to one based on the provision of benchmark-grading guidance for managers. Similarly, Kodak Diagnostics sought to simplify its schemes through the use of generic job descriptions when it found that it had between 300 and 400 different job descriptions covering 600 staff (IRS 1994). The public sector, in particular, has seen major changes in job evaluation. For example, both the organizational restructuring reflected in the emergence of separate executive agencies and the devolvement of responsibility for grading to local authorities under the 1997 national agreement harmonizing white collar and manual conditions have necessitated the search for new job-evaluation systems (IRS 1998a).

None the less, revision stops well short of abandonment. The majority of organizations still have job evaluation with surveys putting the proportion with such schemes at between one-half to three-quarters. Indeed, indicative of the ongoing importance of job evaluation, a significant number of organizations have introduced job evaluation schemes for the first time (Industrial Society 1996).

Changes to job evaluation schemes may reflect in part legislative developments and the need to develop a defence against claims of equal pay for work of equal value. Indeed, it is noteworthy that most organizations now have analytical schemes based upon points-factor rating or factor comparisons (Industrial Society 1996: 8) which would generally provide protection. However, it appears that job evaluation's continued and growing popularity reflects the ongoing importance of the job at workplace level and in the design of personnel policies. Job size remains a key support to grading structures and crucial to more general notions of career development within the organization.

The continued importance of the job is confirmed by developments in grading structures. Again, there have been moves to overhaul such structure as a means of simplifying what are perceived as complex arrangements (IRS 1996a). The extent of changes in pay and grading structures is reflected in a number of surveys which suggests that well over half of the organizations covered have made revisions. An Industrial Relations Services (IRS 1996a) indicated that 55 per cent of the 80 organization covered had altered their grading structure in the last five years. Companies making such alteration include Apricot Computers, Harlow Chemical Company, Birds Eye Walls, Scottish Power and Iveco Ford Truck. A larger Industrial Society (1996) survey of 422 organizations suggests an even higher rate of change, with almost two-thirds signifying change over the last five years.

However, simplification has not generally taken the form of broadbanding schemes. Such schemes still appear to be fairly rare. For example, a Wyatt survey in 1995 of 346 organizations found that only 69 or 20 per cent (Market International 1996: 70) had broad banding. A more recent Industrial Society (1996: 17) survey suggested a higher figure at around one-third, but this is still very much a minority. Moreover, where such banding schemes do exist, they appear likely to cover white-collar staff and managers only, with very few manual workers covered by such schemes (Reissman 1995).

The generally low take-up of broad banding may reflect the difficulties faced by employees and managers in establishing such schemes. For employees, broad banding adds a high degree of uncertainty to pay determination. The transparency and predictability of the traditional service-related incremental steps linked to a given pay rate clearly disappears and much comes to rests on the criteria used to position employees within bands. The Watson Wyatt survey suggests that the most common criterion remains individual performance with all the difficulties (Market Tracking International, 1996: 71) commonly associated with such an approach. Labour-market data emerge as the second most popular mechanism and, given the unevenness and variability of such labour-market pressures across time and space, employee concerns about the vagaries of pay determination may well be exacerbated.

For managers, broad banding places a particular weight on their decision making and judgemental skills. While the establishment of managerial discretion is a key underlying goal of broad banding, the ability to exercise such discretion remains problematic. There may be, for example, a danger of pay drift as managers award overgenerous increases. Guidelines in the form of pay zones within each band, designed to address this issue, run the risk of re-establishing the old bureaucratic and inflexible systems associated with grades.

Pay and the person: competency and skill-based pay

It is not unusual in personnel management to be seduced and diverted by the use of novel practices on the basis of the example of a limited number of high-profile companies. Certainly this appears to be the case in relation to competency-based pay. Time and time again it tends to be the same list of companies quoted as using such arrangements. Any conference or review of the topic is therefore likely to include Volkswagen, ICL, Bass

Brewers, Prudential Assurance Company, Royal Bank of Scotland, Scottish Equitable, National Power Glaxo Welcome (Management Pay Review 1996; Competency Based Compensation Systems, Conference, 15–16 1997, London). The limited number of companies should not, however, obscure considerable variation in the circumstances, rationale, design and operation of such schemes. As a recent review noted, 'Only one major conclusion about competency based pay clearly stands out from the companies looked at – and that is the lack of a common approach' (Management Pay Review 1996).

A number of different circumstances and rationales underlie the use of competency based pay. First, a major organizational restructuring sometimes appears to be the stimulus for its introduction. For example, the merger between Glaxo and Welcome was seen to provide an opportunity to introduce competence pay with its focus on certain behavioural traits as a means of trying to fashion a new organizational culture. Second, shifting product market conditions requiring new employee behaviours can be a catalyst for introducing such schemes. Noteworthy, for example, is that four of the commonly quoted companies are in the finance sector, where deregulation leading to intensification of competition and the pursuit of 'improved quality and customer service' have been explicitly linked to the introduction of such schemes as a way of encouraging and reinforcing behaviour comparative with these goals (IRS 1997).

As for differences in the structure of such schemes, there are variations in the way competencies are linked to pay setting. In some companies, for instance Volkswagen, pay increases are totally determined by competencies, while in others such as Bass and ICL they are only partially related. In addition, the way in which competencies interface with other aspects performance differs. This is reflected in contrasts between organizations in the importance attached to competence as a means of measuring performance relative to other performance indicators. In the Bank of Scotland, for example, competencies play a central part in performance assessment. Elsewhere, competency forms a much smaller part of the assessment. In National, Power, for instance, competencies are just one of 13 performance factors used to generate appraisal targets (Management Pay Review 1996).

The picture is very similar in relation to skills-based pay. A number of well-publicized examples of such schemes can again be cited, including Bayer Diagnostics, Portsmouth Water (IRS 1996b), Remploy, BHS and Blue Circle Cement (IRS 1996c). Moreover, operational differences are once again apparent, particularly in the formality of skills assessment and in the importance of this assessment as a driver of pay increases. In Portsmouth Water, for example, the formality of skills assessment is enhanced by the link with NVQs, while the move to such a linkage has been much slower in Bayer Diagnostic.

Yet perhaps more striking than these 'best practice' examples of competency and skill-based pay is evidence which suggest that the use of such a scheme is extremely limited. It has been noted that the use of skill-based pay is 'still very much in its infancy' (Market Tracking International 1996: 92), while more tangibly an Industrial Society (1998) survey of 344 organizations revealed that only 5 per cent stated categorically that their pay system was competency based, with a further 17 per cent of companies indicating that competency was one component of their pay system. Indeed, there are few signs of any underlying or emergent enthusiasm for such schemes. The same survey found that only 11 per cent of organizations were considering introducing a scheme in the next 12 months, a figure very close to that suggested by a similar Industrial Relations Services (1995) survey.

In the light of this evidence, it naturally becomes pertinent to ask why the current and intended use of such schemes remains so limited. A recognition of the difficulties of designing, implementing and operating such schemes may well be discouraging many organizations. Sparrow (1996), in one of the most systematic critiques of competence pay schemes, highlights some of these difficulties. Distinguishing three main pillars under-pinning any such scheme, he suggests that in practice problems may arise in relation to each. First, the need for organizations to identify the 'correct' competencies forces a reliance of established appraisal techniques which are often not robust enough to support such a process. Second, chosen forms of assessment need to reveal relevant competencies. 'If organizations want to vary rewards to match different competencies, they need to differentiate in-built behaviour from those that can be developed' (Sparrow 1996: 24). This process of differentiation is extremely complex and uncertain, however. Third, managers need to be able to make accurate judgements about revealed competency. Yet, 'in the fast changing world of work we can no longer be sure what being effective will look like . . . What chance has the average line manager got of detecting who has got the right stuff' (Sparrow 1996: 25). Other difficulties can be added. Any attempt to link pay to com-petencies or skills raises employee expectations about training opportunities. However, there is a real danger that the demand for such skills and competencies will exceed the needs of the organizations. In such circumstances, the only viable options are to limit or ration such developmental opportunities, consequently thwarting expectations and poten-tially leading to demotivation. Alternatively, an open-ended commitment can be met, making the process hugely resource intensive and perhaps destabilizing the production process. In Scottish Power, for example, the attempts to adopt the latter approach meant that, on average, employees had 15 days off work on training (presentation 'Working for the Future', DTI-European Commission Conference Glasgow, 28–30 April 1998).

Pay and performance: team and merit pay

Reports of the death of IPRP appear to have been greatly exaggerated. Indeed, rather than diminishing in popularity, the evidence suggests that, if anything, this system may be continuing its onward march. Team-based pay as a response to new ways of working and as a reaction against the individualism of IPRP does not appear to have taken hold.

The impression of declining interest in IPRP noted earlier may be related to a number of factors. The operational difficulties associated with such schemes have been highlighted by a number of commentators. The three main procedural stages of any such scheme have all been seen to generate difficulties (Kessler and Purcell 1992). The setting of performance targets has sometimes been inconsistent within organizations and problematic for certain professional or less skilled occupations where goals have not been easily formulated. The evaluation of performance has given rise to concerns about subjectivity as well as an unwillingness among assessing managers to differentiate between employees as intended. The link between evaluation and pay has also proved unstable with the limited amount of money usually devoted to such schemes seen as unlikely to stimulate improved performance.

Evidence of difficulties has been reinforced by a number of examples of organizations withdrawing their IPRP schemes. BT, for example, suspended its arrangements covering

26,000 managers and professional staff after just 12 months as a consequence of some of the problems highlighted (*Financial Times* 1994). Other organizations, such as the London Boroughs of Brent and Lewisham (Littlefield 1996: 15) and West Dorset Community Trust (Merrick 1995), have similarly jettisoned schemes.

Moreover, the limited research which has been carried out into the impact of IPRP has called into question its effectiveness. This research, usually based upon employee perceptions and carried out in local authorities (Heery 1998), the Inland Revenue (Marsden and Richardson 1994) and a range of other organizations (Thompson 1993), has suggested IPRP is likely to have at best a neutral affect on staff attitudes and behaviour and at worst a negative affect in the form of demotivation.

However, the bad press received by individual performance-related pay does not appear to have dampened the more general enthusiasm or popularity of such schemes. Data generated by an IPD survey (reported in IRS 1998b) highlights this continued interest. It finds that nearly six in ten merit schemes have been introduced in the past five years and concludes that, 'Contrary to the popular belief that organizations are becoming disillusioned with performance pay, and with IPRP schemes in particular, the results strongly suggest that the use of all forms of performance pay is growing'.

The onward march of IPRP should not obscure some managerial concerns about the system, but as in the case of job evaluation and grading this appears to have been reflected in modification rather than abandonment. The IPD survey highlights this fine-tuning, noting that four out of ten of those questioned had overhauled their merit pay schemes since 1995.

The apparent absence of a backlash against IPRP may be related to a number of factors. First, some of the negative impressions associated with the early use of schemes may have been misleading. It is noteworthy, for instance, that much of the discussion and many of the examples at this time were drawn from the public service organizations, where the character of the workforce as well as distinctive financial and political features of the sector were always likely to render such schemes problematic. For example, the conditions under which expectancy theory predicts pay will motivate – clearly defined individual goals, a transparent link between these goals and pay, and employees caring about money – run-up against major barriers in the public services. Setting performance measures is difficult for many employees. The Chair of Brent's Personnel Committee noted, 'I believe PRP sits uneasily in local authorities. How do you measure performance in social services? Is it the number of children in care? What do you measure?' (Littlefield 1996). The link between any such measures and pay is also likely to be weak. As the Audit Commission (1995) stressed, 'As most people in local government cannot increase the income of their employer through good performance, money is not available to fund large scale performance payments.' Finally, the extent to which money, as opposed to intrinsic, job-related features, stimulates public servants may be lower relative to many private-sector groups. As the Human Resource Director of Lewisham stated, 'People are motivated by things other than small salary increases' (Littlefield 1996).

Second, much of the discussion about the (in)effectiveness of such schemes focused upon their motivational impact despite other evidence which suggested that IPRP was being used to pursue a wide range of managerial objectives (Kessler and Purcell 1992). Two sets of goals could be seen to underpin the use of IPRP; first, the 'holy trinity' of traditional pay goals, i.e. recruitment, retention and motivation; and, second, a much more novel set associated with organizational change. This second set was based upon the distinctive capacity of IPRP to influence a variety of behaviours, attitudes and relationships given the procedures and systems needed to operate it. Thus, IPRP has sometimes been seen as a way of developing managerial skills by forcing managers to meet and communicate with staff. It has been viewed as a means of individualizing the employment relationship by explicitly or implicitly marginalizing the role of unions and collective bargaining, forcing an unmediated contact between staff and their managers and providing management with much greater discretion in pay determination. Furthermore, it has been seen as a very powerful mechanism for culture change by sending strong signals about corporate values and beliefs that could be enshrined in individual employee goals and objectives. It is noteworthy, for instance, that many of the IPRP schemes introduced in the late 1980s were in the finance sector which, following deregulation and increased competition, sought to use such schemes as a means on inculcating values compatible with the new operating environment (Lewis 1998). The ongoing popularity of IPRP, despite its limited impact on motivation, might be seen as a confirmation of its ability to further such an extended range of managerial goals.

Third, there is evidence to suggest that managers at least are fairly positive in their views on the effectiveness of IPRP. While much of the earlier research on the impact of IPRP concentrated on employee motivation and therefore on staff perceptions, the more recent IPD survey has focused on managerial views. Managers appear to have a very different view of IPRP to employees, seeing it as leading to improved worker performance, providing a fairer basis for pay determination and encouraging high performers. In the absence of harder data, it appears that the success of IPRP may well depend on who you ask. Clearly, however, such views do not carry equal weight. Given the prevailing balance of power at the workplace, management's positive views of IPRP may help to explain its ongoing use.

Perhaps the most often-repeated criticisms of IPRP is the way in which it might detract from work group co-operation, a concern heightened by the attention paid to the team-working and encouraging consideration of team-based pay. Some organizations have sought ways of rewarding team performance and a number of examples are available. For instance, Ethicon, a manufacturer of healthcare products, introduced such a scheme in the early 1990s, linking pay to the three measures of team performance – output, quality and lead time (IRS 1996d). In the finance sector, Norwich Union and Lloyds Bank have developed systems linking team pay to sales and a measure of customer satisfaction, while at the Benefits Agency team bonuses are given if work groups are seen to make a 'valuable contribution to performance as determined by the local unit managers' (Armstrong 1996).

However, again these cases appear to be fairly isolated (Thompson 1995). More general survey data suggests that team-based pay is not common. An Industrial Society survey (quoted in Market Trading International 1996: 108) found only around 10 per cent of the organization covered was pay related to team performance, a figure which confirmed the earlier findings from a similar IPM (1992), which indicated that only 11 per cent of white-collar staff had team pay. This latter survey indicated a slightly higher coverage of such schemes among manual workers, but the figure still remains barely above a quarter of the organizations (27 per cent).

The limited popularity of team-based pay systems again points to some of the difficulties of operating such schemes in practice. For example, it is not always easy to find clear, viable and meaningful targets or standards for teams, especially if there is no tangible output. Moreover, teams vary greatly in their degree of permanence, with scope to establish a stable link with pay weakened by the degree to which they are temporary. There may also be unevenness in the contribution of team members and the extent to which their activities are genuinely integrated, calling into question whether team output is a genuine result of team effort. As with so many pay initiatives, team-based pay appears to be more attractive in theory than in practice.

Summary and Conclusions

Over recent years, developments in approaches to pay have been characterized by modification and fine tuning rather than radical change. Many of the propositions presented and derived from the new pay rhetoric do not appear to have found much support in terms of managerial practice. Certainly high-profile cases are readily available of organizations which have adopted innovative pay systems and structures. However, more generally, there is little evidence that the job is becoming less important as the basis for grading structures, reflected in the ongoing application of job evaluation and the limited use of broad banding. Competency and skill-based pay appear to have made little headway with the types of IPRP scheme introduced in the late 1980s continuing in use. Even team-based pay, which appears to be so much in tune with prevailing developments in work design, has so far failed to make any significant impression on pay practice.

A range of factors appears to account for the relatively durable nature of British management's approach to pay and certainly the absence of any daring new departures. First, many of the practices falling within the emerging pay rhetoric might be seen as a general reaction to some of the perceived weakness of prevailing techniques. In other words, they represent another swing of the pendulum away from those systems and structures which practice clearly shows to have limitations towards those which, by dint of being abstract and untested, appear to be panaceas. Thus, both competency pay and team-based pay can be seen as a way of dealing with the shortcomings of IPRP and, in particular, its narrow focus on pay-linked tasks to the neglect of other aspects of the job and as undermining teamworking. However, a more careful consideration of these newer techniques highlights the practical problems that can arise when they are pursued. Indeed, this swing of the pendulum perhaps serves to emphasize that there is no perfect approach to pay. Every technique has its strengths and weaknesses.

Second, while choices remain, there are ongoing external pressures which certainly structure choice and may well limit it. Here attention has been drawn to a range of powerful institutional forces which may force or encourage convergence and conformity in approaches to pay. Similarly, it has been suggested that there are certain internal constraints which might limit pay options. The extent to which pay practices are path dependent or embedded in the organization's previous development may have a profound effect on how such practices evolve.

Finally, and related more directly to managerial practicalities, both the incremental and piecemeal nature of developments and the absence of many radical departures may be indicative of a certain threshold beyond which change becomes risky and problematic. Pay will always be a double-edged sword. Its very centrality to the employment relationship makes it a tempting lever for management to use to pursue its objectives. However, the very importance of pay to employees means that, if the organizations get it wrong, serious dysfunctional consequences may follow. As Arrowsmith and Sisson (1999: 67) conclude on the basis of their survey findings, 'organizations had made the simple and straightforward changes (to their pay systems). The next steps needed to put into effect some key aspirations were of a different order of magnitude, making them especially daunting, and potentially involving costs in terms of employee commitment.'

References and further reading

Ahlstrand, B. 1990: *The Quest for Productivity*. Cambridge: Cambridge University Press.

Armstrong, M. 1996: How Group Efforts Can Pay Dividends. *People Management*, 25 January, 22–7.

Armstrong, M. and Baron, A. 1995: *The Job Evaluation Handbook*, London: IPD.

Armstrong, M. and Murlis, H. 1991: *Reward Management*, London: Kogan Page.

Arrowsmith, J. and Sisson, K. 1999: Pay and working time: Towards organization based arrangements? *British Journal of Industrial Relations*, **37**(1), 51–75.

Audit Commission 1995: *Paying the Piper*, London: Audit Commission.

Bloom, M. and Milkovich, G. 1992: Issues in Managerial Compensation Research. In C. Cooper and D. Rousseau (eds), *Trends in Organizational Behavior*, Chichester: John Wiley.

Brown, W. 1989: Managing Remuneration. In K. Sisson (ed.), *Personnel Management in Britain*, Oxford: Blackwell.

Brown, W. and Walsh, J. 1994: Managing Pay in Britain. In K. Sisson (ed.), *Personnel Management in Britain*, Oxford: Blackwell.

CBI 1988: *People at the Cutting Edge*. London: Confederation of British Industry.

Cannel, M. and Wood, S. 1992: *Incentive Pay*. London: Institute of Personnel Management.

Cappelli, P. and Crocker-Hefter, A. 1996: Distinctive Human Resources are Firms' Core Competencies. *Organizational Dynamics*, Winter, 7–22.

Casey, B. Lakey, J., Cooper, H. and Elliot, J. 1991: Payment Systems: A Look at Current Practice. *Employment Gazette*, August, 53–8.

Citizen's Charter: 1991: Cmnd. 1599. London: HMSO.

Deming, W. 1982: *Out of Crisis*. Cambridge: Cambridge University Press.

DiMaggio, P. and Powell, W. 1983: The Iron Cage Revisited: Institutional Isomorphism and Collective Rationality in Organizational Fields. *American Sociological Review*, **48**, 147–60.

Financial Times 1994: 2 February.

Fombrun, C., Tichy, N. and Devanna, M. 1984: *Strategic Human Resource Management*. New York: Wiley.

Fowler, A. 1988: New Directions in Performance Pay. *Personnel Management*, November, 30–4.

Gerhart, B., Trevor, C. and Graham, M. 1996: New Directions in Compensation Research: Synergies, Risk, and Survival. *Research in Personnel and Human Resource Management*, **14**, 143–203.

Gomez-Mejia, L. 1993: *Compensation, Organization Strategy and Firm Performance*. San Francisco: Southwestern Publishers.

Heery, E. 1998: Return to Contract? Performance Related Pay in a Public Service. *Work, Employment and Society*, **21**(1), 73–95.

IRS (Industrial Relations Services) 1994: Developments in Job Evaluation: Shifting Emphasis. *Employment Trends*, 551, January, 10–16.

IRS 1995: Pay Prospects for 1995/96. *Pay and Benefits Bulletin*, 387, November, 5–8.

IRS 1996a: Reviewing and Revising Grading Structures: A Survey. *Employment Trends*, 600, January, 7–13.

IRS 1996b: Skill Based Pay and Multi-Skilling. *Pay and Benefits Bulletin*, 397, April.

IRS 1996c: Skill Based Pay: A Survey. *Pay and Benefits Bulletin* 391, January.

IRS 1996d: Team Reward, Part 2. *Pay and Benefit Bulletin*, 400, May, 2–8.

IRS 1997: Rewarding Competencies at the Bank of Scotland. *Pay and Benefits Bulletin*, 422, April, 2–7.

IRS 1998a: There is Value in Job Evaluation. *Employment Trends*, 665, October, 3–16

IRS 1998b: There's Merit in Merit Pay. *Pay and Benefits Bulletin*, 445, April, 4–6.

Industrial Society 1996: *Job Evaluation*. No. 28, October, London: Industrial Society.

Industrial Society 1997a: *Pay Structures*. No. 39, September 1997, London: Industrial Society.

Industrial Society 1997b: *Reward Strategies*. No. 31, January, London: Industrial Society.

Industrial Society, 1998: *Competency Pay*. No. 43, January, London: Industrial Society.

IPM (Institute of Personnel Management) 1992: *Performance Management in the UK*. London: IPM.

Kanter, R. M. 1989: *When Giants Learn to Dance*. London: Unwin.

Katz, H. 1993: The Decentralization of Collective Bargaining: A Literature Review and Comparative Analysis. *Industrial and Labor Relations Review*, **47**(1), 3–22.

Kessler, I. 1994: Performance Related Pay: Contrasting Approaches. *Industrial Relations Journal*, **25**(2), 22–35.

Kessler, I. and Purcell, J. 1992: Performance Related Pay – Objectives and Application. *Human Resource Management Journal*, **2**(3), 34–59.

Kessler, I. and Purcell, J. 1995: Individualism in Theory and Practice: Management Style and the Design of Pay System. In P. Edwards (ed.), *Industrial Relations, Theory and Practice in Britain*, Oxford: Blackwell.

Kochan, T. and Barocci, T. (eds) 1985: *Human Resource Management and Industrial Relations*. Boston: Little Brown.

LACSAB (Local Authority Conditions of Service Advisory Board) 1990: *Performance Related Pay in Practice*. London: LACSAB.

Lawler, E. 1995: The New Pay: A Strategic Approach. *Compensation and Benefits Review*, July, 14–20.

Lewis, P. 1998: Managing Performance Related Pay Based Evidence from the Financial Services Sector. *Human Resource Management Journal*, **8**(2), 66–77.

Littlefield, D. 1996: Council Swaps PRP for Staff Development. *People Management*, 26 September, 15.

Lupton, T. and Gowler, D. 1969: *Selecting a Wage Payment System*. Research Paper III, London: Engineering Employers' Federation.

Mahoney, T. 1983: Approaches to the Definition of Comparable Worth. *Academy of Management Review*, **8**(1), 14–22.

Mahoney, T. 1989: Multiple Pay Contingencies: Strategic Design of Compensation. *Human Resource Management*, **28**(3), 337–47.

Management Pay Review 1996: Linking Pay to Competencies. *Incomes Data Service*, August, 11–14.

Market Tracking International 1996: *Reward Strategies*. London: Haymarket Business Publications.

Marsden, D. and Richardson, R. 1994: Performance Pay? The Effects of Merit Pay on Motivation in the Public Services. *British Journal of Industrial Relations*, **32**(2), 243–61.

Merrick, N. 1995: NHS Trust Finds Little Employee Support for PRP. *People Management*, 26 January.

Millward, N., Stevens, M., Smart, D. and Hawes, W. 1992: *Workplace Industrial Relations in Transition*. Aldershot: Dartmouth.

National Board for Prices and Incomes 1966: *Payment by Results Systems*. Report No. 65. Cmnd. 3627, London: HMSO.

National Board for Prices and Incomes 1967: *Pay and Conditions for Manaul Workers in Local Authorities, the Health Service, Gas and Water Supply*. Report No. 27, Cmnd. 3230, London: HMSO.

National Research Council 1991: *Pay for Performance*. Washington: National Academic Press.

Pritchard, D. and Murlis, H. 1992: *Jobs, Roles and People*. London: Nicholas Brealey.

PTC (Public Services, Tax and Commerce Union) 1996: *Whatever Happened to National Civil Service Pay*. Research Brief 1, November, London: PTC.

Purcell, J. 1993: The End of Institutional Industrial Relations. *Political Quarterly*, **64**(1), 6–23.

Quaid, M. 1993: *Job Evaluation: The Myth of Equitable Assessment*, Toronto: Toronto University Press.

Reissman, L. 1995: Nine Common Myths about Broadbanding. *HRM Magazine*, August, 79–86.

Rubery, J. 1997: Wages and the Labour Market. *British Journal of Industrial Relations*, **35**(3), 337–66.

Schuler, R. and Jackson, S. 1987: Linking Competitive Strategies with Human Resource Management Practices. *Academy of Management Review*, **1**(3), 209–13.

Schuster, J. and Zingheim, P. 1992: *The New Pay*. New York: Lexington Books.

Smith, I. 1989: *People and Profits*. London: Croners.

Sparrow, P. 1996: Too Good to be True? *People Management*, 5 December, 22–9.

Thompson, M. 1993: *Pay and Performance: The Employee Experience*, Institute of Manpower Studies, Report 258, Brighton: IMS.

Thompson, M. 1995: *Team Working and Pay*. Institute of Manpower Studies, Report 281, Brighton: IMS.

Tolliday, S. 1991: Ford and 'Fordism' in Postwar Britain: Enterprise Management and the Control of Labour 1937–87. In S. Tolliday and J. Zeitlin, (eds), *The Power to Manage*, London: Routledge.

Turner, A. 1996: Link Pay to Performance and We'll Stay on Track. *People Management*, 8 February, 20–2.

Walsh, J. 1993: Internalization Versus Decentralization: An Analysis of Recent Developments in Pay Bargaining. *British Journal of Industrial Relations*, **31**(3), 409–32.

White, M. 1981: *The Hidden Meaning of Pay*. London, Macmillan.

Wood, S. 1996: High Commitment Management and Payment Systems. *Journal of Management Studies*, **33**(1), 53–77.

12

Managing Working Time

James Arrowsmith and Keith Sisson

Working time, along with pay, is the defining feature of the employment relationship. The starting point for most jobs is that time is bought for productive activity. The organization of working time, how it is scheduled and utilized, are fundamental to productivity, motivation and performance. For employers, the arrangement of working-time patterns helps determine the way in which goods and services can be provided. For employees, these working-time patterns shape the very experience of work – its intensity and how it fits with domestic and social life – as well as being a major factor in compensation. It is therefore no surprise that, after pay, working time is one of the most contested areas of workplace industrial relations, and one which has a significant bearing on the job satisfaction, motivation and retention of employees (Millward et al. 1992: 285–8; Cully et al. 1998: 21–2).

Traditionally, working time has been relatively neglected as an area of management interest and academic investigation. Performance management has tended to be considered mainly in terms of pay, training, discipline, motivation and culture, with the organization of working time treated almost as a received framework devoid of scope for strategic choice. For the most part, any debate about working time focused on the issue of working time duration and, typically, would come to the fore when there was a union-led campaign to reduce the working week.

In his classic essay on the significance of time measurement in the emergence of industrial capitalism, Thompson (1974: 61) noted how the calculation and commodification of working time was crucial, first, to the imposition of organized work discipline and, subsequently, to workers' own collective organization and struggle. Campaigns for the ten-hours work day served as a focus for mass mobilization and protest, resulting in successive Factory Acts, from the 1833 Factory Act which, initially covered women and child labourers in the textile industry and which was later, following the 1867 Factory Act, extended to all factory trades and workshops (Hunt 1981).

The duration of working time continued to be a key issue into the twentieth century (see, for example, Bienefeld 1972). The 48-hour week was generally achieved at the end of the First World War, facilitated by the establishment of multi-employer bargaining on a sector basis. The 44-hour week followed after the Second World War. Renewed waves of pressure in 1959–62 resulted in the 42-hour week and after 1964–67 the long-standing union target of a basic week of 40 hours was reached. In 1979 the settlement of yet another dispute over working time in engineering reduced the basic working week to 39 hours with some eight and a half million other manual workers achieving the same standard over the next four years.

Despite these cuts in the basic working week, however, hours worked have remained stubbornly high. Indeed, the UK remains notorious for the long hours of many of its full-time employees, as figures 12.1 and 12.2, which reproduce data from Eurostat's Community Labour Force Survey for 1996, graphically show. The number of full-time male employees in the UK working long hours is especially marked. Although their female counterparts worked fewer hours in comparison with women in other EU member states, they stand out almost as much. The Eurostat data (not presented here) also suggests that the tendency for both men and women in the UK to work longer hours than their EU counterparts applied to most sectors and occupations. Other things being equal, it might have been expected that, under a voluntarist and highly decentralized system, there would have been significant differences from one sector to another. This is not the case, however. A particular working-time culture appears to be pervasive in the UK, despite the various pressures for change.

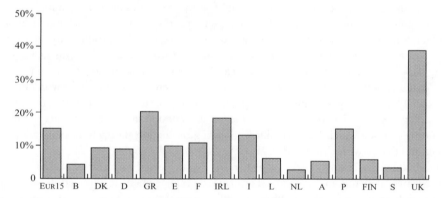

Figure 12.1   Percentage of full-time male employees usually working 46 or more hours a week
Source: Labour Force Survey results 1996, Eurostat

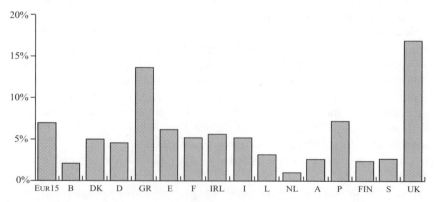

Figure 12.2   Percentage of full-time female employees usually working 46 or more hours a week
Source: Labour Force Survey results 1996, Eurostat

Significantly, too, the engineering workers' campaign in 1989–90 for a 37-hour basic week had nothing like the wider impact of previous ones (for further details, see McKinlay and McNulty 1992). That no wave of similar reductions followed in other industries reflected the wide-ranging changes taking place in the economy and the institutional framework: the decline in the size of manufacturing in general and engineering in particular; increased subcontracting; widespread job insecurity; the increasing feminization of the workforce; the decline and fragmentation of collective bargaining arrangements; and managerial achievements in specifying the working-time agenda to local performance criteria. In the service sectors especially, the distribution of working time had become as important as its duration, if not more so. In the fast-growing retail sector, the notion of a standard working week had all but disappeared.

In recent years, changes in the competitive and regulatory contexts have both intensified the interest in working time and shifted the focus. A harsh competitive environment has led management to see the organization of working time as a major factor in performance. Indeed, in many cases it has been changes in working time arrangements, rather than pay systems, which have been the catalyst for far-ranging changes in work organization and performance management. At the same time, managers are having to respond to demands from an increasingly feminized workforce for family-friendly working hours. They also have to consider the implications of a series of EU Directives dealing with working time, parental leave and the treatment of part-time workers, the first of which was grounded in concerns about the health and safety implications of some of the developing working-time trends. These pressures have already stimulated significant changes in working patterns as well as generating fresh controversies concerning the potential for further working-time change and how it might best be managed.

The focus of the chapter is on the changing significance of managing working time and the considerations forcing it to the top of the personnel management agenda. The chapter begins by considering the greater pressure, both from management and employees, for greater flexibility in working-time arrangements. The second section reviews the main patterns of working time in the UK and assesses the key changes in terms of duration, distribution and variability. The third section considers the limits to the reform of working-time arrangements, highlighting the dilemmas that change in this area poses in the UK. The fourth section discusses the implications of the new regulatory framework of working time. It specifically considers the implications of the recent far-reaching statutory regulations designed to give workers greater protection against long hours and minimum entitlements in terms of annual holidays, raising the possibility that this could lead to a come-back for joint regulation with significant implications for the management of the employment relationship more generally.

Two Kinds of Flexibility

Competition, technology and budgetary constraints

The view that working time is one of the keys to performance reflects ever-increasing competition in the private sector and increasing marketization in the public sector. This has produced significant pressures to introduce greater and more cost-effective variability in working hours as well as, in many cases, to an extension of operating times. In manufacturing, changes in production processes such as cellular team working and just-in-time production have combined with the need to respond to the fluctuating volume and design stipulations of customers to place an increasing emphasis on the flexibility of labour scheduling (Rojot 1989). At the same time, increasing capital intensity provides greater pressures to write off more effectively capital investments in order to reduce marginal costs (Bosch 1995a and b). As a result, employers simultaneously have had to find ways to vary their labour inputs through overtime, variable shift or annualized hours working, and to extend operational time by making additional changes to shift-working arrangements.

Intensifying competition in private services has also had far-reaching implications for working-time arrangements. In food retailing, for example, key developments have been the arrival of the discounters in the early 1990s and the deregulation of opening hours. In such a labour intensive industry, where union organization tends to be low, management have focused both on redistributing total labour hours to cover extended opening, through increased part-time working and the creation of new shifts, and on reducing labour costs, through the removal of hours premia and allowances. All of this has been facilitated by developments in new technologies such as EPOS (automatic scanning at the point of sale) and integrated staff scheduling systems, which have enabled companies to match working time more closely to the highly variable but generally predictable patterns of demand (for further details, see Deery and Mahoney 1994).

Similar trends can be found in financial services and the privatized utilities (gas, electricity, water, telephones), where increased competition following deregulation, coupled with the introduction of new technology, has been the stimulus to change (Walsh 1997; Colling and Ferner 1995). In the former case, computerized data processing has enabled management to separate and centralize 'back-office' work from the branch network which is now largely focused on the selling aspects of customer service. The result has been a substantial programme of branch closures and a significant increase in the size of the part-time workforce, both to staff peak periods in the branches and to cover extended working in the new call centres. In the latter case, companies had striven to improve standards of customer service by introducing new variable shift patterns for key groups of employees such as field engineers, enabling an extension of the available normal working week into evenings and weekends.

In the public sector, it is budgetary flexibility resulting from tightening controls over public spending, together with the introduction of greater managerialism and market testing that have been important catalysts for change (Bach and Winchester 1994; IDS 1997). In local government, for example, almost twice the proportion of temporary workers are employed, at 13 per cent, as in the economy as a whole and two in every five of its workers are part-time. The growing use of temporary and part-time workers has resulted from tight year-to-year budget constraints and the impact of compulsory competitive tendering discussed in chapter 3. Temporary and part-time working in local government therefore reflects the context of uncertainty and pressures to reduce costs. However, work-ing-time flexibility has also been a recent direct concern of the 1997 national harmonization deal for local government staff (IRS 1997). The agreement allowed decentralization to local level of arrangements for determining any premium rates for weekend, overtime and shiftworking. It also introduced the facility to average the newly reduced standard working hours over periods other than a week to meet varying demand for services.

In the NHS, working-time flexibility has long been a prime concern due to the need to reconcile permanent opening with variable levels of demand. The need to make working-time arrangements more acceptable to the workforce owing to recruitment and retention problems associated with relatively low pay, demanding work and the high proportion of unsocial hours has also loomed large (Audit Commission 1997). Especially significant, however, has been the response of local managers to a regime of tight cash limits and highly centralized (but underfunded) pay settlements for groups such as nurses. In effect, they have had little option but to focus on the variables in labour costs under their control, if they are to live within their budgets, which means the numbers of workers employed and the hours that they work.

Pressures for family-friendly working hours

At the same time as the drive for flexibility has led to working time increasingly being seen as a major factor in employers' cost, efficiency and quality strategies, management in some sectors are having to pay more attention to the working time preferences of employees as a result of labour-market changes, skills shortages and difficulties in recruitment and retention. The need to accommodate workers' demands has been most visible in periods of economic growth such as the late 1980s when fears of a demographic timebomb added to employers' tight labour-market woes (NEDO 1989). Of more enduring significance has been the shift in the balance of employment to the service sectors, where it is arguably more possible as well as necessary for management to offer different portfolios of working hours to attract and retain new groups of workers.

Above all, the growth in the labour force participation of women and the expansion of dual-income families and single-parent families, allied to the growing participation of students, has fuelled a demand for patterns of part-time work (Hakim 1997). In retail especially, where there is a long tradition of Saturday working, part-time working has exploded in the wake of longer opening hours, seven-day opening and, in some cases, 24-hour trading. Among the large multiple food retailers, for example, the panel survey being undertaken as part of the Industrial Relations Research Unit's (IRRU) pay and working time project suggests that part-time sales assistants typically outweigh full-timers by more than two to one. The project's case study research finds that shift patterns are set locally and are almost impossible to describe. In superstores with more than 500 employees, for example, there can be almost as many shift patterns as there are workers – with hours ranging from 3 up to 36.5 per week. It is not just women who are working part time either; there are almost as many men who are part-timers as there are male full-time workers. Depending on the local availability of staff, management may be willing to agree to the hours the individual is willing to work rather than seeking to impose their own ideally preferred pattern.

Significantly, the Labour Force Survey shows that most part-timers, particularly women, do not want full-time employment (see table 12.1). Even excluding those in education, eight out of nine female part-time workers and over half of male part-timers said they preferred not to work full time. Patently, such figures need to be treated with a degree of caution as they may not adequately distinguish whether not wanting full-time work is a genuine preference or whether it merely reflects constraints on participation such as

Table 12.1   Reasons for part-time working

Reason	All %	Men %	Women %
Do not want full-time employment	72.0	39.2	79.7
Cannot find full-time employment	11.3	23.7	8.4
Student/at school	14.8	33.2	10.2
Ill/disabled	1.7	3.8	1.2

Percentages may not sum to 100 as totals include those who do not provide a reason.

Source: Labour Force Survey, Summer 1998

difficulties in arranging childcare, poor health or earnings restrictions on retired workers. Another important reservation is to ask 'whether women want part-time *jobs* or jobs with *short hours*' (Ginn et al. 1996: 170); women may prefer to work in jobs with fewer hours, but not to be thereby confined to a part-time sector of the labour market disadvantaged in terms of pay, responsibility, status, and employment conditions (see chapter 6). Even so, it is difficult to escape the conclusion that, for many women with family commitments, the LFS figures pretty accurately reflect a preference for shorter patterns of hours. This is backed up by other data such as the British Social Attitudes Survey, which in 1995 found that only a quarter of part-time employees would work more hours even given the child-care arrangement of their choice (DfEE 1998).

In recent years the focus on family-friendly policies has broadened considerably beyond part-time working and governments have become more actively involved in their promotion. In the words of the UK Government's White Paper on *Fairness at Work*, this comes from the 'need to ensure that as many people as possible who want to work should have the chance to so so' (DTI 1998b: para 5.1). Of course, this not only reflects concerns that organizations are not making the most of the talents potentially at their disposal, but also that there are insufficient openings for groups such as single mothers who might otherwise become the responsibility of the social security system.

In any event, the Government believes that 'To ensure that all parents are better able to balance work and family life, voluntary measures need to be underpinned by a statutory framework' (DTI 1998b: para 5.5). As well as a National Minimum Wage, a package of measures is proposed with which management is going to have to contend, including dealing with the Working Families Tax Credit, a National Childcare Strategy, raising the status of working from home, a wide-ranging review of the operation of existing maternity rights as well as the implementation of the EU Directives covering working time (discussed in the next section), parental leave and equality of treatment for part-time workers.

The Parental Leave Directive is 'designed to facilitate the reconciliation of parental and professional responsibilities for working parents'. Its key points are as follows:

- Men and women workers must have an individual right to at least three months' parental leave for childcare purposes (as distinct from maternity leave) after the birth or adoption of a child up to eight years old to be defined by member states and/or management and labour.

- The conditions of access and detailed rules governing parental leave are to be defined by law and/or collective agreement, and may include a length of service qualification of up to one year, special provisions regarding adoption, provision for notice periods and 'special arrangements to meet the operational and organizational requirements of small undertakings'.
- Workers must be protected against dismissal on the grounds of applying for or taking parental leave, have the right to return to the same or similar job and maintain previously acquired rights.
- Member states and/or management and labour must take the necessary measures to entitle workers to time off from work on grounds of *force majeure* for urgent family reasons in cases of sickness or accident making their immediate presence indispensable, though member states and/or management and labour may specify conditions of access and detailed rules and may limit this entitlement to a certain amount of time per year and/or per case.

A report from the independent 'think-tank' Demos (Wilkinson 1997) confirmed the findings of the DfEE survey in suggesting that relatively few organizations in the UK currently have arrangements for parental leave. In principle, therefore, the impact of the Directive could be considerable. In practice, however, unless the Government also makes provision for parental leave to be paid, the experience of other EU countries suggests there will be little take-up.

The Part-time Directive's main provisions, which follow very closely the understanding reached by the EU social partners under the Maastricht Agreement on social policy, are as follows:

- Part-time workers should not be treated any less favourably than comparable full-time workers.
- Member states, together with the social partners, should identify and review obstacles which may limit part-time work and, where appropriate, remove them.
- A refusal to transfer from full-time to part-time work or vice versa should not in itself constitute a valid reason for termination of employment.
- Employers should, as far as possible, give consideration to requests by workers to transfer from full-time to part-time work and vice versa; to the provision of timely information about the availability of posts in order to facilitate transfers; to measures to ease access to part-time work at all levels including skilled and management positions; and to the provision of appropriate information about part-time working to employee representative bodies.

It is the second and fourth of these provisions which, potentially, management may find most challenging. This is especially so in the case of sectors and occupations with little or no tradition of part-time working.

The Changing Patterns of Working Time

The sections that follow discuss the nature and extent of the principal changes which are taking place in patterns of working time in response to these pressures for greater flexibility.

For the purposes of analysis, these can be distinguished between those relating mainly to the issue of working time duration, and those which focus more on the distribution or variability of working hours.

Changes in the duration of working time

There have been three main types of change in recent years. The first, 'compressed working weeks', has tended to exaggerate the long hours of full-time workers by concentrating working time into longer shifts. The second, predominantly but not exclusively in the service sectors, involves the break-up of working time into shorter blocks for part-time workers. The third relates to the duration of the contract for work rather than to the length of the working day or week itself.

THE COMPRESSED WEEK

A compressed week usually involves the reallocation of hours into fewer and longer blocks of time. For example, one reaction to reductions in the working week in engineering has been to reorganize on the basis of four and a half days a week or nine days out of ten in a fortnight. Typically, this involves a Friday downtime so that employees get the benefit of a longer weekend. This also provides a regular period when essential cleaning and maintenance work can take place. A number of organizations have also moved to 12-hour working as part of wider restructuring involving flexible rostering and annual hours arrangements discussed later. Examples which have been studied in detail include BT (IRS 1995b), Rockware Glass (IRS 1993) and Zeneca Agrochemicals at Yalding (IRS 1994).

Overall, however, the number of organizations with some form of compressed week in the UK is small. According to Labour Force Survey data for 1997 Labour Market Trends, (1997), only 0.9 cent of employees worked a four-and-a-half-day week and only 0.8 per cent a nine-day fortnight. The engineering industry has the largest proportion of employees working a four-and-a-half-day week and transport and communications the largest proportion on a 9-day fortnight.

PART-TIME WORKING

Part-time working is generally taken to mean hours less than the normal basic week, although official statistics often use a definition of 30 hours a week or less. As will be seen from table 12.2, the UK has the third highest proportion of part-time workers among EU countries after the Netherlands and Sweden. The proportion of women working part-time is especially high and is second only to the Netherlands.

Much of the growth in part-time working came in the late 1970s and early 1980s and reflected supply-side considerations – the wish of many employees, especially women, to work part time rather than full time. Employer demand was also important however, and has continued to fuel the growth of part-time work. According to the most recent WERS data, two in five workplaces reported an increase in the employment of part-timers over the previous five years (Cully et al. 1998: 9). One of the main benefits of part-time working

Table 12.2 Men and women employed part time as percentage of each category's total employment, 1985 and 1995

	Total		Men		Women	
	1985	*1995*	*1985*	*1995*	*1985*	*1995*
Belgium	8.6	13.6	1.8	2.8	21.1	29.8
Denmark	24.3	21.6	8.4	10.4	43.9	35.5
Germany[1]	12.8	16.3	2.0	3.6	29.6	33.8
Greece	5.3	4.8	2.8	2.8	10.0	8.4
Spain	5.8[2]	7.5	2.4[2]	2.7	13.9[2]	16.6
France	10.9	15.6	3.2	5.1	21.8	28.9
Ireland	6.5	12.1	2.4	5.5	15.5	23.0
Italy	5.3	6.4	3.0	2.9	10.1	12.7
Luxembourg	7.2	8.0	2.6	1.0	16.3	20.7
Netherlands	22.7	37.4	7.7	16.8	51.6	67.2
Austria	6.7	13.9	1.4	4.0	14.9	26.9
Portugal	6.0[3]	7.5	3.4[3]	4.2	10.0[3]	11.6
Finland	7.8	11.8	4.3	8.1	11.6	15.7
Sweden	25.7[2]	25.8	6.9[2]	10.3	46.0[2]	43.0
United Kingdom	21.2	24.1	4.4	7.7	44.8	44.3
E15	12.5	16.0	3.4	5.2	27.3	31.3

[1] 1995 figures include new Länder
[2] 1987 figures
[3] 1986 figures

Source: adapted and derived from European Commission (1996) *Employment in Europe 1996*

is increasingly seen to be the greater flexibility it makes possible – especially in covering so-called key periods of activity (ACAS 1996: 10–11). These so-called key-time workers are especially significant in energy and water supply, transport and communications, banking and finance, and the public sector (Labour Research Department 1995b: 7–12).

Although part-time working has come to be associated with the service sector, it is not unknown in manufacturing. Table 12.3 shows that a majority of manufacturing workplaces employ at least some part-time workers, although in very few cases do they represent a majority of employees. In this sector, part-time working is most often associated with two main patterns which are particularly prevalent in food, drink and tobacco. The first is the so-called 'early-riser' shift, typically starting between 5.30 a.m. and 6 a.m. and going on to 1 p.m. or 1.30 p.m. The second is known as the 'twilight' shift. This is usually of between four and five hours duration and begins in the late afternoon or early evening (for further details, see IRS 1995a; Labour Research Department 1996).

TEMPORARY WORKING

Temporary working enables employers to vary the total hours worked by changing the numbers employed on contracts of limited or predetermined duration. This can take the form of employing temporary agency workers ('temps') or workers on fixed-term contracts. Around two-thirds of all workplaces have used temporary agency workers or employed

Table 12.3 Part-time work by sector

	Workplaces with no part-time employees %	Workplaces with most employees part-time %
Manufacturing	36	1
Electricity, gas, water	51	0
Construction	39	0
Wholesale and retail	14	43
Hotels and restaurants	3	55
Transport and communications	23	4
Financial services	20	5
Other business services	23	7
Public administration	9	1
Education	0	40
Health	1	50
Other community services	8	51
All workplaces	16	26

Base: all workplaces with 25 or more employees, except column 5, where it is all workplaces five or more years old with 25 employees

Figures are weighted and based on responses from 1,929 managers

Source: Cully et al. (1998: table 2)

staff on fixed-term contracts over the past five years (Cully et al. 1998: 9). Of these, between one-quarter and one-third reported their use to have increased, compared to only one in ten which had decreased their use, with the rest remaining broadly the same. The most affected occupations are the clerical and professional groups (table 12.4), while only a small minority of other categories used either temps or people on fixed-term contracts.

Table 12.4 Use of temporary agency workers and fixed-term contracts, by occupation

Occupation	Temporary agency workers Percent of workplaces employing	Fixed-term contracts Percent of workplaces employing
Managers and administrators	1	6
Professional	5	15
Associate professional and technical	5	6
Clerical and secretarial	17	13
Craft and related	2	3
Personal and protective services	2	5
Sales	0	4
Plant and machine operators	4	2
Other occupations	5	6
None of these workers used	72	56

Note: Base is all workplaces with 25 or more employees. Figures are weighted and based on responses from 1,921 managers

Source: Cully et al. (1998: table 3)

More and more people are experiencing irregular or insecure working patterns as a result of the growing use by employers of temporary forms of employment. In the ten years to 1996, the number of women in temporary jobs increased by 23 per cent and the number of men by 74 per cent (Sly et al. 1997). Temporary employment is now fairly evenly distributed between the sexes, with over 7 per cent of men and approaching 9 per cent of women employees on temporary or fixed-term contracts. According to recent data from the second quarterly LFS survey of 1998, around four in ten male temporary workers and three in ten female temporary workers took such a job only because they could not find a permanent contract. For full-time temporary workers, and those working part time only because no full-time jobs could be found, these proportions of involuntary temporary working are much higher.

The use of temporary workers has traditionally been about filling in for employees absent through illness or maternity leave. However, it is also an increasingly important means by which employers can respond to market pressures through numerical flexibility, reducing or increasing total hours worked through rapid and low-cost changes in employee numbers (Casey et al. 1997; Purcell and Purcell 1998). A significant part of the overall expansion in temporary working may be accounted for by changing practice in the public sector in particular. According to the LFS, more than one in ten public-sector employees are now in temporary jobs, almost twice the proportion of those in the private sector. In the NHS, for example, much of the increased use of fixed-term and 'bank' or agency nurses has been associated with greater short-term uncertainty over budgeting and service contracts (Buchan 1994). However, in the private sector, employers are also increasingly using temporary workers due to increased market uncertainties. For example, the 'partnership' agreements at Rover and the Co-operative Bank (for further details, see chapter 15) facilitate the increasing use of temporary workers by providing some guarantee of employment security for the permanent workforce and by establishing comparable terms and conditions for the temporary staff (IRS 1997).

Changes in the distribution of working time

SHIFT WORKING

Shift working has been the main way in which employers have sought to improve the distribution of working time. Shift working involves the working of two or more periods within the same 24 hours by different employees usually organized in crews or teams. The aim is to increase the coverage of working time beyond the working day of the individual employee, even taking into account overtime. 'Continuous' systems provide cover for the full 24 hours throughout the week; 'non-continuous' or 'discontinuous' systems provide for lesser coverage than this – for example, it may be for 12 or 16 hours out of 24 each day and/or five days out of seven (for further details, see IRS 1995a; ACAS 1996).

Shift working has long been a feature in many sectors in the UK and has been mainly associated with manual workers, above all in transport and manufacturing. Increasingly, however, its net has spread to include non-manual workers in services. Shift working is now very common, for example, in sectors such as banking and finance and in retail, as

Table 12.5   Types of shift pattern by numbers of employees

	All	Men	Women
Two-shift system (early/late or double day)	1,109,000	601,200	500,500
Three-shift working	572,300	386,500	185,900
Sometimes nights, sometimes days	429,200	300,600	128,700
Night shifts	286,200	171,800	128,700
Evening or twilight shifts	178,900	64,400	100,100
Continental shifts[a]	143,100	158,300	14,300
Split shifts	143,100	85,900	71,500
Morning shifts	71,500	64,400	28,600
Weekend shifts	35,800	—	14,300
Other type of shift work	608,100	365,000	257,400
Base: all in employment who usually work shifts[b]	3,577,000	2,147,000	1,430,000

'—' signifies less than 0.5 per cent

Does not include people on college-based schemes

[a]   A continuous three-shift system that rotates more rapidly than conventional three-shift working, e.g. three mornings, then two afternoons, then two nights (with breaks between shift changes), rather than one or more weeks on each shift pattern

[b]   Bases for calculation of percentages exclude a small number of people who did not state their type of shift-work

Source: *Labour Market Trends*, November 1997, LFS60

well as the NHS where it has long been a feature. As will be seen from table 12.5, approximately 3.6 million people 'usually' worked shifts in 1997.

FROM FIXED TO VARIABLE HOURS

The arrangements considered so far involve essentially fixed hours worked on a weekly basis. Most recent attention has focused on arrangements under which hours worked are variable over the day, week or year. It is the extra flexibility that variability brings which, in theory, management might be expected to find especially attractive.

Under 'zero hours' arrangements, the employer calls in 'employees' at short notice as and when there is a need. Employees may even be asked to clock off and so lose pay in quiet periods even though they are required to stay on the premises. The practice, which affected some 0.3 per cent of the workforce in 1997, came to prominence in the early 1990s in the retail and financial sectors especially (for further details, see Neathey and Hurstfield 1996; Cave 1997), and is essentially little different from the casual system prevalent in a wide range of industries in the last century. It has been widely condemned on the grounds that the individual 'employee' has no minimum employment rights whatsoever, and it demonstrates most explicitly the potential for abuse inherent in some forms of flexible working (NACAB 1997). The Government is currently seeking views (in its 1998 White Paper on *Fairness at Work*, para 3.16) on whether 'further action should be taken to address the potential abuse of zero hours contracts and, if so, how to take this forward without undermining labour market flexibility'.

There are two main forms of 'flexi-time'. The first exists mainly for the benefit of employees and is better discussed in the next section. The second form primarily serves the employer. One variant, sometimes known as 'minimum hours' or 'mini-max hours', is primarily found in retail and mainly affects part-time employees. Unlike zero hours, the employee has a contract for a fixed number of hours each week. By agreement with the employee, however, and subject to reasonable notice, the employer can increase the daily or weekly hours up to a pre-set maximum. For example, such arrangements have been introduced into multiple food retailing by Tesco: part-timers can opt to work a fixed core of 10 to 16 hours a week on the understanding that they may be asked to work up to 31 hours a week to cover sickness and other absence. This is subject to special provisions designed to safeguard against casualization, such as minimum guaranteed periods of work and notice required (for further details, see IRS 1996).

Another variation involves 'flexible rostering'. Under these arrangements, the employer can vary the daily or weekly hours around a range. A recent and major example of flexible rostering would be the Customer Service Improvement Programme introduced in BT and covering its engineers servicing domestic customers. Technical and engineering grades are rostered to attend according to four main patterns, with management being able to adjust the starting and finishing times up to an hour each day with debits and credits of up to four hours being accrued (for further details, see IRS 1995b).

In the case of 'seasonal hours', employees work different hours depending on the time of year, with excess hours in one period 'banked' and taken off in lieu in another. Long a feature of agriculture, seasonal hours have emerged in manufacturing and services more generally in recent years. In manufacturing, for example, Blyton (1994: 517–18) quotes the example of Hitachi in South Wales. Since 1991 the standard working week of 39 hours has been modified to meet the extra demand in the run-up to Christmas. Employees work a 42-hour week between August and December and 37 hours a week at other times. Pay, however, remains standardized at 39 hours per week throughout the year.

Arguably, 'annual hours', which bring together a number of practices discussed above such as minimum hours, hours banking, and flexible rostering, represent the most advanced form of change to the management of working time. The basic principle is that working time is defined in terms of the year rather than the week. The employer is therefore better able to match working time to fluctuations in demand for products and services.

In its simplest form, the total number of annual hours is based on the number of weeks in the year multiplied by the number of working hours per week with a deduction for holidays. For example:

52.2 weeks × 39 hours = 2,035.8 hours
less 25 days holiday at (39 hours divided by 5 days) = 195 hours
less 8 public holidays at (39 hours divided by 5 days) = 62.4 hours
Total = 1,778.4 hours

Like shift working, annual hours arrangements differ significantly in the details. Following Blyton (1994: 515–16), however, they are typically one of two types. In the first, the emphasis is on the variability of weekly hours with work periods longer in busy times and shorter during slacker times as in seasonal hours. In the second, rostered hours are less than the agreed annual hours: workers are effectively on call for the non-rostered time and can be required to come into work to cover unforeseen circumstances. The first type has been particularly applied in seasonal demand businesses and the second in continuous process industries (for further details, see IRS 1998a, 1998b).

Commentators have been predicting a significant take-up of annual hours for over a decade (see, for example, Brewster and Connock 1985; Taylor 1994; IRS 1998a). At first sight, there are major attractions in terms of flexibility, costs and productivity. For example, they make possible the closer matching of worked hours to service or production demands, with workers (and supervisors) less likely to anticipate or contrive opportunities for extra-hours working once the direct link with pay is removed. Instead, there is a strong incentive to get work done within the allotted time in order to avoid drawing on any reserve hours. Annual hours can also deliver significant cost savings by reducing overtime working and the hiring of temporary staff. A beneficial productivity effect comes from reducing the underutilization of staff, if the arrangements are accompanied by task flexibility and multiskilling, as has been the case in companies such as Rockware Glass and Zeneca Agrochemicals at Yalding. There may also be gains in terms of employee attendance, motivation and reduced levels of turnover if the scheme is able to provide greater stability for employee earnings.

In terms of coverage, however, annual hours remain very much a minority practice for reasons considered later. Indeed, if anything there appears to have been a decline in the number of employees covered in recent years. LFS data for 1997 (Labour Market Trends 1997: LFS63) suggest that no more than 4.5 per cent of employees worked under such arrangements, whereas a detailed study based on LFS data for 1993 (Watson 1994: 242–4) suggested that twice this number were involved. Overall, the 1993 data suggested there was relatively little difference in the proportion of men and women working annual hours, contrasting sharply with that of the 1997 data, where the proportion of men affected appears to be considerably less than that for women.

EMPLOYEE DISCRETION OVER WORKING-TIME DISTRIBUTION

The changes and developments in the distribution of working time noted above reflect attempts by employers to extend or vary working hours more easily and cost effectively in order to meet their own requirements. Other schemes allow employees greater flexibility and control over the distribution of worked time, within predetermined limits, the most significant of which are flexitime and, more recently, teleworking.

Flexitime allows staff to vary their daily start and finishing times within a defined range. Typically over a month, staff can fluctuate their daily or weekly hours around their contractual working time, carrying a certain amount of accrued credit or deficit hours into the next period. Common in the public- and private-service sectors since the early 1970s, flexitime covers one in ten of all employees with a particular concentration among white-collar groups. According to the Spring 1997 LFS, almost one in five clerical and secretarial workers now have access to flexitime arrangements, in contrast to only 4 per cent of craft and related workers and 3.5 per cent of plant and machine operators.

Home working, the First Findings of the 1998 WERS (Cully et al. 1998: 20) suggest, affects around one in ten of all employees and is more common in the public than the private sector, and for male rather than female employees. Teleworking is a particular and new form of remote working in which staff are based partly or mainly at home but remain technologically connected to the workplace. The Spring 1998 LFS showed that around 102,400 employees work mainly in their own home; approximately 259,000 work in different places but use their home as a base; and a further 240,000 are occasional teleworkers who spend at least a day a week working at home or use it as a base. Around one in five of the first group are in clerical or secretarial jobs, and craft and related occupations are represented to a similar degree in the second. Managers and professionals are well represented in each category, but especially the third where they account for three out of four occasional teleworkers.

In contrast to the routine work tasks normally contracted out to traditional home-workers, telework is generally distinguished by jobs and professions whose work involves a high degree of complexity and discretion. Teleworkers can, in principle, therefore retain or enhance their autonomy in the job and enjoy greater scope to 'flex' their working time around other commitments. Individuals also benefit from not having to travel to work, and this time saved is often shared between the employer and employee, with motivation and productivity improving as a result (Baruch and Nicholson 1997). This is not necessarily or always the case, however, and many teleworkers, particularly those who are in a subcon-tractual relationship with their employer(s), may experience little control over their flow of work and end up working very long hours (Huws et al. 1996).

The Limits to Reform

As the discussion has pointed out, and the details in table 12.6 confirm, significant though many of the changes are, they are clearly nowhere near as widespread as some pundits have proclaimed. Rojot's (1998: 193) judgement, that working time is 'probably one of the most difficult conditions of work to modify or regulate', seems wholly appropriate. A formidable obstacle in moving to annualized working time arrangements, for example, is the complexity of planning and agreeing a mutually acceptable system, one which is able to take account of the inevitable implications for wider pay and grading structures as well as for current working practices. Although difficulties can be minimized by using suitable software packages (IDS 1996), the administration of annual hours can be complex depend-ing on the balance between fixed and flexible hours, the scope for employee choice over holidays and scheduled work shifts, and levels of employee turnover. The reaction of first-line managers and employees can also be off-putting: various worries have been reported about the inconvenience if banked hours are called in at short notice; working excessive hours at certain periods; the effect on earnings of loss of overtime and allowances; reductions in staffing levels; unaccustomed shift patterns; working with unfamiliar work-mates; and the inflexibility of leave when it is rostered into the yearly cycle (see IRS 1998a and b). Awareness of the costs of change might therefore perpetuate a 'make-do' approach to working time, especially in conditions of uncertainty, involving incremental rather than radical alterations. An additional consideration is that changes to established practice can be expensive if they have to be 'bought out' (Bosch 1995a and b).

Yet perhaps the major factor, as Clark (1996) has cogently argued of change more generally, is that there are limits to the amount of flexibility management needs. Nowhere is this more true than of working time. The certainty of knowing that a given number of

Table 12.6   Percentage of employees by type of flexible work arrangement, spring 1997

	All	Men	Women
Employees with a flexible work arrangement[a]	22.0	18.0	26.3
Flexible working hours	10.0	8.8	11.5
Annualized hours contract	4.5	1.5	7.8
Term-time working	4.2	4.3	4.1
Job-sharing	2.1	2.7	1.5
Four-and-a-half-day week	0.9	0.2	1.7
Nine-day fortnight	0.8	0.8	0.9
Zero hours contract	0.3	0.5	0.1
Employees without a flexible work organization	78.0	82.0	73.7
Employees who gave a valid response (thousands) (=100%)	21,250	11,127	10,124
Base: All employees who gave a valid response (thousands)[b]	22,447	11,784	10,663

[a]   Columns add up to more than 100 per cent because respondents can give more than one type of flexible arrangement

[b]   Percentages are based on those people who gave a valid response to the flexible working question. Estimates of levels can be obtained by multiplying the percentages by the base

Source: *Labour Market Trends*, December 1997, LFS63

employees will be available between fixed times is a necessary condition for the most basic forms of operations management. Moreover, any flexibility required is likely to be very specific to the particular types of operations. In an engineering company, for example, just-in-time production is likely to put a premium on extras hours being worked at very short notice, whereas in an industry such as chemicals, characterized by a continuous process, effective three-shift working round the clock is what is most valued. In retail, the peaks and troughs of demand over an increasingly lengthy cycle of seven days a week are massive but predictable, encouraging the development of a plethora of regular part-time shift patterns.

Sectoral differences in labour market characteristics can also be significant in defining the available options for change and reinforcing the operational requirements. Skilled engineering workers, for example, are overwhelmingly male workers looking for full-time secure employment and so part-time and temporary work is less likely to be feasible. In contrast, in the service sector a large proportion of the workforce – secondary earners and those with other household or educational responsibilities – might be willing only to work on a part-time basis. The obligation to tailor working-time arrangements to the needs and preferences of the particular workforce will be even more pronounced in tight labour markets or where there are shortages of particular skills.

It is the segmentation of the labour market which also helps to explain the uneven spread of many of the family-friendly working-time arrangements. In the sectors with few women, such as large parts of manufacturing, little need is seen for such practices. In the sectors in which women's employment is concentrated, part-time employment is widespread, which considerably reduces the need to offer other ways of balancing employment with domestic responsibilities.

In these circumstances, as the authors have argued in detail elsewhere (Arrowsmith and Sisson 1999), the durability of seemingly tried and tested arrangements can itself be a powerful force for conservatism. The outstanding example is overtime working, be it paid or unpaid, which is such a pervasive feature of British working life. The ease and simplicity of overtime working makes it appealing to managers and the premium rates which it can attract offer obvious benefits to employees. The organization of overtime working, which is normally agreed on a voluntary rather than contractual basis, fits easily into the decentralized and informal structure of British industrial relations. It is also supported by the short-term planning horizon of most British businesses and their emphasis on profitability rather than other performance measures such as market share.

In theory, overtime is a very flexible working time arrangement – working hours can be increased to meet exceptional increases in demand without the costs and commitment involved in hiring additional employees. Just as importantly, overtime working can be cut back to respond to downturn periods without having to lose valued skilled staff. In practice, however, the routine use of overtime, especially in combination with low basic rates of pay, risks creating what the DTI (1998a: 3) has called a 'long hours' culture, in which long working hours become established not as the exception but as the norm, with workers depending upon the regular earnings it provides.

The downside of such a culture is felt both by management, which finds itself incurring the regular expense of premium rates for what may be a less productive worked time, and workers, who have to endure long working hours. In Whybrew's (1968: 63) words, 'overtime encourages people to waste time at work'. Workers are prone to resist change in order to protect overtime earnings and managers have little incentive to innovate. Routine overtime can thereby become a force for conservatism, inefficiency and rigidity in the workplace. In fact, for all the talk of technological revolutions, globalization and rapid organizational change, it is extraordinary that the observation made by Flanders (1964: 59–60) some 35 years ago should still ring true today:

> What makes overtime systematic is the almost automatic adjustment in work habits and behaviour that its regular working induces among workers and supervisors alike... the existing level of overtime becomes one of the accepted facts of life. Everyone comes to count on it for the completion of tasks, rather than on some notional 'normal' week... The very regularity of overtime produces the attitudes that will ensure that it is continually needed.

True, many organizations have taken steps to limit the extent of overtime working in recent years (for further details, see IRS 1996). These measures range from restraining strategies of imposing more precise conditions for authorization, tighter budgetary controls and a closer monitoring of absence and scheduling of leave, to more radical elimination strategies involving automation, increasing employment levels (including greater use of part-time, temporary contract and casual staff), new shift-work patterns and, ultimately, annualized hours systems. Yet overtime working remains the practice most characteristically resistant to change (Roche et al. 1996). In the form of 'presenteeism', i.e. unpaid overtime arising from the felt need to be at work (though not necessarily doing work), it now affects not only manufacturing and shopfloor employees, but also services, professions and most grades from the bottom to the very top. Indeed, some chief executives feel that it goes with the job to be the first to arrive and the last to go (see, for example, Harvey 1998).

The New Regulatory Framework of Working Time and Its Implications

The discretion that UK management has had in recent years in deciding its working time arrangements is almost unique among EU member countries. Not only has the legal regulation of working time in the UK been minimal by comparison to that of most of these countries, the decline of collective bargaining has also meant that there has been less other need for employers to seek explicit agreement with their employees (for further details, see Hall and Sisson 1997: 25–6). Less than half the working population now have their terms and conditions of employment determined by collective agreements, including, incidentally, the vast majority of employees who do not already enjoy the paid leave entitlements provided for in the Working Time Regulations (Labour Research Department 1995a: 19–21). Critically, in many sectors such as engineering, multi-employer agreements which were negotiated by employers organizations and unions at national or regional level are no longer in place to set a minimum framework dealing with working time. The current wisdom is that collective bargaining is a matter for individual employers and, where it takes place, should be decentralized to the individual business or decision-making unit.

All this may be about to change. Along with the two EU Directives emanating from the Maastricht social policy process, dealing with parental leave and equality of treatment for part-time workers, the Working Time Directive adds up to the biggest change in the regulatory framework of employment in the UK since the Industrial Relations Act of 1971. To take just the Working Time Directive, the DTI's public consultation document (1998a: Annex E2) estimated that around one-quarter of the workforce in the UK will be affected by its protections and entitlements. Most attention has focused on the 48-hour working week limit, where some 1.7 million people could be affected. In practice, however, it is the annual leave arrangements which are likely to have the most immediate and widespread repercussions. The same document estimated, on the basis of the autumn 1996 LFS figures, that 2.5 million employees had an entitlement to annual paid leave of less than three weeks (a right which came into force in October 1998) and about 3.1 million had less than the four weeks which would become the statutory norm a year later. Around one-third of both of these groups were full-time workers. Many more individuals could be affected if one of the DTI's critical assumptions proves unfounded, i.e. that paid leave on bank and public holidays (or compensatory time off) will count against the new statutory minimum. Many thousands could also be affected by the provision for average pay for holidays in the year the holiday is taken (see Thatcher 1998).

Three particular features of the new regulatory framework are especially worthy of note. One is the that working time now has the legal status of health and safety issues. The second is that there is statutory support for the joint regulation of working time. The third is that there is provision for work is to be adapted to the worker.

Health and safety considerations

British management has long been required to accept that shift work and night work have implications for health and safety (see, for example, the review of the literature in Waterhouse et al. 1992). It is the relationship between the duration of working time and health and safety which has been more hotly debated in recent years. On the basis of the published evidence and their own surveys, organizations as different as the TUC (1995a; 1998) and the Institute of Management (1995; 1996; 1998) have argued that long hours in particular are damaging to health and safety as well as being detrimental to family life.

Ironically, it was the decision of the then Conservative Government to contest the validity of the European Commission's decision to introduce its proposed directive dealing with working time as a health and safety measure under Article 118A of the Treaty involving majority voting which settled the matter. The European Court of Justice decided that, with the exception of the terms restricting Sunday working, the proposed measures were indeed justified on grounds of health and safety, thereby firmly re-establishing the legal link. The current UK Government has accepted this position. In the words of the April 1998 public consultation document (DTI 1998a:)

> The Government considers the Directive to be an important addition to health and safety protections for workers. The Government favours maximum flexibility in implementation but does not believe that this should be at the expense of fair minimum standards and the proper protection of workers from risks of excess working time leading to stress, fatigue and risks to health and safety. (pp. 1–2)

Significantly, the Directive does not just lay down a series of limits and entitlements – i.e. a maximum average working week of 48 hours, including overtime; a maximum average of eight hours night work; a minimum daily rest period of 11 hours; a rest break where the working day is longer than six hours; a minimum rest period of one day a week; and a minimum annual paid leave of three weeks rising to four after a transitional period, with part-time employees receiving pro rata benefits. It also requires health assessments for key groups such as night workers. Furthermore, it emphasizes that, in the wide-ranging flexibilities that are available for 'derogations', the key general principles of recognized health and safety practice have to be taken into account: for example, there must be 'due regard for the general principles of the safety and health of workers'; employees must also be afforded 'equivalent periods of compensatory rest' or 'appropriate protection'; and that, in planning the organization of work, employers must take account of 'the general principle of adapting work to the worker' (for further details, see Hall et al. 1998).

Perhaps of greatest significance for day-to-day practice is the way the Government is proposing to enforce the Regulations which implement the Directive. Unlike its prede-cessor, which proposed to put the onus in the event of alleged non-compliance almost entirely on individual complaints to employment tribunals, the Labour Government is taking a dual approach. In the case of entitlements, for example to rest breaks or to paid annual leave, employees will be expected to exercise their initiative and take any complaint to the employment tribunals. In the case of the limits on working hours, health assessments for night workers, and other night-work provisions, however, the job of monitoring and prosecution is given to the Health and Safety Executive and local authorities, depending on the type of workplace, like other aspects of health and safety legislation. Critically, therefore, individual employees with grievances in these areas will be less exposed.

A come-back for joint regulation?

In line with the approach of EU social and employment interventions more generally, one of the objectives of the Directive is to promote collective agreements or 'agreement between the two sides of industry' wherever possible. The specific way in which the Directive seeks to promote joint regulation is to require national governments to allow employers to define and obtain derogations from certain terms, and to extend some of the stated reference periods for calculating average hours, through agreements made with recognized trade unions. A full list of the so-called flexibilities possible by agreement under the Working Time Regulations is given in table 12.7.

Management's need to secure agreement for more flexible arrangements than the Regulations' basic standards would appear to present unions with a considerable opportunity. For example, there may be an attempt, where they are well organized, to seek to exploit the situation to improve current arrangements. It would be surprising, for example, if there were not attempts to seek a reduction in the working week or an enhancement in some aspect of shift pay, especially where these have been long-standing demands. This, in turn, may lead management to propose their own changes such as flexible rostering or annual hours arrangements.

The key role accorded to collective agreements by the Directive also raises yet again the issue of the UK's structure of collective bargaining touched on in chapters 1 and 15. In other EU member countries, collective bargaining is something which mainly takes place outside the workplace between employers' organizations and trade unions. In practice, it is little different from the legal regulation of employment with the exception that employers and workers, through their organizations, are more actively involved in the decision-making process. In the UK, there are now few multi-employer agreements negotiated by employers' organizations and unions at national or regional level.

Ironically, therefore, UK management now finds themselves at a disadvantage compared to their EU counterparts. Except in sectors where the framework of multi-employer

Table 12.7 Flexibilities possible by agreement under the Working Time Regulations

---

Determining the period of night time during which work is classified as night work (2 [1])
Determining the definition of night worker (2 [1])
Determining the definition of working time (2 [1])
Determining the reference period applicable in respect of the limit on the length of night work (6 [3])
Determining which work involves 'special hazards or heavy physical or mental strain' for night workers (6 [8])
Determining the starting point of a seven-day period for the purposes of applying weekly rest entitlements (11 [4])
Determining the duration of rest breaks where the working day is longer than 6 hours (12 [2])
Determining the start date of the leave year for the purposes of applying annual leave entitlements (13 [3])
Modifying or excluding the application of the regulations concerning the length of night work, daily rest, weekly rest period and rest breaks (23)
Determining the reference period (potentially up to 12 months) in respect of the 48-hour maximum average working week (23)

Regulation number in parentheses

bargaining remains, such as heating and ventilating and engineering construction, they cannot enjoy the flexibilities by collective agreement unless they deal directly with trade union representatives at workplace or company levels.

This is why the UK Government has felt obliged to interpret the provisions of the EU Directive in a way which has further potentially far-reaching implications. Employers can agree working-time arrangements, in the form of 'workforce agreements', with workers who do not already have their terms and conditions of employment set by collective agreement. This represents a further step in the piecemeal process of establishing statutory, but issue-specific, employee representation mechanisms in the absence of representation via recognized unions.

It will be interesting to see how management take to the provisions concerning workforce agreements. At first sight, the idea seems unlikely to be met with much enthusiasm. As chapter 1 observed, the 1980s and early 1990s saw significant numbers of employers rejecting not just collective bargaining but any form of collectivism. Trade unions are also likely to adopt a wary response for fear of undermining their own position.

Yet, if the idea does take hold, a consequence of the provision for workforce agreements could be an increase in joint regulation of employment relations more generally. The regulation of working time, in contrast to redundancies and transfers, cannot realistically be treated as a one-off issue. Given the nature of the issue, it is highly likely that ongoing employee representation will be required, involving not only the making of agreements but also their interpretation and administration. The success of the exercise will also depend on the employee representatives having legitimacy, obliging them to seek mandates from the employees they represent. Most fundamentally, working time is inextricably linked to wider concerns of pay, grading structures, technology and work organization, raising the possibility of an extended dialogue.

Adapting work to the worker

A topic which receives hardly any attention in the regulations implementing the Working Time Directive in the UK is the requirement of Article 13 that member states must 'take the measures necessary to ensure that an employer who intends to organize work according to a certain pattern takes account of the general principle of adapting work to the worker'. Even though it appears in the section of the Directive which deals with night and shift work, this could have far-reaching implications as Article 13 seems likely to have general application. A particular aim of 'adapting work to the worker' is to '[alleviate] monotonous work and work at a predetermined work-rate'. Assembly-line work would appear to be a prime, but not exclusive, target.

The present UK Government, like its predecessor, considers that 'the intention of Article 13 is unclear, but appears to replicate and, to an extent, add to Article 6 (2) (d) of the health and safety framework Directive. To the degree that it differs, it does so principally in respect of the emphasis it places on employers having regard to rest breaks' (DTI 1998a: 35). However, commentators such as Bercusson (1996: 311), who emphasize the importance of the principle of the 'humanisation of work' and quality of working life issues more generally in the development of EU law, regard Article 13 as having a more considerable significance. In fact, one of the most fundamental implications of Article 13, bearing in mind that one of the key objectives of the Directive is to promote social dialogue, would appear to be that employers should consult with employees on the organization of working time. As Bercusson (1996: 34) has argued, this is surely the most obvious way of ensuring that work is 'adapted to the worker'.

Arguably, UK employers are already required to consult on working time and quality of working life issues under the 1977 Safety Representatives and Safety Committees Regulations (which cover unionized workplaces) and the 1996 so-called 'top-up' regulations which extended the principle of consultation to non-union workplaces, though in a more limited form (for further details, see James 1996). Thus the consultation arrangements of the 1996 regulations require employers to consult in good time on matters relating to health and safety at work and go on to specify a number of matters falling within this general duty, such as the health and safety consequences of the introduction of new technology, the introduction of any measures which may substantially affect the health and safety of employees, and the arrangements for nominating or appointing competent persons.

Clearly, however, the possibility of a wider interpretation of 'adapting work to the worker' could lead to a considerable expansion in the range of issues that might be subject to consultation. Among other things, the European Commission's Green Paper *Partnership for a new organization of work* which, as chapter 1 has argued, is widely seen as launching a 'new' European social model, calls for a 'new approach' to working time which embraces 'the adjustment of working time arrangements to the needs of firms or the needs of individual workers' (CEC 1997: 15–17). It also emphasizes that 'The role of workers in decision making and the need to review and strengthen the existing arrangements for workers' involvement in their companies will also become essential issues' (CEC 1997: 15). This anticipated the initiative of the Social Affairs Commissioner, Padraig Flynn, in bringing forward proposals requiring undertakings with 20 or more employees to inform and consult an 'independent and stable employee representative body' over a range of issues including 'changes in work organization and other decisions likely significantly to affect the employees' interests'. The significance which the TUC attaches to the provision comes through clearly in its response to the Government's April 1998 public consultation document: 'The requirement that employers must adapt the work to the worker rather than vice versa is one of the most important provisions of the Directive and ought to underpin its implementation.'

Conclusion

The argument of this chapter can be briefly restated. It is that the traditional view of working time as part of a received framework without scope for strategic choice is increasingly untenable. A range of considerations is forcing working time to the top of the management agenda for action. This includes the growing recognition that working time can be the key to making far-ranging changes in work organization and performance; the pressures for family-friendly hours which reflect an increasingly heterogeneous labour force; the need to ensure that working-time arrangements are compatible with health and safety requirements; and the prospect of greater consultation, both individual and collective, over working time. Underpinning these considerations is an entirely new legal framework of rights and responsibilities associated with what can be seen as the 'new' European social model discussed in chapter 1.

As in other European countries, one of the biggest challenges that UK management will have to confront in these circumstances is how best to balance the often conflicting demands of organizations and employees for flexibility in working time. In some sectors, such as multiple food retailing, public services and the new call centres, working patterns are already being introduced which enable the organization not only to meet its requirements, but also to tap fresh sources of employees such as women returners. Indeed, in some cases, it is working time rather than levels of pay which is proving to be the main instrument of competitive labour-market advantage. In most sectors, however, the traditional pattern of a standard working week prevails, and flexible working practices affect less than one in four of the workforce overall. Many changes have been made at workplace level in recent years, notably in shift patterns and part-time work, but employers on the whole remain slow to adopt a comprehensive approach to working time as a tool for competitive advantage. A combination of existing employees exploiting their new legal rights, when added to competitive pressures in the product market and difficulties experienced in recruiting and retaining appropriate people, could be the necessary catalyst for change which is ultimately in both parties' interests.

A particular problem that the UK faces in managing working time is in changing the long-hours culture. Full-time employees in the UK, both male and female, work by far the longest weekly hours in the EU. Superficially, long hours might be seen as a symptom of a highly efficient and flexible economy. The reality is very different. Not only are long hours a major cause of the high levels of sickness and absenteeism which cost employers so dearly, there is also a strong argument for suggesting that they are a major contributory factor in the relatively poor levels of productivity of many UK organizations. Critically, the availability of long hours encourages the perpetuation of inefficient working arrangements, sloppy management and a lack of investment in technology.

Kicking the long hours habit is not going to be easy. Long hours were identified as a major problem, above all in manufacturing, some 30 years ago by the Donovan Royal Commission Report (1968). In manufacturing, the way ahead has been demonstrated by the experience of companies such as Rockware Glass and Zeneca: some form of annual hours arrangements is necessary which incorporates regular overtime pay into the basic salary so that the fear of the loss of overtime earnings is taken away. Yet annual hours still cover scarcely more than 1 in 20 employees, suggesting that the barriers to their implementation have been considerably underestimated.

Moreover, long hours are not just a manufacturing phenomenon. The disease, it seems, has spread and taken hold throughout British business generally. Most occupations, the Labour Force Survey suggests, are affected to some degree. Crucially, managers and administrators have the highest proportions of those working long hours. So far, most of them have appeared totally impervious to calls either to change their own working-time behaviour or their expectations of such behaviour on the part of their employees. In the circumstances, if the various EU Directives dealing with working time, parental leave and equality of treatment for part-time workers do turn out to be the catalyst for change, they will have been a blessing in disguise, demonstrating that regulation does still have an important role to play in modernizing industrial society.

References and further reading

ACAS 1996: *Hours of Work*. London: HMSO.

Arrowsmith, J. and Sisson, K. 1999: Pay and working time: Towards organization based systems? *British Journal of Industrial Relations*, **37**(1), 51–75.

Audit Commission 1997: *Finders, Keepers: The Management of Staff Turnover in NHS Trusts*. Abingdon: Audit Commission.

Bach, S. and Winchester, D. 1994: Opting out of pay devolution? The prospects for local pay bargaining in UK public services. *British Journal of Industrial Relations*, **32**(2), 263–82.

Baruch, Y. and Nicholson, N. 1997: Home, sweet work: Requirements for effective homeworking. *Journal of General Management*, **23**(2), 15–30.

Beatson, M. 1995: *Labour Market Flexibility*. Employment Department Research Series No. 48.

Bercusson, B. 1996: *European Labour Law*. London: Butterworth.

Bienefeld, M. 1972: *Working Hours in British Industry: An Economic History*. London: Weidenfeld and Nicolson.

Blyton, P. 1994: Working Hours. In K. Sisson (ed.), *Personnel Management: a comprehensive guide to theory and practice in Britain*, Oxford: Blackwell, 495–526.

Bosch, G. 1995a: Flexibility and work organization. *Social Europe*, Supplement 1/95. Luxembourg: European Commission.

Bosch, G. 1995b: Synthesis report. In *Flexible Working Time: Collective Bargaining and Government Intervention*, Paris: OECD, 17–41.

Brewster, C. and Connock, S. 1985: *Industrial Relations: Cost-effective Strategies*. London: Hutchinson.

Buchan, J. 1994: *Further flexing? NHS trusts and changing working patterns in NHS nursing*. London: Royal College of Nursing.

Casey, B., Metcalf, H. and Millward, N. 1997: *Employers' Use of Flexible Labour*. London: Policy Studies Institute.

Cave, K. E. 1997: *Zero Hours Contracts. A Report into the Incidence and Implications of Such Contracts*. Huddersfield: University of Huddersfield.

Clark, J. 1996: *Managing Innovation and Change*. London: Sage.

Colling, T. and Ferner, A. 1995: Privatisation and marketisation. In P. K. Edwards, *Industrial Relations*, Oxford: Blackwell.

CEC (Commission for the European Communities) 1997: Green Paper, *Partnership for a new organization of work*. Bulletin of the European Union, Supplement 4/97, Luxembourg: Office for the Official Publications of the European Communities.

Cully, M., O'Reilly, A., Millward, N., Forth, J., Woodland, S., Dix, G. and Bryson, A. 1998: *The 1998 Workplace Employee Relations Survey: First Findings*. London: Department of Trade and Industry.

Deery, S. J. and Mahoney, A. 1994: Temporal flexibility: Management strategies and employee preferences in the retail industry. *Industrial Relations Journal*, September, 332–52.

DfEE (Department for Education and Employment) 1998. *Equal Opportunities: Childcare, Families and Work*. London: DfEE.

DTI 1998a: Measures to implement provisions of EC Directives on the organization of working time ('The Working Time Directive') and the Protection of Young People at Work ('The Young Workers Directive'). *Public consultation document*, London: DTI.

DTI 1998b: *Fairness at Work*. White Paper presented to Parliament, Cm 3986.

Dex, S. and McCulloch, A. 1997: *Flexible Employment: The Future of Britain's Jobs*. Basingstoke: Macmillan.

Dickens, L. 1995: UK Part-time Employees and the Law – Recent and Potential Developments. *Gender, Work and Organization* (October), pp. 207–15.

Dickens, L. 1997: Exploring the atypical: Zero hours contracts. Review article, *Industrial Law Journal*, **26**, 262–64.

Di Martino, V. 1995: Megatrends in working time. *Journal of European Social Policy*, **5**(3), 235–49.

(Donovan) Royal Commission on Trade Unions and Employers' Associations 1968: Report, London: HMSO.

EOC(NI) (Equal Opportunities Commission for Northern Ireland), 1996: *Report on Formal Investigation Into Competitive Tendering in Health and Education Services in Northern Ireland*. Belfast: EOC(NI).

European Works Council Bulletin 1998: Commission drafts framework Directive on consultation. Issue 17, September/October, 4–7.

Flanders, A. 1964: *The Fawley Productivity Agreements: A Case Study of Management and Collective Bargaining*. London: Faber and Faber.

Forth, J., Lissenburgh, S., Callender, C. and Millward, N. 1997: Family-friendly working arrangements in Britain. *Labour Market Trends*, **105**(10) 387–89.

Ginn, J., Arber, S., Brannen, J., Dale, A., Dex, S. Elias, P., Moss, P., Pahl, J., Roberts, C. and Rubery, J. 1996: Feminist Fallacies: A reply to Hakim on women's employment. *British Journal of Sociology*, **47**(1), 167–73.

Green, F. 1997. Union recognition and paid holiday entitlement. *British Journal of Industrial Relations*, **35**(2), 243–55.

Hakim, C. 1997: A sociological perspective on part-time work. In H.-P. Blossfeld and C. Hakim (eds), *Between Equalization and Marginalization: Women Working Part-Time in Europe and the United States of America*, Oxford: Oxford University Press, 22–70.

Hall, M. and Sisson, K. 1997: *Time for Change: Coming to Terms With the EU Working Time Directive*. London: Eclipse Group Ltd and Industrial Relations Research Unit.

Hall, M., Lister, R. and Sisson, K. 1998: *The New Law on Working Time: Coming to Terms With the 1998 Working Time Regulations*. London: Eclipse Ltd. and Industrial Relations Research Unit.

Harvey, R. 1998: Manager's Maxim Working Hours Survey. *Observer*, 1 November, (Work: 1).

Hunt, E. H. 1981: *British Labour History, 1815–1914*. London: Weidenfeld and Nicolson.

Huws, U., Podro, S., Gunnarsson, E., Weijers, T., Arvanitaki, K. and Trova, V. 1996: Teleworking and gender. *IES Report No. 317*, Brighton: Institute for Employment Studies.

Incomes Data Services (IDS) 1996: Annual hours. *IDS Study 604*, London: IDS.

Incomes Data Services (IDS) 1997: Public sector labour market survey 1997. *IDS Report 751*, December, London: IDS.

Incomes Data Services (IDS) 1998: Flexitime schemes. *IDS Study 642*, London: IDS.

Industrial Relations Services (IRS) 1991: Annualised Hours – The concept of the flexible year. 488, *Employment Trends*, May.

IRS 1993: Annual hours working and harmonisation at Rockware Glass. 543, *Employment Trends*, August.

IRS 1994. Restructuring for growth at Zeneca Agrochemicals, Yalding. 558, *Employment Trends*, April.

IRS 1995a: A hard day's night. 576, *Employment Trends*, January.

IRS 1995b: Customer service drive brings new working patterns to BT. 579, *Employment Trends*, March.

IRS 1996: Flexible workers on call at Tesco. 620, *Employment Trends*, November.

IRS 1997: From here to security? *Employment Trends*, 631, May, 6–12.

IRS 1998a: Flexing the clock part 1: the use of annual hours. 654, *Employment Trends*, April.

IRS 1998b: Flexing the clock part 2: the experiences of annual hours. 655, *Employment Trends*, May.

Institute of Management 1995: *Survival of the Fittest: a Survey of Managers' Experience of, and Attitudes to, Work in the Post-Recession Economy*. London: Institute of Management.

Institute of Management 1996: *Are Managers Under Stress?* London: Institute of Management.

Institute of Management 1998: *The Quality of Working Life: The 1998 Survey of Managers' Changing Expectations*. London: Institute of Management.

James, P. 1996: Mixed responses to new safety consultation rights. *Health and Safety Bulletin*, 245, May, 13–14.

Labour Market Trends 1997: Flexible working arrangements. *Labour Market Trends*, **105**(12), December, LFS63.

Labour Research Department 1995a: Working Hours Survey. *Bargaining Report* 153, September, 19–21.

Labour Research Department 1995b: Working Hours Survey. *Bargaining Report* 154, October.

Labour Research Department 1996: *Flexible Working Time: a Guide for Trade Unionists*.

McKinlay, A. and McNulty, D. 1992: At the cutting edge of new realism: The engineers' 35 hour week campaign. *Industrial Relations Journal*, **23**(3), 205–13.

Millward, N., Stevens, M., Smart, D. and Hawes, W. R. 1992: *Workplace Industrial Relations in Transition: The ED/ ESRC/ PSI/ ACAS Surveys*. Aldershot: Dartmouth.

NACAB (National Association of Citizens Advice Bureaux). 1997: *Flexibility Abused*. London: NACAB.

National Board for Prices and Incomes 1970: *Hours of work, overtime and shift working*, Report No. 161. London: HMSO.

NEDO (National Economic Development Office) 1989: *Defusing the Demographic Timebomb*. London: NEDO.

Neathey, F. and Hurstfield, J. 1996: *Flexibility in Practice: Women's Employment and Pay in Retail and Finance*. Manchester: Equal Opportunities Commission/IRS.

Purcell, K. and Purcell, J. 1998: In-sourcing, outsourcing and the growth of contingent labour as evidence of flexible employment strategies. *European Journal of Work and Organizational Psychology*, **7**(1), 39–59.

Roche, W. K., Fynes, B. and Morrissey, T. 1996: Working time and employment: A review of the international evidence. *International Labour Review*, **135**(2), 129–57.

Rojot, J. 1989: Employers' response to technological change. In A. Gladstone, R. Lansbury, J. Stieber, T. Trew and M. Weiss (eds), *Current Issues in Labour Relations: An International Perspective*, New York: de Gruyter, 29–41.

Rojot, J. 1998: Legal and contractual limitations to working time in the European Union. Review article, *Bulletin of Comparative Labour Relations*, **32**, 193–6.

Rubery, J. and Horrell, S. 1993: The 'new competition' and working time. *Human Resource Management Journal*, **3**(2), 1–13.

Sly, F., Price, A. and Risdon, A. 1997: Women in the labour market: Results from the spring 1996 Labour Force Survey. *Labour Market Trends*, **105**(3), March, 99–120.

Taylor, R. 1994: Management: matter of years, not weeks. *Financial Times*, 23 September.

Thatcher, M. 1998: Clock wise. *People Management*, 3 September.

Thompson, E. P. 1974: Time, work-discipline and industrial capitalism. In M. W. Flinn and T. C. Smout (eds), *Essays in Social History*, London: Oxford University Press (first published 1967.)

TUC (Trades Union Congress) 1995a: *Hard Labour: Britain's Longer Working Week*. London: TUC.

TUC 1995b: *Pushed to the Limit: The Case for the European Working Time Directive*. London: TUC.

TUC 1998: *DTI Public Consultation – TUC Response, Implementation of the Working Time Directive and Young Workers' Directive*. London: TUC.

Walsh, J. 1997: Employment systems in transition? *Work, Employment and Society*, **11**(1), 1–25.

Waterhouse, J., Folkard, S. and Minors, D. 1992: *Shiftwork, Health and Safety: An Overview of the Scientific Literature 1978–1990*. HSE Contract Research Report, 31.

Watson, G. 1994: The flexible workforce and patterns of working hours in the UK. *Employment Gazette*, July.

Whybrew, E. G. 1968: Overtime working in Britain. Research Paper No. 9, Royal Commission, London: HMSO.

Wilkinson, F. and White, M. 1994: Product-market pressures and employers' responses. In J. Rubery and F. Wilkinson (eds), *Employer Strategy and the Labour Market*, Oxford: Oxford University Press, 110–37.

Wilkinson, H. 1997: *Time Out: The Costs and Benefits of Paid Parental Leave*. London: Demos.

Zeytinoglu, I. U. 1992: Reasons for hiring part-time workers. *Industrial Relations*, **31**(3), 489–99.

Part 5

Work Relations

13

Discipline: Towards Trust and Self-discipline?

Paul K. Edwards

There is not that thing in the world of more grave and urgent importance throughout the whole life of man, than is discipline.... Discipline is not only the removal of disorder, but if any visible shape can be given to divine things, the very visible shape and image of virtue.

(John Milton, quoted by Corrigan and Sayer, 1991: 14).[1]

Since the publication of the first edition of this book in 1989, there have been two contrasting trends in the study of discipline. First, the subject, which used to hold an established if scarcely central place in personnel texts, has apparently lost its interest. Texts such as Beaumont's (1993) say nothing about it, while Molander and Winterton (1994) give it two pages. Even Storey's 'critical text' (1995), which sets out to place human resource management in the context of power relationships, excludes discipline from what it calls 'the key practice areas' of HRM. Second, the concept of the organization based on discipline and surveillance, and even the idea of the disciplinary society, has come to prominence through interest in the work of Michel Foucault (see Townley 1994). The core ideas here are that the exercise of discipline is not a discrete activity to be equated with an event like a disciplinary hearing but is achieved continuously through rules and expectations in the very fabric of an organization; that power is similarly not a set capacity but is expressed in continuing relationships; and that new monitoring systems (direct ones such as electronic surveillance in factories and measurements of key strokes per hour in the office, and indirect ones like budgetary controls of managers and other performance-related measures such as league tables of schools) impose increasingly tight disciplinary standards on employees.

The previous versions of this chapter fell between the conventional and the Foucaultian views (Edwards 1989; 1994). They argued that conventional accounts remained at the level of formal discipline and failed to connect it with day-to-day rules that govern behaviour. To that extent they shared part of the Focaultian view (though believing that the point can be well established without resort to Foucault himself). That view sees discipline in many of the practices analysed in other chapters of this book, notably performance management. The present chapter confines itself to a more delimited definition of discipline which is set out below. It argues that discipline in this specific, mundane sense remains more salient than some of the HRM texts seem to believe.

The traditional personnel management texts recognize that discipline is about more than rules and procedures. As one puts it, 'the best discipline is self-discipline, the normal human tendency to do one's share and to live up to the rules of the game' (Strauss and Sayles 1980: 218). Discipline could here embrace any of the many means through which employees are induced to do their share, including reward systems and even training and development. In that sense, the definition is too broad, a point which also applies to the Foucaultian view: if discipline is everywhere, how do we delimit it for analysis? Yet the definition by Strauss and Sayles (1980) is also too narrow in that it assumes that 'doing one's share' is uncontested. Who decides what a reasonable share is, what the rules are, and in what ways breaches of the rules are to be penalized? In any organization there will be differences on these points. A conventional view of discipline describes rules and procedures and assumes that their operation is unproblematic. Yet how people expect to behave depends as much on day-to-day understandings as on formal rules. Workplaces may have identical rule-books, but in one it may be accepted practice to leave early near holidays, in another on Fridays, in a third when a relatively lenient supervisor is in charge, and so on. What the rule is cannot be discovered from the rule-book. Day-to-day experience will create standards which may differ sharply from official rules. It is not even the case that formal rules inscribe managerial expectations while informal standards represent workers' understandings. In some workplaces supervisors have been found to encourage breaches of rules on leaving times (Ditton 1979a). The making of rules is a process in which different levels of management may have different priorities.

The present approach to these issues of the nature of discipline is to identify three faces of discipline. First, discipline in the sense of punishment and correction requires attention because it remains more prevalent than treatments of HRM suggest, partly because there are many organizations which still rely on such traditional practices and partly because even HRM-oriented organizations have not abandoned them. Moreover, conventional treatments say rather little about the extent and nature of punitive sanctions. Second, there is the core field of such texts, the formulation and application of procedures. Some comments are provided, but the reader is referred to a text such as Torrington and Hall (1995: 532–44) for details of the design and operation of procedures. Third, there is the creation in practice of the expectations and understandings that govern behaviour. As Torrington and Hall (1995: 529–30) say, this can involve two aspects:

1 *team discipline*, involving the mutual dependency of all and a 'commitment by each member to the total organization'. As Wickens (1987: 100, italics added) then Personnel Director of Nissan, put it, 'if the Supervisor and his staff have the right relationship and everyone is properly motivated, good time-keeping does not depend on a mechanistic form of time recording but on the *self-generated discipline* within the group'.

2 and *self-discipline*, where a 'solo performer is absolutely dependent on training, expertise and self-control'.

This brings us back to the boundaries of the subject and the Foucaultian view that both team and self-discipline may entail power and manipulation, some of which may be conscious while other parts are deeply entrenched in the organization and are not the deliberate creation of anyone. The present view is that it makes sense to delimit discipline in relation to the *identifiable standards for the behaviour and performance of employees that are produced in organizations (including the formal and informal negotiation of these standards) and the sanctions that may be deployed for their breach.* We need some such delimitation if discipline is not to be equated with any form of pressure, for example from product markets. In the case of school league tables for example, such pressure would be relevant where they were translated into specific expectations on staff that could be enforced by sanctions. They would not be relevant where they were only part of a more general tightening of expectations.

One theoretical point guides the discussion. The recent literature on self-discipline implies that managing through commitment rather than control is a novel idea. In fact, as earlier comments on a natural sense of duty suggest, it has always been part of discipline. An interesting discussion of the parallels between discipline in the military and employment contexts states that 'it is a pattern of behaviour which has been instilled into [the soldier or employee] so that he [or she] no longer thinks of acting otherwise' (Phelps Brown 1949: 48). The theoretical basis of this point has also been long understood. Friedman (1977) identified two broad approaches which he termed direct control (managing through tight discipline) and responsible autonomy (allowing workers discretion). Later work (Edwards 1986; Hyman 1987) established that these approaches, which Friedman tended to present as opposites, were often, indeed normally, combined. Approaches to the management of labour entail a mix of elements rather than the development of self-contained strategies, and they are necessarily uncertain and incomplete because they try to control employees at the same time as releasing their creative potential. Self-discipline is not new, it is not necessarily in opposition to other forms of discipline and, crucially, it is still a form of control because it is part of a relationship in which managers aim to establish authority and regulate the direction of workers' efforts. Control does not necessarily mean a situation ('zero sum' in the jargon) in which workers lose in direct proportion to what managers gain. It means the way in which employees are persuaded to work under managers' authority. Self-discipline is not complete freedom but nor is it merely a trick to persuade workers to work harder. It is one aspect of the ways in which control has to be negotiated.

The chapter begins by examining the development of rules and procedures, thus putting current practice in context and arguing that discipline in the sense of the application of sanctions remains important. It then offers examples of how rules are created in practice, thus displaying the flexibility and negotiability of discipline. These examples are deliberately drawn from studies conducted before the HRM era, for two reasons: they offer a particularly rich picture of how rules are interpreted in practice; and they thus offer a benchmark to assess the effects of HRM in this field. Finally current trends in discipline are reviewed in the light of the question of whether HRM is indeed leading to the withering of traditional ideas of discipline and whether a more insidious and inexplicit set of disciplinary norms is replacing traditional formal discipline.

Disciplinary Rules and Procedures

The origins of discipline

Employers have always needed to ensure the adequate performance of work tasks by their employees. Formal rules became necessary when organizations became large and bureaucratic, with the result that the employer could not oversee operations personally. Pollard (1965: 181–9) has described the disciplinary problems of the early industrial employers: the new factories demanded regular attendance and the carrying out of tasks in the prescribed fashion.

Writers who adopt what Henry (1983: 71) calls a consensus approach have seen such developments as characteristic of an authoritarian approach to discipline. Ashdown and Baker (1973: 5–7), for example, argue that managers saw their own authority as absolute, and imposed discipline in a harsh and arbitrary manner. Since the Second World War, the authors continue, managements have become aware that punitive discipline has adverse effects on morale and efficiency; they have also faced pressure from trade unions, legal restrictions on their powers, and difficulties of recruitment in tight labour markets. As a result, the aim of disciplinary action has become correction instead of coercion, and the administration of policy has been based less on the absolute authority of the employer and more on a democratic approach. Such an interpretation is not limited to 'consensus' theorists. An avowedly radical account of changes in work organization in America sees nineteenth-century work discipline as being based on 'arbitrary command' in which motivation was based on the dictum, 'perform your task correctly or be docked in pay, fired, or, on occasion, beaten'. Under bureaucratic systems of control that have developed since 1945, by contrast, punishment flows 'from the established organizational rules and procedures' and is no longer coercive in purpose or arbitrary in application (Edwards, 1979: 33, 142).

Such interpretations need to be treated with caution. First, they sit uneasily with evidence that in large parts of industry, notably cotton and steel and some areas of coal mining, employers subcontracted sets of operations to skilled workers who were responsible for recruitment, payment, and discipline (Littler 1982). Employers here exercised their authority at one remove. Second, it is hard to conceive all workers being subjected to an identical form of discipline: skilled craftsmen were proud of their skills and independence, and would not have reacted meekly to harsh discipline. Third, standards of regular attendance were enforced slowly and unevenly. Industrialization was a lengthy process in which earlier forms of discipline and control could survive for considerable periods. In Birmingham, for example, it was not until the 1860s that employers were successful in eroding the tradition of taking Monday as a holiday (Reid 1976). Finally, many early employers adopted a paternalistic, and not an overtly authoritarian, approach. Though paternalism involved power relationships as well as a fatherly concern for employees' welfare, it was a means of establishing discipline which relied on many mechanisms other than force (Newby 1977).

Neither should the shift to a corrective approach be exaggerated. One of the assumptions underlying the shift is that, as firms have grown increasingly bureaucratic, old and informal modes of discipline have become unworkable. But bureaucracy is not a product of the period since 1945. Rules emerged in many organizations before then. The railways (see Edwards and Whitston 1994) and the Post Office (Clinton 1984: 45–59) are good examples of organizations with formal and detailed rules specifying workers' duties long before then.

A second assumption is that rates of disciplinary sanction will fall as firms cease to wield the big stick in an arbitrary fashion. Data on the actual use of sanctions, as compared with the fearsome-sounding penalties in rule-books, are rare. But studies of the American textile industry (Gersuny 1976) and the British railways (Edwards and Whitston 1994) point to remarkably similar rates of discipline during the nineteenth and twentieth centuries. The latter study also found that the use of discipline, in both periods, correlated with times of financial exigency. The actual use of penalties thus reflected pressures on managers, and not any automatic progression towards a corrective approach.

All this evidence suggests the danger of making sharp distinctions between punitive and corrective approaches. Any organization is likely to use a mixture of both: even the most punitive management may well remind employees of their obligations, for co-operation cannot be secured by force alone. This suggests an important lesson when current shifts towards self-discipline are considered: the evidence from the past suggests that continuity can be as important as change. It is true, however, that there have been significant changes in procedures for handling discipline.

Formalization of procedures; informality of practice?

As against the view that there was a gradual drift towards a corrective approach, the shift to formal procedures was sudden. Surveys in the 1960s suggested that as many as 90 per cent of establishments had no formal disciplinary procedures (Anderman 1972: 22–4). Yet by 1978, the IPM (1979: 7), in a survey of 273 organizations, found a major change: 98 per cent had written disciplinary procedures for blue-collar workers. Since these tended to be large firms, this figure may exaggerate the growth of procedures. But the Workplace Industrial Relations Survey Series (WIRS) confirms the general picture. Between 1980 and 1990 the proportion of establishments employing at least 25 employees that had procedures for discipline and dismissal rose from 81 per cent to 90 per cent (Millward et al. 1992). The 1998 WERS confirmed this picture and also underlined the extent of procedural justice: virtually all workplaces with procedures allow employees to be accompanied at hearings and permit appeals against managerial decisions (Cully et al. 1998: 14). Procedures have also been widely adopted by non-union firms: 83 per cent of those with no recognized union have a procedure (Millward et al. 1992: 187, 191). Small firms falling below the survey threshold remain, however, relatively informal: only one-third of those with fewer than 20 employees studied by Evans et al. (1985: 30) had a written disciplinary procedure.

A small survey of 70 large organizations in 1991 confirmed the growth of formalization (IRS 1991). Not only did they all have a procedure, but also the systems operated in similar ways reflecting the good practice consolidated in ACAS handbooks. All but one of the procedures allowed for up to one formal oral warning and two written warnings before dismissal or other penalties were applied. And all had an appeals mechanism. A 1995 survey (IRS 1995) confirms this trend.

Explanations of this growth focus above all on the intervention of the law (IPM 1979: 7). The Industrial Relations Act 1971 introduced provisions relating to unfair dismissal, and this legislation has been widely seen as stimulating companies to reform their procedures. Employers interviewed in 1977 felt that the effect of employment protection laws had been to tighten up on recruitment and dismissal arrangements; although they claimed that management's power in discipline had been eroded, they also stressed an increase in the use of proper procedures and a decline in arbitrariness (Daniel and Stilgoe 1978: 37).

The law was plainly not the only influence. As Henry (1983: 102) has argued, legal changes were part of a broader policy of intervention by the state which reflected a belief that formalized and standardized procedures would reduce the number of shopfloor grievances and strikes, thereby contributing to a more general process of industrial relations reform. The influence may not have been all one way. Authors of official and quasi-official reports looked to the practice of progressive firms in drawing up their recommendations. A manager interviewed by Henry (1983: 104) argued that official bodies consulted widely in industry and that they brought together existing practices, saying 'this appears to be what industry does and finds acceptable and therefore this is what we will recommend'. It is unlikely that firms would have responded so rapidly had not legal provisions and advice on what constituted good practice been broadly congruent with ways in which they were already moving.

The growth of formal procedures, particularly in large firms, need not imply formality in practice. A 1992 survey of applications to industrial tribunals (ITs, from 1998, renamed employment tribunals) found that 36 per cent of employers involved in these cases had no procedures while in a further 26 per cent a procedure existed but the case had not in fact gone through it (Tremlett and Banerji 1994: 12). One-quarter of employers involved had changed their organizations as a result of the case, usually by implementing more formal procedures (an illustration of how legal structures can change the nature of 'private justice'). A later study of IT cases found considerable informality and concluded that 'despite the existence of the ACAS Code of Practice and over twenty years of unfair dismissal law, the message is still not getting through to many employers about the necessity for the basic requirements of fairness' such as proper hearings, investigation of the facts and the opportunity for employees to state their case prior to a decision (Earnshaw et al. 1998: 15). Though formalism and due process have spread widely, when it comes to the actual practice of disciplinary action many employers, it seems, do not use their procedures.

Legal changes in the late 1990s may give a further encouragement to formalization. The *Fairness at Work* White Paper of May 1998 proposed three relevant changes: the reduction from two years to one of the qualifying period before an employee has the right to take a case to an employment tribunal; the end of existing ceilings on tribunal awards for unfair dismissal; and the right of any employee to be accompanied at a disciplinary hearing by a trade union official. In addition, the Employment Rights (Dispute Resolution) Act 1998 gives tribunals the right to reduce an award if an employee had not used a relevant procedure and to make a supplementary award if an employer denied the employee use of the procedure. As we will see, informality continues to govern much day-to-day disciplinary activity, but the rules governing significant cases leading to possible dismissal and a tribunal claim are likely to be further formalized by these new legal moves.

The content and operation of procedures

For discipline to be applied effectively, the rules must be clear. Accordingly, most procedures specify the type of conduct which is likely to trigger disciplinary action. It is not, however, possible to be comprehensive: there will always be contingencies that cannot be predicted. Procedures typically do no more than indicate the type of action which is liable to be punished. Such actions fall into two types: very serious misconduct such as theft and violence, which may lead to instant dismissal; and less serious offences such as excessive absenteeism or poor time keeping which will be dealt with intially through warnings and, if performance does not improve, through increasingly severe sanctions.

The main types of action that lead to the operation of discipline seem to be common among small and large firms. Plumridge (1966: 139) found in a survey of 50 organizations that absenteeism was the most common reason, followed by 'incompetence and unsuitability'. Respondents to the IPM (1979: 28–31) survey listed time-keeping, unauthorized absence and poor work standards as the main issues, a result confirmed by later studies (e.g. IRS 1995). The mainly small firms studied by Evans et al. (1985: 27) gave time keeping and absence together as the most common reason, followed by 'incompetence or incapacity in work performance'. The ranking differs among cases going to employment tribunals, where in 1992 39 per cent of cases involved rule breaking or dishonesty, as against 16 per cent of attendance or ill-health (Tremlett and Banerji 1994: 14). It seems that discipline on attendance is relatively likely to be accepted, while penalties for misconduct are more likely to be challenged by the employee.

The operation of a procedure involves many levels of management. Most formal procedures start with action by the immediate supervisor, with higher levels being involved as more severe sanctions are applied. In only 2 per cent of companies surveyed by the IPM (1979: 41) did final authority to dismiss rest with the supervisor, compared with 32 per cent where it rested with the personnel manager and 39 per cent with the factory manager. Underlying these figures is the well-known tendency of the 1970s for authority in the area of discipline to be removed from the supervisor and placed in the hands of the personnel specialist.

Current trends towards the decentralization of responsibility to line managers may suggest a shift in the opposite direction. A study of the handling of absenteeism in 25 organizations certainly found that personnel specialists were increasingly seeing their role as to provide expert advice and support to line managers (see Edwards and Whitston 1993). Yet most of the work of handling discipline remains with the personnel function (IRS 1995).

Decentralization highlights the role of first-line supervisors. They were at one time portrayed as 'men in the middle', caught between workers and management proper, and hence willing to bend or ignore rules. A more realistic view is that supervisors generally espouse broad managerial goals and that they do not differ fundamentally from other managers in seeing the need for discipline (see, especially, Armstrong 1983). They may be less prone to subvert rulings from above than to complain that they are not given sufficient support when they act to assert managerial rights (Edwards and Scullion 1982). During the 1970s it was probably quite common for supervisors to feel that the authority to discipline was being taken away from them. At the same time, of course, they were having to negotiate the day-to-day application of the rules and in doing so may have promoted custom and practice that interpreted the silences of the formal rules or even supplanted them.

During the 1980s a reduction in trade union bargaining power on the shopfloor, together with managerial decentralization, meant that supervisors were probably less likely to perceive a loss of authority over discipline. Case studies in four organizations suggested that there was little problem with a loss of influence (Edwards and Whitston 1993).

Another major influence on the operation of procedures is that of trade unions. Unions' formal involvement appears to be considerable. The WIRS results point to two roles: the representation of individual members (reported by managers in 71 per cent of establishments with procedures); and discussion of the form of procedures, with procedures being agreed in 90 per cent of plants with recognized unions (Millward et al. 1992: 194). Agreement does not necessarily mean substantive negotiation. The IPM (1979: 17) survey, for example, reported that only 38 per cent of respondents negotiated with unions representing blue-collar workers, while only 25 per cent agreed the rules with the unions. Procedures are likely to be agreed with unions, but in most cases this is likely to involve notification and acceptance of a procedure whose shape is set by management, and not negotiation from scratch.

One view of union shop stewards' behaviour is that attempts will always be made to challenge the application of discipline. This appears to be incorrect. First, it implies too narrow a role for the steward. A survey of 1,400 stewards carried out in 1966 reported, 'when asked whether they considered their management reasonably fair in dealing with workers who break rules and disobey orders, 93 per cent of stewards said yes (McCarthy and Parker 1968: 48). As a detailed study of ten workplaces showed, stewards communicate managerial concern about breaches of rules to their members, give warnings about plans to tighten up, talk to members privately and warn them about their behaviour, and provide 'information as to the extent of breaches of rules' (McCarthy 1966: 12).

Second, stewards will not take up cases that they consider to be unreasonable: they may try to persuade members that they are in the wrong, or they may go through the motions of defending them while making it clear to management that they do not agree with the members' claim (see, for example, Batstone et al. 1977: 108–9). Third, as noted above, they are likely to accept the general need for discipline, challenging management only if they feel that the rules have been applied unfairly.

Finally, the role of outside agencies in procedures needs comment. The WIRS data found that reference to bodies outside the individual establishment occurred in about two-thirds of cases. Over the 1980s, two different trends were evident: a growth in reference to management above establishment level (suggesting, note the WIRS authors, concern about public scrutiny of an approach to dismissals and hence a need to check with higher management); and a decline in the use of third parties, with ACAS involvement falling from 29 per cent to 15 per cent of establishments with any reference outside (Millward et al. 1992: 194–6). In Britain, in contrast to the USA, independent arbitration remains rare as the final stage of a procedure. Procedures are more formal but the practice of discipline still leaves a great deal of discretion to management in deciding what is acceptable conduct and how it is to be enforced.

The extent and pattern of discipline

The use of discipline short of dismissal is hard to measure: how serious does a conversation between a manager and a worker have to be before it constitutes discipline? Surveys of employers find that the use of sanctions, in addition to verbal or written warnings, is common: 80 per cent of firms in one survey include such penalties as transfers and downgrading (IRS 1995). Just over 3 per cent of workers were estimated in the 1990 WIRS to be receiving some disciplinary sanction each year (Millward et al. 1992: 200). (Initial results of the 1998 WERS do not include updated figures.) More detailed work using organizational records rather than managerial reports reveals considerable variation. A study of railway workers over the period 1976–87 gave a high figure of ten cases of formal discipline per 100 worker years, but over half the workers studied had experienced no disciplinary cases over this period (Edwards and Whitston 1994: 331). Seifert (1992: 321) reports a study of 13 health authorities in the year 1980/1. There were 0.7 'written warnings or worse' per 100 staff, with a range across the authorities from 0.1 to 2. There are thus considerable variations between individuals and organizations. On the latter, it is to be expected that sectors such as health will use punishment less often than the railways, where work was traditionally organized on quasi-military lines. Yet it remains true that the use of disciplinary sanctions is widespread.

The frequency of dismissal has received more attention. Writing at the end of the 1970s, Daniel and Stilgoe (1978: 59) detected a decline in the use of dismissal over the decade. The WIRS data for the 1980s point to decline followed by an increase: the rate of dismissal fell from 14 per 1,000 workers in 1980 to 9 in 1984, but reached 15 in 1990 (Millward et al. 1992: 201). Longer-term data are not generally available but, as noted above, studies of railways and textiles showed that discipline rates in the 1980s were not markedly different from those in the mid nineteenth century. The assumption that more formalized procedures have led to a secular decline in dismissal rates has little hard evidence to sustain it.

Two studies have examined determinants of the rate of discipline and dismissal. Examining the 1990 WIRS, Edwards (1995) tested the view that the use of HRM will replace reliance on disciplinary sanctions. He could find no support for this view, and concluded that there was no evidence that HRM was associated with a shift away from traditional ways of controlling workers. Instead, he found, as had Deaton (1984) in an earlier study, that rates of disciplinary action were lowest in large plants, and where wages were high and there was a high level of union density. There is thus strong evidence that unions continue to perform their role of providing ways for employees to be managed without the threat of sanctions. And, not surprisingly, large and well-paying firms have alternatives to sanctions.

Some firms are thus far more dismissal prone than others; this reflects not inherent differences between workers but the policies of the firms themselves. In the more progressive companies dismissal is a relatively rare sanction, employed when other means have failed. In others, dismissal or the threat of it remains an important form of control.

Very few studies have examined workers' experience of discipline. A rare example is the interview study with 44 workers by Rollinson et al. (1997: 298). It found that 'for a large proportion of those formally disciplined, the process was not seen as a persuasive one designed to get them to observe rules, but as an event which gave the manager an opportunity to take retribution, or administer a deterrent to limit future transgressions'.

When considering the issue of labour control more generally, the distinction between dismissal for disciplinary reasons and 'normal' labour turnover breaks down. A study of two clothing factories found that over 40 per cent of leavers had been employed for less than six months (Edwards and Scullion 1982). This was associated with very close managerial control of the work process, with disciplinary warnings for poor work performance being commonplace and with very strict control maintained of starting and finishing times. Not only was dismissal an ever-present possibility, but 'voluntary' quitting was also influenced by the control regime: a worker given a couple of warnings, or who found the work pace intolerable, might find leaving the only option. Such quitting helped to reinforce managerial authority because those who might question it did not stay long.

Conclusions

Many accounts speak of a move from punitive to corrective discipline. It is true that procedures have been formalized and it is likely that most organizations operate with basic ideas of due process. However, the rationalization of discipline should not be exaggerated. Simple 'hire and fire' was far from universal in the nineteenth century, rates of disciplinary action have not fallen as fast as might be expected, firms continue to ignore their own disciplinary procedures and, as the study by Rollinson et al. (1997) confirms, workers subject to discipline do not see the process as simply one of correction. Punitive and corrective aspects are intertwined, and traditional modes of discipline remain common.

Discipline in Action

Types of rules

Prescriptive treatments of discipline start from the assumption that all organizational rules have the same status. There are in fact different sorts of rules, which have different origins and are treated differently by people in organizations, and which need not stem from shared interests or perspectives.

In his classic study of a gypsum mine and factory Gouldner (1954) identified three types of bureaucratic rule.

1 'Mock' bureaucracy covers rules that are ignored by all; Gouldner's example is a no-smoking rule that management generally made no attempt to enforce.
2 'Representative' bureaucracy was exemplified by safety rules, to which management devoted considerable attention and against which workers expended few energies, the result being that safety matters were highly bureaucratized and rules were enforced.
3 'Punishment-centred' bureaucracy involves rules that are enforced by one party against another, with sanctions being imposed for disobedience, an example being the rule against absenteeism, which managers wished to enforce rigidly and which workers resented.

Breaches of different rules will be treated very differently in practice. Mock rules are ignored. Representative rules are important to all, so that a worker disobeying a safety rule is likely to be seen, by workmates as well as management, as careless and as requiring some sanction. Punishment-centred rules are imposed, and the group on whom they are imposed may well feel that they are unfair, and may react by trying to evade them, supporting those who are punished and questioning their relevance.

Rules are not, then, all of a piece. Gouldner also stressed (1954: 205) that his types are not fixed: in another organization a safety rule might have a punishment-centred and not a representative character. He also makes an important but implicit qualification about representative bureaucracy. Safety rules can be used to control workers. For example, management introduced a rule preventing movement between parts of the factory that was justified on safety grounds and therefore hard for workers to resist, but its real purpose was to strengthen managerial control over what workers were doing. In addition, management neglected safety interests where these conflicted with the demands of production (a frequent finding: see Nichols 1975). Even 'representative' rules may not serve everyone's interests, and they can be used as a cloak for other things.

Rules, together with the sanctions that go with their breach, are part of wider relations of conflict and control within workplaces. Evidence for the period up to the early 1980s (reviewed by Edwards 1988) showed that informal rules could supplant formal ones. Managers may grant concessions to workers in order to meet production demands, but concessions can rapidly grow into precedents and then into relatively well-established custom and practice rules. These rules will reflect the reality of bargaining power on the shopfloor, and attempts to codify and formalize procedures are unlikely to have much effect on behaviour. It was also assumed that management had the will and the freedom of action to institute reform. But in cases where union organization is weak there may be little felt need among managements to reform, while, where unions are strong, managers may be unable to institute reform that effectively alters behaviour. In addition, the concentration on management leads to the neglect of discipline that can be imposed by unions and work groups. In situations where workers are organized collectively, discipline ceases to be an individual matter but involves bargaining. And the distinction between the two may lie not in the intrinsic nature of an issue but in the approach taken by the parties in respect of any issue. That is, an apparently individual act such as theft may, in fact, stem from collective norms and understandings.

In their study of the docks Mellish and Collis-Squires (1976) found that formal rules on time keeping were ignored, with gangs of workers deciding when to start work and how many workers would be working at any one time. In addition, systematic overtime was worked on a 'task and finish' basis, so that, although workers were supposed to be present for all the overtime period, in practice they went home when the job was finished. Such practices would involve breaches of formal rules such as leaving work without permission and associated clocking offences. The actual rules governing attendance and work conduct were very different from those inscribed in formal rule-books and procedures.

Two points must be entered about this approach. First, Mellish and Collis-Squires (1976) see workers and shop stewards as the main authors of rule bending. Other studies (e.g. Nichols and Beynon 1977: 33) found that managers faced unremitting pressures of scheduling production so as to try to meet cost and delivery targets. In trying to balance different objectives, managers are unlikely to pay close attention to formal rules about workers' behaviour. It is easy to see how they can permit practices such as task and finish to emerge: managers need workers' co-operation to attain production requirements, and may be willing to buy this co-operation with concessions.

Second, studies like that by Mellish and Collis-Squires (1976) imply that all work groups tend to develop collective norms that undermine managerial rules and, while admitting that the docks are in many ways exceptional, they treat their research material as illustrative of a more general phenomenon. Even at the time, however, it was evident that not all, or even most, workers enjoyed the ability to generate custom and practice. We need to consider different types of workplace order.

Varieties of shopfloor relations

This discussion uses studies from the 'pre-HRM' era. It does so to establish the shape of discipline at that time, to act as a benchmark to assess the effects of HRM. But, as argued above, continuity has been a marked feature of the conduct of discipline, and several aspects of the discussion retain their relevance. In particular, the construction of discipline depends on a day-to-day negotiation of order; and how the form of this order varies significantly even though the formal rules may be the same. The cases may be roughly ordered according to the degree to which managerial rules were openly challenged by workers (for details see Edwards 1988).

We may begin with cases used by Mellish and Collis-Squires (1976) to argue that shopfloor rules effectively supplant the rule-book. In such situations there are strong work-group standards of behaviour, and members of the group display a high degree of commitment to these standards. The norms have both a positive and a negative aspect: positive in that certain behaviour is prescribed, and negative in that there are powerful sanctions for nonconformity. A member of a dockers' gang who told management about illicit practices would find himself severely penalized. Attempts to enforce the formal rules are likely to be met with a collective response. Gangs of workers are self-governing and self-regulating.

A second pattern exists where work group control is weaker. Workers are unable to enforce their informal rules against the formal ones, but they enjoy some collective control over their own efforts. Leading examples are studies of workers in engineering factories (reviewed in Edwards 1986, 1988). Workers often develop 'fiddles' which allow them to control the variability of earnings and to attain 'loose' times for their work. Practices include running machines faster than work-study standards allow and starting one job when still booked in on another. There are collective norms about behaviour, notably about not producing too much output for fear of damaging the rate. But these norms are enforced through the relatively informal means of work-group pressures. Though the studies do not describe how disciplinary procedures worked, it is likely that management had more discretion than in the case of strong work groups. Issues such as absenteeism, for example, could probably be handled without the risk of organized reaction. Managements needed, however, to view the workplace regime as a whole. Thus toleration of fiddles may mean that more costly and unpredictable behaviour, like absence and quitting, is constrained (Mars 1982). Although fiddles broke or bent some rules, they contributed to the maintenance of a shopfloor order.

These cases illustrate particularly clearly two themes of general applicability. First, it is not possible to break behaviour down into the normal, which falls within the rules, and the abnormal breaches of rules. Running a machine outside established tolerances, for example, may conflict with a formal rule, but if it increases output without endangering quality standards – as often seemed to be the case – everyone gains. Second, and relatedly, understandings on the shopfloor may help to achieve management's substantive goals even when the formal rules are breached. As Roy (1954) tartly noted many years ago, the image of an economically rational management faced with recalcitrant workers is often an inversion of the truth, for workers often strive to meet production goals despite the rules to which they are subject, while managers can impose rules that actually interfere with production.

In a third pattern, fiddles are still prevalent but management has more power and shopfloor organization is weak or non-existent. The retail and hotel and catering industries (Mars 1982: 66–75) are examples. In Ditton's (1979b) study of a bakery, illicit practices were rife. They included short-changing customers and pilfering the company's goods. Such practices are endemic in sectors where money changes hands and where it is hard to check the quantity and quality of goods. Workers were encouraged by management either directly, for supervisors would often coach them in appropriate ways to fiddle, or indirectly, because basic wages were kept low and workers were provided with plenty of opportunities to fiddle. Managers were well aware of the practices, and occasionally cracked down with dismissals; unlike more strongly organized groups, workers lacked the power to resist. Yet such action had only a temporary effect, for identical practices would soon reappear: 'sacking one workforce and then replacing it with another is merely expensive in recruitment and training' (Ditton 1979b: 101).

In cases of this kind, formal discipline and day-to-day conduct are disconnected. Management can hardly be seen as the custodian of rules that are in the interests of all. Fiddling is endemic, and it is not a matter of applying rules to deal with the minority who step beyond acceptable standards. The rules themselves are applied as the chance of a fiddle's coming to attention dictates. Rules cannot be operated even-handedly between different offences and offenders. And managerial omission and commission encourage the practices which are then penalized.

A fourth type of case occurs where managerial power is considerable and where the opportunities for fiddles are less available than they are in sectors such as hotels. In three plants studied by Armstrong et al. (1981) there were a few informal practices, but management could clamp down on them with confidence. But it was not a matter of the simple application of the rule-book. Managers would bend their own rules when it suited them. For example, fork-lift trucks should have been driven only by qualified drivers, but management successfully argued that workers without qualifications should continue at the job because this was the established custom. Managers can thus impose their own interpretations of rules, which are not necessarily a statement of the rights of the industrial citizen but are instead a set of political resources.

In cases of this kind discipline is highly visible, with workers frequently being admonished for poor work standards. Yet three features temper the image of autocracy. In the plants studied by Edwards and Scullion (1982), first, the rules were applied in very different ways to different groups of workers. Male machine-tenders were supervised in a relatively relaxed way, whereas female production workers were monitored more closely. Even among these workers, however, there were differences: longer-serving employees with valued skills were allowed to bargain over effort standards in ways which would have led to the threat of discipline had they been attempted by less strategically placed groups. Second, there were some escape routes. Thus absence rates were high but managers did not crack down on them, largely because absence imposed few direct costs on them. Third, there were genuine efforts to sustain a paternalist atmosphere, so that, for example, workers who became ill might be driven home by managers. There was also an implicit bargain here, with managers being careful to maintain certain standards of fairness, notably ensuring an even distribution of 'good' and 'bad' work. Discipline was a long way from the corrective model, but neither was it based on straight autocracy.

Before leaving the case of strict managerial control, it should be stressed that authoritarian methods are not limited to small and medium-sized firms. Cavendish (1982: 84) reports an incident while she was working on the assembly-line in a firm employing 20,000 people. A young woman was doing a particularly difficult job and expressing her dissatisfaction by working slowly. She was taken to the supervisor's office and told to work properly or hand in her resignation; she did the latter, and was thus recorded as having left voluntarily. The niceties of disciplinary procedures are a long way from a reality in which workers are weak and uncertain of their formal rights.

The plants described above each employed several hundred workers. But what of smaller firms? Discussing small firms in general, Scase (1995) identifies three main patterns of relationships: autocracy, paternalism and fraternalism. The first is often seen as typical of firms without unions and facing intense market competition. Paternalism means relations of close personal interdependence within a clear division between manager and worker, the farmer and farm-hand being the standard example. By fraternalism is meant the relationship between equals which exists where there is a small distinction between manager and worker, as in the building industry. Each approach will evidently handle discipline differently: autocracy through punishment; paternalism through respect for mutual obligations, albeit with ultimate power residing with the manager; and fraternalism through peer-group expectations.

Straight autocracy is likely to be rare. Ram (1994) considered very small Asian-owned firms. One might expect autocracy to be particularly severe here, as the firms faced intense market competition and the managers could use family loyalties to regulate their female workers. In fact, there was tacit negotiation. Managers could not be too assertive for fear of losing workers and then being unable to meet peaks of demand; and piece-rates were set according to informal understandings and not managerial diktat. Workers were also able to use gender as a resource, for the Asian culture made it hard for male managers to control female workers directly. This certainly did not mean that there was anything like harmony, for there were clear differences of interest between employers and workers, but these differences were handled through what Ram calls a 'negotiated paternalism'. Even in such firms, then, discipline depended on negotiation.

The implication of the above discussion is that the operation of disciplinary procedures by personnel managers is not just a technical matter. It will depend on the broader objectives of management and the situation in which it finds itself. Consider for example the discussion by Strauss and Sayles (1980: 225) of a case in which a disciplinary suspension was withheld because there was a rush of jobs and management needed the worker in question. The authors criticize the decision, arguing that there should be consistency and that the employees learned that the relevant rule would not be enforced. Yet a personnel manager who insisted on procedural correctness in all circumstances would not be popular with other managers trying to meet delivery dates. The application of rules must reflect organizational necessities and the demands and interests of different groups within management, as well as the reactions of workers on the shopfloor. A disciplinary policy which tries to ride roughshod over these realities will be resisted or ignored.

W(h)ither Discipline?

How far does the picture painted above still obtain? Parts of it are evidently outmoded. The use of the docks to illustrate social norms of discipline was always to rely on an exceptional rather than a typical case. The case has been transformed since the late 1980s. As Turnbull and Wass (1994) argue, the abolition of the National Dock Labour Scheme and mass redundancy have destroyed the traditional work culture of the docks. As to what is replacing it, they are sceptical of claims that willing consent has been achieved, stressing instead remaining dockers' perceptions of longer hours and much worsened job security. An atmosphere of fear was found to be widespread. The expectation would then be that social norms had been replaced by managerial regulation. Far from the trend being from a corrective approach towards self-discipline, it was from custom and practice towards a corrective and perhaps punitive managerial discipline.

As for the other patterns discussed above, the most straightforward is that of small firms and other situations where collective worker organization is limited and where union-ization is weak. The approach to discipline in small firms is likely to continue to reflect personalized relationships rather than the deliberate creation of order based on HRM principles. The idea of various forms of negotiated order is likely to continue to capture the realities of discipline here. Earnshaw et al. (1998), in a study of workplace disciplinary procedures in mainly small firms, continually stress a managerial preference for inform-ality, particularly in the early stages of disciplinary action, and the very great problems of establishing consistency of treatment. The same is broadly true of sectors such as hotels and catering. Price (1994: 47) says that 'the overall picture is still one of ad hoc, informal practice which pays scant regard to professional standards'. The picture of discipline in the sector painted by Mars is likely to remain broadly accurate. As the very limited take-up of HRM charted elsewhere in this volume suggests, large sections of the economy are likely to exercise discipline in established ways. A good example is McLoughlin and Gourlay's (1994: 80) study of three non-union firms in high-tech industries. A 'new' approach might be expected here, yet they quote the administration manager in one of them as saying, 'if a secretary has a grievance with her manager she might just as well go [i.e. resign] because he will probably sack her anyway...or agree on terms of departure'. The parallel with the large manufacturing firm studied in the 1970s by Cavendish (1982) and discussed above could not be plainer.

The more difficult issue concerns organizations which may have had some form of informal bargaining in the past but which have been moving towards newer ways of managing discipline. Has self-discipline based on trust really replaced conventional pat-terns? Several initial observations may be made.

First, we have seen that use of disciplinary sanctions does not seem to have changed very much in the recent past. This suggests that acceptance of rules has not notably increased but also that, despite widespread use of the idea of management by fear, sanctions are not an increasing weapon of control. The difficulty, of course, is two-fold: we need some standard against which to assess the data (for example, it could be argued that job insecurity acts as a disciplinary device so that the need for disciplinary sanctions is reduced, with any failure of rates of sanction to decline being seen as evidence that managers are using sanctions more than they might be expected to); and there is likely to be great variation around a national average (so that sanctions might be more common in some situations and rarer in others). On the second of these points, the evidence from WIRS – that HRM practices did not explain rates of discipline, and that the determinants of these rates were much the same as they were in the past – suggests that variability is not as great as might have been expected. On the first, we have no way of assessing different readings of trend data. The safest conclusion is that in general discipline in the sense of the use of sanctions has not decayed but nor has there been an upsurge of the overt use of sanctions.

The second general point is that managers are probably less prone to the tacit acceptance of shopfloor norms than they were in the past. The growing need for efficiency and customer responsiveness suggests that there is less willingness to allow drift. As noted at the start of the chapter, the establishment of performance standards is widespread and the standards embrace the public as much as the private sector (see chapter 10). There is less space for the development and entrenchment of informal practices. This is not to say that discipline now follows managerial preferences. As other chapters in this volume show, many HRM initiatives fail to take root, with reality not matching up to expectation. Among the reasons are the fact that managerial goals are often multiple and conflicting – as when employees are supposed to devote time to customer care and yet meet defined output standards – which allows employees some space to develop their own definitions. Yet it is unlikely that such practices would be allowed to grow into the kinds of customary group norms on behaviour that were familiar in the past.

Third, it is becoming increasingly accepted that simple dualities do not work (see Noon and Blyton 1997: 2). Thus one model asserts that work is now based on trust and commitment, while its opposite emphasizes pressure and stress. As shown in chapters 2 and 15, these extreme views are unsatisfactory and there is a developing approach to issues of empowerment which stresses two points. First, most organizations will fall between the extremes. Second, and more interestingly, increased trust and increased stress are not necessarily opposites. The tendency in many organizations is to implement teamworking or other initiatives which at the same time give employees more discretion but also impose new demands on them. Moreover, employees do not necessarily oppose these demands. Chapter 15 makes these points in the context of debates on direct participation. The discussion here adds to them by relating them to previous debates on discipline and by underlining the conditions under which different possible shopfloor outcomes are likely to emerge.

The relationship to debates on discipline can be spelt out briefly. As this chapter has tried to show, the management of employees has always entailed a balance between control and commitment. Any work organization entails a degree of worker consent, and the key point about the negotiation of rules in the past is not that workers sometimes developed rules that ran counter to managerial preferences. It is that they created an order which enabled the production process to continue as well as allowing workers to create their own social space. Customary rules regulated the order of the workplace, and they often established ways of working which were more efficient than the formal rules.

As for the different types of self-discipline which may emerge, Barker (1993) reports a case study of teamwork in an American printed circuit board plant. He finds that there was team discipline (which would fit the 'positive' side of teamwork) but also that in some respects the team's standards were more demanding than the former managerially imposed ones and that, because they were work-group standards, individual workers found it hard to escape from the demands (the 'negative' element). A study of service workers in the US notes that 'the paradox of empowerment in the service labor process is that while seeming unobtrusive, these forms of control are actually more invasive than more direct means, penetrating into more aspects of workers' psychic and personal lives' (Macdonald and Sirianni 1996: 11). The question is whether such 'invasion' promotes complete acceptance. At one level, the question is unanswerable for we are considering what workers 'really' think; even if workers, when asked, fully endorse managerial goals it is always possible to argue that they have been manipulated in some way. At another, the answer is, 'it depends'. As Noon and Blyton (1997: 131) point out, in some situations, as in the health service, it is perfectly possible for the 'emotion work' required under customer care programmes to be fully consistent with what the employee would have done. In others, there may be a welcome to a change initiative without workers in any way being indoctrinated. The study by Rosenthal et al. (1997) of a TQM initiative in a retail chain shows workers welcoming the scheme and enjoying increased discretion but also being aware of the limits of empowerment and in some respects using the language of customer care to make new demands of management. In other situations, there may be more direct opposition to the language of empowerment. McKinlay and Taylor (1996: 288) report a study of a US-owned telecommunications company in which peer review processes were intended to develop a new and 'totalizing' discipline. Teams were supposed to practise self-discipline, but 'the lack of clear factory-wide rules quickly led to wide variations in disciplinary actions [and discipline came to be seen as] *ad hoc*, arbitrary, and distorted by personality clashes'. Teams 'gradually withdrew from their disciplinary role'.

A good illustration is a study of TQM in two service organizations, a telephone sales office of an airline, and a bank (Taylor 1997). In both cases, workers worked to performance standards which had 'hard' (measurable output) and 'soft' (personal skills) aspects. And they were evaluated by reference to the targets, through customer satisfaction surveys and by direct managerial surveillance. Yet monitoring was not simply a way of making workers work harder. As one supervisor put it: 'I'm not necessarily looking to catch them out when I observe ... I am looking for things to praise ... If I do tell them things, I am only trying to help' (Taylor 1997: 187). Thus monitoring was not just about discipline as a form of control but also entailed a more disciplined and perhaps simply better approach to the task. Taylor also notes that what he terms the 'disciplinary force' (p. 197) of revenue targets was experienced by the telephone sales staff only exceptionally, for example if sales figures were particularly low. And employees found some routes round monitoring, for example learning when the supervisor might be listening to their calls. A study based on participation observation in a call centre also noted numerous ways in which employees could make time for themselves; for example, when they were dealing with credit card payments they could move from their desks and could escape hard performance standards for a while (Pringle and Edwards 1995).

The context of discipline thus seems to have changed. There are more organizations than in the past with explicit performance standards, and there is less space in which largely autonomous shopfloor customs can emerge. Studies such as those just discussed are clear that worker autonomy remains, but also that it exists within relatively narrow limits. The implications are harder to assess. In the past, workers did not necessarily celebrate the power that they enjoyed, for it was often a negative power (the ability to frustrate some managerial goals) and it needed to be exerted to respond to what was seen as potentially unfair or incompetent management. As Batstone et al. (1978) found in a study of a particularly strike-prone plant, most strikes reflected the belief that managers were acting in bad faith and not out of a positive desire to advance specific worker interests. Workers may welcome a more organized and rigorous approach even if it also removes some of the space for custom and practice.

Illustration of this point comes from a further study of TQM (Collinson et al. 1998: 65) in six organizations. It included a survey of employees who were asked how closely they felt that they were monitored and whether the management approach to discipline had grown more or less strict in the previous three years. About 25 per cent of the sample reported being observed or monitored to a great extent, but a larger proportion (43 per cent) experienced monitoring little or not at all. Over 50 per cent the sample felt that discipline had grown more strict. It might be expected that monitoring and strict discipline are parts of a relatively autocratic management style and will be associated with a sceptical view of initiatives such as quality programmes. In fact, when these and other measures of attitudes to management were correlated with views of quality programmes, it was found that they were directly related to them. The authors explain this through the concept of the 'disciplined worker': the employee who accepts the discipline and purpose of a quality management system and the performance standards which go with it. It is also worth noting the parallel with Taylor's (1997) qualitative evidence: TQM does not necessarily mean that workers feel very tightly monitored on a continuing basis.

In respect of organizations successfully deploying TQM and similar schemes, the implication is that discipline is less 'total' than some accounts of modern workplaces imply. But there is none the less a more disciplined and ordered approach to work. It is also crucial to stress that such organizations may remain unusual. In the light of survey evidence that TQM is widely practised, this may seem a surprising statement. Yet detailed implementation is much rarer than espousal in principle. The study just discussed stressed some key conditions, notably a sense of job security, in underpinning workers' acceptance of the disciplines of TQM.

In other situations, discipline may be more assertive. Danford (1998: 61) concludes from a study of Japanese-owned plants in South Wales that 'workers have become more completely subordinated to the supervisor, to the machine and to the intensified pace of production'. By contrast, Elger and Smith (1998: 192) offer a less stark portrait of such firms in Telford, stressing the need for managers to accommodate to workers' preferences and the fact that workers could evade some demands while displaying only 'ritualized compliance' with others. These trends are interpreted through the concept of managerial 'mandate': the right to make decisions, but one qualified by workers' perceptions of fairness. Despite these differences, there is one key similarity between the two studies:

both stress that Japanese-owned firms are not markedly different from their UK-owned counterparts. They both note the absence of what Elger and Smith (1998) term a 'full and coherent package' of management techniques. The implication is that the firms will develop labour policies in general, and on discipline in particular, in response to their specific circumstances: it is not the case that there is a uniform 'Japanese' approach to these matters. This point may help to explain the difference between the studies, for Elger and Smith argue that differences of locality may be important. They are not yet able to say in exactly what way, though it is possible that recruitment and retention issues were especially salient in Telford. Different benchmarks may also be important. Danford (1998) stresses change, reflecting other case-study work based on a long-established, and previously UK-owned, plant. Elger and Smith (1998) compare current reality against a benchmark of uniform Japanese policies being inscribed on a blank slate. In fact, the firms had to adapt to the situation as they found it. It may be that some similar processes were at work in the cases studied by Danford (1998) and that the two sets of cases have a broad similarity. Early studies of Japanese-owned firms established that they had much stricter policies on discipline than their British counterparts (White and Trevor 1983). It may be that the difference has narrowed as British-owned firms have sharpened their management policies but it remains true that Japanese firms are widely noted for their close attention to detail and their lack of tolerance of slack (the point stressed by Danford (1998)). At the same time, they cannot always achieve their aims and in some circumstances they may have to compromise their policies in the face of local labour market and other circumstances, as stressed by Elger and Smith (1998). Be that is it may, what is certainly true is that these studies do not paint a picture of self-discipline or mutually satisfying teamwork in workplaces of this kind.

The tone of the above discussion is deliberately exploratory. The research evidence does not exist to provide a clear picture of discipline, a problem heightened by the fact that different studies use different explicit or implicit benchmarks (for example teamwork as totally 'empowering' or Japanese firms as deploying coherent sets of packages). In particular, it is very hard to explain why different patterns of discipline emerge in different situations, for much of the research focuses on the internal dynamics of specific cases and not on the conditions producing the outcomes described.

Some pointers (drawing in particular on Wright and Edwards 1998; and Collinson et al. 1998) can be offered, however. They may be organized in terms of structural conditions and the process of change.

Structural conditions, promoting a move towards a sense of trust and self-discipline, include the following.

- *Job security* features prominently in accounts of employee involvement schemes, teamwork and of TQM. Where workers have a sense of such security they are the more willing to accept new ways of working and to believe that they can trust managers.
- A *strong product market position* and *the absence of short-term pressures* contribute to job security (and hence indirectly to trust) while also limiting the immediate production pressures that can lead managers into the kind of fire-fighting described in the Motorola case, McKinlay and Taylor (1996: 288). Consider for example the evidence on Japanese firms. Early studies concentrated on large and powerful firms

and it may be that they were able to insulate their workers from immediate pressures. Later work looked at first- and second-tier suppliers where pressures to meet delivery deadlines were more evident and where any ideas of self-discipline, to the extent that they existed at all, may have decayed into managerial diktat, or informal negotiation with workers or an uncomfortable balance of the two.

- A *constructive relationship with unions or other employee representatives* is highlighted in some studies. Note that union presence does not in itself lead to trust, for some of the Japanization studies point to more assertive management policies in union than non-union environments. But the existence of working relationships with unions, or other bodies expressing employee voice, helps to underpin trust relationships. Conversely, the research shows that organizations pursuing union avoidance policies alongside self-discipline send out dangerously mixed messages.

These conditions underpin several processual issues.

- A common one is *top management commitment* to change programmes. This is evidently important, but generic commitment may be undermined by short-term demands, or changes in personnel resulting from reorganization, or many other factors. Commitment does not exist in the abstract, but it is still one condition to ensure that more than lip-service is paid to ideas of self-discipline.
- *Acceptance by middle managers* is a similarly commonly emphasized theme. Its importance in relation to discipline is that it is easy to slip back into a mixture of punitive and corrective approaches. The study by Elger and Smith (1998) neatly illustrates the ways in which shopfloor experience can continue to reflect these approaches rather than any meaningful sense of self-discipline.
- *Workers' responses* to change programmes are also crucial. Where there is a long history of culture change programmes, there is likely to be an air of scepticism. As this chapter has stressed, workers develop their own norms and expectations, and they may not readily endorse concepts of self-discipline, or they may define them in their own ways. Existing employee perceptions are an important and often neglected issue.

Any idea of a progressive trend from punishment through correction to self-discipline is thus too simple. The first two approaches to discipline have not been abandoned, self-discipline could be found well before it began to be proclaimed as a distinctive approach, few companies are likely to claim to practise self-discipline in a developed sense of advanced personnel policies that give workers wide autonomy, and in those that do such discipline may entail a demanding and constrained atmosphere rather than one of freedom.

The informality and negotiation of discipline described in the second section of the chapter have not disappeared. They have changed their nature in some respects, first as a result of the formalization of procedures for handling corrective discipline and second as managements have given more explicit attention to disciplined behaviour and performance standards. But they remain in relatively unchanged form in small firms while in larger organizations there continues to be an area for the negotiation of work standards. Such negotiation reflects the facts that managerial systems of work organization are never as coherent as they seem at first sight and that securing worker co-operation remains an uncertain process.

Demands on workers do seem to have increased. The meaning of 'discipline' may thus have changed. In the past, especially when capitalized, the term meant the first two faces of formal rules and their enforcement. The third face, of day-to-day conduct, was part of a shopfloor reality that was often separate from rules and procedures. As managements have aimed to regulate this reality, they have become more interested in the third face. Self-discipline can be more demanding than a bureaucratic system because it is more difficult for the worker to hide behind the argument that his or her responsibility stops at a specified point. 'New' forms of self-discipline may thus differ from the 'old', not because there is now active commitment when in the past there was none, but because firms have been able to take the world of disciplinary practice and shape it in ways which are more amenable to their own goals. The third face of discipline, which used to exist in a shadowy world of customs and informality, is now more subject to deliberate managerial policy. But it is not directly under management control, partly because the conditions allowing for the sustained use of self-discipline remain rare and partly because workers continue to display ingenuity in developing their own standards of behaviour.

Note

1   The source of this quotation is Hill (1964: 218), who is in turn quoting Milton's *Prose Works*, II, 441. Hill makes the interesting point that Protestant sects saw discipline, which could look like tyranny, as in fact achieving liberty for those whose activities flourished under national unity and peace: the seventeenth-century version of empowerment. The issue of how far discipline is tyranny or liberation, or a blend of the two, is the theme of this chapter.

References and further reading

Anderman, S. D. 1972: *Voluntary Dismissals Procedure and the Industrial Relations Act*. London: Political and Economic Planning.

Armstrong, P. 1983: Class Relationships at the Point of Production: a Case Study. *Sociology*, **17**(3), 339–58.

Armstrong, P., Goodman, J. F. B. and Hyman, J. D. 1981: *Ideology and Shop Floor Industrial Relations*. London: Croom Helm.

Ashdown, R. T. and Baker, K. H. 1973: *In Working Order: a Study of Industrial Discipline*. Department of Employment Manpower Papers 6, London: HMSO.

Barker, J. R. 1993: Tightening the Iron Cage: Concertive Conflict in Self-managed Teams. *Administrative Science Quarterly*, **38**(4), 408–37.

Batstone, E., Boraston, I. and Frenkel, S. 1977: *Shop Stewards in Action*. Oxford: Blackwell.

Batstone, E., Boraston, I. and Frenkel, S. 1978: *The Social Organization of Strikes*. Oxford: Blackwell.

Beaumont, P. B. 1993: *HRM: Key Concepts and Skills*. London: Sage.

Cavendish, R. 1982: *Women on the Line*. London: Routledge & Kegan Paul.

Clinton, A. 1984: *Post Office Workers*. London. Allen & Unwin.

Collinson, M., Rees, C. and Edwards, P. 1998: *Involving Employees in Total Quality Management*. Department of Trade and Industry, Employment Relations Research Series 1. London: DTI.

Corrigan, P. and Sayer, D. 1991: *The Great Arch*. (rev). edn Oxford: Blackwell.

Cully, M., O'Reilly, A., Millward, N., Forth, J., Woodland, S., Dix, G. and Bryson, A. 1998: *The 1998 Workplace Employee Relations Survey: First Findings*. London: DTI.

Danford, A. 1998: Work Organization inside Japanese Firms in South Wales. In P. Thompson and C. Warhurst (eds), *Workplaces of the Future*, Basingstoke: Macmillan.

Daniel, W. W. and Stilgoe, E. 1978: *The Impact of Employment Protection Laws*. London: PSI.

Deaton, D. 1984: The Incidence of Dismissals in British Manufacturing Industry. *Industrial Relations Journal*, **15**(2), 61–5.

Ditton, J. 1979a: Baking Time. *Sociological Review*, **27**(1), 157–67.

Ditton, J. 1979b: *Controlgy*. London: Macmillan.

Earnshaw, J., Goodman, J., Harrison, R. and Marchington, M. 1998: *Industrial Tribunals, Workplace Disciplinary Procedures and Employment Practice*. Department of Trade and Industry, Employment Relations Research Series 2, London: DTI.

Edwards, P. K. 1986: *Conflict at Work*. Oxford: Blackwell.

Edwards, P. K. 1988: Patterns of Conflict and Accommodation. In D. Gallie (ed.), *Employment in Britain*, Oxford: Blackwell.

Edwards, P. K. 1989: The Three Faces of Discipline. In K. Sisson (ed.), *Personnel Management in Britain*, Oxford: Blackwell.

Edwards, P. K. 1994: Discipline and the Creation of Order. In K. Sisson (ed.), *Personnel Management*, Oxford: Blackwell.

Edwards, P. K. 1995: HRM, Union Voice and the Use of Discipline: an Analysis of WIRS. *Industrial Relations Journal*, **26**(3), 204–20.

Edwards, P. K. and Scullion, H. 1982: *The Social Organization of Industrial Conflict*. Oxford: Blackwell.

Edwards, P. K. and Whitston, C. 1993: *Attending to Work*. Oxford: Blackwell.

Edwards, P. K. and Whitston, C. 1994: Disciplinary Practice: a Study of the Railways in Britain, 1860–1988. *Work, Employment and Society*, **8**(3), 317–38.

Edwards, R. 1979: *Contested Terrain: the Transformation of the Workplace in the Twentieth Century*. London: Heinemann.

Elger, T. and Smith, C. 1998: Exit, Voice and 'Mandate': Managerial Strategies and Labour Practices of Japanese Firms in Britain. *British Journal of Industrial Relations*, **36**(2), 185–208.

Evans, S., Goodman, J. F. B. and Hargreaves, L. 1985: *Unfair Dismissal Law and Employment Practice in the 1980s*. Department of Employment Research Paper 53, London: HMSO.

Friedman, A. L. 1977: *Industry and Labour*. London: Macmillan.

Gersuny, C. 1976: 'A Devil in Petticoats' and Just Cause: Patterns of Punishment in Two New England Factories. *Business History Review*, **50**(2), 131–52.

Gouldner, A. W. 1954: *Patterns of Industrial Bureaucracy*. New York: Free Press.

Henry, S. 1983: *Private Justice*. London: Routledge & Kegan Paul.

Hill, C. 1964: *Society and Puritanism in Pre-revolutionary England*. Harmondsworth: Penguin.

Hyman, R. 1987: Strategy or Structure: Capital, Labour and Control. *Work, Employment and Society*, **1**(1), 25–56.

IPM (Institute of Personnel Management) 1979: *Disciplinary Procedures and Practice*. London: IPM.

IRS (Industrial Relations Services) 1991: Discipline at Work 1: the Practice. *Employment Trends*, 493, August, 6–14.

IRS 1995: Discipline at Work: the Practice. *Employment Trends*, 591, September, 4–11.

Littler, C. R. 1982: *The Development of the Labour Process in Capitalist Societies*. London: Heinemann.

McCarthy, W. E. J. 1966: *The Role of Shop Stewards in British Industrial Relations*. Research Paper 1, Royal Commission on Trade Unions and Employers' Associations, London: HMSO.

McCarthy, W. E. J. and Parker, S. R: 1968. *Shop Stewards and Workshop Relations*. Research Paper 10, Royal Commission on Trade Unions and Employers' Associations, London: HMSO.

Macdonald, C. L. and Sirianni, C. 1996: The Service Society and the Changing Experience of Work. In C. L. Macdonald and C. Sirianni (eds), *Working in the Service Society*, Philadelphia: Temple University Press.

McKinlay, A. and Taylor, P. 1996: Power, Surveillance and Resistance. In P. Ackers, C. Smith and P. Smith (eds), *The New Workplace and Trade Unionism*, London: Routledge.

McLoughlin, I. and Gourlay, S. 1994: *Enterprise without Unions*. Milton Keynes: Open University Press.

Mars, G. 1982: *Cheats at Work*. London: Counterpoint.

Mellish, M. and Collis-Squires, N. 1976: Legal and Social Norms in Discipline and Dismissal. *Industrial Law Journal*, **5**(3), 164–77.

Millward, N., Stevens, M., Smart, D. and Hawes, W. R. 1992: *Workplace Industrial Relations in Transition*. Aldershot: Dartmouth.

Molander, C. and Winterton, J. 1994: *Managing Human Resources*. London: Routledge.

Newby, H. 1977: Paternalism and Capitalism. In R. Scase (ed.), *Industrial Society*, London: Allen & Unwin.

Nichols, T. 1975: The Sociology of Accidents and the Social Production of Industrial Injury. In G. Esland et al. (eds), *People and Work*, Edinburgh: Holmes McDougal.

Nichols T. and Beynon, H. 1977: *Living with Capitalism*. London: Routledge & Kegan Paul.

Noon, M. and Blyton, P. 1997: *The Realities of Work*. Basingstoke: Macmillan.

Phelps Brown, E. H. 1949: Morale, Military and Industrial. *Economic Journal*, **59**(1), 40–55.

Plumridge, M. D. 1966: Disciplinary Practice. *Personnel Management*, September, 138–41.

Pollard, S. 1965: *The Genesis of Modern Management*. London: Arnold.

Price, L. 1994: Poor Personnel Practice in the Hotel and Catering Industry: Does It Matter? *Human Resource Management Journal*, **4**(4), 44–62.

Pringle, M. and Edwards, P. 1995: Donkeys in the Age of Smart Machines. *Warwick Papers in Industrial Relations*, 55, Industrial Relations Research Unit, University of Warwick.

Ram, M. 1994: *Managing to Survive*. Oxford: Blackwell.

Reid, D. A. 1976: The Decline of Saint Monday, 1766–1876. *Past and Present*, **71**, 76–101.

Rollinson, D., Handley, J., Hook, C. and Foot, M. 1997: The Disciplinary Experience and Its Effects on Behaviour. *Work, Employment and Society*, **11**(2), 283–311.

Rosenthal, P., Hill, S. and Peccei, R. 1997: Checking Out Service: Evaluating Excellence, HRM and TQM in Retailing. *Work, Employment and Society*, **11**(3), 481–503.

Roy, D. 1954: Efficiency and 'The Fix': Informal Intergroup Relations in a Piecework Machine Shop. *American Journal of Sociology*, **60**(2), 255–66.

Scase, R. 1995: Employment Relations in Small Firms. In P. Edwards (ed.), *Industrial Relations*, Oxford: Blackwell.

Seifert, R. 1992: *Industrial Relations in the NHS*. London: Chapman and Hall.

Storey, J. (ed.) 1995: *HRM: a Critical Text*. London: Routledge.

Strauss, G. and Sayles, L. R. 1980: *Personnel*. 4th edn, Englewood Cliffs, NJ: Prentice-Hall.

Taylor, S. 1997: 'Empowerment' or 'Degradation': Total Quality Management and the Service Sector. In R. K. Brown (ed.), *The Changing Shape of Work*, Basingstoke: Macmillan.

Torrington, D. and Hall, L. 1995: *Personnel Management: HRM in Action*, 3rd edn, New York: Prentice-Hall.

Townley, B. 1994: *Reframing Human Resource Management*. London: Sage.

Tremlett, N. and Banerji, N. 1994: *The 1992 Survey of Industrial Tribunal Applications*. Employment Department Research Series 22, London: ED.

Turnbull, P. and Wass, V. 1994: The Greatest Game No More: Redundant Dockers and the Demise of Dock Work. *Work, Employment and Society*, **8**(4), 487–506.

White, M. and Trevor, M. 1983: *Under Japanese Management*. London: Heinemann.

Wickens, P. 1987: *The Road to Nissan*. London: Macmillan.

Wright, M. and Edwards, P. 1998: Does Teamworking Work? *Economic and Industrial Democracy*, **19**(1), 59–90.

14

Direct Participation

Mick Marchington and Adrian Wilkinson

Introduction

In its various guises, the topic of employee participation has been a recurring theme in British industrial relations and personnel management. Different periods have embraced new forms of participation which have sometimes replaced, and at other times existed alongside, those which were already in place. The wider political and economic environment has had a key influence in facilitating particular forms. In the 1970s, for example, interest was centred around the notion of power sharing through industrial democracy and an influential role was seen for trade unions – even though such ideas were contested by employers and also a subject of controversy within the union movement (Brannen et al. 1976; Brannen 1983). Both the decline in union membership, and influence and changes in public policy conspired to move industrial democracy off the domestic agenda, although more recently British membership of the EU has reawakened interest.

The last 20 years has not seen a decline of participation, however, and managerial interest has never been higher. But this interest has taken a particular form, that of employee involvement (EI). The more recent EI initiatives have been management sponsored and, not surprisingly, have reflected a management agenda concerned primarily with employee motivation and commitment to organizational objectives. EI has focused on direct participation by small groups and individuals, it is concerned with information sharing at a work-group level, and it has excluded the opportunity for workers to have an input into high-level decision making. As such, direct participation is fundamentally different from industrial democracy and indirect participation schemes such as consultative committees which are collectivist and representative in form (Marchington 1995a; Marchington et al. 1992; Wilkinson 1998a, 1998b) or forms of 'social partnership' (chapter 15). In this chapter, we analyse EI and direct participation.

A wide range of factors provides the framework within which direct participation operates, perhaps the most important being product market change. Few would dispute that the product market environment faced by British employers has become increasingly competitive. In the private sector, this is partly the result of globalization and in particular the increased pressure exerted by Japanese and other South-East Asian companies during the period up to the mid 1990s. However, the public sector has not been immune from such forces either, and deregulation and commercialization have been key factors explaining the barrage of initiatives introduced over the last 20 years. The notion of customer choice has also been an important concept in relation to these initiatives. Government policy has also set the scene for wider changes in management approaches. In particular, the free market stance advocated by successive Conservative governments reduced restrictions on employers in order to promote an 'enterprise culture'. This also fitted with political changes in North America, although increasingly this has been at odds with European developments seeking a more uniform social framework. The sole legislative change in Britain has been a requirement in the 1982 Employment Act, that companies employing more than 250 people must include a statement in their annual report indicating the action taken in relation to the provision of information, consultation, financial involvement and practices aimed at promoting economic and financial awareness. However, the actual impact of this policy seems to have been limited. Finally, shifts in the structure of employment in Britain, discussed in chapter 1, away from manufacturing to services and accompanied by a growth in the numbers of part-time and women employees, has raised issues concerning the adequacy of models of participation based on highly unionized male workers in manufacturing. The opportunity for employers to implement direct participation without union opposition has increased significantly.

Whilst each of these factors is important in setting the context within which direct participation can flourish, it is also crucial to examine how these macro-level changes interact with developments at corporate level where business decisions are made. An important influence has been the 'ideas brokers' – consultants and popular management writers – who offer up their interpretation of the changing global market. By the mid 1980s, management thinking recognized that competitive advantage was more likely to be achieved through niche markets with an emphasis on responding swiftly to customer demands (Piore and Sabel 1983). Organizations of the future were encouraged to be flexible, innovative and responsive, rather than seeking economies of scale through mass production. Influential writers such as Drucker (1988), Schonberger (1989, 1990), Peters (1989) and Kanter (1989) all stressed the need to embrace debureaucratization (ending hierarchy and prescriptive rules), delayering, decentralization and the utilization of project-based teams, cutting across functional divides as part of a movement towards this 'new' organization. In a similar vein, the quality movement and the Japanese model also promoted a message of empowerment in which workers were encouraged/required to use their tacit knowledge of the work process to diagnose and possibly implement improvements (Oliver and Wilkinson 1992; Wilkinson et al. 1992; Hill and Wilkinson 1995). Each of these, but particularly empowerment, was viewed as a positive development for employers *and* employees (Cole et al. 1993).

These broad changes have clear implications for the management of employment, work organization and direct participation. Compliance, hierarchy and following rules are no longer seen as relevant for employees who are expected to work beyond contract, exercise their initiative and embrace teamworking. As Walton (1985: 76) put it, managers have now 'begun to see that workers respond best – and most creatively – not when they are tightly controlled by management, placed in narrowly defined jobs, and treated like an unwelcome necessity, but, instead when they are given broader responsibilities, encouraged to contribute, and helped to take satisfaction from their work'. Moreover, better solutions may also be generated. Thus, innovative work practices can increase motivation by providing more interesting work, increasing flexibility and improving individual and organizational performance. In short, through direct participation, employees work harder as well as smarter (Ichniowski et al. 1996).

The notion of 'best practice' HRM (Ichniowski 1990; Pfeffer 1994; Huselid 1995) which arose in the 1990s in the USA made this case even more forcefully, backing it up with an array of sophisticated statistical evidence. More recently, this has been mirrored by some UK research (Patterson et al. 1997). It has been argued that long-term competitive advantage could only be achieved through 'unleashing the power of the workforce' (Pfeffer 1994). Schemes of direct participation and empowerment can be seen as a rejection of a strict division of labour, with workers seen as 'attendants' to machinery, carrying out fragmented and repetitive jobs. Participation practices imply a neo-unitarist approach, which is almost moralistic in tone, and is 'represented as squaring the circle of organizational needs for high levels of employee performance and their own demands for autonomy and self-expression in work' (Claydon and Doyle 1996: 13). A wide array of labels has been attached to these direct participation initiatives: high performance work design (Buchanan 1987), lean production (Womack et al. 1990), high involvement (Lawler 1992), teamworking (Mueller 1994), 'new logic' (Lawler 1996), self-managed teams (Pfeffer 1998) and even 'after lean production' (Kochan et al. 1997). Of course, there is a danger that these initiatives are viewed solely in a positive and upbeat manner, so ignoring the more contested and mundane nature of participation. For example, empowerment, rather than leading to autonomy and self-management, may merely produce greater work intensification, increased stress levels and redundancies. Similarly, teamworking and job redesign can create the potential for conflict and greater interpersonal tensions as opposed to facilitating groups of employees to work together effectively on projects of their own design.

This introduction sets the scene for the remainder of the chapter. First, we review briefly the dynamics of participation, focusing in particular on cycles and waves as competing explanations of how and why participation varies in extensiveness and importance over time. Second, we analyse four separate categories of direct participation, considering in each case some of the major characteristics and problems associated with these schemes in practice. Finally, we evaluate the role of direct participation in general, picking up on a number of key themes and issues relevant to the subject as a whole.

The Dynamics of Participation

Employee participation and involvement are somewhat elastic terms and are amenable to a range of definitions (see, for example, Poole 1986). Brannen (1983: 13) suggests that through participation 'individuals or groups may influence, control, be involved in, exercise power within, or be able to intervene in decision making within organisations'. This is too broad, and it is more helpful if the terms can be deconstructed according to degree, form, level and range of subject matter. Taking the first of these, the degree of involvement indicates the extent to which employees are able to influence decisions about various aspects of management, whether they are simply informed of changes, consulted or actually make decisions. The escalator of participation (figure 14.1) illustrates this point and also implies a progression upwards rather than simply a move from zero participation

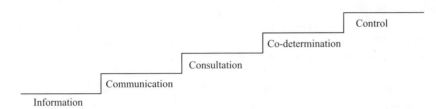

Figure 14.1   The escalator of participation

to workers control. Second, there is the level at which participation takes place: task, departmental, establishment or corporate. Third, the range of subject matter is another dimension; ranging from relatively trivial issues such as canteen food to more strategic concerns relating to investment strategies at the other end of the spectrum. Fourth, there is the particular form of participation. Indirect participation, traditionally associated with the relationship between management and trade unions, is considered in the next chapter. Financial participation relates to schemes such as profit sharing or 'gainsharing' whereby employees participate directly in the commercial success or failure of the organization, usually linking a proportion of financial reward to corporate or establishment perform-ance. Direct participation, the subject of this chapter, is concerned with face-to-face or written communications between managers and subordinates, but involving individuals rather than elected representatives. It is sometimes divided in the American literature between 'on-line' participation (Appelbaum and Batt 1995) where workers make decisions as part of their daily job responsibilities, and 'off-line' participation where workers simply make suggestions off the job. We see empowerment as feeding through all aspects of direct participation to different degrees given that it embraces a very broad range of initiatives (Lashley 1997; Hennestad 1998; Wilkinson 1998a, 1998b).

There have been various attempts to trace the dynamics of participation over time in the UK, the most widely cited being the cycles of control thesis first proposed by Ramsay (1977). He argues that we have seen four broad cycles of interest in participation over the last 100 years. The first began in the late nineteenth century, around the practice of profit sharing. The second and third saw the focus of interest shift to consultative arrangements between management and workers and included the Whitley Committees during and just after the First World War, and the Joint Production and Advisory Committees (JPACs) of the 1940s. In the 1960s and 1970s, attention changed to new forms of participation in the shape of productivity bargaining and worker directors. The reason for this waxing and waning of interest is simple, according to Ramsay (1977). Employers are attracted to the notion of participation only if their authority is under threat from below and, by appearing to share some elements of control, they are able to regain it. Once the threat from labour has abated, management lose interest in participation and allow schemes to fade or to vanish altogether.

This appeared a plausible explanation of some developments in participation, but it has been criticized as a general all-encompassing explanatory theory (Ackers et al. 1992). First, it is essentially rooted in manufacturing and public-sector workplaces and has less relevance where trade unions are weaker. Second, looking principally at extensiveness and interest, it takes a functionalist view, failing to take into account how such schemes are used within the workplace and assuming that the meaning of participation is the same throughout industry. Third, it assumes labour relations are of paramount importance to employers and that control over the labour process is one of their principal objectives. Fourth, it fails to explain more recent developments in direct participation in the 1980s and 1990s (Marchington et al. 1992, Storey 1992; Hyman and Mason 1995; Lashley 1997; Wilkinson 1998b) with a huge array of initiatives in a climate where, according to Ramsay (1977), one would expect decline.

An alternative thesis has been advanced by the authors – termed the 'waves' analysis. The argument here is that a single all-embracing explanation of change is inappropriate, but that participation might be driven by a variety of motives. For example, developments in profit sharing in the 1980s were facilitated by politically driven legal changes which attracted employers as a mechanism to improve recruitment and retention of key staff. Equally, some employers introduce participation for moral or philosophical reasons, and indeed Bougen et al. (1988: 610–11) note that a number of the early profit-sharing schemes did owe a considerable amount to owners who held religious–paternalist views. Other studies have also shown the importance of such deeply held values for the creation of 'progressive' employment practices (Smith et al. 1990). Once the analysis of change in the area of direct participation is broadened to allow for pressures other than organized labour, it becomes possible to look more closely at managerial activities and the differences and conflict between functions. Central to the waves analysis is that internal managerial relations is a key explanation for the ebb and flow of participation initiatives. Indeed, the main argument is that the shape of EI in organizations varies significantly over time, and can be characterized in terms of wave patterns. These are subject to a range of forces, one of the most important being the career aspirations and mobility of managers, and conflicts between different functions and levels in the organizational hierarchy. The impetus behind many participation schemes is the career aspirations of managers in various functions, and the dynamics of participation is also related to the progression of these people, internal political rivalries within management, and supervisory problems in sustaining the schemes. In other words, patterns of EI in particular workplaces owe a considerable amount to relations within management, as much as to relations between managers and workers (Marchington et al. 1993).

Direct Participation in Practice

There is little doubt that direct participation has become more extensive in Britain since the early 1980s just as indirect participation has declined over this period. This was first noted in the 1984 *Workplace Industrial Relations Survey* (Millward and Stevens 1986: 165) and the growth in direct participation became much more apparent by the end of the decade (Millward et al. 1992: 175–6). For example, new EI initiatives were reported at nearly half of all workplaces (employing 25 or more people) in the three years prior to 1990 compared with one-third for the period prior to 1984. The most extensive of these initiatives were team briefing schemes, senior management meetings with employees, employee newsletters and suggestion schemes.

Initial findings from the 1998 *Workplace Employee Relations Survey* confirmed this trend (Cully et al. 1998). Four of the top five 'new management practices and employee involvement schemes' were forms of direct participation. These were: teamworking (65 per cent of all workplaces employing 25 or more people); team briefing (61 per cent); staff attitude survey in the last five years (45 per cent); problem-solving groups such as quality circles (42 per cent). The only other aspect of direct participation in the 16 practices identified was regular meetings of the entire workforce which, at 37 per cent, was rather more extensive than the existence of a workplace-level joint consultative committee, employee share ownership schemes for non-managerial employees, guaranteed training for staff and individual performance-related pay schemes. Whilst noting this increase in the use of direct participation, we also need to be alert to limitations due to definitions and survey design. In the case of teamworking, for example, whilst it was reported in 65 per cent of workplaces, it is instructive to note that in just 5 per cent of these did it take the form of autonomous work groups, those in which team members were given responsibility for their task, jointly decided how work was to be done or appointed their own leader.

Nevertheless, direct participation has been one of the major areas of change in employment relations, coinciding with (and perhaps related to) reductions in collective bargaining scope and coverage in the last 20 years. The growth in extensiveness is not confined solely to Britain, however, and Sisson (1997: 203) notes similar tendencies across much of the rest of Europe to the extent that four out of every five workplaces now have some form of direct participation. Even in the countries of Southern Europe with the lowest coverage (Spain and Portugal), over 60 per cent of workplaces surveyed reported the existence of direct participation. The picture in North America (Cotton 1993) and Australasia (Davis and Lansbury 1996) is also similar.

Despite this, as noted earlier, there are major problems with the terminology which is used to describe direct participation and the range of practices which appear to be subsumed under its banner. Consequently, it is difficult to make precise comparisons about the extent of change over time or the similarity of practices in different countries. For this reason, it is worthwhile to outline briefly the range of practices which are included under the title of 'direct participation'. Drawing upon previous categorizations by the authors (Marchington et al. 1992; Marchington 1995a) and others (Poole 1986; Hyman and Mason 1995), we employ a simple four-fold schema: downward communications; upward problem solving; task participation; teamworking; and self-management. These are differentiated in terms of direction of communication (up, down or lateral), level and scope of subject matter (company-wide, departmental or work group), regularity of involvement (continuing or scheduled at set times) and centrality to the work process (on-line or bolted on). Each of these different categories is now considered in turn.

Downward communications

Downward communications represents the most dilute form of direct participation considered in this chapter, to some extent because of the direction of the communication, but also because, typically, it is 'bolted on' rather than integral to the work process. It takes a number of forms in practice – ranging from formalized written documents distributed to all employees through to face-to-face oral interactions between line managers and their staff – although it has a common purpose to inform and 'educate' employees about managerial actions and intentions. At one level it can be viewed as little more than a mechanism to convey information about a particular issue (e.g. a change to car-parking arrangements or a reminder about work standards), whereas at another level it can be interpreted as an instrument to reinforce management prerogatives and shape employee expectations. More extensive and open management communications are seen as an important precursor to 'fuller' employee involvement by many commentators and as a necessary component in the creation of a more knowledgeable workforce. In the sense that information is rarely neutral, however, the messages conveyed by managers may have a more insidious intent and outcome.

In the past, many workers only discovered what was happening at their workplace through reports in local or regional newspapers, the grapevine or the trade union branch. To the extent that managements now appear more committed to disseminating at least some information, often in advance of public announcements, the growth of direct communications is reflective of more general changes in society. Before the 1980s, it was rare for employers to provide employees with financial information, whereas now it is not unusual, at least for major companies, to issue an employee report to coincide with the publication of annual results. Similarly, many organizations produce newsletters or house journals which contain data about organizational performance, new ventures and product development, as well as the usual mix of information about personnel, sports and social affairs. The use of videos to communicate company-wide information has also been more prevalent, and some organizations set up roadshows and other stage-managed media events for staff. In part, these developments have been stimulated by a desire to ensure that employees receive information direct from management, but also by a feeling that there is a potential link between information disclosure and higher levels of employee commitment to, and identification with, organizational goals. The major criticism of these sorts of technique is that they can induce passive acceptance by employees of managerial statements which are often portrayed as having an objectivity and 'truth' behind them (Tebbutt and Marchington 1997).

Team briefings and other mechanisms for communicating information direct to staff have also become much more widespread over the last 20 years, bringing small, 'natural' groups of staff together at predetermined times (e.g. once a month) to hear direct from their line manager about new developments. Line managers are thus responsible for conveying information and explaining how it relates to their particular functional area, as well as using the briefing session to help build up team spirit. Information is cascaded down the organizational hierarchy, with the original core message being adapted to suit specific audiences. Although the briefings themselves are intended as one-way, downward communications, there is provision for feedback up the line-management chain to clarify issues and ensure that senior managers are aware of employees' feelings. Briefings are not seen as a substitute for day-to-day interactions but are important for ensuring that all staff are provided with regular, relevant, communications. Although the notion of briefings is widely supported, in practice they run into a number of problems. These include: line managers not being able to communicate effectively; information which is irrelevant or not timely; and trade unions seeing briefings as a device to undermine or marginalize their role. These issues are discussed later.

Upward problem solving

Upward problem solving incorporates a range of techniques which are designed to tap into employee knowledge and ideas, typically through individual suggestions or through *ad hoc* or semi-permanent groups brought together for the specific purpose of resolving problems or generating ideas. As with downward communications, these schemes tend to be 'bolted on' rather than integral to the work process and do not take place on a continuous basis, even though they are upward rather than downward in direction. These types of scheme have also grown considerably in extensiveness and importance since the 1980s, and are central to notions of 'soft' human resource management (Storey 1995) and so-called 'bundles' of best practice (MacDuffie 1995; Pfeffer 1998). These practices are predicated on assumptions that employees are a (if not *the*) major source of competitive advantage whose ideas have been ignored in the past or who have been told explicitly that 'they are not paid to think'. Drawing on practices which are rather more extensive in Japanese companies (Oliver and Wilkinson 1992), many British and American organizations have adopted employment and work systems which rely upon employees being able and willing to offer ideas through upward problem-solving techniques. Not only are these practices designed to increase the stock of ideas available to the employer, they are also assumed to help facilitate co-operative relations at work and encourage the acceptance of change. Although clearly offering a greater degree of participation than downward communications, they are also seen by critics as problematic precisely because they encourage employees to collaborate with management in helping to resolve work-related problems and (implicitly at least) to adopt a unitarist perspective. Managers are thus seen not only to 'appropriate' workers' ideas for no extra rewards, they are also able to gain active consent and co-operation in helping to meet organizational goals (Sewell and Wilkinson 1992).

There are two main types of upward problem-solving technique. The first is suggestion schemes which have a long pedigree in the United Kingdom and an even longer history in the USA (Townley 1989: 335). Employees receive financial rewards for their suggestions, with the amount varying depending upon the scheme, and in some cases all those ideas which have some merit gain an award irrespective of the savings which accrue to the organization. Suggestions relating to an employee's own work area are not allowed under the terms of schemes, these being seen as an integral and anticipated part of that person's job. These schemes are a relatively marginal form of employee involvement, but they also have the potential to create bad feelings, especially if the employee making the suggestion feels that their idea merits a higher reward. Moreover, paying for suggestions may encourage an instrumental approach to work whereby employees refuse to offer ideas for improvement unless they are rewarded explicitly.

Problem-solving groups and quality circles constitute the second type in this category of upward communications. These consist of small groups of employees who meet voluntarily on a regular basis to identify, analyse and solve quality and work-related problems. A typical circle would comprise about ten people, drawn either from the same work group or from a range of different areas, who meet under the guidance of a leader, with assistance from one or more facilitators. As with other aspects of direct participation, problem-solving groups are designed to achieve explicit production or service goals (such as productivity improvements or zero defects) as well as improve employee morale and commitment. Quality circles were first observed in Britain in the early 1980s, but have never really operated in that many organizations – certainly compared with team briefing, for example – and even when circles have been introduced into an organization, the take-up rate is not that high (Collard and Dale 1989). Furthermore, it is recognized that there are problems in sustaining circles or problem-solving groups beyond 18 months to two years, once all the immediate problems have been tackled and group members start to question the precise gains which membership will bring in the longer term (Black and Ackers 1988). On the other hand, it might be reasonable to expect that problem-solving groups would have only a limited life-span given the nature of their task and the fact that they are not related directly to workers' on-line participation. There have also been specific problems with quality circles in a number of organizations, most notably in the motor industry, when circles were first introduced, due to trade union opposition to their formation (Starkey and McKinlay 1993). This led to feelings in some quarters that quality circles were being introduced specifically to undermine trade unions (Parker and Slaughter 1988) and to a rejection of all Japanese management ideas because of this concern (Hill 1991).

Task-based participation

Task-based participation represents the third aspect of direct participation, differing from the first two categories in being integral to the job and forming a part of everyday working life. As with certain aspects of upward problem solving, the practices included under this heading have a much longer history, especially under the guise of Quality of Work Life Programs in the USA and Sweden in the 1960s and 1970s (Kelly 1982). This aspect has seen a resurgence in recent times, to some extent due to publications by management gurus such as Tom Peters. These have celebrated more humanistic employment regimes, viewing them not so much as a counter to alienation at work but as a key component in the search for competitive advantage. Cotton (1993: 171), for example, concludes his meta-analysis of research into task-based participation with the view that enriched and enlarged jobs do lead to increased levels of employee satisfaction but not necessarily improved levels of performance.

Delayering and devolution have both increased the pressure on employees to take responsibility for a greater range of tasks than under previous organizational structures, encouraging empowerment and functional flexibility. The removal of demarcations between different groups of workers has also been an issue. In other words, as with all aspects of employee involvement, task-based participation illustrates elements of both 'soft' and 'hard' human resource management, regarding employees not only as resourceful humans but also as workers who have to be controlled in order to minimize costs.

Task-based participation can occur both horizontally and vertically. The former refers to the number and variety of tasks which an individual employee performs at the same skill level in the organization, and this has now become a common feature of many workplaces. The range of tasks may be relatively small and require little if anything in the way of training or skills acquisition, especially on assembly lines where each individual task is straightforward and learned without much difficulty. In these situations, task-based participation may help to alleviate the boredom associated with repetitive routines, and at least offer the opportunity to do something different for a short period of time. In terms of employee involvement, however, the improvements may be minimal; as Herzberg (1972: 118) famously wrote, when 'adding another meaningless task to the existing one, the arithmetic is adding zero to zero'. Vertical task-based participation comprises two different forms: first, where employees are trained to undertake tasks at a different, usually higher, skill level (as in the case of semi-skilled manual workers having responsibility for routine maintenance tasks); second, where employees take on some managerial and supervisory responsibilities (for example, employees take over the planning and design of work as well as its execution). At one level, this can be a genuine attempt to give non-managerial employees more discretion to organize their work in ways which suit them, provided that they meet customer and production requirements. As such it can address anxieties that managers know little about the precise nature of work and would be better allowing employees to plan what they do within agreed parameters. On the other hand, devolving responsibility to employees may do little more than increase their stress levels and the amount of time spent thinking about work, with a detrimental effect on their home and family lives as well as their health (Hochschild 1997).

Teamworking and self-management

The final category is teamworking and self-management, both of which have been central to recent discussions about direct participation and to recipes for 'best practice' HRM. Pfeffer's (1998) list of seven practices which characterize organizational systems which produce 'profits through people' contains self-managed teams – along with other practices such as employment security, high compensation levels linked to performance and extensive training. Again, problems of broad and inconsistent definitions complicate the analysis. Some writers include quality circles in their definition of teamworking, and this really does stretch the credibility of the term. More generally, drawing on a range of definitions (Buchanan 1987; Mueller 1994; Banker et al. 1996; Thompson and Wallace 1996), teamworking and self-management are seen to incorporate the following elements: responsibility for a complete task; working without direct supervision; discretion over work methods and time; encouragement for team members to organize and multiskill; influence over recruitment to the team. Clearly, this form of direct participation is significantly more far-reaching than those considered already, most notably in terms of centrality to work processes and the level and scope of subject matter which are within the control of employees.

Because of this, some analysts would regard self-managing teams as the ultimate in direct participation, a point reinforced by studies which suggest that teams outperform individuals, that teamworking skills are critical to organizational success, and that being a team member is viewed as more beneficial to employees than working in isolation. Yet teamworking is not seen as universally positive. It may increase the pressure on employees to perform, exposing them to the vagaries of their team-mates and to interpersonal tensions. Sinclair (1992), for example, refers to the 'tyranny of teams', whilst Barker (1993: 408) suggests that self-managing teams produce 'a form of control more powerful, less apparent and more difficult to resist than that of the former bureaucracy'. Under a teamworking regime, pressure for performance comes from peers rather than from managers, and whilst some would see this as liberating and generally positive, others would view this as management control at its most subversive and effective because employees take on responsibility for peer surveillance. The fact that teamworking represents the most comprehensive form of direct participation, certainly in its more developed forms, brings the question of control referred to earlier sharply into focus, and it is a point to which we return in a later section of this chapter.

So far, we have considered the dynamics of direct participation and the various forms it takes in practice. In the remainder of the chapter, our purpose is to analyse a number of major themes and issues which relate to direct participation in general, and to focus on three of these: meanings and interpretation; impact and performance; line managers and trade unions.

Meanings and Interpretation

The imprecision in terminology, noted earlier, results in the same term being applied to quite different practices; for example, a team briefing which takes place daily just before a shift commences may take on a quite different meaning for those involved than one which is held on a quarterly basis. The latter could be seen as a bolted-on off-line activity which involves little in terms of time and has minimal impact on daily work, whilst the former is far more significant in relation to everyday work activities. Moreover, even techniques with broadly similar structures and processes may be experienced differently by those involved. For example, in one organization, task-based participation may be part of a broader move to a more progressive style, whilst in another it may be introduced as part of a downsizing package; a desperate struggle for survival with work intensification the outcome and employee compliance with the new regime being achieved because of fear of dismissal. In the latter case, participation is seen not as 'lifeboat democracy' (Cressey et al. 1985) but more as a 'sinking autocracy' (Roberts and Wilkinson 1991). Moreover, the way in which direct participation is introduced can be as significant as the form of participation chosen, and clearly this will affect the perceptions of prospective participants. Analysis based on survey data which is abstracted from organizational context can simplify and gloss over the real meaning and interpretation of these processes (Marchington et al. 1994).

There is a clear polarization in much of the writing on direct participation. On the one hand, it is seen by prescriptive writers as something of a panacea which offers benefits to all (Schonberger 1989; Byham 1991; Foy 1994), part of the re-enchantment of work and the gradual democratization of the workplace. On the other hand, direct participation can be regarded as wholly exploitative, with benefits accruing only to employers (Delbridge et al. 1992; Sewell and Wilkinson 1992). Thus, rather than employees being allocated greater power to do things, the conclusion is that any increase in authority is heavily circumscribed and maintained within the confines of managerial control systems.

Instead of employees being granted greater autonomy and discretion as the proponents of participation and empowerment would argue, the contrary interpretation is that the delegation of responsibility tends to reinforce authority and disciplinary control through more sophisticated means, e.g., electronic surveillance. Under this regime, 'space' is reduced and workers find it difficult to maintain any room for non-productive or idle time, or hide work away for 'rainy days'. Performance is analysed by breaking down the work process into constituent parts, with performance that deviates from set targets being rendered transparent and subject to discipline. Actions which appear to empower employees may actually be disempowering (Collins 1994, 1998). There are also suggestions that workers collaborate in their own exploitation; for example, the neighbour check system at Nissan meant that workers (in their role as internal customers) identified defects caused by other workers and that teams shouldered responsibility by covering for absent colleagues, thus increasing peer pressure (Garrahan and Stewart 1992). Equally, there are contrasting interpretations of whether or not direct participation – at least in its less dilute forms – increases empowerment. Whilst it may lead to a lowering of informal and interpersonal barriers between managers and non-managerial staff, this does little in itself to reduce formal hierarchies or the power of management prerogatives (Wilkinson and Willmott 1994). Rather than gaining greater power, employees assume higher levels of account-ability and responsibility, and can be more easily blamed when things go wrong. From this perspective, empowerment is more significant as rhetoric rather than practice (Delbridge 1998), being little more than the latest example of pseudo-participation (Pateman 1970). Table 14.1 summarizes these contrasting views using a dichotomy between bouquets and brickbats.

Whilst the critics who regard participation as 'management by stress' (Parker and Slaughter 1993) or 'management by sweating' (Kano 1993) have undoubtedly extended understanding, their analyses lack sophistication. As with those who celebrate participa-tion, the critics have also been too eager to accept its rhetoric at face value (Edwards et al. 1997; Collinson et al. 1998). In short, we suggest that the pictures presented are not so much wrong as partial. It is important to recognize the diversity of experience with direct participation, and to not seek an all-encompassing explanation. Many of the critical reviews can be seen as a mirror image of the prescriptive management literature, assuming also that workers are malleable and passive recipients of whatever management desires. Research findings are often polarized into a simple evaluation of participation as *either* increased work effort and intensification *or* more job satisfaction – with no allowance for the fact that much depends on context and processes (Edwards and Wright 1998). There is some evidence that the two can occur simultaneously, with more than one study noting that workers gained improvements and (in some cases) a new lease of life (McArdle et al. 1995; Cappelli et al. 1997). Work might well be more satisfying due to greater discretion over work process whilst at the same time demands are more explicit and rigorous (Clark 1993: 131; Wilkinson et al. 1997a). Adler's (1993) analysis of the General Motors-Toyota Joint Venture at Freemont (NUMMI) argues that the formal work standards developed and imposed by employers are alienating, but that procedures designed by workers in a continuous attempt to improve productivity, quality and skills can humanize even the most disciplined form of bureaucracy (p. 98). Hierarchy and standardization need not build on

Table 14.1   Contrasting meanings of participation

Bouquets	*Brickbats*
Education	Indoctrination
Empowerment	Emasculation
Liberating	Controlling
Delayering	Intensification
Teamwork	Peer-group pressure
Responsibility	Surveillance
Post-Fordism	Neo-Fordism
Blame-free culture	Identification of errors
Commitment	Compliance

Source: Wilkinson et al. 1997a

the logic of coercion but instead on the logic of learning with democratic Taylorism the result (Adler and Cole 1993). Other research has produced contrary findings. In the retail sector, Rosenthal et al. (1997: 493) reported that work was not seen as physically, intellectually or emotionally harder, and indeed the customer-service programme with its emphasis on increasing discretion may have actually reduced the stress of the job.

It is insulting to regard workers as 'cultural dupes' who are convinced totally by managerial ideas and practices (Hill 1995). It may be difficult for workers to disagree with certain discourses in principle – for example, the idea of improving quality – but once the initiative has been implemented there is ample opportunity to contest decisions and shape events. As McKinlay and Taylor (1996: 282) point out, it is misleading to view participation as 'a form of self-subordination so complete, so seamless that it stifles any dissent' and it certainly overstates management power. In their 'Factory of the Future', which is described as having a very favourable setting for corporate ideology to colonize the psyche of the workforce, the cultural terrain remained contested (McKinlay and Taylor 1996: 189). Even British-based Japanese companies, usually seen as the most sophisticated in human resource terms, 'have not solved the "problem" of worker resistance' (Palmer 1996: 141; see also, for the USA, Fucini and Fucini 1990). Consequently, it is unlikely that senior management's interpretation of empowerment is necessarily adopted without challenge or modification by other actors (Wilkinson et al. 1997a). As Thompson and Ackroyd (1995: 633) argue, 'innovatory employee practices and informal organization will continue to subvert managerial regimes'. There is little doubt that, despite the explosion of managerial initiatives designed to elicit greater effort and commitment through new methods of organization or the manipulation of meaning, their success in practice is far from guaranteed.

Impact and Performance

Evaluating the impact of direct participation is tricky for a number of reasons. First, there is a range of measures which can be used to evaluate success – such as an increase in efficiency, a shift in employee attitudes, or changes in the balance of power. There are significant differences between the Quality of Working Life (QWL) movement of the 1960s and the direct participation initiatives of more recent times, with the latter being more pragmatic and business orientated, often linked in with new production regimes and changes in working practices. Workers' needs are typically subordinate to the production or service regime. Given this, it is not surprising that, as Fernie and Metcalf (1995: 405) note, direct participation 'is not necessarily synonymous with co-operative industrial relations and possibly the "caring halo" surrounding EI masks a greater concern for the bottom line'. Second, given that direct participation is only one factor among many which can affect performance, it is difficult to disentangle the impact of direct participation from that of other variables. The notion is that by involving workers in decision making, by making the workplace more democratic and by empowering employees, certain outcomes (e.g. productivity improvements) may result. The problem, according to Cotton (1993: 13), is that 'the process whatever it is, is fuzzy'. Third, even if it were possible to find a significant association between direct participation and performance, it is very difficult to determine the direction of causality. It is just as likely that superior organizational performance leads to more positive employee attitudes as it is that the process of involvement and participation causes employees to work harder and more effectively. As Marchington (1995a: 281) observes, the view 'that direct participation is connected with high levels of commitment and organizational performance is predicated upon a series of assumptions, none of which can be taken for granted. In particular, it assumes that line managers are committed to participation and are able to make it operate effectively in the workplace.'

A number of senior managers and consultants (Wickens 1987; Morton 1994) have made grand claims about the benefits of participation. Cunningham et al. (1996: 152) indicate that their case-study organizations reported benefits in terms of cost savings, improvements in quality and increased employee commitment. However, research on high-performance work teams has identified that the context in which they operate is critical to success. Underpinning work redesign have been more participative decision making, innovative rewards and systematic career planning and development (Buchanan 1994). Work on best-practice HRM also points to the importance of interlocking practices which support and reinforce each other (see Adler 1993; Arthur 1994; Batt 1995; Berg et al. 1995; Ichniowski et al. 1996; MacDuffie 1995). Ichniowski et al. (1996: 299) conclude that a 'collage of evidence suggests that innovative workplace practices can increase performance, primarily through the use of systems of related practices that enhance worker participation, make work design less rigid and decentralise managerial tasks'. They also note that individual work practices have no effect on economic performance but 'the adoption of a *coherent and integrated system* (their emphasis) of innovative practices, including extensive recruiting and careful selection, flexible job definitions and problem solving teams, gainsharing-type compensation plans, employment security and extensive labor–management communication, substantially improve productivity and quality outcomes'. Some British evidence points in the same direction: Patterson et al. (1997) and Wood and Albanese (1995) also report the existence of high-commitment management practices, although primarily in manufacturing rather than services.

There are a number of reasons, however, to adopt a less optimistic interpretation of such studies. As Whitfield and Poole (1997: 757) point out, there are unresolved issues of causality, problems of the narrow base of the work undertaken, concerns that much of the data is self-reported by management, as well as doubts about measures of performance which are used. Even if the data indicate a causal link, we lack understanding of the processes involved and the mechanisms by which practices translate into desired outcomes.

The impact of direct participation on employee attitudes and commitment appears to be influenced by a number of factors, not least the type of scheme which is introduced. In general terms, the more comprehensive and participative the scheme the greater the impact, either in terms of positive effects on employee behaviour or in more critical assessments of the practice, if it is seen to be intrusive and unwanted rather than facilitating and empowering. For example, the impact of downward communications, such as a quarterly team briefing, is typically less than that achieved from a radical restructuring of work which involves a shift to relatively autonomous, leaderless teams. In this case, not only does the latter take up more time, it is also integral to the work process and offers greater opportunity to influence patterns of work and employment relations.

Studies by the authors (Marchington et al. 1992, 1994) have suggested that three sets of factors are important, irrespective of the specific schemes which are implemented. Broadly, it is argued that employee attitudes to direct participation (and EI in general) are dependent upon their prior experiences of particpation and work in general, management's approaches to employee relations, and the recent and projected performance of the organization. Inevitably, these are interrelated to some extent. Prior experiences of participation are crucial to our understanding of employee attitudes, and there are occasions when similar types of scheme are perceived in quite different ways by workers because of this. For example, members of staff who have had relatively little experience of participation are more likely to welcome any initiative which promises to give them some opportunity to become involved, no matter how limited. On the other hand, employees who work for organizations with a long history of EI are prone to react negatively to anything which is seen to offer less than they are accustomed to. Experience of participation may also generate a desire for more – the so-called 'taste for power' hypothesis (Drago and Wooden 1991). On its own, however, prior experience is insufficient to explain attitudes, as so much depends on the way in which employees interpret management's approaches to employee relations in general, as well as in relation to the specific schemes which are being operated. For example, at each of the organizations studied by Marchington et al. (1994: 888), 'employees were less positive about EI where they saw a tightening-up of management styles on the factory floor or in the office'. Conversely, where direct participation was one element in a more integrated set of human resource policies which were delivered by senior managers who were seen to be sincere and trustworthy – illustrated by an open management style and the removal of status distinctions – employees tended to view schemes in a much more positive light. Of course, it is relatively easy for management to maintain a consultative style in an environment where competitive and employment prospects look good, given that there can be a congruence between employee expectations and management style. On the other hand, where the future looks bleak or where there have been spates of redundancies in recent times, it is much more likely that employees will react in a negative manner to attempts by management to introduce direct participation. Not surprisingly, employees are likely to question management's motives and their own interest in schemes which do not appear to offer any hope of long-term security of employment – even if they are packaged as measures which can make work more interesting and enjoyable.

Empowerment is a central issue in considerations of direct participation, but much depends on what one means by empowerment. There is overwhelming evidence that there has not been a significant shift in the locus of power. Comparisons with industrial democracy are somewhat misleading, given that they compare normative expectations of worker directors with the practice of direct participation. If one examined the actual impact of industrial democracy on the lives of rank-and-file workers, it is clear that this was minimal. There is little doubt, of course, that direct participation schemes are set within a strict management agenda which is largely confined to operational issues and does not extend to significant power sharing or involvement in higher-level decision making (Geary 1994; Wilkinson et al. 1997a, 1997b; Edwards et al. 1997; Rees 1998; Wilkinson 1998a, 1998b). However, since neither those implementing schemes intend them to produce radical changes nor those whose working lives it affects expect this, it is hardly surprising to find that significant shifts in power do not take place, or that direct participation fails to resolve contradictions within the employment relationship. It is perhaps too easy to make comparisons between some naive vision of empowerment and the mundane reality, and then dismiss initiatives as either a conspiratorial management trap, or too inconsequential to be worthy of further analysis. If 'full participation' (Pateman 1970) is not on offer, does that mean we should dismiss partial participation as small beer? Drago and Wooden (1991) offer the view that direct, lower-level participation is introduced in order to deflect employee interest away from higher-level managerial issues. A more pragmatic line is arguably more useful. There is some evidence that workers favour the removal of 'sand in shoe' irritations (Morton 1994) – for example, 'over-the-shoulder supervision' – and welcome the opportunity to allocate work among themselves and to address work-related problems. As Gallie and White (1993) suggest, for those involved in quality circles or similar problem-solving groups, the evidence indicated that 'these were highly effective in increasing people's sense of involvement'. This is hardly earth shattering but for employees working in a factory environment, it may represent an improvement in their work lives. Even if workers suspect management motivations – increasing efficiency, rather than employee satisfaction – they can still be well disposed to direct participation. In short, attitudes may be broadly positive, but cautious and guarded, rather than credulous (Wilkinson and Ackers 1995: 86).

The Role of Line Managers and Trade Unions

The prescriptive management literature suggests an optimistic scenario about the role and prospects for line managers who operate under new paradigms of participation. The view is that they move from being holders of expert power to facilitators (or from 'cops to coaches') and hence take on new skills and responsibilities. However, this picture is at odds with research investigating the reactions of line managers and supervisors to direct participation (Bradley and Hill 1983; Klein 1984; Marchington et al. 1992; Denham et al. 1997) some of which suggests that they find participative management to be a burden. As Rathkey (1984) notes 'the more it (participation) existed in the company, the more it might be said that they disliked it' (p. 125). Broadly speaking, we can categorize the responses of line managers into three categories.

First, there is some evidence to suggest that line managers do not believe in the principles underlying direct participation, especially those schemes which are more far reaching. Attempts to involve and empower workers are often regarded as 'soft management' or pandering to the workers, the result of initiatives promulgated by 'long-haired idealists' at head office who have little understanding of the realities of life on the shopfloor where 'a branding iron is seen as a more suitable instrument to work with than any concept of employee involvement' (Wilkinson et al. 1993: 32). This illustrates succinctly the gap between the values of senior management and those of line managers and supervisors.

Second, while some line managers may see the value in principle of direct participation, they have concerns as to its actual operation in the context of current organizational structures and support mechanisms. This relates to conflict between participative practices, such as briefing and quality circles, and the importance of commercial considerations, for example immediate production or customer service requirements. In such a context, employee relations considerations are apt to find themselves secondary to production or service goals. The lack of reward given to line managers for their efforts in this area, and in some cases their lack of skill in implementing new methods due to lack of training, in itself provides telling insights about the relative importance attached to direct participation by senior management and the fact that inconsistent messages are disseminated by them (Fenton O'Creevy and Nicholson 1994: I).

Third, a common anxiety among line managers, especially supervisors, is concern with their own future, whether or not they will continue to have jobs and, if so, the extent to which these are likely to differ dramatically from current activities. A paradox of change operates here. Arguably, jobs at the interface between managers and managed are likely to alter most, but equally these individuals are also required to play a critical change agent role in relation to direct participation. Given a mix of disbelief and agnosticism in their views, and a lack of skills and confidence in their ability, in addition to uncertainty as to the value which senior management attaches to direct participation, it is hardly surprising that problems occur. What is clear from the above analysis, however, is that a major part of the problem is the failure of senior managers to provide appropriate support in terms of training and other systems and structures, rather than blame being placed on the line managers themselves (Edwards and Wright 1998; Cunningham and Hyman 1995).

The relationship between direct participation and trade unions is a complex one. A variety of outcomes is possible, ranging from compatibility or indeed synergy through to tension and competition between management and union representatives to secure influence. Alternatively, the relationship may be relatively unaffected with direct participation and trade unions co-existing because they are seen to operate in quite separate zones. It has been common to suggest that there are a priori reasons why direct participation may marginalize unions; for example, Kumar (1995: 40) argues that new management initiatives (including participation) 'pose serious challenges to unions, threatening their traditional role of defending and advancing worker rights' and have the potential to seriously harm unions. Beale (1994: 120) suggests that participation schemes represent 'a significant challenge to the traditional influence of trade unions in the workplace. Employee involvement programmes provide an alternative source of information, ideas and interpretation of workplace experiences, to that provided by the union.' EI programmes actively promote a new culture in competition with the traditional explanations and culture communicated by the union. A similar view has been taken by Kelly (1988: 265) who argues that 'by linking elements of workers' pay to company performance, providing information about company performance, and encouraging workers to contribute their own ideas for its improvement, the hope is that conflicts of interest can be weakened. Clearly, schemes of this kind, if successful, would pose a considerable threat to the role and possibly to the very existence of trade unions.' There are certainly examples of this taking place where managers introduce a barrage of direct communications – such as briefing or videos – aimed directly at employees with the objective of reducing their dependence on the unions as the main source of information, and making it more difficult for union representatives to challenge management's interpretation of issues.

There have been other examples where employers have not implemented direct participation with the explicit aim of undermining unions, although a consequence of managerial action was to marginalize the union. A more open approach to employee relations which includes a package of direct-participation measures could help to erode distrust, leading employees to identify more with their employer, and hence diminish the role of the union. This may be only temporary if employers are unable to sustain product market success and maintain high wages and benefits. In situations where unions lack membership or recognition, it is possible that a substitution effect takes place in that direct participation fills in the gaps otherwise occupied by trade unions. The obvious UK examples of this are IBM and Marks Spencer which both have reputations for well-developed systems of communication and upward problem solving. Fernie and Metcalf (1995: 404) note that according to WIRS3, most workplaces had some form of communication between management and labour, but that 40 per cent had made an effort to improve employee involvement in the three years prior to the survey, alongside the 'crumbling of collective representation'. However, it should be recalled first that direct participation operates in these organizations together with consultation, and it may not work without this, and, second, on the whole, non-union firms are less likely to operate HRM practices than are unionized workplaces (Sisson 1993).

There are also situations where a degree of complementarity can exist between union organization and at least some parts of the direct-participation mix. In the Employment Department study (Marchington et al. 1992), this occurred at about half of the unionized workplaces, although the links tended to be stronger in relation to indirect participation. In one of the chemical firms studied, part of the process of change included a wide-ranging involvement exercise in which senior managers made extensive efforts to maintain a good working relationship with the senior stewards and not to alienate them by introducing changes without union support. The senior stewards were aware of the potential dangers of being 'incorporated' into management, but saw their involvement in the change programme as essential for the future well-being of their members and the company. In this context, the union representatives who were members of the joint consultative committee were happy for team briefing to be introduced as a vehicle for establishing better internal communications (Wilkinson et al. 1993).

Another scenario is where direct participation and unions run in parallel, with no obvious or overt relationship between them, in a 'dual' approach to the management of employment (Storey 1992: 258; Sisson 1993: 208). In these cases, union representatives may take an agnostic view of schemes such as team briefing, seeing them as largely irrelevant to the union's role and unlikely to affect collective bargaining structure. Indeed, it is difficult for stewards to argue against direct participation which is designed to improve communications, largely because problems relating to breakdowns in information flow are regularly pointed out in attitude surveys as a major concern by employees and unions. Finally, trade unions can also limit the development of direct participation. This situation occurs where employees are suspicious of management intentions in a context of low-trust relations, but also where unions retain the influence and ability to mobilize collective resistance. At the Post Office during the late 1980s, there was significant resistance to team briefing and TQM, partly because union leaders felt it was an attempt to alter and subvert the communication process.

Conclusions

A major theme running through this chapter has been that it is simplistic either to celebrate direct participation as a panacea for organizational ills or equally to dismiss it as a failure because it has made so few inroads into transforming the employment relationship. To celebrate direct participation as empowerment is to ignore the major operational and human obstacles to its implementation (Marchington 1995b) whereas to dismiss participation because it does not fundamentally challenge existing relations between capital and labour is to overstate its potential contribution. Instead, our argument is that so much depends on the context in which direct participation is introduced, in addition to management styles, employee expectations and other human resource processes, as well as on the types of schemes themselves.

Much of the literature assumes a simple differentiation between management and employee perspectives and fails to acknowledge that there are widely differing sets of actors in the workplace – differentiated by function, level in the organizational hierarchy, geographical location, previous educational and work experiences, for example – with different views and ambitions. Marchington et al. (1992) found that direct participation was notable for its diversity and variety in practice, for the use by management of both direct and indirect participation, and for several different types of each form being operational at the same workplace. On some occasions, there appeared to be an overall rationale behind this mix of participation initiatives, but in many cases they were the result of competing initiatives driven by different departments, functions or individuals, overlapping with and directly contradicting each other, and reflecting the quite diverse perceptions of different groups of managers. Although, in the context of direct participation, more certainly does not mean better, recent attempts to develop works councils in organizations which already practise well-established schemes of direct participation might be more meaningful given that both focus on quite different sets of issues and operate at different levels in the organizational hierarchy.

Central to our understanding of employee responses is the issue of trust (Procter et al. 1994/5). A paradox of new management techniques is that whilst they require employee commitment and high-trust relations to make them work, simultaneously they may erode any basis for such relations. This takes us back to the critical issue of context: individuals empowered to make decisions may be unwilling to use their discretion if they feel continually under the watchful eye of 'Big Brother'. This is perhaps most obvious in the public sector as 'technologies of distrust' (Miller 1997) and the audit society (Power 1997) undermine professional judgement, or at least place such judgement under the gaze of rational (accounting) expertise. Not only might such approaches fail to deliver what is expected, they may also lead to dysfunctional and unintended consequences as employees subvert the system and undermine management. Indeed, there is evidence that whilst management may define direct participation in a particular and narrow way, workers themselves can use the discourse of empowerment and quality to bring managers into line with their own expectations, questioning the management agenda and possibly trying to construct their own (Rosenthal et al. 1997; Wilkinson et al. 1997a)

Evidence indicates that most British firms have implemented direct participation in a half-hearted and partial way, adopting techniques in an *ad hoc* and piecemeal manner, and falling short of the holistic, integrated approach which research suggests is required to make EI work effectively. Faddism and fashion in management approaches has been noted by a number of writers (e.g. Gill and Whittle 1993; Huczynski 1993; Hilmer and Donaldson 1996; Micklethwait and Woolridge 1996), and we ourselves have written about this in the area of participation (Marchington et al. 1993). Since there is a relatively low technical base to participation initiatives, compared to information technology or new product design for example, it has been easy for managers to introduce new practices without any substantial professional training or development. Accordingly, acting as a champion for teamworking – for example – might offer managers a cheap and easy 'solution' to problems as well as a route to enhance their own promotion prospects. There is little doubt that the prescriptive management literature underestimates the difficulties in implementing direct participation as well as the costs involved, often ignoring requirements for training, for new reward systems and integration. It could be argued, therefore, that many of the problems with participation are less to do with the concept itself and rather more related to short-sighted or misguided attempts at implementation.

We have seen that participation waxes and wanes over time, taking on different forms at different times, and often with several schemes operating alongside each other at the same workplace. Critics have tended to focus on the problems, and in particular the fact that schemes seem to have a limited shelf-life, in order to argue that these sorts of initiative are destined to fail largely because they are unable to resolve contradictions inherent in the employment relationship. We would not disagree with the conclusion that direct participation is unlikely to transform employment relations fundamentally, and that problems are bound to arise – as with any management practice – once schemes lose their initial appeal, especially if they have been implemented in a faddish and non-integrative manner. On the other hand, it is fascinating to note that managements return repeatedly to the idea of participation in their search for more effective ways to run organizations and to the notion that it makes sense to involve employees in some way or other. This suggests that direct participation does have something to offer, both to employers and employees, but that it may be unrealistic to expect these sorts of scheme to remove problems from work, given that the employment relationship in any organization is built upon both conflict and co-operation.

References and further reading

Ackers, P., Marchington, M., Wilkinson, A. and Goodman, J. 1992: The use of cycles? explaining employee involvement in the 1990s. *Industrial Relations Journal*, **23**(4), 268–83.

Adler, P. 1993: Time and Motion Regained. *Harvard Business Review*, January–February, 97–108.

Adler, P. and Cole, R. 1993: NUMMI V Uddevealla: a rejoinder. *Sloan Management Review*, Winter, 45–9.

Appelbaum, E. and Batt, R. 1995: Worker Participation in Diverse Settings: Does the Form Affect the Outcome, and, if so, Who Benefits? *British Journal of Industrial Relations*, **33**(3), 353–78.

Arthur, J. 1994: Effects of Human Resource Systems on Manufacturing Performance and Turnover. *Academy of Management Journal*, **37**, 670–87.

Banker, R., Field, J., Schroeder, R. and Sinha, K. 1996: Impact of Work Teams on Manufacturing Performance: A Longitudinal Field Study. *Academy of Management Journal*, **39**(4), 867–90.

Barker, J. 1993: Tightening the Iron Cage: Concertive Control in Self-Managing Teams, *Administrative Science Quarterly*, **38**, 408–37.

Batt, R. 1995: Performance and Welfare Effects of Work Restructuring: Evidence from Telecommunications Services, Cambridge, MA: PhD Dissertation, MIT Sloan School of Management.

Beale, D. 1994: *Driven by Nissan? A Critical Guide to New Management Techniques*, London: Lawrence and Wishart.

Berg, P., Appelbaum, E., Bailey, T. and Kalleberg, A. 1995: The Performance Effects of Modular Production in the Apparel Industry. Paper presented at the What Works at Work? conference, January 1995.

Black, J. and Ackers, P. 1988: The Japanisation of British Industry: A Case Study of Quality Circles in the Carpet Industry, *Employee Relations*, **10**(6), 9–16.

Bougen, P., Ogden, S. and Outram, Q. 1988: Profit sharing and the cycle of control. *Sociology*, **22**(4), 607–29.

Bradley, K. and Hill, S. 1983: After Japan: the quality circle transplant and productive efficiency, *British Journal of Industrial Relations*, **21**, 291–311.

Brannen, P. 1983: *Authority and Participation in Industry*. London: Batsford.

Brannen, P., Batstone, E., Fatchett, D. and White, P. 1976: *The Worker Directors*. London: Hutchinson.

Buchanan, D. 1987: Job Enrichment is Dead: Long Live High Performance Work Design, *Personnel Management*, May, 40–3.

Buchanan, D. 1994: Principles and Practices in Work Design. In K. Sisson (ed.), *Personnel Management*, Oxford: Blackwell, 85–116.

Byham, W. 1991: *Zapp! The Lightning of Empowerment*. London: Century Business.

Cappelli, P., Bassi, L., Katz, H., Knoke, D., Osterman, P. and Useem, M. 1997: *Change at Work*, New York: Oxford University Press.

Clark, J. 1993, Full Flexibility and Self-Supervision in an Automated Factory. In J. Clark (ed.), *Human Resource Management and Technical Change*, London: Sage, 116–36.

Claydon, T. and Doyle, M. 1996: Trusting Me, Trusting You? The Ethics of Employee Empowerment. *Personnel Review*, **25**(6), 13–25.

Cole, R., Baadayan, P., Joseph, B. and White, B. 1993: Quality, Participation and Competitiveness. *California Management Review*, **35**(3), 68–81.

Collard, R. and Dale, B. 1989: Quality Circles. In K. Sisson (ed.), *Personnel Management in Britain*, Oxford: Blackwell.

Collins, D. 1994: The disempowering logic of empowerment. *Empowerment in Organisations*, **2**(2), 14–21.

Collins, D. 1998: Is Empowerment Just a Fad? Process, Power and Culture in the Management of Empowerment. *Systemist*, **20**(1), 53–68.

Collinson, M., Rees, C., Edwards, P. and Inness, L. 1988: *Involvement but no Empowerment: a case study analysis of quality management and employee relations*. DTI report.

Cotton, J. 1993: *Employee Involvement*. Newbury Park, CA: Sage.

Cressey, P., MacInnes, J. and Eldridge, J. 1985: *Just Managing: Authority and Participation in Industry*. Milton Keynes: Open University Press.

Cully, M., O'Reilly A., Millward, N., Forth, J., Woodland, S., Dix, G. and Bryson, A. 1998: *The 1998 Workplace Employee Relations Survey: First Findings*. Department of Trade and Industry, London: HMSO.

Cunningham, I. and Hyman, J. 1995: Transforming the HRM Vision into Reality: the Role of Line Managers and Supervisors in Implementing Change. *Employee Relations*, **27**(8), 5–20.

Cunningham, I., Hyman, J. and Baldry, C. 1996: Empowerment: the power to do what? *Industrial Relations Journal*, **27**(2), 143–54.

Davis, E. and Lansbury, R. (eds) 1996: *Managing Together: Consultation and Participation in the Workplace*. Melbourne: Longman.

Delbridge, R. 1998: *Life on the Line in Contemporary Manufacturing*. Oxford: Oxford University Press.

Delbridge, R., Turnbull, P. and Wilkinson, B. 1992: Pushing back the Frontiers: Management Control and Work Intensification Under JIT/TQM Factory Regimes. *New Technology, Work and Employment*, **7**(2), 97–106.

Denham, N., Ackers, P. and Travers, C. 1997: Doing yourself out of a job? How middle managers cope with empowerment. *Employee Relations*, **19**(2), 147–59.

Drago, R. and Wooden, M. 1991: The Determinants of Participatory Management. *British Journal of Industrial Relations*, **29**(2), 177–204.

Drucker, P. 1988: The coming of the new organization. *Harvard Business Review*, January–February, 45–53.

Edwards, P. Collinson, M. and Rees, C. 1997: The Determinants of Employee Responses to Total Quality Management. Working paper.

Edwards, P. and Wright, M. 1998: HRM and Commitment: A Case Study of Teamworking. In P. Sparrow and M. Marchington (eds), *HRM: The New Agenda*, London: Pitman.

Fernie, S. and Metcalf, D. 1995: Participation, Contingent Pay, Representation and Workplace Performance: Evidence from Great Britain. *British Journal of Industrial Relations*, **33**(3), 379–416.

Fenton O'Creevy, M. and Nicholson, N. 1994: *Middle Managers: Their Contribution to Employee Involvement*. Employment Department Research Series No. 28.

Foy, N. 1994: *Empowering People at Work*. London: Gower.

Fucini, J. and Fucini, S. 1990: *Working for the Japanese*. New York: Free Press.

Gallie, D. and White, M. 1993: *Employee Commitment and the Skills Revolution*. London: Policy Studies Institute.

Garrahan, P. and Stewart, P. 1992: *The Nissan Enigma*. London: Cassell.

Geary, J. 1994: Task Participation: Employees' Participation Enabled or Constrained. In K. Sisson (ed), *Personnel Management*, Oxford: Blackwell, 634–61.

Gill, J. and Whittle, S. 1993: Management by Panacea: Accounting for Transience, *Journal of Management Studies*, **30**(2), 281–95.

Guest, D., Peccei, R. and Thomas, A. 1993: The Impact of Employee Involvement in Organizational Commitment and 'Them and Us' Attitudes. *Industrial Relations Journal*, **24**(3), 191–200.

Hennestad, B. 1998: Empowering by de-powering: towards an HR strategy for realizing the power of empowerment. *International Journal of Human Resource Management*, **9**(5), 934–53.

Herzberg, F. 1972: One More Time: How Do You Motivate Employees? In L. Davis and J. Taylor, *Design of Jobs*, London: Penguin.

Hill, S. 1991: How do you Manage a Flexible Firm? The Total Quality Model. *Work Employment and Society*, **5**(3), 397–415.

Hill, S. 1995: From Quality Circles to Total Quality Management. In A. Wilkinson and H. Willmott (eds), *Making Quality Critical*, London: Routledge.

Hill, S. and Wilkinson, A. 1995: In Search of TQM. *Employee Relations*, **17**(3), 8–23.

Hilmer, F. G. and Donaldson, L. 1996: *Management Redeemed: Debunking the Fads that Undermine our Corporations*. New York: Free Press.

Hochschild, A. 1997: *The Time Bind: When Work Becomes Home and Home Becomes Work*. New York: Metropolitan Books.

Huczynski, A. 1993: *Management Gurus*. London: Routledge.

Huselid, M. 1995: The Impact of Human Resource Management Practices on Turnover, Production and Corporate Financial Performance. *Academy of Management Journal*, **38**, 635–72.

Hyman, J. and Mason, B. 1995: *Managing Employee Involvement and Participation*. London: Sage.

Ichniowski, C. 1990: Human Resource Management Systems and the Performance of US Manufacturing Business. National Bureau of Economic Research working paper no. 3449.

Ichniowski, C., Kochan, T., Levine, D., Olsen, C. and Strauss, G. 1996: What Works at Work: Overview and Assessment. *Industrial Relations*, **35**(3), 299–333.

Kano, N. 1993: A Perspective on Quality Activities in American Firms. *California Management Review*, **35**(3), 12–31.

Kanter, R. M. 1989: The new managerial work. *Harvard Business Review*, November–December, 85–92.

Kelly, J. 1982: *Scientific Management, Job Redesign and Work Performance*. London: Academic Press.

Kelly, J. 1988: *Trade Unions and Socialist Politics*. London: Verso.

Klein, J. 1984: Why supervisors resist employee involvement. *Harvard Business Review*, **84**(5), 87–95.

Kochan, T., Lansbury, R. and MacDuffie, J. P. (eds) 1997: *After Lean Production: Evolving Employment Practices in the World Auto Industry*. New York: Cornell University Press.

Kumar, P. 1995: Canadian Labour's Response to Work Reorganisation. *Economic and Industrial Democracy*, **16**(1), 39–78.

Lashley, C. 1997: *Empowering Service Excellence: Beyond the Quick Fix*. London: Cassell.

Lawler, E. E. 1992: *The Ultimate Advantage*. San Francisco: Jossey-Bass.

Lawler, E. E. 1996: *From the Ground Up*. San Francisco: Jossey-Bass.

McArdle, L., Rowlinson, M., Proctor, S., Hassard, J. and Forrester, P. 1995: Total Quality Management and Participation: Employee Empowerment or Exploitation? In A. Wilkinson and H. Willmott (eds), *Making Quality Critical*, London: Routledge.

MacDuffie, J. P. 1995: Human Resource Bundles and Manufacturing Performance: Organizational Logic and Flexible Production Systems in the World Auto Industry. *Industrial and Labour Relations Review*, **48**, 197–221.

MacInnes, J. 1987: *Thatcherism at Work*. Milton Keynes: Open University Press.

McKinlay, A. and Taylor, P. 1996: Through the Looking Glass: Foucault and the Politics of Production. In A. McKinlay, and P. Foucault Taylor, *Management and Organizational Theory*. London: Sage, 173–90.

Marchington, M. 1992: *Managing the Team*. Oxford: Blackwell.

Marchington, M. 1995a: Employee Involvement. In J. Storey (ed.), *HRM: A Critical Text*, London: Routledge.

Marchington, M. 1995b: Fairy Tales and Magic Wands: New Employment Practices in Perspective. *Employee Relations*, **17**(1), 51–66.

Marchington, M., Goodman, J., Wilkinson, A. and Ackers, P. 1992: *New Developments in Employee Involvement*, Employment Department Research Paper No. 2.

Marchington, M., Wilkinson, A., Ackers, P. and Goodman, J. 1993: The Influence of Managerial Relations on Waves of Employee Involvement. *British Journal of Industrial Relations*, **31**(4), 553–76.

Marchington, M., Wilkinson, A., Ackers, P. and Goodman, J. 1994: Understanding the Meaning of Participation: Views from the Workplace. *Human Relations*, **47**(8), 867–94.

Micklethwait, J. and Woolridge, A. 1996: *The Witch Doctors: What the Management Gurus are Saying, Why it Matters and How to Make Sense of it*. London: Heinemann.

Miller, P. 1997: Dilemmas of Accountability: the Limits of Accounting. In P. Hirst and S. Khilnani (eds), *Reinventing Democracy*, Oxford: Blackwell.

Millward, N. and Stevens, M. 1986: *British Workplace Industrial Relations, 1980–1984*. Aldershot: Gower.

Millward, N., Stevens, M., Smart, D. and Hawes, W. 1992: Workplace Industrial Relations in Transition. Aldershot: Dartmouth.

Morton, C. 1994: *Becoming World Class*. London: Macmillan.

Mueller, F. 1994: Teams Between Hierarchy and Commitment: Change Strategies and their Internal Environment. *Journal of Management Studies*, **31**(3), 383–403.

Oliver, N. and Wilkinson B. 1992: *The Japanisation of British Industry*, 2nd edn. Oxford: Blackwell.

Palmer, G. 1996: Reviving Resistance: the Japanese Factory Floor in Britain. *Industrial Relations Journal*, **27**(2), 129–42.

Parker, M. and Slaughter, J. 1988: *Choosing Sides: Unions and the Team Concept*. Boston, MA: South End Press.

Parker, M. and Slaughter, J. 1993: Should the Labour Movement Buy TQM? *Journal of Organizational Change Management*, **6**(4), 43–56.

Pateman, C. 1970: *Participation and Democratic Theory*: Cambridge: Cambridge University Press.

Patterson, M., West, M., Lawthorn, R. and Nickell, S. 1997: *Impact of People Management Practices on Business Performance*. London: IPD Report No. 22.

Peters, T. 1989: *Thriving on Chaos*. London: Pan.

Pfeffer, J. 1994: *Competitive Advantage Through People*. Boston: MA, Harvard Business School Press.

Pfeffer, J. 1998: *The Human Equation: Building Profits by Putting People First*. Boston MA: Harvard Business School Press.

Piore, M. and Sabel, C. 1983: *The Second Industrial Divide*. New York: Basic Books.

Poole, M. 1986: *Towards a New Industrial Democracy: Workers Participation in Industry*. London: Routledge & Kegan Paul.

Power, M. 1997: *The Audit Society*. Oxford: Oxford University Press.

Procter, S., Hassard, J. and Rowlinson, M. 1994/5: Introducing Cellular Manufacturing: Operations, Human Resources and High-trust Dynamics. *Human Resource Management Journal*, **5**(2), 46–64.

Ramsay, H. 1976: Participation: the Shopfloor View. *British Journal of Industrial Relations*, **12**(2), 128–41.

Ramsay, H. 1977: Cycles of Control. Workers Participation in Sociological and Historical Perspective. *Sociology*, **11**(3), 481–506.

Ramsay, H. 1991: Re-inventing the Wheel? A Review of the Development and Performance of Employee Involvement, *Human Resource Management Journal*, **1**(4), 1–22.

Rathkey, P. 1984: Participation and Industrial Democracy: The Shopfloor View. Stockton on Tees: Jim Conway Foundation.

Rees, C. 1998: Empowerment through Quality Management. Employee Accounts from Inside a Bank, a Hotel, and Two Factories. In C. Mabey, D. Skinner and T. Clark (eds), *Experiencing Human Resource Management*, London: Sage.

Roberts, I. and Wilkinson, A. 1991: Participation and Purpose: Boilermakers to Bankers, *Critical Perspectives on Accounting*, **2**, 385–413.

Rosenthal, P., Hill, S. and Peccei, R. 1997: Checking out service: evaluating excellence, HRM and TQM in retailing. *Work, Employment and Society*, **11**(3), 481–503.

Schonberger, R. 1989: *World Class Manufacturing*. London: Hutchinson Business Books.

Schonberger, R. 1990: *Building a Chain of Customers*. London: Hutchinson Business Books.

Sewell, G. and Wilkinson, B. 1992: Empowerment or Emasculation? Shopfloor surveillance in a total quality organisation. In P. Blyton and P. Turnbull (eds), *Reassessing Human Resource Management*, London: Sage, 97–115.

Shaw, K. and Prenneshi, G. 1995: The Impact of Human Resource Management Practices on Productivity. Working Paper No. 5333, Cambridge MA: National Bureau of Economic Research.

Sinclair, A. 1992: The Tyranny of a Team Ideology. *Organization Studies*, **13**(4), 611–26.

Sisson, K. 1993: In Search of HRM. *British Journal of Industrial Relations*, **31**(2), 201–10.

Sisson, K. 1997: *New Forms in Work Organisation: Can Europe Realise its Potential?* Dublin: European Foundation for the Improvement of Living and Working Conditions.

Smith, C., Child, J. and Rowlinson, M. 1990: *Reshaping Work: the Cadbury Experience*. Cambridge: Cambridge University Press.

Starkey, K. and McKinlay, A. 1993: *Strategy and the Human Resource*. Oxford: Blackwell.

Storey, J. 1992: *Developments in the Management of Human Resources*. Oxford, Blackwell.

Storey, J. (ed.) 1995: *Human Resource Management: A Critical Text*. London: Routledge.

Tebbutt, M. and Marchington, M. 1997: Look Before You Speak: Gossip and the Insecure Workplace. *Work Employment and Society*, **11**(4), 713–35.

Thompson, P. and Ackroyd, S. 1995: All Quiet on the Workplace Front: A Critique of Recent Trends in British Industrial Sociology. *Sociology*, **29**(4), 615–35.

Thompson, P. and Wallace, T. 1996: Redesigning Production through Teamworking: Case Studies from the Volvo Truck Corporation. *International Journal of Operations and Production Management*, **16**(2), 103–18.

Townley, B. 1989: Communications. In K. Sisson (ed.), *Personnel Management in Britain*, 1st edn, Blackwell: Oxford, 595–633.

Turner, L. 1997: Participation, Democracy and Efficiency in the US workplace. *Industrial Relations Journal*, **28**(4), 309–13.

Walton, R. 1985: From Control to Commitment in the Workplace. *Harvard Business Review*, (March–April), 77–84.

Whitfield, K. and Poole, M. 1997: Organising Employment for High Performance. *Organization Studies*, **18**(5), 745–64.

Wickens, P. 1987: *The Road to Nissan*. London: Macmillan.

Wilkinson, A. 1998a: Empowerment. In M. Poole and M. Warner (eds), *International Encyclopaedia of Business and Management Handbook of Human Resource Management*, London: ITB Press, 507–17.

Wilkinson, A. 1998b: Empowerment: theory and practice. *Personnel Review*, **27**(1), 40–56.

Wilkinson, A. and Ackers, P. 1995: When Two Cultures Meet: Industrial Relations at Japanco. *International Journal of Human Resource Management*, **6**(4), 849–71.

Wilkinson, A., Godfrey, G. and Marchington, M. 1997a: Bouquets, Brickbats and Blinkers: Total Quality Management and Employee Involvement in Practice. *Organization Studies*, **18**(5), 799–820.

Wilkinson, A., Marchington, M., Ackers, P. and Goodman, J. 1992: Total Quality Management and Employee Involvement. *Human Resource Management Journal*, **2**(4), 1–20.

Wilkinson, A., Marchington, M., Ackers, P. and Goodman, J. 1993: Refashioning the employment relationship: the experience of a chemical company over the last decade. *Personnel Review*, **22**(3), 22–38.

Wilkinson, A., Redman, T., Snape, E. and Marchington, M. 1997b: *Managing with Total Quality Management: Theory and Practice*. London: Macmillan.

Wilkinson, A. and Willmott, H. 1994: Total Quality: Asking Critical Questions. *Academy of Management Review*, **20**(4), 789–91.

Womack, J., Jones, D. and Roos, D. 1990: *The Machine that Changed the World*. New York: Rawson Associates.

Wood, S. and Albanese, M. T. 1995: Can We Speak of High Commitment Management on the Shopfloor? *Journal of Management Studies*, **32**(2), 215–47.

15

Management and Trade Unions: Towards Social Partnership?

Stephanie Tailby and David Winchester

This chapter analyses the changing relationship between management and trade unions in Britain. In particular, it considers the prospects for the development of a qualitatively different form of indirect participation or employee representation – namely, social partnership between employers, trade unions and employees. A number of widely publicized partnership agreements concluded in the 1990s seemed to offer each of the parties significant gains: employers were able to secure a greater degree of job flexibility and a stronger commitment of employees and union representatives to organizational goals; trade unions were offered a more co-operative form of involvement in enterprise-level employment regulation; and employees were promised greater employment security and the opportunity to participate in new forms of consultation.

The debate on the meaning of social partnership, however, has produced a variety of conflicting interpretations of its essential features and its significance for the future of employment relations. There is little agreement between trade union leaders, employers, politicians and academics on the contribution that social partnership might make to the reform of industrial relations. There is disagreement also on the extent to which partnership agreements represent an innovative form of enterprise-employment relations, the prospects for their diffusion across different sectors, and their sustainability under different product and labour-market conditions. Finally, there is an ambiguous relationship between the rhetoric and practice of recent British partnership agreements and the more deeply rooted institutional expressions of social partnership found in many member states of the European Union.

These issues will be explored in the following way. First, the political and economic background to the debate on social partnership will be outlined. It will be argued that major shifts in public policy and economic conditions over the last few decades have eroded trade union organization and power, and constrained employers' ability to realize the anticipated benefits of collective bargaining reforms and new human resource management policies. Second, the principles of social partnership, and the practice of partnership agreements revealed in case study and survey evidence, will be outlined and assessed in the light of the wider academic debate. Finally, the prospects for the diffusion and sustain-ability of partnership agreements will be reviewed alongside broader conceptions of social partnership, and in the light of differences in the legal and institutional context in Britain and other European countries.

Background to the Partnership Debate

The political and economic context

Over the last 30 years, the organizational strength and ideological values of trade unions, and the personnel policies and practices of employers, have changed more decisively in Britain than in most advanced capitalist countries. These changes can be explained partly by the sharp fluctuations in government policies, designed to reform the system of industrial relations, and erratic shifts in government economic policies. Both aspects of government policy were influenced by the increasing pressure of international competition arising from the policies of multinational companies and the movement towards economic integration in the European Union.

More than 30 years ago, the Royal Commission on Trade Unions and Employers' Associations was established by a Labour Government in response to the widespread belief that trade union power was the root cause of the Britain's economic malaise. Its Report (Donovan 1968) disappointed many critics by offering a strong defence of the role of trade unions within a largely voluntarist industrial relations system. None the less, it recom-mended that management should take the initiative in the reform of collective bargaining at establishment or enterprise levels. The subsequent reforms in pay structures, work organization and procedural agreements were implemented in an uneven and piecemeal manner in the 1970s, but they led to some important changes in British industrial relations.

First, the reforms contributed to a decisive shift away from industry-wide or multi-employer bargaining in the private sector. In sharp contrast to the legally regulated 'dual system' of industry-level collective bargaining and establishment- and enterprise-level employee representation found in most other European countries, the reforms speeded up the movement towards single-employer, enterprise-level bargaining, dependent on the willingness of employers to recognize trade unions. Second, the process of bargaining reform – alongside the significant programme of employment legislation introduced by the 1974–79 Labour government as part of its 'social contract' with the TUC – strengthened trade union organization and legitimacy. In large workplaces especially, trade union recognition was extended to non-manual employees, including senior grades of staff. Also there was a growth in the coverage of the closed shop, and the increasing number of shop stewards were provided with more generous facilities and time off for union duties. These developments could be seen as a form of 'enlightened managerialism' by personnel directors, based on the calculation that an increase in trade union legitimacy was a prerequisite for wide-ranging reforms that would strengthen overall management control by securing more predicatability in industrial relations (Fox 1974; Purcell 1979). As Purcell and Sisson (1983) argued, however, the scope of collective bargaining reform was limited. Only a minority of employers developed a 'sophisticated consultative' employment-relations management style designed to maximize union co-operation in the achievement of enterprise goals through extensive consultative procedures. In the majority of work-places, the pragmatic and opportunistic 'standard modern' management style did not transform the typically adversarial patterns of bargaining.

The political and economic context of management–union relations in the 1980s and early-1990s could scarcely have been more different. A lengthy, continuous period of Conservative government – first elected after the widespread industrial conflict of the 'winter of discontent' in 1979 – facilitated the introduction of monetarist economic policies, restrictive union legislation, public-sector privatization and compulsory competi-tive tendering, and labour-market reforms. In combination, these measures dramatically reversed the gains in organizational strength and influence that trade unions had made in the previous decade. The policies – and the free-market ideology on which they were based – were designed explicitly to undermine trade union influence in the workplace, and to exclude it altogether from national political representation. This marked a sharp break with the broad political consensus embracing all post-1945 governments in Britain, and had no counterpart elsewhere in Europe.

Employers' policy options

The policies of Conservative governments obviously increased the freedom of employers to experiment with industrial relations policies. Some chose to flout established bargaining procedures and impose new working practices and harsher work regimes on their work-force. Notable examples of 'macho-management' occurred in the nationalized industries where the government was willing to underwrite the costs of disruption caused by aggressive employers' policies in strongly unionized sectors. More generally, employers were willing to work with trade unions, rather than confront or bypass them. Such strategies of co-operation, however, were an indication of the increasing fragility and defensiveness of workplace trade unionism in the economic context of the time (Legge 1988). The deep recession of the early 1980s was followed by a period of strong economic growth in the mid 1980s and another very harsh recession in the early 1990s. High levels of unemployment and widespread job insecurity in manufacturing industries encouraged many forms of concession bargaining. Employers were able to cut labour costs through job losses and changes in working practices, and to minimize the resistance of trade unions – already weakened by punitive legislation – by increasing the real earnings of their slimmed-down workforce.

From the mid 1980s onwards, some employers sought an alternative path of industrial relations reform through new human resource management (HRM) policies. As the origins, aspirations and limitations of HRM are discussed in considerable detail in chapter 1, the focus here is on two more limited questions. First, to what extent did the principles and practices of HRM challenge the legitimacy of trade unions and the traditional pluralist values of British industrial relations, given that they had already been eroded significantly by Conservative government policies by the mid 1980s? Guest (1989) argued that the values of HRM are both unitarist, in that they assume 'no underlying and inevitable differences of interest between management and workers', and also individualist, in that they emphasize 'the individual – organization linkage in preference to operating through group or representative systems' (p. 43). He also argued that of the four policy goals of

HRM – strategic integration, quality, flexibility and commitment – it was the last which presented the greatest challenge for trade unions (Guest 1995). If employers succeeded in winning hearts and minds of their employees, the oppositional role of trade unions would become less tenable.

Whilst it is possible for employees to develop a dual commitment to their employer and to their union, Guest (1995) suggested that this is most likely within 'a positive industrial relations climate . . . in which both the company and union have distinctive roles' (pp. 115–16). For example, the dual system of employment relations in Germany embodies a formal, legal distinction between issues covered by collective bargaining between unions and employers' associations at sectoral level and other issues enshrined in the law and practice of works councils at enterprise and establishment levels. Whilst this has not resolved all of the problems raised by the concept of dual commitment, it has provided a coherent framework for the development of social partnership in Germany. As will be argued later, the absence of a comparable legal and institutional framework in Britain means that the dual commitment of employees – as well as broader conceptions of social partnership – are dependent largely on employers' values and priorities.

The second issue concerns the relationship between the 'hard' and 'soft' variants of HRM, and the extent to which the latter posed major problems for British managers, as well as for trade unions. As the discussion in chapter 1 indicates, many employers were unable or unwilling to make the considerable investment necessary to develop and sustain a high-commitment model of HRM (Marchington and Parker 1990). This requires managers to treat employees as a resource whose contribution should be maximized through training and other measures designed to cement the psychological contract, and to encourage high commitment and high performance. This implies a fair system of pay and rewards, due process in the handling of grievances, extensive employee communication and involvement and, perhaps most critically, some measure of employment security (Purcell 1993).

It is clear that the attraction of soft HRM policies was based partly on employment relations policies and practices developed in other countries and exported in modified form in the policies of foreign-owned multinational companies. For example, the employment practices of large Japanese manufacturing companies were based on long-term relations with their core employees. Similarly, high levels of productivity in German manufacturing industry have been sustained partly because the constraints on employers' freedom to hire and fire encouraged investment in the upgrading of workforce skills to achieve 'functional flexibility' in production (Streeck 1992). In contrast, management prerogatives have been far less constrained in Britain; this was the case in the 1970s, and even more so in the 1980s when Conservative governments weakened the already limited job protection rights enjoyed by employees and encouraged the decollectivization of industrial relations.

Whilst a range of employers' policy options can be set out in schematic form, some appear to be more compatible with the economic, political and legal environment in Britain in the 1980s and early 1990s than others. For example, Hyman (1997) provides a matrix of ideal–typical employer regimes, based on Streeck's (1987) delineation of two fundamental issues facing employers (see Guest 1995 for a broadly similar typology). The first is whether to attempt to exclude unions from the regulation of the employment relationship or to seek to integrate them. The second presents a choice between the 'extension of status', or a 'return to contract', in the management of employees; that is, between an approach that integrates employees as members of the enterprise, or one that seeks flexibility by emphasizing labour's disposability and job insecurity.

The bottom right-hand quadrant in figure 15.1 locates the traditional pattern of organized industrial relations in Britain. Hyman uses the term the 'regulated market' to denote its essential features; namely, the employer's insistence on the formal right to hire and fire 'which is in practice constrained by collective employee pressure' (Hyman 1997: 323). In the top left-hand quadrant is soft HRM which, in idealized form, provides employees with the employment security and other benefits which might diminish their attachment to independent trade union representation. In the late 1980s and early 1990s, the challenge posed by HRM to the traditional role of trade unions was widely debated by academics and by trade union leaders. By the late 1990s, however, attention had turned to the prospects for a reconfiguration of the relationship between trade unions and management along the lines of social partnership (labelled 'micro-concertation' in Hyman's 1997 article). This conceptualizes the possibility that management and employee representatives could seek a trade-off between employment security and collaboration in initiatives to improve the flexibility, quality and productivity of work. The potential interest of employers in such a realignment of employment relations policies will be explored later, but the interest of trade unions in social partnership can be readily understood. By the mid 1990s it was clear that there had been a sharp decline in organized industrial relations in Britain that confronted trade unions with very serious problems.

Trade unions and the decline in organized industrial relations

Whilst there are no unambiguous measures of the strength or effectiveness of trade union organization and policies, quantitative data on membership, union recognition and the coverage of collective bargaining offer convincing evidence of the developing crisis facing British trade unions since the early 1980s. Reviewing the period of strong union growth in the 1960s and 1970s, Bain and Price (1983) described a 'virtuous circle of cause and effect in which the more that unions obtain recognition and succeed in participating in job regulation, the more likely they are to increase their recognition and deepen their participation in job regulation' (p. 18). In contrast, the evidence of the last two decades suggests a vicious circle of membership decline, reduced participation in collective bargaining and an increased incidence of union derecognition.

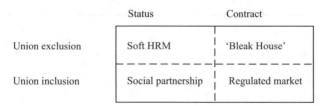

Figure 15.1 A typology of employer regimes
Source: adapted from Hyman (1997: 323)

Aggregate union membership has declined every year since the peak of around 13 million in 1979 to less than 7 million today. Trade union density (that is, union membership expressed as a percentage of potential membership in employment) exceeded 55 per cent in 1979, but had fallen to less than one-third of the workforce by the mid 1990s. Data collected by the Labour Force Survey indicate that union density among employees stood at 30.2 per cent in 1997 (Cully and Woodland 1998: 355).

The links between union membership, recognition and collective bargaining can be illuminated by the series of Workplace Industrial Relations Surveys that allow comparisons of data over time. As table 15.1 indicates, there has been a continuous and significant decline between 1984, 1990 and 1998 in the proportion of establishments with union members and with recognized unions, as well as in union membership density, and in the proportion of employees covered by collective bargaining. The authors of the 1990 survey described the decline in the coverage of collective bargaining from 71 per cent in 1984 to 54 per cent in 1990 as 'one of the most dramatic changes in the character of British industrial relations' revealed by the surveys (Millward et al. 1992: 93). Since the surveys in this period excluded establishments with fewer than 25 employees, the findings exaggerated the coverage of the collective bargaining in the economy overall (see table 1.4 in chapter 1 for data on the strong association between workplace size and union membership, density and recognition).

An important explanation for the decline in union membership and the coverage of collective bargaining focuses on the changing structure of industry and the composition of employment. This argument was elaborated by Millward et al. (1992) in the conclusion of the 1990 survey

> The decline of heavy manufacturing industries with their concentrations of male manual workers, the tendency towards smaller workplaces, the steady rise of the service sector, the contraction of the public sector, the rising proportion of overseas-owned workplaces, the increase in part-time employment – all these changes worked against trade union membership.   (p. 356)

The concentration of employment growth in the 1980s in smaller-scale establishments and private service industries clearly has presented the unions with significant challenges, for it is among such workplaces that management attitudes are likely to be most hostile towards union membership and representation (Tailby et al. 1997).

The effect of compositional changes, however, provides only a partial explanation for the retreat of organized industrial relations. First, the marked differences in union density

Table 15.1 Trade union presence, membership, recognition and collective bargaining coverage, 1984, 1990 and 1998

		Percent	
	1984	*1990*	*1998*
Establishments with union members	73	64	53
Union membership density, all employees/establishments	58	48	36
Establishments with recognized trade unions	66	53	45
Employees covered by collective bargaining	71	54	n/a

Source: Millward et al. (1992: 58–9, 94) and Cully et al. (1998: 15)

found at the beginning of the 1980s – between production and service industries, male and female employees, and between manual and white-collar workers – have been largely evened out as membership density in the 1980s and 1990s has declined more rapidly in areas of previous union strength (Cully and Woodland 1998: 357). Second, there is evidence of a more general hardening of management attitudes towards trade unions in the last decade. Whilst surveys in the late 1980s and early 1990s found that the derecognition of unions was relatively rare in Britain, its incidence had increased (see Gregg and Yates 1991; Millward et al. 1992: 362; Claydon 1996). The analysis of the 1990 WIRS findings suggested that a precipitatory factor in some instances had been the termination by employers of industry-wide bargaining arrangements (Millward et al. 1992: 74). As Clark and Winchester (1994: 712) argued, this amounted to a *de facto* derecognition of unions as industry-wide bargaining agents, and its effect was to render the local union increasingly dependent on its direct appeal to employees or, indeed, to employers, at establishment and company level. Where union membership was low or falling, recognition proved difficult to safeguard and sustain. Thus, recognition in some instances may have simply withered away for lack of employee and employer support. Claydon (1998: 184), however, pointed out that the incidence of derecognition increased in the early 1990s, spread to a wider range of industries and employee groups, and in some sectors (for example, the oil industry) indicated a strategic decision on the part of management.

Millward's (1994) analysis showed that rates of union recognition were lower among newer workplaces established in the 1980s than among those established earlier (pp. 28–9). The differences could not be explained by the size or industry composition of the sample of newer workplaces; indeed, the decline in the rate of recognition among newer workplaces was most marked within manufacturing industry. Millward (1994) suggested more general causes, including the removal of statutory support for recognition in 1980 and 'the decline in the presumption by managements and the state in favour of collective bargaining between trade unions and employers' (p. 29).

This raises the question of the extent to which employers have sought to reconstruct employment relations in the mould of soft HRM discussed earlier. Findings from the third Workplace Industrial Relations Survey in 1990 suggested a marked contrast of employment regimes between unionized workplaces and those typical of the growing non-union sector of the economy. Among the small and medium-sized workplaces which dominate the non-union sector, the management of employment relations appeared to be largely unaffected by the prescriptions of HRM. Indeed, the clock seemed to have been turned backwards (Millward et al. 1992: 363–4; Millward 1994). Thus Sisson's (1993) analysis of the WIRS results for the non-union sector led him to apply the label of the 'bleak house' to denote the resemblance with the employment regimes of the Dickensian era. Management prerogative was largely unconstrained and employment security was minimal. Employers enjoyed the freedom to remain in business by neglecting workforce health and safety, 'flexing' wages downwards and treating labour as a commodity to be hired and discharged as market conditions dictated.

In contrast, the unionized sector had more equitable employment practices: there was less use of individual performance pay, more formal job evaluation, and less extreme differentials between the highest and lowest paid. Workforce reductions were no less common, but they were less likely to be implemented through compulsory redundancy. Disciplinary dismissals were far less common, and procedural formality in handling employee grievances and disciplinary matters was much more likely (Millward et al. 1992: 363–4). Union members were represented in their direct dealings with management, and could indirectly participate in the determination of their pay and other employment conditions covered by collective bargaining. Moreover, the transposition of EU Directives into British employment law imposed on employers which recognized trade unions, although not on those that did not, the obligation to consult employee representatives on a number of issues, including collective redundancies and transfers of ownership. Acknowledgement of the decline in union recognition, coupled with European Court of Justice rulings on the inadequacy of British legislation, forced the issue of the growing 'representation gap' on to the political agenda in the early 1990s, where it has remained ever since, as will be discussed later.

The results of the 1990 WIRS found only limited evidence of fully developed soft HRM in either the unionized or non-union sectors, but elements of the model were more common in the former. In particular, there had been a substantial increase in the use of channels of direct communication between management and employees in the unionized sector, and the techniques adopted were more likely to allow a process of two-way communication than those found in non-union workplaces (Millward 1994: 90 and see chapter 14).

An optimistic interpretation of these findings was expounded in TUC literature; that is, unions were a force for progressive developments in the employment relationship and as such their presence should be welcomed by managers (TUC 1994). The interpretation of the data by Millward (1994: 90) was more pessimistic. He noted that the decline in union recognition and collective bargaining had been accompanied by a decline in the incidence of joint consultative committees and a diminution in the role played by unions within them. Managers in unionized establishments appeared to have been developing direct channels of employee communication in preference to previous structures of joint consultation. The case-study evidence of Storey (1992) also indicated that managers had been investing in new forms of direct communication and consultation whilst neglecting, rather than attacking, the old union-based structures of consultation and bargaining, perhaps in the hope that they might 'wither on the vine' (see also Smith and Morton 1993, and Cully et al. 1998).

From this perspective, trade unions in the 1990s were faced with a dual challenge. They had to ward off efforts to marginalize their role in the workplaces and sectors in which they retained a reasonably strong presence, and to renew their efforts to organize employees in the growth areas of employment, that is the more difficult recruitment territory of the private service sector. The latter was pursued through a series of organizing initiatives in national unions, culminating in the TUC conference on 'New Unionism' in 1996 (Heery 1997) and, by this time, the increasing expectation of a Labour election victory encouraged union leaders to develop proposals for a new legal framework for union recognition.

The TUC also pursued closer links with the CBI and other business interest groups and began to develop its proposals for social partnership, defined broadly in terms of 'union cooperation with the modernization of British industry on the basis of flexible working and investment in skills' (Heery 1998: 344). This initiative was encouraged by a widespread belief that Conservative governments' policies of deregulation had produced increasing inequality, job insecurity and grievances arising from work intensification that were likely to have negative consequences for economic performance. Survey evidence had revealed that HRM initiatives designed to increase employees' trust, and their commitment to enterprise goals, had achieved only modest success (Kessler and Undy 1996). Thus, the embryonic idea of social partnership advanced by the TUC met with at least qualified approval from some employers who were seeking ways to change the climate of industrial relations in their organizations. Indeed, a number of employers had already negotiated partnership agreements designed to create a broader conception of common interest between managers, employees and trade union representatives.

Social Partnership: Principles and Practice

The idea of social partnership, which until recently had an 'alien ring for the English reader' (Ferner and Hyman 1998: xv), moved centre stage in the debate on the reconstruction of British industrial relations in the late 1990s. This was encouraged by a number of developments, but especially by the reform of the Labour Party and the redefinition of its relationship both with trade unions and the business community in the period prior to the change of government in May 1997. The pre-election commitments of the 'New' Labour Party showed much continuity with the preoccupations of the Conservative administration and, in the words of McIlroy (1998: 541), an accommodation to the idea that 'globalization had rendered demand management, an interventionist state and expansionary policies redundant'. Differences with the Conservatives centred mainly on supply-side economics and the measures required to upskill Britain's workforce and to enhance enterprise competitiveness.

In the run-up to the 1997 election, and after attaining office, New Labour reiterated the Conservatives' commitment to labour-market flexibility. Extensive legal regulation of employment was ruled out as inimical to business efficiency and, for electoral and other considerations, a commitment was made to retain much of the 1980s industrial relations legislation (Dickens and Hall 1995). Nevertheless, in advocating a 'third way' in economic management, New Labour acknowledged and sought to redress some of the economic and social costs of deregulation. The New Deal programme and related measures were introduced to reduce social exclusion and to wean the long-term unemployed, single parents and others off welfare and into work. New individual and collective employment rights were proposed in the White Paper *Fairness at Work* (1998) to provide a more positive legal framework to encourage employee commitment and adaptability. Some of the policies and rhetoric followed from the government's more positive commitment to the European Union and its decision to end the British opt-out from the social chapter of the Maastricht Treaty. Other policies were home grown, such as the national minimum wage and new procedures covering union recognition. On the latter issue, and despite the opposition of the CBI, the IPD and other employers' organizations to any legislation designed to assist trade union recognition where it was opposed by employers, the White Paper stressed the need to promote partnership between employers and employees, and emphasized the potential role of ACAS conciliation in overcoming employers' resistance (McCarthy 1999: 14).

Whilst social partnership has been presented as a framework for public policy, its meaning and significance for employment relations in Britain remain uncertain. Ferner and Hyman (1998) have noted that in continental European countries where the idea of social partnership has deeper roots, it is not a synonym for industrial harmony and peace; indeed, 'the term is often most familiar in countries with the strongest traditions of militancy and class conflict'.

> What the idea of 'social partners' implies . . . is, first a societal recognition of the different interests of workers and employers; second, an acceptance – indeed encouragement – of the collective representation of these interests; and third, an aspiration that their organized accommodation may provide an effective basis for the regulation of work and the labour market. Implicit also is the notion that encompassing organizations (Olson 1982) and centralized regulation are the optimal features of an industrial relations system. (Ferner and Hyman 1998: xv–xvi).

In Britain, the interest in social partnership followed the substantial disorganization of industrial relations noted earlier. It is not surprising, therefore, that the concept's meaning has been construed in relatively narrow terms. To date, almost all discussion has been focused on company and workplace employment relations. Thus, 'partnership at work' – rather than the broader conception of 'social partnership' – has attracted most interest, and in many accounts social partnership has been interpreted mainly as an attempt to create a more consensual and collaborative relationship between employers, employees and their representatives, and a joint commitment to achieve common goals and mutual benefits. Indeed, the parameters of the British partnership debate have been sketched by New Labour which, since attaining office, has encouraged business leaders more actively than union leaders to participate in the process of government policy formulation, and has 're-legitimized collectivism but on one central condition: that it be imbricated with management objectives' (McIlroy 1998: 543).

The TUC and many individual union leaders have championed the philosophy of social partnership since the early 1990s. This enthusiasm has to be interpreted, of course, against the backdrop of complete political exclusion in the 1980s, dramatic membership decline and the marginalization of workplace influence discussed earlier. TUC partnership proposals emphasize the positive contribution that a new, and more accommodative, trade unionism can make to the management of change, facilitating greater competitiveness and the generation of secure and rewarding jobs (TUC 1994; 1996). As such they can be read as an attempt to 'define a role for trade unionism which balances its central concern to represent employees' interests with a productivist appeal to employers and government' (Claydon 1998: 180). In the run-up to the May 1997 general election and subsequently, the message has been that the unions 'want to be taken seriously as part of the solution to the country's problems rather than seen as a problem themselves' (TUC 1998).

There are many critics of partnership, however, on both the right and the left of the political spectrum. Thus, the novelty of the arrangements proposed, their desirability for enterprise and business, the possibility of achieving a significant reconstruction of union–management relations in the partnership mould, and the efficacy of partnership as a strategy for trade union renewal, have each been questioned. The following discussion first summarizes the principles of partnership expounded by its main advocates, especially the TUC. Second, it examines the content of a number of partnership agreements and the motivation and priorities of the management and union negotiators involved. Third, it evaluates the significance of these agreements in the light of survey evidence on the diffusion of the partnership approach and academic critiques of the partnership philosophy.

Partnership principles

The TUC has envisaged partnership operating at national, enterprise and workplace levels. Its *Partners for Progress* policy statement explained the former as 'Government discussing issues with employers and trade unions on a fair and open basis where a common approach can reap dividends' (TUC 1997a: 1). To date, however, the relatively modest proposals for national-level tripartite discussions on economic and social policy issues have been largely unheeded by the New Labour government: party strategists and ministers 'continue to worry such a move would be seen as a return to the discredited failures of the 1960s and 1970s' (Taylor 1998). Consequently, most attention has focused on the TUC's proposals for social partnership at the workplace.

These proposals are based on a simultaneous appeal to a business interest in efficiency and an employee interest in secure and rewarding employment (Claydon 1998: 188). The presumption is that both sets of interests can be achieved if companies reconfigure their product-market strategies and employee relations systems to meet the prevailing competitive conditions. Following the logic of some of the HRM literature, the TUC suggests that the key to enterprise success now comes from 'companies producing the high quality goods and services, that their customers want and having the positive flexibility to respond rapidly to change' (TUC 1997b: 3). This demands employment practices which achieve a 'worldclass workforce with the skills to produce high quality, high value added products and services and to respond to rapid technological change' (TUC 1994: 5).

In the TUC's view, the fact that too few employers have recognized their self-interest in upmarket restructuring arises principally from the deregulatory thrust of government policy since the 1980s. Short-term cost cutting and get-rich-quick capitalism have been encouraged, fuelling insecurity among employees and limiting their commitment to the enterprise (TUC 1996). Thus in the TUC's view, there is a strong case for new regulatory structures; the enactment of minimum labour standards to 'encourage the worst employers to treat employees as people rather than disposable assets'; and a partnership approach at work which is inclusive of unions and consensual in orientation (TUC 1994; 1996). The argument is that consensus is possible because employers and employees both stand to gain from a high value-added product-market strategy, and also that a union presence is necessary to 'exercise restraint on employer prerogatives' and ensure the fairness of treatment at work that such a strategy demands (TUC 1994: 9).

Social partnership at the workplace 'means employers and trade unions working together to achieve common goals such as fairness and competitiveness . . . it is a recognition that although they have different constituencies, and at times different interests, they can serve these best by making common cause wherever possible' (TUC 1997a: 1). There are, in the TUC view, four main components in such an approach (Monks 1998: 176–8). The first concerns employment security and new working practices. Employers who reject a hire-and-fire regime have an incentive to invest in the upgrading of workforce skills and will in turn achieve 'true flexibility'; that is, employees with the skills and motivation to respond positively to changing requirements. The second involves giving employees a voice in their own companies; they should have a right to basic information about their company and, since it is important for employers to listen to staff views when taking decisions, consultation procedures are required. For consultation to be meaningful it must be representative in nature and, preferably, based on the union channel. It should be undertaken with a view to reaching agreement on a wide range of topics, including major business issues such as mergers and takeovers. The third component covers fair financial reward and the recognition that workers should be able to choose to bargain collectively over their wages. The fourth concerns investment in training which enhances employees' ability to work flexibly and efficiently in responding to change and signals the employer's commitment to employee development.

There is considerable overlap and cross-referencing between the TUC's proposals and those of the Involvement and Participation Association (IPA), an organization with business and union sponsors which has existed since the late nineteenth century as a pressure group for the promotion of partnership in industry (see Coupar and Stevens 1998). Both organizations view partnership in pluralist terms. Whilst they do not envisage the eradication of conflict at work, they nevertheless presume that harsher competitive conditions and new, high-performance work regimes have increased the need and the scope for collaboration. The IPA (1996: 2) argues that unions and employers now have many common goals, for example, in the areas of health and safety, training, quality and performance, which can be achieved through joint action. To set partnership in motion, the IPA advises the parties to come together to agree certain joint aims: a joint commitment to the success of the enterprise, a joint effort to build trust, and a joint declaration recognizing the legitimacy of the role of each party (IPA 1996: 4; 1997: 4). More specifically, unions and management are urged to rethink their approach in four key areas in order to make partnership work.

The areas identified conform broadly with the TUC's partnership proposals, but there are significant differences of interpretation in terms of the concessions deemed to be necessary. On the issue of 'sharing in the success of the organization', for example, the IPA (1996) identifies as the key challenge for management the need to ensure that the division of the rewards of enterprise success (and failure) is seen to be fair; excessive pay increases for senior executives are deemed unhelpful as these 'sour the atmosphere' (p. 7). But it urges that unions must accept the shift away from traditional pay bargaining and the introduction of a greater element of performance-related reward. The IPA regards collective employee representation as fundamental to the partnership approach: employees have a basic right to representation and their involvement in corporate decision making – which is desirable to enhance the legitimacy of management decisions – can only be achieved through representative structures (IPA 1997: 14–15). In contrast with the insistence in union literature that 'real partnership can only work where there is an independent trade union' (for example, Usdaw 1998: 6), the IPA (1996: 2, 1997: 17) argues, however, that the single-channel, union-only model, is no longer adequate, not least because union presence is weak or non-existent in a majority of workplaces in Britain. The IPA implies that new structures of representative consultation may provide the most effective means of bridging the representation gap and of extending the partnership approach in non-union and unionized contexts alike. The works council system of indirect employee representation established in many continental European countries appears to be a favoured model (see Coupar and Stevens 1998).

The IPA and the TUC have been the most active proselytizers of the partnership approach to relations at work in Britain in the 1990s. As this review of their proposals suggests, both organizations conceptualize the approach in pluralist and collectivist terms whilst making concessions towards the unitarist aversion to conflict and, in the case of the IPA, towards HRM's emphasis on individualism in the management of the employment relationship (Ackers and Payne 1998). New Labour government ministers have used 'partnership' more loosely, as a synonym (or prescription) for co-operative relations between firms, between employees and management, and between business and government. It is the last of these spheres of partnership that the New Labour administration has been most anxious to cement. Thus in the area of industrial relations reform, the Government has moved cautiously, proposing individual and collective employment rights alongside the 1980s legislation on industrial conflict in a system of checks and balances – or reciprocal rights and obligations – designed to promote workplace co-operation with a 'progressive' business agenda (McCartney 1998). Nevertheless, the pre-election opposition of the CBI to the union recognition proposals was followed by talks with the TUC that produced only very limited agreement. The Joint Statement signed by the leaders of both organizations could not disguise their differences, and it seems unlikely that the provisions of the Employment Relations Bill (published in January 1999) will secure the co-operation of employers or enable unions to deal effectively with its absence (McCarthy 1999). Critics of the overall social partnership project of the TUC cite this as further evidence that vindicates their scepticism.

Partnership in practice

A number of employers have embraced enthusiastically the partnership concept, and some of the best-publicized partnership agreements were concluded before the TUC had set out its own policy proposals. The New Deal negotiated by unions and management at the Rover car company in 1991/2, for example, included job security commitments in return for greater flexibility and the extension of teamworking. Given the history of adversarial bargaining in the company, this agreement was widely cited as an 'example of the new consensual approach to industrial relations apparent across British manufacturing industry' (Taylor 1994, cited in Scarborough and Terry 1996: 13). Early agreements were concentrated in manufacturing and the privatized utilities, but interest in partnership has since spread to organizations in retail, finance, and in the public services (see IDS 1998; IRS 1997). This section examines four agreements to establish management and union objectives, the processes through which the partnership deals were negotiated and implemented, and the perceived benefits and costs of the substantive changes achieved.

UNITED DISTILLERS

Marks et al. (1998) investigated the work reforms and employee relations innovations pursued at the Scottish production sites of companies operating in the international spirits industry (see also IDS 1998). They report that management initiatives were focused on the need to enhance enterprise competitiveness by reorganizing production to secure greater flexibility, efficiency and innovation in response to changing product market conditions.

Many firms have experimented with teamworking, but management at United Distillers (owned by Guinness, now merged with Grand Met) recognized the need to support their ambitious change programme by moving from 'low trust' to 'high trust' work relations. The company's plants are highly unionized and management's approach to labour relations in the past had been 'simultaneously adversarial and indulgent' (Marks et al. 1998: 212). Hardline policies had been pursued, but the existence of a relatively strong workplace union often persuaded managers to make concessions in the interests of maintaining production.

The change programme, planned by senior operational executives and introduced from 1994, linked innovations in corporate structure (the decentralization of decision making and empowerment), work organization (teamworking in place of traditional work practices), and industrial relations (a partnership approach to the management of employee relations). This programme was initiated in a difficult industrial relations context of plant closures and redundancies. Management recognized the need to offer some assurance of employment stability and better workforce communications in order to support the development of high-trust relations. Thus, when negotiations on a 'positive partnership' deal were opened with the unions, the company offered a package centred on a three-year 'job security' guarantee of no compulsory redundancies. In spite of the rhetoric of partnership, however, 'the entire initial bargaining agenda was set exclusively by the company; the unions were not allowed to present their agenda, and substantive negotiations were not allowed to progress until the principle of a three-year (pay) deal had been accepted' (Marks et al. 1998: 213). Management insisted that it was an 'all-or-nothing' package which included commitments to teamworking, greater flexibility, skills training and culture change.

Marks et al. (1998) suggest four reasons why union full-time officers supported the management initiative. First, they viewed involvement in change as preferable to opposition which would mean, in effect, leaving the management of change to management. Second, they saw 'engagement' with the proposals as the only means of exercising any influence over the change process – that is, of prohibiting the marginalization of union influence. Third, engagement offered the possibility of raising issues of union concern, such as the quality of working life. Finally, the lead union negotiator was an active supporter of 'a more integrated, strategic and collaborative role for the unions' (Marks et al. 1998: 214). The shop stewards and employees, however, were far less enthusiastic and the package was initially rejected. Whilst the workforce recognized the need for the company to be competitive, they were not confident that management would protect their interests in implementing the proposed changes. The absence of majority support for strike action nevertheless led to the agreement by default.

Marks et al. (1998) report that the changes have proved to be 'highly successful' for the company which has reaped significant improvements in productivity and competitiveness (p. 218) and they argue that 'work reform efforts underpinned by a wider set of HR policies and joint involvement by management and unions' are the most likely to be successful for companies (p. 223). In support of this conclusion they note that the changes in working practice pursued by United Distillers' principal competitor (Allied Distillers Ltd), which did not involve the HR department or the unions, was unsuccessful. The benefits for workers include an employment security guarantee, which was extended for a further three years in 1997, and Marks et al. (1998) also found that employees were favourably disposed towards teamworking and most of the associated training. Also they report management's view that employees are now better able to represent their own interests, individually and through teams and other structures of representative consultation (p. 218). The involvement of workplace union representatives in grievance and disciplinary issues, however, has been reduced.

Trade union involvement was crucial in the change programme. Given the initial industrial relations context, management could not easily bypass the unions; in fact, they needed union support to persuade employees to accept the proposed changes. The partnership agreement has – in the immediate term at least – consolidated the unions' institutional presence. Full-time officials have secured an enhanced role in corporate decision making, although there are some doubts about their ability to set – rather than simply respond to – the business agenda (Marks et al. 1998: 222). The scope of the shop stewards' role and plant-level bargaining, however, have been squeezed by the direct dealings between the HR director and full-time union officials, and by the decentralization of decision making to plant level which has increased the discretion enjoyed by local management. Moreover, direct participation through teamworking, and representative participation through consultative committees focused on a business-led agenda, have been elevated at the expense of union–management negotiations. The fragmentation of decision making and, in particular, the enhanced autonomy of local managers, however, have created their own problems. Management assertiveness in disciplinary and other matters has threatened the pursuit of high-trust relations. Marks et al. (1998) suggest that these difficulties have been recognized by senior company executives who may be obliged to make changes and institute a greater formality into the conduct of workplace relations.

Welsh Water

The partnership agreements pursued by Welsh Water (*Dwr Cymru*) have received much publicity – especially from the publication jointly authored by a senior manager and Unison official (Thomas and Wallis 1998). Formerly a regional public utility, Welsh Water was privatized in 1989 and is now part of the Hyder plc utilities group. Its industrial relations practices were rooted in the procedures and traditions of local government of which it was a part until 1974 when the regional water authorities were created. National bargaining arrangements persisted for the three main groups of manual, craft and staff grades, and the local management input into the determination of pay and conditions was very limited.

Under the aegis of a new board and senior management, including a personnel director who was a former full-time union official, a culture-change programme was initiated. In the run-up to privatization, two key foundations were put in place: a joint project to involve the unions in changing working practices; and a strong commitment to management development and training. The latter emphasized the importance of 'management style', and recruitment was tailored to support an organizational culture of involvement. In the preparations for privatization, senior union officers discussed with the personnel team how arrangements could be developed following the termination of national bargaining. Both sides had independently consulted academics at Templeton College, Oxford, and had been convinced that a 'sophisticated consultative model' (Purcell and Sisson 1983) offered a better way forward than the ritual of annual national pay negotiations which often failed to meet the expectations of both employees and managers.

Four partnership agreements have been concluded by management and full-time union officers. The first, in 1991, proposed a new pay formula based on increases in the retail price index, a Welsh labour market factor, and an element of profit-related pay. It also identified seven action areas: a single-table, representative council; new work patterns – including a more flexible arrangement of the working week, and a company-specific annualized hours system; the harmonization of other conditions; monthly pay; a unified pay structure; productivity improvement through flexible working between groups, skill enhancements and increase in employees' responsibilities for roles formerly undertaken by supervisors; and a 'no compulsory redundancy' policy.

The package was hailed as a breakthrough in union management relations; a move away from an adversarial structure of annual pay negotiations towards greater trust in relations between management, unions and employees, based on job security (Thomas and Wallis 1998). Management expectations that job security would be reciprocated by increased employees' co-operation in organizational and technological change, however, were not realized. An employee survey conducted 18 months after the signing of the 1991 agreement revealed that only one-third of manual and craft grades considered that it had had any impact on them. This finding was followed by intensive efforts to convince employees that they had obligations to increase flexibility. A series of 'partnership road-shows' and videos was organized.

The second partnership agreement in 1993 implemented the pay formula agreed in the first, developed proposals on a unified pay structure and on performance reviews for all staff, and reiterated the commitment to employment security – even though 'the necessity to achieve manpower reductions was recognised by all parties – a difficult step for the trade unions traditionally committed to defending jobs' (Thomas and Wallis 1998: 164). The agreement was approved by a majority of three to one after local managers and union representatives explained its content using an agreed script and a video. This joint communication strategy was developed even further in the preparations for the third agreement reached in 1995; 'senior personnel staff and full-time union officials undertook a series of joint roadshows, meeting small groups of staff... the views of over 75 per cent of the staff were heard and more importantly listened to' (Thomas and Wallis 1998: 164).

Managers and full-time union officers define the purpose of partnership in terms of the need to meet more stringent customer requirements, partly by increasing employee enthusiasm and commitment to the enterprise. The benefits to the company include enhanced flexibility in the area of working hours; improvements in quality, cost and customer service; and the willingness of employees to work with subcontractors, temporary and agency staff. Apart from greater job security, many workers have benefited from harmonization of conditions, improved consultation and from the empowerment of staff and work teams that, it is claimed, offers 'a greater degree of freedom than ever before in controlling their own working lives' (Thomas and Wallis 1998: 166). None the less, to the disappointment of managers, employees still expected to be materially rewarded for their enhanced job responsibilities.

The partnership agreements seem to have offered relatively few direct benefits for the trade unions. Whilst the three agreements have been endorsed by substantial and increasing majorities of staff, Thomas and Wallis (1998: 167–8) stress the scale and difficulty of the adjustments that had to be made by the trade unions:

> the consensual nature of partnership restricts the number of opportunities for union officials to demonstrate publicly their value to the membership ... set-pieces such as the annual pay negotiation are eliminated ... the role of trade unions therefore needs to move into new territory by helping the organisation to become more effective and dealing with the problem of achieving significant manpower reductions.

The accusation of 'collaborating with the enemy' was not unknown, and union officials had to be able to demonstrate that co-operation could work to the mutual benefit of all. As Kelly (cited in Ball 1998), noted some unions that were unwilling to make such adjustments to their role were derecognized by the company.

Blue Circle Cement

Redundancies accompanied the introduction of integrated working and annualized hours at Blue Circle Cement's production sites from the late 1980s. The company secured significant productivity gains but also encountered union resistance at each of its plants. A consultant's report in 1995 advised that additional job shedding was required to reap further efficiency gains. The company was sensitive to the impact on customer confidence of any industrial action. Its new personnel director approached the unions with the offer of discussions, not on the changes proposed, but on the ways in which these might be achieved. Early 'think-tank' talks were followed by the formation of a company-wide action team (CWAT) comprising works managers, staff association representatives, shop stewards from each site, senior stewards and senior company managers. Agreement on the draft of a Way Ahead agreement was reached by the autumn of 1996. This was presented subsequently as a 'framework for constructive employment relations' supportive of the company's objectives on its 'journey towards excellence' (IDS 1998: 10). Its principal elements were a rolling three-year pay deal, harmonization of terms and conditions, payment linked to skills acquisition, and employment security. The last entails a company commitment to avoid compulsory redundancy as a means of labour shedding, and a commitment from employees to co-operate with training and development, flexible working and redeployment where necessary.

In this, as in other 'partnerships', management and union negotiators have been assiduous in their efforts to enlist and maintain employee interest in the progress of discussions through joint presentations, new consultative structures and so on. A considerable investment has been made also in workforce partnership training. At the end of 1998, over 600 employees had attended a course convened by consultants and the GMB union on the behaviours required by the new work and industrial relations approach. Senior management and union representatives in public have been evangelical in their support of the partnership approach and the transformation of industrial relations that has been achieved at their company. At the same time the union representatives have confessed to the flak that they have received from members and activists for their enthusiastic embrace of a closer working relationship with management.

Tesco

The partnership agreement concluded between the supermarket group, Tesco, and the shopworkers' union, Usdaw, in March 1998 was hailed by Labour Government ministers as 'a milestone in the government's drive for greater co-operation in the workplace' and by the general secretary of the TUC as 'dispelling the myths about trade unionism' (cited in the *Guardian* 1998). To the extent that previous pioneer agreements were concentrated in manufacturing and the privatized utilities, the agreement is distinctive in a number of respects. Tesco has an above-average union density for the retail trade and the largest number of trade union members among its workforce of any private-sector organization. Over half of the retail staff (85,000 out of the total of 150,000) are members of Usdaw, the only union recognized by the company. Yet workplace union organization has been weak, at least in comparison with the traditions of manufacturing. Usdaw's principal role has focused on the national negotiation of pay and conditions. At the workplace level its role has been confined to employee representation in grievances and disciplinary matters, rather than the joint regulation of working practices. Moreover, while most partnership agreements have been developed at a time of crisis, and have taken the form of a trade-off between employment security and job flexibility, the Tesco agreement was concluded at a time of unprecedented commercial success for the company (*Guardian* 1998; *Financial Times* 1998).

The agreement arose from a series of workshops involving senior managers, union officials and lay representatives, organized by Michael Allen of the Cranfield School of Management. He argues that senior management wanted to move away from the 'polarized and inflexible structures' of the annual negotiations, especially the union membership ballot on pay and conditions offers, which clashed with the company's organizational culture of innovation and flexibility in responding to changes in the competitive environment. The leadership of Usdaw partly shared Tesco's frustration with the adversarial rituals of national negotiations, and accepted the evidence of employee attitude surveys that its members wanted a broader agenda of consultation and negotiation (Allen 1998).

The partnership agreement replaces traditional union bargaining over pay with a three-tier structure of consultation with much wider terms of reference. Consultative staff forums are to be created in all 586 Tesco stores. The members of these workplace-level forums are to be elected by all store employees, allowing for the involvement of non-union members for the first time, though a place will be reserved for a union representative and a store manager. The store forums will send representatives – who must be Usdaw members – to three regional forums, and these will elect a national forum. The national forum will discuss major business issues and will be responsible for the annual review of pay and conditions. Its proposals on the latter will be approved or rejected by the regional forums.

The advantages of the partnership agreement for Usdaw include Tesco's commitment to be 'more energetic' in encouraging new employees to join the union, the potential for influence in regional and national consultation on 'business issues', and the example that the deal may set to other retail employers where membership is weak or non-existent. The risk, of course, is that the end of pay bargaining, coupled with the universal franchise of employee participation, will reduce the significance of Usdaw for members and potential members. The company has indicated its desire for a speedier employee agreement to proposed changes in operating procedures than allowed for by the bureaucracy of union procedures. Employees may therefore be committed to arrangements which encourage co-operation at the expense of more detailed consideration and discussion of their interests. Moreover, one of the aspirations at the core of the agreement – that trade union representatives should understand and promote the business goals of Tesco – may test the spirit of co-operation that developed during its negotiation (Allen 1998).

Evaluation and Future Prospects

Partnership agreements have been hailed as an innovative and progressive development in union–management relations, not least by the union representatives and managers involved in their negotiation and by Labour Government ministers (see McCartney 1998). Other observers, however, have questioned the novelty of the agreements, the gains that employees and their representatives derive from them, and the prospects and desirability of a wider diffusion of the partnership approach (see Kelly 1996, 1998; Overell 1997; Claydon 1998). What light do the exemplar agreements explored above, and other survey data, shed on these conflicting assessments?

In terms of their substantive content, partnership agreements embrace a fairly familiar checklist of employment relations and HRM practices; for example, union co-operation in more flexible work patterns, teamworking, the introduction of annualized hours and the harmonization of terms and conditions of employment. Job security guarantees have been identified as the hallmark of partnership agreements by many of its advocates, although they have not featured in all such agreements (see the case of Tesco above). In most cases they amount to relatively limited management commitments to avoid the use of compulsory redundancy as a means of labour shedding – a fairly familiar practice in organizations that can attract sufficient candidates for early retirement and voluntary redundancy with enhanced severance payments. Moreover, in some partnership agreements, trade unions and employees are required to co-operate with measures which make the avoidance of compulsory redundancy easier, including the acceptance of the company's use of subcontracted, temporary or short-term contract staff (see the Welsh Water case above).

The process of negotiating partnership agreements seems to have some distinctive and innovative features. First, negotiations have focused on relatively long-term horizons; for example, three-year rolling agreements designed to create a more stable framework for reforms and to minimize the impact of adversarial annual pay bargaining. Second, the language of agreements often reflects the discourse of soft HRM, although there is an emphasis on 'jointism', shared aspirations and commitments, and also on openness and trust between the parties. Third, in a number of cases, the services of consultants and business school facilitators have been employed to assist the negotiators in creating a broad consensus on potential reforms and the outline of initial agreements. Finally, there has been a considerable investment of time and resources in joint union–management presentations, publicity videos and roadshows designed to proselytize the benefits of partnership agreements to shop stewards and employees whose initial enthusiasm has often been limited.

In combination, these features of different phases of the negotiation process amount to the most distinctive characteristic of recent partnership agreements. In many cases, the language and rhetoric of agreements, and the close involvement of trade union officials in the management and legitimation of organizational culture-change programmes, imply an ideological break with past practice. It can be argued, of course, that most unions are involved in co-operative relationships with management for most of the time, and that partnership agreements exhibit many of the characteristics of the new-style single-union agreements of the mid 1980s (Kelly 1996). What is new, perhaps, is the degree of trade union consensus around the principles of partnership; there are relatively few echoes of the acrimonious debate over new realism and the legitimacy of single-union agreements that divided TUC affiliated unions in the mid 1980s (Winchester 1988).

Whilst it is difficult to evaluate systematically the outcome of partnership agreements, managers have enthusiastically reported business benefits in terms of quality and productivity improvements. IPA-sponsored research, reporting the views of managers and employee representatives in 54 of its members' organizations, found an indirect but positive link between partnership practices and organizational performance outcomes. The former were associated with employee attitudes and behaviours which were in turn associated with positive employee relations outcomes (lower labour turnover, absence and conflict), relatively high internal performance (productivity, quality and innovation) and good external performance, such as sales and profits (Guest and Peccei 1998). These findings must be treated with some caution as they are based on the subjective reports of respondents who may be personally committed to partnership, and employees views' were not sought. Nevertheless, the conclusion that partnership is beneficial for business has been widely reported, and this should encourage further research on the complex links between employment relations and labour productivity (see Cully et al. 1998; TUC 1998).

Trade unions and employees often cite enhanced security of employment as the principal benefit of partnership agreements, and the IPA study suggests that it is the key to the performance improvements reported by organizations (Guest and Peccei 1998: 42). It must be noted, however, that most partnership agreements were negotiated at a time of low and declining unemployment, with shortages of skilled and qualified staff in many organizations. Their employment security clauses have not prevented job losses even in this relatively benign economic environment. The case of the Rover car company indicates the limits and precariousness of employment security clauses. With overcapacity in the global motor industry squeezing profits, Rover's German owner, BMW, insisted on further flexibility concessions, and an agreement on substantial job losses, from its workforce in late 1998 and early 1999 as the price for the survival of the Longbridge factory.

Finally, greater direct participation and autonomy over work, together with a collective voice in organizational decision making, are seen by enthusiasts as the hallmark of the partnership approach. Whilst Guest and Peccei's (1998) research for the IPA found both sets of practices to be strongly associated with organizational performance gains, it also revealed a relatively low uptake of these practices among the organizations surveyed. IPA members are more likely to be committed to the partnership ideal than most companies, yet only a minority (28 per cent) were reported by either the manager or the employee representative as having made a high degree of progress towards partnership. Trade union presence was reported by 72 per cent of the whole sample, and was found to be positively associated with representative participation and influence over employment decisions, although not over organizational policy issues. The finding that levels of union recognition were lowest among those organizations which reported substantial progress towards partnership, however, must be a source of concern for union supporters of the approach (Guest and Peccei 1998: 31).

This assessment of the substance, process and impact of enterprise-level partnership agreements can be linked with wider questions concerning the meaning of social partnership in Britain. It was argued earlier that partnership agreements emerged in a distinctive political context: that is, towards the end of a long period of Conservative government characterized by policies of deregulation; and at the beginning of a period of Labour government associated with a rhetorical, if ambiguous, commitment to partnership. Whilst government ministers have enthusiastically embraced the idea of enterprise partnership agreements, they have distanced themselves from the more comprehensive expressions of social partnership found in many member states in the European Union, and have indicated their opposition to some of the social policy proposals developed by the European Commission.

In comparison with most EU member states, there is no legal or institutional framework supporting social partnership in Britain. Whilst leaders of the TUC and the CBI may choose to meet more often than a decade ago, their status and role as social partners is very limited and, at industry or sectoral level, trade union and employers' representatives rarely engage in collective bargaining or in institutionalized forms of consultation. Whilst the higher profile attached to national and sectoral social dialogue in the EU may encourage some initiatives in Britain, neither employers' associations nor trade unions possess the same degree of legitimacy and organizational experience as many of their continental counterparts for such a role.

At the enterprise level, it has been possible for employers and trade unions to conclude a small number of innovative partnership agreements, as noted above, but they exist in an institutional vacuum. The diffusion of such agreements – or indeed any forms of collective bargaining or employee consultation and representation – will be dependent largely upon employers' initiatives. It will also be constrained by the representation gap that exists in half the workplaces in Britain. In this context, the decision of the Labour Government to oppose the European Commission's 1998 draft Directive aimed at 'establishing a general framework for informing and consulting employees' in all EU member states diminishes the prospects for the development of a widespread commitment to social partnership in Britain; in most other EU member states, legally regulated works councils and similar consultative arrangements have provided a crucial institutional support for the development of social partnership (Rogers and Streeck 1995).

The potential impact of union recognition legislation on the scale of the representation gap in Britain – and on the climate of employment relations more generally – is difficult to predict. In early 1999, a few well-publicized recognition agreements were couched in the language of partnership, and were accompanied by trade union commitments to work with management to improve the competitive position of the companies. At the same time, there was evidence that other employers were willing to pursue aggressive policies of resistance to union recognition campaigns, or to establish employee forums and consultative committees as an alternative to trade union recognition (Taylor 1999).

It is almost certain that the crumbling edifice of Britain's previously voluntarist employment relations system will be eroded further by the Government's decision to end its predecessor's opt-out from the social chapter, and its desire to participate more positively in the process of European economic integration. Also, it is likely that there will be a partial convergence between British employment relations policies and practices and those of a new European social model (see chapter 1). It is possible, however, that the convergence will result more from an erosion of the values and policies associated with social partnership in continental Europe – as the combined impact of EMU and the single market exacerbates the problem of high labour costs and structural unemployment – than from the Labour Government's modest and business-friendly employment relations and partnership proposals.

References and further reading

Ackers, P. and Payne, J. 1998: British Trade Unions and Social Partnership: Rhetoric, Reality and Strategy. *The International Journal of Human Resource Management*, **9**(3), 529–49.

Allen, M. 1998: All-inclusive. *People Management*, 11 June, 36–42.

Bain, G. S. and Price, R. 1983: Union Growth: Dimensions, Determinants and Destiny. In G. S. Bain (ed.), *Industrial Relations in Britain*, Oxford: Blackwell.

Ball, C. 1998: Partnership principle is New Labour's big idea to sweeten relations at work. *Guardian*, 8 August.

Clark, J. and Winchester, D. 1994: Management and Trade Unions. In K. Sisson (ed.), *Personnel Management: A Comprehensive Guide to Theory and Practice in Britain*, Oxford: Blackwell.

Claydon, T. 1996: Union Derecognition: A Re-Examination. In I. Beardwell (ed.), *Contemporary Industrial Relations: A Critical Analysis*, Oxford: OUP.

Claydon, T. 1998: Problematising Partnership: The Prospects for a Co-operative Bargaining Agenda. In P. Sparrow and M. Marchington (eds), *Human Resource Management: The New Agenda*, London: Financial Times/Pitman.

Coupar, W. and Stevens, B: 1998: Towards a New Model of Industrial Partnership. In P. Sparrow and M. Marchington (eds), *Human Resource Management: The New Agenda*, London: Financial Times/Pitman.

Cully, M., O'Reilly, A., Millward, N., Forth, J., Woodland, S., Dix, G. and Bryson, A. 1998: *The 1998 Workplace Employee Relations Survey: First Findings*. London: Department of Trade and Industry.

Cully, M. and Woodland, S. 1998: Trade Union Membership and Recognition 1996–97: An Analysis of Data from the Certification Officer and the LFS. *Labour Market Trends*, July, 353–64.

Dickens, L. and Hall, M. 1995: The State: Labour Law and Industrial Relations. In P. Edwards (ed.), *Industrial Relations: Theory and Practice in Britain*, Oxford: Blackwell.

Donovan 1968: Report of the Royal Commission on Trade Unions and Employers' Associations. Cmnd 3623, London: HMSO.

Fairness at Work 1998: Department of Trade and Industry White Paper, Cm 3968, London: Stationery Office.

Ferner, A. and Hyman, R. (eds) 1998: *Changing Industrial Relations in Europe*. Oxford: Blackwell.

Financial Times 1998: 15 March.

Fox, A. 1974: *Man Mismanagement*. London: Hutchinson.

Gregg, P. and Yates, A. 1991: Changes in Wage-setting Arrangements and Trade Union Presence in the 1980s. *British Journal of Industrial Relations*, **29**(3), 362–76.

Guardian 1998: 14 March.

Guest, D. 1989: Human Resource Management: Its Implications for Industrial Relations and Trade Unions. In J. Storey (ed.), *New Perspectives on Human Resource Management*, London: Routledge.

Guest, D. 1995: Human Resource Management, Trade Unions and Industrial Relations. In J. Storey (ed.), *Human Resource Management: A Critical Text*, London: Routledge.

Guest, D. and Peccei, R. 1998: *The Partnership Company: Benchmarks for the Future*. London: Involvement and Participation Association.

Heery, E. 1997: Annual Review Article. *British Journal of Industrial Relations*, **35**(1), 87–109.

Heery, E. 1998: The Relaunch of the Trades Union Congress. *British Journal of Industrial Relations*, **36**(3), 339–60.

Hyman, R. 1997: The Future of Employee Representation. *British Journal of Industrial Relations*, **35**(3), 309–36.

IDS (Incomes Data Services) 1998 *Partnership Agreements*. IDS Studies 656, October.

IPA (Involvement and Participation Association) 1995: *Welsh Water: Towards Industrial Partnership. Putting it into Practice*. No. 3, London: IPA.

IPA 1996: *Towards Industrial Partnership: A New Approach to Relationships at Work*. London: IPA.

IPA 1997: *Towards Industrial Partnership: New Ways of Working in British Companies*. London: IPA.

IRS (Industrial Relations Services) 1997: Partnership at Work: A Survey. *Employment Trends*, 645, December, 3–24.

Kelly, J. 1996: Union Militancy and Social Partnership. In P. Ackers, C. Smith and P. Smith (eds), *The New Workplace and Trade Unionism*, London: Routledge.

Kelly, J. 1998: *Rethinking Industrial Relations: Mobilization, Collectivism and Long Waves*. London: Routledge.

Kessler, I. and Undy, R. 1996: *The New Employment Relationship: Examining the Psychological Contract*. Issues in People Management, No. 12, London: Institute of Personnel Development.

Legge, K. 1988: Personnel Management in Recession and Recovery. *Personnel Review*, **17**, 3–69.

McCarthy, Lord 1999: *Fairness at Work and Trade Union Recognition: Past Comparisons and Future Problems*. London: The Institute of Employment Rights.

McCartney, I. 1998: In All Fairness. *People Management*, 17 December, 38–40.

McIlroy, J. 1998: The Enduring Alliance? Trade Unions and the Making of New Labour, 1994–1997. *British Journal of Industrial Relations*, **36**(4), 537–64.

Marchington, M. and Parker, P. 1990: *Changing Patterns of Employee Relations*. London: Harvester Wheatsheaf.

Marks, A., Findlay, P., Hine, J., McKinlay, A. and Thompson, P. 1998: The Politics of Partnership? Innovation in Employment Relations in the Scottish Spirits Industry. *British Journal of Industrial Relations*, **36**(2), 209–26.

Millward, N. 1994: *The New Industrial Relations*. London: Policy Studies Institute.

Millward, N., Stevens, M., Smart, D. and Hawes, W. R. 1992: *Workplace Industrial Relations in Transition*. Aldershot: Dartmouth.

Monks, J. 1998: Trade Unions, Enterprise and the Future. In P. Sparrow and M. Marchington (eds), *Human Resource Management: The New Agenda*, London: Financial Times/Pitman.

Olson, M. 1982: *The Rise and Decline of Nations*. New Haven: Yale University Press.

Overell, S. 1997: Harmonic Motions. *People Management*, 11 September, 24–30.

Purcell, J. 1979: A Strategy for Management Control in Industrial Relations. In J. Purcell and R. Smith (eds), *The Control of Work*, London: Macmillan.

Purcell, J. 1993: The End of Institutional Industrial Relations. *Political Quarterly*, **64**(1), 6–23.

Purcell, J. and Sisson, K. 1983: Strategies and Practices in the Management of Industrial Relations. In G. S. Bain (ed.), *Industrial Relations in Britain*, Oxford: Blackwell.

Rogers, J. and Streeck, W. (ed) 1995: *Works Councils: Consultation, Representation, and Cooperation in Industrial Relations*. London: University of Chicago Press.

Scarborough, H. and Terry, M. 1996. Industrial Relations and the Reorganization of Production in the UK Motor Vehicle Industry: A Study of the Rover Group. *Warwick Papers in Industrial Relations*, 58, February, Warwick: Industrial Relations Research Unit, Warwick Business School, University of Warwick.

Sisson, K. 1993: In Search of HRM. *British Journal of Industrial Relations*, **31**(2), 201–10.

Smith, P. and Morton, G. 1993: Union Exclusion and the Decollectivization of Industrial Relations in Contemporary Britain. *British Journal of Industrial Relations*, **31**(1), 97–114.

Storey, J. (ed.) 1989: *New Perspectives on Human Resource Management.* London: Routledge & Kegan Paul.

Storey, J. 1992: *Developments in the Management of Human Resources.* Oxford: Blackwell.

Streeck, W. 1987: The Uncertainties of Management and the Management of Uncertainty. *Work, Employment and Society,* **1**(2), 317–49.

Streeck, W. 1992: *Social Institutions and Economic Performance.* London: Sage.

Tailby, S., Pearson, E. and Sinclair, J. 1997: *Employee Relations in the South West.* London: ACAS.

Taylor, R. 1998: Tide set to turn for TUC as delegates gather by the sea. *Financial Times,* 14 September 1998.

Taylor, R. 1999: An Unlikely Reunion. *Financial Times,* 4 March 1999.

Thomas, C. and Wallis, B. 1998: Dwr Cymru/Welsh Water: A Case Study in Partnership. In P. Sparrow and M. Marchington (eds), *Human Resource Management: The New Agenda,* London: Financial Times/Pitman.

TUC (Trades Union Congress) 1994: *Human Resource Management: A Trade Union Response.* London: TUC.

TUC 1996: *Your Stake at Work: TUC Proposals for a Stakeholding Company.* London: TUC.

TUC 1997a: *Partners for Progress: Next Steps for the New Unionism.* London: TUC.

TUC 1997b: *Take Your Partners: The Business Case for a Union Voice.* London: TUC.

TUC 1998: *Productivity and Partnership. TUC Response to McKinsey.* London, TUC.

Usdaw (Union of Shop, Distributive and Allied Workers) 1998: *Social Partnership.* Executive Council Statement to the 1998 Annual Delegate Meeting.

Winchester, D. 1988: Sectoral Change and Trade Union Organization. In D. Gallie (ed.), *Employment in Britain.* Oxford: Blackwell.

Index

Abernathy, W., 48
absenteeism, 323, 326, 328, 330
ACAS, 33, 74, 155, 248, 295, 297, 321, 322,
    324, 373
Ackers, P., 343, 348, 355, 377
Ackroyd, S., 6, 45–6, 63, 185, 352
action learning, 198, 207–11
Adams, K., 5, 18
Adler, N, 230
Adler, P., 351–2, 353
age discrimination, 142, 150
agency work, 295–6, 297
Ahlstrand, B., 277
Albanese, M. T., 59, 60, 353
Alexander, G. P., 197
Algera, J., 113
Allen, J., 75
Allen, M., 382–3
Anderman, S. D., 321
Anderson, N., 133
Anglo–Dutch model, 225–6, 228
annual hours, 299–302, 306
Appelbaum, E., 343
apprenticeships, 179, 180, 260–1
Argyris, C., 210, 231
Armstrong, D., 96, 97
Armstrong, M., 243–5, 252, 258, 260, 265, 274,
    282
Armstrong, P., 323, 329
Arnold, J., 131
Arrowsmith, J., 270, 276, 284, 302
Arthur, J. B., 15, 63, 353

Arthur, M. B., 220
Arthur, W., 125
Arttachariya, P., 230
Ascher, K., 72, 80
Ashdown, R. T., 320
Ashton, D., 178, 190
assessment centres, 127–9
asset management, 45, 46, 63
Atkinson, J., 71, 74, 80, 107, 151
Audit Commission, 281, 291
Auluck, R., 160–1
authority, 320, 323–4, 330, 350
autocracy, 329, 330, 334
autonomy, 4, 53, 334, 342, 353, 379
Avery, R. D., 103

Bach, S., 7, 14, 18, 247, 290
Bachman, R., 77
Badger, B., 208
Bain, G. S., 369
Baker, K. H., 320
Ball, C., 381
Banerji, N., 322, 323
Bank of England, 30
Banker, R., 349
banking sector, 30, 148, 186, 282
Barker, J., 349
Barker, J. R., 333
Barlow, G., 249, 253, 255–6
Barocci, T., 272
Baron, A., 243–5, 252, 258, 260, 265
Barrick, M. R., 126

Barsoux, J-L., 228
Bartlett, C. A., 129
Bartolome, F., 223
Bartram, D., 126
Baruch, Y., 301
Batstone, E., 324, 334
Batt, R., 343, 353
Beale, D., 356
Beaumont, P., 77, 317
Beaver, G., 197
Becker, B., 15, 23
Beer, M., 247, 251
Bell, D., 97
Benbow, N., 233
Bentham, J., 255
Bercusson, B., 307–8
Berg, P., 353
Berggren, C., 53
Bevan, S., 154, 241, 243, 247
Beynon, H., 327
Bhavnani, R., 141–2
Bienefeld, M., 287
Black, J., 348
Blau, P., 70
Blinkhorn, S., 126
Blue Circle Cement, 279, 381
Blundell, R., 181
Blyton, P., 299, 332, 333
Boak, G., 208
Boam, R., 116
Bognanno, M., 116
Bolwijn, P. T., 130
bonus payments, 267, 268
Bosch, G., 290, 301
Boston, S., 152
Bougen, P., 344
Bowen, D. E., 133
Bowles, M., 254
Boyatzis, R. E., 116
Boydell, T., 197
Bradley, K., 355
Brannen, P., 340, 342
Braverman, H., 6
Brennan, J., 132
Bretz, R., 254
Brewster, C., 300
Britain, 187–9, 199–213; career management,
    221–2, 225, 229, 232–3, 236
Brockner, J., 52
Brown, C., 47, 141

Brown, W., 9, 265–6
Bruegel, I., 141, 151, 153
Buchan, J., 297
Buchanan, D., 342, 349, 353
budgetary constraints, 289–91
buffer stocks, 48, 49, 50
Burawoy, M., 6
bureaucracy, 50, 51, 70–1
bureaucratic control, 6–7, 82, 320, 326
Burgoyne, J., 197, 198
Burke, R., 230
business plan, 94–5, 98–100, 106
business process re-engineering, 44, 46–8, 50,
    55–7, 64
business services (growth), 75–6, 79
business strategies, 27–9, 212–14, 271, 275–7;
    manpower planning, 99–100, 104, 106–8
Butler, P., 85
Buxton, T., 186
buyers, 77–83
Byham, W., 350

cadres, 228
Calás, M., 58
Cameron, E., 253
Cameron, I., 160, 163
Cameron, K., 52
Campbell, A., 6
Cannell, M., 190, 269
Cannon, T., 235
capitalism, 55, 70, 71, 287
Cappelli, P., 14, 45, 276, 351
career: breaks, 162; development, 51–2, 223–4;
    management, 218–36
Carlton, I., 248, 252, 253
Carroll, S. J.,108
Carter, S., 235
Casey, B., 267, 297
Cave, K. E., 298
Cavendish, R., 330, 331
CBI, 84, 144, 188, 200, 269, 272, 372, 373, 377,
    385
cellular manufacturing, 28, 49–50, 290
champion role, 58, 60–2, 64
Champy, J., 50, 55
Chan, A., 230
Chandler, A., 70
change agent, 58–9, 61, 62
Chatman, J. I., 133
Chen, C., 253

Child, J., 57
childcare, 156, 162, 292
Chisholm, L., 187
Cianni, M., 197
Civil Service, 73, 80, 84, 140, 156, 276
Clark, I., 78
Clark, J., 9, 13, 15, 301, 351, 371
Clark, L., 153
Clarke, K., 151, 181
Claydon, T., 342, 371, 374–5, 383
Clegg, C. W., 57
Clinton, A., 321
Clutterbuck, D., 209–10
coaching, 207, 209–10
Coates, G., 254
Cockburn, C., 105, 151, 153, 159–62
Coe, M., 52
Coe, T., 232
Coffield, F., 187
cognitive tests (selection), 126
Cole, R., 341, 352
Colgan, F., 153
Collard, R., 347
collective bargaining, 9, 11, 20, 24, 31, 34–6,
    188; equality and, 152–3, 155; pay systems,
    266, 269–70, 282; social partnership, 365–72,
    385; working time, 289, 304, 306–7
Collin, A., 201
Colling, T., 71–2, 74, 80–1, 83, 139, 151, 152,
    290
Collins, D., 350
Collinson, D., 154, 158–9, 177
Collinson, M., 9, 54, 177, 334–5, 351
Collis-Squires, N., 327–8
Commission for Racial Equality, 139–40, 142–5,
    148, 150, 156
commitment, 3, 5, 7, 11, 14, 130, 185, 230–1,
    253, 368; HRP and, 101, 104; lean
    organization, 44, 46, 48, 52–3, 55–6, 59, 61,
    63
compensation, 155–6, 279
competencies, 112, 114–16, 196, 201–3; based
    pay, 273–4, 278–80; core, 5, 8, 15, 71, 99–
    100, 174, 202, 243, 277
competition, 45, 56, 289–91
competitive advantage, 5, 34–5; direct
    participation, 341–2, 347; learning
    organization, 173, 177, 184, 187, 190
competitive strategy, 15, 93, 272; in learning
    organization, 173, 183–6, 188, 190

compliance approach, 137, 146–51, 153–6
compulsory competitive tendering, 13, 27–8,
    71–3, 85, 149, 157, 290, 367
computers, 58, 80, 105–8, 215, 290
Connock, S., 300
Constable, J., 195, 199, 203–4
Constable, R., 13
content analytical interview, 124, 125
contingency theory, 53, 272, 276
contracts: extended organization, 70–86; *see also*
    compulsory competitive tendering;
    outsourcing; subcontracting
control, 17–19, 63, 343; bureaucratic, 6–7, 82,
    320–1, 326–7; costs, 14, 46; surveillance, 7,
    45, 53, 177, 255–6, 317, 333; *see also* discipline
Cooper, C., 229
Cooper, D., 127, 128
Copeland, L., 146
core competencies, *see* competencies
core-periphery model, 71, 84
Cornelius, E. T., 118
corporate strategy, 93, 98–100
corrective approach, 320–6, 330, 336
cost, 14, 29, 48, 53, 71; of labour, *see* labour;
    overheads, 46, 50, 52; reduction, 50–1, 80–1,
    85, 106
Costa, P. T., 127
Cotton, J., 345, 348, 352
Coulson-Thomas, C., 232
Coupar, W., 52, 376
Cowling, A., 97
Cox, A., 81, 84
Coyle, A., 153, 157, 160
Coyle-Shapiro, J., 82
Cressey, P., 30, 350
Crites, J. O., 223
critical incident analysis, 114, 124–5
Crocker-Hefter, A., 276
Crompton, R., 159
Cully, M., 3, 20, 22–6, 37, 74–5, 140, 147, 183,
    249, 287, 294, 296, 300, 321, 344, 370–2, 384
culture, *see* organizational culture
Cunningham, I., 353, 356
Cunninson, S., 152
Curran, M., 158
customers, 50, 62, 333, 341
Cytrynbaum, S., 223

Dale, B., 347
Dale, M., 116

Dalton, G. W., 223
Danford, A., 334, 335
Daniel, W. W., 57, 58, 322, 325
Darmon, I., 178
Darrah, C., 105
data protection, 33, 257
Davidson, M., 229, 230, 235
Davis, E., 345
Davis, H., 73
Dawson, P., 54
Dean, J., 19
Deaton, D., 325
decentralization, 46, 58, 323–4, 379
decision-making, 71, 78, 131, 157–8, 178, 242–3, 340, 379
Decker, P. J., 118
Deery, S. J., 290
delayering, 47–8, 50–2, 56–8, 62, 207, 269, 348
Delbridge, R., 7, 53, 350–1
Deming, W. E., 200, 246, 269
Dench, S., 182, 184
Denham, N., 355
deregulation, 74, 187, 290, 341; labour market 31–2, 46; pay, 279, 282; social partnership, 372, 375, 385
Derr, C. B., 220, 224–5
Derrida, J., 43
development: career management, 218–36; learning organization, 173–91; of management, 195–215
devolution, 348, 349
Dex, S., 142, 152
Dickens, L., 18, 139, 144–6, 149, 151–3, 156, 158–9, 162, 373
Dickerson, A. P., 187
Dickson, W. J., 114
Digings, L., 79
DiMaggio, P., 276
Dipboye, R. L., 125
direct participation, 16, 35, 340–59
disability, 138–9, 143, 159, 162; legislation, 32, 142, 147–8, 150, 155, 161
discipline, 54, 255–6, 317–37
discrimination, 130; equal opportunity policies, 137–64; *see also* age discrimination; disability; race/racial equality; sex discrimination
dismissals, 321–5, 329
DiTomaso, N., 253
Ditton, J., 318, 329
division of labour, 7, 31, 342

divisionalization, 28, 83
dock workers, 331
Doeringer, P. B., 102
Dohse, K., 53
Donaghy, R., 149, 152
Donaldson, L., 358
Donovan Commission, 11, 13, 309, 366
Dopson, S., 51, 233, 235
Dore, R., 212
double-loop learning, 175, 210
downsizing, 46–8, 50–2, 56, 58, 62, 130, 207
downward communications, 345–6, 353
Doyle, M., 19, 342
Drago, R., 354, 355
Dreilinger, C., 52
Dreyfuss, J., 119
Drucker, P., 5, 98, 341
Druker, J., 74, 83
Du Gay, P., 75
Dunne, J., 75, 76
Dutton, G., 210
Dyer, L., 14

Earnshaw, J., 322, 331
Edmonds, J., 189
education: qualifications, 183, 199–202, 206–7, 228, 230; VET, 179–81, 187
Edwards, J. E., 108
Edwards, P., 9, 334–5, 351, 354, 356
Edwards, P. K., 196, 211, 317, 319, 321, 323–9 *passim*
Edwards, R., 6, 320
Elger, T., 334–5, 336
Elliott, L., 185
employees: appraisal, 7, 241–61; career management, 218–36; involvement, 21, 49, 53, 340–59, 384; job satisfaction, 4, 51, 53, 213, 231, 351; recruitment and selection, 111–33; share owners, 21, 267, 345; working time, 25–6, 185, 287–309; *see also* commitment; discipline; empowerment; pay; psychological contract; workforce
employers, 36, 143, 182, 367–9; *see also* CBI
employment: agencies, 117–18; changing patterns, 23–6; equality, 137–64; legislation, 30–3, 148, 150, 322, 372; protection, 78, 83, 86, 322; rights, 29, 32–3, 148, 322; system/ strategy, 100–3; tribunals, 31, 142, 305, 322–3
employment relations, 17–18, 20–1, 28; discipline, 317–37; extended organization,

employment relations *Continued*
81–4; legislation, 31, 33, 188, 371;
participation, 340–59; social partnership, 14,
340, 365–86; voluntarism, 9, 30–3; working
time, 287–309; *see also* industrial relations
empowerment, 7–8, 35, 184, 219; direct
participation and, 341–3, 350–2, 354;
discipline and, 333, 335; in lean
organizations, 48–51, 53, 54, 56–7
EMU, 29–30, 34, 386
enterprise culture, 45, 51, 71, 213, 341
equal opportunities, 35, 137–64
Equal Opportunities Commission, 139, 141–3,
145, 148, 155–6
equal pay, 147–50, 154–5, 159, 270, 277
Eraut, M., 178, 180, 182, 191
Escott, K., 157
ethics, 127
ethnic minorities, 32, 139–62 *passim*
European Central Bank, 30
European Commission, 16, 34–6, 150, 154, 156,
305, 308, 385
European Court of Justice, 153–4, 156, 305, 372
European Foundation, 16, 21–2, 23
European social model, 31, 34–6, 308, 386
Europeanization (challenges), 29–36
evaluation, 213, 383–6
Evans, K., 179
Evans, M., 52
Evans, P., 223, 225–7
Evans, S., 74, 321, 323
excellence, 44, 45, 52, 53
expectancy theory, 131–2, 281
extended organization, 7, 46, 70–86
external career (management), 220–3
external labour market, 94, 100–2, 162, 222
external recruitment, 117–19
externalization, 5, 27–8
Ezzamel, M., 52, 58

facilitator, 58, 60–2, 184, 347, 355
Fagan, C., 141
Fagenson, E., 230
family-friendly policies, 10, 18, 156, 289, 291–3,
302
Fell, A., 16–17, 62
Felstead, A., 71, 76, 78, 151, 182
Fenton O'Creevy, M., 356
Ferner, A., 71, 74, 290, 373–4
Fernie, S., 352, 357

Ferris, G. A., 125
Fevre, R., 152
fiddles, 328, 329
Figart, D. M., 162
financial services, 62, 290
financial systems, 8, 78–9
Findlay, P., 241, 249, 251, 255–6
Finegold, D., 173, 179
firm-specific skills, 5, 101–2, 270
Fiske, D. W., 123
Fitzgerald, G., 81
fixed hours, 298–300
Flanders, A., 11, 303
Fletcher, C., 116, 244, 246, 254, 258
flexible firm, 7, 59, 71
flexible specialization, 53
flexible working, 299–302, 306
Flood, P. C., 72
Flynn, P., 308
Fombrun, C., 272
Fordism, 101, 177, 185
forecasting (manpower planning), 94–6
Foster, C., 71
Foucault, M., 7, 53, 255, 317
Fowler, A., 269
Fox, A., 366
Foy, N., 350
French, S., 260
Friedman, A. L., 319
Fröhlich, D., 22
Fryer, R. H., 181
Fucini, J., 352
Fucini, S., 352
full-time work, 249, 288, 291, 293–4, 302, 304
Fullerton, J., 145
functional flexibility, 53, 348, 368
Furnham, A., 252, 254, 258

gain-sharing schemes, 274, 343
Gallie, D., 7, 19, 26, 355
Garrahan, P., 7, 53, 351
Gaugler, B., 128
Geary, J., 354
Gerhart, B., 276
gender, 25–6, 32; equal opportunities, 137–64
passim; *see also* men; women
German model, 225, 226, 228
Gershuny, J., 75
Gersuny, C., 321
Ghoshal, S., 129

Gier, J. A., 124
Gilbert, K., 149, 152
Gilbert, T., 84
Gill, D., 246, 247
Gill, J., 358
Ginn, J., 292
globalization, 29, 45, 55, 340, 373
GMB union, 189, 381
Goffee, R., 72, 218, 220, 232–3, 235
Goldberg, L. R., 127
Gomez-Mejia, L., 271
Gooch, L., 18
Goold, M., 6
Gouldner, A. W., 326–7
Gourlay, S., 331
government (social partnership), 366–9
grading structures, 277–8
Graham, L., 53
Graham, M., 276
Grant, D., 11
Grant, R., 5
Green, A., 187
Green, F., 151, 182, 183
Greenslade, M., 146
Greer, C. R., 96, 97
Gregg, P., 371
Greuter, M., 113
Grey, C., 50, 55–7, 64, 248, 255–6
Griffiths, R., 13
Griffiths, W., 13
Grint, K., 55, 57, 246, 252, 256–7, 260
Guest, D., 11, 14–15, 52, 59, 82, 93, 98, 218, 220, 231, 236, 367–8, 384–5
Gunz, H., 223

Hackett, G., 144, 148, 158
Hackman, R., 251
Hakim, C., 291
Hall, L., 11, 16–18, 34, 98, 108, 236, 251, 254, 318
Hall, M., 156, 304, 305, 373
Hamel, G., 5, 72, 93, 99
Hammer, M., 50, 55
Hammond, V., 138
Hampson, I., 196
Handy, C., 13, 195, 199, 203, 218, 258
Hannah, L., 70
Harrison, A., 72
Harrison, B., 80, 81
Harrison, R., 180

Harvey, R., 303
Hassell, N., 82
Hawthorne studies, 63, 114
health and safety, 32, 304–5, 307–8
Healy, G., 255–6, 260
Heery, E., 152, 281, 372
Hendricks, R., 55
Hendry, C., 95, 100–2, 104, 175–6
Hennestad, B., 343
Henry, S., 320, 322
Hercus, T., 94, 98
Herriot, P., 52, 130–1, 197, 224, 232, 233, 235–6
Herzberg, F., 348
hidden persuader, 58, 60, 61
hierarchical organization, 70, 71, 82
Highhouse, S., 252, 253
Hill, J., 125
Hill, S., 341, 348, 352, 355
Hilmer, F. G., 358
Hitner, T., 139
Hochschild, A., 349
Holbeche, L., 51–2
Holland, L., 159
Holtermann, S., 153
home working, 162, 300–1
Hooper, N., 73
Hope-Hailey, V., 18
Horrell, S., 145
hours of work, 287–309
Howard, C., 52
Howell, K., 253
Huczynski, A., 358
Huffcutt, A. I., 125
human resource management, 11–16, 44–5
human resource planning, 93–109
Humphries, J., 151
Hunt, E. H., 287
Hunter, J., 80
Hunter, J. E., 126
Hunter, L., 74
Hurstfield, J., 298
Huselid, M., 15, 23, 59, 63, 342
Huws, U., 301
Hyman, J., 344, 345, 356
Hyman, R., 14, 17, 319, 368–9, 373–4

Ichniowski, C., 15, 342, 353
Iles, P. A., 116, 128, 133, 160–1
in-tray exercises, 128
incomes policy, 268

indirect participation, 35, 340, 343, 357
industrial relations, 8, 10, 30, 59, 83; legislation, 304, 322; social partnership, 365–86; Research Unit, 9, 75, 145, 146, 152, 291
Industrial Society, 10, 182, 246–50, 253, 275, 277–9, 282
Industrial Training Boards, 181–2
industrial tribunals, 32, 155, 322
information and communication technologies, 44, 50, 55, 56, 57–8
information systems, 105–7, 108
information technology, 80–1, 215
Inkson, A., 52
innovation, 27, 70, 99, 129, 230, 232
Institute of Management, 51, 232–3, 305
Institute for Manpower Studies, 71
Institute of Personnel and Development, 4, 5, 10, 11, 13, 18
Institute of Personnel Management, 96–7, 112, 201, 246–7, 282, 321–3
internal career (management), 220, 223–4
internal contractor, 59–60, 61, 62
internal labour market, 100–2, 162, 214, 222
internal market, 28
internal recruitment, 116–17
internal resources of firm, 93
internalization, 270
interpreter role, 58, 60
interviews, 113–14, 119–20, 123–5
Investors in People, 145, 182, 206, 248
Involvement and Participation Association, 53, 376–7, 384
Izraeli, D., 230

Jackson, S., 15, 202, 272
James, M., 86
James, P., 308
Janz, T., 124
Japanese model, 3, 334–5, 341; career management, 222, 225, 227, 229, 236; lean organization, 44–6, 59, 62–3; management development, 211–13
Javidan, M., 5, 99
Jeffery, M., 156
Jenkins, R., 157–8, 163
Jewson, N., 139, 153, 157–8, 160–1
job: analysis, 113–16, 129; competence, *see* competencies; description, 6, 49, 112, 114–16, 129, 273; evaluation, 6, 154, 265–6, 273, 275, 277–8, 281; performance, *see* performance;

profile, 112; satisfaction, 4, 51, 53, 213, 231, 351; security, 14, 22–3, 53, 61, 63, 77–8, 84, 213, 219, 289, 335, 378, 380, 383; segregation, 141–2, 151–2, 160; sharing, 162, 302
Johnson, C., 126
joint consultative committees, 345, 357, 372
Joint Production and Advisory Committees (JPACs), 343
joint regulation, 13, 20, 26; of working time, 289, 304, 306–7
Jones, A., 128
Jones, C., 175–6
Jones, D. T., 13
Jones, G., 159
Judge, T. A., 125
just-in-time production, 44–5, 47–50, 52–5, 290, 302

kaizen, 44, 48–50, 53, 61, 229
kanban system, 50
Kandola, R., 145
Kane, J., 253–4
Kano, N., 351
Kanouse, D., 259
Kanter, R. M., 44, 219, 269, 341
Katz, H., 270
Keep, E., 8, 173, 175, 179–80, 185, 187
Kelley, M., 80, 81
Kelly, E. L., 123
Kelly, J., 10, 14, 348, 356, 383–4
Kemp, N. J., 57
Kessler, I., 82, 250, 270, 276, 280–1, 373
Kettley, P., 51, 257, 258
Kinder, A., 126
Kinnie, N., 44, 47, 51–2, 55, 58, 61
Klein, J., 355
Kmieciak, Y. M., 132–3
knowledge sharing, 185
Kochan, T. A., 14, 34, 272, 342
Kodz, J., 185
Koike, K., 176
Kolb, D., 175, 178, 186
Kotter, J. P., 232
KPMG, 185, 243
Kumar, P., 356
Kumpe, T., 130

labour, 54–5, 94–5, 104–5, 107; costs, 6, 77–8, 81, 86, 108, 274, 290–1, 367; productivity, 23, 30, 35, 47, 53, 277

labour market, 72, 85–6, 95, 103–4, 276; deregulation, 31, 46; equality, 137–64; external, 94, 100–2, 162, 222; internal, 100–2, 162, 214, 222; occupational, 101, 105; segregation, 141–2, 220; technical/industrial, 101
labour process tradition, 6–9, 53
Lane, C., 77, 225
Lansbury, R., 345
Laribee, J., 82
Lashley, C., 197, 343, 344
Latham, G. P., 124
Latin model, 225, 227, 228–9
Laurent, A., 225
Lawler, E. E., 251, 271, 342
Lawrence, B., 221
Lawrence, P., 228
Leach, B., 161
lean organization, 43–65, 342
lean production, 48–50, 52–5
learning: accreditation of prior, 201; action, 198, 207–11; organization, 173–91
Ledwith, S., 18, 153
Lee, G., 151, 152
Legge, K., 6, 11, 14–15, 45, 48, 50, 53, 55, 58–9, 61, 64, 243, 367
Lewis, P., 243, 250, 282
Lewis, R., 74
Lewis, S., 18, 253
Liff, S., 99, 105, 146, 158, 161–3, 234
Lindley, P. A., 126
Lipman-Blumen, J., 160
Lippitt, G., 197
Littlefield, D., 281
Littler, C. R., 320
local government: equal opportunities, 145, 149–50; services, 72, 79–80, 85–6, 276–7, 281, 290
Lockwood, J., 232
Loden, M., 146
Long, P., 246–9, 254
Longnecker, C., 252
Lonsdale, C., 81, 84
Lovenduski, J., 159
Ludwig, D., 252
Lupton, T., 272, 276

Maastricht Treaty, 34, 293, 304, 373
Mabey, C., 6, 133, 175, 190, 203
McArdle, L., 53, 351

McCabe, D., 55
McCarthy, Lord, 373, 377
McCarthy, W., 9, 324
McCartney, I., 377, 383
McColgan, A., 152
McCormick, E. J., 114
McCormick, R., 13, 195, 199, 203–4
McCredie, H., 128
McCrudden, C., 150
McCulloch, A., 142, 152
McDaniel, M. A., 125
Macdonald, C. L., 333
MacDuffie, J. P., 23, 27, 59, 63, 347, 353
McGeevor, P., 132
McGivney, V., 181, 187, 190
McGovern, P., 220, 235, 253, 254
McGregor, D. C., 4, 246
McIlroy, J., 373, 374
MacInnes, J., 57, 74
Mackay, L., 115
Mackenzie, K., 218, 220, 236
McKersie, R. B., 45
McKinlay, A., 7, 256, 289, 333, 335, 348, 352
McLoughlin, I., 331
McNulty, D., 289
McRae, R. R., 127
Maguire, M., 159, 178, 180
Mahoney, A., 290
Mahoney, T., 264, 265
management, 232–4; control, 6–8; development, 195–215; by objectives, 247, 248; social partnership, 365–86
Management Charter Initiative, 195, 200–3, 212, 214
managerialism, 10, 290, 366
Mangan, J., 107
Mangham, I., 195, 199
manpower planning, 93–109
manual work, 25, 85, 184, 188, 249, 268
manufacturing, 23–6, 44–6, 179, 185, 289
Manwaring, T., 117, 159
Maples, J., 188
Marchington, M., 3, 9, 36, 51, 58–62, 85, 251, 340, 344–6, 350, 353–5, 357–8, 368
Margerison, C., 246
Marginson, P., 6, 9, 27, 57, 74, 84
market testing, 71, 77, 80, 84–5, 157, 290
marketization, 270, 289
Markow model, 96, 97
Marks, A., 377–9

Marquardt, M., 177, 178
Mars, G., 328, 329
Marsden, D., 179, 260, 281
Marshall, J., 235
Marsick, V., 209
Martell, K., 108
Martin, G., 219
Martinez, L. M., 64
Mason, B., 344
Mason, D., 153, 158, 160–1
mass production, 48, 59, 341
Mayhew, K., 8, 185, 187
Meager, N., 71, 74
Mellish, M., 327–8
men, 229–30; hours of work, 288, 291–2, 295, 297–8
mentoring, 60, 181, 207, 209–10, 212
mergers and acquisitions, 27, 45, 185–7
merit pay, 280–3
Merrick, N., 281
meta-analysis, 123, 126, 128, 348
Metcalf, D., 352, 357
Metcalf, H., 189
Meyer, A., 231
Michaels-Barr, L., 82
Micklethwait, J., 358
Miles, I., 75
Miles, R., 15, 99, 152
Miller, D., 145, 162, 163
Miller, P., 358
Millward, N., 3, 13, 16, 62, 64, 75, 269, 287, 321, 324–5, 344, 370–2
Milne, S., 185
Mitchell, L., 202
Mitev, N., 50, 55–7, 64
Moingeon, B., 5
Molander, C., 317
Mole, G., 208
monitor role, 60, 61
monitoring, 54, 333
Monks, J., 375
Moralee, L., 142
Morgan, D., 196
Morton, C., 353, 355
Morton, G., 372
Mount, M. K., 126, 258
Mueller, F., 342, 349
multinational companies, 27–30, 366, 368
multiskilling, 22, 53, 56, 300
Mumford, A., 197, 209

Mumford, E., 55, 58
Munro, A., 188
Munro Fraser, J., 115
Murlis, H., 265, 272–3
mutual dependency, 77–8, 86, 318

National Economic Development Office, 96, 291
National Health Service, 28, 72–3, 85, 138–9, 149, 178, 291, 297–8
National Minimum Wage, 31, 33, 86, 156, 270, 292, 373
Naylor, M., 229
Neathey, F., 298
networks/networking, 70–1, 96, 117, 209
New Deal, 377
New Labour, 45–6, 373–5, 377
Newby, H., 320
Newell, H. J., 62, 233, 235
Newell, S., 123, 125, 127, 128, 129
Newton, T., 241, 249, 251, 255–6
Nichols, T., 327
Nicholson, N., 220, 233, 301, 356
Nixon, B., 197
non-manual work, 141, 249, 268–9
Noon, M., 332, 333
Nordic model, 31, 34
Nowack, K., 210

occupational labour market, 101, 105
O'Doherty, D., 95
Oliver, N., 47, 49, 59, 341, 347
Ollerearnshaw, S., 143
OPEN framework, 116
opportunism, 71, 77, 78, 79
Opportunity 2000 campaign, 138, 144, 153, 158, 234
Oram, M., 55, 57
O'Reilly, C. A., 132
organizational culture, 7, 48, 59, 127, 133, 190, 220, 279; change, 60, 190, 197, 243, 336, 384
organizational self-interest, 137, 144–6, 150, 151–3
organizational structure, 74, 81–3, 107, 230, 272
Osterman, P., 23, 35, 102
Ostroff, C., 133
Oswick, C., 11
Oughton, J., 80
outsourcing, 7, 71–7, 80–1
Overell, S., 383

overheads, 46, 50, 52
overtime, 290, 303, 327

Paddon, M., 79
Palmer, G., 352
Panoptican, 7–8, 255–6
parental leave, 147, 156, 289, 292, 304
Parker, C., 125
Parker, M., 53, 348, 351
Parker, P., 9, 368
Parker, S. R., 324
part-time work, 20, 23–6, 31, 103, 181, 249;
    equal opportunities, 141, 145, 147, 156, 162;
    trends, 289–96, 302, 304
participation, *see* direct participation; indirect
    participation
partnership, 35, 53–4, 188–9, 297; *see also* social
    partnership
Pateman, C., 351, 355
paternalism, 320, 330
Patterson, M. G., 16, 342, 353
pay, 23–4, 30, 141–2; bonus, 267, 268; equal,
    147–50, 154–5, 159, 270, 277; national
    minimum, 31, 33, 86, 156, 270, 292, 373;
    performance-related, 7, 14, 21, 159, 243–8,
    260, 264, 266–70, 273–6, 280–3, 345, 376;
    remuneration systems, 264–84
Payne, J., 181, 377
Payne, T., 128
Peccei, R., 52, 384–5
Pedler, M., 175, 197, 209, 211
peer review process, 333
Pekruhl, U., 22
Pemberton, C., 52, 197, 224, 232–3, 236
penalties, 318–27, 329–30, 332, 336; avoidance,
    137, 146–51, 153–6
Penn, R., 105
pensions, 32, 86
performance: appraisal, 7, 21–2, 241–61; direct
    participation, 350, 352–5; related pay, *see* pay;
    working time and, 287–309
Perrons, D., 141, 151, 153
Perry, P. J. C., 182
person specification, 112, 114–16, 130
personality tests, 8, 119–21, 126–7, 132–3, 249
personnel management: in extended
    organization, 70–86; lean organization,
    43–65; in perspective, 3–37
Peters, T., 22, 44, 71, 341, 348
Pettigrew, A., 213–14

Pevotto, A. E., 183
Pfeffer, J., 15–16, 342, 347, 349
Phelps Brown, E. H., 319
Philips, A., 151
Phizacklea, A., 152
piecework schemes, 267, 268, 269
Pike, A., 85
Pil, F. K., 23, 27
Piore, M. J., 48, 53, 102, 341
Pirani, M., 141
Plowden, F., 71
Plumridge, M. D., 323
Pollard, S., 70, 320
Pollert, A., 81
Poole, M., 13, 47, 59, 342, 345, 353
Porter, L., 251
Porter, M., 5, 99
Position Analysis Questionnaire, 114
Powell, G. N., 103
Powell, W., 276
power, 80, 157–8, 161–2, 340; relations, 174,
    184, 188, 234, 320; *see also* control;
    empowerment
Power, M., 358
Prahalad, C. K., 5, 72, 93, 99
predictive validity, 121, 123, 125–6, 128, 133
pregnant workers, 147, 156
prescriptive tradition, 4–10, 21
Price, L., 331
Price, R., 369
Pringle, M., 334
Pritchard, D., 265, 272–3
Pritchard, S., 81–2, 84
Private Finance Initiative, 85
private sector, 73–4, 83, 85
privatization, 13, 27, 29, 51, 80, 223, 276, 290,
    367, 379–80
problem-solving, 128, 181, 184, 209–11, 265;
    upward, 346–8
Proctor, S., 6, 45–6, 63, 185, 358
product development, 174, 346
productivity, 23–4, 30, 35, 47, 53, 277
profit, 6, 8, 46, 56, 77; sharing, 21, 267, 270,
    343, 344
promotion, 51, 95, 218–19, 221, 223, 228
'prospector' strategy, 99
psychological contract, 7, 15, 52, 59, 208, 368;
    career management, 231–2, 234–5; extended
    organization, 81–2; recruitment/selection,
    125, 131, 133

psychological testing, 125–7
psychometric approach, 112–33
public sector, 269, 290; contracts, 72–4, 79–81, 83, 85–6
punitive approach, 318–27, 329–30, 332, 336
Purcell, J., 15, 17, 59, 63, 83, 160, 270, 280–1, 297, 366, 368, 379
Purcell, K., 297
Purdie, E., 229

Quaid, M., 277
quality, 7, 11, 48–50
quality circles, 21, 53, 345, 347–9, 355
questionnaires (recruitment), 114

race/racial equality, 32, 139–62
Raelin, J., 210
Raffe, D., 179
Rainbird, H., 173, 179, 180, 188
Rainnie, A., 74
Ram, M., 9, 74, 117, 330
Ramsay, H., 343, 344
Raper, P., 182
Rathkey, P., 355
rational planning model, 100, 102
recruitment, 111–19, 129–33
Redman, T., 257, 258
redundancy, 23, 48, 51, 56, 78, 354, 371, 378
Rees, C., 44, 46–8, 53–4, 58, 60–4, 354
Regini, M., 185
regulation, 30–3, 77–9, 304–8, 369
Reich, M., 47
Reich, R., 29
Reichers, A.E., 231
Reid, D. A., 320
Reilly, P., 97
Reissman, L., 278
reliability criteria, 119–21, 123
religious discrimination, 147, 150, 154
remuneration systems, 264–84
repertory grid, 114, 116
representative participation, 35, 379
representative rules, 326, 327
resource-based theory of firm, 5, 93, 276
resources: equal opportunities, 137–64; human resource planning, 93–109; recruitment and selection, 111–33
reward systems, 21, 22, 274–7, 318
Reynold, A, 177, 178
Rice, D., 52

Richardson, R., 281
Roach, S. S., 46, 65
Roberts, I., 350
Robertson, I. T., 124, 126–8, 133
Robinson, S. L., 233, 234
Roche, W. K., 303
Rodger, A., 115
Roethlisberger, F. J., 114
Roffey Park Management Institute, 51
Rogers, J., 385
Rojot, J., 290, 301
Rollinson, D., 325, 326
Roman–Germanic model, 31, 34
Rose, M., 105
Rosenthal, P., 333, 352, 358
Rothwell, S., 57, 98
Rousseau, D. M., 233, 234
Rowe, K., 251
Roy, D., 329
Rubery, J., 102–3, 141, 151, 159, 265, 269
Rucker plan, 274
rules, 318, 320–31
Ryan, P., 179

Sako, M., 76
Salaman, G., 160, 190, 203
Sayles, L. R., 318, 330
Scanlon plan, 274
Scarbrough, H., 5, 13, 99, 177, 185, 377
Scase, R., 72, 218, 232, 235, 330
Schein, E., 220, 224
Schmidt, F. L., 126
Schmidt, N., 126
Schneider, B., 132, 133
Schön, D., 210
Schonberger, R., 341, 350
Schuler, R., 15, 99, 202, 272
Schuster, J., 271
Scott, A., 9, 141
Scullion, H., 9, 323, 326, 329
Secker, J., 149, 152
Seddon, V., 160
Seifert, R., 325
selection, 111–12, 119–33
self-actualization, 53
self-appraisal, 254, 260
self-development, 4, 198, 208, 212, 219
self-discipline, 55, 318–19, 321, 331, 333, 335–7
self-employment, 142, 147, 208

self-interest, 71, 85; organizational, 137, 144–6, 150, 151–3
self-managed careers, 219, 235
self-management, 342, 349–50
Senge, P., 174, 180, 184
seniority, 101, 160, 201, 207
Senker, P., 182
services sector, 23–6, 62, 72–3, 75–6, 79, 141, 179, 185, 289–91
Sewell, G., 53, 347, 350
sex discrimination, 32, 138–43, 146–7, 149, 156
sexual harassment, 150, 155, 160
Shackleton, V. J., 123, 125, 127–9
share ownership, 8, 21, 187, 267, 345
Shaw, J., 141
Sheehey, P., 13
shift working, 290–1, 295, 297–8, 302, 304–5
shop stewards, 324, 357, 378, 379
shopfloor workers, 268–9, 328–31
short-termism, 8, 9, 46, 58, 78, 187
Shutt, J., 79
Silver, M., 107, 195, 199
Simpson, R., 253
Sinclair, A., 349
single-loop learning, 175, 186
Sirianni, C., 333
Sisson, K., 3, 4, 8, 13–14, 17, 27, 29, 74, 83–4, 98, 196, 211, 219, 243, 270, 276, 284, 302, 304, 345, 357, 366, 379
Skapinker, M., 210
skills, 45, 151, 260–1; based pay, 273, 278–80; firm-specific, 5, 101–2, 270; human resource planning, 95, 99–107; multiskilling, 22, 53, 56, 300; *see also* learning; management development
Slaughter, J., 53, 348, 351
Sloman, M., 248, 252, 253
Sly, F., 142, 297
Smallman, C., 196
Smircich, L., 58
Smith, C., 8, 334–5, 336, 344
Smith, D., 197
Smith, I., 268
Smith, M., 122, 132
Smith, P., 197, 372
Smith, W. H., 258
Snape, E., 257, 258
Snell, M., 154
Snow, C., 15, 99
Social Action Programme, 35

Social Chapter, 30, 156, 373, 385
social contract, 366
social justice, 16, 64, 144, 145
social partnership, 14, 15, 188–9, 340; management and trade unions, 365–86
social security, 148, 292
socialization, 116, 125, 133
Sofer, C., 218
Solomos, J., 163
Sonnenfeld, J. A., 222
Soskice, D., 173
Sparrow, P., 3, 36, 51–2, 85, 116, 280
Stability and Growth Pact, 30
Stageman, J., 152
stakeholders, 8, 43, 47–50, 187
Starbuck, W., 99
Starkey, K., 348
Starks, M., 74
Stemp, P., 197
Stevens, B., 52, 376
Stevens, M., 344
Stewart, P., 7, 53, 351
Stewart, R., 51
Stiles, P., 52
Stilgoe, E., 322, 325
Storey, J., 11–12, 29, 58, 64, 98, 108, 188–9, 195, 203, 211, 213, 222, 229, 236, 243, 246–9, 253, 260, 317, 344, 347, 357, 372
Strassman, P., 50
Strauss, G., 318, 330
Streeck, W., 189, 368, 385
Stringfield, P., 254, 258
Stuart-Smith, K., 259
subassemblies, 48–9
subcontracting, 27, 46, 70–86, 173, 289
Sunday working, 32, 305
supervision/supervisors, 51, 323–4
supporter role, 60
surveillance, 7, 45, 53, 177, 255–6, 317, 333
Swieringa, G., 175, 178

Tack, W. L., 210
Tailby, S., 370
Tarbuck, M., 57
task and finish practices, 327, 328
Tate, W. V., 197, 201
Tavistock Institute, 182
Taylor, B., 151
Taylor, F. W., 111
Taylor, K., 18, 253